DOWN FROM OLYMPUS

DOWN FROM OLYMPUS

ARCHAEOLOGY AND
PHILHELLENISM IN
GERMANY, 1750-1970

Suzanne L. Marchand

PRINCETON, NEW JERSEY

PRINCETON UNIVERSITY PRESS

COPYRIGHT © 1996 BY PRINCETON UNIVERSITY PRESS

PUBLISHED BY PRINCETON UNIVERSITY PRESS, 41 WILLIAM STREET,

PRINCETON, NEW JERSEY 08540

IN THE UNITED KINGDOM: PRINCETON UNIVERSITY PRESS, CHICHESTER, WEST SUSSEX

ALL RIGHTS RESERVED

LIBRARY OF CONGRESS CATALOGING-IN-PUBLICATION DATA

MARCHAND, SUZANNE L., 1961–

DOWN FROM OLYMPUS: ARCHAEOLOGY AND PHILHELLENISM IN GERMANY,

1750–1970/SUZANNE L. MARCHAND.

P.   CM.

INCLUDES BIBLIOGRAPHICAL REFERENCES AND INDEX

ISBN 0-691-04393-0 (ALK. PAPER)

1. GERMANY—INTELLECTUAL LIFE—18TH CENTURY.   2. GERMANY—

INTELLECTUAL LIFE—19TH CENTURY.   3. GERMANY—INTELLECTUAL

LIFE—20TH CENTURY.   4. ARCHAEOLOGY—GERMANY—HISTORY.

5. ENLIGHTENMENT—GERMANY.   6. ART, GREEK—INFLUENCE.

7. NEOCLASSICISM (ART)—GERMANY.   8. CIVILIZATION, CLASSICAL.   I. TITLE.

DD193.5.M37   1996

938′.0072043—dc20   95-53324 CIP

THIS BOOK HAS BEEN COMPOSED IN BERKELEY MEDIUM

PRINCETON UNIVERSITY PRESS BOOKS ARE PRINTED ON ACID-FREE PAPER

AND MEET THE GUIDELINES FOR PERMANENCE AND DURABILITY OF THE

COMMITTEE ON PRODUCTION GUIDELINES FOR BOOK LONGEVITY

OF THE COUNCIL ON LIBRARY RESOURCES

PRINTED IN THE UNITED STATES OF AMERICA BY PRINCETON ACADEMIC PRESS

1 3 5 7 9 10 8 6 4 2

For Victor

CONTENTS

ILLUSTRATIONS

ACKNOWLEDGMENTS

PERHAPS philhellenic nostalgia continues to intrigue me precisely because the modern world has offered me such a wealth of intellectual and personal delights. This does not mean, however, that I have been insensible to Greece's charms, past and present, which I first encountered as a result of a visit to the Peloponnese with my parents in 1981. My attraction to that country has been renewed in recent years by my sister Jean's pursuit of a career in classics and marriage to a Greek citizen, who has graciously introduced us to the delights of postclassical Greece. But, as a student at UC Berkeley, I developed a stronger fascination for German intellectual history, perhaps because the cultural achievements and predicaments of this modern nation bear more heavily on the world in which I live. In pursuing this field, first at Berkeley, and then at the University of Chicago, I have been inspired by some marvelous teachers, among them Martin Jay, David Sorkin, Jan Goldstein, Michael Geyer, John Boyer, Samuel Jaffe, and George W. Stocking, Jr.

Thus, when I came back to the Greeks, I did so with a particular interest in the German appropriation of classical antiquity and in the history of disciplines, the latter a particular specialty of the University of Chicago. I planned an extensive study of German philhellenism, based both on familiar and prosaic texts, printed sources, and archival records. Fortunately, as a result of a pioneering expedition to the archives in 1987, funded by a summer grant from the Institute for European History, I discovered early in my research both the constraints I would face and the rich documentary material available for the student of the history of archaeology. I chose to focus my attention on this field of thought, which I believed would offer unique insight into the institutional, as well as intellectual, rise and fall of German philhellenism. I hope that this book justifies this initial decision.

In 1989–90, I took advantage of a Social Sciences Research Center grant to do extensive research at the archive of the Deutsches Archäologisches Institut (DAI), the Berlin-Dahlem Staatsarchiv, the Handschriftsabteilung of the Berlin Staatsbibliothek, the Merseberg Zentrales Staatsarchiv (now defunct), the Potsdam Zentrales Staatsarchiv, the Politisches Archiv, Auswärtiges Amt, in Bonn, the archive of the Römisch-Germanische Kommission in Frankfurt, the Bundesarchiv, Koblenz, and the Warburg Institute, London. Thanks to a summer research grant from Princeton University, I was able to return to some of these old haunts in 1993; at that time, I also visited the Bayerisches Hauptstaatsarchiv in Munich and the Archiv der Akademie der Wissenschaften in Berlin. A postdoctoral grant from the Center for European Studies, Harvard University, in 1994–95 allowed me to visit the

Zentralarchiv der Staatlichen Museen zu Berlin and to complete final revisions on the manuscript with full use of the splendid Widener Library. And finally, a Stanley J. Seeger fellowship from the Program in Hellenic Studies at Princeton funded a long-awaited trip to examine the archives of the DAI office in Athens. I would like to express here my deepest appreciation for the kind assistance offered me at all of these institutions, and my thanks to H. D. Schmidt-Ott and Helmut Becker for allowing me access to the papers of Friedrich Schmidt-Ott and C. H. Becker. I am most grateful to Theresa Jaeger Ried for permission to publish her father's portrait and to Ms. Ried and the Houghton Library for allowing me to publish material from the papers of Werner Jaeger. Most especially, however, I would like to thank the staff of the DAI, who have borne my many requests with patience and solicitude.

But archival research alone did not make this book; I have also to thank the staffs of numerous libraries, whose resources I exploited to the best of my abilities. Among these are: the British Library, the Berlin Staatsbibliothek, the Regenstein Library, the Widener Library, the Bayerische Staatsbibliothek (Munich), the Firestone Library, and the Louisiana State University Library, on which I depended while writing up my thesis. I have also made profitable use of photo libraries; I would particularly like to thank Else Schwichtenberg at the Bildarchiv, Preußischer Kulturbesitz, Jörn Grabowski of the Zentralarchiv der Staatlichen Museen, and Rainer Köppe at the Meßbildarchiv.

I owe an unpardonable debt to the many friends and colleagues who have read and commented on this manuscript; their expertise, criticism, advice, and encouragement enriched and improved this project enormously. I am deeply indebted to those who read the entire manuscript: Rachel Lauden and Thomas Broman, whose acute readings forced me to sharpen my argument; Hagen Schulze, who shared his expertise in modern German history; and most especially Peter Brown and Anthony Grafton, whose vast erudition and constant reassurance have been invaluable in keeping me going. I would also like to thank Peter Lake, Robert Darnton, Daniel Rodgers, and the other members of the Princeton History Department who offered me intelligent advice on polishing the manuscript for publication. In addition, many other scholars were kind enough to read chapters or sections, and to offer me helpful comments and criticism: I have particularly to thank Hans Aarsleff, Josine Blok, Philippe Burrin, Susan Crane, James Hankins, Klaus Herrmann, Sally Humphreys, Klaus Junker, Bruce Kuklick, Arno Mayer, Alain Schnapp, and Bonnie Smith. In addition, presentation of chapters at the History of Human Sciences Workshop, University of Chicago, the German Studies Association Conference in Minneapolis, the Hellenic Studies Seminar, Princeton, and the Center for European Studies, Harvard, have all helped me to formulate my thoughts and arguments. Eva Giloi and Martin

Rühl helped to straighten out the footnotes and bibliography. Gavin Lewis, my superb copy editor, has saved me from many miscues, and prevented me from indulging my passion for Germanic phrasing.

Finally, no scholarly project, this one included, can be completed without the support of friends and family. In the former category, I would like to thank my friends from Haste House, Berkeley, Hyde Park, Chicago, LSU in Baton Rouge, Berlin-Dahlem, Princeton, and Cambridge, Massachusetts. But I owe my most heartfelt gratitude to my family, which has endured me and my project, day in, and day out, for more years than I care to count. My parents offered me everything a scholar–daughter requires: no book could possibly repay them for sharing with me their wisdom, curiosity, common sense, diligence, humanity, and compassion. My most profound thanks, however, go to my husband, Victor Stater, who provided the title for this book and the love, humor, and inspiration that allowed its author to write it, revise it, and, at last, let it go.

ABBREVIATIONS

AA	*Archäologischer Anzeiger*
AA zur AZ	*Archäologischer Anzeiger zur Archäologischen Zeitung*
ADAI	Archiv des Deutschen Archäologischen Instituts, Athens
AZ	*Archäologische Zeitung*
BAdW	Berlin, Archiv der Akademie der Wissenschaften
BHStA	Bayerisches Hauptstaatsarchiv, Munich
BM	British Museum, London
BGAEU	Berliner Gesellschaft für Archäologie, Ethnologie und Urgeschichte
BSB	Berlin, Staatsbibliothek
DAI	Deutsches Archäologisches Institut
DAI	Archiv des Deutschen Archäologischen Instituts, Berlin
DGEA	Deutsche Gesellschaft für wissenschaftliche Erforschung Anatoliens
DGfV	Deutsche Gesellschaft für Vorgeschichte
DOG	Deutsche Orient-Gesellschaft
GStAPKB	Geheimes Staatsarchiv, Preußischer Kulturbesitz, Berlin
IfAK	Institut für archäologische Korrespondenz
JbdesDAI	*Jahrbuch des Deutschen Archäologischen Instituts*
KaEET	Kommission für die archäologische Erforschung der Euphrat- und Tigrisländer
KBA	Koblenz, Bundesarchiv
KMK	Kultusminister-Konferenz
KWG	Kaiser-Wilhelm-Gesellschaft
MdesDAI,A	*Mitteilungen des Deutschen Archäologischen Instituts, Athen*
MGH	*Monumenta Germaniae Historica*
MZStA	Merseberg, Zentrales Staatsarchiv
PA/AA/K	Bonn, Politisches Archiv, Auswärtiges Amt, Kulturabteilung
PZStA, AA/K	Potsdam, Zentrales Staatsarchiv, Auswärtiges Amt, Kulturabteilung
PZStA, AA/R	Potsdam, Zentrales Staatsarchiv, Auswärtiges Amt, Rechtsabteilung
PZStA, RMfWEV	Potsdam, Zentrales Staatsarchiv, Reichsministerium für Wissenschaft, Erziehung und Volksbildung
RGK	Römisch-Germanische Kommission

RGK	Archiv der Römisch-Germanischen Kommission, Frankfurt am Main
RGZM	Römisch-Germanisches Zentralmuseum
RLK	Reichslimeskommission
StMBZ IM	Staatliche Museen zu Berlin, Zentralarchiv, Islamisches Museum
StMBZ VAM	Staatliche Museen zu Berlin, Zentralarchiv, Vorderasiatisches Museum
StMBZ AS	Staatliche Museen zu Berlin, Zentralarchiv, Antike Sammlungen
WI	Warburg Institute, London

INTRODUCTION

Our idealistic "Griechheit" will hardly be understood by a
future race of utilitarians, or it will be understood only as we
today understand the enthusiasm for the Crusades.
(*Ferdinand Gregorovius*)

I S IT POSSIBLE to comprehend the utopian zeal with which the Germans of the Enlightenment sought to resurrect and recreate the forgotten truths and beauties of ancient Hellas? Can we now fathom the chi-
liastic aestheticism that brought Schiller to remark, on contemplating a
piece of Greek sculpture: "Man brought something here into being, that is
more than he himself is, that hints at something greater than his own species [*Gattung*]—does this perhaps prove, that [man] is now less than he
will be?"[1] An otherworldly aura, produced by the exquisite beauty of German Romantic poetry and the brilliance of German Romantic philosophy,
surrounds this world of rapturous Graecophilia, making it seem remote
from and nobler than our own world of anti-aestheticizing belles lettres and
careerist specialized scholarship. Yet the world that produced Goethe's *Faust*
and Schiller's *Über die ästhetische Erziehung des Menschen* (*Letters on the
Aesthetic Education of Man*) also called forth the *Gymnasien*, the regimented
classical secondary schools that served as exclusive credentialing institutions
for the bureaucracy and free professions, and that warren of research seminars and experimental laboratories known as the University of Berlin. The
founders of these educational institutions shared Schiller's admiration for
the ancients and his belief in the possibility of human self-transformation
through the cultivation of the arts and sciences; they simply put the emphasis on scholarship (*Wissenschaft*) as the proper means to understand
and appreciate the Greeks. If, ultimately, it was this group's organizational
zeal and intellectual curiosity that transformed the relationship between
Germans and ancient Greeks over the course of the nineteenth century,
their promise to revitalize German culture too, was underwritten by the
aestheticized image of the Greeks bequeathed by the *Goethezeit*. To re-
count the fate of German Graecophilia, then, is not to mourn the diminution of poetic passions or the onset of utilitarian intolerance. To investigate
the wider history of philhellenism, is, rather, to describe the ways in which

In the epigraph, "Griechheit" was also the name of a well-known reading circle composed
of poets and scholars which was founded in the late eighteenth century. See chapter 2.
[1] Schiller quoted in Nikolaus Himmelmann, *Utopische Vergangenheit: Archäologie und Moderne Kultur* (Berlin, 1976), p. 193.

the triumph of historicized classical scholarship over poetry and antiquarian reverie gradually eroded the very norms and ideals that underwrote philhellenism's cultural significance.

Since the publication of Eliza May Butler's *The Tyranny of Greece over Germany* in 1935, the obsession of the Schillerian German literary and scholarly elite with the ancient Greeks has become an accepted—if severely underanalyzed—cliché. Few would, I think, dispute Butler's claim that the ancient Greeks did indeed entrance the educated elite, particularly in Protestant Prussia, and continued to do so long after the *Goethezeit* (age of Goethe) and Greek War of Independence. The elective affinity Germans of the late eighteenth century discovered between themselves and the supposedly noble, naive Greeks became a constantly recurring motif that resounded through the pages of German prose, poetry, and scholarly literature, down (at least) to 1945. But Butler's book, treating only a handful of innovative philosophers and poets, did not examine philhellenism's humanistic sources and pedagogical and scholarly emanations, aspects of the phenomenon essential to an understanding of the sociopolitical means by which this "tyrannical" trope achieved and then preserved its hegemonic cultural position. Writing self-consciously against Nazism's amoral aestheticization of politics and the "otherworldly" irresponsibility of contemporary German writers, Butler did not observe the eminently worldly processes at work in the evolution and degeneration of this Graecophilic tradition. Nor could she, in 1935, clearly comprehend the overall social significance and cultural consequences of the rise and fall of this national obsession for Germany—and by extension, for those cultures that shared some of its educational institutions and cultural norms—in the modern era.

Standing, as we do, at the end of this Graecophilic epoch, the time has perhaps come for a reassessment of German philhellenism's rise and fall, and a consideration of the problem from a different perspective than that presented in Butler's book. Primarily concerned with relationships between sociopolitical phenomena and cultural forms, this book places its focus on institutional developments rather than on individual actors, and on the social functions of Graecophilia rather than on the specific achievements of the scholars and artists under scrutiny. This divergence from the more conventional literary mode springs from my conviction that biographical vignettes, as variable as they are, fail to grasp aspects of German admiration for the ancient Greeks that make this obsession a significant element in modern cultural history as a whole. Most crucially, these works overlook a momentous change in the movement's social function that took place during the nineteenth century. The first German philhellenes borrowed their ideals—self-cultivation, disinterested contemplation of the beautiful, good, and true, admiration of the ancients—from aristocratic models; but the incorporation of nineteenth-century philhellenism into the founding ideals of Prussia's new research universities, secondary schools, museums, and art academies after 1810 universalized these values and in effect imposed them on generations of middle-class Germans. After the Napoleonic Wars, the Romantic generation's cultural successes and political failures were clearly evident in the entrenchment of philhellenism in state-supported educational and cultural institutions, on the one hand, and the silencing of supporters of the Greek revolution on the other. As the century progressed, philhellenism became more and more the conventionalized predilection of the educated middle class (*Bildungsbürgertum*), inextricably linked to the academy and the state bureaucracy. By 1871, Graecophilia had become part of the national patrimony, though eulogies to Athens thereafter frequently papered over a widening gap between a conservative aesthetics and the dynamic forces of specialized scholarship. We would risk overlooking this new and highly significant role of philhellenism in German society, if we were to treat its history only in terms of the activities of individuals.

This emphasis on the social functions and institutional attachments of the Greek ideal should not be construed as an attempt to reduce antiquity's role in modern politics, literature, and scholarship to a purely sociological— or cynical—one. If I emphasize self-interest and downplay intellectual virtuosity and personal commitment, it is not because I have overlooked the passionate devotion to Greek culture that inspired men like Ulrich von Wilamowitz-Moellendorff and Wilhelm Dörpfeld to take up classical scholarship. Nor am I unaware of the role that Greek themes played in the work of nonspecialists such as Arnold Böcklin, Stefan George, and Martin Heidegger, to take just a few examples. But innumerable writers have already described the particularities of these Graecophiles, without, in general, recognizing the debts they owed to the elitist culture of academic neoclassicism. It is my task here, on the other hand, to examine the ways in which individuals such as these were members of what might be loosely termed a "cultural interest group," which sought to defend and preserve the waning social and intellectual credibility of Graecophilia. Philhellenism as an institutionally generated and preserved cultural trope, rather than as a personal passion, lies at the heart of this analysis.

My conviction that philhellenism must be understood, at least in part, as an institutionally entrenched extension of the European humanistic tradition will perhaps illuminate another dimension of this book's form, and that is its focus on the cultural history of classical archaeology. I am convinced that Greek art lies at the center of German philhellenism, and archaeologists, in the nineteenth century, were responsible for discovering, interpreting, and popularizing ancient art. Art was the one realm in which, by the later eighteenth century, the "ancients" had not been definitively defeated by the "moderns," and hence provided an ideal source for neohumanist pedagogical philosophy. The model for self–cultivation (*Bildung*), and the emblem of the nation's rise to museological and intellectual maturity, classical sculpture provided an easily readable image of the society for which the liberal nationalists yearned. And then, of course, there was Winckelmann, the towering example of the man who had fused passion and knowledge, or, flesh and the ideal, in the recent words of Alex Potts.[2] If this Romantic hero had associated Greek art with democracy and suggested it as an antidote to the baroque, Frenchified culture of the German courts, by 1830 the revolutionary political implications of admiring Greek art had been lost. Even nineteenth-century historicism made little headway against the conventional, normative proclamations of Greece's aesthetic superiority. Both scholars and artists celebrated its unique achievements.

But if classical art offered opportunities for agreement between "ancients" and "moderns," archaeology as a scholarly discipline clearly has its origins in "modern" institutional and intellectual contexts. The first German intellectuals to make the study of ancient art their metier were committed to the romantic, neohumanist ideal. But their faith in the possibility of the re-creation of this world grew steadily fainter as the institutionalization, nationalization, and professionalization of the study of classical art progressively exposed the tenuousness of Winckelmann's conclusions about the universality (that is, lack of national mannerisms), serenity (lack of emotional turpitude), and grandeur (lack of ornamental frivolity) of Greek art. Moreover, the demands of "disinterested" scholarship, as well as the defense of established privileges, encouraged classicists and especially archaeologists after 1870 to cultivate a new kind of social legitimacy beyond the neohumanist justification of individual enrichment, one that now exalted the benefits of scholarship for the state. In the last decades of the century, as archaeology shifted its operations from Greece and Rome to Asia Minor and Germany itself, it contributed powerfully to the destruction of both the Romantics' idealized portrait of Hellas and the humanists' elitist *Bildungsideal*. Archaeology is also important in having launched a methodological challenge to the hegemony of philology; as it developed means of "reading" objects rather than texts, it threatened philology's monopoly on the interpretation and even definition of culture, heretofore an attribute only possessed by literate civilizations. Finally, in seeking to defend their social position by opposing educational reforms after the 1890s, the classical archaeologists began to make use of visual aids to demonstrate the glories of Hellas—and of German archaeology. The neo-Romantic aestheticism of some of this material provided the next generation with a set of idealized images of antiquity that were appropriated to dignify racial, as well as cultural, elitism.

---

[2] Alex Potts, *Flesh and the Ideal: Winckelmann and the Origins of Art History* (New Haven, Conn., 1994).

Uniquely shaped by the linkages forged in the post-Napoleonic period between Graecophile aesthetics, specialized scholarship, and state power, the history of classical archaeology, then, is an ideal arena in which to observe and document the series of clashes between neohumanist *Bildung*, "disinterested" *Wissenschaft*, and German nationalism in the last two centuries. In addition, the discipline affords the best documentation available about philhellenism's "external" profile. The high cost and diplomatic entanglements of grand-scale excavation made archaeology the object of much academic-bureaucratic correspondence, and hence it is possible to study in careful detail the process by which scholars, in pursuing their scientific interests, defending their judgments, and defending the cultural institutions built on both interest and taste were (not at all unwillingly) drawn into the realm of what the Germans call *Kulturpolitik*. I fully realize that, in the attempt to comprehend these "external" processes of mediation between the world of thought and the world of political decision-making and social action, I have slighted description of the "internal" development of archaeology as a scholarly field. This is above all the result of my determination to focus on the evolving relationships between humanistic scholarship and the state, rather than to write a history of the discipline of classical archaeology. Disciplinary histories have accorded us the important insight that the differentiation of fields of knowledge requires the articulation of specific objects of analysis to which expert opinion must be applied. It is now time to confront the wider social, cultural, and political implications and consequences of the expansion and new prestige of this sort of expertise in the modern world.

Thus, if this study sheds some light on the meaning of philhellenism's rise and fall for modern Germans, I hope that it will also provoke discussion among intellectual historians about the peculiar cultural conditions that divide us from our early modern predecessors. Recent studies have emphasized the origins of what we once believed to be nineteenth-century ideas and social developments—such as historicism, nationalism, professionalization, or antifeminism—in the eighteenth century and beyond. Though much of this work is very fine, it frequently fails to appreciate the dramatic alterations in Europe's *institutional* landscapes after 1800. Here, the *scale* and *systematic development* of what one might call democratizing forces (such as the rise of mass politics and literacy, the development of communications technology, the new accessibility of institutions of higher learning) on the one hand, and the progressive pressures of scientific and professional specialization on the other, shaped nineteenth-century intellectual life in essential, but little discussed, ways. Without the materialist mechanism of Marxist base/superstructure analyses, now long outdated, it seems, we intellectual historians have lost our ability to connect the changing nature and function of ideas with the new tools, patrons, professional considerations, audiences, and forms of communication that enabled them to become effectual actors in the cultural realm. Establishing the process by which ideas become active forces, and conversely, events or structural factors effect changes in thought, has ever been the intellectual historian's nightmare, one from which I'm afraid we shall never fully awaken. But we in the modern field are particularly obliged not to ignore the traces of these processes of negotiation, mediation, and reproduction that remain and can be recovered; if we overlook the role played by institutions and interest groups in the process by which ideas become effectual and identifiable elements of national consciousness and institutionalized authority, we miss a critical dimension of modern cultural history.

It is also crucial, now, that we begin to work synthetically, to fit our particular objects of study into the larger sweep of complementary, or competing, sociocultural developments. No ideal is an island: each depends on a complex of other ideals, institutions, ideologies, and interest groups for its self-definitions and properties of internal cohesion. Particularly in the period after 1870, during which modernization took divergent paths in various European nations, specific social, economic, and political constellations shaped each country's cultural institutions in important ways. Where political oversight or extensive and continuous patronage intruded into the realm of cultural production (as in the case of school systems or grand-scale scientific projects), most especially, analysis should begin by inspecting the position and function of each ideal in its national intellectual ecosystem.

Philhellenism is no exception to this rule. To understand its social, political, and cultural contours, I found it necessary to investigate rival tropes—for example, orientalism and Germanophilia—and rival pedagogies—clerical and utilitarian—against which philhellenism delimited its intellectual territory and defined its sociocultural aims. Like "Hellas," the "Orient" and "Germandom" were by no means fixed, stable concepts whose interrelationship, once demarcated in the late eighteenth century, remained preserved in imperialist or racist amber. While I applaud the efforts of Edward Said and Martin Bernal to elucidate the operation of these prejudicial Western tropes, I am convinced that the changing parameters and cultural salience of the three geocultural concepts I sketched above depended heavily upon domestic developments that Said and Bernal do not take into account. If I have had to sacrifice international comparisons for the sake of illuminating the peculiarities of the German case, I hope I have provided future comparativists food for thought, and American and English readers a synthetic overview of a field still largely inaccessible to those who do not read German. Once we have reconstructed the thicket of competing ideas and cultural forces our actors inhabited, we will perhaps come to better appreciate the uneven topography of the forest.

This attempt to understand the changing cultural salience of German philhellenism has entailed two additional sacrifices on my part. In focusing on institutional developments, I have attenuated my treatment of those largely excluded from the cultural-political contests of the modern era in Germany, most notably, Catholics and women. We need only mention Ludwig I of Bavaria to be reminded that philhellenism was not confined to Prussia. But Catholic piety restrained attempts to link Bavaria (and also Austria) to Greece without the mediation of Rome; even Ludwig I, as Friedrich Thiersch confided to August Böckh, was torn between fierce loyalty to the Church and Prussian-style free scientific inquiry.[3] German philhellenism partook so heavily of that peculiar form of secularized Lutheranism known as "secularized Protestantism" (*Kulturprotestantismus*) that in 1862 the biographer of the philologist F. A. Wolf felt he had to correct the pervasive impression that Greek was exclusively the language of Protestantism.[4] In addition, the basic institutions of neohumanism—the *Gymnasium* and the philological seminar—were borrowed from the north, and their integration into the Catholic lands occurred less as an abrupt shift in state policy than as a continuation of eighteenth-century classicism.[5] Throughout the Second Empire and into the Weimar period, Berliners controlled central neohumanist institutions like the Deutsches Archäologisches Institut and the Royal Museums. Catholics rarely participated in their activities, sometimes by choice, sometimes by sociological coincidence (there were few Catholics in academia in comparison to their numbers in the general population), sometimes by deliberate exclusion.

Regrettably, too, I will be unable to devote much attention to the women who, by and large, were excluded from participation in neohumanist endeavors and institutions.[6] Classical *Bildung*, as conceived and implemented by Wilhelm von Humboldt, was strictly for boys. If a few women appeared on the periphery—as all-important links between senior scholars and ambitious neophytes, or as audience members at public lectures, or as assistants and copyists—there was no German equivalent of Jane Harrison or Amelia Edwards. Their absence here should not be taken as license to forget their

[3] Thiersch to Böckh, 20 September 1828, in Max Hoffmann, *August Böckh* (Leipzig, 1901), p. 250. See also Manfred Landfester, *Humanismus und Gesellschaft im 19. Jahrhundert* (Darmstadt, 1988), p. 10.

[4] J. F. J. Arnoldt, *Friedrich August Wolf in seinem Verhältnisse zum Schulwesen und zur Pädagogik*, vol. 2 (Braunschweig, 1862), p. 362.

[5] On the origins of the philological seminar in Bavaria, see Rudolf Pfeiffer, "Klassische Philologie," in *Geist und Gestalt: Biographische Beiträge zur Geschichte der Bayerischen Akademie der Wissenschaften*, vol. 1: *Geisteswissenschaften* (Munich, 1959), pp. 113–39. Thiersch, who was instrumental in this process, traveled throughout Germany and the Low Countries in the early 1830s as Ludwig's commissioner for improvement of the school system, and composed a three-volume treatise on educational reform that argued for Bavaria's adaptation of the Prussian system. On classical scholarship in Bavaria, see Anthony Grafton, "The Origins of Scholarship," in *The American Scholar* 48 (Spring 1979): 242–46.

[6] Bonnie Smith's forthcoming book will, I hope, fill this lacuna in the literature, at least for the historical profession. More work, however, remains to be done here.

crucial roles in enabling the existence of the world of "pure scholarship" or their reprehensible exclusion from participation in this world as independent actors. Rather, the reader should assume that women frequently played the sort of part in classical studies assumed by Eduard Gerhard's wife Emilia, who helped him with his work, writing and reading for him when he was weary or ill, entertaining his guests, and running his household so that he could dedicate his time to the pursuit of "pure" knowledge and "ideal" art forms. In expressions like that of Reinhart Kekulé von Stradonitz, that Emilia Gerhard "lived for her husband," we should see an exaggerated but revealing indication of the position these women were expected and compelled to hold.[7] The partial exclusion of Catholics and the nearly total exclusion of women from this world are, I think, sufficient indictments of the blind spots in this classicist community's "universal humanism" to make further comment on this point redundant.

Finally, a word about what I have termed the "decline" of philhellenism, which is, in fact, the principal subject of this book. I hasten to note that one can never predict pedagogical, scholarly, and aesthetic movements, and it would certainly be premature to declare philhellenism, as well as humanistic *Bildung*, dead and gone.[8] Since Roman times, the "ancients" and "moderns" have displaced and then replaced one another as cultural idols, and the future may well hold similar reversals of interest and taste. But classical antiquity will not easily recover its former nimbus of universality, nor will classicists recover their status as disinterested providers of culture without a considerable change in modern outlook; the ambiance of social exclusivity and irrelevance still hangs heavy around Olympus. The weight of demystifying scholarship—both about the ancients and about their modern advocates—is now formidable. Thanks, too, to the Nazis' unscrupulous exploitation of Romantic-era linkages between aesthetic normativity, disinterested science, and state power, it is unlikely that the Bundesrepublik would now wish to claim that its citizens possess some sort of special access to the *Geist* of the ancient Greeks. Unquestionably, the academically inclined will still cultivate their Latin and Greek, but, *with respect to German cultural institutions*, philhellenism has faded from view. *Pace* Gregorovius, Germans have not become uncomprehending utilitarians, but have remade their norms, as well as the entire complex of social and cultural institutions that develop and distribute them. It is to the exploration of this process of intellectual and institutional transformation that the author devotes the following volume.

[7] Reinhart Kekulé von Stradonitz, *Eduard Gerhard* (Berlin, 1910), p. 9.

[8] The *Gymnasium* remains the gateway to membership in an ever-expanding *Bildungsbürgertum*; if some have begun to worry about the overproduction of *Akademiker*, parents are still anxious to enroll their children in the "classical schools."

DOWN FROM OLYMPUS

THE MAKING OF A CULTURAL OBSESSION

In those days, nothing but the Beautiful was divine . . .
(Friedrich Schiller)

ABOVE ALL, the Germans admired the Greeks because the Greeks admired, cultivated, and exemplified the beautiful. Friedrich Schiller was only one among many German Enlightenment figures whose Graecophilia stemmed chiefly from his conviction that to be Greek was to worship beauty, and to live a beautiful life, free from the disfiguring conventions and restrictions of the modern world. Schiller's poem, "Die Götter Griechenlands" ("The Gods of Greece"), first published in the literary journal *Der Teutschen Merkur* (*The German Mercury*) in 1788, contrasted the happy, harmonious, and exquisitely beautiful world inhabited by the Greek deities with the calculating, joyless, and antiartistic present day; a metaphoric north wind had frozen Greece's blossoms, and her riotous crowd of friendly divinities had been replaced by one distant and jealous God. But, as Schiller's critics were quick to point out, the poet's paean to Hellas contained contemporary political implications; if the poem's melancholic paganism first enraged Christian writers, a year later, others began to link his praise for Greece's divine humans to the outbreak of the French Revolution.[1] Rather puzzled by this criticism, and horrified by the Terror, Schiller completed a second version of the poem in 1793, whose central premise is contained in the epigraph above. In the second version, Schiller explicitly offered art as the proper form for the commemoration of Hellas, and implicitly charged his contemporaries with the obligation to compensate for the loss of this earthly paradise by its celebration in "song." "What is to live eternally in song, must lose here its [earthly] life," the new poem concludes.

Most commentators contend that Schiller's revisions mark the abandonment of enlightened Prometheanism for Romantic aestheticism; Schiller is taken to task for retreating from politics into the cultural sphere, for making individual self-transformation the prerequisite for political change, as he seems also to do in the series of letters published as *Über die ästhetische Erziehung des Menschen* (*Letters on the Aesthetic Education of Man*—1793).

---

[1] See, e.g., Friedrich Stolberg's response to Schiller's poem in Dieter Schmidt, ed., *Schillers Werke*, vol. 3 (Frankfurt, 1966), pp. 188–94.

It may indeed be the case that Schiller, like many of his countrymen, was persuaded by events in France (and by Edmund Burke) to take a skeptical view of pure reason and political revolution. But this does not mean that the social criticism implied in Schiller's *Aesthetic Letters* and both versions of his "Gods of Greece" lacked force and transformative effects. The exaltation of a cultural epoch in which "nothing but the Beautiful was divine" in the highly religious, baroque world in which eighteenth-century German Graecophiles lived did represent a challenge to the status quo. That this was a cultural, rather than a political revolution like the one occurring simultaneously in France, owes both to the more limited aims of reform-minded German intellectuals, and to the more repressive state in which they lived. Over the years, historians have often lamented the unwillingness of this generation of Germans to confront political issues head-on, without recognizing that by avoiding political confrontations, the poets and thinkers of the Golden Age were able to accomplish something more feasible given their small numbers, and something they wanted more passionately than political change: the remaking of German culture and cultural institutions. Even this "revolution" was halting and reversible; but the legacy of the Schillerian attack on the Frenchified, courtly culture of the old regimes was lasting, and laid the basis for the creation of the secularized, specialized cultural world of post-unification Germany.

Schiller and his friends, of course, owed a great debt to the humanist tradition, in which Greek contributions to the arts and sciences had long been recognized. But unlike most humanists, German philhellenes did not like to emphasize their dependence on a long tradition of scholarly erudition, or to acknowledge the intermediary function of Rome. This is only one of the many ironies of German philhellenism, that it owes some of its greatest debts to Latin writers and Roman copies of Greek statuary, to Italian humanists and French philosophes; access to things Greek was almost always mediated by the wider culture of Latin learning. But the Germans wished to see themselves as rediscoverers of a lost Arcadia and pioneers of a new kind of pedagogy. And the development of Germany's national self-identification with the Greeks, precisely in its explicit rejection of the culture of "Augustan" neoclassicism, did create a new complex of ideas and ambitions. The singling out of Greece and its rhetorical elevation above Rome were distinctly the product of late Enlightenment social and political conditions, and the extraordinary group of influential intellectuals who shaped this fetish cast a long shadow over German cultural developments in the two centuries to follow.[2] It is the task of this chapter to describe the

---

[2] It was precisely the familiarity of the Italian city and the prevalence of "Augustan" neoclassicism in courtly circles that inclined the German Romantic generation to focus its affections on Greece. Walter Rüegg, "Die Antike als Begründung des deutschen Nationalbewußtseins," in *Antike in der Moderne*, ed. Wolfgang Schuller (*Xenia*, Heft 15) (Konstanz, 1985),

confluence of intellectual, social, and political currents that produced what the Germans would call "neohumanism," whose most characteristic feature, I argue, is its passionate, and nearly exclusive, obsession with Greek beauty.

Greece and Rome were not, of course, the only historical models available to the intellectuals of the Romantic era. They might, for example, have chosen to stake claim to the legacy of the ancient Israelites, as did the English revolutionaries, or to the traditions of the Goths, who did enjoy a certain celebrity in intellectual circles before 1819, thanks to the efforts of literary figures like Klopstock, Novalis, and Heinrich von Kleist. But by the middle of the eighteenth century, Enlightenment skepticism and absorption in the question of the origins of language had revived a Lucretian vision of man's emergence from nature, debilitating the myth of Adam as universal ancestor and desacralizing the role of the Jews in human history.[3] More importantly, perhaps, the ancient Hebrews could not offer the sorts of visual representations of the "natural" world that fired the antibaroque aesthetic imagination and complemented the secular, utopian politics of the late Enlightenment;[4] the iconic power of Greek statuary for the generation of the 1790s should not be underestimated. Finally, the actual presence in German towns and cities of religious Jews made the appropriation of their ancient past problematical.[5] Among the *Bildungsbürger*, the study of the German language was impeded by its association with practical, rather than erudite, schooling and by the post-Renaissance (and post-Reformation) disdain for the culture of the Middle Ages. Moreover, the stress laid upon hermeneutical self-understanding by Wolf, Humboldt, and Schleiermacher underwrote the conviction that classical antiquity remained the proper content for *Bildung*: one had to step into another linguistically constructed world to comprehend one's own. Like the orientalists, the Germanists increased their numbers and professionalized their scholarship; the latter would, at the end of the century, lead a popular revolt against neohumanist education itself.

---

p. 281; Anthony La Vopa, "Specialists Against Specialization: Hellenism as Professional Ideology in German Classical Studies," in *German Professions, 1800–1950*, ed. Geoffrey Cocks and Konrad H. Jarausch (New York, 1990), pp. 30–36; R. S. Turner, "Historicism, *Kritik*, and the Prussian Professoriate, 1790 to 1840," in *Philologie und Hermeneutik im 19. Jahrhundert*, vol. 2, ed. Mayotte Bollack and Heinz Wismann (Göttingen, 1983), pp. 455–56.

[3] Paolo Rossi, *The Dark Abyss of Time: The History of the Earth and the History of Nations from Hooke to Vico*, trans. Lydia G. Cochrane (Chicago, 1984), pp. 267–69; Frank Manuel, *The Broken Staff: Judaism through Christian Eyes* (Cambridge, 1992), pp. 162ff.

[4] Hebrew poetry, on the other hand, was widely revered, most notably by Herder and Lessing.

[5] This problem could, however, be finessed to some extent by ignoring Jewish history, literature, and scholarship since the diaspora, as did Herder and the biblical scholar J. D. Michaelis. Manuel, *The Broken Staff*, pp. 252–69.

But at the moment that reform-minded, aestheticizing nationalists set out in search of an ancient, exemplary ideal, the medieval German world was at once too exotic and too prosaic to suit their needs.

Greece, on the other hand, the powerless and almost extinct nation whose dignity and influence depended solely on its cultural legacy, appealed to the German *Bildungsbürger*, the young man seeking to rise by means of sheer intellect and hard work. Unquestionably, it was men of this ilk who, in the late eighteenth century, endowed German philhellenism with its characteristic aesthetic tenets and sociopedagogical form. Theirs was a generational revolt against religious repression, aristocratic airs, and social immobility; but it was especially a *cultural* revolt, launched by intellectuals whose primary interests lay in the free—but well-funded—cultivation of the arts and sciences and the universalization of nonutilitarian, aristocratic education.[6] Greece appealed to this group not because democracy was born there, or because the Athenians possessed unique freedoms—though these aspects lent Athens charm in some eyes—but because the ancient Greeks had achieved the pinnacle of artistic beauty and scientific genius. The foremost "political" aim of the first Graecophiles was the reconfiguration of German cultural institutions, not the overthrow of the state, and we should not be surprised that having succeeded in the former endeavor, they were not particularly eager to participate in the latter. For, once institutionalized, philhellenism became part of the political landscape of Prussia, and then the *Kaiserreich*; it is undoubtedly telling that its final displacement would require another generational and cultural revolution: the student movement of the 1960s and 1970s.

Over the course of a century and more, German philhellenism moved from left, to liberal, to right, and from the fetish of young outsiders to the credo of aged academicians. Nonetheless, many aspects of eighteenth-century philhellenism proved long-lasting, and left their stamp on German neohumanism and its institutions. The shaping and entrenchment of this common cultural philhellenism rests in large measure on the efforts of three men, on whom, partly from the need to confine the vast reaches of this subject to manageable proportions, this chapter will focus. Johann Joachim Winckelmann, Friedrich August Wolf, and Wilhelm von Humboldt, all figures familiar to German cultural historians, owed much to their milieux, but also were responsible for reformulating the aesthetic, pedagogical, and "scientific" theories and practices of their day to suit new social purposes. Each used his particular variety of philhellenism to counter an unappealing modern world with a stately new model for future generations. The ways in which each of these highly influential men formulated his

[6] English philhellenism, of course, shares important similarities with the German version. See Frank M. Turner, "Why the Greeks and not the Romans in Victorian Britain?" in *Rediscovering Hellenism: The Hellenic Inheritance and the English Imagination*, ed. G. W. Clarke (Cambridge, 1989), pp. 61–82.

Greek ideal were in many respects complementary, and the common as-cetic, moralizing, and elegiac qualities of their thought could not but exert a heavy influence on humanistic education and research. Each, in his own way, contributed to the institutionalization of German admiration for Greek beauty, and, at the same time, to the elaboration of modes of scholarly inquiry that would make this admiration all but impossible to uphold.

J. J. Winckelmann: The Asceticism of Philhellenist Aesthetics

Whether we begin by investigating the origins of German philhellenism, the inspiration for the development or archaeological inquiry, or the fundamen-tal premises of the history of art, we must commence with Johann Joachim Winckelmann. Winckelmann, the poor, self-educated student of Greek lit-erature who discovered in Rome the sublimity of Greek art, acquired con-siderable cachet with the publication in 1755 of his *Gedanken über die Nachahmung der griechischen Werke in der Malerei und Bildhauerkunst (Re-flections on the Imitation of Greek Masterpieces in Painting and Sculpture)*, and even greater prestige with the appearance of his *Geschichte der Kunst des Alterthums (History of Ancient Art)* in 1764. Of course, Winckelmann was not without predecessors; in the artistic realm as in the philological, admiration for the ancients dated back at least to the late medieval period, and had, of course, been the hallmark of the Renaissance. By the time he arrived in Rome in 1755, French and British architects and antiquarians had already produced massive tomes on the subject of Greek art; many of these men had even seen the monuments in Greece, something Winckelmann could never be persuaded to do. By the mid-eighteenth century, handbooks of Greek history were not rare items in Europe, and several French scholars had developed stylistic characterizations of ancient Mediterranean art simi-lar to that which Winckelmann would propound in his *Geschichte der Kunst des Alterthums*. Winckelmann, then, hardly merits the exalted title Goethe later lavished upon him: Columbus to the undiscovered continent of the Greeks he was not.[7]

Yet Winckelmann's vibrant literary style, his rise from Saxon pauper to world-renowned connoisseur and scholar, and his violent end at the hands of his Italian lover, ensured that his work would appeal to scholars and Romantic poets, followers of the enlightenment as well as cultural national-ists. Even if his work was less than wholly original and considerably less than scientifically accurate, the uniqueness of his character and the near

---

[7] See Arnaldo Momigliano, "George Grote and the Study of Greek History," in idem, *Con-tributo alla storia degli studi classici* (Rome, 1955), pp. 213–31; Norbert Miller, "Winckelmann und der Griechenstreit: Überlegungen zur Historisierung der Antike-Anschauung im 18. Jah-rhundert," in *J. J. Winckelmann, 1717–1768*, ed. Thomas W. Gaehtgens (Hamburg, 1986), pp. 239–64, esp. p. 243.

1. The great philhellene J. J. Winckelmann examines an engraving of a Greek nude. Portrait by Anton Maron, 1768. © Bildarchiv, Preußischer Kulturbesitz, 1996

eroticism of his descriptions of Greek sculpture insured that his works would be read by many succeeding generations of Germans. Winckelmann's great popularity with such influential thinkers as Herder, Lessing, Schiller, Goethe, and Humboldt made him the subject of their frequent, reverent mention. Moreover, in part as a result of the accolades of these poets and thinkers, veneration of the philhellene was bequeathed to the nineteenth century as a quasi-national legacy. Goethe's paeans to Winckelmann's originality helped to fulfill his own 1805 prediction that the passionate, ever-striving, and prematurely deceased hero, like Achilles, would exert a powerful allure from beyond the grave.[8]

---

[8] J. W. von Goethe, "Winckelmann," reprinted in Johann Winckelmann, *Geschichte der Kunst des Altertums* (Vienna, 1934), p. 486.

Part of Winckelmann's initial appeal lay in the social implications of his aesthetic predilections, though he himself, existing on the patronage of first Saxon then Roman nobles, never explicitly advocated social change. His Greeks lived in a world without confining clothes or disfiguring diseases, where children were raised to be beautiful and nature revealed its beauties unabashedly before all.[9] The sculptor was meant to represent sublime ideas, not particular (aristocratic) individuals, the painter to "have the fire that Prometheus stole from the gods awakened in him" by painting only noble allegorical themes.[10] His axiomatic praise for the "noble simplicity and serene grandeur" of the perfectly formed Greeks heralded a social revolution against the baroque, aristocratic tastes and values of the old regime. " [T]he cure [for the corruption of society]," as Ludwig Curtius indicates, "which for Rousseau was the return to nature, for Winckelmann was the return to the Greeks. Here essential humanness [allgemeine Menschheit] was to be found, in which, without consideration of status or role, the noble and beautiful in each person was recognized and cultivated."[11]

For Winckelmann's younger contemporaries, nature, in the form of the Greeks, called for the freeing of individual genius from the bondage of artificial social distinctions and overrefined courtly behavior, and they did not miss his insistence that freedom—according to Winckelmann's definition, extant in ancient Greece—was an essential prerequisite of national artistic greatness.[12] Winckelmann's Greeks looked not unlike this generation's image of themselves; youthful, creative, self-sufficient, yearning for self-fulfillment, passionate, uninterested in short-term success or eventual salvation. In the modern world, however, such men were undervalued and their creativity cramped by tyrants of less artistic and more calculating mien; Winckelmann, Herder lamented, was just one of many talented Germans who, dragged down by "slave work," found it preferable to escape into the totally foreign, free world of the Greeks.[13] This association of the Greeks with nature, genius, and freedom, and of the modern world with the unnatural, the overspecialized, and the tyrannical was perhaps Winckelmann's most significant contribution to German philhellenism.

If one attraction of Winckelmann's work was its critical and reformist

---

[9] J. J. Winckelmann, Gedanken über die Nachahmung der griechischen Werke in der Malerei und Bildhauerkunst (Stuttgart, 1969), pp. 6–18.

[10] Ibid., pp. 10–13, 38–39.

[11] Ludwig Curtius, "Winckelmann," in idem, Humanistisches und Humanes: Fünf Essays und Vorträge (Basel, 1954), p. 58. Henry Hatfield notes that the comparison between Winckelmann and Rousseau dates back to Diderot, who contrasted them in his "Salon de Paris" (1765). Henry Hatfield, Winckelmann and his German Critics, 1755–1781 (Morningside Heights, N.Y., 1943), p. 16, n. 130.

[12] See, for example, Winckelmann's treatment of this requirement in his Geschichte der Kunst, p. 130, where he conveniently disregards the practice of slavery in Greece.

[13] See Herder's "Denkmal Johann Winckelmanns" (1777), reprinted in Winckelmann's Geschichte der Kunst, pp. 426–28.

stance, however, a contradictory social position could also be derived from the Graecophile's conception of art as a historical and national-cultural product. Instead of discussing the merits of single works by individual artists, Winckelmann described *the* art of *the* Greeks as an entity unto itself, with its own rules and properties. Making art dependent on its surrounding climate and geography, as well as on the political culture in which it developed, Winckelmann implied that only certain nations of temperate climate and suitable racial stock could produce beautiful art; and only certain facial types, he argued, made fit subjects for beautiful art.[14] Thus the achievement of artistic beauty was less the product of workmanship and expression than of a kind of special revelation, available only to a people chosen by nature as well as God.[15] Like Vico, Winckelmann conceived of human (and art) history as a cyclical rather than a progressive evolution; cultures appear as isolated, autonomous organisms, passing through successive stages of birth, flowering, and decay. Far from Romantic prophecies of eventual world harmony, Winckelmann's *Geschichte der Kunst des Alterthums* sketches a fatalistic chronicle of the waxing and waning of cultural wholes of the sort perfected by Oswald Spengler.

Against the normative spirit of his writings, Winckelmann's art history also opened the possibility of an evaluation of the meaning of objects apart from their aesthetic value. Building upon the work of virtuosi like the Comte de Caylus, Winckelmann sorted objects according to national styles and chronological sequences. His categories owed more to his considerable knowledge of Greek literature than to his quite narrow familiarity with original sculpture; the few monuments he did see in person were largely Roman copies of freestanding, post-Periclean Greek works. But he had studied plenty of ancient gemstones, coins, and figurines in Dresden, and after resettling in Rome, he jealously collected as many artifacts and engravings as time and his patron allowed.[16] Wolf Lepenies has compared the German art historian's emphasis on observation and careful descriptions, but rejection of rote classification, to the work of the eighteenth-century naturalist Buffon.[17] Like Buffon, Winckelmann can be said to have revitalized painstaking study of form by giving it a new, quasi-evolutionary meaning; in this

----

[14] See *ibid.*, pp. 146–48. George Mosse suggests that Winckelmann is the correct starting place for a history of racialist thought in Germany. See Mosse's *Toward the Final Solution: A History of European Racism* (Madison, Wis., 1985).

[15] Alexander Demandt, "Winckelmann und die alte Geschichte," in Gaehtgens, *Winckelmann*, p. 303.

[16] See Maria Grazia Lolla's excellent chapter in her recent Cambridge University doctoral dissertation: "'Monuments' and 'Texts': Antiquarianism and Literature in Eighteenth- and Early Nineteenth-Century Britain" (1996).

[17] Wolf Lepenies, "Fast ein Poet: Johann Joachim Winckelmanns Begründung der Kunstgeschichte," in idem, *Autoren und Wissenschaftler im 18. Jahrhundert* (Vienna, 1988), pp. 95–98.

way, Winckelmann's work points ahead to the historicizing typologies of the mid- to late nineteenth century.

If Winckelmann's writings helped to usher in a new respect for and interest in the study of objects, however, he also shared with many of his contemporaries a sort of aesthetic predilection for words over things, mind over matter, and the creative formulation of ideals over the exact copying of nature. This predilection was a pan-European phenomenon, evolving over the course of the eighteenth century as philosophers began to challenge the scholarly predominance of the detail-absorbed antiquarians and *érudits*. It was shared by neoclassicists and early Romantics; Edward Young and Lord Shaftesbury in England, Diderot in France, and Kant and Herder in Germany rejected the French Academy's principles for assessing the value of works of art, which were based on the mimetic attributes of the work and its subject matter, and emphasized instead the artist's creative powers. As one critic describes it, a "missionary zeal" seized critics of rococo superficiality and sensuousness all over Europe. Rejecting the visual deceptions and dense ornament of the courtly art of their day, they found in antiquity timeless, simple, and communicable truths.[18] This vogue in aesthetic thought gave art a purpose beyond merely pleasing the spectator: because art expressed ideas behind the surface forms, art could—and possibility here implied normativity—reach down into the soul of the spectator and *form* him.

In Germany, the Pietist emphasis on inwardness and individual self-discipline, horror of material comforts, and tendency to exalt sentimental (but restrained) emotionality exacerbated this trend toward greater solemnity and purer form. In spite of his admiration for the sensuous qualities of Greek sculpture, Winckelmann's essays dwell not on the particularities of the objects, but rather on their ideal forms. His instructions on creating beautiful art, derived from Aristotle's account of the compositional style of the painter Zeuxis, required the artist to select the best parts of several different models and mold these together into a whole, more beautiful than nature itself. Winckelmann very specifically outlawed mere copying from nature; this was the flaw in the work of Dutch painters as well as in the "cold" realism of his own countrymen.[19] In his *Geschichte der Kunst des Alterthums* he noted that even in Greece, bodies as they occurred in nature were rarely perfect, leading Greek artists to develop a new compositional style:

> these wise artists behaved like good gardeners, who graft different shoots of the finest sorts onto one branch; as a bee drinks from many flowers, likewise

---

[18] Hugh Honour, *Neoclassicism* (Harmondsworth, Middlesex, 1968), pp. 19–20; see also Rensselaer Lee, *Ut Pictura Poesis* (New York, 1967).

[19] Carl Justi, *Winckelmann und seine Zeitgenossen*, vol. 1 (1943; reprint ed., Hildesheim, 1983), p. 433; Hatfield, *Winckelmann*, p. 9.

[the Greek] concept of beauty was not reducible to individual, particular beauties . . . but [Greek artists] sought the beautiful in uniting many beautiful forms [*Körpern*]. They purified their images of all personal characteristics, which would divert our minds from the truly beautiful.[20]

This exaltation of nonmimetic composition and its accompanying emphasis on the departicularizing of the artist's representation of ideal beauty runs through Winckelmann's work and underlies his claim for the universal significance of Greek art. As usual, Winckelmann's counterexample is baroque art, specifically that of Bernini, which takes its "degenerate" forms immediately from nature and appeals only to the unsophisticated mob of spectators who are pleased by superficial visual trickery. Greek forms, on the other hand, appeal not to our "lusts" (*Wollust*), which are particular and highly variable, but to our understanding, which, in Winckelmann's view, is the faculty most likely to produce universal concurrence in judgments of taste.[21] In sum, Greek art is great because, appealing to the mind rather than merely to the senses, it refers least of any national style to its particular context and is most likely to occasion universal agreement that it is beautiful.

It is hard to resist the conclusion that Winckelmann, despite his vivid descriptions and homoerotic sensibilities, was in matters of taste not only a Platonist but also something of an ascetic. He preferred drawing to painting, contour to color, nakedness to clothing, smooth surfaces to ornamentation. He lauded white above all other colors and water above all other substances, for these were the purest forms matter could take.[22] In fact, the less matter-like art was, for Winckelmann, the more it conformed to the supreme exemplar of the beautiful, God. "The highest beauty is in God," he averred, "and the conception of human beauty will be more perfect, the more it is thought to be in accordance and agreement with the highest Being, which we differentiate from matter by means of the concepts of unity and indivisibility."[23] Winckelmann, his great nineteenth-century biographer Carl Justi commented, was horrified by ornamentation without a sublime thought behind it, and he was always urging painters to become less illu-

---

[20] Winckelmann, *Geschichte der Kunst*, p. 155.

[21] Ibid., pp. 139–47.

[22] In describing the contradictions in Winckelmann's discussion of the "high" style, Alex Potts has recently captured this asceticism in one lovely phrase: "The most immediate and powerful impact on the spectator is effected by an almost substanceless image that is purged of the very variety, emotive expressiveness, and sensual appeal conventionally taken to constitute the interest of the visual image." Potts, *Flesh and the Ideal: Winckelmann and the Origins of Art History* (New Haven, Conn., 1996), pp. 111. Potts then enters into a highly interesting discussion of the relationships between this depiction of the "high" style and Winckelmann's homoerotic narcissism; ibid., pp. 132ff.

[23] Winckelmann, *Geschichte der Kunst*, p. 149.

sionistic and more poetical or allegorical.[24] It would be unfair to say that Winckelmann, who could also wax rhapsodic over select paintings, was wholly unappreciative of the sensuous pleasures of the visual arts, but even here he awarded top honors to Raphael, Poussin, and Anton Mengs—masters, he argued, of drawing and allegorical composition. It is highly probable that the Saxon tutor would have endorsed the nineteenth-century adage cited by Rudolf Haym in his biography of Wilhelm von Humboldt, that Raphael would have been a great painter even had he been born with no hands.[25]

Lessing's *Laokoon* (1766) owes a number of debts to Winckelmann, not least its view of the sculpture itself. Both Lessing and his Graecophile predecessor note that whereas in Virgil's account of the tale, Laocoon lets out a terrible cry, the sculpture depicts the sufferer with closed lips. Lessing uses this difference in representation to draw a distinction between the oral and visual arts. Yet if Lessing's pivotal aesthetic treatise liberates sculpture and painting from the French Academy's doctrine of *ut pictura poesis*,[26] he has clearly created a new hierarchy of the two separate forms: the "picturesqueness" of painting cannot compare to the wholeness, movement, and expressiveness of poetry. As E. H. Gombrich once suggested, "the more one reads *Laokoon*, the stronger becomes the impression that it is not so much a book about as against the visual arts."[27] Another critic has even accused the dramatist of displaying a "fear of images";[28] in any event, Lessing's treatment of Greek art simply exacerbated the tendency in Winckelmann's work to equate the beautiful with the nonmaterial.

Herder, too, though he believed that there was no single standard for beauty in the arts, still emphasized form over color, sculpture over painting, and both poetry and music over the visual arts. In part four of his *Kritische Wäldchen* (*Critical Groves*—1769), Herder recommended that the student learn to form himself by standing before the works of Phidias and Lysippus with his eyes closed, simply *feeling* "the first ideas of beautiful nature, of fine forms of expression and handling, in this holy darkness."[29] In fact, darkness plays a major role in Herder's work on aesthetic perception; he frequently refers to Diderot's *Lettre sur les aveugles* (1749), praising its de-

---

[24] Justi, *Winckelmann*, 1:444; see also the last section of the *Gedanken*, entitled "Allegorie," and his treatise on painting, *Versuch einer Allegorie* (Dresden, 1766).

[25] See Rudolf Haym, *Wilhelm von Humboldt: Lebensbild und Charakteristik* (Osnabrück, 1856), p. 231.

[26] See Lee, *Ut pictura poesis*.

[27] E. H. Gombrich, "Lecture on a Master Mind: Lessing," in *Proceedings of the British Academy* 43 (1957): 140.

[28] See W. J. T. Mitchell, *Iconology* (Chicago, 1986), pp. 113ff.

[29] Johann Gottlieb Herder, "Kritische Wälder," in idem., *Sämtliche Werke*, vol. 4, ed. Bernhard Suphan (Berlin, 1878), p. 157.

piction of the superior imaginative powers of the blind.[30] Diderot had argued that the man born blind had fewer fixed forms cluttering up his imagination and thus sensed heat, weight, sound, and time better than the ordinary man; Herder added a characteristically Pietist emphasis on the fleeting world of illusory appearance. Were we all blind, he speculated, we could abandon our alienating attachments to appearances and understand ourselves more clearly. Our language itself could be purged of abstract words and "painterly descriptions" so that we, like the blind man, could feel the powers of the soul working within us, for while bound to the visible world, "we are too distracted [zerstreut], too thrown out of ourselves, to think about it."[31] Though Herder wished simply to give each art form its own particular criteria of perfection, his stress on the distracting and illusory nature of seeing stands as a testimony to the introspectiveness and idealism of his unintentional hierarchy of the arts.[32]

Immanuel Kant's *Critique of Judgment* (1791) departed radically from Enlightenment aesthetics but retained, importantly, the ascetic, neoclassical predilections of Kant's antecedents. In this third critique, so central to Romantic thought, Kant shifted the focus of aesthetic inquiry from the stimulus to the stimulation itself, from the qualities of the object to the harmony or "fit" of the feeling occasioned by the experience of the object with the patterns of the mind. Kant located the cognitive process of aesthetic apperception between those of a priori logic and a posteriori reason; the judgment of art and nature was supposed to bridge the gaps left by the previous two critiques between subjectivity and universality, nature and freedom, theoretical knowledge of phenomena and practical reason, and to serve as a kind of propaedeutic for the application of the categorical imperative.[33] To provide this bridge, however, Kant had to tackle the problem raised by Winckelmann, and more recently, by David Hume: how can judgments of taste be authoritative when different judges invariably disagree about which objects are beautiful? Kant's solution to this problem of rampant, observable subjectivity in judgments of taste leaves his theory of art slanted heavily against "illusory" and "sensory" arts like painting. The essential element of art, for Kant, is its formal purposiveness—only this trains the mind for moral ideas. Only delineation, form, admits of universal commu-

---

[30] See esp. ibid., 8:96ff. Diderot's essay can be found in *Œuvres complètes*, vol. 4 (Paris, 1978), pp. 1–127.

[31] Herder, "Studien und Entwürfe zur Plastik," in idem, *Sämtliche Werke*, ed. Bernhard Suphan, 33 vols. (Berlin, 1877–1913), 8:96–97.

[32] For a much more sophisticated reading of Herder's aesthetics, see Robert E. Norton, *Herder's Aesthetics and the European Enlightenment* (Ithaca, N.Y., 1991), especially pp. 216–32.

[33] On the subject of making judgments of taste as a kind of analogue for judging whether one's will is good, see Ted Cohen, "Why Beauty Is a Symbol of Morality," in *Essays in Kant's Aesthetics*, ed. Ted Cohen and Paul Guyer (Chicago, 1982), pp. 221–36.

nicability; elements such as ornament, color, tone, introduce "empirical satisfaction" (charm or emotion) and thus only distract from judgments of beauty.[34] Like Lessing and Herder, Kant considered poetry the highest form of art; enjoyment of the nonvisual arts gave greater scope for the free exercise of the imagination and thus approximated most nearly the experience of moral action.

Herder, Kant, and Lessing, like Winckelmann, preferred sculpture to other visual arts, especially sculpture that depicted the human body. Winckelmann's exaltation of the human form may have originated in the French Academy's hierarchy of subjects, reaching from history painting at the top to landscape and still life at the bottom. He might have found the same predilections in his study of ancient and Renaissance aesthetics, or in his early training in theology (after all, God created man in his image). But after 1755, it was clearly Winckelmann's passion for the genre that younger writers echoed. Lessing's distaste for painting has already been noted. Herder, too, preferred sculpture to painting; for the former, he contended, re-created something essential and eternal, the human form, while painting merely pleased the eye with its lovely illusions.[35] Kant, who seems to have studiously ignored the painting collections accessible to him in Königsberg, ranked sculpture above painting and its kindred "illusory" arts (landscape gardening, the decoration of interiors, and "the art of tasteful dressing"), as only in this genre could moral, universal ideas be represented.[36] Goethe, who was able even to appreciate landscape painting, argued that sculpture deserved the high regard accorded to it "because it can and must bring representation to its highest point, for it strips away from man all that is not essential to him."[37] And Hegel argued that the human body provided both the form and content of classical art, a unity of internal and external that made classical sculpture equivalent to true art in its essential nature.[38] With the connivance of such revered cultural figures, Winckelmann's Platonic Pygmalionism would leave its traces on succeeding generations of German art historians and aesthetes, who were slow to rescind this identification of true beauty and Greek sculpture.

In large measure as a result of Winckelmann's influence, the aesthetic philosophy of the late eighteenth century exalted Greek art as the symbol

[34] See Immanuel Kant, *Critique of Judgment*, trans. J. H. Bernard (New York, 1951), p. 170 (sec. 52); pp. 58–62 (secs. 13 and 14). For some remarks on the social implications of Kant's asceticism, see Pierre Bourdieu, *Distinction: A Social Critique of the Judgement of Taste*, trans. Richard Nice (Cambridge, Mass., 1984).

[35] Herder, *Werke*, 8:120–26.

[36] Walter Kaufmann, *Goethe, Kant, and Hegel: Discovering the Mind*, vol. 1 (New Brunswick, N.J., 1991), pp. 149–53. Kant, *Critique of Judgment*, pp. 164–69, 68–73 (secs. 51 and 17).

[37] Goethe, "Über Laocoon," in *Werke*, vol. 12 (Hamburger Ausgabe; Munich: 1981), p. 59.

[38] See Hegel, *Aesthetics*, vol. 1, trans. T. M. Knox (Oxford, 1975), p. 434.

and embodiment of humankind's true, free, uncorrupted nature. But just as Rousseau recognized that insuperable barriers prevented modern man from actually returning to the state of nature, German Romantics like Herder, Schiller, and Goethe acknowledged that the ancient world as such could not be recaptured. Slavish imitation of the Greeks would be of no avail, they contended; only the Greek spirit (*Geist*) could be re-created, in forms suitable to the modern age. "Everyone should be Greek in his own way! But he should be Greek!" Goethe cried.[39] Thus in *Faust*, part 2, though the hero conjures up and even weds Helen of Troy, he cannot possess her, and she disappears, leaving him holding only her veil. This short episode has been invoked by every generation of Germans since Goethe to symbolize the true nature of the German-Greek relationship: a marriage in spirit alone, an unsatisfied and unsatisfiable longing, a noble if deeply melancholy resignation to what Nietzsche once called mere "metaphysical solace"[40]—although, as we will see, the later nineteenth century saw the rise of a new thirst to consummate this marriage by actually possessing the spiritual goods of Greece. As we move first to a discussion of the development of classical philology and then to the institutionalization of neohumanist pedagogy, we would do well to keep in mind the peculiar asceticism and aestheticism of this Graecophilia, captured so profoundly in the image of Faust clutching Helen's veil.

F. A. Wolf and the Ascension of *Altertumswissenschaft*

If German philhellenism was marked by aesthetic asceticism and deep aversion to courtly tastes, it was also shaped to a great degree by the German university culture of the post-Enlightenment. Since the Reformation, a number of important German humanists had occupied university professorships, and the international culture of gentlemanly collectors and text critics did indeed depend in myriad ways on princely patrons. But in the early modern era, humanism's "republic of letters" had never been exclusively academic, nor were all of its sustaining funds provided by heads of state. Of course, as aristocratic patronage receded and universities gained greater respectability in the later eighteenth century, humanists sought niches in the academic world. But nowhere so much as in late Enlightenment Prussia did humanistic scholarship gravitate so quickly toward the

[39] Johann Wolfgang von Goethe, "Antik und Modern," in *Die schönsten Aufsätze Goethes*, ed. Horst Oppel (Recklinghausen, 1948), p. 493.

[40] For a recent example, see Walter Leifer, *Hellas im deutschen Geistesleben* (Herrenalb, Schwarzwald, 1963), p. 95. Nietzsche's comment comes in *Zarathustra*, part 4 (1886), reproduced in Francis Golffing's translation of his *The Birth of Tragedy and the Genealogy of Morals* (New York, 1956), p. 14.

universities, and nowhere were so few respectable humanists left outside state institutions. Though Bismarck, like the lesser members of his bureaucracy, attended a *Gymnasium*, it is hardly thinkable that he might have produced a multivolume commentary on Homer, as did his contemporary William Gladstone. As Heinrich Schliemann would discover to his intense annoyance, nineteenth-century Germany had little but contempt for humanists lacking professional credentials.

Importantly, academic study of the ancient world was from the outset dominated by scholars trained in philology, the art of textual emendation and interpretation. Already a respected occupation in the medieval world, philology made the transition from religious to secular texts during the Renaissance with its lofty status intact; as esteemed members of the learned estate (*allgemeiner Gelehrtenstand*), classical philologists played an important role in perpetuating the estate's culture of eloquent and erudite Latin learning.[41] In the Germanies, the close ties established by Luther and Melanchthon between classical and biblical studies also made philology a crucial component of theological inquiry; the gradual adoption of Roman Law, too, made the study of Latin and the history of Roman institutions vital to members of the juridical faculty.[42] If, as nineteenth-century scholars would contend, philology in this premodern era remained a *Hilfswissenschaft*, an ancillary, subordinate, science, their achievements depended in many ways on the mass of technically brilliant and historically exacting philological scholarship produced by their sixteenth-, seventeenth-, and eighteenth-century predecessors.[43]

By the end of the eighteenth century, new interest in the ancients, especially in the Greeks, aroused by new translations of the Homeric poems (there were six between 1754 and 1793),[44] well-publicized voyages to the Peloponnese, and Winckelmann's reveries, opened the prospect of independent academic standing and, correspondingly, improved social status, for classical specialists. That this portent was fully realized owes much to the work of Friedrich August Wolf, with whom nineteenth-century classical scholarship—described by Wilamowitz as the completion of "the conquest of the ancient world by scholarship"[45]—properly commences. The oft-related tale crediting Wolf with being the first student to matriculate in

[41] Turner, "The Prussian Professoriate," p. 453.

[42] See James Q. Whitman, *The Legacy of Roman Law in the German Romantic Era: Historical Vision and Legal Change* (Princeton, N.J., 1990).

[43] For novel insight into this complex baroque world and its castigation by later critics, see Anthony Grafton, *Defenders of the Text: The Traditions of Scholarship in an Age of Science, 1450–1800* (Cambridge, Mass., 1991); Momigliano, *The Classical Foundations of Modern Historiography* (Berkeley, Calif., 1990).

[44] John Edwin Sandys, *A History of Classical Scholarship*, 3 vols. (New York, 1964), 3:8.

[45] Ulrich von Wilamowitz-Moellendorff, *History of Classical Scholarship*, trans. Alan Harris (London, 1982), p. 105.

philology is apparently apocryphal.[46] But Wolf's determined rejection of theological training did clearly herald a new determination on the part of classicists to wrest pedagogy and scholarship from clerical control. Wolf may not deserve credit for pioneering historical philology, but his fusion of neohumanist pedagogical tenets with a rigorous method of source criticism, a pugnacious secularism, and a single-minded devotion to the glorious Greeks amounted to a clear declaration of philological autonomy. His widely read Latin study of Homer, published in 1795, provided, as Anthony Grafton has described, "the manifesto of the German historical spirit, the charter of classical scholarship as an independent discipline."[47]

Born in 1759, F. A. Wolf undoubtedly owed much of his precocity to his father, a schoolteacher; at the age of six, Wolf already knew some Greek and a good deal of Latin and French.[48] As a student at Göttingen, Wolf refused to apprentice himself to the world-famous classicist there, C. G. Heyne, and instead retreated to his study where he performed feats of self-discipline reminiscent of medieval monastic practices. Like Heyne, who slept only two nights a week for six months in an attempt to read all the classical authors as swiftly as possible, Wolf is said to have staved off sleep by denying himself heat, submerging his feet in cold water, and binding up one eye (to rest it, while the other read on).[49] But beyond hard work and intelligence, Wolf required a patron, for, as Heyne had warned him upon his matriculation, the study of classical philology for its own sake set Wolf on "the straight road to starvation."[50] Instead of applying to Heyne, the obvious choice, Wolf in the 1780s sought and won the support of the Prussian education administration, at the time headed by the reform-minded minister K. A. von Zedlitz.[51] In 1783, Wolf accepted Zedlitz's offer of a position as professor of pedagogy and philosophy at the University of Halle. The troubled, overly theoretical pedagogical seminar soon collapsed, but in 1787, to his great delight, Wolf was allowed to fashion a philological seminar to replace it. His new program of study explicitly disavowed any connection to pedagogical theory and aimed instead at the production of expert classical scholars.[52]

[46] Rudolf Pfeiffer, *History of Classical Scholarship from 1300 to 1850* (Oxford, 1976), p. 173.

[47] Anthony Grafton, Glenn W. Most, and James E. G. Zetzel, "Introduction," in F. A. Wolf, *Prolegomena to Homer, 1795*, trans. Grafton, Most, and Zetzel (Princeton, N.J., 1985), p. 29; see also Grafton, "Prolegomena to Friedrich August Wolf," *Journal of the Warburg and Courtauld Institutes* 44 (1981): 103–9.

[48] Anthony La Vopa, *Grace, Talent, and Merit: Poor Students, Professional Careers, and Professional Ideology in Eighteenth-Century Germany* (Cambridge, 1988), p. 311.

[49] David Constantine, *Early Greek Travellers and the Hellenic Ideal* (Cambridge, 1984), p. 85.

[50] Quoted in Sandys, *History of Classical Scholarship*, 3:52.

[51] For details on Wolf's early career, see J. F. J. Arnoldt, *Friedrich August Wolf in seinem Verhältnisse zum Schulwesen und zur Paedagogik*, vol. 1 (Braunschweig, 1861), pp. 45–59.

[52] La Vopa, *Grace, Talent, and Merit*, pp. 313–15. The basic form of the pedagogical seminar had in turn been borrowed from the theologians. See Hans Aarsleff, *The Study of Language in England 1780–1860* (Minneapolis, 1983), p. 180.

Not only would this approach produce the top-ranking classicists of the next generation, but the seminar itself provided a much-imitated organizational model for the new or reorganized universities of the nineteenth century.[53]

Paradoxically, Wolf's Halle seminar commenced its activity in the midst of agitation by reform-minded educators for "dead language" instruction to be replaced with lessons in the sciences and other "useful" subjects.[54] Wolf too wished to see higher education reformed—but felt that universities already taught too many "useful" subjects and instead should dedicate their efforts to the pursuit of knowledge for its own sake. An ardent Graecophile, Wolf was also contemptuous of the aristocracy's eclectic tastes and superficial cultivation; his ascetic attitude toward teaching and scholarship betrays the same antipathy for ornamentation, sensuality, and sloth discernible in Winckelmannian aesthetics. In Wolf, too, there is a palpable antiutilitarian spirit: he deplores the worldly ambitions of those seeking to use their knowledge for personal gain and applauds the unselfish pursuit of "disinterested" learning. Students today, Wolf wrote in an 1803 memorandum for Civil Cabinet director K. F. Beyme, lack self-discipline and heartfelt interest in their studies, a condition that in turn has caused the decline of scholarly instruction. "The great majority [of students]," Wolf complained,

> see their studies as a kind of manual labor, and have no further goal than receiving a post by passing the usual exam—and the craving arises from this to spend the hours that remain after writing their exercises in the most pleasurable [*lustig*] way possible. Their lectures are also chosen on these grounds. . . . There are only a very few, select souls who really have a deep interest in their chosen field.[55]

Wolf was anxious that his philologists provide a counterexample to this crass materialism and self-indulgence; ironically, his faith in the power of philological study to instill self-discipline, idealism, and nobility of character continued to be echoed by many civil servants and free professionals of the later nineteenth century, to whom *Gymnasium* Greek and Latin drills had become merely the means to lucrative white-collar careers.

Wolf's two major works, his *Prolegomena ad Homerum* (*Prolegomena to Homer*—1795) and his *Darstellung der Altertumswissenschaft* (*Classical Scholarship: A Summary*—1807) did not mark significant departures either

---

[53] The universities of Berlin and Bonn (established in 1810 and 1811, respectively), followed this form, as did many other European and American universities. On American borrowings, see Carl Diehl, *Americans and German Scholarship, 1770–1870* (New Haven, Conn., 1978).

[54] See Lenore O'Boyle, "Klassische Bildung und soziale Struktur in Deutschland zwischen 1800 und 1848," *Historische Zeitschrift* 207, no. 3 (December 1968): 58.

[55] Wolf quoted in Helmut Schelsky, *Einsamkeit und Freiheit: Idee und Gestalt der deutschen Universität und ihrer Reformen* (Reinbeck bei Hamburg, 1963), p. 54.

in philological method or in the interpretation of Homer.[56] But in combining the systematic approach to textual interpretation pioneered by the biblical scholar J. G. Eichhorn and contemporary thinking on the Homeric question, Wolf demonstrated the fundamental importance of the establishment of authentic texts to interpretations of their history, authorship, and meaning, and hence provided a justification for philological, as opposed to philosophical, expertise.[57] In addition, though Wolf borrowed his view of poetic composition from Herder and others, he was the first to show how the history of the Greek language could be used to verify his claims. Access to the Greek mind was to proceed by means of strict attention to linguistic, grammatical, and orthographic detail; as Rudolf Haym described the method, "Wolf made the most precise determination of the letter [of the text] the indispensable prerequisite for understanding the spirit and the beautiful substance [Schönheitsgehalt] of the ancients."[58] It is the establishment and legitimation of this professional, dispassionate, exacting approach to Greek texts that must be attributed, above all, to Wolf; if he pined for the Peloponnesian past as ardently as did Schiller or Keats, he expressed his ardor in wholly unpoetic terms.

In the Prolegomena, Wolf subjected the ancient recensions of the epic poems to a thorough historical investigation; to use his own metaphor, he put the manuscripts on trial, attempting to determine the conditions of their appearance and, ultimately, their proximity to the irrecoverable urtext.[59] In seeking to establish the textual history of the poem, Wolf found novel ways to use his profound knowledge of ancient sources. For example, to buttress his contention that the poems acquired written form only in the mid-sixth century B.C., under Pisistratus, tyrant of Athens, he used historical linguistics to show interpolations in the earliest manuscripts, commonsensical reasoning about the constraints of oral poetry, and a carefully defended argument from silence (classical commentators found no mention of writing in the Homeric poems).[60] At once self-effacing and self-promoting, Wolf's Prolegomena keeps up a running commentary on the work of the philologist himself, what he knows and what he suspects, what authorities he trusts and what leaps in logic he is allowed. One might even say that it is more an introduction to the mental world of the academic philologist than to that of Homer, who figures in the work only as a distant voice, speaking from the murky depths of an illiterate—and hence irrecoverable—age.

Wolf's Altertumswissenschaft explicitly excluded from its domain many of the cultures we now believe constitutive of the ancient world. His

[56] See Grafton, *Defenders of the Text*, pp. 214–43.
[57] See Grafton, "Introduction," in Wolf, *Prolegomena*, pp. 18–26.
[58] Haym, *Humboldt*, p. 71.
[59] See Wolf, *Prolegomena*, pp. 44–45.
[60] Ibid., e.g., pp. 62–63, 122, 93.

Darstellung separated Greeks and Romans from Egyptians, Jews, Persians, and other "Orientals," describing only the first two in the list as possessing "a higher *Geistescultur* (intellectual culture) of their own." The latter, he argued, had only reached the level of "bürgerliche Policirung oder Civilisation [policed civility or civilization]."[61] Wolf underlined the necessity that a culture possess security, order, and leisure in order to develop noble perceptions and knowledge—conditions not, apparently, met by the Egyptians or Persians. It was especially vital that a culture develop a literature of its own, one issuing from the nation as a whole, rather than from a caste of bureaucrats or accountants. Here Wolf had to resort to some bizarre digressing to justify his exclusion of the Jews—their art was too unappealing to European tastes, he argued, to be included with that of the Greeks and Romans.[62] Thus, Greek and Roman civilization constituted *Altertum* (antiquity) as a whole, while other ancient peoples were consigned to being "Barbari."[63] Several pages later, Wolf narrowed his field of vision again, confining the Romans to rhetorical, martial, and especially curatorial successes; if, to their credit, they had recognized the greatness of Greek culture, "the Romans," he wrote, "were not a people of original talents."[64] By the end of the piece, Wolf has advanced to the position that knowledge of any other people besides the Greeks is not essential, for only the Greeks manifest the ostensibly fundamental qualities of "true humanness."[65]

But if the recovery of the spirit of the Greeks required precise, historical interpretation of texts, Wolf also enjoined his students not to ignore the contribution that knowledge of subfields like epigraphy and numismatics could make to the reconstruction of the ancient world. In his *Prolegomena* Wolf had announced his view "that exact knowledge of the Greek language is not sufficient equipment for understanding the poems of farthest antiquity in terms of the talent and genius of their authors."[66] *Altertumswissenschaft*, for Wolf, encompassed twenty-four disciplines, from grammar to geography, all of which, theoretically, the student should master in order to help decipher the evidence given by a text. Wolf differentiated between six "first-class" disciplines (linguistic, metrical, and grammatical), and eighteen belonging to the "second class" (including numismatics, history, geography, and several kinds of archaeology), thus making manifest his own

---

[61] F. A. Wolf, "Darstellung der Altertumswissenschaft," in *Kleine Schriften*, vol. 2, ed. G. Bernhardy (Halle, 1869), p. 817.

[62] Ibid., pp. 817–19. In his university lectures, Wolf frequently depreciated the Jews as "the nation that the Greeks described as having invented nothing at all." See Arnoldt, *Wolf*, 2 (Anhang): 394.

[63] Wolf, "Darstellung," p. 819.

[64] Ibid., p. 821.

[65] Ibid., p. 887.

[66] Wolf, *Prolegomena*, p. 73.

hierarchy of words and things.[67] One commentator has argued persuasively that the articulation of *Altertumswissenschaft* was in fact part of an "expansionist program" launched by philologists in search of social legitimacy, and may have even preserved for philology a dominant position in the academy after the first flush of enthusiasm for the field had passed.[68] Whether intentionally expansionist or not, Wolf's program succeeded in joining philology to other sorts of historical inquiry in a way that preserved textual interpretation's predominance. By the time of his death in 1824, Wolf's vision had prevailed; the "road to starvation," classical philology, had become the recognized foundation for professionalized humanistic scholarship.

Wolf's triumph, of course, was neither immediate nor complete. Competing philological schools, like that of Gottfried Hermann, persisted, and especially outside Prussia, neohumanist ideals were never realized to the extent nostalgic professors of the 1890s and 1900s believed they had been. But Wolf was well placed to exert great influence on future generations of university students and scholars. The next section will show how Wolf's friendship with Wilhelm von Humboldt resulted in the institutionalization of Wolf's text-critical method (together with Humboldt's neohumanist pedagogy) in the Prussian *Gymnasien* and universities. Yet Humboldt was not Wolf's only well-placed admirer; as we have seen, Wolf had already earned the patronage of K. A. von Zedlitz in the early 1780s, and by the turn of the century, he was advising Civil Cabinet head K. F. Beyme on arrangements for a new institute of higher learning to be built in Berlin.[69] Goethe, who had multiple ties to the Saxon court, hid behind a curtain to hear Wolf's lectures, and in 1796, Wolf was offered the premier position in classics in Europe: the chair at the University of Leyden. He declined, and continued to lecture at Halle until the French occupation of the city in 1806 abruptly ended his tenure. In 1809, he accepted the first professorship of *Altertumswissenschaft* at the University of Berlin. Though he produced little original scholarship after leaving Halle, his very capable and energetic students, including the important philologist August Böckh and the long-serving Prussian bureaucrat Johannes Schultze, carried his legacy into lecture halls and ministerial offices all over Germany.

Wolf's insistence that his Halle seminar not be encumbered by lessons in pedagogical theory but rather dedicate its efforts to the pursuit of philological expertise contributed to the turning inward of the university community after 1800. Wolfian haughty insistence on "disinterestedness" and scholarly autonomy imbued philology, and *Altertumswissenschaft*, with a kind of social detachment rare among eighteenth-century scholars, many of whom

[67] Arnoldt, *Wolf*, 1:82. For Wolf's definition of archaeology, see chapter 2.

[68] Turner, "The Prussian Professoriate," p. 469.

[69] Schelsky, *Einsamkeit und Freiheit*, p. 311.

had depended on the patronage of aristocrats or income from a second job outside the university.[70] Eighteenth-century professors, too, had generally been esteemed for their lecture skills rather than for their independent research. By the turn of the century, however, as R. Steven Turner has shown, the concept of "discovery" had undergone significant democratization; the creation of new knowledge increasingly seemed to lie within the powers of every industrious scholar, not just geniuses like Descartes and Newton.[71] Soon publications became the measure of scholarly stature; by the 1830s, at the latest, most professors legitimated their efforts on the basis of the evaluation of their published work by other specialists, rather than according to their appeal to a wider public.[72] Classical scholarship in particular quickly evolved what might be called a higher form of snobbism; disdain for dilettantism and popular appeal followed close on the heels of philology's acquisition of autonomy.[73]

As university entrance became more and more dependent on passage through the classical *Gymnasium*, candidates for teaching posts and civil servants came increasingly from aristocratic or educated bourgeois families, and the combination of greater social exclusivity, specialization, and the emphasis on strict scientific procedure drew the interests of academics and laymen further and further apart.[74] Within academia, however, this increasing distance from the population at large worried few; on the contrary, Wolf's rather elitist approach to the ancients came to represent the proper means to preserve the pure essence of *Altertum*. As Rudolf Haym boasted in 1856, Wolf had rescued classical studies from the perils presented by the bellelettrist, "humanized" humanism of Heyne, which had posed "a clear danger that one would neglect criticism for the sake of aesthetics, that one would stop being painstaking in order to become witty, popular, and pleasing, and that one would distance oneself more and more from the true spirit of antiquity, the more one disseminated it and attempted to make it accessible for modern comprehension."[75] Accessibility, already in Wolf's day, but especially in Haym's, signified superficiality, inauthenticity, and incomprehension; the Greeks really spoke only to the expert philologist.

Wolf's painstaking and determinedly nonpopular method had helped to

---

[70] See La Vopa, "Specialists Against Specialization," p. 41.

[71] R. Steven Turner, "University Reformers and Professional Scholarship in Germany, 1760–1806," in *The University in Society* vol. 2, ed. Lawrence Stone (Princeton, N.J., 1974), pp. 495–531.

[72] R. S. Turner, "The Growth of Professional Research in Prussia, 1818 to 1848: Causes and Consequences," in *Historical Studies in the Physical Sciences* 3 (1971): 172.

[73] Turner suggests that among philologists, hostility toward nonspecialists was already apparent by 1810; "The Prussian Professoriate," pp. 467–68.

[74] See Charles McClelland, *State, Society, and University in Germany, 1700–1914* (Cambridge, 1980), pp. 156, 198–99.

[75] Haym, *Humboldt*, p. 70.

give classical philology in Germany an independent, if elitist, new character. Wolf's distaste for theology, and his disdain for all but the Greeks and
Romans, soon became hallmarks of the professional (particularly Prussian)
classicist. His dedication to the production of "disinterested," nonpopular,
historical scholarship and his contempt for comparative, ethnographic, and
broadly philosophical questions cast a long shadow over German *Altertumswissenschaft*.[76] Wolf may not have created much new knowledge about
the ancients, but he struck a scholarly pose much imitated by his descendants. Thus to our evocation of the ascetic, idealist quality of German philhellenism we can add the post-Winckelmannian dominance of elite, expert,
and philosophically unadventurous university philologists over the study of
the ancient past, a condition that would further delay the confrontation
between German scholars and the material world of the glorious Greeks.

Wilhelm von Humboldt: Neohumanism, Nationalism, and the Prussian Bureaucracy

Manfred Fuhrmann has convincingly argued that for Winckelmann, as for
Herder and perhaps Goethe, the comparison between the Greeks and the
moderns mattered more than the juxtaposition of Greeks and Germans.
The era of the Napoleonic Wars, however, brought the latter comparison to
the fore, blending the spirit of pedagogical and social reform with that of a
new German cultural nationalism, born of the common struggle to defeat
the French invaders.[77] Fuhrmann is probably correct, though Winckelmann's key passage in the *Gedanken* advocating imitation of the Greeks
occurred in the context of a description of the great services to German
culture rendered by Elector Augustus the Strong of Saxony in bringing
Greek art to Dresden; also, Winckelmann, like Lessing and Herder, frequently coupled his criticism of the lack of Greek imitators with disgust for
French cultural hegemony in the German-speaking lands. But during the
darkest hours of the Revolutionary Wars, German identification with the
Athenian Empire—politically fragmented, conquered by force of arms, but
united by a single language and spirit—became much more palpable, and

[76] Already in 1829, Wolf's colleague Friedrich Schleiermacher criticized Wolf for his dogmatic, purely historical interpretations and his insensitivity to the experiential and individual
dimensions of communication. Friedrich Schleiermacher, "Über den Begriff der Hermeneutik
mit Bezug auf F. A. Wolfs Andeutung und Asts Lehrbuch," *F. D. E. Schleiermacher: Hermeneutik und Kritik*, ed. Manfred Frank (Frankfurt, 1977), pp. 310–20.

[77] Manfred Fuhrmann, "Die 'Querelle des Anciens et des Modernes,' der Nationalismus und
die deutsche Klassik," in *Deutschlands kulturelle Entfaltung: Die Neubestimmung des Menschen*,
ed. Bernhard Fabian, Wilhelm Schmidt-Biggemann, and Rudolf Vierhaus (Munich, 1980),
pp. 49–67.

much less obviously the property of one generation of upstarts. In the shadow of Prussia's defeat in the Battle of Jena in 1806, German philhellenism underwent a profound change; its antiaristocratic aspects were transformed into pronational sentiments, and a new form of pedagogy, built on the notion of *Bildung*, made its peace with the state and the status quo.

We can only touch here on the subject of eighteenth-century pedagogy, which has been treated in detail by many others.[78] By the third quarter of the century, a number of reform movements had emerged that sought to cast off what was seen as lifeless, unnatural, and unprofessional pedagogy, practiced mainly by young, ill-prepared, and often impoverished clergymen. New systems were proposed by Enlightenment reformers such as Pestalozzi, Herbart, and Basedow, all indebted in one way or another to John Locke and to Rousseau's *Emile* (1762), all similarly hostile to court life and the legally regulated society of orders. In many ways, neohumanism was just another expression of this same discontent with "mechanical" upbringing, designed to rob men of their natural individuality. But neohumanism, with its persistent advocacy of Greek models and Renaissance norms, was more historically oriented than other sorts of reformist pedagogy, more critical of utilitarian goals, and also more self-consciously aestheticizing. And finally, in practice, neohumanism, despite its radically individualist rhetoric, was not as egalitarian as many other reform programs. In place of birth or social function, neohumanism, the credo of the emergent *Bildungsbürgertum*, assessed the individual on the basis of particular cultural capabilities, the acquisition of which proved increasingly difficult for the lower orders to attain.[79]

The driving force behind the institutionalization of neohumanist pedagogy was Wilhelm von Humboldt, a Brandenburgian nobleman who served a brief but seminal term as head of the newly created Sektion für Kultus und Unterricht (Educational and Ecclesiastical Affairs Section) of the Prussian Interior Ministry between February 1809 and July 1810. From a very early age, Humboldt had virtually equated sound pedagogy with the study of the ancients;[80] reading ancient texts provided him with a means of communing with great, self-educated individuals as well as a way of disciplining his mind. In the 1790s, Humboldt's circle of close friends included Wolf and Schiller, both of whom were to help shape his educational philosophy. If

[78] See, for example, La Vopa, *Grace, Talent, and Merit*; Friedrich Paulsen, *Das deutsche Bildungswesen in seiner geschichtlichen Entwicklung*, 4th ed. (Leipzig, 1920); James Van Horn Melton, *Absolutism and the Eighteenth-Century Origins of Compulsory Schooling in Prussia and Austria* (Cambridge, 1988).

[79] See McClelland, *State, Society, and University*, pp. 113–14; La Vopa, *Grace, Talent, and Merit*, pp. 396–98.

[80] On Humboldt's early classicism, see W. H. Bruford, *The German Tradition of Self-Cultivation* (Cambridge, 1975), pp. 1–2.

Humboldt convinced Wolf that *Altertumswissenschaft* should be an organic science of man, striving for "knowledge of human nature as a whole," Wolf persuaded Humboldt that authentic understanding of the Greeks required detailed philological study.[81] Schiller, who continued to produce a stream of literary reflections on his epoch's fall from Edenic antiquity, convinced the young nobleman of the usefulness of the Greek example as an antidote to the social and political fragmentation of the present. The poet's equation of human advancement, freedom, and beauty, however, led Humboldt more and more to identify appreciation of the Greeks with the ideal of individual self-cultivation, thereby drawing him away from, rather than into, the public sphere. His brief tenure of office on the Berlin Court of Appeal (January 1790–May 1791) had convinced him that service to the despotic, mechanical state merely stifled man's natural process of creative self-realization, and he resolved to, as it were, cultivate his own garden.[82] In a letter to a friend, Wolf doubted whether Humboldt would ever return to political office in Prussia: "The Greeks absorb him completely," he explained.[83]

But Humboldt did consent to take on a quite different sort of public office; in 1802, he became Prussian ambassador to the Holy See, a position that allowed him the opportunity to live amongst the antiquities of Rome and to devote much time to his own scholarly pursuits. He left Rome for Berlin in 1808 less to come to the aid of German *Kultur* than to take care of family property that now lay in territory occupied by the French; but, having returned to Prussia, he could not resist being drawn into the projects for the reform and revitalization of the state that followed Napoleon's defeat of the Prussians at the Battle of Jena in 1806.[84] The reforms of 1806–12 were led by two enlightened administrator-nobles, Karl von Hardenberg and Karl Freiherr vom Stein, and included the freeing of the serfs, the granting of a limited form of citizenship to Jews, some economic and fiscal reforms, and the reorganization of the bureaucracy. In the process, the new department of the Interior Ministry for educational and ecclesiastical affairs was created, and Humboldt, who was well known to Stein and Hardenberg, was offered the position. The scholarly, self-absorbed Graecophile was a rather unusual choice to head the new bureau for, until the mid-eighteenth century, spiritual matters had largely been delegated to church bodies (*Konsistoria*), and down to 1808, educational institutions (especially primary and secondary schools) had remained largely under clerical control.[85] But,

---

[81] Peter Bruno Stadler, *Wilhelm von Humboldts Bild der Antike* (Zürich, 1959), p. 58.

[82] Bruford, *Self-Cultivation*, pp. 16–17.

[83] Quoted in Haym, *Humboldt*, p. 87.

[84] See Sweet, *Wilhelm von Humboldt: A Biography*, vol. 2: *1808–1835* (Columbus, Ohio, 1980), pp. 4–11, 21.

[85] In 1738, the first actual minister for "geistliche Sachen" was appointed within the Department of Justice; in 1764, the position was divided in two to allow equal representation of Lutheran and Calvinist faiths. See Eduard Spranger, *Das Ministerium der geistlichen und Unterrichtsangelegenheiten* (Berlin, 1917), p. 3.

in the wake of crushing defeat by the French, the reformers felt the time had come for the articulation of a new relationship between the state and the schools, and that Humboldt, despite the fact that many of his contemporaries suspected him of being a pagan,[86] was just the man to reform Prussian *Geist*.

Prussia's collapse had induced Humboldt, too, to accept the necessity of reform from above. Now more than ever the state appeared to him a necessary evil, the only means of redeeming Prussia and asserting the spiritual power of German culture. He took up his new duties, which included the supervision of schools, universities, the art and science academies, cultural associations, and the Royal Theater,[87] determined to enhance and extend *Kultur* by making the Prussian state the patron and protector of the educational ideal he had himself pursued. In this spirit he attempted to take the financing of education out of the hands of local communities and transfer responsibility to the central state.[88] He implemented a requirement that prospective university students pass the *Abitur*, a state-wide school-leaving exam characterized by strenuous translations from Greek and oral as well as written tests to be completed in Latin. The *Abitur* could only be administered by classical schools designated as *Gymnasien*; these then became the sole university preparatory institutions (and remained so down to the end of the century) and, consequently, the required choice for all aspiring state servants, teachers, and free professionals, including even dentists.[89] Humboldt initiated the mandatory testing of candidates for teaching posts in secondary schools, restricting the town councils' choices of instructors to those with a *Gymnasium* education.

Finally, Humboldt designed the University of Berlin, founded in 1810. Continuing a trend begun in the eighteenth century and strongly endorsed by both Kant and Wolf, Humboldt elevated Berlin's philosophical faculty (containing philology and its related disciplines, philosophy proper, and the natural sciences) above the more "practical" faculties of medicine, law, and theology. Within the philosophical faculty, he subordinated the natural sciences to the humanities, fearing that the former would otherwise slide into mindless empiricism.[90] And, by offering large salaries and new prestige, Humboldt brought to Berlin brilliant young scholars in all fields, but especially in classical philology, which he hoped to make the centerpiece of his grand new institution. Berlin quickly became known as an *Arbeitsuniver-*

---

[86] Ibid., pp. 6–7.

[87] Ernst Müsebeck, *Das preußische Kultusministerium vor hundert Jahren* (Stuttgart, 1918), p. 38.

[88] Humboldt's plan to institute a direct school tax, however, failed, and the burden of payment remained on the communal governments. See Spranger, *Ministerium*, p. 9.

[89] Until 1834, however, a loophole allowed some to enter the university by passing an entrance exam. See Paulsen, *Das deutsche Bildungswesen*, pp. 126–27.

[90] Ibid., p. 189; Turner, "Growth of Professional Research," p. 152; Haym, *Humboldt*, pp. 274–75.

sität, an institution for industrious, mature, and unsocial scholars such as Wolf and Humboldt themselves had been.[91] By the time Humboldt left the ministry in June 1810, it would not be too much to say that he had made neohumanist *Bildung* the cultural philosophy of the Prussian state.

What, exactly, was Humboldt's conception of *Bildung*? Blending the rigorous individualism of Rousseauist pedagogy with the "republican" aspirations of the humanist tradition, Humboldt concluded that the sound formation of social morals depended upon the individual's self-transformative progress from natural immaturity to self-willed citizenship. *Bildung* celebrated the diverse talents and characters of individual humans; it promised the intellectual overcoming of anomie and the liberation—at least internally speaking—of the individual from a "mechanical" and compartmentalized external world. "One-sidedness" was the terrible debility *Bildung* sought to cure—at least in males; "one-sidedness" in women, Humboldt thought, was not necessarily a bad thing.[92] But *Bildung* also intended to bind its male graduates together in civic harmony and loyalty to the state. Humboldt envisioned a society in which education, not property ownership or birth, made men deserving of freedom and citizenship. Convinced that the French Revolution had miscarried because it failed to revolutionize the inner man,[93] he dwelt so single-mindedly on spiritual emancipation that he overlooked external, material constraints on human development. Thus his meritocratic vision contained both egalitarian and elitist elements, a combination whose consequences would prove far-reaching.[94]

Given his commitment to individualized self-development, Humboldt, even more than Rousseau, was reluctant to dictate the proper content of *Bildung*; in fact, in his 1809 report to the king on his plans for reorganizing elementary education, he explicitly argued that the need to make education useful to all classes required that instruction be directed at the sharpening of intellectual skills, not the conveyance of any particular content.[95] But Humboldt the humanist did, consistently, argue that "man" should somehow form the content of *Bildung*; and after about 1800, partly as a result of his encounters in Paris with French debates on the nature and history of language and partly as a result of Wolf's encouragement of his philological endeavors, he began to develop a means to use language to ground a com-

---

[91] Charles McClelland, " 'To live for Science': Ideals and Realities at the University of Berlin," in *The University and the City: From Medieval Origins to the Present* (New York, 1988), pp. 181–97.

[92] See Humboldt to C. Diede, summer 1826, in Wilhelm von Humboldt, *Humanist without Portfolio*, trans. Marianne Cowan (Detroit, 1963), p. 345.

[93] Jean Quillien, *G. de Humboldt et la Grèce: Modèle et Histoire* (Lille, 1983), p. 52.

[94] See La Vopa, *Grace, Talent, and Merit*, pp. 390–98.

[95] Humboldt, "Bericht der Sektion des Kultus und Unterrichts, Dezember 1809," in *Wilhelm von Humboldts Werke*, ed. Albert Leitzmann et. al, 17 vols. (Berlin, 1903–36), 10:205–6.

prehensive, historico-philosophical "critique" of man. Languages were not imminent in the order of things, or given by God; they were human products, he argued. More specifically, they were the products of nations of native speakers, and their structures embodied each nation's character. Although all languages were man-made, Humboldt maintained, some remained closer to nature (here, the nature of man's mind) than others, and the Greek language—like Greek art forms for Winckelmann—exhibited unparalleled transparency and universality. Humboldt would later offset this methodological contraction of humanistic study with a gradual expansion of its content;[96] but in 1806–09, residing mostly in Rome and prompted to reconsider the past glories of the Greek polis by the collapse of the Holy Roman Empire, Humboldt was still a long way from his later studies of American Indian and Javanese languages.[97] Thus the conception of *Bildung* Humboldt activated upon his appointment to the ministry combined his enduring admiration for the Greeks with an evolving commitment to language as the key to comprehending mankind and creating the well-rounded individual.

There is no better demonstration of this intersection of aesthetic Graecophilia with scientific concentration on language than Humboldt's 1806 essay, "Latium und Hellas, oder Betrachtungen über das klassische Alterthum" ("Latium and Hellas, or Observations on Classical Antiquity"). Here Humboldt—who does not actually discuss "Latium" at all—argues that the Greeks had developed the most natural, and at the same time, the most ideal sculpture; poetry that like no other raised reality to ideality; religion stripped of idolatry and idealizing man; universally enviable mores; and a polity that fostered good breeding and wealth without plunging itself into oligarchy or plutocracy.[98] This is, of course, hardly a departure from the views of contemporary aesthetes and scholars, but in the second half of

---

[96] He would retain, however, both his presumption that language was constitutive of thought, and his further presumption that the "inner fixity" of inflected languages, now exemplified by Sanskrit, made them superior forms of communication (and by extension, made their speakers superior thinkers and communicators). See Hans Aarsleff's extremely helpful "Introduction" in Wilhelm von Humboldt, *On Language: The Diversity of Human Language-Structure and its Influence on the Mental Development of Mankind*, trans. Peter Heath (Cambridge, 1988), esp. pp. xxvi–xxxii, lx–lxv.

[97] Humboldt *had* shown earlier signs of wishing to depart from his narrow Graecophile frame. But as in his unpublished essay of 1795, "Plan einer vergleichenden Anthropologie," the young aristocrat practiced an enlightened form of comparative "anthropology" in the style of Montesquieu or Kant rather than an embryonic form of the "scientific" comparative linguistics of Bopp or Silvestre de Sacy. See Sweet, *Humboldt*, 1:142–45, 181–91. Humboldt's essay is reprinted in *Humboldts Werke*, 1:377–410. On Humboldt's revived interest in antiquity between about 1806 and 1808, see Quillien, *Humboldt*, pp. 63–68.

[98] See Humboldt, "Latium und Hellas oder Betrachtungen über das klassische Altherthum," in *Humboldts Werke*, 3:136–64.

the essay, Humboldt took something of a new turn. Rather than subscribing to the view that all cultural forms—poetry, religion, art, politics—represent different expressions of the *Volksgeist*, Humboldt argued that the key to understanding all of these forms, and of national character as a whole, can only lie in the study of language.[99] Thus language is both a key to essence and to historical development; it "is at once a convenient means to grasp character, a mediator between the fact and the idea, and since it is formed from general, or at least dimly perceived, principles and is usually also formed from preexisting prejudices, it offers not only a means to compare many nations, but also a means to trace the influence of one [nation] on another."[100] Humboldt's vaguely stated conclusion—which he and his fellow bureaucrats would put into practice—is that only language offers modern man the opportunity both to appreciate historical distance and to grasp the Greek ideal.

Humboldt did not, however, want classical philology to drive out all other subjects; his lesson plans, in fact, granted ample hours to the two most prominent rivals for curricular centrality: religion and German studies. Humboldt the presumed heathen opposed elimination of religious training from the schools, a stance that contributed to the quick reconsolidation of clerical control of lower education after 1820.[101] The *Gymnasium* curriculum set out by Humboldt and his followers in 1811 (revised in 1816) offered more hours of German education than did the official plan of 1882.[102] Yet inclusion in the neohumanist curriculum extracted a price from these would-be master subjects; they were admitted as aspects of Humboldtian *Bildung*, a pedagogical principle intrinsically hostile to the Germanist reformers' practical orientation and the Church's emphasis on moral conformity. Opposing the "mechanical" and hierarchical allocation of knowledge offered by utilitarian reformers and the "external" imposition of faith demanded by clerical bodies, Humboldt infused the school system with his generation's commitment to *Zwecklosigkeit*, *Innerlichkeit*, and *Wissenschaftlichkeit* (nonpurposiveness, inwardness, and scholarliness).

But how was this nonutilitarian, secular, inner *Bildung* to be taught? Would it really be taught to all students? The traditional aim of instruction in the classics, to refine compositional style, figured rather small in Humboldt's pedagogical program. Students were to treat classical texts as historical creations rather than as sources from which one might borrow rhetori-

---

[99] Ibid., p. 166.

[100] Ibid. Compare Friedrich Schlegel's extremely influential application of this same reasoning to the language and culture of the Indians in his *Über die Sprache und Weisheit der Indier* (1808) in idem, *Studien zur Philosophie und Theologie*, ed. Ernst Behler and Ursula Struc-Oppenberg, Kritische Friedrich-Schlegel-Ausgabe, vol. 8, part 1 (Munich, 1975), pp. 105–433.

[101] Sweet, *Humboldt*, 2:39.

[102] Wilhelm Vesper, *Deutsche Schulgrammatik im 19. Jahrhundert* (Tübingen, 1980), p. 26.

cal flourishes; he was adamant that they learn to read and interpret original texts, for him the only means to proper historical understanding. As all male students were to attend the *Gymnasium*, whether or not they intended to continue their educations at university, all would partake of this historico-philological learning. Importantly, however, for Humboldt, this educational program applied only to boys; as James Albisetti has shown, Humboldt's reforms did not include provision for the creation of *Gymnasien* (or any other sorts of secondary schools) for girls. Like the vast majority of other nineteenth-century administrators and educators, Humboldt apparently believed nonutilitarian, neohumanist *Bildung* a philosophy suitable for males alone.[103]

Although Humboldt had hoped to create a natural progression from the self-enriching *Bildung* of the *Gymnasium* to the strict *Wissenschaft* of the university without burdening the former with the specialized concerns of the latter, his greater successes in encouraging scientific research in the universities exerted a regrettable ripple effect on secondary education. *Gymnasium* teachers, who were now required to study philology at the university, tended to hand on the specialized text-interpretive skills and the detail-fetishism they learned in the seminar to their young students.[104] Grammar study increased beyond the bounds of practicability, but was staunchly defended by the humanist professoriate, which was convinced of grammar's value as, in Hegel's words, "elementary philosophy."[105] Particularly as classical grammar was introduced into the lower grades of the *Gymnasien*, which came to serve as a kind of terminal general education for many non-university-bound students, the reforms' failure to provide multifaceted, individually tailored education made itself manifest. Not surprisingly, then, by the 1840s, the neohumanists were suffering from the same sort of attack on their lifeless, drill-oriented lessons that they had launched against the Latin schools of the eighteenth century.

The philologists were not alone in retreating from the spirit of reform after 1819–21; the Prussian bureaucracy led the way. Humboldt's replacement, Friedrich Schuckmann, distrusted the university community and education based on pure reason, rather than on religious belief. Thus the further implementation of reform during Schuckmann's tenure (1810–17) was left to subordinates who retained their commitment to Humboldtian principles, despite the increasing hostility of the king and court to neo-

---

[103] James Albisetti, *Schooling German Girls and Women: Secondary and Higher Education in the Nineteenth Century* (Princeton, N.J., 1988), pp. 15, 18–19.

[104] Anthony Grafton, "Polyhistor into *Philolog*: Notes on the Transformation of German Classical Scholarship, 1780–1850," in *History of Universities* 3 (1983): 169–70.

[105] Quoted in Georg Jäger, *Sozialgeschichte des deutschen Unterrichts an höheren Schulen von der Spätaufklärung bis zum Vormärz, Schule und literarische Kultur*, vol. 1 (Stuttgart, 1981), p. 29.

humanism's egalitarian implications.[106] Karl Freiherr von Altenstein, who had occupied important posts in the reform-era governments of Stein and Hardenberg, in 1817 became the first head of an independent Ministerium der Geistlichen, Unterrichts- und Medizinal-Angelegenheiten (Ministry of Spiritual, Educational, and Medical Affairs—hereafter referred to as the Ministry of Education). Initially inspired by Fichte's call for national unity, Altenstein grew more and more enamored of Hegelian philosophy, which he raised to the level of an official state dogma. But Altenstein's tenure as minister of education (1817–40) saw both the onset of severe budget shortages and the revival of what Eduard Spranger called "a patriarchal conception of the state which harkened back to the feudal-church relationships of the sixteenth century"[107]—a reaction against both secularization and centralization, especially in lower education, whose cultural consequences will be considered in later chapters.

Importantly, it was during this era of princely reaction that the fate of the modern Greeks became, briefly, a matter of grave concern for intellectuals and governments across Europe. In the Germanies, a small propaganda campaign in favor of Greek independence—led by two university professors—was already under way when in March 1821, a small Greek force commanded by Alexandros Ypsilantis crossed the Pruth river into Turkish Moldavia. This sortie was quickly halted, but it set off a series of uprisings and bloody battles that culminated in the declaration of an independent Greek state in 1828.

Educated Europeans responded immediately; Germans in particular—many of them fired by their *Gymnasium* educations—took up the Greek cause with great enthusiasm. Undoubtedly, many of the *Bildungsbürger* who championed the cause were also attracted by the obvious parallel to be drawn between the repressive Ottoman Empire and the post-Napoleonic German states. The central features of early pro-Greek propaganda lay in condemnation of Turkish barbarism and appeals to fatherland, freedom, and (Christian) faith; harkening back to the liberalism of the reform era, the invocation of *Vaterland* and *Freiheit* here represented deep discontent with the states' recent reactionary turn. By the summer of 1821, volunteers began to gather in many German cities and pro-Greek sentiment had seized the universities. But in August and September, the philhellenes' hopes that the German states would back the Greeks were crushed. Fearing that the Greek revolt would breathe new life into nationalist and democratic endeavors, Count Clemens von Metternich pressed the German states to curb philhellenist activities. Particularly in Prussia and Austria, but also in Bavaria,

---

[106] Müsebeck, *Preußisches Kultusministerium*, p. 151; Spranger, *Ministerium*, pp. 10–11; Ute Preuß, *Humanismus und Gesellschaft: Zur Geschichte des altsprachlichen Unterrichts in Deutschland von 1890 bis 1933* (Frankfurt, 1988), pp. 7–10.

[107] Spranger, *Ministerium*, p. 15.

Saxony, and elsewhere, the authorities issued prohibitions on the mustering of volunteers, on the formation of associations for the purpose of financing the cause, and even, in some states, on public expression of support for the Greeks.[108] To the apparent disgust of their wider following, the disillusioned leaders of the movement in areas under censorship retreated from the cause, rather than risking the hardships of imprisonment or exile.[109]

As Christoph Hauser has shown, in the southwestern German states that tolerated pro-Greek associations and publications, the Greek war opened a new age of bourgeois-liberal political organization, preparing its supporters for the more openly political battles of the 1830s and 1840s.[110] In the north, too, even the efficient administrators of the Prussian state were unable to stamp out literary paeans to the Greeks, or even informal money-raising groups, whose members included important state servants like Wilhelm von Humboldt and Field Marshall Neithardt von Gneisenau.[111] But clearly, already by late 1821, the first phase of political philhellenism had ended, and all danger that the revolution might spread from the Greeks to their spiritual kin in central Europe had passed. After this initial spurt of excitement, organizational efforts largely moved to London, Zürich, and Paris, and German contributions were largely of a humanitarian nature.[112] Once again, philhellenism had failed to spark political change.

Interestingly, as Hauser shows, the Christian faith of the Greeks—as against the "barbaric" beliefs of the Turks—was used heavily in attempts to raise funds for the cause, while, at least in the southwest, the glories of Greek antiquity played a rather minor role.[113] Apparently, the "continuity thesis," as Michael Herzfeld terms the claim for modern Greece's inheritance of ancient ideas and practices, was thought less likely to enthrall the wider public than political, religious, and emotional appeals. Continuity was, however, clearly the presumption of those Graecophiles who hotly refuted the many bitter accounts of the wholly unclassical behavior of the Greeks penned by disillusioned soldiers.[114] In the imaginations of the *Bildungsbürger*, the Winckelmannian image of Greece unquestionably re-

---

[108] Christoph Hauser, *Anfänge bürgerlicher Organisation: Philhellenismus und Frühliberalismus in Südwestdeutschland* (Göttingen, 1990), pp. 42–45.

[109] Ibid., pp. 49–51.

[110] Ibid., especially pp. 234–42.

[111] Johannes Irmscher, "Der Philhellenismus in Preußen als Forschungsanliegen," in *Sitzungsberichte der deutschen Akademie der Wissenschaften zu Berlin* (Klasse für Sprache, Literatur und Kunst), 1966, no. 2, p. 39.

[112] Hauser, *Anfänge*, pp. 98–110.

[113] Ibid., 205–7.

[114] Michael Herzfeld, *Ours Once More: Folklore, Ideology, and the Making of Modern Greece* (Austin, Tex., 1982), pp. 10–21; Gustav Heydemann, "Deutscher und britischer Philhellenismus: Ein Vergleich," in *L'Anchità nell' ottocento in Italia e Germania*, ed. Karl Christ and Arnaldo Momigliano (Bologna and Berlin, 1988), pp. 377–78.

mained uppermost, and was supplemented by the lyrical poetry and romantic death of George Gordon, Lord Byron, who perished in the battle for Greek liberty at Missolonghi in 1824. Byron—personified as Euphorion, son of Faust and Helen of Troy, in part two of Goethe's epic—was read and widely admired in the Germanies—though Goethe's skepticism about Byron's unrestrained dedication to the achievement of political freedom through violence may well have been shared by his fellow philhellenes.[115] If the grandeur of antiquity did not figure prominently in propaganda, it was surely one of the obsessions Byron shared with his elite German readership.

Thus, thanks to Byron, the censors' inability to prevent the publication of literary tributes to Greece, and the armchair Graecophiles' unwillingness to accept criticisms of the modern Greeks, German Romantic philhellenism was not substantially altered by the Greek revolution. Once Greek independence was established, and particularly after Otho I, a member of the royal house of Wittelsbach, assumed the Greek throne in 1832, philhellenism again became a relatively inoffensive taste—though Graecophiles continued to carry a whiff of left liberalism into the 1840s.[116] By then, republicans and liberal reformers had turned elsewhere for their issues and models, leaving the modern Greeks to fight their own battles and the ancients to the expert tending of the professional philologists.

In the universities, many classicists had defended the Greek cause, at first openly, then more quietly. They now returned to explorations of the ancient past and professional debates, which raged with particular virulence during the decade of the 1820s. Still, the defenders of the princely status quo kept a watchful eye on the intellectual elite, and on the *Gymnasien*, frequently suspected of disseminating republicanism and pantheism.[117] In their own defense, classicists felt the need to underline their political irrelevance, as did Friedrich Creuzer in 1839:

---

[115] See William J. McGrath, "Freedom and Death: Goethe's *Faust* and the Greek War of Independence," in *Rediscovering History: Culture, Politics, and the Psyche*, ed. Michael Roth (Stanford, Calif. 1994), pp. 102–20.

[116] For a discussion of Bavarian philhellenism and the role of the house of Wittelsbach in Greece, see Wolf Seidl, *Bayern in Griechenland* (Munich, 1981).

[117] The effects of reaction were reflected in the 1837 emendation of the 1812 secondary-school *Lehrplan*. The new curriculum guidelines reduced Greek instruction in the *Gymnasium* from fifty to forty-two hours, math from sixty to thirty-three hours, German from forty-four to thirty-three hours, and natural science from twenty to sixteen hours, and increased Latin lessons from seventy-six to eighty-six hours. This attempt to revive the model of the Protestant Latin schools of the sixteenth century against the "pagan" humanism of Humboldt and Wolf was continued in the post-1850 era. Manfred Landfester, *Humanismus und Gesellschaft im 19. Jahrhundert* (Darmstadt, 1988), pp. 69–71. The 1812 curriculum also prescribed thirty hours of history and geography and twenty hours of religious instruction. See Paulsen, *Das deutsche Bildungswesen*, pp. 125–26, 129.

Philologists are just as patriotic as anybody else, they participated equally in the recent Wars of Liberation (militatum abierunt), but they are said to be, it is said here and there, republicans. Yes, so we are—but [republicans] in the free city of scholars, and in the world of civil society, we know better than anyone else the crimes and evils of the ancient republicans. Yes, we are republicans, and we teach our students to seek Plato's unfettered [herrenlos], free virtue. But we are also Christian philologists; we know that God made men free through grace, we have learned and teach these [principles]: Subordinate yourself to the authorities, and render unto Caesar, that which is Caesar's.[118]

As the Greek War of Independence faded from view, academic neohumanists progressively stripped philhellenism of its social and political aspirations in order to maintain their tenuous hold on new cultural institutions, a price the philologists, at least, were certainly willing to pay.

If provincial and clerical forces reasserted themselves, particularly in primary education, however, neohumanism had left an indelible mark on education in Prussia and in the German states as a whole. Humanists—mostly philologists by training—held the top university posts; Gymnasium-educated men, by the 1830s, began to dominate the civil service and free professions; and links established as early as 1809–10 between neohumanism and nationalism, secularization, centralization, and individualism withstood, on the whole, the countermeasures of the Vormärz bureaucracy. Thanks especially to Winckelmann, Goethe, and Schiller, the study of the Greeks had taken on the quality of a redemptive return to mankind's origins;[119] thanks to Wolf and Humboldt, this vision had become an official academic and bureaucratic creed. The philhellenists were fortunate, too, that the revival of Greece in Germany coincided with victory over Napoleon, newfound Europe-wide respect for German scholarship, and the flowering of German poetry, philosophy, and philology; but they were less fortunate in the swift and sure reconquest of institutional control by the forces of reaction. The aestheticism of German philhellenism made the Greeks exemplary symbols of the "disinterested" pursuit of knowledge and models for cultural renewal, but not powerful exemplars of republican resistance to the reconsolidation of aristocratic and monarchical power. The art historians, philologists, and pedagogical theorists of ensuing decades would reap the consequences of the institutionalization of this peculiarly ascetic obsession.

[118] Friedrich Creuzer, "Ueber das Verhältniss der Philologie zu unserer Zeit" (1839), in Verhandlungen der zweiten Versammlung deutscher Philologen und Schulmänner in Mannheim (Mannheim, 1840), p. 18.

[119] Lionel Gossman, Orpheus Philologus: Bachofen versus Mommsen on the Study of Antiquity, Transactions of the American Philosophical Society, vol. 73, pt. 5 (Philadelphia, 1983), p. 75.

FROM IDEALS TO INSTITUTIONS

Nowhere else as in Germany did humanism, then historicism
so swiftly, one after another, receive such passionate devotion.
(*Karl Reinhardt*)

IF IN 1936, Friedrich Meinecke needed two long volumes to trace the origins of German historicism, it is probably safe to say that the completion of any comprehensive history of humanism, today, would require many more volumes and the enlistment of a team of scholars. For humanism is a much older and richer tradition than is historicism, and its historiography—written mostly by classicists and Renaissance scholars—is vast. But humanism's fortunes in the modern world have been less explored than those of historicism, which, combining humanistic practices with ideas and methods borrowed from the sciences, contributed heavily to the remaking of the study of antiquity without entirely destroying key aspects of the older tradition. Perhaps nonclassicists have found the subject dauntingly complex; perhaps modernists have been so blinded by the twentieth-century apotheosis of the natural sciences that they have consigned the world of the humanists to the mists of obscurity. In any event, even Arnaldo Momigliano, who brilliantly blazed this historiographical trail, devoted only disparate essays to the subject, and I too will have to content myself with providing an account of one important aspect of the modern fate of German neohumanism: the contribution of archaeology to the rise and fall of its philhellenic fixation. If I cannot hope to match Meinecke's encyclopedic achievement, this is partly the result of some of the processes I describe. One of the unintended consequences of the specialization of humanistic scholarship is that it has become impossible for a single scholar to write its history.

Perhaps a few remarks will suffice to clarify the problem of neohumanism's debts to and divergences from the humanist tradition that preceded it. Since their origin in the Renaissance and Reformation, the *studia humanitatis* have offered potentially conflicting claims about their ends: the encounter between modern men and ancient texts was to produce both knowledge about the ancient world and the ability to imitate ancient achievements. In effect, the humanist believed in the exemplariness of the classical past and the comparative degeneracy of his day, but also in the self-transformative capabilities of modern individuals. The worldly anthropomorphism of a Pico della Mirandola differed greatly from the Neoplatonism of a Marsilio Ficino and the Lutheran intellectualism of a Phillip Melanchthon, but all are considered "humanists" by virtue of their conviction that reading the ancients gave individuals the tools to remake themselves for the better. The seventeenth-century French and English "quarrels" between the "ancients," who believed that the Greek and Latin models could never be surpassed and their exemplariness would be ruined by wearisome, nit-picking scholars, and the "moderns," who insisted that knowledge had progressed and that modern men could authenticate and enhance ancient texts by careful philological and historical study, exposed some of the underlying contradictions in humanism's ambitions. By the early eighteenth century, as Joseph Levine has demonstrated, the collective weight of more than two hundred years of philological and antiquarian inquiry threatened to overwhelm the student whose aim was imitation and eloquence: in the 1710s, Alexander Pope developed a headache just thinking about the mass of texts he would need to consult to complete his translation of the *Iliad*.[1] In many ways, the flourishing of specialized philology and the great expansion of the elite student body in the next century simply exacerbated and exposed these inherent contradictions between learnedness and liveliness.

On the other hand, the reassertion of Renaissance norms in an age of increasing economic modernization and expanded literacy should also draw our attention to the novelties of "neo"-humanism. In the Germanies, by the mid-eighteenth century, humanistic learning had actually lost much of its prestige to the newer, more empirical disciplines (the natural sciences, the study of administration and statecraft [*Staatswissenschaft*]); Latin usage had dropped off, and, even at a reputable institution such as the University of Marburg, the Greek language retained merely "a shadow existence."[2] As the case of F. A. Wolf demonstrates, humanistic learning was seen very much as a countermeasure to ward off Enlightenment utilitarianism and "mechanical" classification. Greece's paganism was as important to Wolf as it was to Schiller and to von Humboldt; German neohumanism was, at least initially, very much an attempt to ground a secular, national-cultural identity, not to perform the traditional task of reconciling the ideas of the ancients with the precepts of Christianity. Perhaps it was this aim that predisposed neohumanists to prefer meticulous philology to the speculative philosophical systems of Hegel and Schelling. In any event, German neohumanism was by no means simply a continuation of an older tradition; as we saw in the last chapter, it was very much shaped by a small group of highly talented and

[1] Joseph M. Levine, *The Battle of the Books: History and Literature in the Augustan Age* (Ithaca, N.Y., 1991), p. 197.

[2] Gisela Wirth, *Die Entwicklung der alten Geschichte an der Philipps-Universitvät Marburg* (Marburg, 1977), p. 77.

ambitious scholars in the course of their attempts to remake Germany's cultural institutions.

As much excellent recent scholarship has shown, Renaissance and baroque humanists owed many of their mannerisms and mores to the court culture of their princely patrons. But, in the endeavors of early modern humanists to extend their activities and secure their social status, we can also see the prototypes of some familiar academic forms: the grant proposal, the letter of recommendation, the endowed chair. Early modern museum keepers like Ulisse Aldrovandi of Bologna had constantly to flatter his numerous benefactors for funds to enhance his collection and subsidies to permit him to publish the fruits of his labors. Humanists and courtiers exchanged letters introducing visiting students and peers, and verifying their social and intellectual credentials.[3] The early eighteenth-century English humanists Thomas Hearne and Henry Dodwell pursued their studies as dependent residents on the estate of Sir William Cherry.[4] Antiquarians and natural historians, whose business was the collection and study of objects, were particularly dependent on wealthy patrons. Travel required time as well as money, given the scattered nature of (mostly private) collections; as Herder commented in 1777, those who complained of the incompleteness of Winckelmann's art history had failed to consider the costs of a journey to see the artworks in Naples, to say nothing of the expense of visiting other worthy monuments dispersed across the continent.[5] Winckelmann was compelled to change his religion as well as his country of residence to gain access to the collections he wished to study. As the personal client of Cardinal Albani, Winckelmann was more, not less, dependent on political events and the whims of fashion than were his archæologist descendants.

But here, precisely, the differences between early modern and late modern humanism, produced by institutionalization, professionalization, and technological modernization, are evident, and national divergences are important. As Paula Findlen's book on early modern science museums shows, most of these "institutions" did not outlast their originators; modern museums, by contrast, were envisioned as *permanent, national* collections whose funding was not to be dependent on the whim of a single patron. In some ways, the nationalization and bureaucratization of the earlier system of interpersonal patronage simply translated the flattering of rulers into appeals to enhance the prestige of the state. But the evolution of (sup-

---

[3] Paula Findlen, *Possessing Nature: Museums, Collecting, and Scientific Culture in Early Modern Italy* (Berkeley, Calif., 1994), pp. 346–65, 129–46.

[4] Levine, *Dr. Woodward's Shield: History, Science, and Satire in the Augustan Age* (Ithaca, N.Y., 1991), pp. 182–83.

[5] Herder, "Denkmal Johann Winckelmanns" (1777), reprinted in Johann Winckelmann, *Geschichte der Kunst des Altertums* (Vienna, 1934), p. 442.

posedly) impersonal systems by which the client's credentials could be judged changed the methods individuals employed to gain favor as well as the social significance of scholarly advance. Finally, the vastly increased *scale* of specialized scholarship in a world of hierarchically organized laboratories and, to take an example we will return to frequently, the grand-scale overseas archaeological excavation, transformed patronage relationships in multiple ways. Permanence, bureaucratization, specialization, and increased scale abstracted and nationalized dependency relations between patrons and clients. We should not ignore the cultural consequences such changes brought in their train.

Of course, the transformation of patron-client relations occurred at different rates and with different degrees of completeness in Italy, the Germanies, England, France, and America. In nineteenth-century Prussia, liberal anxieties about the corrupting influence and uncertain duration of private patronage and willingness to submit to bureaucratic supervision resulted in greater dependence on financing by the central state than anywhere else in Europe. Similar concerns and pressures helped to induce imitation of this model in the other German states before 1871. The high value placed on research, and the tradition of academic self-administration— though not always honored by the states—resulted in enormous gains in specialized knowledge, and made the German universities objects of veneration, not only for the *Bildungsbürgertum* at home, but also for educated elites abroad. But state-supported specialization also had its costs, for ultimately, the expense and complexity of "disinterested" scholarship made it impossible to pursue as an amateur, outsider, or "internal émigré." As we will see, the idiosyncrasies of German state patronage played a major role in the development of classical archaeology, and the decline of German philhellenism.

In the last chapter, we examined the origins of philhellenic neohumanism as it made the transition from private passion to institutionalized ideal. If its prescriptive elements linked philhellenism in this era to dangerous liberal nationalist politics, the state's incursion into the cultural sphere at this particular juncture secured the victory of nonthreatening, historicist philology over the socially and politically destabilizing aspects of humanistic *Bildung*.[6] Emphasis on philological exactness helped to set up a hierarchy of inexpert, expert, and more expert Graecophiles; professionalization concentrated research on a narrowly defined set of questions, and political advocacy on the advancement of the interests of *Philologen* (both *Gymnasium* teachers and university classicists). A profound transformation in the study and disposition of antiquity and antiquities commenced as the

---

[6] See Steven Moyano, "Quality vs. History: Schinkel's Altes Museum and Prussian Arts Policy," *The Art Bulletin* 72, no. 4 (December 1990): 605–7.

insecurities of aristocratic patronage and extra-university existence gave way to the founding of permanent cultural institutions.

In this chapter, then, the narrative begins to shift its focus from individuals to institutions, in the hope that in this way nineteenth-century humanism's departures from earlier endeavors can best be captured. In the course of tracing the transformation of the scholarly practices and social status of "Archäologie," this book's focus on the study of ancient art will also become more obvious. By surveying the development of three nineteenth-century institutions central to post-Winckelmannian archaeology—the university chair, the national archaeological institute, and the national museum—I hope I can throw some light on both the social costs and the scholarly benefits of the midcentury constriction of philhellenism.

Academic Philologists and the Interpretation of Objects

Since the end of the eighteenth century, few scholars have accepted the appellation "antiquarian" with good grace. The interpretation of texts had always been the central concern of the humanist tradition, but as long as text criticism remained something of a gentlemanly art, the less lettered collectors—perforce gentlemen as well—were not so habitually scorned. In the nineteenth century, however, "antiquarian," like "dilettante," became synonymous with "amateur" and "fumbler"; the early modern virtuosi who—supposedly—collected according to whim and organized information according to arbitrary criteria served this later age as scapegoats for the missteps of humanistic science. In fact, premodern antiquarians had garnered a wealth of information on ancient chronology, religion, economic relations, and art from the coins, intaglia, gemstones, pots, and small statuary they collected; if they erred in their interpretations, or failed to recognize forgeries, it must be remembered that, in a world before photographic reproductions, public museums, railroads, and travel stipends enormously increased the accessibility of objects, their bases for comparison were much less broad and reliable. Though it frequently denied its antiquarian legacy, "scientific" archaeology inherited much from the world of the antiquarians, not least of which was its entanglement with philology.

Philology's centrality for neohumanist thinkers simply accentuated an already existing hierarchy between texts and artifacts. From Wolf on, the interpretation of artifacts was thought to be an inferior means to acquire knowledge of ancient life because unlike writing, objects communicated information in an indirect way.[7] As Goethe remarked regretfully in 1827,

---

[7] Wolf, "Darstellung der Altertumswissenschaft," in *Kleine Schriften* vol. 2, ed. G. Bernhardy (Halle, 1869), p. 829, also pp. 836–37.

"One still trusts the letter more than the vivid figural evidence."[8] If objects could be treated like texts, however, the philologists concurred, they could perhaps still yield accurate and useful evidence about the ancient past. When early nineteenth-century classicists set down the principles for "scientific" archaeology, then, they attempted to apply the text-critical methods popularized by Wolf to the interpretations of art and artifacts. And they did not hesitate to advertise their philological, rather than antiquarian, allegiances. Eduard Gerhard, founder and long-time director of the Prussian-financed Institut für archäologische Korrespondenz (Corresponding Society for Archaeology) in Rome, defined archaeology as "the philology of monuments". In 1849, Otto Jahn used the same analogy to indicate archaeology's backwardness: it was essential, he argued, that future generations learn to interpret the "language of artworks" with the rigor and attention to detail philologists had long applied to their texts.[9]

One recent commentator has asserted, with good cause, that the use of this analogy simply masked the reduction of Winckelmannian aesthetics to an empty, oft-repeated formula and the privileging of written sources over the study of actual works of art.[10] But this emphasis on philological parallels also masked considerable confusion about archaeology's proper subject matter, an issue still muddied by the use of the term "Archäologen" to refer both to ancient art historians and to architecturally (or anthropologically) trained excavators. As we have seen, Winckelmann's *Geschichte der Kunst des Alterthums* left room both for purely historical analyses of forms and for the aestheticizing study of singular works of art. Appellations were even more confused in Wolf's *Darstellung*, where "Archäologie" is used to describe both the venerable field of *antiquitates* (the study of ancient art) and the study of political, legal, and economic structures, in the manner of the Roman "antiquarian" Varro.[11] In 1834, Heidelberg professor F. G. Welcker

[8] Quoted in Max Wegner, "Geschichte der Archäologie unter dem Gesichtspunkt der Methode," *Studium Generale* 17 (1964): 197.

[9] Otto Jahn, "Über das Wesen und die wichtigsten Aufgaben der archäologischen Studien," *Berichte über die Verhandlungen der Königlichen Sächsischen Gesellschaft der Wissenschaften zu Leipzig* 2 (1848): 224.

[10] Stephanie-Gerrit Bruer, *Die Wirkung Winckelmanns in der deutschen klassischen Archäologie des 19. Jahrhunderts*, Akademie der Wissenschaften und der Literatur Mainz: Abhandlungen der Geistes- und Sozialwissenschaftlichen Klasse, no. 3 (Stuttgart, 1994), pp. 52–57.

[11] Wolf, "Darstellung," pp. 840–41. To some extent, Böckh as well as H. L. Heeren, B. G. Niebuhr, T. Mommsen, and even Max Weber belong to this tradition. See Arnaldo Momigliano, "New Paths of Classicism in the Nineteenth Century," *History and Theory*, suppl. vol. 21 (1982): 3–31; Karl Christ, "Theodor Mommsen und die 'Römische Geschichte,'" in idem, *Römische Geschichte und Wissenschaftsgeschichte*, vol. 3: *Wissenschaftsgeschichte* (Darmstadt, 1983), pp. 26–73; and Momigliano's review of Alfred Heuß, *Theodor Mommsen und das 19. Jahrhundert*, in *Secondo Contributo alla Storia degli Studi Classici* (Rome, 1960), pp. 421–27.

made the modern definition of archaeology cover "remains [*Altherthümer*] of public and private life and all the arts, sciences, and institutions," but emphasized that no consensus had emerged on the manner in which such remains should be studied. "Nowadays," he wrote, "it often seems unclear whether by archaeology one means exposition [*Erklärung*] or history, or both."[12]

At the heart of this confusion were the conflicting neohumanist urges to provide normative models and "disinterested" scholarship. Was it possible to introduce historicizing criticism into the study of Greek art without diminishing its universal significance or disregarding its unique beauties? Wolf had protested against restricting archaeological attention to beautiful art and consigning the rest to the care of *Alterthumskrämer* (antiquities peddlers). Even the ugly, he felt, could be instructive.[13] But Wolf believed that artifacts should receive aesthetic as well as historical treatment. The estimation of the beauty of artworks as such, "not simply as monuments of antiquity," was part of a holistic *Wissenschaft* that would triumph over a merely cerebral *Gelehrsamkeit* (erudition).[14] Similarly, Welcker, well versed in mythology, iconography, and, unusually, philosophy, rejected the notion that one might treat all objects with equal indifference to their quality as a kind of superficial and turgid pedantry.[15] Jahn, pressing for a lawlike historical treatment of artifacts, superficially divorced archaeology from aesthetics in arguing that the task was to study all of art, not merely beautiful art. He then had to justify the exclusion of "Handwerk" (crafts) such as tables, pots, and even architecture, which he accomplished by declaring their forms to have been dictated by necessity, subtly reintroducing the Kantian conception of nonutility as the criterion of beauty.[16] Despite his expansive interests, Jahn never concealed his special passion for Greek masterpieces.[17]

And yet, in the universities, historicism was gaining the upper hand, thanks in good part to the relentless promotion of *Sachphilologie* by August Böckh. Appointed professor of rhetoric at the University of Berlin in 1811, Böckh was a highly influential teacher as well as an important personage in

[12] Welcker, "Aus der Anzeige von K. O. Müllers Handbuch der Archäologie 1830 die vorangehenden allgemeinen Bemerkungen," in idem, *Kleine Schriften*, vol. 3 (Bonn, 1850), pp. 336–37.

[13] Wolf, "Darstellung," p. 828.

[14] Ibid., p. 850.

[15] Wilfred Geominy, "Die Welckersche Archäologie," in *Friedrich Gottlieb Welcker: Werk und Wirkung*, ed. William M. Calder III et al., *Hermes*, vol. 49 (Stuttgart, 1986), p. 243.

[16] Jahn, "Über das Wesen," p. 214. For more detailed information on Jahn and his generation, see the essays collected in *Otto Jahn (1813–1868): Ein Geisteswissenschaftler zwischen Klassizismus und Historismus*, ed. William M. Calder III, Hubert Cancik, and Bernhard Kytzler (Stuttgart, 1991).

[17] Renate Schlesier, *Kulte, Mythen, und Gelehrte: Anthropologie der Antike seit 1800* (Frankfurt, 1994), p. 39.

court and bureaucratic circles; his students (including Karl Otfried Müller, Theodor Mommsen, Richard Lepsius, J. G. Droysen, and Ernst Curtius) would dominate the study of antiquities in Germany until late in the century. As a philologist, Böckh was distinguished by his perpetual emphasis on the necessity of studying the ancient, and especially the Greek, past in its entirety. One had to comprehend ancient law, customs, religion, art, economics—the entire life of the *Volk*—as well as Greek grammar and vocabulary in order to achieve a complete understanding of the Greeks. This dedication to the material and cultural aspects of antiquity was generally known as *Sachphilologie* or *Realphilologie*, to distinguish it from studies more exclusively concerned with language usage and grammar, which went under the rubric *Wortphilologie*. A staunch monarchist but forceful defender of the autonomy of science, Böckh the *Sachphilologe* helped to promote as well as to shape nineteenth-century archæological inquiry.[18]

For Böckh, Greek art reflected the beauties of nature; its foundation and source, however, Böckh stressed, lay in Greek religion. Winckelmann, too, had indicated the process of selection from nature performed by Greek artists, but he did not define their guiding ideals as religious conceptions. Even less would the Saxon aesthete have agreed that "Art is a product of religion," one of many possible externalizations of an ur-historical, sublime life force.[19] Böckh, like many of his romantic contemporaries, linked the production of art to a kind of subconscious, naive expression of communal beliefs; like Hegel—whose philosophical method he rejected—he insisted upon the universalizing function of the nature-worshipping Greeks in preparing the way for the true world religion, Christianity (which could never have sprung from narrow, nationalistic Judaism).[20] Thus Greek art, for Böckh and Hegel, was bound up with religion in at least two ways: it was a sensual manifestation of the *Volksgeist* at any particular point in time, and it was a kind of humanistic revelation, prefiguring in art what would later be realized in the (Pietist) spirit. Introducing a dynamic, progressive element into Greek history—its culmination in German Christianity—but retaining a healthy measure of nostalgia for the unsurpassable beauty of Greek art, these two extremely influential contributors to midcentury reaction were instrumental in raising the study of Greek art from mere antiquarianism toward independent membership in the humanities.

If Hegel and Böckh tied Greek art to other manifestations of the Greek "spirit," Karl Otfried Müller took it in the direction of Rankean national history. As Josine Blok has recently argued, Müller's work grew out of his

[18] Böckh was a strong backer of the overseas collecting activities of both Gerhard and Lepsius. Maximilian Hoffmann, *August Böckh* (Leipzig, 1901), pp. 64, 98.

[19] See Böckh, *Encyklopädie und Methodologie der philologischen Wissenschaften*, ed. Ernst Bratuscheck, 2d ed. (Leipzig, 1886), pp. 447, 412.

[20] See, e.g., ibid., p. 273.

Pietist-Romantic faith in the authenticity and autonomy of the *Geist* of each folk.[21] Historians, he argued, must begin by presupposing a transcendental world of belief, but then must recognize that its particular forms are always rooted in the mental life, physical conditions, and linguistic forms of a tribe of believers.[22] Against leading scholars in the field, including Welcker, Böckh, and Friedrich Thiersch, Müller insisted upon the autonomous development of Greek art and religion from the diverse characteristics of the region's clans [*Stammcharaktere*], which he carefully isolated from simultaneous and uninterrupted oriental and Egyptian traditions.[23] For Müller, comparative linguistics might show prehistorical connections between Greeks and orientals, "But the gods, the worships, the mythi of the Greeks in their distinctive character, assuredly belong to a totally different period, a period of separate development, in which there was even no external, compact, national whole."[24] Thus the philologist defended his exclusive concern with the Greeks on linguistic and professional grounds; the Greeks might have borrowed ideas, but these only became meaningful and researchable when they were reformulated as precise, Greek, concepts. But clearly the philologist's Graecocentrism was also derived from aesthetic, religious, and quasi-racist preferences.[25] Exemplary in every way, for Müller, the Greeks stood alone.

Martin Bernal is undoubtedly right to underline Müller's role in the narrowing of classical scholarship in the mid-nineteenth century. His mistake, however, is to attribute this narrowing exclusively to "racism" rather than to a similarly fateful combination of cultural nationalism, philological skepticism, institutionalized philhellenism, *and* the beginnings of racialist thought.[26] Bernal also overlooks the importance for Müller, and for the

---

[21] See Josine Blok, "Quest for a Scientific Mythology: F. Creuzer and K. O. Müller on History and Myth," *History and Theory*, suppl. 33 (1994): 26–52.

[22] Karl Otfried Müller, *Introduction to a Scientific System of Mythology*, trans. John Leitch (1899; reprint ed., New York, 1978), p. 176.

[23] See, e.g., Müller's review of Heinrich Meyer, *Geschichte der bildenden Künste bei den Griechen* (1824) and Friedrich Thiersch, *Ueber die Epochen der bildenden Kunst unter den Griechen* (1825), in *Karl Otfried Müllers kleine deutsche Schriften*, ed. Eduard Müller, vol. 2 (Breslau, 1848), pp. 315–98. Welcker refuted Müller's contentions explicitly in a long review of *Ancient Art* published in the *Rheinisches Museum* in 1834; see Welcker, "Aus der Anzeige von K. O. Müllers Handbuch der Archäologie 1830," pp. 329–52, esp. p. 335.

[24] Müller, *Introduction*, pp. 220–21.

[25] See, e.g., ibid., pp. 21, 166–67.

[26] See Martin Bernal, *Black Athena: The Afroasiatic Roots of Classical Civilization*, vol. 1: *The Fabrication of Ancient Greece, 1785–1985* (New Brunswick, N.J., 1987), pp. 308–16. It should be noted that Bernal quotes Müller almost exclusively from secondary sources. For Müller's account of Egyptian cultural autonomy, uncomplimentary though it is, see Müller to P. W. Forchhammer, 9 June 1831, in Müller, *Briefe aus einem Gelehrtenleben, 1797–1840*, vol. 1, ed. Karl Svoboda (Berlin, 1950), pp. 152–56, and Müller, "Ueber den angeblich ägyptischen Ursprung der griechischen Kunst," in *Müllers kleine Schriften*, 2:525.

classicist community as a whole, of the seminal methodological debate of the 1820s: the so-called Creuzer Affair. The Creuzer Affair was instrumental in delegitimizing comparative studies and, effectively, marking the end of romantic philhellenism, and Müller played a central role in it. Born in 1771, Friedrich Creuzer, like other contemporary scholars—for example, Humboldt, Friedrich Schlegel, or F. G. Welcker—made important studies of the Orient and the Mediterranean, of Indo-European culture as well as classical antiquity. But his dislike of historicist, text-critical scholarship and his suspicious association with Catholicism and Hegelian philosophy turned much of the world of specialist philology—especially in Berlin—against him. Though some remnants of Creuzerian ideas made their way into archaeological circles, the historicist text critics' victory in this methodological skirmish was of considerable consequence for the developmental course of German *Altertumswissenschaft*, and deserves a short digression here.

Like many another philologist of his generation, Friedrich Creuzer began his studies intending to become a Lutheran pastor. A student at the University of Jena in the rambunctious 1790s, Creuzer delved into Kantian philosophy, read enlightened biblical criticism, and listened, rapturously, to all of Schiller's lectures.[27] It was, however, the Romantic historian of law, Friedrich von Savigny, who convinced Creuzer to undertake a teaching career, and introduced the young scholar to his other protégés, the brothers Wilhelm and Jakob Grimm. Creuzer moved from the University of Marburg to the chair of philology and ancient history at the University of Heidelberg in 1804; here he joined a circle that included the Grimms, the Catholic mythographer and journalist Joseph von Görres, and the brothers Friedrich and August Schlegel. Görres and the Schlegels awakened Creuzer's interest in India and the Near East; the Grimms undoubtedly contributed to his fascination with local antiquities. Already at the time he completed the manuscript of his most widely read book, *Die Symbolik* (first edition 1810–11), Creuzer apparently suspected that his ambitious account of the history of religious experience would not content the historicists; having begun with the symbol as the primordial embodiment of thought and sensory experience, Creuzer traced the elaboration of symbols into myths, and myths into religions, which became increasingly rational as history progressed and civilization moved from East (India) to West (Greece). He had known, Creuzer later insisted, that this sort of inquiry would be reviled by those "who are exclusively interested in deconstruction [*decomponiren*], and in making everything that trustworthy history and religious conscious-

---

[27] Friedrich Creuzer, *Aus dem Leben eines alten Professors*, part 5, vol. 1 of *Friedrich Creuzer's Deutsche Schriften* (Leipzig, 1848), pp. 10–27. On Jena in the 1790s, see Theodor Ziolkowski, *German Romanticism and Its Institutions* (Princeton, N.J., 1990).

ness hold to be eternal and unchangeable into uncertain fluctuations [*Fluc-tion*], in order that we admire their keen understanding and heroic daring and that they may now be able to build the throne of their egoism in the midst of a general nihilism."[28] He had not, however, expected that the "egoists" would triumph.

The bitterness of Creuzer's retrospective prophesy was undoubtedly a function of the virulent campaign launched against him. A. C. Lobeck attacked Creuzer's philological probity; Johann Voß's *Anti-Symbolik* (1824) contained a plurality of "proofs" that Creuzer was a crypto-Catholic and deluded by dilettantish oriental mysticism.[29] Some critics, however, were less savage, but more influential. If K. O. Müller denounced Creuzer for basing his account of India's ur-religion on little more than ancient rumors, and for failing to recognize the essential differences that separated Hellenic and Egyptian *Geist*, he also praised Creuzer for his insightfulness.[30] But Müller's *Prolegomena zu einer wissenschaftlichen Mythologie* (1825—translated into English as *Introduction to a Scientific System of Mythology*) piled argument upon argument against comparative history-writing, and against incautious speculation about the preliterate past, a sin Creuzer had certainly committed. If for Creuzer, historical inquiry was not limited to the inspection of written testimony, for Müller, and even more for his younger contemporary Leopold von Ranke, the arrival of writing marked the boundary beyond which secure judgments could not be made. In reviewing another popular cross-national interpretation of artistic symbolism, Müller asked: "Can that which is commonly grasped purely externally, without understanding the language, without attempting to trace out religious concepts, ever provide a solid basis for scientific knowledge?"[31] The most influential critic of Creuzerian prehistorical comparativism and speculation, Müller reconfirmed Winckelmann's pronouncements on the autochthony of Greek culture and insisted upon archaeology's conformity to the dictates of philological historicism.

Müller's most significant contribution to the development of the study of Greek art was his *Handbuch der Archäologie der Kunst* (1830—translated into English as *Ancient Art and Its Remains*), which one of his successors, a half-century later, was to call "an epoch-making handbook, its system au-

[28] Creuzer, *Aus dem Leben eines alten Professors*, p. 55.

[29] See the documents collected in Ernst Howald, *Der Kampf um Creuzers Symbolik: Eine Auswahl von Dokumenten* (Tübingen, 1926), esp. pp. 39–41, 130ff.

[30] See Müller's 1821 review of Creuzer's *Symbolik* in *Müllers kleine Schriften*, 2:3–20; also, Blok, "Quest for a Scientific Mythology," pp. 32–37.

[31] Müller, review of C. A. Böttiger, *Ideen zur Kunst-Mythologie: Erster Cursus* (1826), in *Müllers kleine Schriften*, 2:50. For Ranke's views, see Donald R. Kelley, "Mythistory in the Age of Ranke," in *Leopold von Ranke and the Shaping of the Historical Discipline*, ed. George G. Iggers and James M. Powell (Syracuse, N.Y., 1990), p. 6.

thoritative down to the present day."[32] For Müller, art, like other emanations of human *Geist*, could only be understood as a product of *national*
particularities. "Like all higher intellectual activities," he had written in
1820, "like the unconscious development of language, like beliefs and
myths and poetry, [art] belongs essentially to the people [*Volk*]."[33] In the
Handbuch, he proffered a strictly Kantian definition of pure, nonsensual
beauty, and insisted upon the autonomous development of Greek styles,
despite the nation's many contacts with the Orient.[34] Greek art owed its
perfections primarily to the optimal blend of the natural and supernatural
in Greek religion; the glories of Greek sculpture were a function not of
political freedom, but of spiritual harmony.[35] The philologist consigned to
an appendix his discussion of "nations not of Greek race," including the
Egyptians, Semites and Syrians, and Indians. All of these benighted nations
had failed to reach or shape Greek artistic splendor, he claimed, the Egyptians because their architectonic forms were too utilitarian, the Semites because their art was too decorative, the Indians because their few plastic
arts were too sensuous.[36] Müller did not mind if others devoted their talents
to pursuing these divergent national traditions; one of his most brilliant
students, Karl Richard Lepsius, became nineteenth-century Germany's
greatest—but strictly historicist—Egyptologist. But clearly, for Müller and
his descendants, comparative studies of art and mythology could not offer
any real insight into historical developments. In the wake of this historicizing trend, wide-ranging *érudits* like Creuzer, Welcker, and even Böckh himself increasing came to seem strangers at the philhellenist feast, as the other,
slightly older generation of neohumanists, such as Humboldt and Friedrich
Schlegel went to their graves.

Müller himself came to regret the philological narrowing that followed
the Creuzer Affair, and the somewhat similar battle between the *Sachphilologe* Böckh and the *Wortphilologe* Gottfried Hermann.[37] In an 1833
letter to Eduard Gerhard, he expressed the hope that Gerhard's work would
inspire German *Philologen* to pursue new and deeper studies of art—"or at
least the latter [philologists] have only themselves to blame if they stay on
the old, barren, totally overcrowded meadows while the most delightful

[32] Karl Bernard Stark quoted in Bruer, *Die Wirkung Winckelmanns*, p. 101.

[33] Müller, "Ueber den angeblich ägyptischen Ursprung," p. 524.

[34] *Ancient Art and Its Remains*, ed. F. G. Welcker, trans. John Leitch (London, 1852), pp. 4–
10, 106.

[35] Ibid., pp. 9–11.

[36] Ibid., pp. 183–226. Müller never explicitly gives racial inferiority as his reason for excluding the Egyptians from participation in the making of Greek culture, though at one point
he describes the former as the Caucasians nearest the Negro type (ibid., p. 184).

[37] Hermann's sharp criticisms of Böckh's linguistic skills divided the philological community of the 1820s and 1830s, but Hermann, unlike Creuzer's critics, did not succeed in discrediting his opponent. Hoffmann, *Böckh*, pp. 48–61.

fields are opened and made accessible to them," he wrote.[38] A political liberal, Müller also opposed the exiling of the "Göttingen Seven," in part because he believed it would destroy the honor and prestige of the university to which he belonged.[39] But, once begun, specialization and depoliticization were hard to reverse, and ironically, both contributed to archaeology's emergence as an independent study of "real things" [Realien], a fully historicized category that included knowledge of artifacts, art, topography, architecture, legal and economic affairs, and history. Under this definition, archaeology could be saved from the "arbitrariness" of antiquarianism and the unscientific speculativeness of the mythographers, and lay claim to academic respectability alongside the philologists.

Philologists, however, were slow to acknowledge the need for expert training in Realien; many early archaeologists owed their appointments to their royal patrons, not to university faculties. Both Ernst Curtius, who had been tutor to the Prussian crown prince, and Eduard Gerhard owed their Berlin appointments to imperial decree.[40] In 1842, the University of Berlin vetoed Karl Richard Lepsius's application for a teaching position on the grounds that there was no need to include Egyptology in the curriculum; upon his return from an exceedingly successful collecting and recording tour in Egypt, however, the faculty did not object to the king's appointment of the now famous historian to a new Berlin chair.[41] Eventually, the rapidly increasing pace of scholarly production did induce faculties, where funds permitted, to add an additional position dedicated to Sachphilologie. In 1856, for example, the University of Göttingen decided to fill the professorship once held by the eighteenth-century polymath J. G. Gesner with two scholars, one (Hermann Sauppe) to handle "the exegetical-linguistic side of philology" and another (Ernst Curtius) to represent "the real [side of philology] (archaeology, art history, mythography, constitutional history, geography)."[42] But, as few new positions were opened until after 1871, and as

[38] Müller to Gerhard, 26 February 1833, in Müller, Briefe, p. 189.

[39] See his letter to Ernst Herbert Reichsgraf zu Münster (20 February 1838) and to Gerhard (25 June 1838), ibid., pp. 329–36, 343. The "Göttingen Seven" were liberal members of the faculty of the University of Göttingen who refused to pledge an oath to the new king of Hanover, who had just abrogated the state constitution. Their protest failed, and three of them were forced into exile.

[40] See Adolf Borbein, "Klassische Archäologie in Berlin vom 18. bis zum 20. Jahrhundert," in Berlin und die Antike, ed. Willmuth Arenhoevel and Christa Schreiber (Berlin, 1979), p. 129; Reinhard Kekulé von Stradonitz, Eduard Gerhard (Berlin, 1910), pp. 6–10.

[41] M. Rainer Lepsius, "Richard Lepsius und seine Familie—Bildungsbürgertum und Wissenschaft," in Karl Richard Lepsius (1810–1884), ed. Elke Freier and Walter F. Reineke, (Berlin, 1988), pp. 37–39.

[42] Jochen Bleicken, "Die Herausbildung der alten Geschichte in Göttingen: Von Heyne bis Busolt," in Die klassische Altertumswissenschaft an der Georg-August-Universität Göttingen, ed. Carl J. Classen (Göttingen, 1989), pp. 106–7.

philologists continued to see archaeology as a subordinate, auxiliary field, rather than as an autonomous equal, archaeology had to await the rise of grand-scale, state-funded excavations and the expansion of the Royal Museums to gain its full measure of academic respectability and social prestige.

Grudgingly, however, as French and British archaeologists brought home new, ever larger, treasures, and as photography and railroads simplified the reproduction and transport of images and artifacts, philologists grew more and more interested in the study of ancient *Realien*. It must be said, too, that archaeological adventures appealed more strongly to the bureaucracy and the general public than did even the finest text editions. Thanks to the success of his expedition, Lepsius became a popular lecturer and trusted bureaucrat. The letters he sent to Berlin during his visits to Egypt and Ethiopia were published for popular consumption, and the collection of lithographs, architectural drawings, and inscriptions his team amassed during this trip appeared in twelve volumes so luxuriously heavy as to be almost impossible to lift off the library shelves. At one point in his career, Lepsius held the offices of full professor at the University of Berlin, general secretary of the Deutsches Archäologisches Institut, editor of the *Zeitschrift für ägyptische Sprache und Altertumskunde* (*Journal for the Study of Egyptian Language and Antiquities*), director of the Egyptian Museum, and director of the Royal Libraries. And Curtius, as the next chapter will show, became an equally powerful scholar-bureaucrat, whose public lectures drew enormous crowds.

Importantly, archaeology possessed something philology did not: an immediate, visual, means to gain access to the beautiful. Art was one realm in which readers *expected* scholars to pick favorites and wax eloquent, and classical sculptures offered easily "readable" symbols of the neohumanist pedagogical promises. Classical scholars frequently looked to art to counterbalance their own anxieties about the effects of the ever-advancing scholarly division of labor; later in the century, the virtues of the holistic, direct apprehension of Greek sculpture would be repeatedly touted in response to attacks on the drudgery of *Gymnasium* language lessons. Thus, despite the rapid obsolescence of Winckelmann's work as a source of factual information, archaeologists throughout the nineteenth century proudly advertised their descent from this aestheticizing ancestor. Beginning in 1831, commemoration of his birthday became the occasion for the recapitulation of archaeology's origin in the normative aesthetics of the German Golden Age.[43] It would be the great challenge of German archaeology to reconcile

---

[43] See, e.g., Eduard Gerhard, *Winckelmann und die Gegenwart nebst einem etruskischen Spiegel* (16th program of the Archaeological Society in Berlin on Winckelmannstag) (Berlin, 1856). On the spread of Winckelmannstag celebrations, see Wolfgang Schiering, "Zur Geschichte der Archäologie," in *Allgemeine Grundlagen der Archäologie*, ed. Ulrich Hausmann, *Handbuch der Archäologie*, vol. 1 (Munich, 1969), p. 46.

its passionate, and efficacious, attachment to Winckelmannian philhellenism with the historicist conventions of professional classical scholarship.

Intellectually, then, the years after 1820 were marked by the narrowing
of humanism's horizons and the triumph of philological historicism; the
poetic and political elements of philhellenism were largely displaced by
strict scholarly decorum, though Greek art did not lack for rapturous admirers. At the same time, the social world in which the classicists moved
narrowed. As noted above, many of the first generation of neohumanist
Altertumswissenschaftler—Niebuhr, Humboldt, Friedrich Schlegel—spent
the greater parts of their careers outside the university system. In the next
generations, there are hardly any examples of this (C. J. von Bunsen is one
exception). Particularly in classics, respectable intellectual activity was becoming more and more defined by university affiliation, and as this occurred, private lives too were interlaced with professional bonds. In general,
autobiographical accounts and eulogies contain very little in the way of
personal information; except for glimpses into political behavior where it is
unavoidable, as in the cases of Welcker or Mommsen, or chance comments
on professorial eccentricities, the picture painted is one of ceaseless toil, of
a Spartan life-style fully commensurate with the Pietist-ascetic dedication
to learning advocated (and practiced) by F. A. Wolf. Perhaps by leading
such puritanical lives, nineteenth-century classicists managed to survive to
great age, especially those who did not venture too far from home. Creuzer
lived to be eighty-seven; Immanuel Bekker to be eighty-six. Mommsen died
in 1903 at the age of eighty-six; Böckh and Ernst Curtius were eighty-two,
and Welcker was eighty-four, when their careers ended. The relatively
young age at which these philologists had received their positions meant
that they held their chairs for extraordinarily long periods. Bekker held his
Berlin post for sixty-one years; Böckh lasted fifty-six years in Berlin, while
Creuzer occupied his Heidelberg chair for fifty-four years.[44] Its formative
experiences in the era of Humboldt's reforms, this cohort of classicists held
positions of influence and prestige into the 1860s, exerting an undeniable
drag on innovation.

The classicist community in the nineteenth century was more than durable; it was inbred. Its very high proportion of father–son-in-law relations
suggests that daughters of the *Bildungsbürgertum* still came with a dowry,
now intellectual rather than monetary in nature. Moriz Haupt married the
daughter of his teacher Gottfried Hermann; Wilamowitz married Theodor
Mommsen's daughter Marie; two members of the Olympia excavation team,
Paul Graef and Wilhelm Dörpfeld, married daughters of the excavation's
leading architect, Friedrich Adler. In a feat of perhaps unparalleled kinship

---

[44] John Edwin Sandys, *A History of Classical Scholarship*, 3 vols. (New York, 1969) 3:65, 97,
85. A similar phenomenon is discernible for the generation born between about 1848 and
1860. See below, chapter 8.

loyalty, Ernst Curtius married a colleague's widow in 1850 and her sister in 1853, after his first wife's death, while his brother Georg married a third sister from the same family. The philologist Hermann Usener married Lili Dilthey, sister of the classicist Carl Dilthey and the philosopher Wilhelm Dilthey, Usener's dearest friends.[45] Richard Schöne wisely married a daughter of the successful publisher Hermann Härtel, who had printed Schöne's dissertation; when she died in childbirth, he married her sister.[46] Numerous other examples could be given. The point is that social and familial ties recapitulated intellectual ones, further isolating the classicists from unfamiliar ideas and experiences. Small wonder, then, that the vigor and determination of the school reform movement of the 1880s and 1890s took them almost completely by surprise.

Thus German classical scholarship between about 1820 and 1870 veered away from the socially progressive educational program of Humboldt and turned its attention to specialized studies, and particularly to painstaking linguistic analysis or the collection of materials for national histories to be composed in the wiser (and less repressive) future. The universities, and especially the University of Berlin, were unquestionably the cultural institutions from which appropriate understanding of the Greeks emanated. Beyond the universities, however, German *Altertumswissenschaft* was evolving in a location even more remote from the social and political realities of midcentury Prussia: Rome.

Origins of the Institut für Altertumskunde

By the time Winckelmann arrived in Rome in 1755, signs of new interest in the arts of the ancient world were rife. In 1738–39, Lord Sandwich, a member of the Society of Dilettanti, sailed around the Aegean, bringing back to England a shipload of antiquities. Almost accidentally, Richard Jenkyns suggests, the Dilettanti, originally a rakish aristocratic social club, became the first patrons of new, serious study of Greek culture, beginning with the publication of volume 1 of James Stuart and Nicholas Revett's *Antiquities of Athens* in 1762.[47] Between 1731 and 1740, again from 1745 to 1765, the Bourbon royal house in Naples conducted a series of excavations at Herculaneum, as well as digging at Pompeii and Stabia from 1748 and 1749, respectively. Duke Philip of Parma also conducted excavations, and in 1760 founded a museum of antiquities;[48] the continuing popularity of archaeol-

[45] Momigliano, "New Paths of Classicism," p. 38.

[46] Ludwig Pallat, *Richard Schöne: Generaldirektor der Königlichen Museen in Berlin* (Berlin, 1959), p. 38.

[47] Richard Jenkyns, *The Victorians and Ancient Greece* (Cambridge, Mass., 1980), pp. 4–5.

[48] Carlo Pietrangeli, "Archaeological Excavations in Italy, 1750–1850," in *The Age of Neo-Classicism* (London, 1972), pp. xlv–xlvii.

ogy among the nobles of this city is paid tribute in Stendhal's *Charterhouse of Parma* (1839). Already by the third quarter of the eighteenth century, the large numbers of excavators at work in the Papal State were required to have official permission to dig on public land and to give a portion of their finds to the Holy See.[49] These and other activities produced three notably influential works: the *Antichità di Ercolano esposte* (8 vols., 1757–1792), Stuart and Revett's *Antiquities of Athens*, and the Comte de Caylus's *Recueil d'antiquités égyptiennes, étrusques, et romanes* (1752). The *Description de l'Égypte*, the ten-volume masterpiece that communicated the results of Napoleon's Egyptian expedition, was printed between 1809 and 1828; its beautiful engravings gave European readers their first detailed impressions of ancient Egyptian monuments. Inspired by such a wealth of new publications, art enthusiasts like, most famously, Lord Elgin, went off to plunder classical sites, in search of model masterworks that might improve modern taste; and even Lord Byron, by highlighting Elgin's depredations in his popular poem, *Childe Harold's Pilgrimage*, contributed to the new fascination for ancient art and obsession with its ownership.[50]

This pan-European phenomenon, so optimally reflected in the extravagant excavations of Rome funded by the city's Napoleonic occupiers,[51] expressed itself in increased interest in ancient artifacts and customs in the German-speaking lands as well. Few Germans, however, reached Greece before the Greek War of Independence; many academic scholars—including Winckelmann, Wolf, Böckh, Bekker, Gottfried Hermann, Welcker, and even Heinrich Brunn (d. 1894)—avoided the perilous trip altogether. Böckh, who also failed to visit Rome, maintained, half-jokingly, that he knew what Greece and Rome had looked like in antiquity, and that was enough for him.[52] K. O. Müller's trip to Greece in 1839–40 promised a new marriage of site observation, exact measurement, and geographical commentary, but Müller fell victim to sunstroke while collecting inscriptions at Delphi and died before he could publish his results. Those who did venture the risk were largely aristocrats of adventurous demeanor like Baron von Riedesel, who made a desultory visit to the mainland in 1768 (Winckelmann was meant to accompany him but demurred at the last moment), and Baron Otto von Stackelberg, who was captured there by pirates in 1813.[53]

[49] Ibid., pp. xlvii–xlviii.

[50] On Byron and Elgin, see William St. Clair, *Lord Elgin and the Marbles* (London, 1967), pp. 187–89.

[51] See Ronald T. Ridley, *The Eagle and the Spade: Archaeology in Rome during the Napoleonic Era* (Cambridge, 1992).

[52] Walter Rehm, *Griechentum und Goethezeit: Geschichte eines Glaubens* (Leipzig, 1936), p. 6.

[53] On Riedesel, see David Constantine, *Early Greek Travellers and the Hellenic Ideal* (Cambridge, 1984), pp. 128–46; on Stackelberg see Wilhelm Barth and Max Kehrig-Korn, *Die Philhellenenzeit* (Munich, 1960), p. 15. Stackelberg did, however, participate in a dig paid for by Ludwig I of Bavaria at Aegina.

If Riedesel and Stackelberg differed from most other German philhellenists in actually having visited Greece, in many other ways they were typical of the generation of nonacademic early archaeologists resident in Rome during the *Vormärz* (the period between 1815 and the March revolutions of 1848). Both possessed the three essential qualities shared by all these men: money, good connections, and aesthetic enthusiasm. Energetic aestheticism was needed to push projects ahead, though in later years it might be said that desire for scientific respectability and personal recognition replaced aesthetic enjoyment as collections were amassed and the collectors aged. Private wealth was required to finance such early exploits as Lord Elgin's "excavation" in Athens, and was in relative abundance in Rome, which had long been a vital part of the young aristocrat's grand tour. Connections, especially those made official by appointment to diplomatic posts, allowed well-to-do scholars easy entry into court circles. As early as 1806, Crown Prince Ludwig of Bavaria had deputized Bishop Häffelin to buy art for his collection in Rome; a number of Ludwig's later buyers were able to convince the monarch to finance excavations in pursuit of finer acquisitions.[54] It should be recalled that Humboldt, as Prussian ambassador to the Holy See between 1802 and 1808, did his best to promote German scholarship and art in Rome, though he rarely visited museums or galleries and thought excavation of antiquities to be a kind of sacrilege, sacrificing the imagination to the mere increase of knowledge.[55] Humboldt's successors, most notably the Roman historian B. G. Niebuhr and the pious and prolific scholar C. J. von Bunsen continued this tradition with such ardor that a contemporary Frenchmen suggested that they served as envoys not only of the Prussian state to the Papal State but also of German science to Roman antiquity.[56]

Rome during the *Vormärz* was not a place in which educated men of like interests could easily miss one another; as an envious twentieth-century archaeologist put it, the city was then "free from the *profanum vulgus* of today's flood of foreigners."[57] In 1823, several of these young enthusiasts

[54] Raimund Wünsche, "Ludwigs Skulpturenerwerbungen für die Glyptothek," in *Glyptothek München, 1830–1980*, ed. Klaus Vierneisel and Gottlieb Leinz (Munich, 1980), pp. 23–83.

[55] Rudolf Haym, *Wilhelm von Humboldt: Lebensbild und Charakteristik* (Osnabrück, 1856), p. 230; Bruford, *German Tradition*, p. 21.

[56] Quoted in Dr. E. Loch, "Das Deutsche Archäologische Institute," in *Unterhaltungsbeilage zur Täglichen Rundschau*, no. 92 (20 April 1904), p. 366, in DAI, Nachlaß Dörpfeld, Kasten 14, Mappe 3. Other states similarly combined scientific and governmental posts. August Kestner, for example, a devout student and collector of antiquities, served as Hanoverian ambassador; he also mediated between the Pope and the British royal house, which had no representative of its own in Rome. Adolf Michaelis, *Geschichte des Deutschen Archäologischen Instituts, 1829–1879* (Berlin, 1879), p. 8.

[57] Eugen Petersen, "Adolf Michaelis," *Zeitschrift für bildende Kunst* 36 (1911): 193.

came together to form a reading circle devoted to the study of ancient art and mythology. The society's founding members were August Kestner (son of Charlotte Kestner, Goethe's model for Lotte in *Werther*, and Hanoverian ambassador to the Holy See), Stackelberg, and two students, Eduard Gerhard and Theodor Panofka. Apparently, these German dilettanti were particularly intrigued by ancient cults of Apollo, and thus took on the title *Hyperboreisch-Römische Gesellschaft* (Hyperborean-Roman Society), in honor of the mythical northern Hyperboreans among whom Apollo supposedly dwelled during the winter.[58] With the exception of Gerhard, none of these men were particularly well schooled or interested in philology (and, not surprisingly, only Gerhard was respected in academic circles). But they were all anxious to see, and catalog, as many ancient artworks—Roman, Etruscan, and Egyptian, as well as Greek—as possible; despite their sincere Graecophilia, all these well-traveled men maintained serious interests in other forms of art. Kestner's eclectic collection, greatly admired by his many visitors, included terracottas, bronzes, paintings, Egyptian artifacts, and his own sketches.[59] The others aspired to the same sort of ecumenical aestheticism, in more and less scholarly forms.

Not satisfied with a private association, the Hyperboreans soon developed a plan to turn their personal connections and wide-ranging tastes to scholarly ends and to make Rome the collecting point for all European work on monuments. Their plans, however, initially foundered, owing both to lack of funds and to Ambassador Bunsen's fear that the founding of such an organization might offend the Pope or Italian scholars.[60] The association was still contemplating its next move when the Prussian crown prince (later Friedrich Wilhelm IV) arrived in Rome in late 1828. Fortunately Gerhard was selected to show the prince the wonders of the city, and, after three weeks of concerted lobbying, Gerhard and Bunsen at last convinced him to serve as protector of a new, international Institut für archäologische Korrespondenz.

The new society held its first meeting on 21 April 1829, with three diplomats presiding: the Duc de Blacas (French ambassador to Naples) as honorary president, Bunsen as general secretary, and Kestner as archivist. Full members of the IfAK included Leopold von Ranke, the Danish sculptor Bertel Thorwaldsen, Goethe, and the architects K. F. Schinkel and Leo von Klenze, as well as many French and Italian scholars and artists. As K. O.

[58] Marie Jorns, *August Kestner und seine Zeit, 1777–1853* (Hanover, 1964), p. 201.

[59] Ibid., pp. 213–14, 313.

[60] Eugen Mercklin, "Archäologische Institute," in *Forschungsinstitute: Ihre Geschichte, Organisation, und Ziele*, vol. 1 ed. Ludolph Brauer et al. (Hamburg, 1930), p. 282; Michaelis, *Geschichte*, pp. 21–22.

2. The Institut für archäologische Korrespondenz, as seen by its members. Marquand Library, Department of Rare Books and Special Collections, Princeton University Libraries.

Müller described his visit to a meeting of the IfAK in 1839, "There one can easily have to speak four languages in a quarter of an hour."[61] As the title implied, the institute's main purpose was the collection and publication of drawings and information conveyed to it by scholars, antiquarians, and collectors. Rather than hoping to exhume unknown treasures, the institute desired, as its statutes proclaimed, and the frontispiece for its *Monumenti inediti* suggested, "to gather and make known all archaeologically significant facts and finds—that is, from architecture, sculpture and painting, topography, and epigraphy—that are brought to light in the realm of classical antiquity, in order that these may be saved from being lost, and by means of concentration in one place may be made accessible for scientific study."[62] This statement, as well as the institute's self-limitation to the study of

---

[61] Müller, quoted in Jorns, *August Kestner*, p. 303. For more on the early IfAK, see Adolf Michaelis, *Geschichte des Deutschen Archäologischen Instituts, 1829–1879* (Berlin, 1879), pp. 24–37.

[62] Quoted in Mercklin, "Archäologische Institute," p. 282.

Greece and Rome, would have to be significantly altered in the years to come.

With the founding of the institute, an important change came over the Hyperboreans, no longer a society of private individuals pursuing their personal interests but now an institution devoted to the advancement of knowledge. A directorate (*Direktion*, later *Zentraldirektion*) was formed, consisting of a general secretory and several subsecretories in charge of Italian, French, and German members; in 1856 and in 1885, reforms both expanded the directorate and created new hierarchies. But in the 1830s, as in decades to come, the directorate's first priority was the raising of funds. In his *Thatsachen des Archäologischen Instituts in Rom* (The Actual Situation of the Archaeological Institute in Rome [1832]), designed to raise much-needed funds from the Prussian court, subsecretary Gerhard ascribed the lack of progress in his field since the days of founding father Winckelmann to the basic incapacity of the individual scholar to overcome the inherent difficulties of the field:

> In the museums where original artifacts are piled up, no one knows where these came from; one has to be wary of the depictions that are produced in engravings, as one can only verify the true form of the work by means of comparison with the real thing; finally, with good reason, one rarely dares to describe the relationship of the individual work to the totality of all available monuments, for no one is in a position to survey the whole mass. Winckelmann . . . had to exclude from consideration the monuments across the seas and within the earth; in a field in which the material has increased vastly since his time, hardly any new approach [to the material] has appeared; his successors, proceeding in isolation, likewise cannot achieve this—should one then give up on furthering any sort of science, because to do so is impossible for any single person?[63]

Naturally, Gerhard's answer was "no," and his proposal was clear: if archaeology were ever to merit comparison to "the highly refined study of the literary monuments [*Sprachdenkmäler*] of antiquity,"[64] it would have to become a supraindividual, semibureaucratic endeavor. Given the vastness of the mission, Winckelmann's legacy would have to be carried out by means of a scientific, bureaucratically organized division of labor.

In addition to propounding this novel organizational vision, Gerhard, ardent Winckelmannian though he remained, also guided the IfAK into unfamiliar artistic and historical territory. As one eulogist remarked, the decisive moment in Gerhard's scientific career was his invitation to take part in Lucien Bonaparte's dig at Volcenti in 1829, during which excavators

---

[63] Gerhard, *Thatsachen des Archäologischen Instituts in Rom* (2d ed., Berlin, 1834), p. 21.
[64] Ibid.

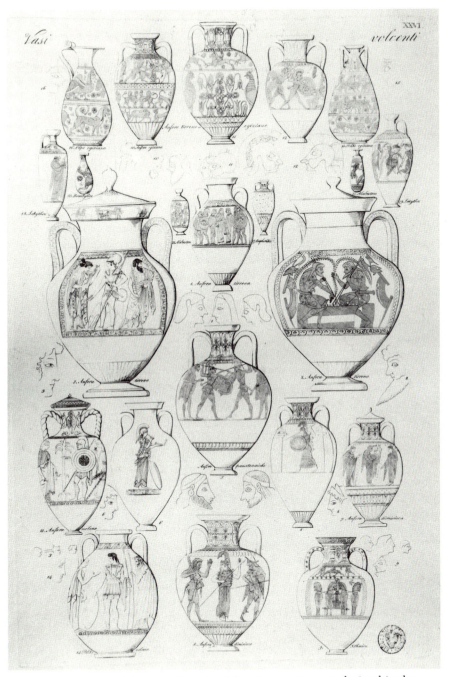

3. A selection of the vases from the Volcenti excavations, as depicted in the *Monumenti inediti*. The IfAK artist was particularly concerned to show differences in the rendering of the faces of warriors. Marquand Library, Department of Rare Books and Special Collections, Princeton University Libraries.

extracted over three thousand painted vases from the gravesite. Gerhard's scholarly study of these vases, published in the institute's Italian-language journal in 1831, showed that these artifacts, unlike the difficult to date and rare monumental marbles, could be used to trace the continuous development of classical art.[65] "All art-historical knowledge must proceed from the masterpieces of sculpture," Gerhard argued in an essay of 1858; but other genres, too, should be represented in educational collections, including pottery, architecture, and coins. Emphasizing both the pedagogical importance of "a vibrant and elevating impression [*Anschauung*]" and the scholarly imperative that all artistic materials be put in a historical frame,[66] Gerhard was instrumental in broadening the academic and popular conception of classical art.

In his yearly reports on the state of archaeological studies printed in the journal of the Archäologische Gesellschaft (an elite but not exclusively learned society founded by Gerhard to foster popular admiration for classical art in Prussia), the IfAK director did not dwell on the newly discovered beauties of a few select masterpieces. Instead Gerhard turned his attention to the stumbling blocks to scholarly progress—lack of trained personnel, the greed of private collectors, rare and poor illustrations, and shortages of funds.[67] But two additional impediments loomed larger in Gerhard's conception than these technical, organizational, and monetary difficulties: the blithe ignorance of classical art demonstrated by philologists, and the lack of Prussian archaeological triumphs in the Mediterranean. Without sufficient funds or political power, Gerhard could do very little to remedy the latter situation. He did, however, campaign vigorously for the demise of German philological one-sidedness, recognizing that the flourishing of archaeology depended directly upon the philological community's willingness to share its access to the Greek and Roman *Geist* with the students of classical art.

Of course, archaeological achievements also depended on the IfAK's income. At first, the institute was financed largely by private subscriptions and donations; from 1832, at the urging of Alexander von Humboldt, the Prussian state also contributed small amounts, a benevolence that was never granted without some reference to the institute's diplomatic function.

---

[65] Eduard Gerhard, "Rapporto intorno i vasi volcenti," in *Annali dell'Instituto di Corrispondenza Archeologica* 3 (1831): 5–218; Karl Friedrichs's elegy quoted in "Wissenschaftliche Vereine," in *AA zur AZ* 25, no. 222 (June 1867): 81–3; Kekulé, *Gerhard*, p. 12.

[66] Eduard Gerhard, "Ueber archäologische Apparate und Museen," in *AZ* 16, nos. 116, 117 (August–September 1858): 210.

[67] E.g., [Gerhard], "Archäologische Gesellschaften," in *AZ, Beilagen* n.s. 6 (June 1848): 85–94.

In 1833, Minister of Education Karl Freiherr von Altenstein urged the Finance Ministry to approve the King's request for a yearly subsidy of 420 talers for the IfAK. "The state cannot be indifferent toward an organization of such excellent [international] standing," Altenstein wrote, "and surely may, when it needs immediate assistance, make modest expression of this."[68] After 1833, the state continued to provide yearly subsidies, although funding was never guaranteed. Between 1838 and 1842, the sum fell to 300 talers; 1842–47 saw a rise to 800 talers (enough for the first secretary's salary), paid from the king's privy purse, plus an additional 540 talers, added in 1845 to pay the wages of Wilhelm Henzen, the second secretary.[69] On recommending the addition of this position, the Minister of Education Johann Eichhorn, usually no friend to scholars, echoed Altenstein's commendation of the institute, adding that it was also concerned with "the enhancement of Your Royal Majesty's artistic and scientific collections." The benefits accruing to the patron of such a redoubtable body surely exceeded the costs, Eichhorn wrote, particularly as its expanded activities had made it a gathering point for archaeologists of all nations. "It seems to me important," Eichhorn added, "not simply with regard to scholarship, that our government secure a closer relationship to the archaeological institute in Rome."[70]

Despite the encouragement of the cultural bureaucracy and the agitation of institute members, however, the IfAK did not officially become a Prussian state institution until 1871. In 1859, the institute's subsidy (now at 4,500 talers and soon raised to 5,840 talers) was switched from the privy purse to the state budget—but was still considered a "temporary" expense.[71] Moreover, Gerhard's grand publishing plans could rarely be realized for lack of funds, and institute members feared for the continuation of their subsidy in times of frequent budget shortfalls. In response, scholars began to emphasize the Germanness of the IfAK in their appeals for funds and to underline its salutary contribution to the cultural refinement of the Fatherland. Al-

---

[68] Altenstein to Finance Ministry, 18 March 1833, MZStA Rep. 151-IC/7108. Altenstein had himself suggested this subsidy to the king; see Altenstein to Friedrich Wilhelm III, 16 February 1833, MZStA 2.2.1/21317, pp. 2–3, reminding the latter of the institute's connections with big-name European scholars. This sum (420 talers) was hardly princely; it amounted to about twice the paltry stipend artists received from the Berliner Kunstakademie in the same era. See Joachim Grossmann, *Künstler, Hof und Bürgertum: Leben und Arbeit von Malern in Preußen, 1786–1850* (Berlin, 1994), pp. 26–27.

[69] See Friedrich Wilhelm IV to Eichhorn, 7 January 1842 and 3 February 1845; also Education Ministry to Finance Ministry and Friedrich Wilhelm IV, 27 December 1853, all in ibid., Rep. 151 IC/7108.

[70] Eichhorn to Friedrich Wilhelm IV, 16 January 1845, ibid.

[71] See Raumer to Friedrich Wilhelm IV, 11 May 1858, ibid. 2.2.1/21317, pp. 60–61.

ready in 1860, the IfAK statutes had expressed an obviously uninternational aim—"especially to prepare staff to direct the Roman IfAK and teachers of archaeology for our national universities."[72] This explicit policy change, and the provision in 1859 of stipends for young archaeologists, marked another step away from the Hyperborean tradition toward the era of nationally segregated "schools" in Rome and Athens devoted to the training of museum officials, conservators, and teachers for the home country. Over the next few years, too, something of a generational revolution took place in Rome; the years 1865–69 saw the death of many of the more internationally minded scholars and generous patrons of the *Vormärz*, such as Welcker, Jahn, de Luynes, and Gerhard; and in 1865, the IfAK's second director and intellectual heir to this generation, Heinrich Brunn, took a professorship in Munich. The Hyperborean age of private patronage, cosmopolitan partnership, and dilettantish aestheticism was clearly nearing its end.[73]

Gerhard had himself foreseen some of the changes underway at the time of his death. As precise measurements progressively displaced flowery descriptions in the pages of professional journals and new digs opened not only in Greece and Italy, but also in Syria, Russia, and many German states, Gerhard noted the disappearance of a kind of romantic passion in the art-historical community. In 1857, the IfAK director observed sadly that classical scholars like Curtius and Wilhelm Henzen seemed more charmed by inscriptions than by artworks,[74] and in the following year, he identified another worrying departure from Winckelmannian aestheticism: the sight of classical art was becoming commonplace. The exoticizing tastes promoted by "modern *Bildung*," Gerhard lamented, were driving classical archaeologists into dilettantry or obsolescence:

> Greek antiquity and the study of its monuments are from [modern *Bildung's*] standpoint stale goods. Some representatives of so-called classical archaeology, who like us have required some time to catch up to Italian scholarship, are in danger of seeming deficient, if they do not want to take into the bargain Celtic and American graves, Gothic churches and Byzantine diptychs, carved ivories and chasubles, all the techniques of the most ancient Orient and the most recent Occident; but who today has any desire to apply the most serious and fundamental scholarship to this colorful crowd of far-flung objects?[75]

In the flush of recent acquisitions and expanded exposure to ancient art, Gerhard forecast both the popular demise of Graecophilia and scholarly resistance to its death.

[72] Quoted in Mercklin, "Archäologische Institute," pp. 285–86.
[73] Schiering, "Zur Geschichte der Archäologie," p. 46; Gerhard Rodenwaldt, *Archäologisches Institut des Deutschen Reiches, 1829–1929* (Berlin, 1929), p. 10.
[74] Gerhard, "Allgemeiner Jahresbericht," in *AA zur AZ* 15 (1857): 22.
[75] Gerhard, "Allgemeiner Jahresbericht," ibid., 16 (1858): 148–49.

4. If the IfAK devoted most of its attention to vases and sculptures, it did occasionally depict architectural remains, as in this assemblage of Etruscan sepulchral monuments. Note the variety of monuments depicted and the paucity of technical details. Compare to illustration 28. Marquand Library, Department of Rare Books and Special Collections, Princeton University Libraries.

Finally, in the wake of the Italian wars of unification, a full-scale campaign to make the IfAK a state institution was mounted, but ran up against the stolid opposition of the Prussian Finance Minister, Otto von Camphausen, who insisted that this legal change would have to be approved by the Pope and hence would make the IfAK's decisions in the future dependent on the papal government's concurrence. The change in status, he argued in a later letter, would also exacerbate the "jealousy" of the Italians, resulting in worsened conditions for German scholars resident in Rome.[76] The Ministry of Education countered with a masterpiece of combined patriotic boasting and extortion, informing the king that, given the current high level of nationalist sentiment in Rome, it was likely that a private institution like the IfAK would be dissolved by the Italians, who would then re-create the organization on their own, inferior, terms.[77] The King took the archaeologists' part, and on 18 July 1870, the day before the outbreak of the Franco-Prussian War, he approved the Prussian takeover of the institute with a yearly budget amounting to 5,840 talers.[78]

Yearly subsidies, however, were not the sum total of the Prussian state's contribution to archaeological inquiry. Not only were sundry, though small, amounts awarded to Gerhard and others to defray additional publishing costs, but already in the 1840s, requests for the funding of archaeological expeditions began to trickle in. The most significant of these was Richard Lepsius's plan to view, and especially to collect, antiquities in Egypt, which he promised to donate to the Egyptian Museum, at that time a small museum of Egyptian casts housed in the Monbijou Palace.[79] Backed by two of the King's closest advisers, Bunsen and Alexander von Humboldt, Lepsius played on German classical scholarship's renown, and the Prussian state's backwardness in funding new exploits, to win Friedrich Wilhelm IV's support for his trip. "It seems," he wrote in 1842, "that for *Germany*, for which above all other nations scholarship has become a calling, and which has not yet done anything to further scholarship since the key to the ancient land of wonders was found [Champollion's decipherment of the hieroglyphs], the time has come to take up this task from her perspective and to lead on

---

[76] Finance Ministry to Mühler (Education Ministry) 9 June 1868, and Finance Ministry to Education Ministry and Bismarck, 27 September 1868, both in MZStA, Rep. 151 IC/7108.

[77] Mühler to Wilhelm I, 30 December 1868, ibid.

[78] Wilhelm I to Staatsministerium (Bismarck), 18 July 1870, ibid., 2.2.1/21317, p. 134. The final statute was approved on 2 March 1871.

[79] The Egyptian Museum was formally created in 1828; in its early years, it contained largely artifacts from the private collection of General Heinrich von Minutoli. After 1850, the collection was moved to the Stüler Building of the New Museum, which was totally destroyed during World War II. See also Marchand, "The End of Egyptomania," forthcoming in Wilfried Seipel, ed., *Ägyptomanie: Europäische Ägyptenimagination von der Antike bis heute* (Milan, 1996), and essays in Freier and Reineke, *Lepsius*.

toward a solution."[80] This combination of praise and chastisement had the desired effect, and Lepsius soon sailed for Cairo.

Lepsius's three-year expedition cost a total of 34,600 talers, plus an additional 9,100 talers for shipping of finds paid in 1847, and 50,000 talers granted by the king in the same year to subsidize Lepsius's publications (with an additional 18,000-taler supplement in 1856), to which one might also add the 15,000-taler wedding gift that the king gave Lepsius upon his return from Egypt, for a grand total of 126,700 talers, quite a hefty sum in the 1840s.[81] Friedrich Wilhelm IV also provided the IfAK Egyptologist with a personal recommendation to Muhammad Ali, officially the Turkish pasha or viceroy of Egypt and that country's de facto independent ruler. The Prussian king also sent along a number of fine porcelain vases as Lepsius's student and biographer Georg Ebers put it, "in order to lay the viceroy himself under an obligation and to secure for the expedition the favor of that monarch."[82] Grateful for his government subsidy, Lepsius celebrated the monarch's birthday at the pyramid of Cheops, leaving behind a commemorative inscription in hieroglyphs carved directly into the Egyptian tomb.

However much it cost, Lepsius's expedition (1842–45) proved a smashing success. Lepsius's blanket *firman* (excavation permit) and extremely cheap labor force (at Fayoum he hired 108 men to work at 20 pfennigs per day) seemed unimaginable boons to the Egyptologist of the next generation, for by the 1860s, the French-dominated *Service des antiquités* had taken over the distribution of sites and finds.[83] Ernst Curtius, on whom Lepsius's example was not lost, later testified that this state-funded expedition marked a new departure both for science and for the Prussian state. Lepsius, Curtius reported, had always been proud "that he was allowed to be the one who unfurled the Prussian banner in a distant part of the world and was permitted to inaugurate a new era of science and art in the Fatherland."[84] While the imperialist nations were greedily consuming exotic territories, Curtius implied, the noble Prussians would venture overseas only to study the great civilizations of antiquity—and to take home a modest number of finds for further contemplation.

Lepsius himself had stressed the *historical* purpose of his trip, in contrast

---

[80] Richard Lepsius, "Denkschrift über die auf Befehl Seiner Majestät des Königs Friedrich Wilhelm IV zu unternehmende wissenschaftliche Reise nach Aegypten," 24 May 1842, in BAdW, Kap. VIII, II-VIII, p. 260.

[81] Georg Ebers, *Richard Lepsius: A Biography*, trans. Zoe Dana Underhill (New York, 1887), pp. 165, 229; Olfers (General Director of the Museums) to Friedrich Wilhelm IV, 14 April 1847; Education Ministry to Finance Ministry, 20 August 1847, and 25 October 1856, in MZStA Rep. 151 IC/7135, pp. 39–41, 45, and 111, respectively.

[82] Ebers, *Lepsius*, pp. 136–37.

[83] Ibid., pp. 143–44.

[84] Ernst Curtius, "Richard Lepsius," in *Unter drei Kaisern* (Berlin, 1889), p. 156.

5. Richard Lepsius raises the Prussian flag over the pyramid of Cheops, 1842. The hieroglyphs around the edges repeat the inscription in honor of Friedrich Wilhelm IV that Lepsius carved into the pyramid itself. © Bildarchiv, Preußischer Kulturbesitz, 1996.

to French and Tuscan "journeys of discovery"; Lepsius, after all, had begun his career as a classical philologist, absorbing from his teachers in Göttingen and Berlin the historicist particularism, philological exactitude, and critical skepticism pervasive in that field. He thought of himself very much as a historian, operating with philological methods, and as a collector of historical data. As his teacher K. O. Müller emphasized the internal coherence of Greek cultures, so Lepsius stressed the autonomy of Egyptian civilization, and the necessity that serious students in the field possess the ability to read the Egyptian monuments in addition to the familiar classical and biblical texts. This was already an important achievement, opening up Egypt and the Orient to specialized, historicist inquiry, and closing these regions off, at the same time, to the cross-cultural speculations of the philologically unfit. But Lepsius had also established an important precedent for German archaeologists to imitate: as Ernst Curtius suggested, Lepsius had showed the museum curators how to free themselves from their dependence on chance acquisitions by means of archaeological reconnaissance and state backing for "science."[85] If this lesson was slow in impressing itself on the Prussians, when it did strike home in the 1870s, the stage was set for the mutually advantageous cooperation of excavators, museum bureaucrats, and the central state.

Museum Modernization and German Unification: The Rise of Richard von Schöne

Museum collections in midnineteenth-century Europe were almost uniformly understaffed, badly housed, poorly funded, and disorganized by any definition of that term. But the situation in the Germanies was particularly dire. Lacking not only a centralized cultural administration and colonies, but also generous private patrons, the Royal Museums in Berlin were slow in acquiring impressive artistic and scientific collections. In Italy, the public could visit grand collections of artworks under the administration of either the municipal governments or the Church; in England and the United States, private patrons donated generously to national museums and trusts;[86] and in France, the state had continued the Revolutionary and Napoleonic policy of decreeing artwork of sometimes questionable ownership "national" treasures. Spurred by the Revolution's confiscations and Napoleon's invasions, colonial exploits and the Great Exhibition of 1851, over the course of the nineteenth century the other European nations increased their holdings at a furious pace.

In the German states before 1800, the collection of classical art was impeded by aristocratic penury, limited opportunities and enthusiasm for travel to southern Europe, and, in Prussia, by large investments in the military. There were, of course, important princely collections, like that of Augustus the Strong in Dresden, and between 1742 and 1770, Friedrich II increased Prussia's holdings considerably by purchasing several large collections of antiquities, including the famous bronze "Praying Boy".[87] Just after the turn of the century, Crown Prince Ludwig of Bavaria (later Ludwig I) began to amass an impressive collection of classical vases and sculptures for display in his lavish neoclassical Glyptothek, and in Prussia, plans were made for the building of a grand new museum in close proximity to the

<hr />

[85] Curtius, "Lepsius," p. 156.

[86] Bequests of private collections to the national museum seem to have been frequent in Britain. On the self-financing tactics of the Metropolitan Museum, see Kenneth Hudson, *Museums of Influence* (Cambridge, 1987), pp. 55–57.

[87] On Friedrich's collections, see Renate Petras, *Die Bauten der Berliner Museumsinsel* (Berlin, 1987), pp. 28–30.

6. The library of August Kestner in Rome. Note the many and varied art objects that surround the diplomat-antiquarian hard at work. Kestner Museum, Hannover.

royal palace (see illustration 34). Well-to-do scholars who had been to Rome brought back antiquities to decorate their homes: Wilhelm von Humboldt displayed his acquisitions at his villa in Tegel, outside of Berlin, according to the current fashion among Italian noblemen,[88] and Hyperboreans like August Kestner simply surrounded themselves with bits and pieces of the ancient past. But in the early 1820s, just as German collectors began to compete with other Europeans in the antiquities market, budgetary shortfalls required both Bavaria and Prussia to forgo purchasing expensive masterworks. The early administrators of the Prussian Royal Museums, the Egyptologist Adolf Erman later reported, had agreed to buy what was cheap, allowing the expensive, prize pieces go to London and Paris. Much to Erman's disgust, they had filled in the gaps with plaster casts.[89]

Writing in 1929, Erman was unjust to judge and condemn the actions of the *Vormärz* generation by the values—and museum budgets—of his day. Before about 1870, even academic classicists did not consider the exhibition of original artifacts essential; as the interpretation of ancient artworks re-

[88] Gudrun Calov, *Museen und Sammler des 19. Jahrhunderts in Deutschland, Museumskunde* 38 (1969): 169.

[89] Adolf Erman, *Mein Werden und mein Wirken: Erinnerungen eines alten Berliner Gelehrten* (Leipzig, 1929), p. 122.

mained firmly tied to classical texts, and since their appreciation still depended largely on their aesthetic value rather than their historicity, plaster casts satisfied most visitors.[90] While visiting Dresden in 1789, Friedrich Schlegel was stunned by the cast collection belonging to Winckelmann's friend A. R. Mengs; Schlegel later claimed that the impressions he formed on his repeated return visits to the collection provided the basis for his studies of classical antiquity.[91] The displaying of plaster casts became very popular after Welcker's creation of the Akademisches Kunstmuseum in Bonn (which was, incidentally, housed in the university library, in close proximity to the relevant texts) in 1827.[92] The practice would serve the needs of the Berlin museums very well, for, though short on income, the museums wished to display only truly beautiful masterpieces, not items of purely historical interest. Since, as we have seen, classical sculpture, for Germans of this generation, best exemplified the beautiful in art, it is hardly surprising that the new Berlin museums would be awash in sculptures, or that the founders would find pristine, pure white casts perfectly acceptable for contemplative purposes.

Originally, the Romantic architect K. F. von Schinkel had conceived the Altes Museum as a "temple" dedicated to the worship of art, rather than as a visual textbook for the display of art-historical types.[93] As members of the planning committee for the new museum, both Wilhelm von Humboldt and professor of architectural history Alois Hirt vetoed historical arrangement on the grounds that there were too many gaps in the royal collection to make this practicable.[94] The museum's central rotunda was stocked with statues of the Greek gods in imitation of the Pantheon, and it was here that the Pergamum marbles would first be exhibited after their arrival in Berlin in 1879. But soon after the opening, a new set of aims was added to that of the institution's founders. Initially, the building was meant to house antiquities and paintings; in decades to come, numerous subsidiary "collections"

[90] The use of casts as pedagogical instruments in art academies dates at least to the end of the seventeenth century; their use in the instruction of university students began about a century later. The Prussian state first embraced the idea of a wider-ranging cast museum (at the University of Bonn) immediately after the Napoleonic Wars, in order to display casts of artworks and rare plant and animal specimens appropriated (and not returned) by the French. Wolfgang Ehrhardt, *Das akademische Kunstmuseum der Universität Bonn unter der Direktion von Friedrich Gottlieb Welcker und Otto Jahn* (Opladen, 1982), p. 13.

[91] Ernst Behler, "Einleitung," in *Kritische Friedrich-Schlegel Ausgabe*, vol. 1, pt. 1: *Studien des klassischen Altertums*, ed. Ernst Behler (Munich, 1979), p. xcv.

[92] Schiering, "Zur Geschichte der Archäologie," p. 106. See also Ehrhardt, *Das akademische Kunstmuseum*, p. 70.

[93] On Schinkel's conception of the museum, see Ziolkowski, *German Romanticism*, pp. 318–37; Moyano, "Quality vs. History."

[94] Huberta Heres, "Archäologische Forschung und die Aufstellungen der antiken Skulpturen im Alten Museum 1830 und 1906," *Forschungen und Berichte* 27 (1989): 246–47.

or "departments" were organized under the administrative control of the Royal Museums. Some of these, like the *Antiquarium* (antiquities other than sculpture) were housed in Schinkel's building; others, like the *Islamische Abteilung*, were not. In 1833, Eduard Gerhard was appointed archaeologist to the museum, and, depending upon K. O. Müller's *Handbuch*, the Hyperborean began to impose a semihistorical organization on the classical collections.[95] His appointment resulted in a great expansion of the museum's collection of minor arts[96] and of plaster casts. While at first these had been employed to provide copies of unobtainable masterpieces for contemplation, increasingly, under Gerhard, they functioned as pedagogical exemplars, filling in gaps in historical sequences.

When August von Stüler's Neues Museum opened in 1859, this historical orientation was clearly in evidence: the entire first floor of the building was occupied by the cast collection.[97] The Egyptian collection was moved from the Monbijou Palace, and took up residence in the basement of the Neues Museum. Here Lepsius's acquisitions were shown to impressive effect, set off against walls decorated with actual Egyptian motifs; by selecting some of the most beautiful and characteristic of these motifs, Lepsius wrote, the museum simultaneously saved money on artistic composition, offered the public an attractive and accurate portrayal of Egyptian art, and protected itself against the "peevish art critic" who might otherwise criticize the murals.[98] Lepsius's reply to General Director Olfer's recommendations for a historical progression of rooms nicely illustrates this evolution from Schinkel's concept toward the more insistent historicism of later years; "This [historical succession] has always been before my eyes, also in [the monuments'] collection, although I do not believe that this principle should be pedantically carried into every particular."[99] Lepsius, strict historicist that he was, also filled in exhibition spaces with plaster casts; his beautiful Egyptian Court, destroyed in World War II, represents a transitional phase between the palatial showcase of the Glypthotek and the period rooms of twentieth-century museums.

[95] Ibid., p. 250.

[96] The collection's expansion was in large part due to the generosity of three IfAK associates, Panofka, Ludwig Ross, and Gerhard, who donated their collections at their deaths in 1855, 1860, and 1869, respectively. See Ernst Curtius, "Das Antiquarium," in *Zur Geschichte der Königlichen Museen in Berlin: Festschrift ihres fünfzigjährigen Bestehens am 3. August 1880* (Berlin, 1880), p. 130.

[97] Petras, *Bauten der Berliner Museumsinsel*, pp. 68–72. By 1921, when Theodor Wiegand arranged for their transport to the university museum, the museum owned at least twenty-five hundred of these items. Max Kunze, "Die Ausstellungen der Berliner Antikensammlung," *Forschungen und Berichte* 27 (1989): 224.

[98] Richard Lepsius, *Discoveries in Egypt, Ethiopia, and the Peninsula of Sinai in the Years 1842–1845*, ed. Kenneth R. H. MacKenzie, 2d ed. (London, 1853), pp. 385–86.

[99] Lepsius to Olfers, 11 July 1845, quoted ibid., pp. 376–77.

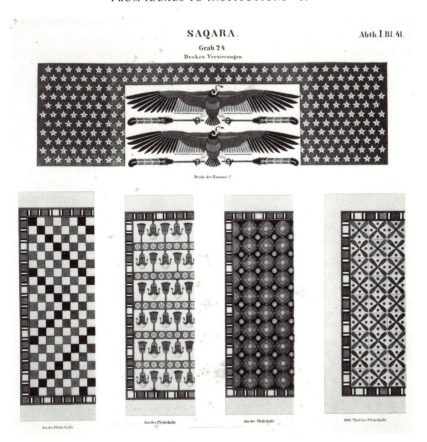

7. Egyptian motifs copied from two tombs at Saqqara. These designs, reproduced in color in Lepsius's *Denkmäler*, were used to decorate the galleries of the Egyptian Museum in Berlin.

The Egyptian Museum proved quite popular, opening just before a short bout of Egyptomania—induced mostly by Georg Ebers's exceedingly popular novel, *Eine ägyptische Königstochter* (*An Egyptian Princess*—1864)—struck the German public.[100] But by and large, the new museums provided little space for the exhibition of nonclassical artifacts, and few spokesmen arose to combat this state-sanctioned prejudice. In 1869, the art historian Herman Grimm praised Ernst Curtius for pleading publicly the cause of the museums, but wondered aloud, "since Curtius speaks in eloquent language in favor of Greek art, as if there were no other kind, who will take up the task of standing beside him and arguing the case for German and Italian

[100] On German Egyptomania, see Marchand, "The End of Egyptomania."

art? . . . We may wish to look at the splendor of ancient Greek: but not of that alone!"[101] The German Ethnography Museum, where prehistorical artifacts (including Schliemann's collection) were housed, opened only in 1886 and, as later chapters will show, few Near Eastern, Asian, or Indian artifacts were displayed in prominent places until after World War I. We can perhaps get some sense of the relative popularity of artifacts from different regions and periods by surveying a catalog of cast copies for sale by the museums in 1893. It offered 165 Egyptian items, 337 medieval and Renaissance sculptures, 106 modern sculptures, 141 ethnographic or prehistorical items, 64 Near Eastern works, and 807 Greek and Roman works.[102] But by 1893, the German artistic palate had already undergone several decades of diversification; at midcentury, classical works, and especially sculpture, remained unchallenged as the exemplary art for public display.

In addition to the limitations of the collections, the character of the museum administration itself slowed the expansion and modernization of the collection. Dominated by royal cronies and rich benefactors and wedded to a Byzantine organizational structure that fostered internal rivalries, "this fatal administrative arrangement," as Mommsen called it, impeded acquisition even when funds were available.[103] The six separate museum departments could only recommend purchase of artifacts; these requests then had to receive approval from a museum-wide reviewing committee, the general director, the crown prince (as protector of the museum), and the Ministry of Education. Administrators spent little time on museum affairs and their assistants were badly paid.[104] Given such conditions, despite a substantial operating budget (58,000 talers), the Prussian museums did not initiate an aggressive acquisition policy until after the founding of the Second Reich.[105]

With the close of the wars of unification, however, the backwardness of the "nation of poets and thinkers" in the cultural and scientific realm became an embarrassment to the National Liberals. In the early 1870s, they were the dominant party in the Reichstag and, with the help of Crown Prince Friedrich and the expanding Prussian bureaucracy, made great at-

[101] Herman Grimm, "E. Curtius über Kunstmuseen," *Preußische Jahrbücher* 25 (1869): 619, 622.

[102] *Verzeichniss der in der Formerei der Königlichen Museen käuflichen Gipsabgüsse* (Berlin, 1893).

[103] See Mommsen's speech before the Reichstag on 16 March 1876, reprinted as "Über die Königlichen Museen," in idem, *Reden und Aufsätze* (Berlin, 1905), p. 233.

[104] Their salary was still only 2,400 marks a year in 1879. See ibid., pp. 229–30, 238–41. By comparison, in 1879, the average industrial worker earned 71 marks a week, or 3,692 marks a year, down from 85 marks a week or 4,420 marks a year in 1873–74. See B. R. Mitchell, *European Historical Statistics, 1750–1970* (New York, 1978), p. 72.

[105] Richard Schöne, "Die Gründung und Organization der Königlichen Museen," in *Zur Geschichte der Königlichen Museen in Berlin*, p. 46.

tempts to modernize German cultural institutions, sometimes with the co-operation of the university elite, and sometimes, as in the case of attempts to expand the study of the applied sciences, in the teeth of academic opposition.[106] The Liberals, and especially the men of letters among them, as John Craig has shown, were anxious to annex Alsace, and to Germanize the university there; the time had come, at last, for the creation of the *Kulturstaat*, the state based on shared culture, that liberal nationalists had longed for since the 1820s.[107] In the 1870s and 1880s, a flurry of governmental activity created new institutions and para-academic organizations, including the Physikalisch-Technische Reichsanstalt (Reich Physical and Technical Institute), devoted to improving precision measurements (useful both for science and commerce), and the Orientalisches Seminar at the University of Berlin, dedicated to training Germans for consular service in the East. At the same time, numerous older institutions under Prussian supervision were reorganized, staffed with aggressive bureaucrats, and—when Bismarck and the conservatives permitted—given new funding. Exuberant at the German army's swift victories, the National Liberals were eager to crown military success with cultural modernization.

Not all funding for new institutions came from the Reich or the states; private support was also essential, particularly for institutions with commercial or technical orientations. Some attempt was made to cultivate private support for nonutilitarian organizations as well, and in some fields (like the study of oriental art), it remained the major form of patronage. But after 1870, private contributions never played a very significant role in the acquisition of *classical* antiquities, and archaeologists quickly shifted their demands for institutional reform and increased patronage back to the state, which did not disappoint them.

In the 1870s, the museums' acquisition budget swelled to previously unimaginable proportions. The acquisition fund was increased from 20,000 talers to 108,000 talers in 1873, plus an additional 100,000-taler subsidy, which was repeated often in years to come:[108] over the next thirty years, one commentator notes, the museums received over eight million marks in state subsidies for acquisitions, on top of progressively increasing budgeted allowances.[109]

Bureaucratic reform, however, did not prove so easy. When General Di-

[106] See Alan Beyerchen, "On the Stimulation of Excellence in Wilhelmian Science," in *Another Germany: A Reconsideration of the Imperial Era*, ed. Jack R. Dukes and Joachim Remack (London, 1988), pp. 139–68.

[107] John E. Craig, *Scholarship and Nation Building: The Universities of Strasbourg and Alsatian Society, 1870–1939* (Chicago, 1984), pp. 29–30.

[108] Schöne, "Gründung und Organization der Königlichen Museen," p. 55.

[109] Karl Hammer, "Preußische Museumspolitik im 19. Jahrhundert," in *Bildungspolitik in Preußen zur Zeit des Kaiserreiches*, ed. Peter Baumgart (Stuttgart, 1980), p. 271.

rector Ignaz von Olfers retired in 1869, the administration was left in the hands of Count Guido von Usedom, a personal friend of Wilhelm I. Usedom had made his career as a diplomat; located in Italy during the *Vormärz*, not surprisingly, he had been a regular participant in the activities of the IfAK. As general director, Usedom saw his purpose as that of making the museums serve the "cultivation, education, and edification" of the nation, a cause he attended to chiefly by making copies of paintings (especially Italian works) and casts available for distribution in the universities and higher schools.[110] A half-century earlier, Usedom's neohumanist endeavors would have satisfied the nation's wants, but in the wake of the founding of the Reich, his connoisseurship credentials no longer sufficed. In 1872, nationalist historian Heinrich von Treitschke attacked Usedom's dilettantry in the *Preußische Jahrbücher*, accusing the government of treating his position simply as an honorific post.[111] Theodor Mommsen, though directing his fire at the institutional causes of the deficiencies of the Royal Museums, which he compared to a badly bleeding body, also deplored the "damage done by individuals"—under which category he undoubtedly included the efforts of the beleaguered count.[112] Privately, Ernst Curtius, too, worried that despite the efforts of the new minister of education and the crown prince Friedrich, Prussia's cultural affairs were in the hands of incompetent courtiers. "The most cherished advisers are half-educated people," he wrote, "whose ideas can be approved in high places with no break in daily routine."[113] Within the museums, Usedom's aggressive young underlings tired of his administrative sluggishness and began to circumvent his authority. From the standpoint of all of these critics, the greatest sin of the general director lay not only in his lack of ambition, but also in his unwillingness to function purely as an administrator, leaving curatorial decisions to specialists—both of which failings would be remedied by the accession of Richard Schöne.

Born in 1840, Richard Schöne had a first career as an artist, a youthful pursuit that brought him to Rome and into the circle of the Hyperboreans. In the mid-1860s, he switched callings and began to study archaeology, in which field he received his *Habilitation* in 1868. He lectured briefly at the university in Halle, but in 1872, he made a final career change, accepting a position in the Ministry of Education under the new liberal minister, Gustav von Goßler. In his first five years in the ministry, Schöne played a major role in reforming the Academy of Arts, the Academy of Architecture, and the Higher School of Music, as well as in the reorganization of the Royal

---

[110] Pallat, *Schöne*, p. 114.
[111] Ibid., p. 110.
[112] Mommsen, "Museen," pp. 234, 229.
[113] Ernst to Georg Curtius, 27 February 1872, in *Ernst Curtius: Ein Lebensbild in Briefen*, ed. Friedrich Curtius (Berlin, 1903), p. 618.

Museums.[114] A common theme in all these reform efforts was the strengthening of the role of the Prussian Ministry of Education and its allies in the universities against inexpert provincial officials, whose nepotism and narrow-mindedness disgusted the young Schöne.[115] Like his contemporary Friedrich Althoff, the powerful undersecretary in charge of university matters, Schöne believed in *dirigiste* cultural politics, and both were indeed instrumental in making German *Kultur* a nationally administered entity.

In the museums, Schöne helped to institutionalize the appointment of experts, to head the separate departments. In 1880, his hard work, and some crafty intriguing, earned Schöne Usedom's vacated directorship, a position he combined with that of Education Ministry museum liaison until his retirement in 1905. During his quarter-century tenure, Schöne proudly presided over the greatest expansion of the Royal Museums to date, in terms of acquisitions, funds, and personnel; under his leadership, the number of museum sub-departments swelled from six to seventeen.[116] As early as 1880, he described the new opulence of the museums as an accomplishment Wilhelm von Humboldt would have seen as the fulfillment of all his wishes, and he continued throughout his life to see museum acquisitions as a barometer of national *Bildung* as well as international standing.[117]

In fact, Schöne's museological philosophy differed considerably from that of Humboldt, who believed that the Royal Museums' function lay in displaying great art. Schöne, on the other hand, wanted the museums to keep up with scholarly developments. In appointing department heads, he passed over older, less productive scholars, favoring Berlin full professors (and thereby exacerbating the tendency to office accumulation). He presided over the reorganization of older collections, the publication of new, more scholarly guidebooks, and especially the acquisition of original, and monumental, artifacts. Though his first love remained Greek sculpture, Schöne replaced the classicizing aestheticism of the pre-1870 museums with a rather more historicist organizational scheme and a host of new artifacts Humboldt undoubtedly would have not thought suitable for display.

Appropriately, given his commitment to expand Berlin's holdings and keep pace with scholarly developments, Schöne became a vigorous proponent of archaeological excavation, especially in Asia Minor, where the prospects of acquisitions were highest; the former IfAK member spent untold hours arranging monies, permissions, and personnel for archaeologists. When archaeologists required bureaucratic pressure to wrest funds from the Kaiser, the Finance Ministry, or the Foreign Ministry, Schöne could

[114] See Pallat, *Schöne*, pp. 45ff.

[115] Ibid., p. 106.

[116] At the time of Schöne's retirement, the museums employed approximately fifty scholars with civil-service rank. Erman, *Mein Werden*, p. 189.

[117] Richard Schöne, "Die Gründung und Organization," p. 58.

always be counted on to defend their interests. For not only did archaeological excavation assist the Royal Museums in enhancing national *Bildung*—the newfound consonance of interests between the institute and the museum administration blessed the latter's ambitions with the legitimacy of scholarly inquiry. The museum bureaucracy's compact with scholars elevated its purposes beyond those of greedy speculators, also allowing it to argue its service in rescuing artifacts from destruction by uncultivated natives. In later years, the museum administration's self-aggrandizing quest for acquisitions would simply intensify the excavation mania induced by the institute's positivistic desire to accumulate information. Bred a Hyperborean, Schöne would die a specialist in archaeological procurement.

But Schöne, who only died in 1922, remained, throughout his career, a committed philhellene. One might easily have said of him, as he did of the excavator Carl Humann in 1896: "Above all, the grandeur and sublimity of Greek culture filled his soul; to bring its monuments out of oblivion into the light of day, to make them accessible for scholarly study and awe-filled contemplation in the present, to ornament the capital city of the restored Reich with them—that was what he strove for with all his heart."[118] Like K. O. Müller and Eduard Gerhard, Schöne combined the tastes of a Romantic humanist with the specialized talents and bureaucratic instincts of a midnineteenth-century *Bildungsbürger*. And, like the others, he created the conditions for the perpetuation and reproduction of his passion after he himself retired from the field. If philhellenism persisted longer in Germany than elsewhere, it is this underappreciated generation of institution builders that deserves a large share of the credit—and blame.

---

[118] Richard Schöne, "Zur Erinnerung" (1896), in *Der Entdecker von Pergamon: Carl Humann*, ed. Carl Schuchhardt and Theodor Wiegand (Berlin, 1931), p. 10.

THE VICISSITUDES OF GRAND-SCALE ARCHAEOLOGY

> Men come and go. He who participates in academic activity is
> able to take comfort in the hope that when he lays down his
> work, another will take it up, perhaps a lesser, perhaps a
> better [scholar]; he always has the privilege, more than any
> other, of extending his work beyond his lifetime.
> (*Theodor Mommsen*)

LIFE IS SHORT, art is long, quoth Goethe's pedantic Dr. Wagner, defending scholarly virtuosity against the doubts of his mentor Dr. Faust. Dr. Wagner, however, could only conceive of the achievement of lasting fame in individual terms; and even the much wiser Faust sought insight into the mysteries of nature and God for the sake of satisfying his own will to know, not—to use a favorite positivist metaphor—to contribute a brick to the edifice of Knowledge. By the mid-nineteenth century, however, specialization had proceeded so far that even exceptional scholars like Theodor Mommsen had concluded that one man's career and talents would prove insufficient to the task of reconstructing classical antiquity, as it had really happened. Hopes ran high that full restoration could *eventually* be completed; the first step, however, was to amass and "clean up" all the source materials. As collective editing projects like the *Corpus Inscriptionum Graecorum* and *Monumenta Germaniae Historica* (*MGH*), got under way, leading scholars became small-time bureaucrats and dispensers of patronage in their own rights. The age of "big scholarship" had begun.[1]

It was apparently Mommsen himself who coined the term "big scholarship," and he was one of few members of his generation to express his anxieties about its deleterious social and intellectual effects. "Big scholarship" ('*Großwissenschaft*'), the Roman historian mournfully declared in 1890, was the scholarly complement to the development of big industry (*Großindustrie*) and the big city (*Großstadt*), and shared with these two a common, bureaucratic, social structure. *Großwissenschaft* could not be executed by one man alone in his study, but rather required a division of labor,

---

[1] There are examples of earlier collective projects; e.g., the revision of Camden's *Britannia*, 1694–95. Joseph M. Levine, *The Battle of the Books: History and Literature in the Augustan Age* (Ithaca, N.Y., 1991), pp. 327–36.

in which the scholar's role was to *direct* the activity of a host of subordinates.[2] "Big scholarship" required specialized technical training, bureau-
cratized administration, corporate or state funding, and political neutrality.
It was everything *Bildung*, in Mommsen's view, was not and should never
be; but it was the wave of the future. If *Bildung* was about the cultivation of
the individual personality, *Großwissenschaft* was about its suppression. The
effacement of divergent interests and experiences had provided a solution to
the depredations of dilettantism at the cost of opening a glaring gap between education and scholarship.

The advent of "big scholarship" induced both intellectual and institutional changes in archaeology, classical studies, and German philhellenism.
Grand-scale overseas excavation provided archaeology with an admiring
public and a vast collection of new materials on which to exercise its expertise. But "big scholarship"'s ambition to accumulate exhaustive knowledge,
and the emulation of natural science's methods that accompanied it, contributed to the disappearance of the normative aestheticism intrinsic to neohumanist *Bildung*: the specially trained excavators of Assur and contribut-
ing editors to the Pauli-Wissowa *Realenzyklopädie des klassischen Altertums*
were hardly the well-rounded citizens Humboldt had envisioned.[3] Perhaps
more importantly, the dynamics of specialized science increasingly made
the maintenance of Germany's international scientific prestige in classical
studies dependent on lucrative state patronage, amenable diplomats, and
sympathetic bureaucrats. National funding, professional credentialing, and
bureaucratization, in turn, diminished the cosmopolitan orientation of organizations like the IfAK and the participation of connoisseurs in art-
historical studies. Paradoxically, as archaeology took a historicist direction,
"disinterested" pursuit of knowledge grew more and more reliant upon national, extra-academic organizations like the Royal Museums and Foreign
Ministry; appropriately, this odd liaison would contribute much to the simultaneous increase of archaeology's status and diminution of the Winckelmannian ideal.

But curiously, the very *Bildungsbürger* whose activities fueled this state-
funded scholarly dynamism were also anxious to promote inertia in the
social sphere. Having risen to positions of cultural prominence by virtue of
their hard work and intellectual gifts, they sought to maintain the same
system of semimeritocratic Humboldtian principles in the face of expanding
bureaucracies and increasing industrialization. For both practical and self-
interested reasons, they insisted that occupation of posts in the bureaucracy, teaching corps, and free professions remain tied to university atten-

---

[2] Mommsen, "Antwort an Harnack, 3 Juli 1890," in idem, *Reden und Aufsätze*, (Berlin,
1905), pp. 209–10.

[3] For a full discussion of the fate of neohumanist education in an age of "big science," see
chapter 4.

dance, and that university admission remain dependent on the successful completion of courses at the classical *Gymnasium*. Thus, only those who had completed their nonutilitarian Greek and Latin training could hope to ascend to these higher cultural spheres, although, of course, the political and military institutions of the Reich remained firmly in the control of Junker aristocrats and Bismarckian conservatives. To stave off school reform and to ensure the expansion of their specialized projects, the *Philologen* would gradually take on the colors of this reactionary environment.

Correspondingly, neohumanist rhetoric altered its tactics and its goals to better suit an era of social conservatism and scholarly dynamism. The replacement of classical-language studies with practical secondary-school training, warned the philologist Georg Curtius in 1849, threatened to unseat "everything that gives human life higher value and a certain sanctity [*Weihe*]." "Art, literature, and scholarship would be laid so low that they perhaps would never revive."[4] Thirteen years later, Curtius was still defending philology against allegations that it was merely "dead erudition or idle playing with ideas." "But it might be pointed out, here," he continued, "that a science like philology also aims at goals and is occupied with big projects whose completion can in no way be a matter of indifference for the intellectual life of our age."[5] The change in Curtius's appeal is characteristic of the neohumanists' increasing emphasis on the prestige won by scholarly feats over the personal enrichment students received from the deep and careful study of the ancients. As archæologists began to provide sensational new proofs of Germany's *national* scholarly virtuosity, and as specialized journals expanded to proffer the detailed results of historicist *Großwissenschaft* to the expanding academic elite, the Humboldtian vision of a population widely cultivated in the arts and sciences and free from one-sidedness grew increasingly faint.

Ernst Curtius and the Excavations at Olympia

Like his brother Georg, Ernst Curtius was in many ways a product of the Altenstein-Eichhorn era of religious conformity and positivist historicism. Heavily influenced by Hegel but still committed to making philology, rather than philosophy, the *ur*–university discipline, Ernst Curtius saw in Greek culture a universality comparable to that of Christianity; the role of the Germans, he maintained, was to reconcile and realize the two forces.[6] Per-

---

[4] Georg Curtius, "Ueber die Bedeutung des Studiums der classischen Literatur," (1849) in idem, *Kleine Schriften*, vol. 1, ed. E. Windisch (Hildesheim, 1972), p. 107.

[5] Georg Curtius, "Ueber die Geschichte und Aufgabe der Philologie," (1862), ibid., p. 111.

[6] Ernst Curtius, "Der Weltgang der griechischen Cultur," in idem, *Alterthum und Gegenwart* (Berlin, 1877), pp. 59–77.

8. The historian and "victor of Olympia," Ernst Curtius. Deutsches Archäologisches Institut, Berlin.

haps it was Curtius's combination of philhellenism, Christian piety, and German nationalism that attracted huge crowds to his public lectures on the art and history of Athens. His 1844 lecture on the cultural geography of the Acropolis is said to have drawn an audience of 950, including the crown prince (later Wilhelm I) and princess, who were so impressed that they hired Curtius to tutor their eldest son (the future Friedrich III).[7] Hearing him lecture decades later, the young Egyptologist Adolf Erman ridiculed the gushy sentimentalism (*Schwärmerei*) of "Ernst Curtius, the ever-enthusiastic; when, with a jerk, he raised his eyes to the heavens and then spoke rapturously of 'the Greeks,' I simply could not take him seriously."[8] But in the years before about 1880, Curtius's ecstatic delivery impressed students and the broader public alike.

Curtius belonged not only to the university community but also to the court. Over the course of his life he not only acquired a prized faculty chair at the University of Berlin and high office in the Prussian Academy of Sciences, but he also received from his personal friends, the Hohenzollerns, honors rarely bestowed on scholars, including the *Pour le mérite* and the Order of the Red Eagle (second class).[9] Although Curtius preferred his

---

[7] Manfred Landfester, *Humanismus und Gesellschaft im 19. Jahrhundert* (Darmstadt, 1988), p. 53.

[8] Adolf Erman, *Mein Werden und mein Wirken: Erinnerungen eines alten Berliner Gelehrten* (Leipzig, 1929), p. 120.

[9] His awards were enumerated, in the course of giving him another one, by Goßler in a letter to the Kaiser, 23 November 1890, MZStA 2.2.1–19930, pp. 80–81.

pupil, the liberal crown prince Friedrich, to the rest of the Hohenzollern household, he continued to visit, petition, and praise the royal clan down to his death in 1896. Curtius was clearly no great friend of democratic causes; he disliked Catholics and disapproved of partisan politics in general. Still, he was neither a rabid nationalist nor an anti-Semite; he belonged more to an aristocratic world of neohumanist ideals and small-scale, patrician politics than to the sword-rattling, pan-German era that was dawning at the time of his passing. But, in the last decades of his career, Curtius the courtier-scholar became one of the nineteenth century's great *Großwissenschaftler*, and took upon himself a thoroughly modern cause: the obligation of the state to invest in cultural affairs.

As an apprentice *Sachphilolog*, Curtius had studied with each of the three great *Altertumswissenschaftler* of the *Vormärz*: F. G. Welcker, K. O. Müller, and August Böckh. In 1837, he had traveled to Athens, where he served as tutor to the Brandis family, while Georg Brandis advised King Otho, the new ruler of Greece (and a member of the Bavarian house of Wittelsbach). While in Greece, Curtius met and traveled with the great geographer Karl Ritter, from whom he undoubtedly acquired his interest in ancient topography and demography.[10] Curtius was still in Athens when his favorite teacher, Müller, arrived on his first (and last) visit to the Peloponnese. Müller's death from sunstroke in August 1840 touched the young student deeply, and he left Greece soon thereafter for Rome, where he studied briefly with Gerhard.[11] In 1841, he returned to Berlin, finished his doctorate, and began the highly successful course of lectures that eventually secured for him the position of court tutor.

As tutor to crown prince Friedrich Wilhelm (crowned only in 1888), Curtius introduced his pupil to the glories of ancient Greece—and the German neoclassical revival. The two toured Berlin, so that the prince could see Schinkel's masterpieces and the atelier of the "Prussian Praxiteles," C. D. Rauch.[12] However, Curtius, remarkably, did not require that his pupil learn Greek, or even the finer points of the Latin language; it is noteworthy that Prince Friedrich remained an ardent Graecophile, while Wilhelm II, compelled by his tutor to learn Greek and Latin grammar, was easily convinced that neohumanistic education was not essential to the perfecting of German culture. In fact, Curtius owed much of his later organizational facility to his early success in winning over his pupil—whom he once described as "lovable and as moldable as wax"[13]—to his philhellenic cause. For this private

[10] Adolf Michaelis, "Ernst Curtius," *Biographisches Jahrbuch und Deutscher Nekrolog* 1 (1897): 57.

[11] For Curtius's reaction to Müller's death, see his letter to his parents, 7 August 1840, in *Ernst Curtius: Ein Lebensbild in Briefen*, ed. Friedrich Curtius (Berlin, 1903), pp. 232–38.

[12] Franz Herre, *Kaiser Friedrich III: Deutschlands liberale Hoffnung* (Stuttgart, 1987), pp. 30–31.

[13] Ibid., p. 32.

patron would be instrumental in assisting Curtius to establish the necessity of state support for "big scholarship."

The outbreak of the 1848 Revolution in Berlin found Curtius still ensconced in the royal palace, a position he clearly preferred to that of revolutionary in the street; but soon thereafter, his tutoring duties complete, Curtius embarked on an academic career. In 1856, he landed a philologist's chair (for *Realien*) in Göttingen, where he wrote his very popular multivolume *Griechische Geschichte* (1857–67). Twelve years later, he was called back to Berlin, to occupy Gerhard's chair, and to direct the Antiquarium (later Antikensammlung) the section of the Royal Museums in charge of all antiquities excluding sculptures and casts. Perhaps most significantly, during this period Curtius developed close personal as well as professional ties to the Prussian military. His cooperative work with J. A. Kaupert, director of the cartographic section of the General Staff, resulted in the publication of influential topographical studies of ancient Attica and Athens, and also attracted for Curtius, and through him, for the IfAK, the personal interest and patronage of Helmuth von Moltke, chief of the General Staff in the Prussian military, himself an avid student of ancient geography.[14] Notwithstanding his impressive list of exalted positions and ambitious projects, at the time of the Reich's founding Curtius remained unsatisfied; for the Romantic scholar still cherished an unfulfilled dream. He wished to use the advanced techniques of German classical studies to reclaim the sacred site of Olympia from the depredations of nature and time.

The idea of excavating Olympia was hardly Curtius's invention; others, most crucially Winckelmann, had longed to unearth this renowned ancient complex. Curtius had visited the forsaken valley of the Morea, in which Olympia lay, in 1838 and 1840, and had lamented that the "sultry, unhealthy atmosphere" and swarms of tormenting insects reminded one more of the sufferings of the modern Greeks in their battles for independence than of the gay pageantry of the ancients.[15] In 1852, in a well-attended public lecture in Berlin, Curtius developed a plan to redress this sad situation, to do homage to the great Winckelmann, and to expose once more the great works of the ancients to the light of day. Blending together religious

[14] Michaelis, "Ernst Curtius," p. 70; Gerhard Engelmann, "Johann August Kaupert, 1822–1899," in *Berichte zur Deutschen Landeskunde* 42 (1969): 78. Curtius's unofficial alliance with the military would later become routine practice. Moltke permitted Kaupert first to collaborate with Curtius on his historical atlases and then to work with the IfAK on other assorted mapping projects down to the time of Kaupert's death in 1899. See Engelmann, "Kaupert," pp. 82–84; Rodenwaldt, *Archäologisches Institut des Deutschen Reiches, 1829–1929* (Berlin, 1929), p. 30. When the state funded research into the *limes*, or Roman frontier fortifications, in 1892, it specified that the work be supervised by a team of military cartographers and civilian excavators, a clear legacy of the Curtius-Kaupert joint effort. See below, chapter 5.

[15] See Rudolf Weil, "Geschichte der Ausgrabung von Olympia," in *Olympia: Die Ergebnisse der von dem deutschen Reich veranstalteten Ausgrabung, Textband I: Topographie und Geschichte*, ed. Ernst Curtius and Friedrich Adler (Berlin, 1897), pp. 101–8; Curtius quoted, p. 106.

and humanistic rhetoric, he called on his countrymen to support his quest to revive this admirable ancient model. "What lies there in those dark depths," he intoned, "is life of our life. If other emissaries of God have gone out in the world and preached greater forms of peace than the Olympic truces, Olympia remains for us today a holy place, and we ought to take up, in our world, illuminated by pure light, [Olympia's] flights of inspiration, unselfish patriotism, devotion to art, and joyful energy that endures despite all life's cares."[16] Duty—to God and antiquity—called German scholars to realize Winckelmann's dream.

A few weeks later, hoping his years at court would not be wasted, and perhaps taking Richard Lepsius's recent triumphs in Egypt to heart, Curtius submitted a proposal to the Prussian Foreign Ministry and Education Ministry for permission and funds to perform such a worthy exploration. In this memorandum, Curtius emphasized the national and scholarly benefits to be gained from an excavation at Olympia. Like Gerhard's *Thatsachen* of 1832, Curtius's 1853 proposal contrasted the great increase in dilettantish collecting to the modest gains in scientific knowledge made since the eighteenth century. Digs in Greece, he wrote, with the exception of the excavations at Athens (directed by the Greek Archaeological Society), were "isolated, unprincipled, and therefore relatively limited in success." The problem was that the job was too big for the French, who had already started digging elsewhere, and the Greeks possessed "neither the interest nor the means" to do a major excavation. But modern Germans, Curtius argued, had every reason to look on this project as a contribution to the enhancement of their own culture. "Germany has herself inwardly appropriated Greek culture," he argued; "the spirit of Greek antiquity has pervaded German scholarship; German art since Schinkel has begun to make the laws of Greek building its own. We recognize as a vital objective of our own *Bildung* that we grasp Greek art in its entire, organic continuity."[17]

Curtius went on to elaborate the very encouraging prospects for a successful dig, emphasizing especially the fine cache of inscriptions certain to be found. He estimated the cost of the excavation at twelve hundred talers a month, for a trial period of three months.[18] Charmed by the idea, the king gave Curtius preliminary approval to negotiate with the Greeks, and the Athens embassy began making inquiries about excavation rights on his behalf in late 1853.[19] However, negotiations over permissions were prolonged apparently by Prussian attempts to get around Greece's monument protec-

---

[16] Curtius quoted in Adolf Boetticher, *Olympia: Das Fest und seine Stätte* 2d ed. (Berlin, 1886), p. 63.

[17] See Curtius's (untitled) memorandum, 8 August 1853, PZStA AA/R 70191, pp. 5–9.

[18] Ibid., pp. 6b, 8b.

[19] On the King's approval, see Walter Leifer, *Hellas im deutschen Geistesleben* (Herrenalb, Schwarzwald, 1963), p. 272; on the negotiations of the embassy, see, e.g., Thiele (Athens embassy) to Foreign Ministry, 13 October 1853, and 11 June 1854, in PZSTA AA/R 70191.

tion laws.[20] Negotiations were nearly concluded when the Crimean War began, and the ensuing period of political instability in Greece convinced Prussian diplomats that the project should be further postponed. Curtius's proposal was still languishing in forgotten Foreign Ministry files in 1868, when he returned to Berlin and broached the subject anew.

Bismarck feared entanglement in Greek affairs, and also resented spending money on scientific frivolities. Furthermore, he opposed on principle any plan backed by the liberal Crown Prince Friedrich, and believed that cultural affairs should continue to be left in the hands of individual German states. He was therefore content to allow Curtius's plan to molder indefinitely. The chancellor especially opposed state funding for a dig that promised no material benefit for Prussia, as the Greek laws against exportation of art objects seemed to ensure. Undoubtedly following his instructions, in February 1868 the Athens embassy reported that this was not an auspicious moment to negotiate a profitable agreement.[21] In March, Bismarck passed this judgment on to Wilhelm I, adding that the Greek king should not be approached on the matter. Should he intervene on Prussia's behalf, the chancellor warned, this too would undermine the already unstable Greek cabinet: "Without a doubt the opposition would use the [Olympia] project as a welcome nationalist issue to turn against the leader of the present government."[22] But, for once, Bismarck was fighting a losing battle, for by July 1869, the Prussian ministries of Education, War, and Foreign Affairs all favored reopening Olympia negotiations.[23]

Finally, in October 1869, on his way to attend the opening of the Suez Canal, Crown Prince Friedrich visited King George in Athens and personally expressed his wish "that the governments of both sides could join together in a common endeavor for the sake of enlivening Greek antiquity, namely by means of excavations."[24] In Athens, the prince, steeped in Byronic philhellenism, also condemned Lord Elgin's depredations; throughout the negotiations, he would continue to oppose attempts to violate the Greek ban on the exportation of antiquities. "When through such an international cooperative venture a treasure trove of pure Greek art works . . . is gradually acquired," he told the Education Ministry in 1873, "both states will receive the profits, but Prussia alone will receive the glory."[25] Arranging

[20] See Education Ministry, Finance Ministry, and Admiralty to Friedrich Wilhelm IV 7 February 1854, MZStA 2.2.1-20771, pp. 7–10; and Goltz (General Staff) to Friedrich Wilhelm IV 7 March 1856, in PZStA AA/R 70191; Weil, "Geschichte der Ausgrabung," p. 108.

[21] Wagner (Athens Embassy) to Foreign Ministry, 15 February 1868, ibid., pp. 52–54.

[22] Bismarck to Wilhelm I, 3 March 1868, MZStA 2.2.1–20771, pp. 124–25.

[23] See Education Ministry, Foreign Ministry, and War Ministry to Wilhelm I, 17 July 1869, ibid., p. 131.

[24] Letter from Crown Prince to Ambassador von Wagner (Athens), 18 October 1872, quoted in Weil, "Geschichte der Ausgrabung," p. 109.

[25] Crown Prince to Minister of Education Falk, 29 January 1873, quoted ibid.

an agreement that suited the scholars and his own liberal idealist aspirations, the crown prince did not, perhaps, realize that he was setting a precedent to be widely imitated (if not always honored) in cultural treaties to come. Given the strictures of the German philhellenic tradition, he simply could not have demanded from the Greeks recompense beyond the fame such endeavors would bring to his "barbarian" land.

In spite of administrative and imperial intervention, however, negotiations dragged on. In April of the following year, Curtius reported to his brother: "The matter of Olympia has now, again, after its adventurous travels through all the ministries, landed back before the king, and it will soon be decided whether or not an undertaking of such an ideal character as the uncovering of the temple area can be executed in the absence of egotistical secondary objectives."[26] To further this "ideal" project, again Curtius took to the podium where, in 1872, he made a masterful appeal, deploying the rhetoric of neohumanist "disinterestedness," while expressing flattering hopes for Germany's standing as a patron of scholarship and art. The lecture began with an obligatory invocation of the Greeks, and especially of Athens, the first state to recognize *Bildung* as the best preparation for citizenship. Curtius acknowledged that Greek science and art had been free products of the *Volksgeist*, in no way dependent on the state; but times had changed, and today, scholars could not do without state help to secure their source materials. "Is it right that we allow noble works of human *Geist* to lie in the earth and molder?" he queried. Of course not; it was the state's *duty* to help scholars rescue the past from the depredations of time.

Curtius's next salvo bears quoting at length, for it shows both the historian's debts to philhellenist, antiutilitarian asceticism, and the recasting of these ideals as national necessities:

> As I see it, the state ought to proclaim publicly its dedication to science and art. This should not be the sort of [support] offered by the courts of Alexandria and Pergamum, for, wanting to pursue outside goals and glorify themselves, they always had some other end in view. Rather, [support] should be offered in the true Hellenic sense, that one love the good for its own sake. Here, art and science are not seen as luxuries, which after real state needs have been met also deserve some consideration, but as the noblest part of the life of the nation, which may not be neglected without great injury, as an inexhaustible source of vitality and an indispensable counterweight to the ceaseless quest for possessions and profit.[27]

It was the responsibility of the state to prevent culture from falling prey to market forces and mores; if Germany were to escape the fate of the "deca-

---

[26] Curtius to Georg Curtius, 4 April 1870, in Friedrich Curtius, *Ernst Curtius*, p. 592.

[27] Ernst Curtius, "Die öffentliche Pflege von Wissenschaft und Kunst," (1872) in idem, *Alterthum und Gegenwart*, p. 128.

dent" worlds of Alexandria and Pergamum, it would have to accept the disinterested pursuit of the arts and sciences as an essential aspect of national identity and a permanent category in the state's budgets.

The effects of Curtius's rhetorical blandishments are difficult to gauge, but by 1873, both Wilhelm and King George were ready to sign an excavation treaty, and the Reichstag, dominated by National Liberals, was ready to allocate the necessary funds. Regrettably for Curtius and his backers, a final agreement was again delayed by the unexpected intervention of the maverick archaeologist Heinrich Schliemann. Schliemann, temporarily unable to dig at Hissarlik as a result of his difficulties with the Turks,[28] requested permissions to excavate at Olympia and Mycenae. He offered the Greek government terms identical to those suggested by the German team, but also threw in a promise to build a lavish museum in Greece, in which his Trojan and Greek finds would be housed after his death. Initially the Greek parliament took Schliemann's side, partly, as Bismarck had predicted, as a means to express opposition to Prime Minister Dimitrios Voulgaris, and, for a time, it seemed the private scholar would triumph. But in March 1874, Curtius and the architect Friedrich Adler were dispatched to Athens with a note from the crown prince to King George. This personal embassy evidently inspired George to act, and in April 1874, he signed the excavation treaty, agreeing even to provide the archaeologists with new roads to improve access to their site; the Germans were also permitted to open a DAI branch office in Athens. As Crown Prince Friedrich had stipulated, the Germans received the right to excavate Olympia and to publish and photograph the finds, but only to export casts and duplicates of such artifacts as the excavators desired.[29] In forcing through this "disinterested" archaeological treaty against Bismarck's opposition, Curtius and the crown prince snatched a liberal triumph from the teeth of *Realpolitik*, but also established a new form of "cultural" diplomacy susceptible to manipulation by the state.

Excavations at Olympia commenced, at long last, in October 1875. But, both in Greece and in Germany, the project continued to be controversial; in Greece, nationalists denounced their government for allowing foreigners to excavate Greek treasures and spread rumors that the Germans were shipping artifacts back to the Reich.[30] In Germany, grumbling over the all too generous provisions of the treaty threatened the project, as the Reichstag was required to approve new monies for its continuation at the conclusion

---

[28] See chapter 5.

[29] See Weil, "Geschichte der Ausgrabung," pp. 110–13. Not until 1887 was the German ambassador Joseph Maria von Radowitz able to acquire doubles from Olympia for his nation's collections. Theodor Wiegand, "Zur Geschichte der Ausgrabungen von Olympia," *Sitzungsberichte der Preußischen Akademie der Wissenschaften*, Phil.-hist. Klasse (1926), p. 21.

[30] Boetticher, *Olympia*, pp. 69–70.

of the three-month trial period. Fortunately for the excavators, in late December, after more than two months of unrewarding digging, they uncovered a large number of marble pedimental sculptures and the remains of a winged Nike, which they attributed to the sculptor Pananios. In his memoirs, Count Radowitz described the relief felt by supporters of the dig—including the crown prince—at having learned of these finds. "Now," he wrote, "the necessary measure approving additional subsidies [for the excavation] could be brought before the Reichstag with the prospect of a successful conclusion."[31] In their memorandum read before the Reichstag, the excavation's directors had sufficient confidence in the progress of their work to advertise their contributions to Bildung: "For the knowledge of classical antiquities, which is the foundation of all higher education in Germany, an abundance of new material has already been obtained," they claimed; moreover, continuing state patronage was justified in light of the popularity and patriotism of their project. "With rare unanimity," the memorandum argued, "[the German people] have recognized the project as a national endeavor; even among those who follow the excavation reports without having special knowledge or affection [for the subject], there is a clear feeling that Germany, after the great successes of its statesmen and military leaders, can find no better way to celebrate its triumphs than through the free and unselfish furthering of this sort of peaceful endeavor [Friedenswerkes]."[32] Impressed by these claims, the deputies approved 150,000 marks to continue the excavations.

In the royal palace, Kaiser Wilhelm himself followed the progress of the dig with great interest. Bismarck, on the other hand, very likely one of those Curtius accused of harboring "egotistical secondary objectives," remained discontented with the unrewarding treaty and insensitive to arguments about the dig's great service to science. He was unable to stop the payments, however, as the excavation was financed from the Kaiser's privy purse as well as from the Reich budget.[33] By 1880, with 661,000 marks already spent and the excavators requesting an additional 90,000 marks, the chancellor had had enough. On January 19, Bismarck refused to sign on the new appropriation, informing the treasury that the German state had done its part for science, and it was now time to step aside and allow someone richer to

---

[31] Joseph Maria von Radowitz, Aufzeichnungen und Erinnerungen aus dem Leben des Botschafters Joseph Maria von Radowitz, vol. 1 (1839–1877), ed. Hajo Holborn (Osnabrück, 1967), p. 348.

[32] "Denkschrift, betreffend die Ausgrabungen zu Olympia," in Stenographische Berichte über die Verhandlungen des Deutschen Reichstages (1876) Anlagen, vol. 3 (Berlin, 1876), p. 433.

[33] In 1873, the Prussian finance minister had balked at the notion that Prussia should fund the campaign; like Bismarck, he did not think "scholarly results" merited such large expenditures. See Camphausen to Falk (Education Ministry), 13 March 1873, PZStA 70191, pp. 106–7.

pay for the project.[34] Despite Wilhelm's avowal that stopping the excavations at the halfway point "would be a sin against art and scholarship,"[35] Bismarck poured out his complaints to his imperial employer. "The German Reich," he protested, "has performed an important and a very selfless service to international scholarship, as the bearing of all costs of these fertile investigations proves. If others should take over the continuation of this service, Germany's share in [bringing forth] the results for scholarship as a whole will be no less than it is today, and we will also still be able to acquire casts of finds."[36] Bismarck advised against the use of the Kaiser's privy purse to pay for such an unprofitable enterprise, particularly since the Reich needed to maintain the fund to compensate invalids and war veterans. Even Wilhelm, however, saw through his chancellor's pathetic appeal and demanded that at least eighty thousand marks go to the excavators.[37]

The Kaiser was absolutely adamant in his support for Olympia. As he told Cabinet Minister von Wilmowski in a letter of 26 February, he greatly resented Bismarck's refusal to release funds for the dig:

> The artistic treasures that come to light each day are of such significance for the history of the ancient world as [they are] for art itself that other states would consider themselves lucky to spend twice the money for their possession. . . . Every one of us remembers having heard about the Olympic Games in his youth, and what an interesting, nay, charming, impression, they made on him. And now that we have the remains of whole cities of the great past, as described by the traditional storytellers, standing before our eyes, should we not complete so great an enterprise, hardly half-finished, simply because of the money?! That would be unworthy of Prussia![38]

To no avail, Bismarck later tried to shift the burden of publication costs for the expedition onto the separate provinces, a move blocked by the Prussian education and finance ministers, who persuaded Wilhelm to dip again into his privy purse.[39] The archaeologists, invoking national pride, international

---

[34] Bismarck to Scholz (Treasury), 19 January, 1880, reprinted in Wiegand, "Olympia," p. 15.

[35] Kaiser to Bismarck, 11 February 1880, reprinted ibid., p. 15.

[36] Bismarck to Kaiser, 24 February 1880, MZStA 2.2.1-20772, pp. 88–96; also printed (without marginalia) in Wiegand, "Olympia," pp. 16–18.

[37] See Wilhelm's marginalia to Bismarck's letter, 24 February 1880, MZStA 2.2.1-20772, pp. 88–96, and also his approval for the funds to be paid from his privy purse, Kaiser to Foreign Ministry 28 February 1880, ibid., 2.2.1-20882, p. 98.

[38] Kaiser quoted in Karl Griewank, "Wissenschaft und Kunst in der Politik Kaiser Wilhelms I. und Bismarck," in *Archiv für Kulturgeschichte* 34, no. 3 (1952): 305–6.

[39] See Bismarck's letter of 23 June 1882 reprinted in Wiegand, "Olympia," p. 19; and in delayed reply, Goßler and Scholz (Finance Ministry) to Kaiser, 4 June 1886, and Wilhelm I to Education Ministry and Finance Ministry, 23 June 1886, both in MZStA 2.2.1-20773, pp. 11–17, 24.

scholarly status, and the philhellenic tradition, had found their way to the Kaiser's heart—and to his pocketbook.

Excavations at Olympia began in 1875 and continued until 1881. This was indeed grand-scale archaeology; in 1880, at least five hundred workers were hired to ensure completion of the systematic dig.[40] The Olympia excavators also did their utmost to make their dig rigorous and scientific, in contradistinction to Schliemann's treasure-hunting exploits. As Adolf Borbein has argued, the excavators constructed their excavations as if they were conducting a scientific experiment, seeking to make their conclusions free from the vagaries of "accidental discoveries."[41] As part of this endeavor, a trained architect, Friedrich Adler, accompanied the dig; he was soon joined by his protégé (and son-in-law) Wilhelm Dörpfeld, whose architectural inquiries proved to be the most consequential, as well as the most controversial, achievement of the expedition. For in discovering what he considered to be a homogeneous era of clay-brick construction, Dörpfeld provided a new means to prehistorical dating;[42] a kind of cultural stratigraphy could be deduced from variations in construction techniques. Similarly, another young archaeologist, Adolf Furtwängler, was brought to Olympia to make a systematic study of small finds; in the process of inventorying thousands of bronzes, potsherds, and figurines, Furtwängler perfected a method for prehistorical stylistic categorizing. Dörpfeld and Furtwängler, two students steeped in technical and formal—rather than humanistic or philological—knowledge, were to prove the unlikely heroes of Winckelmann's dream.[43]

The sheer quantity of artifacts uncovered at Olympia would surpass all expectations for a modern-day dig. In 1879, Georg Treu, the on-site excavation director, reported that since 1875, 1,328 stone sculptures, 7,464 bronzes, 2,094 terra-cottas, 696 inscriptions, and 3,035 coins had been found.[44] But the Germans failed to find much in the category most prized by the state bureaucrats, the *Gymnasium*-educated public, and even the archaeologists themselves: monumental sculpture of the high classical era (with the exception of the much-publicized Hermes of Praxiteles and Nike of Pananios). After their initial discovery of numerous pediment fragments from the temple of Zeus, the German team increasingly filled its reports with discussions of architectural and ethnographic material rather than ar-

[40] Karl Christ, *Von Gibbon zu Rostovsteff: Leben und Werk führender Althistoriker der Neuzeit* (Darmstadt, 1972), p. 81.

[41] Borbein, "Klassische Archäologie in Berlin vom 18. bis zum 20. Jahrhundert," in *Berlin und die Antike*, ed. Willmuth Arenhövel and Christa Schreiber (Berlin, 1979), p. 138.

[42] Carl Schuchhardt, *Schliemann's Excavations*, trans. Eugenie Sellers (Chicago, 1974), pp. 34–35.

[43] See chapter 4.

[44] Georg Treu, "Die Ausgrabungen zu Olympia," report no. 37 (1879), in MZStA 2.2.1-20772, pp. 58–61.

9. Panoramic view of the Olympia dig site, ca. 1880.

Deutsches Archäologisches Institut, Athens.

10. One of the Olympia excavation's proudest finds was the Nike of Pananios, shown here from two directions.

tistic works, invariably securing the importance of these humbler artifacts by citing relevant passages of Pausanias.[45] In 1876, Curtius celebrated the discovery of an "idealized head" from the east pediment of the temple, "deeply damaged, but of unmeasurable value." Although he considered it impossible that the entire scene could be restored, as excavators had so far discovered little more than "individual crumbs from antiquity's table," this find did give him hope that inch by inch, the most important aspects of the whole could be reconstructed.[46] But by 1880, Curtius himself expressed

---

[45] See, e.g., Wilhelm Dörpfeld, "Die Ausgrabungen von Olympia," report no. 36, in *AZ* 37 (1879): 123.

[46] Curtius, "Die Ausgrabungen von Olympia," report no. 10, in *AZ* 34 (1876): 216.

disillusionment. Painful gaps in the reconstruction of Olympia's art, Curtius admitted, would have to remain; many beautiful works could not be resurrected from the ruins. "If we had known about this ruinous condition from the outset," the aging philhellene mused, "we would hardly have approached the excavation of the Altis [the sacred precinct of Zeus] with such high hopes." The sheer volume of excavated artifacts made the disappointments of the dig easier to bear, Curtius claimed, and his final accounting of the important (that is, sculptural) finds was indeed impressive: eighty-seven statues (torsos), of which forty-four were over life-sized and forty-three were described as Roman; and forty-two heads (plus the Hermes and the Nike). "The main achievement, however, is not the individual pieces, but the whole, the resurrected vista of the whole area of Olympia. . . ."[47] In an age of scholarly collations and cooperative ventures, appropriately, the emphasis was placed on the *vraisemblance* of the panorama rather than on the beauty of particular works of art.

That is not to say, however, that the broader public embraced this view without equivocation. Though the costly first edition of the excavation report was quickly sold out, the disappointment of one reviewer of the post-excavation publications seems to have been widely shared. The huge cache of bronzes discovered, he wrote, citing Adolf Furtwängler's scholarly report, "are, apart from a few significant pieces of representational art, on the whole merely ancient rubbish, small objects that were worthless then or single fragments of larger objects."[48] As Education Minister Gustav von Goßler indicated, most of the material discovered at Olympia bore on relatively unknown eras of early Greek history, and thus could not be presented to the public without full scholarly comment (as Goßler thought possible, we can infer, for grand sculpture). "Perhaps the far greater significance of the undertaking," he told Bismarck, underscoring the need for full and Reich-funded publication of the results, "lies in the great increase in our knowledge of the more ancient steps in the evolution of Greek sculpture, architecture, and also language, an increase that can only contribute to the common benefit of larger and larger circles and achieve general significance when communicated through scholarly explanation."[49] Ironically, the long-thwarted excavation of Olympia, which, as German archaeologists never tired of repeating, had been a cherished dream of Winckelmann's, had brought to light material inaccessible—and, the implication was, unappealing—to the man of general neohumanist *Bildung*.

[47] Curtius, "Die Ausgrabungen von Olympia," report no. 44, in *AZ* 38 (1880): 110–13.
[48] Unsigned review of Adolf Furtwängler, "Die Bronzen von Olympia," in *Beilage zur Allgemeinen Zeitung*, 15 October 1880; DAI, Nachlaß Furtwängler, Kasten 11.
[49] Goßler to Bismarck, 10 July 1882, reprinted in Wiegand, "Olympia," p. 20.

Pergamum, Professionalization, and the Vicissitudes of "Big Archaeology"

With the founding of the Second Reich, the IfAK, which had worked so hard at becoming a Prussian institution, suddenly found itself nominated for promotion to a *Reichsinstitut*. It was Curtius, more than anyone else, who had carried to its logical end the process begun by Humboldt of binding together the interests of career philhellenists and the German nation; his Olympia campaign had helped to usher in an age in which cultivating "spiritual" ties with the Greeks came to be seen as a state obligation. And it was he who made the most forceful public plea for the Reichstag's approval of the IfAK's transformation into the Deutsches Archäologisches Institut (DAI) in an 1872 article in the *Preußische Jahrbücher*.[50] But this cause had a corollary; in the essay, the court favorite linked the founding of the new national body to new projects of archaeological expansion in the East, to be launched from a newly created IfAK branch office in Athens. In arguing this case, Curtius concocted a fateful alliance between Germany's established scholarly primacy, its emerging industrial strength, and its imperialist expectations:

> The time is ripe. In the whole Orient, as far as educated men live, it is expected that Prussia will make good its new position of power in honorable and strong representation of the interests of art and science in the classical lands. . . .
> Everywhere they see us as the progenitors of greater enterprises, without our being able to promise these. Can one imagine what could be achieved if our available energies could be harnessed together in the right way: the steam power of the navy, the technical know-how of the General Staff, the expertise of archaeologists and architects![51]

Though Curtius himself had very little interest in leading the IfAK to new triumphs in Asia Minor, his descendants would happily obey this injunction to conquest.

If by the 1880s, Greece was becoming a feasible destination for German travelers (Baedeker's first volume on Greece appeared in 1883), Asia Minor still remained largely unexplored and intimidatingly exotic. This hesitancy to venture beyond Constantinople was reinforced by Bismarck's Orient policy, which depended on the persistence of an undisturbed Russian-British-French rivalry and studious neutrality on the part of Germany and Austria. Finally, excavations in the Ottoman Empire required great physical stamina, and after Schliemann's imperious treatment of Turkish officials, necessi-

---

[50] Apparently the Bavarian ambassador to Rome, Graf Tauffkirchen, also strongly backed this plan, wishing to see that the interests of non-Prussian archaeologists were also officially recognized. Griewank, "Wissenschaft und Kunst," p. 300.

[51] Quoted in Michaelis, "Ernst Curtius," p. 75.

tated an artful sort of diplomacy that would have been unimaginable to the Hyperborean generation. The archaeological *Drang nach Osten* would require closer, more regularized ties to the state bureaucracy than Curtius's position at court allowed him and, for its full flowering, a diplomatic policy unencumbered by Bismarckian balance-of-power politics. Expansion into Asia Minor would demand, in short, the full articulation of archaeology as *Großwissenschaft*, and as quasi-imperialist practice.

When Carl Humann, a Prussian-trained engineer, first visited Asia Minor in 1864, his mission was not the recovery of past civilizations but rather the plotting of modern transportation networks. Having departed northern Europe for the sake of his health, Humann had accepted a post in the service of Grand Vizier Fuad Pasha, whom he advised on railway and road routes into the 1870s.[52] Like the telegraph expert and later president of the Deutsche Bank Georg Siemens, and Helmuth von Moltke, who mapped Asia Minor for the Prussian General Staff, Humann was representative of a generation of rough and ready pioneers in the East. Unlike Siemens and Moltke, however, Humann did not return to Germany to amass a fortune or become a hero; he stayed in Asia Minor and became an archaeologist.[53]

But Humann was an archaeologist cut of an entirely different cloth than those belonging to the universities and the IfAK. He had little use for philologists, whom he considered effete incompetents.[54] Predictably, given this antipathy, his relations with the scholarly set in Berlin were not always harmonious; Alexander Conze, for example, demanded a systematic and careful approach whose slowness aggravated the impatient on-site excavator.[55] But Humann's connections in the Ottoman Empire extended from the Turkish court down to local officials and workmen, reaching a depth and sensitivity far beyond that of the neohumanist ambassadors. His adeptness in trafficking with Turks of all stations earned for him the nickname "Viceroy of Asia Minor," and the very important esteem of the director of the Turkish Museums, Hamdi Edhem Bey.[56]

In later years, Humann's patriotic devotion to enriching the Fatherland was widely acclaimed. Without question, Humann *was* determined to bring

---

[52] Doris Pinkwart, "Carl Humann," in *Archäologenbildnisse*, ed. Reinhard Lullies and Wolfgang Schierung (Mainz, 1985), p. 69.

[53] On Siemens, see Karl Helfferich, *Georg von Siemens: Ein Lebensbild aus Deutschlands großer Zeit* (Berlin, 1921); on Moltke, see Fedor von Koeppen, *Moltke in Kleinasien* (Hannover, 1883).

[54] See Carl Schuchhardt, "Ein Jahr bei Carl Humann," in *Der Entdecker von Pergamon*, ed. Carl Schuchhardt and Theodor Wiegand (Berlin, 1931), p. 97. For fear of being labeled a "philologist," Schuchhardt refused to tell Humann of a rather severe injury to his knee; ibid., p. 98.

[55] Ibid., pp. 110–11.

[56] This appellation was coined by the German ambassador in Constantinople, Joseph von Radowitz. See Edward Schulte, "Carl Humann," in *Neue Deutsche Biographie* 10 (1974): 33.

the glories of Pergamum home to the Reich, but, reading the DAI president's letters celebrating Humann's service to the Royal Museums ("whose antiquities collections will, thanks to *you*, begin a new epoch")[57] and the posthumous tribute of the museum director to Humann's patriotism,[58] one cannot help but feel that the desires of Berlin were partly projected onto the expatriate in Asia. One might better surmise, paraphrasing another eulogist, that Humann found in Conze (and the Reich) a doctor to cure his "chronic Pergamum-longing,"[59] and, by the same token, the Reich found in the adventure-seeking Humann a solution to its yearning for original and monumental Greek sculpture.[60]

As early as 1871, Humann had tried to interest the Prussians in a dig at Pergamum, but Curtius, to whom Humann had sent two fragments of a monumental relief, had been too absorbed in his plans for Olympia to be a successful advocate. Humann, however, did what digging he could with private funds and continued his agitation. In 1878, he finally succeeded in attracting the attention of Alexander Conze, the new director of the Royal Museums' sculpture collection. Perceiving great promise in the Hellenistic site, Conze immediately enlisted Richard Schöne, then a prominent young official in the Education Ministry, to help organize a grand endeavor. Working around Museum Director Usedom, the two secured the backing of the crown prince and a royal grant of fifty thousand marks, to be matched by the museums, as well as the collusion of the German embassy in Constantinople. The whole plan was hushed up until 1880, when Conze triumphantly presented the results of the dig to the Prussian Academy of Sciences. By then, two things had been accomplished. First, Usedom's stubborn resistance to an aggressive acquisitions policy had resulted in his early retirement and replacement by Schöne. Second, by 1880, the Turkish government had sold the local property to Humann and conceded its one-third share of the finds to the Berlin museums in exchange for the paltry sum of twenty thousand francs, hardly suspecting what it had given away.[61]

---

[57] Conze to Humann, 28 September 1878, in DAI, Nachlaß Humann, Kasten 1.

[58] Richard Schöne, "Zur Erinnerung," in Schuchhardt and Wiegand, *Der Entdecker von Pergamon*, p. 10.

[59] Otto Kern, "Karl Humann," in *Voßische Zeitung* 15 April 1896, morning ed., first suppl., in DAI, Nachlaß Humann, Biographische Mappe.

[60] Despite all the rhetoric touting Humann's great contribution to knowledge the IfAK could not bring itself to list him as "Gelehrter" but accepted his membership merely as "Architekt." Otto Kern, "Ernst Curtius und Karl Humann," in *Deutsche Literaturzeitung* 34, no. 29 (10 May 1913): 1161.

[61] Pallat describes Schöne's 1878 report to the finance minister in which he stressed "that the whole matter be handled in strict secrecy, in order not to let the Turkish officials discover the significance of the finds" (p. 138). Under Turkish law, in 1878 one-third of the finds went to the excavator, one-third to the property owner, and one-third to the Turkish government. See also Conze to Humann, 16 July 1878, and Conze to Humann, 28 September 1878, both in DAI, Nachlaß Humann, Kasten 1; and Bülow to Wilhelm I, 20 December 1879, MZStA 2.2.1-20772, pp. 64–65. In a letter to Schliemann, Humann confirmed the twenty-thousand-

In the first year of excavation, Humann sent home ninety-four slabs of the large frieze and thirty-five of the smaller frieze from the enormous altar, built by Attalus II to commemorate his victory over the Galatians (Celts who had settled in Anatolia in 184 B.C.). The large frieze, known as the *Gigantomachia*, represents the battle of the gods against the giants, as described in Hesiod's *Theogony*, and has become one of the best-known and most admired works of ancient art. In addition to this extremely important material, Humann also sent home many statues, busts, and other items, packed in 462 crates; his first shipment weighed a total of 350 tons.[62] Excavations at Pergamum continued until 1886; a second campaign lasted from 1901 until Conze's death in 1915, and a third was just beginning when the Nazis came to power in 1933.

Education Minister Falk's first report of the excavation's achievements to the Kaiser captures both the importance of the sculptures to the Reich's self-conception as a European *Kulturnation*, and the general contemporary aesthetic disapprobation of the "baroque" altar:

> If [the altar] does not belong to the era of the full flowering of ancient art, on the other hand, it . . . has preserved surprising information on a heretofore little-known area of Greek art history. It is, however, of particular significance that the collection of the museums, which was until now very poor in Greek originals, consisting mostly of works from the Roman era, now possesses a Greek work of art of dimensions that are equal (or nearly) to the great rows of Attic and Asia Minor sculptures in the British Museum.[63]

By 1880, two large fragments of the *Gigantomachia* were on view in the Royal Museums; the Kaiser himself had viewed them even before Conze's address to the academy.[64] At the Berlin Art Academy's one hundredth-anniversary exhibition in 1886, an enormous semicircular panorama of the acropolis at Pergamum dwarfed the exhibit of the Olympia sculptures. The highlight of the exhibition was the "Pergamene Celebration" in which fifteen hundred costumed artists reenacted Attalus II's triumph; the costumes scarcely concealed the obvious parallel between the victory of Attalus over the Celts and that of Bismarck and Moltke over the French.[65] In 1902, a new museum exclusively devoted to the Pergamum treasures opened in

---

franc price (Humann to Schliemann, 9 February 1890 in Ernst Meyer, ed., *Heinrich Schliemann: Briefwechsel*, vol. 2: (1876–1890) (Berlin, 1958), p. 350. Carl Schuchhardt, who was assisting Humann at the time, later insisted that the cost for the final third was twenty thousand *Turkish* francs, or 18½ marks. See Schuchhardt, "Carl Humann zum 100. Geburtstag," *Forschung und Fortschritte* 15, no. 1 (1 January 1939): 16.

[62] Schöne, "Zur Erinnerung," p. 2.

[63] Falk to Wilhelm I, 20 June 1879, MZStA 2.2.1-20772, pp. 48–50.

[64] Conze to Humann, 7 January 1880, DAI, Nachlaß Humann, Kasten 1.

[65] Max Kunze, "Carl Humann—Vom Ruhm und Nachruhm eines deutschen Ausgräbers," *Forschungen und Berichte* (Staatliche Museen zu Berlin) 31 (1991): 154.

11. Karl Humann and Richard Bohn, showing off some of their monumental finds at Pergamum. © Bildarchiv, Preußischer Kulturbesitz, 1996.

Berlin. In general, the procurers of the Pergamum Altar were greeted with greater and more nationalistic fanfare than the excavators of Olympia had received just a few years before; on his triumphal visit to Berlin in 1880, Humann "was received like a general who has returned from the battlefield, crowned with victory."[66] Curtius's contribution to the progress of scholarship would indeed win him the title of "Olympic victor" from the professoriate, but for the Reich bureaucracy, full possession of artifacts was obviously the better part of archaeological valor.[67]

Like Humann, Alexander Conze was no Hyperborean. Having studied with Eduard Gerhard, very early in his career Conze had turned his attention to pre-Periclean art, and can in fact be credited with the identification

[66] Kern, "Karl Humann."

[67] Kern, "Ernst Curtius und Karl Humann," p. 1159. When his Olympia funds were briefly blocked owing to the bureaucracy's absorption in the Pergamum dig, Curtius bitterly remarked: "They revel in this accidental mass of originals and feel they have equaled London." Quoted in Kunze, "Carl Humann," p. 156.

of the Geometric style of pottery in 1862.[68] Conze had himself headed an important series of short digs at Samothrace between 1873 and 1875, funded by the Austrian government. Perhaps more important than his own scientific contributions, however, was Conze's promotion of architects like Humann and Dörpfeld (whom Conze appointed DAI Athens director in 1887) and his agitation to expand German archaeological efforts beyond the Mediterranean. Here, Conze and his colleagues were not bound by the "disinterested" philhellenism of the Olympia treaty, and it was even possible for Conze, in an 1898 speech to the Prussian Academy of Sciences, to praise Lord Elgin. He predicted, rightly, that Germany "would not be spared some of what has been said about Lord Elgin after his death";[69] but he did not even briefly consider offering the Turks the Pergamum finds and retaining only the glory for the museums and the Reich.

Rather than organizing great "peaceful endeavors," Conze hoped to use his powerful bureaucratic positions to increase his nation's commitment to specialized scholarship. His insistence upon full study of the "physiognomy" of each site, without regard to the artistic value of excavated fragments, helped to redefine archaeology as a technical science of painstaking historical reconstruction rather than a humanistic and aestheticizing study of ancient artwork. For Conze, all manner of available material might be used to reconstruct the ancient past; all objects were equal in the eyes of the "scientific" archaeologist. Where no texts existed to guide the scholar, objects could provide an alternative means of historical documentation, for like Winckelmann, Hegel, and Burckhardt, Conze believed that works of art expressed something essential about the people who had created them—a belief that in Conze's case extended also to humbler artifacts. This was the grand scientific vision Conze wished to realize. In the name of "big archaeology," the Germans were to seize "the exalted task of uncovering and comprehending whole cities and landscapes in their entirety . . . from images, inscriptions, and all manner of minor art forms down to the most insignificant potsherd, to bring forth, with the united energies of [many] scholars, the finer characteristics of the grand picture."[70] For Conze, the aim of archaeology was to reconstruct the everyday life of the Greeks, not to revive models for imitation, a significant revision of the philhellene's relationship both to Hellas and to his own age.

Already in his letters to Humann in the 1870s, Conze had stressed the necessity of collecting all evidence, whatever its size and value, in order to

[68] Adolf Borbein, "Alexander Conze" in Lullies and Schierung, *Archäologenbildnisse*, p. 60; Hans Dragendorff, *Alexander Conze: Gedächtnisrede gehalten am Winckelmannstag 1914* (Berlin, 1915), p. 6.

[69] Conze, "Pro Pergamo," reprinted in *Entdeckungen in Hellas: Reisen deutscher Archäologen in Griechenland, Kleinasien, und Sizilien*, ed. Heinrich Alexander Stoll (Berlin, 1979), p. 492.

[70] Conze, "Dezember: Winckelmannsfest," in *AA* 3 (1902): 167.

12. Work proceeds at Pergamum. When possible, the German excavators hired local Greeks to carry out their digs. Deutsches Archäologisches Institut, Athens.

allow for a full postexcavation reconstruction of the site. His instructions to Humann included the exhortation not to devote all his efforts to finding single works of art, but rather to keep in view the whole structure of the altar, the true object of inquiry.[71] During the negotiations over the finds in September 1878, he urged Humann to settle on the basis of a holistic, historical principle: the Germans would receive everything belonging to the era of the great altar, a solution perhaps less agreeable to the royal curators but necessary for scientific study. Similarly, in his address to the Academy of Sciences, Conze clearly indicated that the object of archaeological inquiry should be the entire temple complex, including the market area and the walls. It was not sufficient, he insisted, to simply grab the monumental sculptures and run; science required that the city as a whole, including its waterworks and its street plan, be studied in detail. Conze considered the study of the "physiognomy" of Pergamum vital, too, because the Hellenistic city fit historically between Athens and Rome, and thus filled a historiographical gap.[72]

[71] Conze to Humann, 16 July 1878, in DAI, Nachlaß Humann, Kasten 1.
[72] See Conze's "Pro Pergamo," pp. 475–92.

The highly expressive Pergamum sculptures, the Berlin archaeologist believed, could also serve as a means to battering down the Winckelmannian aesthetic prejudices that had blinded even Sculpture Gallery curator Adolf Bötticher to the importance of Hellenistic culture.[73] Following his visit to view the altar in 1880, the Russian novelist Ivan Turgenev had mused in print: "At the sight of all these irrepressibly fine wonders, what becomes of all our accepted ideas about Greek sculpture, its severity, serenity, about its confinement within the borders of its particular art, of its classicism—all those ideas which have been inculcated on us as indubitable truths by our instructors, theoreticians, aesthetes, by the whole of our training and scholarship?"[74] Two years later, Jacob Burckhardt, an early admirer of Hellenistic art, exulted in a letter to a friend: "This discovery has thrown the archaeologists' system into confusion! The narrow aesthetic is shaken at its roots, everything that has been written about the pathos of the Laocoon is waste paper, now that we have experienced this frightful event."[75]

Yet these two avant-garde intellectuals overestimated the damage suffered by the classical ideal in German circles, and even Conze's announcement in 1897, that the public had corrected its "all too low opinion of an age of decline, to which, until only very recently, it could not bring itself to attribute great works of art," proved premature.[76] In 1912, the art historian Arnold von Salis felt the historicist battle had not yet been won against those who had labeled the altar "decadent" and/or "baroque." "Even today the classical ideals still have such binding force that the appreciation of other trends can prevail only with much effort against the power of received artistic perceptions," Salis lamented.[77] Conze had persuaded his contemporaries to appreciate the historical importance of the altar and the patriotic significance of its arrival in Berlin; he had not convinced many of them of its beauty.

Conze's appointment to the position of DAI general secretary in 1881 marks a crucial turning point in the evolution of the institute. His Pergamum experience had taught him that a new "professional" scientific ethos would require continuous and substantial state support, both financial and diplomatic. Grand-scale excavation was the profession's future, but

[73] Adolf Erman reports that Bötticher opposed exhibiting the altar in the Royal Museums; see Erman, *Mein Werden*, p. 121.

[74] Ivan Turgenev, "Pergamos Excavations: A Letter to the Editor of *European Herald*" (1880) in *Ivan Turgenev: Literary Reminiscences and Autobiographical Fragments*, trans. David Magarshack (New York, 1958), p. 291.

[75] Burckhardt quoted in Felix Stähelin, "Einleitung des Herausgebers," in *Jacob Burckhardt: Gesamtausgabe*, vol. 13 (Stuttgart, 1934), p. 16.

[76] Conze, *Pergamon* (Berlin, 1880), p. 13.

[77] Arnold von Salis, *Der Altar von Pergamon: Ein Beitrag zur Erklärung des hellenistischen Barockstils in Kleinasien* (Berlin, 1912), p. 6.

13. The Pergamum Altar in its first home, the Altes Pergamonmuseum
© Bildarchiv, Preußischer Kulturbesitz, 1996.

to excavate a cultural whole required technical expertise and long-term commitment; Rome could not be dug in a day. With Conze's ascension, this scientific and administrative conviction was raised to the status of an institutional dogma, which has retained its authority until the present day.

As the first Pergamum campaign came to a close, Conze launched an all-out campaign to reform the institute to conform to his new program. Beginning in 1885, he repeatedly petitioned Reich officials for the necessary funds to convert DAI officials from lay volunteers into professionally trained, salaried bureaucrats. His efforts had to commence with the reclassification of his own job. When he joined the DAI, its general secretaryship, in true Hyperborean style, was an honorary, unsalaried position,[78]

---

[78] Bismarck was probably to blame for the government's reluctance to meet Conze's requests. See correspondence in PZStA AA/R 37794, esp. "Motive zu den Abänderungsvorschlägen" by Foreign Ministry representative Humbert (n.d.), pp. 140–47. Conze's salary for 1887 was set at 11,100 marks. See Foreign Ministry to Conze, 6 April 1887, PZStA AA/R 37794, pp. 62–63.

14. DAI General Secretary Alexander Conze takes care of some bureaucratic correspondence, under the exotic conditions of the Ottoman Empire. Deutsches Archäologisches Institut, Berlin.

with relatively few bureaucratic duties: it is said that Conze's predecessor, Richard Lepsius, at the height of his activity wrote about eighty institute-related letters over a three-month period.[79] Conze made the job a full-time occupation, with much time spent on bureaucratic correspondence; by the 1920s, this correspondence consumed most of the general secretary's waking hours, leaving little time for independent scholarship.[80] Importantly, he also greatly diminished the significance of Rome and the influence of Italian scholars by holding all meetings of the central directorate in Berlin and acceding to Bismarck's demand that the institute's official language be changed from Italian to German. In ensuing decades, this shift away from

[79] Georg Ebers, *Richard Lepsius: A Biography*, trans. Zoe Dana Underhill (New York, 1887), p. 211.

[80] See chapter 8.

the patrician cosmopolitanism of Rome before 1850 would become even more pronounced.

It should be noted that with Conze's recategorization as a salaried official, he formally became an employee of the Foreign Ministry; and though he continued to consider himself a scholar above all, this new designation was neither unimportant in his conception of his own responsibilities nor inconsequential in his direction of the institute. For in addition to increased funding,[81] "big archaeology" also required virgin sites on which to realize its holistic vision. Italian nationalism was too strong and Greek excavation laws too rigid for either Mediterranean territory to offer great promise, particularly given the Education Ministry's primary interest in stocking the Royal Museum. Pergamum had opened the door to the East, however, and through it coursed a generation of German archaeologists, capitalizing on improved German-Ottoman relations, and, after 1888, on the personal friendship established between Wilhelm II and Sultan Abdul Hamid II. All this, however, would require close collaboration with Foreign Ministry representatives abroad and the articulation of scientific archaeology as a key element in cultural diplomacy. Professionalization, here, required of the classicist an unprecedented form of bureaucratic savoir faire.

In 1886, Conze himself arranged early retirements for the proponents of the old beaux arts tradition and the genteel internationalism of the *Vormärz*.[82] It was high time national and scientific concerns took the stage; "The practices [*Weise*] of the once international institute," Conze later reflected, "had been allowed to continue all too long."[83] Many years later, Gerhart Rodenwaldt would describe the ensuing confrontation of *Realpolitik* and romantic aestheticism as a "tragic conflict."[84] If tragic, however, this conflict was also inevitable, for the DAI had become divided into two camps, each with an essentially different view of archaeology's aims. The Munich art historian Heinrich Brunn, who spent much of his early career at the IfAK, had complained in 1873 that the central directorate was dominated by philologists and historians: Even the archaeological work of [Ernst] Curtius," he wrote, "does not really run in the same direction as the activities of the institute."[85] Most of Conze's opponents resided in Rome and belonged to an older generation of Hyperborean archaeologists; like the Swiss classicist J. J. Bachofen, who had many friends among them, they

---

[81] The DAI budget for 1888–89 totaled 130,005 marks, in comparison to its 1870 budget of 5840 talers (the equivalent of 17,520 talers at the rate of 1 taler = 3 marks.) "Etat für das DAI auf das Etatsjahr 1888/9" in MZStA, Nachlaß Althoff, AI-Nr. 197, pp. 28–29.

[82] See Conze to Wolfgang Helbig, 22 January 1886, DAI Nachlaß Conze, Kasten 2a.

[83] Conze, *Unsern Kindern*, p. 46.

[84] Rodenwaldt, *Archäologisches Institut*, p. 33.

[85] Brunn to Bavarian Education Minister, 25 March 1873, in BHStA, MK 14245.

disliked "modernism" in scholarship and resented the power plays of the Berliners.[86] As ousted Second Secretary Wolfgang Helbig later described, he and First Secretary Wilhelm Henzen had been displaced by a new species of narrow-minded scholar-bureaucrats:

> Near the end of the seventies, new men found entry into the Berlin central directorate whose horizons were narrow, unlike any of the earlier members. They pronounced the institute a bureaucratic organization, which broke with the tradition that had previously determined the evolution of the institution. The new general secretary, Alexander Conze, made himself unloved through his dogmatic judgments. In his oral and written remarks he used a tone that Henzen and I were not accustomed to. And so, we took our leave.[87]

"The so-called reform of the institute," Helbig added, "immediately made a negative impact on our relations with the Italians," an accusation Conze admitted to be true.[88] But Conze was not willing to sacrifice the support of the Reich and the progress of scholarship to the maintenance of genteel social connections. German national feeling and Conze's professionalizing tactics now coalesced in a policy characterized by relative insensitivity to the importance of international sociability.

By the late 1880s, then, archaeology was increasingly becoming "big scholarship," despite the protests of scholars like Carl Robert, who, astoundingly, resigned his post at the University of Berlin in order to register his protest against the age of advancing bureaucratization and de-aestheticization. In 1891, Robert, now at the University of Halle, devoted his *Winckelmannstag* address to decrying this trend. "Scholarly work cannot be pursued in the same way as the postal and telegraph service," Robert insisted, "and one should not confuse those who perform scholarly labor with the laborers on excavations in Asia Minor. . . ."[89] Robert worried, as did his friends at the Rome institute, that overspecialization would destroy the unity of his field and the integrity of its artistic comprehension. What he did not yet understand was that the expanding ambitions of professional archaeology, and the contracting social foundations of classical learning, would soon provide a hospitable climate for the reconciliation of "armchair" archaeologists and field laborers, whose images of Greek art were not, after all, so very irreconcilable.

---

[86] See Bachofen to Heinrich Meyer-Ochsner, 24 January 1862, in *Johann Jakob Bachofens Gesammelte Werke*, vol. 10: *Briefe*, ed. Fritz Husner (Basel, 1967), p. 252.

[87] Helbig statement dated 10 February 1911, included in Wangenheim to Civil Cabinet, 3 March 1911, MZStA 2.2.1-21319, pp. 103a–103e.

[88] Ibid.; Conze to Foreign Ministry, 25 May 1887, PZStA AA/R 37795, pp. 135–37.

[89] Robert quoted in Otto Kern, *Hermann Diels und Carl Robert: Ein biographischer Versuch* (Leipzig, 1927), pp. 84–85.

Developments in Archaeological Writing from the *Vormärz* to the Fin de Siécle

When archaeologists such as Heinrich Brunn and Johannes Overbeck decided to write histories of Greek art in the 1850s, it became quickly apparent that the Winckelmannian tradition would prove a poor model for their endeavors. Indeed, as early as 1778, C. G. Heyne had determined that Winckelmann's art history contained a sufficiently large number of errors of historical fact and judgment as to be effectively useless.[90] Factual errors, however, did not immediately doom Winckelmann to the art-historical dustbin, and he continued to be reverently invoked by specialists throughout the nineteenth century. Yet as the century wore on and artifacts from numerous regions and epochs made their appearance, the inadequacy of Winckelmann's generalizations about the formal attributes of Greek art, drawn for the most part from literature, became more and more evident. In the course of the next decades, discussions of "style" replaced arguments over beauty, and gave art historians both a much wider range of subjects for study and a narrower set of issues to address.

The rise of stylistic analysis revolutionized art historical as well as archaeological thinking, and consequently has been discussed in detail by numerous historians. But art historians, anxious to identify the philosophical principles that underlie the autonomy of their field, frequently fail to examine the technical skills early art historians learned from their antiquarian predecessors and the practical pressures they faced over the course of their careers as museum curators, catalogers, and connoisseurs. In addition, in celebrating the emancipation of their field from aesthetic judgments, art historians often underestimate the extent to which new excursions into less hallowed epochs like the baroque or the Gothic issued from nationalist desires to raise northern traditions to equal standing with the Italian Renaissance. The rise of stylistic thinking, then, might be better understood in the context of the confrontation of older, antiquarian practices with new, nationalist, museological imperatives and professional convictions.[91] And this confrontation might be more easily observable in the field of archaeology, than in the much better-known history of the study of painting.

The style criticism of the later nineteenth century was shaped by many forces, but the basic conception of artistic style is probably best traced to three humanist interpretive practices: philology, paleography, and numismatics. Philological emendations and authentications depended on the

---

[90] Heyne quoted in Alexander Demandt, "Winckelmann und die alte Geschichte," in *Johann Joachim Winckelmann, 1717–1768*, ed. Thomas W. Gaehtgens (Hamburg, 1986), p. 302.

[91] See my remarks in "Professionalizing the Senses: Art and Music History in Vienna, 1890–1920," in *Austrian History Yearbook* 21 (1985): 23–57.

same principle of historically bounded styles of expression that came to be de rigueur in art history. But, as Carlo Ginzburg has noted, the different status accorded to copies of works of art and copies of literary texts made this philological–art-historical analogy dysfunctional in practice: whereas texts could be accurately reproduced to yield true copies, nothing but the original work of art was considered to be authentic.[92] Once one knew the formal "language" of an era, one still had to be able to recognize the idiosyncratic rendering of the individual letters of the alphabet. Thus, archaeological authenticity required both the lexical sophistication of the philologist as well as the visual adeptness of the paleographer—or numismatist. The study of coins and carved gems—so important to early modern collectors and virtuosi—clearly contributed much to the understanding of the development of different sorts of modes of representation. Winckelmann, the heir to all these practices, was already able to provide a sophisticated discussion of the different handling of drapery, hair, and expression characteristic of each age in his *Geschichte,* the *ur*-model for later stylistic analyses.

But it is also evident that older humanistic models underwent considerable change as new demands, and vastly increased new materials, pressed curators and connoisseurs to shift their sights from the individual work of art to the type. The inclusion in museum collections and art histories of objects for which no inscription had been preserved and about which no literary source spoke demanded that some means of labeling the objects be found. As the collecting of authentic antiquities became an international sport, forgers as well as scholars learned to recognize telling marks of age and provenance. Here the nonaestheticizing typologies created by architects like Karl Philipp Moritz (1737–93; professor of classics at the Berlin Academy of Arts), Aloys Hirt (who lectured first at the Berlin Academy of Architecture and then at the University of Berlin on the history of art and architecture), and Gottfried Semper (author of *Der Stil*), undoubtedly provided important models for painstaking comparisons of structures and decorative details.[93]

The natural sciences, too, played an important role in the articulation of formalist style analysis. It has been suggested that Semper derived his evolutionist taxonomy from George Cuvier's exhibit of animal skeletons at the Jardin des plantes,[94] and Adolf Furtwängler, whose eye for stylistic distinc-

[92] Carlo Ginzburg, "Clues: Roots of an Evidential Paradigm," in idem, *Clues, Myths, and the Historical Method*, trans. John and Anne Tedeschi (Baltimore, 1989), p. 109.

[93] Adolf Borbein, "Klassische Archäologie in Berlin," pp. 104ff. See also Anthony Vidler, *The Writing of the Walls: Architectural Theory in the Late Enlightenment* (Princeton, N.J., 1987). On Semper, see Michael Podro, *The Critical Historians of Art* (New Haven, Conn., 1982).

[94] See Rosemary Bletter, "Post to Pillar" (review of Wolfgang Hermann, *Gottfried Semper*) in *Times Literary Supplement*, no. 4,321 (January 24, 1986): 97.

tions was widely acclaimed, when asked what he owed to his instructors in
Altertumswissenschaft, replied "nothing at all," giving full credit instead to
his reading of Semper's *Der Stil* and Darwin's *The Expression of Emotion in
Animals and Man*.[95] It should not be forgotten, too, that Giovanni Morelli,
alias Ivan Lermolieff, the eccentric Italian senator responsible for the reat-
tribution of hundreds of European paintings in the third quarter of the
nineteenth century, was by training a physician. Morelli appraised paintings
with a kind of medical or criminological attention to minutia, discerning
"the master's hand" in the subconscious mannerisms of the rendering of
insignificant body parts such as earlobes and fingernails.[96] It is the architectural and natural-scientific elements that gave modern style criticism its
distinctive precision and aesthetic self-restraint.

Nineteenth-century philosophy, too, helped to form modern style criticism: in Hegel's hands, Winckelmann's history of ancient art was transformed into a philosophy and history of aesthetic perception. Each of the
three "stages" of art (preclassical, classical, and postclassical) was made to
carry philosophical weight (from unconsciousness to self-consciousness to
unhappy consciousness); a corresponding aesthetic valuation (symbolic
representation, inadequate to express spirit; beauty in naive-natural representation; sentimental overripeness); a political estimation (tyranny; positive freedom; negative freedom); a religious character (mysticism; natural
religion; skepticism); and an evaluation of national vigor (weakness in division; united national strength; dissolution and dependence). Michael Podro
has underlined the differences between Hegel's conception of art as part of
reflective thought and the views of other writers who made art an extension
of social behavior or an active influence in creating the cultural conditions
of its age.[97] But with respect to the elaboration of the conception of "style,"
all of these fledgling art-historical efforts shared the historicist conviction
that certain styles were only possible in certain places, at certain times. This
historio-philosophical presumption was crucial to the development of stylistic analysis, and to articulation of archaeology as a *historical* science.

To add a final complication, when one looks to contemporary literature
for an explanation of the emergence of the new formalistic approach, the
answer most frequently given is not an intellectual innovation, but rather a
technical novelty: the invention and increasing use of photography. The use
of photography by archaeologists had been pioneered, not surprisingly, by

[95] Ludwig Curtius, "Erinnerungen an Adolf Furtwängler," *Münchner Neueste Nachrichten*, 4
November 1927, in DAI, Nachlaß Furtwängler, Biographische Mappe.

[96] Edgar Wind, "Critique of Connoisseurship," in idem, *Art and Anarchy* (Evanston, Ill.,
1985), pp. 30–46.

[97] See Podro, *Critical Historians of Art*, pp. 17–43. I cannot hope to do justice to the rich-
ness of Podro's account here.

Schliemann in the 1870s: Equally unsurprisingly, however, professional archaeologists had hesitated to employ this new medium until after the dual forces of Morellian methodology and anti–school reform popularization combined to raise the social significance of visuality in the late 1890s.[98] Thereafter, however, photography became an instrumental as well as transformative part of the study of the ancient world. "With the help of photography," wrote Michaelis—who had initially opposed the substitution of the camera for the draftsman's pen—in 1908, "we have learned to see afresh, and if the whole of modern archaeology has taken a decisive turn toward stylistic analysis and evolution, this is not least the work of photography."[99] Furtwängler also gave mechanical reproduction much credit for allowing the sort of "objective" comparison of details upon which formalist studies rested.[100]

Whether it owed most to the humanist practices, philosophical preoccupations, or new technological possibilities, formalist style criticism helped to solve the practical dictates of authentication, labeling, and dating, formidable tasks for archaeologists and museum curators facing avalanches of new acquisitions. But style criticism's usefulness in resolving practical problems of interpretation, authentication, and self-legitimation in turn contributed to the limiting of its intellectual aspirations and cultural implications. Morelli's formalistic positivism, for example, drew attention away from traditional *sachphilologische* interests in cultural history to the inspection of techniques of artistic execution. Morelli also had little interest in "unscientific" discussions of beauty. In a letter to his close friend A. H. Layard, the famed British excavator of Nineveh, Morelli described the aims of his recent work:

> I want to show there that the total impression of a work of art is not enough;
> and that to recognize the works of a great master with certainty, it is necessary
> to know beforehand all the *forms* that are proper to this master, and in order to
> recognize and to know how to appreciate these forms correctly, it is necessary
> to have learned the grammar of artistic language. Aesthetics and what is today
> called cultural history has nothing to do with the science of art.[101]

---

[98] See Gerhild Hübner, "Bild als Botschaft: Das antike Erbe Athens in fotographischen Zeugnissen des 19. und 20. Jahrhunderts," in *Fotogeschichte* 8 (1988): 11–26; Hans Christian Adam, "Heinrich Schliemann und die Photographie," in *Das Land der Griechen mit der Seele suchen: Photographien des 19. und 20. Jahrhunderts* (Cologne, 1990), pp. 38–41.

[99] Michaelis, *Ein Jahrhundert kunstarchäologischer Entdeckungen*, 2d ed. (Leipzig, 1908), p. 296. Hübner, "Bild als Botschaft," p. 11.

[100] Adolf Furtwängler, *Masterpieces of Greek Sculpture*, ed. Al. N. Oikonomides (Chicago, 1964), p. vii.

[101] Morelli to Layard 1886, (date obscured) in BM, Layard Papers, Add. Mss. 38965, pp. 53–55.

If many art historians—especially those of Hyperborean cast—disliked Morelli's narrow concentration on formalistic elements,[102] they could not deny that his method provided the strictest guidelines so far established for attribution and authentication. That they could not change the terms of the debate, however, is indicative of the new importance style analysis had assumed in the age of "big archaeology."

Style-historical thinking complemented the historicist urge to treat topics in national contexts, as well as new attempts to discover the "real" processes of historical change. Ancient historians like Theodor Mommsen, Richard Lepsius, and Eduard Meyer scrutinized the practical motivations, environmental factors, and superstitious foibles of the ancients as they might have studied their contemporaries; sharing their liberal colleagues' antipathy for party politics and religious sectarianism, they attempted to remove all traces of partisanship from their texts. Their aim was not, however, to deny the presence of subjectivity in the construction of histories, nor was it to make ancient texts irrelevant to present events.[103] In all three of these cases, but particularly in that of the "Orientalists" Lepsius and Meyer, the goal was to rid *Altertumswissenschaft* from the last vestiges of Romantic *Schwärmerei* and theological contamination. Mommsen, famously, was attacked by both J. J. Bachofen and Ferdinand Gregorovius for attiring his ancient Romans in unflattering, modern Prussian garb;[104] but it was he, rather than one of these Romantics, who received a Nobel Prize in 1902 and whose work is still read with profit today.

For historians of Greece, this midcentury "realism" was a bit harder to carry off. If Ernst Curtius opened his *Griechische Geschichte* (1857–67) with a long discussion of the geographical perfections of Hellas, he also could not restrain himself from a passionate tribute to Greece's uniquely sublime spiritual development, which he attributed largely to the glories of Greek grammar.[105] As Curtius's contemporary Herman Grimm testified in

---

[102] For example, Bode, *Mein Leben*, vol. 1 (Berlin, 1930), pp. 57–63. Bode's real venom, however, is reserved for Morelli's unthinking epigones; Michaelis, *Ein Jahrhundert kunstarchäologischer Entdeckungen*, p. 297.

[103] James Whitman, "The Last Generation of Roman Lawyers in Germany," in *The Uses of Greek and Latin: Historical Essays*, ed. A. C. Dionisotti, A. Grafton, and Jill Kraye (London, 1988), pp. 211–25; Renate Schlesier, *Kulte, Mythen und Gelehrte: Anthropologie der Antike seit 1800* (Frankfurt, 1994), pp. 65–99; John A. Wilson, *Signs and Wonders Upon Pharaoh: A History of American Egyptology* (Chicago, 1964), p. 112.

[104] For Bachofen's critiques of Mommsen, see Lionel Gossman, *Orpheus Philologus: Bachofen versus Mommsen on the Study of Antiquity*, Transactions of the American Philosophical Society, vol. 73, pt. 5 (Philadelphia, 1983); on Gregorovius, Hanno-Walter Kruft, "Der Historiker als Dichter: Zum 100. Todestag von Ferdinand Gregorovius," *Bayerische Akademie der Wissenschaften, Philosophisch-Historische Klasse: Sitzungsberichte 1992*, no. 2, p. 9.

[105] Curtius, *The History of Greece*, trans. Adolphus William Ward, vol. 1 (New York, 1892), pp. 27–36.

the pages of the *Preußische Jahrbücher*, "The Greece whose history Curtius
tells lies a long way away from the Roman Empire of Mommsen, where the
wind blows and bad weather dominates, and which reminds one of today's
prosaic national economy."[106] Not surprisingly, though specialized scholars
soon found fault with Curtius's history, it was a great popular success, in
France and England as well as in Germany; only in the 1890s did it begin to
lose favor as readers, now familiar with the prehistorical Greece discovered
by Schliemann and the Hellenistic art of Pergamum, turned to the less aestheticizing works of Eduard Meyer, Julius Beloch, and Jacob Burckhardt.[107]
In writing the history of the less aestheticized Hellenistic era, Curtius's contemporary J. G. Droysen was much more successful in illuminating the
Realpolitik of the Greek world. But as Arnaldo Momigliano has shown, in
the realm of cultural affairs, Droysen could not carry out his historicist
principles—he remained convinced of the incomparability of Attic high
classicism.[108] Continuing the line from Wolf and K. O. Müller, the heirs to
the Prussian tradition of specialized, historicist philology led the retreat
from speculation and comparativism, without, however, completely abandoning the aesthetic idealization of the Greek world.

In art-historical writing, this tendency expressed itself in the transformation of the study of mythology into form criticism, the expansion of inquiry
into epochs previously impugned as being unripe or decadent, and the widening of the material basis upon which criticism was exercised. One of the
few Romantic holdouts, F. G. Welcker, in 1857, condemned attempts to
reduce the study of mythology to pure classification; daringly, he agreed
with Creuzer that a mythographer needed a feeling for the religious, for
Greek "belief," to truly appreciate the cultural products of the Peloponnese.[109] Several years earlier, however, Eduard Gerhard had already chosen
the "philological" over the "philosophical" study of mythology,[110] and even
if Creuzer's legacy lasted longer at the IfAK than in Prussian universities,
here too the emphasis shifted from the origins and meanings of mythological figures to the preliminary securing of the integrity of source materials,
by means of dating, authenticating, and classifying Greek forms. Of course,
this shift in focus owed much to the archaeologists' desire to demonstrate

---

[106] Herman Grimm, "E. Curtius über Kunstmuseen," *Preußische Jahrbücher* 25 (1869): 616.

[107] Karl Christ, "Ernst Curtius und Jacob Burckhardt: Zur deutschen Rezeption der
griechischen Geschichte im 19. Jahrhundert," in *Antichità nell'ottocento in Italia e Germania*,
ed. Karl Christ and Arnaldo Momigliano (Bologna and Berlin, 1988), p. 223. For an early
critique of Curtius, see Konrad Bursian, *Geschichte der classischen Philologie in Deutschland von
den Anfängen bis zur Gegenwart*, vol. 2 (Munich, 1883), pp. 1146ff.

[108] See Arnaldo Momigliano, "J. G. Droysen: Between Greeks and Jews," in idem, *Essays in
Ancient and Modern Historiography* (Middletown, Conn., 1977), p. 314.

[109] Welcker, *Griechische Götterlehre*, vol. 1 (Göttingen, 1857), pp. vi–vii, 79–82. See below,
chapter 9 on Wilamowitz's return to Welcker's view.

[110] Gerhard, *Griechische Mythologie* (Berlin, 1854), pp. 1–2.

their virtuosity in the art of reading forms; just as Lepsius emphasized the centrality of familiarity with hieroglyphic and Coptic over biblical (and classical!) sources partly as a means to ensure the professional independence of Egyptology, the archaeologists narrowed their questions to underscore their unique proficiencies.

No one was so important in this narrowing and sharpening of archaeological style analysis than Heinrich Brunn, long a resident of Rome and IfAK associate. In a number of important books and essays, ranging from 1846 to 1893, Brunn attempted to trace the translation of mythological characters into the "language" of artistic form and to pave the way for the elaboration of a historical sequence of forms drawn directly from the monuments.[111] If Brunn's important *Geschichte der Griechischen Künstler* (*History of Greek Artists*—1853–59) still depended almost exclusively on literary testimony to determine its division of Greek artists into schools, by 1878, the Munich professor was using his eye for anatomical details to attempt to place unlabeled sculptural fragments in chronological sequence, determine their place of origin, and even to guess at their authorship. In a short essay published in the proceedings of the Bavarian Academy, Brunn "proved" that a *kouros* recently donated to the British Museum by Lord Strangeford belonged not only to the late Archaic period but also to the school of the Aegina pediment sculptor. Brunn's argument depended on the observation that in creating the *kouros* the archaic artist was obliged to adhere closely to the "system of forms" he had learned; hence, slight formal differences in individual sculptures could be used to arrange a stepwise sequence and locational index of Archaic artistic developments. The handling of ribs, muscles, and knees helped Brunn to identify the provenance of his *kouros*, particularly where "certain anomalies" in the rendering of body parts confirmed his comparisons with other similar forms.[112]

Not surprisingly, given both the pervasiveness of the comparison of the study of artistic forms to the procedures of text criticism, and the prevalence of historicism among philologists, midcentury archaeologists like Brunn insisted upon the strict delineation of national boundaries for the development of art. Already in his *Künstlergeschichte*, Brunn described the nationally defined formal conventions that constrained the art production of each age.[113] In an important essay of 1856, "Ueber die Grundverschiedenheit im Bildungsprincip der griechischen und ägyptischen Kunst" ("On the Fundamental Differences in the Formative Principles of Greek and

[111] On Brunn's importance, see Adam Flasch, *Heinrich Brunn: Gedächtnisrede* (Munich, 1902).

[112] Brunn, "Archäologische Miscellen," in *Sitzungsberichte der K. Bayerischen Akademie der Wissenschaften*, Phil.-Hist. Kl., 1872, vol. 2, p. 533.

[113] See, e.g., *Geschichte der Griechischen Künstler*, 2 vols. (Braunschweig, 1853; Stuttgart, 1859), 1:110.

Egyptian Art"), he demonstrated the social and climatic conditions that produced completely different ideas about art in these nations.[114] Many years later, he would reiterate this claim in a rather more provocative way: "Not even the most zealous student of things Semitic," he contended in 1893, "would dare to speak of a limited influence of the Semitic language on Greek. In precisely the same way, the Greeks borrowed from the Asiatics the artistic alphabet [*Schrift der Kunst*], but in art too, from the beginning they spoke their own language."[115] Proceeding to discount the possible effects of Assyrian and other oriental forms, and explicating the limited reciprocal influence of Greek art on the "petrified forms" of the East, Brunn concluded his argument with a general statement on the nontransferability of artistic forms. "That this effect [Greek on oriental] remained partial can be explained on internal grounds: each *Volk* observes the human form with the eyes of its own individuality and therefore is very little susceptible to foreign influences."[116] Like the art historians Alois Riegl, Adolf Hildebrand, and Heinrich Wölfflin, Brunn had succeeded in converting formalistic description into history of art at the cost of converting art history into a history of essentialized national *mentalités*.

But the narrowing of focus and rejection of universal norms that accompanied the rise of style analysis also had the effect of conferring new *historical* importance on periods once thought to be unripe or decadent, and material objects previously rejected as inappropriate for artistic study. Most prominent of the eras to receive new attention from German and Austrian art historians after 1870 were those surrounding the two cultural epochs most celebrated by previous generations, the Periclean Golden Age, and the Italian Renaissance, that is, the archaic and hellenistic periods on the one hand, and the Gothic and the baroque eras on the other.[117] In the universities, this change was quite gradual—in 1892, art history was represented at the University of Berlin by two specialists in Italian painting and one classical archaeologist. But, pressed onward by the combined forces of vast new museological acquisitions, specialization, and in some cases, nationalism, by the 1880s and 1890s, art historians had began to explore the little-known areas of late antiquity and the baroque, European prehistory and ancient Mesopotamia. If positivist historicism narrowed the range of questions, it also expanded archaeology's purview.

In part as the result of the omnivorous collecting of the later nineteenth

---

[114] Brunn, "Ueber die Grundverschiedenheit im Bildungsprincip der griechischen und ägyptischen Kunst," in *Rheinisches Museum für Philologie* 10 (1856): 158–59.

[115] Brunn, *Geschichte der Griechischen Künstler* 2:73.

[116] Ibid., p. 115.

[117] On the archaic period, see Glenn W. Most, "Zur Archäologie der Archaik," in *Antike und Abendland* 35 (1989): 1–23; on the popularity of the Pergamum marbles, see Michaelis, "Ernst Curtius," p. 78.

century, art historians and archaeologists also felt the need to expand their evolutionary schemata to include art forms besides sculpture. As chapter 1 indicated, the generation of Lessing and Kant had given pride of place within the plastic arts to the representation of the human form in three dimensions by means of freestanding sculpture. Their successors retained this ascetic preference for the white, nude, and usually male form; cast collections became so popular after 1850, that when Aby Warburg surveyed the situation in 1909, he turned up the information that 109 collections could be found in Germany in that year, some of them with inventories in the thousands.[118] If art-historical interest shifted to paintings sometime after midcentury, sculpture long remained the genre of choice for "archaeologists." But here, the diminution of sculpture's status owes in large part to the actual execution of archaeological excavations after 1870, during which, as we have seen, the uncovering of intact masterpieces proved extremely rare; one could not hope to trace out full historical sequences on the basis of sculpture alone.

Thus, after 1870, pottery and the minor arts began to play an important role in archaeological treatises. Particularly in the pre-Homeric era, pottery often formed the basis for the dating of graves, settlements, and other objects found in the same area. Digs frequently yielded no other artifacts in sufficient quantities to establish eras of occupation or the origins of the settlers, and as regional pottery typologies were elaborated over the course of the later nineteenth century, this stylistic evidence became more and more an index of ethnic encounters as well as time elapsed. The discovery of early Archaic grave urns at the Dipylon Gate site in Athens in 1863, for example, spurred the recognition of a previously unappreciated "Geometric" era stretching between the Mycenaean and archaic epochs, and gave birth to new speculations about possible links between proto-Greek and Indo-Germanic civilizations.[119] Humble objects lent themselves more easily to positivistic sequencing and national typologizing than did monumental sculpture.

In field archaeology, style-historical thinking privileged the specialized technical skills and willingness to relocate to "uncivilized" sites in the East that made excavators valuable to the museums and the academic community, but also made them unsuitable as interpreters of meaning. Far from the Reich's libraries and lacking in the strict philological training demanded of the professoriate, the site archaeologist himself was expected to make his

[118] See Warburg's report dated 26 May 1909, in WI, Wuttke, no. 72. He counted 3,800 casts in Düsseldorf, 2,271 in Berlin, 1,600 in Dresden, and 1,500 in Munich.

[119] See Alexander Conze, "Zur Geschichte der Anfänge griechischer Kunst," in *Sitzungsberichte der Kaiserlichen Akademie der Wissenschaften in Wien* (Phil.-Hist. Kl.) 64 (1870): 505–34; and idem, "Zur Geschichte der Anfänge griechischer Kunst," ibid., vol. 73 (1873): 221–50.

15. The vase collection of the Neues Museum in the late nineteenth century; an iconographer's dream. © Bildarchiv, Preußischer Kulturbesitz, 1996.

reports as accurate, succinct, and theory-free as possible.[120] Lepsius, the anti-aestheticizing student of Müller, was instrumental in institutionalizing an austere, analytical method of Egyptological research; this "German school" advocated careful, historicist classification of observations, in contrast to the "French school," whose members prided themselves on their

---

[120] The discrepancy in the styles of excavators and interpreters is clearly reflected in the *Jahrbuch des DAI*, in which the main articles down to the First World War were still largely iconological investigations of Greek and Roman sculpture, vases, and mosaics, while site reports, stressing street plans, water channels, and measurements were printed in the *Archäologischer Anzeiger*, an information sheet attached to the *JbdesDAI*. The explosion of new digs, acquisitions, and archaeological activity is witnessed by the fact that by 1906, the *AA* had overtaken the *JbdesDAI* article section in length; in 1912, the ratio was 706 pages in the *AA* to just 344 pages of *JbdesDAI* articles.

aesthetic sensitivity and holistic comprehension.[121] Alexander Conze's demand for thoroughgoing "physiognomic" investigations of building complexes contributed much to this, as did the pronouncements of Schliemann's "scientific" excavator Wilhelm Dörpfeld.[122] As trained architects, rather than historians or philologists, increasingly took over the supervision of excavations, archaeological reports began to include more measurements and discussions of building materials than interpretations of objects or rhapsodies on the splendors of ancient form. Like Carl Humann, Dörpfeld was more interested in uncovering structures than in exposing the meaning or glorifying the form of Greek cultural objects. Dörpfeld himself once told the architect-archaeologist Armin von Gerkan that what he could not measure or specify, particularly artistic considerations, did not interest him.[123] In imitation of these two anti-aesthetic, architecturally oriented excavators, on-site archaeologists took to carefully recording details and dimensions, postponing historical generalizations until an exacting description of the site and the stylistic categorization of the artifacts was complete. Style history delayed the reevaluation of the history of the classical world in light of its newly discovered surrounding cultures and internal fissures; it was easier, cognitively and practically, to classify than to reconceptualize the European past.

Classification also took less time than historical reappraisal, and time, for on-site archaeologists—particularly those at work in the Ottoman Empire—was of the essence. Duty to scholarship and to the state called archaeologists to proceed with excavation as rapidly as possible and to delay analysis of meaning for the future, a practice that the art critic Karl Scheffler later caricatured as *Anhäufungspolitik*, or the policy of heaping things up.[124] In Babylon, for example, Robert Koldewey dug winter and summer, with between 200 and 250 workers, leaving himself little time to appraise individual pieces. The eccentric architect was anxious to finish this dig, central to his plan for the systematic excavation of all of Mesopotamia, before German-Turkish relations degenerated, and permits were apportioned to rival nations. The Berliners remained unimpressed by Koldewey's discovery of colored tile reliefs and enjoined the excavator to look for inscriptions,[125] and a quarrel with the cuneiform philologist Friedrich Delitzsch further accelerated digging rather than deliberation.

But some archaeologists, particularly those devoted to the study of an-

---

[121] Erman, *Mein Werden*, pp. 113–14, 162–63; Wilson, *Signs and Wonders*, p. 109.

[122] See Conze, "Pro Pergamo."

[123] Armin von Gerkan, "Wilhelm Dörpfeld," in *Gnomon* 16 (1940): 428.

[124] Silke Wenk, ed., *Auf den Spuren der Antike: Theodor Wiegand, ein deutscher Archäologe* (Bendorf am Rhein, 1985), pp. 25–26.

[125] Walter Andrae, *Babylon: Die versunkene Weltstadt und ihr Ausgräber, Robert Koldewey* (Berlin, 1952), p. 145.

cient *art*, remained unimpressed by the results of "big archaeology," and recognized that stylistic studies, in spite of their professional utility, did not make any apparent contribution to that other important facet of the neohumanist project, *Bildung*. In 1886, the art historian Herman Grimm (son of Wilhelm Grimm) complained to the Education Ministry that the Winckelmannian vision of universal art history as a single, coherent field of study had been lost as IfAK archaeologists and academic classicists grew more and more isolated in their specialized areas. "They consider the material—which should be only secondary—the main thing, rather than the spirit, and, instead of devoting themselves to the study of the whole evolution of art, they consign themselves either to cataloging work or to the search for new material, which no one will ever look at."[126] The specialization and positivism of these new archaeologists, warned the author of a highly aestheticizing biography of Michelangelo, would distance the profession more and more from the pedagogical task entrusted to it. "For most of the classical [*Gymnasien*] and nonclassical [Realschulen] secondary schools," he wrote, "the material is not relevant, but rather the method." Therefore, archaeologists should take heed, lest they go the way of their colleagues in that venerable neohumanist discipline, philology. For classical philology, Grimm announced ominously, "has declined into a mindless cult of words without meaning, and the sound intuitions of the *Volk* will rise up against it."[127] German archaeologists had acquired new state funding, autonomous scholarly standing, and enhanced international prestige only to arrive at a further dilemma: how could the increasing specialization, professionalization, and bureaucratization of classical studies be reconciled with the perpetuation of antiquity's traditional pedagogical and normative functions?

[126] Hermann Grimm to Education Ministry, 6 February 1886, MZStA, Nachlaß Althoff, AI-197, pp. 1–4.
[127] Ibid.

TROUBLE IN OLYMPUS

Everyone should be Greek in his own way!
(*Goethe*)

TO BE A GREEK GOD, or a nineteenth-century German philologist, meant that one observed the heroic strivings of mortals from sublime heights, rousing oneself occasionally to beat back assaults on Olympian privileges. In the last decades of the century, the classicist establishment faced a series of institutional and intellectual challenges to its hegemony, to which it responded with all the generosity and willingness to compromise of an offended Hera. We have surveyed the means by which the classicists themselves consented to or connived in the abandonment of Romantic Graecophilia; as a result of the specialization of scholarship, the development of grand-scale excavation, and the rise of radical nationalism, scholars were compelled to abandon the long-cherished belief that antiquity formed a single conceptual and cultural entity. Here, however, we have to examine the resistance the classicist establishment mounted to the reform of educational institutions in accordance with these changes, and the persistence, in an era of positivism and historicism, of deeply ingrained philhellenic habits and convictions. Even if it had become acceptable to devote effort to the study of Roman-German pots and Mesopotamian dwellings, it was not possible to remove Greece as the affective epicenter of antiquity, for Graecophilia underwrote the institutional coherence of classical scholarship as well as the social and pedagogical centrality of the *Gymnasium*. Put bluntly, philhellenism had become a matter of social self-preservation at the same time that its philosophical and aesthetic tenets could no longer embrace the wealth of new material revealed by the spade.

Paradoxically, the most significant intellectual challenges to neohumanist academe were issued by two of the century's greatest admirers of the Greeks. Operating in entirely different spheres and inspired by very different motivations, Heinrich Schliemann and Friedrich Nietzsche lent to their explorations of classical antiquity something that had been missing from *Altertumswissenschaft* since the Romantic era: passion. Though Nietzsche was trained as a philologist, and Schliemann grew more and more concerned about scientific procedure over the course of his career, it was not their scholarly credentials but their outsider status and untamed "genius" gained them admirers. Schliemann and Nietzsche taught their audiences to distrust the bookish Graecophilia of the *Gymnasien* and professoriate and to look elsewhere for the "real" splendors of Hellas. Though their lessons really only hit home after both had gone to their graves, these two maverick philhellenes provided alluring new ways of making the Greek past present that challenged the cultural dominance of the professional philologist.

If Nietzsche and Schliemann threatened established classicists by opening Greece to new, nonphilological, sorts of inquiry, the growing movement for secondary-school reform challenged the institutional hegemony of classical-language training—which still, in 1890, consumed 46 percent of classroom time at this level of education.[1] School reformers wished to diminish the role of Greek and Latin training, to advance the teaching of modern subjects, and to break the monopoly of the *Gymnasien* over university entrance. Although reformist ideas had been born with neohumanism itself, the end of the *Kulturkampf* and the commencement of imperialist endeavors ushered in an era of severe criticism of the numbing effect of the study of classical grammar, the physical debilitation of young Germans caused by overburdening them with classwork, and the paltry representation of natural sciences, modern history and languages, physical education, and above all German studies, in the secondary-school curriculum. As Friedrich Paulsen later described, the wars of unification and Germany's rise to world power had sparked new interest in the life of the present, at the cost of a diminution of concern for classical antiquity. "The forces that came to play a decisive role in the age of Bismarck," he claimed, "were very different from those that had stamped German character in the age of Goethe. . . . Youth, following the presentiment that is unique to it, turned its attention to new things: sports and games, voyages of discovery and colonial conquests, ironclads and motor-cars, technical inventions and scientific discoveries."[2] A moderate defender of reform, Paulsen did not condone the increasingly radical critiques of the *Gymnasien* by nationalists and leaders of the youth movement. But by the time Paulsen took on the youth movement standardbearer Ludwig Gurlitt in 1905, the advocates of moderation had already been eclipsed by a wide spectrum of uncompromising ideologues.[3]

To their credit, many classicists recognized that their ideals no longer corresponded to historical realities and had lost their appeal for the majority of German schoolboys. They could not relinquish, however, the claim

---

[1] James Albisetti, *Secondary School Reform in Imperial Germany* (Princeton, N.J., 1983), p. 23.

[2] Friedrich Paulsen, *Das deutsche Bildungswesen in seiner geschichtlichen Entwicklung*, 4th ed. (Leipzig, 1920), p. 131.

[3] For Paulsen's view of Gurlitt, see Friedrich Paulsen, *An Autobiography*, trans. Theodor Lorenz (New York, 1938), pp. 477–78.

that preservation of the ideal of Greekdom was the sine qua non of German *Kultur*; those who demanded greater utility simply did not understand the higher purposes of classical education. That the classicists of the 1890s responded to the critique of the "relevance" of their studies with smug self-righteousness, and to the critique of their loyalty to the German nation with oaths and pledges, says a good deal about their social conscience; that most assumed that the answer to Nietzsche's fundamental question—what was the value of scholarship for modern-day life?—was self-evident indicates their naïveté. The school reform controversy marks a turning point in the history of German philhellenism, for the historicist rhetorical strategy that classicists developed in this era to preserve their cultural hegemony completely failed to satisfy their students, who began to look elsewhere—to the poetry of Hugo von Hofsmannsthal and Stefan George, the travel writing of Gerhart Hauptmann, and the painting of Arnold Böcklin—for a "true" understanding of the Greeks. Even the archaeologists' attempts to revivify antiquity through *Anschauungsunterricht* (perceptual training) in the *Gymnasien* only partly captured their young audience's attention. If the heroic excavations of Schliemann and the vitalist philosophy of Nietzsche signal the onset of neohumanism's intellectual decrepitude, the school-reform controversy marks the beginning of the end of institutionalized philhellenism.

Heinrich Schliemann's Brave New World

The uncontested hero of modern classical studies in the popular mind, Heinrich Schliemann conducted his philhellenic quests in a peculiarly unmodern manner. Schliemann's excavations did not really herald the coming age of bureaucratically organized, nationalist archaeology; he paid for his own digs with private funds, arranged (or disarranged) digging agreements with host governments in his own name, and stored his collection in his own home in Athens until he had negotiated a satisfactory agreement on its exhibition with the German Ethnography Museum.[4] But Schliemann, whose progress from rags to riches to Trojan ruins has become a fantastically popular German variation on the Horatio Alger fables, in fact played an important part in the development and especially the popularization of grand-scale archaeology. Due partly to the negative example he set for academically trained archaeologists and partly to the publicity his discovery of preclassical sites received, Schliemann helped to validate the late nineteenth-century articulation of archaeology as an independent science of objects. But in so doing, like Nietzsche, he also reintroduced into the study

[4] See Ernst Meyer, ed., *Heinrich Schliemann: Briefwechsel*, vol. 2 (Berlin, 1958), especially for the years after 1881.

of the classics a kind of speculative urge incompatible with the positivist historicism of his day.

Schliemann first visited Greece and Asia Minor in the mid-1860s. Owing to his notorious mendacity, it is impossible to determine whether he had really dreamt of discovering Troy since his childhood, as he claimed in his autobiographical accounts.[5] But in the nineteenth century, the existence of a real, historical Troy was not a matter of widespread conviction; if, as we have seen, philologists like F. A. Wolf cast doubt over the existence of a single, historical Homer, the material reality of an epic city was doubly hard to credit. As A. H. Sayce remarked in 1883, the "destructive criticism" of the previous fifty years had resulted in a pervasive "spirit of skepticism" in the interpretation of ancient sources.[6] The Homeric poems, for the average philologist of the age, represented a moment in European intellectual development, not a literal account of ancient geography, warfare, or private life. Schliemann's choice of sites reflected what had become a scientifically unacceptable faith in the testimony of the ancients; he dug for Troy beneath the Roman and Greek city of Ilion, whose location had never been in dispute. Thus Schliemann's search for Troy, though not at all unprecedented, seemed to contemporaries less a scientific endeavor than a treasure hunt, a characterization that the ceaseless self-promoter abetted by loud advertisement of his discoveries of "Priam's Treasure" and his lonely sufferings on the plain of Ilion.

The romance of his quest attracted wide, if often critical, press coverage, provoking wide public interest, as well as the wrath of the Turkish government. Schliemann's battles with the Turks are legendary, but the implications of these skirmishes for later archaeological negotiations have not been drawn. In 1870, without the permission of local authorities, Schliemann began to dig at Hissarlik, and almost immediately incurred the Turks' wrath. The wealthy ex-businessman attempted to buy his site, but discovered that the Turkish minister of public instruction, Safvet Pasha, had shrewdly purchased the property under Hissarlik a short time before.[7] Schliemann was then compelled to spend the next eight months attempting to convince the minister that he had only the interests of knowledge at heart; as the excavator complained to the American ambassador in Constantinople, he resented this delay, imposed by a man "who ought to think it a great favor from

---

[5] William M. Calder III, "A New Picture of Heinrich Schliemann," in *Myth, Scandal, and History*, ed. William M. Calder III and David A. Traill (Detroit, 1986), p. 28.

[6] A. H. Sayce, "Preface," in Heinrich Schliemann, *Troja: Results of the Latest Researches and Discoveries on the Site of Homer's Troy* (New York, 1884), p. vi. See also Peter Goessler, "Professor Wilhelm Dörpfeld zum Gedächtnis," in *Wilhelm Dörpfeld* (Berlin, 1940), p. 12; Leo Deuel, *Memories of Heinrich Schliemann* (New York, 1977), p. 12.

[7] Schliemann to Wayne MacVeagh (U.S. ambassador in Constantinople), 24 January 1871, in *Schliemann: Briefwechsel*, 1:178–80.

heaven that during his administration the great problem of Troy was solved."[8] The Turks certainly did not think it a favor when Schliemann, who did at last receive an excavation permit in 1871, proceeded to send his entire collection of finds to Greece. To convey their discontentment, they responded by suing the expropriator for ten thousand francs. Hoping to win sympathy for his future plans, Schliemann paid fifty thousand francs to the Cultural Ministry in Constantinople toward improvement of the Imperial Ottoman Museum,[9] but the Turks, it seems, were not greatly impressed by his generosity. Thereafter, Schliemann experienced great difficulty in arranging digging permits; at Hissarlik, he was carefully watched by armed guards, and he was refused permission to measure or sketch the site until late in 1882, supposedly to protect the secrecy of a military installation six kilometers away.[10] As a private citizen, Schliemann had to perform his own negotiations and could exert only as much pressure as his personal connections and finances allowed. Although individually arranged and funded digs continued to occur regularly down to 1914, after Schliemann's travails, most archaeologists would look to scholarly or state agencies to represent their interests. By the same token, after Schliemann, the Foreign Ministry in Berlin itself would try to dissuade amateurs from excavating abroad, fearing that privately organized excavations might jeopardize exportation agreements and permissions for future digs for government-supervised scientists. The lesson Schliemann learned too late about the importance of unruffled relations with the host country would soon become the shared conviction of the scholarly and diplomatic establishments.

If Schliemann's sensational finds at Hissarlik vexed the Turks, his exploits also called forth disdain from the halls of academia. Theodor Mommsen called Schliemann a "truffel hound"; Curtius accused him of being a botcher and a confidence trickster.[11] The archaeologists Adolf Furtwängler and Georg Loeschke wrote two books about Mycenaean pottery without consulting the site's excavator or viewing his collection, which was on display in the Ethnographic Museum in Berlin by 1882.[12] Schliemann was not, of course, the sort of man German scholars found easy to include in their circle. He was independently wealthy, and had never studied philology; he wrote for a popular audience, and he held no official post. Most shocking, he cared little for the sort of monuments the Hyperboreans treasured. "You

---

[8] Schliemann to MacVeagh, 12 March 1871, ibid., p. 184.

[9] Carl Schuchhardt, *Schliemann's Excavations*, trans. Eugenie Sellers (Chicago, 1974), p. 9.

[10] William A. McDonald, *Progress into the Past: The Rediscovery of Mycenaean Civilization* (Bloomington, Ind., 1967), p. 39; Wilhelm Dörpfeld, *Troja und Ilion: Ergebnisse der Ausgrabungen in den vorhistorischen und historischen Schichten von Ilion, 1870–1894* (Athens, 1902), p. 12.

[11] On Mommsen, see J. H. Ottaway, "Rudolf Virchow: An Appreciation," *Antiquity* 47 (1973): 103; on Curtius, Calder, "Heinrich Schliemann," p. 34.

[12] Hartmut Döhl, *Heinrich Schliemann: Mythe und Ärgernis* (Munich, 1981), pp. 46–47.

must know," his long-suffering overseer at Mycenae reported to the Greek Archaeological Society in 1876, "that he eagerly demolishes everything Roman and Greek, in order to lay bare the Pelasgian walls. If we find Greek or Roman vases, he looks at them in disgust, and if such fragments come into his hands, he lets them fall."[13] And Schliemann himself provoked controversy; his first dig on the Trojan plain took place at Bunarbashi, a site he excavated, it seems, only to prove that it was *not* Troy, and to show Curtius, who had propounded this theory, to be in error.[14] When classicist academics refused to credit his literal interpretation of the epics, he accused them of "beastly spite," and sought solace in the general public's approval.[15]

But in addition to being a popular hero, Schliemann also wanted to be accepted by German scholars, and this schizophrenia led him to seek out specialists like Conze, to visit Curtius's Olympia excavations, and eventually to hire away the DAI's young architect, Wilhelm Dörpfeld. While the classicist community continued to malign—or at least ignore—Schliemann until just before his death in 1890, however, he did win the backing of a quite different sort of *Bildungsbürger*: the adventurers and medical doctors who pioneered the study of anthropology and prehistory in Germany. Schliemann arranged a first meeting with Rudolf Virchow in 1875 in order to consult the pathologist, whose polymath accomplishments also included extensive studies of prehistory, about the owl-headed face-jars Schliemann had found at Mycenae. In 1879, Virchow accompanied Schliemann to Hissarlik. Convinced that Schliemann had correctly identified the location of Troy, Virchow did his best to enhance the scholarly world's appreciation of Schliemann—or at least to prevent it from ignoring him completely.[16] The close friendship of the two virtuosi resulted in mutually beneficial joint vacations, like their Nile trip of 1888, during which Schliemann made a number of swift digs and Virchow measured Egyptian heads, ancient and modern.[17] In addition to their antipathy for Berlin classicists, the two shared a preoccupation with material culture and the preliterate world rare for educated men of their era.

Professional classicists had been particularly loathe to accept Schliemann's attempts to validate the historical testimony of Homer; while most came grudgingly to appreciate the historical value of his finds—especially

---

[13] Stamatakis quoted in Emil Ludwig, *Schliemann: The Story of a Gold-Seeker*, trans. D. F. Tait (Boston, 1931), p. 168.

[14] Hartmut Döhl, "Schliemann the Archaeologist," in Calder and Traill, *Myth, Scandal, and History*, p. 103. The geographer H. Kiepert and Helmuth von Moltke also credited this hypothesis; the Austrians under J. G. von Hahn had also recently completed a dig at this site. Dörpfeld, *Troja und Ilion*, p. 1; Schuchhardt, *Schliemann's Excavations*, pp. 18–19, 26.

[15] Deuel, *Memories*, p. 6.

[16] Döhl, *Schliemann*, pp. 50–53.

[17] Ibid., p. 334.

those at Tiryns—they long resisted the excavator's attempts to use evidence drawn from the epics to identify specific artifacts with poetical descriptions.[18] In part, their scruples were well warranted; after Schliemann's death, it was generally agreed that the level he had believed to be Homeric Troy in fact belonged to a much earlier age. But they seem to have found his arguments particularly difficult to swallow because the artifacts he excavated looked so crude, so "un-Greek." This is particularly evident in discussions of the Mycenaean finds, whose dates and stylistic reference points were so uncertain. Writing in 1876, Arthur Milchhöfer rejected comparisons to Assyrian, Phoenician, and Corinthian art, but conjectured an Asiatic origin for the style, as it was clearly not a product of "autonomous Greek art."[19] Curtius could not believe that the rude "pre-Hellenic" pottery and overrefined "post-Hellenic" gold pieces Schliemann had uncovered could possibly belong to the same era; the rich and diverse cache of finds found in Mycenae's circular pit, he argued, suggested a long-maintained treasury, rather than royal shaft graves.[20] The director of the DAI branch office in Athens, Ulrich Köhler, suggested that the "un-Greek, barbarian stamp" of the finds was partly responsible for classicists' initial mistrust of Schliemann's discovery; how could such strange and unlovely objects have been found on Greek soil? "The astonishing, shocking, I may even say anguishing quality of these finds lies not in their oriental characteristics but in their exclusively oriental character. In seeing them, one has the feeling as if one were suddenly thrown into a foreign, barbarian world in which one searched in vain for a familiar face, for an accustomed article."[21] Even if scholars rejected his claims to exact literary correlations, Schliemann had complicated the problem of understanding the origins of true "Greekness" by opening up the prehistorical world to stylistic inquiry; his demonstrations of Egyptian-Mycenaean stylistic commonalities, too, could only vex the heirs of K. O. Müller.

Not coincidentally, then, Schliemann the Graecophile was lionized in anthropological circles as nowhere else, for his researches took him deep into the human past, beyond the reaches of written language, into a realm in which philology-based *Altertumswissenschaft* was of no use. As Schliemann wrote in a report on his findings of 1873, "apart from the monuments of

---

[18] See, e.g., Conze's review of Schliemann's *Mykenae* in *Göttingische Gelehrte Anzeigen*, 27 March 1878, pp. 385–406. Even Schliemann's friend Virchow approached this question of proof with care; we will never know if the king who ruled the Burnt City of Troy was actually Priam, Virchow wrote in 1881, but Priam and Ilium "will remain the designations upon which our thoughts fasten." Virchow, "Preface," in Schliemann, *Ilios: The City and Country of the Trojans* (New York, 1881), p. xv.

[19] Arthur Milchhöfer, "Die Ausgrabungen in Mykene," in *MdesDAI*, A 1 (1876): 327.

[20] Ernst Curtius, "Griechische Ausgrabungen, 1876–1877," *Nord und Süd* 1 (1877): 91–100.

[21] Ulrich Köhler, "Die Grabanlagen in Mykene und Sparta," *MdesDAI*, A 3 (1878): 4.

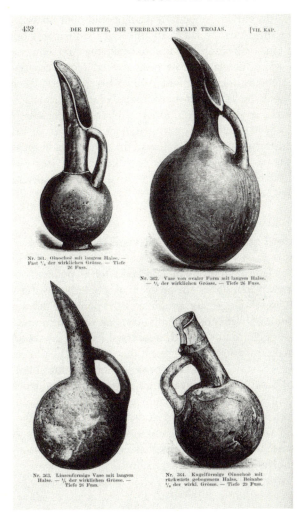

Nr. 361. Oinochoë mit langem Halse. — Fast ¼, der wirklichen Grösse. — Tiefe 26 Fuss.

Nr. 362. Vase von ovaler Form mit langem Halse. — ¼, der wirklichen Grösse. — Tiefe 26 Fuss.

Nr. 363. Linsenförmige Vase mit langem Halse. — ¼, der wirklichen Grösse. — Tiefe 26 Fuss.

Nr. 364. Kugelförmige Oinochoë mit rückwärts gebogenem Halse. Beinahe ¼, der wirkl. Grösse. — Tiefe 29 Fuss.

16. Page from Schliemann's *Ilios* (1883). Note the humbleness of the objects, despite their origin in what Schliemann then thought was Homeric Troy.

timeless value I have brought to light, with these newfound artifacts, I have discovered a new world for archaeology." When the forthcoming account and photographs of his finds appeared, and if the "civilized" world treated his evidence fairly, he continued, all remaining doubts about the existence of Troy would disappear, and he would finally be rewarded for his "super-human exertions, hardships, and gigantic expenditures."[22] Schliemann's self-aggrandizing statement echoed the resentment of like-minded men in the anthropological sciences toward the classicists, who would criticize

[22] Schliemann's report "Ausgrabungen in Troia," dated 24 May 1873, in *Schliemann: Brief-wechsel*, 1:229–30.

their amateurish procedures but whose book learning could offer no assistance in understanding this "new world." An outsider, Schliemann belonged to neither camp but was perhaps the first to shake the confidence of classicists, particularly when his claim to have discovered Troy was reasserted so forcefully after his death by Dörpfeld. And, as his correspondence suggests, he quickly became the hero of those enamored of unclassical ages, where documentation was scarce and conventional aesthetics inapplicable.[23]

Paradoxically, the man who sought to confirm Homer's veracity made his main contribution in illustrating the insufficiency of the literary tradition as a means to demarcate the nature-culture divide. The discovery of Troy was the beginning of the end of philological hegemony over the study of ancient *Kultur*.

The Philology of the Future and the Positivism of the Present

Reflecting on his *Birth of Tragedy* more than a decade after its publication, Friedrich Nietzsche correctly identified "the problem of scholarly investigation" as the central and most "dangerous" problem of the book. He did not specify the precise community "endangered" by his essay, though in these late musings he did argue that the book had "addressed itself to artists or, rather, to artists with analytical and retrospective leanings."[24] At the time of its composition, however, Nietzsche had been professor of classical philology at the University of Basel, and it is clear from private correspondence before and after the volume's publication that Nietzsche had in fact intended his book to reach—and unsettle—an audience of fellow philologists. If he advocated an antihistoricist, philosophical form of philological inquiry, in 1872 Nietzsche still thought of himself as a member of a community of professional scholars of Greek language and literature. But his attempt to articulate an overarching explanation of the causes of Greek genius that would serve as an antidote to the historicist sterility of his fellows had taken the Basel philosopher beyond textual testimony: the book's additional attempt to enunciate a program for the achievement of German cultural primacy simply underlined its departure from convention. Nietzsche meant to criticize the establishment to which he belonged from a presentist and Wagnerian point of view. In so doing, he unwittingly joined together three cultural projects that would later unite forces against the philhellenist establishment: the liberal-nationalist desire to crown the victory of 1871

---

[23] For a good example, see Theodor Schreiber (professor, University of Leipzig) to Schliemann, 14 July 1885 (ibid., 2:220–21) on Schliemann's inspiration to this student of the art of Alexandria in the Ptolemaic era.

[24] Nietzsche, "A Critical Backward Glance," in idem, *The Birth of Tragedy and The Genealogy of Morals*, trans. Francis Golffling (New York, 1956), p. 5.

with lasting "cultural and spiritual unification" (innere Reichsgründung), the modernist and Germanophile campaign for school reform, and the avant-garde attack on philistinism. If Nietzsche had hardly an inkling of what he had wrought, the classicist establishment, at the height of its prestige and influence, most certainly failed to recognize the seriousness of Nietzsche's challenge. *The Birth of Tragedy* was ignored and its author was reviled partly because Nietzsche was an "embarrassment" to the guild, but especially because the clearly antiphilological position he took up was not yet a serious threat. The *Gymnasium* had become the accepted gateway to university education and white-collar careers, philosophical faculties teemed with specialists in Greek and Latin grammar, collections of classical casts were to be found in every medium-sized German city, and the great excavations at Olympia and Pergamum were just around the corner. Attempts at a real response to Nietzsche's aims would only come in the 1890s, when the school reform movement had begun to eat away the social and political foundations of philological hegemony. But the context in which the book appeared and the controversy it generated should illuminate the philhellenic world of the 1870s, and prepare us for the classicist reaction to new challenges in the 1890s.

The Birth of Tragedy, its author tells us, was composed in the midst of two kinds of emotional turbulence: observation of and participation in the Franco-Prussian War, and ardent devotion to the music of Richard Wagner. Nietzsche did not detail, however, a third sort of mental turmoil evident in his volume: his attempt to come to grips with the professional position he had suddenly attained at the age of twenty-four. As Carl Pletsch has recently described, Nietzsche's ambivalent attitude toward the classical philologists of his day has its origins in his experiences at Schulpforta, where he thrived on academic discipline and, at the same time, enthusiastically pursued private studies in philosophy and the arts.[25] Throughout his college career, he continued this pattern, seeking the kudos that came with demonstrations of philological rigor as well as pursuing the deeper truths offered by Arthur Schopenhauer and the materialist philosopher Friedrich Albert Lange. He both admired his mentors and thought them lacking in creativity and courage; he thought philology the noblest of callings, but believed ninety-nine out of a hundred contemporary scholars had chosen the field for the wrong reasons (emulation of teachers, lethargy, simple breadwinning).[26] If, as James Whitman has argued, *The Birth of Tragedy* can been seen as an over-exuberant celebration of the "magisterial" tradition in German academia, it was clearly also a denunciation of contemporary positivist practice; against

---

[25] See Carl Pletsch, *The Young Nietzsche: Becoming A Genius* (New York, 1991), esp. pp. 46–62.

[26] See his sketch for one of the "Untimely Meditations" entitled "Wir Philologen," in *Friedrich Nietzsche: Werke in Drei Bände*, vol. 3 (Munich, 1966), pp. 323–24.

the backdrop of the highly specialized and impersonally technical phi-
lological writing of the second half of the century, Nietzsche's attempt to
introduce poetic and philosophical insights into the interpretation of the
Greek world looked revolutionary, not reactionary. This—in addition to
Nietzsche's paeans to the equally revolutionary Wagner—explains why the
only establishment figure to respond to the volume called his remonstrance
Zukunftsphilologie! (*Philology of the Future!*), not *Vergangenheitsphilologie
Philology of the Past*). The future-oriented injunction "Soyons de notre siècle," which Nietzsche proposed to his friend Erwin Rohde as a motto for
their philological faction,[27] was precisely the aspect of *The Birth of Tragedy*
that most irritated the soon-to-be satrap of *Altertumswissenschaft*, Ulrich
von Wilamowitz-Moellendorff, and resulted in his denunciation of this antihistoricist enterprise.

In spite of his debts to earlier poets, philosophers, and teachers, which
numerous commentators have detailed,[28] Nietzsche's *Birth of Tragedy* was a
highly unconventional piece of classical scholarship. Nietzsche argues that
the need for fictional self-creation and the equally compelling urge to self-
dismemberment, represented by the gods Apollo and Dionysus, are the
drives that account for human culture. The Greeks before Euripides and
Socrates managed to strike an elegant balance between these two impulses
in tragic theater. Since then, however, the Apollonian *principium individua-
tionis* has predominated, alienating man from the primary, universal world
beyond appearances. Man needs appearances—a fundamental one of which
is language—to save him from Dionysian self-annihilation, Nietzsche argues, but the prelinguistic realm of music is our primordial home.[29] If we
fail to see this side of the Greeks, we eschew their practical pessimism for a
rapacious "Alexandrian" theoretical optimism that sacrifices life and art for
a kind of knowledge that can never satisfy our longing for truth.

Clearly, this argument has normative implications for scholarly praxis.
Like Rousseau, Nietzsche makes desires that transcend needs and abilities
the source of human unhappiness and weakness; like Goethe, he finds the
will to know the most sublime and the most dangerous aspect of human
desires. Like both of these thinkers, Nietzsche incorporated into his work
numerous autobiographical elements; as a result, he frequently employs the
figure of the philologist to symbolize the Faustian frustrations of the modern world. "[Modern man] remains eternally hungry," he writes, "the critic
without strength or joy, the Alexandrian man who is at bottom a librarian

[27] Quoted in Pletsch, *Young Nietzsche*, p. 90.

[28] See, e.g., James Whitman, "Nietzsche in the Magisterial Tradition of German Classical
Philology," *Journal of the History of Ideas* 47, no. 3 (July–September 1986): 453–68; M. S. Silk
and J. P. Stern, *Nietzsche on Tragedy* (Cambridge, 1981), pp. 1–30.

[29] See Nietzsche, *Birth of Tragedy*, p. 46.

and scholiast, blinding himself miserably over dusty books and typographical errors."[30] Like the positivist philologist, modern man found himself in a Faustian predicament; just as knowing the lifeless, disconnected facts about the past would never result in the rebirth of ancient Greece, tearing off nature's veils would never tell man what he most wanted to know. A healthier, more beautiful life required self-reflective understanding of this search as in itself hopeless, but also part of the process of generating necessary illusions. If, as Nietzsche writes in perhaps the most famous phrase in the book, "the world is only justified as an aesthetic phenomenon," philology is only justified as a means to self-creation; historicism diverts this creative energy into unproductive and debilitating channels.

This attack on historicism was combined with an attack on Greek beauty. By making music-drama the key to Greek aesthetic sensibility, and by denying the applicability of "beauty" to this form,[31] Nietzsche subverted traditional accounts of Greek genius that made fifth-century Athens the model for German emulation. As M. S. Silk and J. P. Stern have shown, Nietzsche's admiration for the archaic style of Aeschylus and disdain for Plato and Sophocles challenged the ideal of classical beauty still dominant in academic circles.[32] Moreover, he portrayed the Golden Age as the opening of a long period of artistic degeneration—more evidence of what Wilamowitz called his "taking pleasure in pure contradiction" (*Freude am Urwiderspruch*).[33] Clearly, Nietzsche's Wagnerian aesthetic could not be easily reconciled with a conventionalized philhellenism that lavished its highest praise on the sculptures of Phidias and Praxiteles.

Finally, Nietzsche made a new and compelling case for his book's reformulation of the Winckelmannian project of marrying investigations into Greek aesthetics to new plans for German cultural revival.[34] It seems that Nietzsche believed his book to be crucial to Germany because it was there that the greatest chance of exploding the Alexandrian, Socratic, optimistic cult of man as searcher after knowledge existed. Thanks to Kant and especially to Schopenhauer, it was possible to recognize the limits of our knowledge and the other world beneath that of appearances; Wagner's Dionysian music and Germanic mythologizing, moreover, gave hope for the return of tragic art, and the founding of the Reich for the rebirth of Greek tragedy— or even, a wholesale return to fifth-century Greece, in German form. But this return to the Greeks, as usual, could not be accomplished by mere

---

[30] Ibid., p. 112.

[31] Ibid., p. 97.

[32] Silk and Stern, *Nietzsche on Tragedy*, p. 37.

[33] Wilamowitz, *Zukunftsphilologie! Zweites Stück: Erwidrung auf die Rettungsversuche für Fr. Nietzsches "Geburt der Tragödie"* (Berlin, 1873), p. 15.

[34] See, e.g., *Birth of Tragedy*, p. 16.

imitation. Nietzsche believed that the German spirit was pure and vigorous enough to eliminate alien myths and elements grafted onto it by force. In a passage echoed by many later writers, he argues:

> It might be thought that the battle should begin with the eradication of all elements of Romance culture. Our victory in the last war might be taken as an encouraging sign, yet it is merely external: the internal challenge must be sought in the desire to prove ourselves worthy of our great predecessors, Luther as well as our best artists and poets. But no one should think that such battles can be fought without one's household gods, one's mythic roots, without a true "recovery" of all things German.[35]

Roman and French culture would have to be stripped away, were the founding of the Reich to be completed "internally." These mediating, pan-European forms simply thwarted Germany's ability to imitate the Greeks. One could see this imperative to prune away foreign graftings as the intellectual equivalent of Bismarck's demand for the Germanization of the DAI, but Nietzsche's passage portrays national self-creation as a process not of institution building, but of mythmaking. In making healthy cultural self-production dependent on the sort of "monumental" histories he thought most advantageous, Nietzsche left existing institutions and conventional canons of proof behind for a world beyond the reach of words and wholly obscure to the disinterested, fact-collecting scholar. Here what mattered was life, German cultural purity, and power, not historical accuracy or scientific proof.

Not surprisingly, this unconventional book called forth an unconventional book review. Appearing in mid-1872, Ulrich von Wilamowitz-Moellendorff's *Zukunftsphilologie!* detailed with considerable relish all of Nietzsche's misinterpretations of Greek texts and lack of evidence for his claims. Nietzsche, Wilamowitz charged, not only had failed to understand Homer, Plato, Pindar, Aristotle, and Euripides, he had also done violence to the great German philhellenes of recent times, including Winckelmann, Lessing, and Goethe. But Wilamowitz found Nietzsche's general approach and attitude toward his subject matter and his lack of respect for his professional forbears to be the most objectionable aspect of the book. He wanted nothing to do with this metaphysician-journalist, a man wholly lacking in love of truth and proper humility, whose dedication to Wagnerism had led him to construct an ahistorical picture of Attic drama. "This is precisely the opposite," Wilamowitz argued,

> of the scholarly direction, that the heroes of our, and in fact every real field of knowledge have traveled. [These heroes] were not blinded by any presupposition about the end result and, loyal to truth alone, progressed step by step from

[35] Ibid., p. 140.

finding to finding. They conceived each historically conditioned phenomenon only by examining the assumptions of the age in which it developed, in order to see its meaning in light of its historical necessity. Their historical-critical method, which at least in principle has become the common property of the field, is the precise opposite of a sort of inquiry that must find confirmation of its dogmatic assumption in all ages. This [opposition] could not have escaped even Herr Nietzsche's notice. His way out of this [problem] is to ridicule the historical-critical method, to insult every aesthetic viewpoint that does not support his views, and to call the age in which philology in Germany was raised to never before imagined heights (especially by Gottfried Hermann and Karl Lachmann) "a wholesale misunderstanding of the study of antiquity."[36]

One can hardly hope to find a more pious tribute to positivistic philology. Wilamowitz, who in the course of this scholarly controversy described his intention to "stand at my post just as I did before the walls of Paris,"[37] clearly felt Nietzsche's book to be a sort of declaration of scholarly civil war. It did not matter so much to Wilamowitz if the philosopher spun out his tale of Greece and India, Wagner and Sophocles, to a popular audience, but he could not be permitted to remain in the lectern, "where he ought to teach scholarship. Let him gather tigers and panthers around his knees," Wilamowitz continued, "but not Germany's young philologists, who ought to learn, through the asceticism of self-effacing work, to search for truth alone, to free their judgment through willed humility, so that classical antiquity may grant them that singular sort of immortality, [which] the favor of the Muses promises. . . ."[38] Nietzsche, Wilamowitz asserted, had made mockery of philology as a science, but he had also imperiled the inheritance of the classics and the "favor of the Muses"; the Basel philosopher was a threat not just to the profession, but to German culture as a whole.

This emotional defense of "scientific" classical philology and old-fashioned philhellenism provoked two different sorts of responses from the pro-Nietzsche camp. One characteristically self-serving salvo came from Wagner, who published an open letter of thanks and praise to Nietzsche in a sympathetic newspaper, the *Norddeutsche Allgemeine Zeitung*, on 23 June 1872. Wagner's letter must have assured Wilamowitz that his identification of the dangerousness of Nietzsche's book had been correct, for it proved to be a direct attack on the entire philological establishment. This caste, the composer argued, contributed nothing to *Bildung* or art and had no purpose save the production of more useless *Gymnasium* teachers and professors,

---

[36] Wilamowitz, *Zukunftsphilologie! Eine Erwiderung auf Friedrich Nietzsches 'Geburt der Tragödie'* (Berlin, 1872), p. 8.

[37] Letter from Wilamowitz to his mother, quoted in Uvo Hölscher, *Die Chance des Unbehagens: Drei Essais zur Situation der klassischen Studien* (Göttingen, 1965), p. 15.

[38] Wilamowitz, *Zukunftsphilologie!*, p. 32.

who destroyed rather than encouraged their students' admiration for the Greeks. Sublimely positioned above the masses like Indian Brahmins, Wagner asserted, philologists should be expected to make divine pronouncements; "And in fact, this is what we are waiting for; we are waiting for a man to emerge from this wonderful sphere and tell us, without learned phrases and ghastly citations, what the initiated, beneath the veil of their researches, so incomprehensible to us laymen, are doing, and if this is worth the upkeep of so expensive a caste."[39] *Gymnasium* philologists had nearly killed the composer's admiration for the Greeks, and in spite of Wilamowitz, they spoke only to a small group of like pedants and note-shufflers; they had done nothing at all to improve art or advance truth. Nietzsche, on the other hand, though his scholarship was solid, spoke to the world beyond the philologists' guild; only his sort could insure that German *Bildung* escaped "cretinization" and contributed to the new nation's achievement of its noble goals.

Nietzsche appreciated Wagner's support, but quickly recognized that Wagner's letter would in fact produce effects amongst the philologists contrary to those intended. Consequently, he joyfully accepted his friend Erwin Rohde's offer to write a scholarly defense of *The Birth of Tragedy* to be circulated within the guild.[40] Rohde, who had already given the book a glowing review in the *Norddeutsche Allgemeine Zeitung*, had, like Nietzsche, been a student of the philologist Friedrich Ritschl at the University of Bonn, and now held an associate professorship at the University of Kiel. Like Ritschl, Rohde disapproved of Wagner's uninformed attack on the whole discipline of philology; unlike Ritschl and Wilamowitz, however, Rohde did not suspect that Nietzsche's book represented a challenge of the same order. A refutation of Wilamowitz, he wrote to Nietzsche, did not require a denunciation of philology as such; "rather, the aim of my essay can only be to . . . maintain the linkage between historical and philosophical inquiry as the final goal of philology, and to deprive the philologists of the pretext of the unphilological aspects of your piece."[41] Decorum and diplomacy, too, he said, inclined him to avoid an all-out attack on the antiphilosophical philologists of Berlin and Leipzig. But what Rohde produced proved to be the manifesto of a small heretical group of philologists who, after this debacle, would find themselves even more marginalized within or excluded from academia than they had been previously. A descendant of the out-of-

[39] Wagner to Nietzsche, 12 June 1872 (published in *NAZ* 23 June 1872), in *Nietzsche: Briefwechsel: Kritische Gesamtausgabe*, vol. 2/4: *Briefe an Friedrich Nietzsche, Mai 1872–Dezember 1874*, ed. Giorgio Colli and Mazzino Montinari (Berlin, 1978), p. 16.

[40] Nietzsche to Rohde, 18 June 1872, in *Nietzsche: Briefwechsel*, vol. 2/3: *Friedrich Nietzsche, Briefe Mai 1872–Dezember 1874*, pp. 11–12; for Rohde's offer, see Rohde to Nietzsche 15 June 1872, in *Nietzsche: Briefwechsel*, 2/4:26–27.

[41] Rohde to Nietzsche, 12 July 1872, p. 40.

favor "dilettante" Friedrich Creuzer and the mentor of Walter F. Otto, the neo-Romantic scholar of Greek religion, Rohde made the case for the necessity that philology abandon its obsession with trivial facts in favor of the pursuit of deeper truths. His defense of Nietzsche had at its center a justification of "the philology of the future" and the seeds of generational revolt.

Rohde's *Afterphilologie (Anal Philology)* did, however, mean to defend Nietzsche's scholarship against Wilamowitz's criticisms, and did so ingeniously, if not to the satisfaction of the establishment. Rohde denounced Wilamowitz's philistinism and pedantry, but also sought to show up his opponent's lack of philological skills and deficient familiarity with ancient Greek texts. He engaged in extensive bouts of shoe-on-the-other-footism, demonstrating that Wilamowitz had failed to grasp the meaning of texts that Nietzsche had understood perfectly well but neglected to cite in his own behalf. Most importantly, Rohde set up a rival model of "true" philology to that of the Berlin school, which he described as "a parody of all authentic philology, a horrible distortion of sensible criticism, a truly anal philology."[42] Philology of Wilamowitz's sort was merely obsessed with the trivia of antiquity, and could offer nothing but lifeless, meaningless, and fragmentary accounts of the past; it might be able to prove its facts—though Rohde was highly skeptical of this—but it could offer no insight into what Rohde called "the highest prize of the study of antiquity, an understanding of the noblest works of art, which themselves could be fruitful in leading the way to an artistic existence."[43] Wilamowitz's attempt to save philology from Nietzsche's depredations had been buttressed by a false and naive understanding of the field's true mission. That Nietzsche's work was in tune with "the noblest strivings of the present" in no way invalidated it as scholarship; he could both be "an authentic philologist" and, in Nietzsche's own self-description, "a citizen of that which is to come."[44]

Wilamowitz, however, was not convinced. His reply to Rohde, which appeared in early 1873, sarcastically praised the philologist for having sacrificed his intellect and scholarly honor for his great friend Nietzsche. In fact, Wilamowitz had discovered a number of points on which Rohde's explanation contradicted Nietzsche's actual statements, and he predicted (rightly) that the two "philologists of the future" would soon have a falling-out of their own.[45] Naturally, Wilamowitz had resented the aspersions cast on him by Rohde, and he refused to buy the argument that deeper truths did not have to be documented directly. "Thank God," he ruminated, "that I do not have the wisdom to comprehend in the reporting of a story what is not

---

[42] Rohde, *Afterphilologie: Sendschreiben eines Philologen an Richard Wagner* (Leipzig, 1872), p. 12.

[43] Ibid., p. 9.

[44] Ibid., p. 48.

[45] See Wilamowitz, *Zukunftsphilologie! Zweites Stück*, p. 8.

reported in it."[46] Wilamowitz concluded his second response with a new profession of his faith in the lawful and rational development of the world, whose secrets had step by step been revealed by centuries of scholarship. He would not endure the destruction of the gains made by hard work and genius "in order for a drunken dreamer to take a strange, deep look into the Dionysian abyss."[47]

Nietzsche himself felt that Wilamowitz had understood him "neither in the whole nor in the parts" and attributed his opponent's hostility to his Berlin training. But in the same letter in which he expressed this view, he also recognized the loneliness of his position and the probable fruitlessness of Rohde's defense, and predicted that Wilamowitz would, through his opposition to himself and his friend, win a professorship somewhere (as in fact he did in 1879).[48] Already on 26 June 1872, Nietzsche had told Ritschl that he felt less like an honorary member (*Ehrenmitglied*) of the Leipzig Society (of philologists) than like an "embarrassing member" (*Schandemitglied*), "For I have seen myself in the mirror Herr Wilamowitz has held up for me, and become conscious of the whole hideousness of my physiognomy."[49] Perhaps this was facetious; Nietzsche clearly despised the Berlin philologists who had condemned him, above all "Wilam Ohne Witz," whom he also denounced, in a private letter, as "an insolent-Jewish, sickly boy."[50] If he had been anxious to defend his designation as philologist, or better, to let Rohde do this for him, he recognized that the professionals would never forgive him for having made the lay public his primary audience.[51] He was deeply hurt when no students arrived to study with him in the winter of 1872 and seems also to have regretted the slights directed at the University of Basel on his account; he even briefly considered abandoning academia to become a full-time Wagnerian acolyte.[52] When Wagner encouraged him to stay on at the university, he requested that he be transferred to a chair of philosophy (but was denied); thenceforth, he renounced philology as a scholarly pursuit, though he continued to teach the subject until he left the university in 1879.

The Birth of Tragedy controversy clearly marked a turning point in Nietzsche's self-conception and his relationship to scholarly institutions and ideals. His scattered essays in the years following the debacle consistently attacked the asceticism of "lifeless" positivist science and the mediocrity of

---

[46] Ibid., p. 15.
[47] Ibid., p. 23.
[48] Nietzsche to Rohde, 8 June 1872, in *Nietzsche: Briefwechsel*, 2/3:7–8.
[49] Nietzsche to Ritschl, 26 June 1872, ibid., p. 17.
[50] Nietzsche to Gustav Krug, 24 July 1872, ibid., p. 30.
[51] See Nietzsche to Malwida von Meysenburg, 7 November 1872, ibid., pp. 81–82.
[52] See Nietzsche to Richard Wagner, mid-November 1872, ibid., pp. 89–92.

contemporary institutions of higher learning.[53] In his last works, the analogous "ascetic" types of scholar and priest stand opposed to the "healthier," happier, higher types who cultivate life and art (or life as an art). As the prophet of life, Zarathustra is a kind of antiphilologist.

In attempting to make philology a life-embracing, nation-building, and artistic enterprise, Nietzsche had in fact laid the foundations for the next generation's attacks on his field for precisely these same failings. This critique of positivist historicism would be taken up by reformers outside the philhellenic establishment, who came to similar conclusions by other means, and within the *Bildungsbürgertum*, Nietzsche's attack on the failings of workaday philology would lie at the core of subsequent calls for change. According to the philologist Eduard Fränkel (1888–1970), the encounter with Nietzsche's philosophy was the event most accountable for the intellectual gulf that separated his generation of 1914 from the generation that had gone before.[54] It would not be too much to say that with *The Birth of Tragedy*, antipositivist philhellenism was also born. Its maturation, however, would require several more decades, during which social and political opposition to the pedagogical status quo would also be added to the classicists' woes.

The Historicist Response to School Reform

Nietzsche's volleys aside, the generational revolt given voice in the 1890s did not arrive unheralded. Preceding decades had seen the development of semi- or nonclassical secondary education in response to rising demand for a "real" or "modern" school curriculum. The second half of the nineteenth century witnessed the rise of a confusing array of "modern" schools; year by year, these gained ever more popularity and increasing enrollments, if little recognition from the universities and central bureaucracy. The *Realschulen* catered to the new entrepreneurial and commercial classes, while, as Fritz Ringer has argued, after 1870, *Gymnasium* education became increasingly the preserve of the old *Mittelstand* (such as lower officials, teachers, and shopkeepers), and of course, the *Bildungsbürgertum*.[55] In the 1860s, the *Gymnasien* enrolled 69 percent of secondary students; in 1890, this total had dropped to a still considerable 60 percent, but the *Realschulen* were

---

[53] See, e.g., Nietzsche, "Wir Philologen;" idem, "Über die Zukunft unserer Bildungsanstalten," also in *Nietzsche: Werke*, 3:175–264.

[54] Hugh Lloyd-Jones, "Nietzsche and the Study of the Ancient World," in *Studies in Nietzsche and the Classical Tradition*, ed. James C. O'Flaherty, Timothy F. Sellner, and Robert M. Helm (Chapel Hill, N.C., 1976), p. 1.

[55] Fritz Ringer, *Education and Society in Modern Europe* (Bloomington, Ind., 1979), pp. 74ff.

gaining fast. Between 1890 and 1914, the number of *Oberrealschulen* (nine-year modern schools, in which French and English took the place of classical languages) in Prussia increased from 37 to 111, while *Realschulen* (seven-year schools with no Latin) leapt from 138 to 180. *Realgymnasien* (nine-year modern schools that taught a great deal of Latin) increased from 76 to 187. By contrast, the *Gymnasien* and *Progymnasien* (seven-year, rather than nine-year classical schools) added only 13 to their number in the two decades before the war. Their numbers—367 in 1914—and the privileges of their graduates, however, remained considerable.[56]

The rising number of these modern schools, most of which still administered a healthy dose of the classics, the increasing number and social standing of their present and former students, and especially the rising number of resentful *Realschule* teachers, produced a reaction against the social and cultural *Gymnasium* monopoly. This discontent with the pedagogical status quo was expressed most forcefully by new advocacy groups like the Realschulmännerverein, the Verein für Schulreform, and the Verein für Förderung des lateinlosen höheren Schulwesens (The Association of Modern Schoolmen, the Association for School Reform, and the Association for the Advancement of Secondary Schooling Without Latin). Naturally, these groups appointed their own heroes—like the German philologist cum prophet Paul de Lagarde—and leaders. Lagarde abhorred the very idea of *Bildung* and ridiculed the fascination of the *Gymnasien* with antiquity.[57] Friedrich Lange, president of the *Realschulmänner*, also fulminated over the obsolete, stifling "scholasticism" of the *Gymnasium*-educated bureaucracy and professoriate: humanism, "now stiff and cold," survived only by dint of collusion between the state and an elite clique of obscure men.[58] Though Lagarde and Lange undoubtedly spoke for the radical right wing of the school reform movement, their criticisms of *Gymnasium* neohumanism were reflective of wider, and ever-increasing, social dissatisfaction with Wilhelmine educational institutions.

Like the classicists, many of their more moderate critics invoked the great era of Humboldt and Goethe, glorifying, however, the artistic and patriotic successes of the age rather than its scholarly progressiveness. The ultimate correctness of Humboldt's educational ideal was not in question. Rather, it was claimed that the classicists, especially the philologists, had rendered it sterile. For example, in his memoirs, Count Harry Kessler described how Latin and Greek teaching in the schools had become a means of disciplining, rather than cultivating, individuals. Thus philology "had ac-

---

[56] Albisetti, *Secondary School Reform*, pp. 84, 288.

[57] Fritz Stern, *The Politics of Cultural Despair* (Berkeley, Calif., 1961), p. 74.

[58] Friedrich Lange, "Wiedergeburt: Eine Neujahrsbetrachtung," in *Reines Deutschtum: Grundzüge einer nationalen Weltanschauung* (Berlin, 1893), pp. 57–58.

quired an independent function and usurped, as it were with satanic majesty, the throne of the old ideal of humanism."[59] Friedrich Paulsen stressed the historicity of Humboldt's interest in Greek, certain that the nobleman would not have pressed the subject on modern students for whom the language lacked all utility.[60] Many who favored reform still could not bear to attack the Greeks. One advocate of expanded art history lessons in the schools, for example, defended his position by arguing that an understanding of modern (by which he meant mostly German) art would underscore the eternal value of Greek forms, proving "that the much-maligned dogma of classical antiquity is really something more than a hallucination of the philologists, and that behind this stands the truth."[61]

By the late 1880s, the Prussian Education Ministry, which had studiously ignored the reform movement, could no longer deny the existence of a major current of opposition to its policies. In 1888, the National Liberal education minister, Gustav von Goßler, had received a petition requesting a school conference from the Verein für Schulreform containing more than twenty-two thousand signatures, many of them of notables. Soon thereafter, the ministry of education admitted to the Prussian Landtag that it had received 344 proposals for educational reform between 1882 and 1888, but used the occasion to poke fun at the stranger schemes rather than to take serious note of the widespread discontent indicated by this avalanche of petitions.[62] Meanwhile, another, less negligible, proponent of school reform had begun to agitate for curriculum change: the new Kaiser, Wilhelm II. Wilhelm, who was still relatively close to his restrictive, heavily philological education (he finished *Gymnasium* in 1877), felt that German national consciousness was being smothered under what he called in his memoirs "the fossilized, antiquated philological curriculum" of the secondary schools.[63] He also hoped, as he announced to his principal advisers in April 1889, that the schools could be used to stamp out Social Democracy, instilling instead of classical grammar pious docility and patriotic solidarity.[64] In the face of popular pressure and the railings of the Kaiser, Goßler at last agreed to call the much-demanded school conference, hoping to use it to buttress his own resistance to the aspirations of the reformers.[65]

[59] Quoted in R. H. Samuel and R. Hinton Thomas, *Education and Society in Modern Germany* (London, 1949), p. 18.

[60] Albisetti, *Secondary School Reform*, p. 109.

[61] Hans Dipthmar, *Gymnasialarchäologie oder allgemeine Kunstgeschichte? Ein Beitrag zur Frage der Kunsterziehung am humanistischen Gymnasium* (Zweibrücken, 1907), p. 6.

[62] Friedrich Lange, "Aus der Praxis der Schulreform I," in *Reines Deutschtum*, p. 189.

[63] Wilhelm II, *The Kaiser's Memoirs*, trans. Thomas R. Ybarra (New York, 1922), p. 183.

[64] Christoph Führ, "Die preußischen Schulkonferenzen von 1890 und 1900: Ihre bildungspolitische Rolle und bildungsgeschichtliche Bewertung," in *Bildungspolitik in Preußen zur Zeit des Kaiserreiches*, ed. Peter Baumgart (Stuttgart, 1980), p. 196.

[65] Albisetti, *Secondary School Reform*, p. 193.

By any reckoning, the number of reform-minded participants invited to the 1890 conference was far outstripped by that of their opponents. Goßler and his powerful under secretary Friedrich Althoff seem to have been inclined to allow some reforms to pass, especially the relaxation or abandonment of requirements for Greek study.[66] Wilamowitz, however, would not consent to such a disastrous change in the *Gymnasium* curriculum. He had not opposed the addition of modern subjects, the philologist insisted, recounting the conference's backstage proceedings in his 1928 autobiography: "But without Greek, German *Bildung*—to which all of us [not only philologists] are indebted for the intellectual advances of the nineteenth century—goes to rack and ruin. It was a good thing," he continued, "that [Adolf] Harnack and I saved Greek at that time. Naturally [we did so] before the conference began, through negotiations with the ministry, for the rhetorical battles that occur at such large gatherings have nothing but ornamental value."[67] During the conference itself, however, the Education Ministry's plans to pacify its critics by means of a few Bismarckian-style reforms from above were dashed by the unexpected behavior of the Kaiser, who insisted in his keynote address to the conference that German language, literature, geography, and history become the basis of all secondary school instruction. "We want to educate our pupils into young Germans," he affirmed, "not young Greeks and Romans." Classical education formed physically inferior, decadent thinkers rather than healthy, patriotic doers; the *Gymnasien* menaced the success of the Reich's *Weltpolitik*.[68]

The support of the young Kaiser emboldened the reform movement, and Wilhelm was perfectly content to take credit for the battle he had won "against desperate opposition from the philologists inside and outside the ministry and school circles. Unfortunately," he confessed, "the reform did not take the shape I had hoped, and did not lead to the results I had expected."[69] One reason for the failure of reform efforts was the formation during the 1890 conference itself of a powerful counterreform organization, the Gymnasialverein, boasting a membership of more than two thousand by early 1891.[70] Not numbers, however, but social prestige and bureaucratic connections made the *Gymnasialverein* a formidable opponent to even the Kaiser's plans, for it counted among its backers Mommsen, Wilamowitz, Curtius, Harnack, Schöne, Conze, and Dörpfeld. The 1892 curriculum guidelines for *Gymnasien* reflected some change: Latin was reduced from seventy-seven to sixty-two hours and German increased from twenty-one to

---

[66] Arnold Sachse, *Friedrich Althoff und sein Werk* (Berlin, 1928), p. 318.

[67] Wilamowitz, *Erinnerungen, 1848–1914*, 2d ed. (Leipzig, 1928), p. 252.

[68] See Wolf von Schierbrand, ed. and trans., *The Kaiser's Speeches: Forming a Character Portrait of Emperor William II* (New York, 1903), pp. 212–17 (quotation, p. 214).

[69] *The Kaiser's Memoirs*, pp. 185–86.

[70] Führ, "Die preußischen Schulkonferenzen," p. 205.

twenty-six hours, but a Latin essay was still required on the *Abitur*, and the *Abitur* was still required for university entrance.

In 1900, a somewhat more ideologically balanced school conference at last accorded *Oberrealschule* and *Realgymnasium* graduates the right to attend universities in Prussia; all other states of the Reich had adopted this reform by 1908.[71] The *Gymnasien*, now permitted to return to its classical predilections, raised their Latin hours once more. Still, lingering prejudices and status-group mores kept the *Gymnasien* at the heart of elite education. In 1905, only 4 of 105 members of the Prussian General Staff had had an *Oberrealschule* or *Realgymnasium* education, and in 1914, 59 percent of university entrants still held leaving certificates from *Gymnasien*.[72] In Prussia in 1911, 103,850 of 160,237 total secondary-school students attended a *Gymnasium*.[73] The comments of the patriotic German philologist Gustav Roethe in 1905 may be taken as reflective of the biases of the educated elite as a whole: "Variety in education is in itself a great virtue. That doesn't change the fact that the intellectual leadership [*geistige Generalstab*] will for long, even always . . . have to be educated in the schools of Greece and Rome. Governmental proclamations can certainly put various kinds of cultivation on equal footing, but they can't make them equal in value."[74]

There can be no doubt that many professors and *Gymnasium* teachers believed school reform to herald the onset of a cultural crisis of the first order. To cite just one example, in 1892 Wilamowitz argued that school reform's threat to the normative power of antiquity posed "a grave danger to the intellectual and moral health of our *Volk*, or even more, to all human culture."[75] The great fear, of course, was that the debasement of secondary education would drag down university scholarship as well, and by the 1880s, there were clear signs that rising interest in modern education at the lower levels had seeped into the higher spheres. Between 1860 and 1883, the University of Leipzig reversed its emphasis in language course offerings: in 1860, twenty-five courses were offered in classical and sixteen in nonclassical languages, but in 1883, the balance favored the latter, with twenty-six courses, to classics' total of seventeen.[76] Even within the philosophical faculty, enrollments in classicist-dominated humanities dropped, from 86.4 percent to 62.9 percent between 1841 and 1881, while math and science

[71] Ringer, *Education and Society*, p. 39.

[72] Samuel and Hinton Thomas, *Education and Society*, p. 45; Albisetti, *Secondary School Reform*, p. 288.

[73] Ute Preuß, *Humanismus und Gesellschaft: Zur Geschichte des altsprachlichen Unterrichts in Deutschland von 1890 bis 1933* (Frankfurt, 1988), p. 20.

[74] Gustav Roethe, *Humanistische und nationale Bildung* (2d ed., Berlin, 1913), p. 4.

[75] Wilamowitz, "Philologie und Schulreform," p. 115.

[76] Maurice Jacob, "Etude comparative des systèmes universitaires et place des études classiques au 19ᵉ siècle en Allemagne, en Belgique, et en France," in *Philologie und Hermeneutik im 19. Jahrhundert*, vol. 2, ed. Mayotte Bollack and Heinz Wismann (Göttingen, 1983), p. 121.

enrollments increased from 13.6 percent to 37.1 percent during the same period.[77] In 1890, according to figures provided by Fritz Ringer, the number of regular faculty engaged in teaching modern languages exceeded, for the first time, the number devoted to teaching ancient ones; but the humanities in general, though losing enrollments relative to the natural sciences, long managed to retain low student-faculty ratios by banking on their prestigious record of accomplishments. "Even during the late nineteenth century," Ringer writes, "German humanists apparently succeeded more fully than their colleagues in the natural sciences in making the case for research to the ministries."[78] If they could not prevent the inclusion of new, and especially applied, sciences in the university faculties, or the defection of their students to the pursuit of "utilitarian" careers, the humanists could at least insulate themselves against the consequences of relative social and institutional decline.[79]

The most influential general response to the challenges of the reformers was formulated by Wilamowitz. As we have seen, Wilamowitz played a major role in the 1890 conference, and according to his student Werner Jaeger, was brought by Althoff to the University of Berlin in 1896 "to restore on the university level what had largely been lost on the secondary level of German education: the life-giving contact of young minds with the spirit of antiquity."[80] To this end, Wilamowitz undertook the translation of numerous Greek plays, the delivery of many public lectures, and the composition of a widely used *Gymnasium* Greek primer, in which the philologist laid out many of his responses to the school reformers' attacks. In the introduction to this *Griechisches Lesebuch* (1902), Wilamowitz acknowledged that, given the scholarly findings of recent decades, it had now become impossible to return to Winckelmannian aestheticism; nor did the argument that Greek served best as mental discipline still apply. "Thus we learn Greek," he wrote, "exclusively in order to read Greek books."[81] But this, for the histor-

---

[77] J. Conrad, *Das Universitätsstudium in Deutschland während der letzten 50 Jahre* (Jena, 1884), p. 136. The overall rate of growth in enrollments in the humanities amounted to 275 percent between 1836 and 1882, as compared to 1007 percent for the sciences. Ibid., p. 137.

[78] Fritz Ringer, "A Sociography of German Academics, 1863–1938," *Central European History* 25, no. 3 (1992): 258; figures from table, pp. 254–55.

[79] As Ringer notes, however, this situation changed sometime after the turn of the century, as the natural sciences began to catch up to the humanities in numbers of positions, and the student-faculty ratio in the humanities climbed swiftly. Surely some of this decline began before the outbreak of the Great War, but it is also clear that the war itself and its aftermath provided the setting for the humanities' fall from grace. See ibid., pp. 254–58; see also chapter 8, below.

[80] Jaeger, "Classical Philology in Berlin," in idem, *Five Essays*, trans. Adele M. Fiske (Montreal, 1966), p. 58. Althoff made the appointment conditional upon Wilamowitz's agreement to give inspiring weekly lectures on classical subjects to the general public, a duty Wilamowitz performed willingly and effectively for nearly three decades.

[81] Wilamowitz, "Vorrede," in idem, *Griechisches Lesebuch*, vol. 1 (2nd ed. Berlin, 1902), p. iv.

ically minded philologist, was no small thing, for Greek *Geist* defined the entire period between the sixth century B.C. and the fourth century A.D.; Hellenism's unique status as world-historical culture belonged to the realm of reality, not that of romantic fantasy.[82] In addition, Greek political thought offered helpful lessons for future citizens: by studying Aristotelian political philosophy, Wilamowitz argued, "[the student] can become familiar with the essence of things and the fundamental conditions and final ends of the social order, which are everywhere the same, without the intrusion of the complexities of modern life and the catchwords of modern party opinions."[83] Finally, for Wilamowitz, an archetypical exemplar of secularized Protestantism, the Greeks gave students inspirational access to Christian beliefs: "Epictetus and Marcus [Aurelius] and Posidonius and Aristotle and Plato: they all take different paths, but their goal is the same: they all show the way to God."[84]

Wilamowitz intended to make universal his appreciation of the historical importance of Greek culture, and to separate this from the technical tasks performed by experts. "Philology is for philologists," he insisted; "*Hellenentum*, that which is eternal, is for everyone who wants to come, see, and understand."[85] But the Berlin professor could not sanction the resurrection of classicizing aestheticism, which continued to be popular among *Philologen* and armchair archaeologists.[86] Wilamowitz repeated many times his warnings against attempts to return to the Schillerian worldview, now made impossible by the progress of specialized scholarship.[87] But as an 1897 public lecture—celebrating Wilhelm II's birthday—revealed, Wilamowitz had another reason for rejecting this kind of classicism, namely, fear of its appropriation by social (and cultural) revolutionaries. Wilamowitz opened his speech by denouncing those who believed in the delusion of a Golden Age to come, and especially those who spread this vision amongst the "masses who have no judgment." History taught the foolishness of optimism:

> There is no need for speculation: the world has learned the lesson that things do not always go forward, that breakthroughs made by human endeavor that seem to be permanent and secured can also be lost. Culture can die, for it has died at least once before. The jackals howl in Ephesus, where Heraclitus and Paul preached; in the marble halls of hundreds of cities in Asia Minor, the thorns proliferate and only a handful of stunted barbarians cower. . . . Anyone

[82] Ibid., p. v.

[83] Ibid., p. viii.

[84] Ibid.; on Wilamowitz and the Christian tradition, see Arnaldo Momigliano, "New Paths of Classicism in the Nineteenth Century," *History and Theory*, suppl. vol. 21 (1982): 55–57.

[85] Wilamowitz quoted in Hölscher, *Chance des Unbehagens*, p. 24.

[86] See Preuß, *Humanismus und Gesellschaft*, pp. 54–55; see below.

[87] See, for example, Wilamowitz, "Philologie und Schulreform," in idem, *Reden und Vorträge* (3d ed., Berlin, 1913), pp. 98–119.

who has wandered, contemplatively, through the Roman forum must have felt instinctively that the belief in eternal, continuous progress is a delusion.[88]

Moreover, history taught that the Romans had idolized the Greeks for no better reason than that their own culture had fallen into decline, and that this fantasy had done nothing to revivify Rome. "When antiquity is made an absolute, binding model for art and life, it is dangerous for both, because it is a delusion," Wilamowitz warned.[89] A sort of pessimistic historicism, the philologist felt, provided a strong defense against both materialist optimists (like the school reformers and socialists) and aestheticizing classicizers like his old foe Friedrich Nietzsche.

As we have seen, Wilamowitz, the highest-paid Prussian professor in his day, possessed exceedingly wide influence both in academia and in ministerial circles.[90] His vast erudition and fine writing style have been praised by many, and his historicist defense of the importance of antiquity still seems the most sensible argument for classical education today. But Wilamowitz's strict rejection of "dilettantism"—including comparative work—and all that smacked of Nietzsche's vitalistic *Lebensphilosophie* (life-philosophy) also prevented German academic exploration of the irrational side of Greek thought and the aspects Greek culture shared with other cultures at precisely the moment that others (e.g., Jane Harrison and James Frazer in England, Lewis Henry Morgan in America, and Fustel de Coulanges in France) were just beginning to investigate such topics. The Berlin philologist was instrumental in the sidelining of two significant German scholars who were moving in these "anthropological" directions, Herrman Usener and Erwin Rohde. Wilamowitz criticized Usener and his religious-historical school (including Aby Warburg and Hans Lietzmann) for overemphasizing "superstition"; though he recognized the merits of Rohde's enormous study of Greek religion (*Psyche*, 1894), he could not embrace a former friend of Nietzsche.[91] As Renate Schlesier has recently claimed: "Under the aegis of Wilamowitz's unimpeachable authority, anthropology (and comparative mythology as well) was laden with anathema."[92] If Wilamowitz's historicism did shore up, at least in the eyes of the all-important cultural bureaucracy, the universal importance of Greek culture, this did not occur without significant consequences for German scholarly thought.

Of course, in the sword-rattling years after the ascension of Wilhelm II,

---

[88] Wilamowitz, "Weltperioden," ibid., pp. 122–23.

[89] Ibid., p. 11.

[90] William M. Calder III and Alexander Kosenina, eds., *Berufungspolitik innerhalb der Altertumswissenschaft im wilhelminischen Preußen: Die Briefe Ulrich von Wilamowitz-Moellendorffs an Friedrich Althoff (1883–1908)* (Frankfurt, 1989), p. 120, n. 502; p. 129, n. 540.

[91] See Renate Schlesier, *Kulte, Mythen und Gelehrte: Anthropologie der Antike seit 1800* (Frankfurt, 1994), pp. 195–213, 314–15.

[92] Ibid., p. 315.

even so successful a defense of Greece's universal significance did not suffice; classical *Bildung's* determinedly nonutilitarian (*zwecklos*) orientation became a liability rather than an asset in its struggle to maintain a dominant position in German culture. Even the members of the Gymnasialverein recognized the need to show their Kaiser and countrymen that the study of the Greeks was spiritually, at least, "useful" (*zweckmäßig*) and irreproachably German. For the Greek philologist Friedrich Leo, the question: "What use is [Greek] for life?" was one not of usefulness for *external* life but of vital sustenance for the German soul. The nineteenth-century quest for Greekness (*Drang nach dem Griechischen*,) Leo averred, was bound up with the elemental, essential forces in German culture; "The rise of German national culture was in fact born from the Renaissance of the Greek."[93] Another neohumanist advocate refuted a reformer's contention that the *Gymnasium* "transplanted students from a tender age to the soil of Italy and Greece and by means of continual preoccupation with Greek and Romans distanced them from the history and literature of their own folk and Fatherland." On the contrary, the author argued, the study of the ancients taught the virtues of heroic self-sacrifice for the sake of the nation.[94] No contradiction existed between humanistic and national *Bildung*, for these defenders of the status quo; the classical world held the keys to national self-recognition.

By the later nineteenth century, as Beat Näf has shown, debates about Greek democracy had taken on new importance, partly as a result of George Grote's great twelve-volume *History of Greece* (1846–56). Grote, a banker by trade, a liberal parliamentarian, and a member of the radical philosophical circle around J. S. Mill, exemplified for monarchist Germans the "interested" historian, and his enthusiastic defense of democracy seems to have provoked the expression of much skepticism about Greek exemplariness in the political realm.[95] In general, it seems, conservative German scholars praised Athenian democracy when it strengthened the state, and reviled democratic rule when they perceived it to threaten the state's security; Eduard Meyer, Wilamowitz, Hans Delbrück, and K. J. Beloch, as Näf shows, all shared this conviction to greater or lesser extent.[96] Robert von Pöhlmann—a conservative monarchist of the purest stripe—composed a two-volume *Geschichte des antiken Communismus und Sozialismus* (*History of ancient Communism and Socialism*—1893–1901) to show how the rule of the

---

[93] Friedrich Leo, "Die Bedeutung des Griechischen für die Deutsche Kultur," *Neue Jahrbücher für Pädagogik* 16 (1913): 57–58, 62.

[94] E. Neuburger, "Gymnasium und Vaterlandsliebe," *Süddeutsche Blätter für höhere Unterrichtsanstalten* 2, no. 3 (February 1894): 30.

[95] Beat Näf, *Von Perikles zu Hitler? Die athenische Demokratie und die deutsche Althistorie bis 1945* (Bern, 1986), pp. 36–43.

[96] Ibid., pp. 60–80.

masses had caused the degeneration of Athenian democracy into class warfare, inequality, unfreedom, and military lassitude. Pöhlmann's extensive popular writings attempted to convey the same antidemocratic answer to the "social question," their relevance undergirded by his claim that the history of the ancient city-states provided better, clearer lessons in patriotism than did German history itself.[97] But in the late nineteenth century as in its first half, German scholars were much more likely to praise Athens for its great cultural feats than to denounce it for its political experiments. For the cultural elite, state-sponsored cultivation of the arts and sciences remained Athens's greatest selling point.

On the defensive after decades of institutionalized intellectual hegemony, philologists and historians like Wilamowitz, Leo, and Pöhlmann sought refuge in a kind of aristocratic conservatism and self-serving (though not necessarily insincere) nationalism. Like their colleague Hermann Diels, they did not believe that scholarship alone could save their culture from decadence, but an attempt had to be made to ward off Nietzschean anarchy in thought and social-democratic "chaos" in politics. In a speech before the Prussian Academy of Sciences in 1902, Diels warned against the recurrence of an "Alexandrian" split between art and scholarship, between the antiscientific, purely subjective world of Wagner, Nietzsche, and Schopenhauer, and the objective, anti-individualist world of the pursuit of knowledge. His advice to his fellows, however, entailed no compromises with reformers and prophets, but simply more popularization of scholarly conclusions and accomplishments—without respect to "the opinions of the day."[98] Emphasizing Prussia's long tradition of supporting the pursuit of nonutilitarian knowledge, Diels did not see any reason to take the critics of specialized scholarship seriously. Accustomed to holding the central position in German cultural life, the German philological mandarins were not about to accept criticism from outsiders with Stoic equanimity.

Archaeology and School Reform: The Importance of *Anschauung*

The response of archaeologists to the challenges posed by reformers was somewhat different than the historicist defenses of the philologists, and, importantly, rather more successful in appealing to discontented youths and alienated prophets. In part, this divergence was the product of archaeology's increasing independence from philology, and in part it was the result of archaeology's ability to take advantage of the increasing prominence of

---

[97] Ibid., pp. 101–3; Preuß, *Humanismus und Gesellschaft*, pp. 34–37.

[98] Hermann Diels, "Festrede" (23 January 1902), in *Sitzungsberichte der Königlich Preußischen Akademie der Wissenschaften zu Berlin* (1902): 25–42 (quote, p. 42).

visual culture to reinvigorate philhellenism. Particularly in Berlin, philologists had retreated from the study of *Realien* as the pursuit of "big archaeology" got under way; at the same time, archaeologists, eager to establish formal and chronological sequences, reminded themselves of the primary importance of understanding "the language of art." The onset of the school reform movement, however, gave the two disciplines a common cause, and, coupled with the younger science's recent triumphs in Greece and Asia Minor, helped to persuade philologists to look more benignly on the science of the spade.[99] For, following the much-publicized arrival of the Pergamum altar, many philologists began to recognize the importance of archaeology to the project of revitalizing antiquity, a recognition that, curiously, produced a kind of reaction against historicism and de-aestheticization, playing into the hands of those who did not want to give up on the beauty and normativity of Greek art.

It was not by chance that those who supplied the central ideas and texts for the archaeological defense against reform came from Munich, and were products of south German classicism and the Roman Hyperboreans. The leading figure was certainly Munich professor and Glyptothek director Heinrich Brunn, the same Brunn responsible for perfecting the application of formalist studies to Greek art history. In 1885, Brunn's address as rector of the university, "Archäologie und Anschauung" ("Archaeology and Perceptual Understanding"), articulated a new program for classicist counter-reform, linking progress in the professionalization and social standing of archaeology to the fortunes of humanistic education *tout court*. It was time, Brunn claimed, for archaeology to declare its independence from philology, and for philologists to realize that archaeological expertise consisted in knowledge of a wholly separate, artistic, sphere:

> If we expect from the philologist that he first of all eagerly study his authors as the source material for his scholarship, we should by the same token demand from the archaeologist that he first immerse himself in his sources, that is, in monuments, in the most extensive way. If the philologist explains his authors as much as possible in their own terms, from their individual qualities, so it

---

[99] Predictably, Wilamowitz was one of the first to make this realization, and to see archaeology—when not merely concerned with technical details—as a means to combat the narrow, purely textual interests of many of his fellows. But even this wide-ranging scholar could not relinquish his favoritism for philological methods in the study of art. Recalling a long-past trip to Olympia with Dörpfeld in 1928, Wilamowitz contended that "archaeology, as the study of all monumental remains, including those that have formed the whole character of the region, is at least equal in value to the older philology, based solely on language and literature, but for the purposes of art history or even the history of artists remains less rewarding than the old-fashioned study of grammar." Wilamowitz, *Erinnerungen*, p. 220. For his rejection of stylistic inquiries, see Wilamowitz to Althoff, 4 August 1892, and 12 February 1897, in Calder and Kosenina, eds., *Berufungspolitik*, pp. 94, 131.

appears obvious that the archaeologist also proceeds in his explanations from the monument itself.[100]

Brunn did not exclude the use of literary sources in interpreting ancient artwork, but aimed at a strict science of forms "that cannot be allowed to be inferior to the systematically-based knowledge of language in the field of philology."[101]

The barriers to the evolution of such a science, Brunn continued, lay in the one-sidedness of *Gymnasium* preparation, which trained only the ear (the organ philologists depend on), neglecting the eye (needed for archaeological, as well as mathematical understanding). Not archaeology as a discipline but *Anschauung* as a mode of understanding, he insisted, deserved a place in the curriculum. It was important for students to acquire feeling for forms and spaces by learning to draw, and photographs and models of artwork should be introduced alongside poetry and prose to give students a sense of the communicative possibilities of various types of human expression. Brunn concluded his argument for proper schooling of the eye with a telling condemnation of the withering away of *Altertumswissenschaft* under the domination of philological specialization, adding a corresponding recommendation that archaeology, the younger and long-subordinated sister discipline, step in to revive and rescue humanistic education:

> It is not to be denied that philology now is pursued not enough as a science of antiquity as a whole [*Altertumswissenschaft*], but rather, one-sidedly, as a science of language [*Sprachwissenschaft*], and that thereby it has suffered great losses to its influence as a method of humanistic *Bildung*. Leading representatives of the field have faced up to this admission, in order to link it to the suggestion that it is now the task of archaeology to intervene for the sake of [*Altertumswissenschaft*'s] advancement and expansion and to fill the gaps that regrettably still exist.

Brunn ended this section by reasserting the rights of archaeologists for independence, social status, and governmental recognition: "For what archaeology now claims for itself," he wrote, "it no longer demands only for itself, but in the general interest of the expansion of humanistic *Bildung*."[102]

Brunn's student and successor Adolf Furtwängler also contributed heavily to the development of *Anschauungsunterricht* and its application to the defense of the beleaguered Greek ideal. Furtwängler's 1893 classic, *Meisterwerke der griechischen Plastik* (*Masterpieces of Greek Sculpture*), provided a style-historical undergirding for Winckelmannian aesthetic intuitions and prejudices. Rather than chastising Winckelmann for his mistakes

---

[100] Heinrich Brunn, (rectoral address, 21 November 1885) (Munich, 1885), p. 9.
[101] Ibid., p. 10.
[102] Ibid., pp. 19–20.

or condemning Roman copies for their "corrupt" borrowings from Greek forms, in this very popular volume, Furtwängler returned "masterpieces" like the Apollo Belvedere and the Rondini Medusa to center stage by underlining their status as records of Western art-historical development. Furtwängler, who had spent the first years of his career making inventories of vast numbers of prehistorical bronzes, Mycenaean pots, and Greek gemstones, exhibited relative disdain for written sources and depended instead upon his extremely keen eye. If this approach (in addition to his Catholicism and his caustic personality) precluded a warm welcome for his book in the academic community, it made the Bavarian art historian's work appealing to a larger audience.[103] As Adolf Michaelis commented in 1908, Furtwänglerian style criticism in combination with archaeological explorations gave substance to the names recorded by Pausanias and Pliny: "From the pits of the ever-inquisitive, spade-wielding archaeologists, blood has flowed into the veins of the artists, who had previously roamed about as pale shades in the Hades of the written tradition. . . ."[104]

Appearing in the middle of the school reform furor, Furtwängler's *Meisterwerke*, depending upon skilled *Anschauung*, symbolized the emancipation, in Brunn's terms, of the eye from the ear, of the "living" image from the dying word, and of archaeology from the toils of philological dependence. Adolf Trendelenburg, reviewing the work for the *Kölnische Zeitung*, correctly anticipated that Furtwängler's high-handed treatment of literary sources would preclude a warm welcome for his book in academic circles. But the philosopher also praised Furtwängler's contributions to the appreciation of ancient art, which, thanks to the growing art education movement and the publicity accorded to recent excavations, was gaining popularity:

> Interest [in the classics] is growing not only in the schools, which more and more strive to enliven classwork by drawing on works of art, but also among those whose educational experience and position in life have until now given them no contact with antiquity. Thus archaeological discoveries may count on interest outside the circle of professionals and strictly scientific work may also appeal to a wider public.[105]

Like Brunn, Furtwängler also coauthored a heavily illustrated school textbook on Greek and Roman sculpture (*Denkmäler griechischer und römischer*

103 [A. Trendelenburg], "Meisterwerke der griechischen Plastik," in *Kölnische Zeitung*, 24 December 1893), in DAI Nachlaß Furtwängler, Kasten 11.

104 Adolf Michaelis, *Ein Jahrhundert kunstarchäologischer Entdeckungen*, 2d ed. (Leipzig, 1908) p. 301.

105 [Trendelenburg], "Meisterwerke." Both the *Vossische Zeitung* and the *Leipziger Zeitung* similarly noted the popular appeal of Furtwängler's subject. Richard Engelmann, "Die neuesten Untersuchungen ueber antike Kunstgeschichte," in *Sonntagsbeilage zur Vossische Zeitung* no. 5, 1894 and *Leipziger Zeitung* 1893, both in DAI, Nachlaß Furtwängler, Kasten 11.

Skulptur [1898]), which strove to assuage complaints about "dry-as-dust" approaches to antiquity by substituting images for words.[106] Furtwängler's was not the only educational effort of this kind. "What inspires our youth is not increased knowledge, but heightened *Anschauung*," an advertisement for *Seemans Wandbilder*, a poster series of classical artworks, asserted. "The teacher will accomplish much more if he knows how to work not only on the intellect, but also on the powers of perception. What can be won through *Anschauung* should not be conveyed through words."[107] The aim of these posters, as one advocate noted, was not to "burden" students with memorizing archaeological minutiae, but to bring before their eyes master-pieces, and especially the exemplary forms created by "those who thirsted for beauty, the Greeks."[108]

If the appreciation of *Anschauung* began among the Bavarian art histo-rians, the Berliners were not slow to recognize the idea's attractions. As Gerhart Rodenwaldt later attested, DAI director Alexander Conze also cher-ished the hope that his organization's excavations could play a significant role in resuscitating *Gymnasium* education.[109] In 1889, the DAI chief re-reported to Bismarck that in addition to his overseas exploits, he was renew-ing his efforts to secure good relations between the institute and the home-land, "with the consciousness that the institute was founded and now exists for the pursuit of professional study but also aims at making [its pursuits] useful for the whole of German *Kultur*. . . . A practical conclusion drawn from this must be that, beyond the professional scholarly character of work and publications, we must seek various ways to strengthen vital links to those circles in Germany that are in the best position to carry the results of our work into German cultural life as a whole. These are, without doubt, the *Gymnasium* circles."[110] True to his word, Conze promptly initiated a campaign to reach out to the beleaguered *Gymnasium* supporters. In 1890, he introduced a column in the institute's *Archäologischer Anzeiger* (*Archae-ological Gazette*) entitled "Gymnasialunterricht und Archäologie" ("Gym-nasium Instruction and Archaeology") to report on methods and materials available for classroom instruction; the DAI itself was quickly drawn into the process of developing visual materials—maps, posters, and slides, often

---

[106] Teachers gathered at the Weimar Art Education Day of 1903 declared Furtwängler's textbook ideal for use in *German* lessons, in which Greek art would only be taught "insofar as it has become an essential and indispensable element of our national culture." Julius Sahr, review of *Denkmäler griechischer und römischer Skulptur* in *Zeitschrift für den deutschen Unter-richt* 19 (1905): 468–69.

[107] Announcement of *Seemans Wandbilder* (1895) in BHStA, MK 14846.

[108] Karl Tittel, "Künstlerischer Wandschmuck in der Schule," in *Neue Jahrbücher für Pädagogik* 8 (1905): 514, 510.

[109] Gerhart Rodenwaldt, *Archäologisches Institut des Deutschen Reiches, 1827–1929* (Berlin, 1929) p. 45.

[110] Conze to Bismarck (DAI yearly report), 29 June 1889, PZStA AA/R 37799, pp. 81–87.

described as *Anschauungsmittel* (visual aids)—and distributing them to needy *Gymnasien*.[111]

Anschauungsunterricht provided a vital link between the interests of professional archaeologists and an aggressive revitalization program designed to deflect changes advocated by proponents of school reform. In 1897, the DAI contined this campaign, inviting representatives to the Dresden Philologists' Convention to gather for two meetings on archaeological instruction in the schools. The account of the event in one of Munich's leading newspapers suggests that the wider public, too, understood archaeological *Anschauungsunterricht* as a contribution to the regeneration of the arts and humanities. Many had a role to play in artistic education, the article proclaimed—artists, publishers, museum keepers, and the like; but all these efforts would be in vain were the younger generation not taught to see, to understand "the language of forms." The simplicity and rigor of Greek art suited it especially to this pedagogical task, so vital to the resuscitation of the humanities. "In our opinion," the article concluded, "the representatives of humanistic *Bildung* are losing a valuable weapon in the battle against the attacks of the fanatical proponents of usefulness [*Nützlichkeitsfanatiker*] if they do not accept the help offered by archaeology in the most comprehensive way possible."[112] To this writer, at least, the links that Brunn, Furtwängler, and Conze had sought to forge between archaeology, the art education movement, and humanistic revitalization were obvious as well as urgently desired.

But archaeologists did not mean to limit their popularizing efforts to the younger generation. Beginning in the late 1880s, the DAI, backed by the Ministry of Education and the museum administration, instituted a program of short courses in archaeology for *Gymnasium* teachers, offered in Berlin and Bonn. In 1888, Baden also began to offer such courses, and the idea soon spread to Saxony, Bavaria, and Austria. In 1891, trips to Italy, Greece, and later Asia Minor for *Gymnasium* instructors commenced; in 1893, grants for this purpose were available through the DAI.[113] By 1908, the institute had apparently negotiated a deal with Germany's biggest steamship company to offer half-price tickets to *Gymnasium* instructors who organized their Mediterranean trips through the DAI.[114] As one enthusiastic advocate argued, by proffering personal, immediate experience of the

---

[111] Rodenwaldt, *Archäologisches Institut*, p. 45; see also the discussion of the Institute's role in "Philologenversammlung," *AA* in *JbdesDAI* 8 (1893): 57–63.

[112] "Archäologie und Gymnasium," in *Beilage zur Allgemeinen Zeitung*, 16 October 1897, in BHStA, MK 14846, Mappe 15433.

[113] Eugen Mercklin, "Archäologische Institute," in *Forschungsinstitute: Ihre Geschichte, Organisation und Ziele*, ed. Ludolph Brauer et al. (Hamburg, 1930), 1:289.

[114] Bavarian Cultural Minister to rectors of humanistic *Gymnasien*, 14 October 1908 (secret!), in BHStA, MK 11007.

classical world, these trips were an optimal means of reviving interest in the classics. "Lucky he," wrote this contributor to the Gymnasialverein's journal, *Neue Jahrbücher für Pädagogik*, "who imprints on his heart the unobscured sight of beauty and energy, those eternal guardians of the tomb of classical antiquity, so deeply that he brings it back unextinguished to his prosaic hometown and into the stuffy atmosphere of the classroom. For his enthusiasm will enliven the ancient prose writers as fresh water [revives] the dry Jericho rose."[115] In addition, claimed the writer, heading off reform-minded critics, such trips built ethical character and allowed sites of major events in German history to be viewed; travel to the South was a good way to awaken new appreciation for the Fatherland.[116] The archaeologists—and their patrons in the Reich bureaucracy—must have been pleased that their investments in *Anschauung* had reaped such eloquent rhetorical rewards.

This new emphasis on visual experience permitted Greek achievements to be more widely and swiftly conveyed, and also allowed the circle of those fit to defend the classics against criticism to be broadened. In 1889, Straßburg professor and DAI member Adolf Michaelis contrasted the narrow, declining appeal of Greek grammar to the vitality of art, which could be appreciated by all who earned their expertise by frequenting museums or rambling amongst the ancient ruins:

> From various camps a powerful attack against classical studies as the foundation and heart of German *Bildung* is being organized, which has as its most obvious cause the frequently dry-as-dust, purely grammatical, purely formal treatment of classical authors in our *Gymnasien*. But the study of ancient art offers material of unsurpassable educative power for all and can also serve as leaven for outmoded kinds of philology. Even Wilhelm Scherer [see chapter 5] once said that classical Greek *Bildung*, that is, the sense for the beauty of Hellenic poetry and art, has its best home in archaeology's lecture halls. But far beyond the lecture halls stand the museums, the temples, the ruins of the great cities of the classical lands. Whoever is at home in them will be especially able to preach the gospel of beauty at home.[117]

No longer, it seems, could the distribution of *Bildung* be left to the lecture halls; those who had immersed themselves in Greek art could spread the neohumanist "gospel" as well.

Perhaps this attempt to widen archaeology's circle of proselytes and neophytes also explains its adoption of a new saint: Heinrich Schliemann. It may not be possible to decide whether the German academy's embrace of

---

[115] Johannes Teufer, "Über klassische Studienreisen," *Neue Jahrbücher für Pädagogik* 2 (1899): 419–20.

[116] Ibid., pp. 421–23.

[117] Adolf Michaelis, "Die Aufgaben und Ziele des Kaiserlichen Deutschen Archäologischen Instituts," *Preußische Jahrbücher* 63 (1889): 49.

17. Unable to afford original sculptures, the Royal Museums devoted considerable space to the display of plaster casts. Here, the Niobe Room of the Neues Museum as it appeared in 1906. © Bildarchiv, Preußischer Kulturbesitz, 1996.

Schliemann after about 1885 owed more to the vexatious amateur's increasing solicitude for specialists, to archaeology's greater appreciation for nontextual evidence, or to Schliemann's unquestionable public appeal in an era of populist challenges to classicist hegemony. Certainly, Schliemann, whose "discovery" of Troy had been based on well-known, if little-trusted, texts (Pausanias, Strabo, Homer), had made laudable advances in the development of nonliterary forms of proof. The majority of classicists eventually recognized the virtues of Virchow's anthropological studies of ritual burials and Dörpfeld's architectural insights (though many quarreled with their results). To these gains, Schliemann had added careful typological studies of Mycenaean pottery types, weapons, and tools. It was thanks to Schliemann, as well as to Conze, that the pursuit of the greatness of the Greeks shed its ascetic aestheticism for a positivistic historicism better suited to the specialist dictates and diplomatic requirements of "big archaeology."

But it was not his services to digging technique or prehistorical dating that earned the Mecklenburger new respect. Schliemann offered the besieged classicist establishment three important, nonintellectual assets. The first was the Trojan treasures, which he at last presented to the Reich in 1881, apparently in exchange for becoming the third honorary citizen of

Berlin, after Bismarck and Moltke.[118] Secondly, he offered classicists his philhellenic, fairy-tale life story, which was particularly appealing after his death in late 1890. In that year, Carl Schuchhardt's enthusiastic but intellectually respectable biography appeared; Schuchhardt's *Schliemann* proved very popular until replaced by Emil Ludwig's Weimar-era biography, which reveled in Schliemann's triumphs over the university professors. Finally, Schliemann was perhaps the best-known and most admired classicist of his day: archaeologists who came to respect his scholarly work also hoped his popularity would help to bridge the widening gap between the philhellenist ideal and the German general public.

Proofs of the classicists' change of heart are not difficult to find. In 1891 Ernst Curtius, who had once called Schliemann a confidence trickster, prepared a eulogy for the excavator in which he added the excavator to an exclusive list of great German Graecophiles: "How often are we told today that the lively interest in classical antiquity, which inspired the age of Lessing, Winckelmann, Herder, and Goethe, has died out. Yet with what excitement did educated people on both sides of the Atlantic follow every step of Schliemann?"[119] In a private letter, archaeologist Georg Hirschfeld thanked Schliemann for allowing scholars to peer into the distant Greek past. "But I do not esteem any less," Hirschfeld continued, "the finds that through your exertions have given new life to or even awakened the interest of thousands in Greek antiquity."[120] Schliemann's digs always figured prominently on the agenda for summer and vacation *Gymnasium* courses, and whenever German archaeological triumphs were boasted of, Schliemann's work was included alongside that of Curtius, Humann, and Conze.[121] As a final tribute to the amateur excavator's adoption by the establishment, in 1893, Kaiser Wilhelm II announced that the Prussian state would now finance a DAI dig at Hissarlik.[122]

The classicist establishment would never consent to the cooption of Nietzsche as they did Schliemann: the former, after all, was an academic apostate, the latter, something of a convert. But in invoking *Anschauung*, archaeologists came closer than their historicist colleagues in making their peace with a new generation of poets and thinkers whose aspirations led far behind the regeneration of neohumanism the classicists desired. Perhaps most ominous was the vitalistic aestheticism of Brunn's student and erst-

---

[118] Ludwig, *Schliemann*, pp. 242–44.

[119] Quoted in Deuel, *Memories*, pp. 352–53.

[120] Hirschfeld to Schliemann, 24 January 1886, in *Schliemann: Briefwechsel*, 2:232.

[121] See the column titled "Gymnasiumunterricht und Archäologie," in the *Archäologischer Anzeiger* section of the *JbdesDAI* during the 1890s.

[122] Dörpfeld gives Schöne and Virchow most credit for the Reich's intervention, and notes that the first increment amounted to thirty thousand marks. See Dörpfeld, *Troja und Ilion*, pp. 17, 21.

while friend, Julius Langbehn. Langbehn, who had studied archaeology and prepared a doctoral thesis under Brunn at the University of Munich, had been initially refused a DAI stipend, in part because of his deficient philological skills.[123] Despite the attempts of Brunn and even Mommsen to further Langbehn's classicist career, the arrogant young man turned to self-cultivation and prophecy, publishing in 1890 the exceptionally successful *Rembrandt als Erzieher* (*Rembrandt as Educator*). Here Langbehn elevated Brunn's complaints about the one-sidedness of humanistic education to an overall condemnation of German academia and bookish intellectualism. "The letter kills," he declared, "the picture is alive."[124] For Langbehn, deeply influenced by Nietzsche, no mere reform in *Gymnasium* pedagogy would suffice. His call was not to revivify neohumanist *Bildung* but in some sense to overcome it: to reinvent German culture from the ground up. If archaeology, at least to some extent, could revitalize the classics by means of grand-scale excavation and a new pedagogical program, the ascetic, aristocratic, and philological philhellenism that spawned the "science of the spade" could not respond to this final, ever more loudly voiced, demand.

[123] Stern, *Politics of Cultural Despair*, p. 101.
[124] Quoted ibid., p. 127.

EXCAVATING THE BARBARIAN

Here we will always be barbarians!
(*A wise Goth in Italy, in Felix Dahn*, Ein Kampf um Rom
[1876])

IN HIS LOVELY ESSAY, "Eighteenth-Century Prelude to Mr. Gibbon," Arnaldo Momigliano describes the increasing desire of enlightened antiquarians and scholars "to penetrate below the Roman surface of Western Europe," to discover particularized, nonuniversal ancestors.[1] This new impulse, as Momigliano recognized, was spurred both by discontent with conventional narratives and by anti-Roman sentiment, which sprang from a multitude of locally variable sources. In the Protestant German states, of course, "Rome" had long represented clerical corruption and ultramontane conspiracy; once Prussia began its battles against the hegemony of the Habsburg Empire, and the educated elite its campaigns against aristocratic court culture, "Rome" took on additional unpleasant connotations. But if some Germans, like Herder, did put considerable effort into uncovering early Germanic culture, most late eighteenth- and early nineteenth-century intellectuals looked to Greece to provide an alternative to Rome-centered cultural history, or to the Orient to create a new "spiritual" trajectory. By 1810, Rome, Germandom, Greece, and the Orient had all become ideological markers as well as historical entities, available for politico-philosophical appropriation as well as for new applications of specialized expertise.

As the Prussian reaction set in after 1820, the study of Germandom undoubtedly suffered most from political restraints on academic freedom and from economic privation; its general paucity of texts and lack of aesthetic appeal also disadvantaged the field in the competition for state patronage and academic status. Yet, in an era of slowly expanding state resources, liberal nationalism, and undisputed classicist hegemony, clashes between students of Graeco-Roman, Germanic, and oriental antiquity were rare. In part, as we shall see, this was because the nonclassical fields depended upon systems of patronage and professional training beyond the neohumanist strongholds of the philosophical faculty and the *Gymnasium*. In part, too,

---

[1] Arnaldo Momigliano, "Eighteenth-Century Prelude to Mr. Gibbon," (1976) in idem, *Sesto Contributo alla storia degli studi classici e del mondo antico*, vol. 1 (Rome, 1980), p. 257.

mid-century scholars generally still shared the eclectic tastes of the Golden Age, even if specialization made it increasingly difficult to contribute to more than one field. Until the unification of Germany made institutional centralization, "cultural and spiritual unification," and the democratization of higher education national imperatives, the three fields enjoyed relatively pacific, if inequitable, coexistence.

By the century's close, however, unification had made the study of early Germandom safe for state-employed scholars, and the nation's new "friendship" with the Ottoman Empire offered new opportunities for scholarly work on biblical—and especially classical—sites in Asia Minor. Of course, classical archaeologists were some of the first to wish to extend their activities into these areas beyond the philologists' pale; hopes ran high that connections between the Orient, Central Europe, and the Mediterranean world, previously only suggested by comparative linguistics, could be established archaeologically, and a new, perhaps prehistorical, basis for the history of the ancient world discovered. What these scholars had not anticipated, however, was resistance to attempts to impose their professional control on the study of the Fatherland and the exploitation of the Orient. Paradoxically, in order to prevail in these domestic and foreign struggles, these "disinterested" scholars would need to become increasingly dependent on the central state; and this would create new resentment against neohumanist classicism, rather than grant it new purchase.

In this chapter and the next, then, we will investigate the consequences of rising interest in the preclassical world for neohumanist cultural institutions. Although we will not be dealing directly with philhellenism, we will be able to observe the cultural position held by the Greeks with respect to other, much-discussed ancient "nations," namely, the Romans and early Germanic peoples in this chapter, and the Egyptians, Assyrians, and Hebrews in the next. Once again, we will be concerned not with the general European fascination with the "primitive" and the "oriental," born of Enlightenment universalism, Romantic nostalgia, and imperialist racism, but rather with the specific conditions under which Germans came to interest themselves in these aspects of the ancient past. Only by observing at close range the institutional and intellectual processes that shaped Germans' perception of their own early history and of oriental antiquity will we appreciate the deeper ironies of Germanophilia and the peculiarities of German orientalism, and thereby gain further insight into the changing cultural status of German philhellenism.

Strangely, these two stories seem to point in opposite directions; the uniqueness of Germanic prehistory, many have argued, lies in its politicization and its adoption of racist conceptions, while German orientalists, according to Edward Said, stand apart from French, English, and American colleagues because of their peculiarly nonpolitical, almost exclusively "classical" interests.[2] We will leave discussion of this latter point for the next chapter, but let me here anticipate the single answer to this double puzzle. At the heart of both the politicization of prehistory, and the "disinterestedness" of German orientalism stands the sometimes complementary, more often confrontational, relationship of each field to the institutionalized admiration of classical antiquity. Although, as these chapters will underline, German cultural institutions—secondary schools, university philosophical faculties, museums—long ignored oriental philology and especially Germanic prehistory, this does not mean that either the Goths or the Orient lost their appeal to the wider population; on the contrary, theological faculties pursued orientalist studies with relish, and extra-academic associations devoted enormous efforts to the collection and preservation of German historical materials.[3] But institutional segregation shaped these fields, both intellectually and socially, and when, after about 1885, the upsurge of radical nationalism, the progress of imperial conquest, and the challenges of the school reform movement inclined bureaucrats and classical scholars to attempt to include these areas in their purview, a maze of parallel institutions and antiestablishment hostilities was already in place to make centralization impossible and conflict inevitable.

This is particularly true of prehistory. From the outset, *Vorgeschichte* was a field replete with antinomies, many of them the result of its subordinate relationship to *Altertumswissenschaft*. First, *Vorgeschichte* aspired to be both a scientific and a patriotic pursuit: even those who sought to professionalize the discipline retained this double identity. Second, prehistory combined natural-scientific and historical-philological modes of inquiry; though its first patrons and much of its theoretical basis came to it from the natural sciences, *Vorgeschichte* aspired to categorization with the *Geisteswissenschaften*. Third, a large majority of nineteenth- and early twentieth-century prehistorians held degrees in Germanic or classical philology, though the field defined itself as treating only preliterate cultures. Finally, the study of prehistory in Germany was split along geocultural lines, dividing *Germania romana* (the area of Germany once occupied by the Romans) from *Germania libera* (the remaining, never-conquered area). Thus the central prehistorical bodies grew up with the collective adjective "Roman-German" in their titles, an adjective that papered over the ideological differences between those who studied the remains of a "foreign" power on German soil, and those who dedicated themselves to indigenous artifacts—but also staked their scholarly careers on the study of "barbarians."

The importance of this final ideological antinomy will require us to open

[2] Edward W. Said, *Orientalism* (New York, 1978), p. 19.

[3] The great popularity of two historical novels, both written by scholarly experts—Georg Ebers's *Eine ägyptische Königstochter* (Berlin, 1864) and Felix Dahn's Gothicizing *Ein Kampf um Rom* (Leipzig, 1876)—clearly illustrates the public's fascination for these nonclassical epochs.

this chapter by briefly investigating the important topic of Germany's volatile relationship to Rome. The contrasting pair Rome–Germany was not invented by proto-Nazi racists, but has its roots in Renaissance humanism, and its full, cultural elaboration in the second half of the nineteenth century. Although I cannot hope to do justice, here, to all aspects of this story, it is critical that we acquire some understanding of the centrality of interpretations of Rome's decline and Germandom's role therein, for these issues played a central role in the evolution of prehistorical archaeology in Germany, and indirectly, in the history of German philhellenism. Without comprehending Rome as the antithesis to Germany—representing civilization but also the corruptions of Christianity that provoked Luther's revolt, the continuity of the classical tradition but also the superficial dilettantism of the aristocratic grand tour—it is difficult to understand the assortment of resentments, longings, and self-conceptions that prehistorians invested in early Germandom. At the risk of pushing the point too far, one might say that the contradictory relationship between Rome and Germandom, not the adoption of racial biology, is the key to German prehistory's *Sonderweg* ("separate path").

By emphasizing the prehistorians' institutional and sociological disadvantages, as I do in this chapter, I do not mean to excuse them from charges of dilettantism or, later, racial prejudice. But it does seem to me that studies of the anthropological sciences in Germany have largely failed to appreciate the ways in which the subordinate status of prehistory, as the exemplary form of "interested" and "amateur" inquiry, shaped the discipline's history and practice. In part, this failure stems from our long-lasting presumption that the nation must be the only relevant unit of analysis; German intellectual historians, in particular often overlook the redundancies and rivalries of parallel local, provincial, and national cultural institutions, which did not, by any means, disappear with the founding of the Second Reich in 1871.[4] But we have also largely bought into a post–World War II Manichean dichotomy between "politicized" pseudoscholarship and "disinterested" pure scholarship that has obstructed our understanding of their dialectical interdependency. Rather than simplifying the historian's tasks, these misconceptions have made it more difficult to understand prehistory's simultaneous liability to political appropriation and its entrenched positivistic orientation on the one hand, and on the other its internal fragmentation and ambivalent relationship to neighboring disciplines, most notably classical *Altertumswissenschaft* and physical anthropology.

Later in this chapter, then, I would like to sketch the institutional devel-

---

[4] James Sheehan made this point some time ago in his important essay, "What Is German History? Reflections on the Role of the Nation in German History and Historiography," *Journal of Modern History* 53 (1981): 1–23.

opment of German prehistory as a means to redress some of these imbalances. I hope that by underlining its internal rifts, contested ends, and pariah status with respect to nineteenth-century humanist academe I will illuminate the conditions that made it so attractive for Nazi exploitation and yet so impossible to bring under the control of one national agency.

Romandom and Germandom

In an 1860 speech entitled "Rom und die Deutschen" ("Rome and the Germans"), Ernst Curtius argued that the Germans hated Rome more and were more hated by Rome than any other people, "and thus [the two peoples] could never simply go their separate ways, thus the idea that Rome was the world's metropole struck deeper roots in Germany than elsewhere."[5] The prominent Greek historian emphasized the essential differences that made Roman culture difficult for Germans to assimilate, but assured his audience that they had now done so to such an extent that Rome was no longer "the oracle in matters of finer cultivation."[6] Coming from one of Prussia's foremost classicists and champions of the IfAK/DAI, such a virulent attempt to distance Germandom from the great center of humanist learning might seem surprising; but Curtius was in fact drawing on a long tradition of anti-Roman remarks. Emboldened by German scholarship's recent triumphs, Curtius revived, in terms befitting a midcentury, Protestant, cultural nationalist, the memory of Roman conquest and Germanic resistance, of the threat to German culture and liberties presented by Rome's universal "civilizing" mission. Like most other Romantic philhellenes, Curtius could not maintain the aura of disinterested grandeur when discussing Rome. While the examination of Greek civilization remained a relatively uncontroversial realm in which for classicists to display their professional credentials and aesthetic predilections, the history of the Roman Empire was fraught with fundamental questions about Germany's autonomy, identity, and world-historical role.

As several commentators have noted, the ideologically loaded opposition of Rome and Germandom has its beginnings in Aenaes Silvius Piccolomini's unsavory depiction of the early Germans, *De situ, ritu, moribus et conditionibus Teutoniae descriptio* (1458).[7] Piccolomini (later Pope Pius II) drew on Tacitus's *Germania*, a Roman text little known before 1458; but if Tacitus

---

[5] Curtius, "Rom und die Deutschen," (1860) in idem, *Altherthum und Gegenwart* (Berlin, 1877), p. 42.

[6] Ibid., p. 50.

[7] Volker Losemann, "Aspekte der nationalsozialistischen Germanenideologie," in *Alte Geschichte und Wissenschaftsgeschichte: Festschrift für Karl Christ*, ed. Volker Losemann and Peter Kneissl (Darmstadt, 1988), pp. 257–58.

had intended to paint a flattering picture of the uncorrupted Germans, Piccolomini used the text to set up a contrast between Renaissance civility and German barbarity. His treatise both infuriated German humanists and introduced them to a text they could mine for their own purposes. Conrad Celtis began lecturing on the *Germania* at the University of Vienna in 1497. Then, in the wake of the publication of the *Annals* in 1515, fellow German patriots like Ulrich von Hutten gave new attention to Germanic antiquity, and especially its newly minted *Ur*-hero, Arminius (Hermann the Cheruscan), the victor over the Roman Varus in the battle of the Teutoburg Forest in A.D. 9.[8] This humanist literature dwelt on themes that were to prove remarkably durable: the Germanic love of liberty, so passionate as to outweigh material or personal concerns, and so fatal to the creation of a united anti-Roman front, was set against Roman tyranny, greed, love of luxury, and calculating pragmatism, all flaws that both explained that nation's success in conquest and prepared it for its falls from grace. In the next four centuries, Tacitus's texts would continue to play the central role in arguments over German customs, morals, cultural achievements, and property rights—yet another proof, if one were still necessary, of the enduring cultural power of humanistic thought and scholarship in the modern age.

After the Thirty Years' War, the question of the nature of the early Germans, and their relationship to the Romans, lay largely dormant; Arminius was not the proper hero for a particularist age. In the second half of the eighteenth century, however, the debate was reopened by Protestant intellectuals eager to oppose the Francophile neoclassicism of the poet J. C. Gottsched and his influential circle and inspired, no doubt, by Friedrich II's recent victory over Austria. The Pietist poet F. G. Klopstock intertwined patriotic mythology and prayers for poetic revival in his Pindaric odes; Klopstock and the pastor and philosopher J. G. Herder greeted the forged bardic poetry of "Ossian" and the first edition of the *Nibelungenlied* (1782) most enthusiastically, finding in this simple folk poetry the essence of autonomous Germanic culture. As usual, Herder ran ahead of his time in denouncing the enervating effect of Roman conquest on Germanic culture.[9] But as we have seen, contemporaries, like Lessing, who ridiculed the "witty courtier" Virgil for his inferior imitations of Homer,[10] were pleased to de-

---

[8] R. Kuehnemund, *Arminius, or the Rise of a National Symbol in Literature* (Chapel Hill, N.C., 1953), pp. 11–19.

[9] K. Düwel and H. Zimmermann, "Germanenbild und Patriotismus in der deutschen Literatur des 18. Jahrhunderts," in *Germanenprobleme in heutiger Sicht*, ed. Heinrich Beck (Berlin, 1986), pp. 375–95; Ekkehard Hieronimus, "Von der Germanen-Forschung zum Germanen-Glauben: Zur Religionsgeschichte des Präfaschismus," in *Die Restauration der Götter: Antike Religion und Neo-Paganismus*, ed. Richard Faber and Renate Schlesier (Würzburg, 1986), p. 246.

[10] Theodore Ziolkowski, *Virgil and the Moderns* (Princeton, N.J., 1993), pp. 76–79.

nounce the Romans in the course of paying homage to the more glorious Greeks. If German patriotism meant quite different things to Pietist visionary Klopstock and the cosmopolitan Graecophile Lessing, they could at least agree that Rome represented the antithesis of "truly German" values and ends.

During the Napoleonic Wars, the seal was set on this revivified German–Roman dichotomy. Though confiscated by the Austrians in 1809, Heinrich von Kleist's newly written play (*The Battle of Arminius*) offers striking confirmation of the new emotional purchase of this incident. Intended to serve as anti-French propaganda,[11] the play emphasizes the moral depravity of the Romans, as against the selfless, unflinching virtue of the big, blond barbarians, and contains language that seems more appropriate to the period after 1871—when the play was added to the repertoire of major theaters—than to the "enlightened" age in which it was written.[12] Mme de Staël's extremely influential *De l'Allemagne* (1813) opened with her renowned division of Europe into three great races: the Latins, the Germans, and the Slavs. The Latins were defined by having "received their civilization and language from the Romans"; the German nations, on the other hand (including the Germans, Swiss, English, Swedes, Danes, and Dutch) "had almost always resisted the yoke of the Romans; they were civilized later, and exclusively by Christianity; they passed directly from a kind of barbarism into Christian society. Their most vivid memories are those of chivalric times, of the spirit of the Middle Ages."[13] Like Kleist, the Genevan Protestant Staël intended her essay to serve as anti-French propaganda, lauding the cultural achievements and high morals of the so-called "barbarians;"[14] it was important for both to begin their encomia by emphasizing Germanic resistance to Roman tyranny, and, where possible, the unity of the Germanic tribes. And they were not alone. Between 1807 and 1814, attempts were made to found journals with the names *Germania*, *Hermann*, and *Thusnelda* (Hermann's queen), and at least seventy-two publications were devoted to the Teutoburg Forest battle between 1809 and 1900.[15]

---

[11] Kuehnemund, *Arminius*, p. 87.

[12] In Hermann's final speech, following his bloody victory over Varus, the victorious Cheruscan urges his fellows to continue the battle until Rome itself is destroyed, for this "Mordbrut" (breeding ground of murder) will give the nations no rest, "until the robbers' nest is completely destroyed, and nothing but a black flag waves over a desolate heap of ruins." Heinrich von Kleist, "Die Hermannsschlacht," in idem, *Sämtliche Werke* (Munich, 1967), p. 752. See also Volker Losemann, "Arminius und Augustus: Die Römisch-Germanische Auseinandersetzung im deutschen Geschichtsbild," in *Römische Geschichte und Zeitgeschichte*, vol. 1: *Caesar und Augustus*, ed. E. Gabba and K. Christ (Como, 1989), pp. 133–34.

[13] Mme de Staël, *De l'Allemagne*, vol. 1, 2nd ed. (Paris, 1835), pp. 1–2.

[14] See John C. Isbell, *The Birth of European Romanticism: Truth and Propaganda in Staël's "De l'Allemagne," 1810–1813* (Cambridge, 1994).

[15] Kuehnemund, *Arminius*, p. 95; Losemann, "Arminius," p. 135.

One of Germaine de Staël's central claims was that the Germans, rather than playing the role of civilization's destroyers, were now at the forefront of cultural innovation. Her favorable treatment of the early German tribes was supported by the earlier work of Montesquieu, Voltaire, and Gibbon, all of whom emphasized the *internal* collapse of Rome, rather than its destruction by barbarian invaders. Gibbon, though no admirer of Germanic "barbarism," had elaborated in elegant detail the philosophes' insight that the introduction of Christianity—as well as luxurious living and arbitrary rule—had undermined antiquity's essentially this-worldly spirit.[16] These claims converged very nicely with the Hegelian conceits that the classical world had collapsed under the weight of its own contradictions, and that *Geist* had completed its process of self-formation in the "Germanic-Christian" world. This dialectical logic, combined with the obvious domestic difficulties of the French, Ottomans, and Austrians, seemed to point to the inevitable rise of the "Germans"—often including the English and Scandinavians—to world power. Such speculations gave scholars like the historian Georg Gervinius confidence that German principles (individualism, national particularism, Protestantism) would be the leading principles of the modern age.[17] By contrast, then, corporatism, universalism, and Catholicism—all "Latinate" principles—belonged implicitly to the past, a claim that fit very well with new discussions of moral and social "decadence," in which the ancient Romans were often paired with the modern French. That the "rise" of one "race" was closely linked to the moral, political, and social "decline" of the other seemed to be proved by Germany's swift victory over France in 1870–71. The Rome–France comparison, secured by the cultural propaganda of the Napoleonic Wars, still echoed through the triumphal rhetoric of this new era, as Ferdinand Gregorovius's immediate reaction to the outbreak of the Franco–Prussian War demonstrated. In 1870, this free-lance historian, whose neo-Romantic diaries (*Wanderjahre in Italian* [*Italian Travels*—1856–77]) were second only to Goethe's Italian journal in inspiring German yearning for southern climes, wrote, with apparent relish: "The Latin world is sinking, the Germanic, after a long interlude, is once more on the rise."[18]

After 1870, "Rome," more than ever, came to signify antinationalist tyranny, elitism, and ultramontanism, and its symbolic defeat grew increas-

---

[16] Walther Rehm, *Der Untergang Roms im abendländischen Denken* (1930; reprint eds., Darmstadt, 1966), pp. 97–109.

[17] Heinz Gollwitzer, "Zum politischen Germanismus des 19. Jahrhunderts," in *Festschrift für Hermann Heimpel*, vol. 1 (Göttingen, 1971), p. 296.

[18] Gregorovius quoted ibid., p. 341. See also Jens Petersen, "Das Bild des zeitgenössischen Italien in den *Wanderjahren* von Ferdinand Gregorovius," in *Ferdinand Gregorovius und Italien: Eine kritische Würdigung*, ed. Arnold Esch and Jens Petersen (Tübingen, 1993), pp. 88–89. Thanks to Irène Kruse for this reference.

ingly important to the establishment of German cultural autonomy and the completion of "cultural and spiritual unification." Since the early modern era, learned Germans—Ulrich von Hutten, Luther, Hermann Conring— had registered their opposition to the implementation of Roman law in the Germanies; defended by the historical school of Friedrich von Savigny in the 1820s and 30s, Roman law came under new attack after 1840 by those, like Otto von Gierke and Georg Beseler, who favored a return to "Germanic" law.[19] The onset of the *Kulturkampf*, the Risorgimento's failure to put an end to Papal politics, and the founding of the Catholic Center party simply intensified anti-Roman polemics: in an era in which loyal Catholics were presumed to be opponents of the German state, "Rome" took on a seditious air. Among art critics, a consensus emerged that Rome had lost its significance for the maturation of German artists; in 1889, Wilhelm Porte argued that they could easily dispense with a trip to Rome: "They could just as easily go to another lovely place where the wine is good and cheap and where life is gay."[20] This is precisely the era, as we have seen, in which archaeologists, too, began to forego Rome for more exotic locales, and in which the German bureaucracy demanded that the DAI print its journal in German rather than in Italian. In law and politics, in art and scholarship, the nationalization of German institutions entailed the sloughing off the last vestiges of the "universal" culture centered in Rome.

Of course, German philology and *Altertumskunde* (the study—not science!—of antiquities) both reinforced and profited from this emerging north–south cultural essentialism. The brothers Grimm provided a great deal of material upon which a "deep" history of Germandom could be based; in 1870–71, the Germanic philologist Karl Müllenhoff attempted to provide an even longer national trajectory in his popular multivolume *Deutsche Altertumskunde*. Based exclusively on written sources, the first volume of *Deutsche Altertumskunde* scrutinized the work of ancient Greek geographers, poets, and philosophers for evidence of early encounters with Germanic peoples. Wilhelm Scherer, reviewing the volume for the *Preußische Jahrbücher*, imagined the casual browser's reaction to the book: "For heaven's sake, where do the [Germanic] antiquities begin? What do all these Greeks have to do with German *Altertumskunde*?"[21] Scherer, however, did not fail to recognize Müllenhoff's attempts to give Germanness a long and venerable history; for both scholars, the quest for German historical self-consciousness in the present required that an autonomous German es-

---

[19] Gollwitzer, "Zum politischen Germanismus," pp. 294–95.

[20] "Rom und die deutsche Kunst," in *Frankfurter Zeitung*, 15 December 1889, in MZStA, Nachlaß Althoff, AI-Nr. 197, p. 30.

[21] Wilhelm Scherer, "Zur deutschen Alterthumskunde," *Preußische Jahrbücher* 28 (1871): 178.

sence be discernible *before* the Roman conquests divided it in two.[22] This Germanic idea, for Müllenhoff, lay behind Germandom's centuries-long "struggle with Rome," and it was the recognition of the tenacity of these quixotic resisters (and the fulfillment of their "idea" in the present) that gave *Altertumskunde* its purpose.[23] Scherer reiterated this conviction in concluding his review:

> The ancient, unique element, that long fueled the resistance against the Roman spirit [*dem römischen Wesen*], in order finally to triumph over it in war, [this element], which despite many metamorphoses still endures in the present, has been one of the most important factors in recent great deeds. And it is to represent and comprehend this element in a more complete, multifaceted, and deeper way than has previous been done that seems to me the task of German *Altertumskunde*, whose completion we await from Müllenhoff.[24]

It was perhaps Felix Dahn, however, who contributed more than any other of his contemporaries to the elaboration of the "Gothic," anti-Roman type. Dahn, an actor's son, had learned to read from an edition of Schiller's works, but as a university student in the 1850s had abandoned the cosmopolitanism of the *Goethezeit* for the national particularism of the historical school of law. In 1863, he was appointed associate professor of the history of law at the University of Würzburg, and in 1872 was called to a chair at Königsberg; but throughout his long life, he continued to write not only multivolume, positivist works on prehistoric and medieval Germandom, but also a huge corpus of ballads, plays, poems, and historical novels.[25] His *Ein Kampf um Rom* (*A Struggle for Rome*, 1876), one of the most-read books over the next fifty years, and said to appeal especially to adolescent boys, was instrumental in popularizing the image of the corrupt power politics of the Romans and the noble sufferings of the encircled Germans.[26]

Dahn's novel is set in A.D. 526, and opens with a solemn discussion among the Goths of the impending death of their heroic king (and the conqueror of Italy) Theodoric. The succession is a problem; Theodoric's grandson Athalarich suffers from inherited, feminizing ailments and an overbearing mother who arouses the Goth's suspicion by writing Greek and speaking Latin: "I doubt that she thinks Gothically," one compatriot avers.[27] The Roman villain of the piece, Cethegus, is slick, loves luxury, and

---

[22] See, e.g., Karl Müllenhoff, *Deutsche Altertumskunde*, vol. 1, ed. Max Roediger (2d ed., Berlin, 1890), pp. x–xi.

[23] See, for example, ibid., p. ix.

[24] Scherer, "Zur deutschen Alterthumskunde," p. 183.

[25] On Dahn's life, see Herbert Meyer, *Felix Dahn* (Leipzig, 1913).

[26] Klaus von See, *Die Ideen von 1789 und die Ideen von 1914: Völkisches Denken in Deutschland zwischen Französischer Revolution und Erstem Weltkrieg* (Frankfurt, 1975), pp. 93–96.

[27] Dahn, *Ein Kampf um Rom*, vol. 1, (12th ed., Leipzig, 1885), p. 10

has lost his faith to skeptical philosophy; he hates the naïveté and stupid heroism of the Goths, but pretends to befriend them in order to betray their cause. Dahn contrasts the decadent vices of Cethegus to the selfless virtues of the handsome young Goth Totila; beyond these two caricatures, based on those already current of Augustus and Arminius, the book is extremely rich in stereotypes and parables typical of German reflections on decadence, ancient and modern. Perhaps most striking is Dahn's version of the venerable topos of the *furor teutonicus*, the irrational, self-destructive passion of the German soldier defending his nation without hope of victory.[28]

The heroic stoicism of the dying Goths in losing the final *Kampf um Rom* marks the acceptance of the "barbarian" as positive national ancestor in the realm of popular culture: the increasingly frequent invocation of Richard Wagner's operas by German nationalists provides further proof that descent from "barbarians," by the 1880s, had become less an embarrassment than a point of pride. This shift in self-conception predates, but only slightly, the acceptance of Germanic prehistory as a legitimate subject of scholarly interest. We should not be surprised, then, that this field, too, was deeply shaped by the slow acceptance of the anti-Roman "barbarian" as Germany's cultural ancestor, and that its foremost nationalist, Gustav Kossinna, would find no yoke so unbearable as that of the condescending classicists. For institutionally, as well as intellectually, the classical tradition, and the will to fight free of its norms and limitations, shaped the study of Germanic antiquity; but perhaps even more frustrating for nationalists like Kossinna, Germanic archaeology was also shaped by the same fatal flaw that had brought Arminius, at last, to his knees: inter-German particularism. Excavating the barbarian world, like many other contemporary German plans for self-aggrandizement, meant fighting a war on two fronts.

Central Institutions, Local Allegiances:
The Antinomies of *Vorgeschichte*

Scientific *Vorgeschichte*, like a number of other things, came to Germany late, after it had already taken hold in Scandinavia, France, and England. Very significantly, the first prehistorians trained as such grew up in the twilight hours of Humboldtian humanism and came of age in an era of increasingly illiberal nationalism. But this fin de siècle generation, whose racist presumptions are widely known, could hardly be treated as the first *Vorgeschichtler*. The field's ideological roots undoubtedly reach back into

---

[28] On the *furor teutonicus*, and the evolution of German self-conception as "barbarians," see Klaus von See, "Der Germane als Barbar," *Jahrbuch für Internationale Germanistik* 13, no. 1 (1981): 42–72.

the Reformation era, during which German and Italian humanists traded claims about the costs and benefits of the Germanic conquests.[29] Though the main source of information here remained textual, with Tacitus's *Germania* playing the major role, by the seventeenth century, a few of the many scholars trying to explain natural curiosities and the Bible's logic had begun to suspect that material evidence might be used to supplement the ancient written sources. Unconventional sources, of course, were particularly important for northern Europeans, whose history received little coverage in Greek and Latin texts, and who wished to separate their course of development from that of the Catholic south; it was Protestant Scandinavians like the Danish collector Ole Worm (1588–1654) and the Englishman William Camden (1551–1623) who pioneered the historical study of local artifacts.[30] In the Germanies, by the later eighteenth century, the publication of local *Chronik*, collection of folk tales and local artifacts, and the study of early German poetry coalesced in an antiaristocratic amalgam known as *Altertumskunde*, bounded more by geographical area than by methodological difference or historical periodization. In the next decades, the nascent nationalism provoked by French occupation and the Wars of Liberation contributed greatly to the popularity of *Altertumskunde* and won for it important patrons in the Prussian bureaucracy and in princely courts. In spite of the changes the field would undergo over the course of the nineteenth century, German *Altertumskunde* would long retain the impress of the provincial Romanticism and cultural patriotism of the period between about 1793 and 1819.

Altertumskunde would also, importantly, retain the institutional structure of the *Verein* (association) which, unlike a guild, corporation, or estate, was a freely formed group, without birth or status requirements. Such organizations appeared all over Germany in the mid- to late eighteenth century to bring together members of the middle classes for purposes as diverse as prison reform and choral singing, poor relief and gymnastics, and have been seen by historians as key instruments of bourgeois cultural and social self-assertion.[31] *Vereine* devoted to cultural affairs typically emphasized practical and/or particularist interests, though some of the associations founded during the wars and the reform era also expressed grander aims. The Thüringisch-Sächsische Verein für Erforschung des vaterländischen Alther-

---

[29] Hieronimus, "Germanen-Forschung," pp. 242–43.

[30] Ibid., p. 244; on Worm and Camden, Alain Schnapp, *La conquête du passé: Aux origines de l'archéologie* (Paris, 1993), pp. 160–67, 139–42.

[31] See Thomas Nipperdey, "Verein als soziale Struktur in Deutschland im späten 18. und frühen 19. Jahrhundert: Eine Fallstudie zur Modernisierung I," in idem, *Gesellschaft, Kultur, Theorie: Gesammelte Aufsätze zur neueren Geschichte* (Göttingen, 1976), pp. 174–205; Wolfgang Hardtwig, "Strukturmerkmale und Entwicklungstendenzen des Vereinswesens in Deutschland, 1789–1848," in *Vereinswesen und bürgerliche Gesellschaft in Deutschland*, *Historische Zeitschrift*, suppl. vol., n.s. 9 (1984): 14–47.

tums und Erhaltung seiner Denkmäle (Association of Thuringia and Saxony for the Study of Our Ancient Past and the Preservation of its Monuments—TSV), for example, was founded in 1819 by Richard Lepsius's father, and included Goethe, both von Humboldts, the brothers Grimm, and 350 other members of the Saxon haute bourgeoisie.[32] The presence of such important members of the liberal literary estate in the *Vereine* points not only to the breadth of their appeal, but also to the intertwining of poetry, patriotism, and a sort of participatory (if not always republican) ethos; here, investigations of ancestors were frequently combined with an antiabsolutist emphasis on ancient Teutonic loyalties, a reading of history that had ominous implications for feudal Prussia as well as for Napoleonic France.[33]

If some historical *Vereine* harbored reformist convictions, most proved politically innocuous, and were founded by the dozen in virtually every German-speaking state between 1810 and 1870, usually with the encouragement and endorsement of local princes and notables. Saxony, for example, boasted not only the TSV, but also *Vereine* in Bernburg, Blackenburg, Burg bei Magdeburg, Dessau, Eisleben, Köthen, Stendal, Herzberg/Schweinitz, Sangerhausen, Torgau, Weißenfels, and Zeitz.[34] The pursuits of these organizations were diverse and rarely limited to a single period (*Altertumskunde* covered everything before the Napoleonic Wars) or modern "field," but encompassed all aspects of the regional past, including the study and protection of "monuments," folkloric studies, history, prehistory, classical archaeology, and even geography. The medium for the transmission of *Verein* information was the locally published journal or newsletter, which appeared irregularly in many localities; publication in any case lagged behind the acquisition of objects, an activity suited much more to localist self-representation than to pan-nationalist or purely scholarly pursuits.[35] Beginning with the Sammlung Schlesischer Altertümer (Silesian

[32] Friedrich Schlette, "Die Anfänge einer Ur- und Frühgeschichtsforschung in Halle bis zur Gründung des Provinzialmuseums," *Jahresschrift für mitteldeutsche Vorgeschichte* 67 (1984): 23; Rainer M. Lepsius, "Richard Lepsius, und seine Familie—Bildungsbürgertum und Wissenschaft," in *Karl Richard Lepsius (1810–1884)*, ed. Elke Freier and Walter F. Reinecke (Berlin, 1988), p. 32.

[33] See Jost Hermand, *Old Dreams of a New Reich: Volkish Utopias and National Socialism*, trans. Paul Levesque (Bloomington, Ind., 1992), pp. 8–21. For an intriguing discussion of the historical *Vereine*, see Susan Crane, *Collecting and Historical Consciousness: New Forms for Collective Memory in Early Nineteenth-Century Germany* (Ph.D. diss., University of Chicago, 1992).

[34] Schlette, "Anfänge einer Ur- und Frühgeschichtsforschung," p. 23.

[35] See Celia Applegate, *A Nation of Provincials: The German Idea of Heimat* (Berkeley, Calif., 1990), pp. 48–52; Hermann Heimpel, "Geschichtsvereine einst und jetzt," in *Geschichtswissenschaft und Vereinswesen im 19. Jahrhundert*, ed. Hartmut Boockmann et al. (Göttingen, 1972), pp. 45–73. In 1909, Karl Schumacher, director of the Römisch-Germanisches Zentralmuseum, was still complaining about this tendency for inventories to remain unpublished. See his "Aus südwestdeutschen Museen," in *Prähistorische Zeitschrift* 1 (1909): 90–97.

Antiquities Collection) in Breslau (1818) and the Bonn Museum für Rheinisch-Westfälischer Altertümer (Museum of Rhenish and Westphalian Antiquities—1820), a large number of local museums were founded throughout the Germanies to display the history of the *Heimat* and to cele-brate the industry of the *Vereine*.[36]

During the Napoleonic Wars, the Prussian court and bureaucracy had demonstrated new interest in Germanic history and artifacts; as early as 1798, Friedrich Wilhelm III had given over a gallery in the Monbijou Palace for the display of "national" antiquities. His collection, acquired mostly before 1820, consisted partly of purchases and partly of "gifts of patriot-ically and scientifically minded private persons."[37] The Bonn museum had received the enthusiastic support of Chancellor Prince Karl August von Hardenberg, who instructed the museum's director, Wilhelm Dorow, to im-prove the collection "so that it will serve the purposes of youth education, historical research, and preservation of valuable monuments [and] will in-spire and nurture the sense of the significance of our fatherland and the history of the past [*Vorzeit*]."[38] Freiherr Karl vom Stein projected for the *Vereine*, many of which he helped to found, the central role in the collec-tion, editing, and publication of source materials for a total history of the German *Volk*. Stein's document series, the *Monumenta Germaniae Historica* (MGH), founded in 1819, quickly became the personal preserve of the ar-chivist, bureaucrat, publicist, and historian George Heinrich Pertz, and then was put under the professional supervision of Roman historian Theodor Mommsen; its history, in fact, provides rich testimony to the short-lived bureaucratic enthusiasm for popular, patriotic antiquarianism.[39]

As the reform period gave way to a new era of aristocratic isolationism, and as classical philology gained preeminent status in secondary schools and university philosophical faculties, the German states, in fact, began ac-tively to discourage the study of "national" antiquities and history and to

---

[36] There were still at least 143 in Germany in 1927. See Karl Schumacher, "Das Römisch-Germanische Central-museum von 1901–1926," in *Festschrift zur Feier des 75 jährigen Beste-hens des Römisch-Germanischen Centralmuseums zu Mainz 1927* (Mainz, 1927), p. 64. It would be wrong, however, to compare these local museums to the art and sculpture galleries being erected at the same time; local historical museums were by and large tiny, dank, ill-lighted rooms in abandoned castles or university buildings; inventories were scarce and hours of opening short.

[37] See Leopold von Ledebur, *Das Königliche Museum vaterländischer Alterthümer im Schlosse Monbijou in Berlin* (Berlin, 1838), p. v.

[38] Hardenberg to Dorow, 4 January 1820, quoted in Reinhold Fuchs, "Zur Geschichte der Sammlungen des Rheinischen Landesmuseums," in *Rheinisches Landesmuseum Bonn: 150 Jahre Sammlungen* (Düsseldorf, 1971), p. 31.

[39] See J. R. Seeley, *Life and Times of Stein*, vol. 2 (Boston, 1879), pp. 452–60. On Pertz, see Annedore Oertel, "Georg Heinrich Pertz," in *Berlinische Lebensbilder*, vol. 4: *Geisteswissen-schaftler*, ed. Michael Erbe (Berlin, 1989), pp. 87–108.

encourage the study of distant, and safely dead, epochs and achievements. If literary figures continued to treat "Gothic" themes, the lower schools largely left the Germanic tribes out of their history lessons.[40] In the universities, professors generally concluded their courses on the history of the Germanies with the Peace of Westphalia in 1648; Heinrich von Treitschke, appointed lecturer at the University of Leipzig in 1859, was one of the first to offer courses on more recent events.[41] Preference for classical antiquity went hand in hand with an aestheticizing impulse, which militated against the academic acceptance of early Germanic arts and crafts. As early as 1822, Wilhelm Dorow's museum fell out of favor with the Prussian education minister, Freiherr von Altenstein, and with the Bonn University scholars who had been appointed to oversee the museum. The professors, most of them philologists, particularly wished Altenstein to clear the museum of Dorow's nonclassical artifacts, which they thought overly large and ugly.[42] Dorow's position was eliminated; thereafter, his collecting and digging activity had to be done during vacations from his new job with the Foreign Ministry. Reflecting on this period of stagnation, provincialism, and increasingly dominant classicism, Dorow described the frustrations of the patriotic amateur: "People then had . . . no sympathy for national antiquities; they dreamed only of art works, of museums of Greek and Egyptian antiquities."[43]

Indeed, as we have seen, the Prussian Royal Museums, opened in 1830, aimed at the aesthetic rather than the historical education of the population; in imitation of the Louvre and the British Museum, the Berlin collection emphasized masterworks of classical antiquity (often presented in cast form) and excluded the works of unlettered peoples, including prehistoric Europeans. The other German princes followed suit: Ludwig I of Bavaria completed the all-classical Glyptothek in 1829; the dukes of Baden dedicated the Kunsthalle in Karlsruhe in 1846, and the kings of Württemberg and Saxony opened galleries in 1843 and 1855, respectively.[44] If Vereine and local museums continued to receive some state patronage, their budgets were tiny compared to the salaries paid to academics and the funds expending on the building of new art museums—and they could be made even tinier if the associations failed to curb the sorts of cultural nationalism the states had fostered before the reactionary era set in. In 1828, the TSV was frozen out of the Prussian state budget; the Education Ministry's communication announcing the cessation of funding explained that "the society has

[40] Hieronimus, "Germanen-Forschung," p. 248.

[41] Andreas Dorpalen, *Heinrich von Treitschke* (New Haven, Conn., 1957), p. 49.

[42] Wolfgang Ehrhardt, *Das akademische Kunstmuseum der Universität Bonn unter der Direktion von Friedrich Gottlieb Welcker und Otto Jahn* (Opladen, 1982), p. 31.

[43] Dorow quoted in Fuchs, "Geschichte der Sammlungen," pp. 75–76.

[44] James J. Sheehan, "From Princely Collections to Public Museums," in *Rediscovering History: Culture, Politics, and the Psyche*, ed. Michael S. Roth (Stanford, Calif., 1994), pp. 175–76.

withdrawn its activity too much from provincial interests, which alone can secure for it a vital role."[45]

The exclusion of Germanic studies from prestigious cultural institutions undoubtedly reinforced the field's antiestablishment self-conception and localist preoccupations; political sanctions, combined with low status in the emerging intellectual hierarchy, compelled the *Vereine* in the post-1820 period to retreat from grand claims and nationalist rhetoric into data collection. In 1837, the journal of the newly-founded Verein für hessische Geschichte und Landeskunde reported modestly on the present-day function of the historical *Vereine*, which were now "attempting to direct the particular history of individual areas, which partly escapes and partly must remain unconsidered by the historian who has all of Germany in view."[46] A year later, Leopold von Ledebuhr, keeper of the Monbijou collection, cheerfully acknowledged that he could do no better than organize his catalog according to the provincial locations in which objects had been found: "patriotic" *Altertumskunde*, he averred, could not yet separate objects of Roman, Slavic, German, and oriental origin, or give them anything like a secure chronology.[47] Ledebuhr's accumulation of objects without daring to organize them provides a nice example of an emerging socio-intellectual division of labor, under which interpretation was left to the academically trained experts, while modest amateurs merely collected material for some future history. As few experts were available to take on the tasks of interpretation and synthesis, this situation produced a typologizing meticulousness and antispeculative propensity that continue to be characteristic of German prehistorical thought today.[48]

If interpretation fell to the experts, and collecting to the amateurs, it was also clear that a certain sort of segregation in subject matter was under way. Classical remains, especially texts, were clearly the province of the academy; in an era in which academic historians were touting their "scientific" aims and specialized research skills, it seemed reasonable to assume that without philological training, one could not correctly read documents, or understand their testimony about the ancient world. The excavation of tumulus graves, restoration of local monuments, and collecting of folklore, on the other hand, seemed to require no special skills, and could safely be left to amateurs.[49] Insofar as humanist scholars were interested in local artifacts, they concentrated on the Roman material from the Rhineland and

---

[45] Friedrich Schlette, "Anfänge einer Ur- und Frühgeschichtsforschung," p. 24.

[46] "Einleitung," *Zeitschrift des Vereins für hessische Geschichte und Landeskunde* 1 (1837): i.

[47] Ledebuhr, *Das Königliche Museum*, p. viii.

[48] See Heinrich Härke, "All Quiet on the Western Front? Paradigms, Methods, and Approaches in West German Archaeology," in *Archaeological Theory in Europe: The Last Three Decades* ed. Ian Hodder (New York, 1991), pp. 187–222. Many thanks to Peter Brown for supplying me with a copy of this essay.

[49] Heimpel, "Geschichtsvereine," p. 63, n. 41.

Bavaria; but even this area was generally thought unfit for scholarly attention. In his memoirs, Ulrich von Wilamowitz-Moellendorff recalled that in his schooldays in the late 1860s, "Only dilettanti troubled about German antiquities of Roman date."[50] The *limes*, the series of Roman fortifications on the empire's German frontier, however, marked a greater divide in academic respectability as well as in cultural geography, both of which contributed to the creation of lasting distrust between western and eastern German historical *Vereine*. As early as the 1830s, the Mittelfränkisches Verein had made it clear that from its perspective, the *limes* formed the frontier of Germanic civilization against the West, rather than, as the more classically inclined Rhinelanders and Bavarians believed, the barricade erected by the civilized Romans against the barbarians of the East.[51] Such attempts to define to Germanic culture's "true" patrimony were the stuff that the interagency enmities of twentieth-century, state-supported prehistory were made on.

In the wake of Friedrich Wilhelm IV's ascension to the Prussian throne in 1840, liberals were offered new opportunities for nationalist agitation. Numerous members of the educated middle classes, scholars, students, journalists, teachers, and lower-level bureaucrats, called for cultural and political unification and an end to princely absolutism. Not surprisingly, the historical Vereine, which drew their members from this sector of the population, were also caught up in the patriotic fervor of the 1848 revolutions, so much so that, at least in the west, the desire to overcome the provincialism of the past outlasted the collapse of the Frankfurt Assembly. In 1852, spearheaded by two mural painters at the Bavarian court, the brothers Ludwig and Wilhelm Lindenschmit (also the leaders of the Verein zur Erforschung der rheinischen Geschichte und Altertümer [Association for the Study of Rhenish History and Antiquities]), a general meeting of *Vereine* in Mainz decided that the time had come for a central museum for Roman-German antiquities (Römisch-Germanisches Zentralmuseum—RGZM).[52] As Ludwig's son later explained:

> The Black-Red-Gold [republican] age had gone up in smoke, the vision of a
> Germany united under one king had dissipated, but in a hundred thousand

---

[50] Ulrich von Wilamowitz-Moellendorff, *Erinnerungen, 1848–1914* (2d ed., Leipzig, 1928), p. 87. The Romantic philologist Friedrich Creuzer did devote considerable time to Roman-German antiquities; see, e.g., his review of fifteen works on south German *Altertumskunde* in *Jahrbücher der Literatur* (Vienna) 117 (1847): 169–95.

[51] Arnold Esch, "Limesforschung und Geschichtsvereine: Romanismus und Germanismus, Dilettantismus und Facharchäologie in der Bodenforschung des 19. Jahrhunderts," in Boockman, *Geschichtswissenschaft und Vereinswesen*, p. 182.

[52] At precisely the same time, Baron v. Aufseß and another contingent of *Vereine* founded a central museum for medieval and Christian artifacts in Nuremberg, thus neatly dividing German history into Roman and non-Roman halves.

hearts the flame of pure patriotism burned still and the yearning for the unification of the German *Stämme* lived on. . . . The drive for brotherhood and political unity found rapid expression in almost all social gatherings and caused learned societies to incorporate this mentality. As a further sure sign of the spiritual community of all Germans, in 1852 the Deutsches Museum in Nuremberg and the Römisch-Germanisches Zentralmuseum in Mainz were founded by the Union of German Historical and Antiquarian Societies.[53]

Ludwig, the foremost Lindenschmit, hoped that centralization would both provide scientific benefits and increase nationalist sentiment. Collecting all relevant material in one place, he believed, would allow for comparative study of artifacts, an essential step toward determination of the boundaries of Germandom, Slavdom, and Celtdom.[54] According to Lindenschmit's plan, local groups would contribute their findings to the central institute; both sides would benefit from the scientific insights generated by coordination, and the public would learn to appreciate the cultural achievements of its ancestors.

A number of obstacles, however, stood in the way of the creation of a central institution in a decentralized—indeed, not yet unified—nation. Decades of local preoccupation and numerous snubs from the state had not been without their effect on the historical *Vereine*. As Jakob Grimm had discovered in 1846, the greatest obstacle to centralization lay in the jealousies of the local collectors; no collectors, museums, or *Vereine* were willing to donate their objects to his projected *Zentralantiquarium*.[55] Lindenschmit had recognized this problem, and his RGZM, accordingly, depended on the use of casts, copies, and drawings for its exhibitions, thus circumventing the problem of extracting originals from local collectors. But, as the founding father himself admitted in 1866, even these measures had failed to make the RGZM a success. Establishing the museum had actually done little to overcome the provincial loyalties of amateur collectors and permit a total view of national prehistorical conditions.[56] *Vorgeschichte*, in this era, was far from the "supremely national science" that Gustav Kossinna would claim it to be a half-century later.

The second major problem faced by the RGZM was funding. Predictably, state subsidies were thin on the ground during the 1850s and 60s. By 1856,

[53] Quoted in Kurt Böhner, "Das Römisch-Germanische Zentralmuseum—Eine vaterländische und gelehrte Gründung des 19. Jahrhunderts," *Jahrbuch des Römisch-Germanischen Zentralmuseums, Mainz* 25 (1978): 1.

[54] Gero von Merhart, "Das Römisch-Germanische Zentralmuseum: Rückblick und Ausblick," *Festschrift des RGZM in Mainz zur Feier seines hundertjährigen Bestehens 1952*, vol. 3 (Mainz, 1953), p. 195.

[55] Ibid., p. 195.

[56] Ludwig Lindenschmit, "Die deutsche Altertumsforschung," *Archiv für Anthropologie* 1 (1866): 47.

the museum was receiving small amounts from Hessen, Saxony, and Austria (a total of about 750 talers); in 1857, Prussia was persuaded to add 200 talers to this total.[57] After unification, the prospects for increased funding of national cultural institutions improved considerably, but as must be stressed, no national Ministry of Culture existed in Germany until the Nazi period (though as time went on, the Prussian Ministry of Education increasingly attempted to function as such); culture was still officially the provenance of the separate states. In 1878, a proposal by the Prussian Education and Finance ministries to raise the Reich's contribution to the RGZM from six thousand to fifteen thousand marks (the equivalent of five thousand talers) received the Kaiser's approval. This proposal, however, contained an important proviso, one that would dog the RGZM down to the collapse of imperial Germany: the museum would only be allowed to purchase items, whether newly discovered or already held in collections, that the provincial museums did not want. "This appears to be our only way," wrote the Prussian bureaucrats, "to exert influence over the central museum in Mainz and to prevent the now existing, disadvantageous financial competition of [the RGZM] with our own institutions."[58] At the very moment in which the Reich was seeking to consolidate the achievements of Bismarck's wars of unification, Prussian cultural policy only reinforced the stubborn localism of the *Vereine*.

Thus by the 1870s and 1880s, prehistorical work in Germany remained the preserve of local amateurs, jealous of attempts by centralizers to expropriate their finds and dependent on private and local government patronage for their activities. Most early Germanic material was housed in provincial museums or private collections; digs at local sites were still conducted mostly by amateurs, and finds remained the property of the landowners. As an extra-academy avocation, the collection of prehistorical artifacts was hardly distinguished from local history and folklore: it, too, depended on the sense of a communal past and a simple—but noble—ancestry, and it reaffirmed first local, then national ties. As we have seen, this provincial orientation was intrinsic to the world of the *Vereine*; we should not be surprised that it did not suddenly vanish with the coming of Bismarck and the Franco-Prussia War.

But in the wake of unification, German *Altertumskunde* had begun to acquire new academic respectability and social status. In the universities, several important classical philologists of the 1840s and 50s—Karl Lachmann, Georg Curtius, and Moriz Haupt—had undertaken studies of early

---

[57] Gustav Behrens, "Das Römisch-Germanisch Zentralmuseum von 1927 bis 1952," *Festschrift des RGZM*, 3: 183. Fr. Olfers (General Director of the Berlin Museums) to Geheimrat Freine, 9 September 1856, in MZStA 2.2.1/20515, pp. 7–8.

[58] Education and Finance ministries to Wilhelm I, 6 April 1878, in MZStA 2.2.1/20515, pp. 38–39.

18. Interior of the Bronze Age Room of the Römisch-Germanisches Zentralmuseum, Mainz. The artifacts, many of them copies of objects in other museums, might have been humble, but the museum's decoration was quite elaborate. Römisch-Germanisches Zentralmuseum, Mainz.

Germanic texts; as specialization accelerated, their students would be scholars of the Germanic world alone. In the next two decades, the novels and artifact-rich histories of Felix Dahn and Karl Müllenhoff inspired new forays into the Middle Ages. Pressed by nationalist sentiment, accelerating specialization, and the dropping away of biblical presumptions about human origins, academic philologists, archaeologists, and physical anthropologists began to probe the preclassical past for evidence of early settlements, skull types, and cultural achievements. Entering this field in the 1870s, they found it densely populated by *Verein* amateurs and sorely afflicted by particularist sentiments and lack of interpretive rigor. A young Germanist like Gustav Kossinna, a student of Müllenhoff and Rudolf Henning, could find plenty of material, piled in local museums or described in *Verein* publications, for his purposes; if, as some have suggested, Kossinna created prehistory's first "paradigm," he did so simply by superimposing a set of questions and aims borrowed from Germanic philology onto the typological positivism of the local associations.[59]

The new notoriety of national *Altertumskunde*, of course, had much to do with external political events; campaigns to neutralize Catholics and socialists, Germany's entry into the arena of imperialist exploits, the formation of Pan-German pressure groups, and the emergence of the school reform movement all contributed to the formulation of a more explicitly nationalist sort of German studies which, it was hoped, would help to complete the process of "cultural and spiritual unification." In 1897, Rudolf Virchow, physician, prehistorian, and general polymath, advocated concentration on questions of national, rather than international or provincial, interest;[60] Virchow had also been the prime mover behind the founding of a national museum for ethnography in 1886. In 1898, the Leipzig "Anthropo-Geographer" Friedrich Ratzel published a popular volume entitled *Deutschland: Einführung in die Heimatskunde* (*Germany: Introduction to the Study of our Homeland*) in which he urged his countrymen to abandon their particularist loyalties and embrace as "home" the entire region between the Rhine and the Vistula.[61] If Virchow, like Theodor Mommsen, owed allegiance to the liberal nationalism of 1848, Ratzel, a strong proponent of migrationist colonialism, already had one foot in the illiberal twentieth century. Just as the liberal strongholds, the states and city governments, had lost their momentum for progressive change after Bismarck's "reform from above" projects of the 1870s and 1880s, localist liberals after 1879 were never able to regain control of patriotic rhetoric. Those who would reap this particular whirlwind were aggressive Education Ministry bureaucrats like Richard Schöne and Friedrich Althoff, and a handful of Germanophile academics and publicists. As national patronage and considerations of national prestige were introduced from the top, the liberal vision of a popular, nationalist *Heimatkunde* was transformed in response to the dictates of the central state, the rhetoric of radical patriots, and the demands of "big scholarship."

The metamorphoses undergone by the three major nineteenth-century liberal organizations devoted to *Altertumskunde* are characteristic of this shift. In style and substance, all three of the organizational movements con-

[59] See Günther Smolla, "Das Kossinna-Syndrom," *Fundberichte aus Hessen* 19–20 (1979–80): 1–9; on Henning (a Germanist and Rudolf Virchow's son-in-law) see Smolla, "Gustaf Kossinna nach 50 Jahren: Kein Nachruf," *Acta Praehistorica et Archaeologica* 16–17 (1984–85): 10. I am grateful to Professor Smolla for sharing his work and thoughts with me.

[60] Karel Sklenar, *Archaeology in Central Europe: The First 500 Years* (New York, 1983), p. 146.

[61] Friedrich Ratzel, *Deutschland: Einführung in die Heimatkunde* (Leipzig, 1898), p. 314.

sidered here must be described as "top-down" projects: in spite of liberal rhetoric, the initiative for their creation came from professional scholars, and their memberships were overwhelmingly composed of social elites with close ties to high bureaucratic and political circles. One of these organizations has already been described; the IfAK/DAI, its interests chiefly classical until very late in the century, also figures prominently in the history of the development of research into prehistory. The social status of the members of the other two bodies—the Reichslimeskommission (Imperial Commission for the Study of the *limes*—RLK), and the Berliner Gesellschaft für Archäologie, Ethnographie, und Urgeschichte (Berlin Society for Archaeology, Ethnography, and Prehistory—BGAEU)—did not differ greatly from that of the DAI. But all three organizations fought bitterly among themselves for control of the new, centralized institute for German prehistory authorized by the Reichstag in 1899.

Perhaps the most genuinely "popular" of these three bodies was the RLK, a loose confederation of local archaeologists and antiquarians dedicated to studying the remains of the Roman fortifications in Germany. The idea for the commission had come from Theodor Mommsen, whose systematizing instinct had led him to propose a Reich-funded cooperative effort as early as the mid-1870s. But Bismarck, Mommsen's archenemy, had allowed the liberal deputy's proposal to languish in advisory committees, just as he had shelved Curtius's plans for Olympia in the 1850s.[62] Shortly after the Iron Chancellor's retirement, however, Mommsen resurrected his idea in a speech to the elite Archäologische Gesellschaft zu Berlin, in which he lamented the lack of coordination between Germany's "separate fatherlands" and the consequent "all too blank pages of Roman-German prehistory."[63] His plan, backed by Helmuth von Moltke, called for the joint direction of excavations and publications by civil and military officials, and Mommsen carefully stressed the import of both centralized administration and local research. In conclusion, the eminent historian recommended the founding of a national institute for Roman-German archaeology, a suggestion he would live to rue.

Even before Mommsen's speech, the Prussian Education Ministry had pressured the Foreign Ministry to broach the subject of *limes* work with the southwestern German states.[64] By mid-December 1890, Education Minister Goßler had organized a conference on Roman-German archaeology. His sketch for the Limeskommission took over many of Mommsen's general

[62] Karl Griewank, "Wissenschaft und Kunst in der Politik Kaiser Wilhelms I. und Bismarcks," *Archiv für Kulturgeschichte* 34, no. 3 (1952): 301.

[63] Theodor Mommsen, "Die einheitliche Limesforschung," *Reden und Aufsätze* (Berlin, 1905), pp. 347, 344.

[64] Goßler to Caprivi, 14 June 1890; and Falcke (Foreign Ministry) to Goßler, 24 September 1890, both in PZStA AA/R 37861, pp. 4–10 and pp. 38–39, respectively.

ideas: his more detailed administrative structure called for the division of the territory into *Streckenkommissionen* (section committees) and of the costs by the number of Roman *castella* (fortresses) occurring in each section. Goßler estimated the total cost of the project at eighty thousand marks, then a considerable sum for prehistorical work, but far from the final Reich contribution, which came to two hundred thousand marks for the first five years.[65] *Limes* research, which continued on a smaller scale into the 1930s, like Stein's historical project, provided an opportunity for local amateurs to participate in a larger patriotic-scientific project of the type Mommsen himself had dubbed "big scholarship." Contributors invested so much energy in these excavations that by 1905, the organization's director Ernst Fabricius was receiving complaints about overfull storehouses from local museums and appeals from scholars for access to the as yet unpublished data; controversies over ownership and overly industrious accumulation had prevented this local/central joint venture from producing much in the way of synthetic results.[66]

Mommsen's praise for local research, in fact, had proved in practice to be rather backhanded. His assessment of the sluggish progress made by the *Vereine* seems to have been based on a knowledge of "professional" publications only, and his coorganizers, especially in southern Germany, were museum officials, military men, and other bureaucrats, rather than *Verein* leaders, which left the RLK open to attack by southern separatists and *Verein* populists.[67] In Württemberg and Bavaria, *Vereine* reacted with skepticism to a project that seemed to promise Prussian tutelage. Some feared archaeological projects would be engineered to allow Prussians to spy on southern activities; such suspicions prompted Munich professor of classical archaeology Heinrich Brunn to warn Mommsen against the political consequences of too close a cooperation with the Prussian military. "An invasion of Prussian General Staff officers, who comb every corner of Bavaria," Brunn wrote, "could easily make an unpleasant impression in certain high quarters."[68] The Bavarians and Württembergers eventually did join the RLK, but their extreme circumspection, twenty years after the founding of the Reich, suggests that a general consensus about the Fatherland and its past was still some time away.

The BGAEU, like the RLK, was largely the creation of one prominent

---

[65] Goßler to conference participants, 16 December 1890, ibid., pp. 56–57; "Der römische Grenzwall in Südwest-Deutschland" *AA* in *JbdesDAI*, 7 (1892): 6.

[66] Ernst Fabricius, "Denkschrift über die Behandlung der Einzelfunde aus den Grabungen der Reichs-Limeskommission," 5 August 1905, in BHStA, MK 14467.

[67] Rainer Braun, "Die Anfänge der Limesforschung in Bayern," *Jahrbuch für fränkische Landesforschung* 42 (1982): 65.

[68] Ibid., pp. 60–66 (Brunn quoted, p. 66); also, idem, "Die Erforschung der 'Teufelsmauer' in Württemberg bis 1890," *Fundberichte aus Baden-Württemberg* 10 (1985): 71, 75.

scholar—in this case, Rudolf Virchow. Derived from the Versammlungen der deutschen Naturforscher und Ärzte (Conferences of German Natural Scientists and Doctors), which had met yearly since 1822, the BGAEU was founded in 1869. Not surprisingly, then, this society was largely composed of doctors, whose interest in ethnographic and anthropological evidence extended little further than the evolution of skeletal types and the distribution of diseases. In the next quarter-century, the founding anatomists and pathologists increasingly gave way to men with total devotion to anthropology and prehistory, though due to the slow reception of these fields in the university curriculum, these scholars were still initially trained in medicine, geography, German philology, or classics. For many years, the BGAEU remained the premier ethnographic research institute, cultivating increasingly good relations with the Prussian ministries of education and trade.[69] As Germany's imperial activities commenced, however, new groups developed interest in ethnographic issues and objects. Like the RLK, the BGAEU often treated local organizations with sovereign disdain; not only did it oppose the opening of new local museums (fearing fragmentation of the material), but the society's statutes explicitly forbade the granting of membership to these amateur "Landsleute" (provincials), despite their frequent reporting of local work and finds to the president.[70] Again, like Mommsen's organization, the BGAEU put enormous efforts into the collection of artifacts and data, and considerably less into the encouragement of their dissemination, interpretation, and display.

Like Virchow himself, the BGAEU displayed a political as well as a positivist side. Despite its penchant for publishing charts and tables, and its cautious treatment of generalization about ethnogenesis, the society still looked forward to the application of its anthropological work to colonial administration in Africa and the South Seas, and Virchow himself hoped that his organic scientific method would help to consolidate political unification by becoming the basis for a liberal and nondenominational cultural community.[71] But in spite of having become the ethnographic society most respected by scholars and the state, just twenty years after its founding the society, paradoxically, began to lose its steam. The 1890s saw the deaths of

[69] See Christian Andree, "Geschichte der Berliner Gesellschaft für Archäologie, Ethnographie, und Urgeschichte," in *Festschrift zum hundertjährigen Bestehen der BGAEU, 1869–1969*, vol. 1 (Berlin, 1969), pp. 24–57, passim; the Ministry of Trade apparently looked out for the interests of the society from the beginning, convincing railroad magnates to build their tracks around grave sites.

[70] Ibid., p. 39; also, Brigitte Rüster, "Geschichte des Museums von 1884 bis 1912," *Jahresschrift für mitteldeutsche Vorgeschichte* 67 (1974): p. 76.

[71] Andree, "Geschichte der BGAEU," p. 72; Walter Bußmann, "Rudolf Virchow und der Staat," in *Vom Staat des Ancien Regime zum modernen Parteienstaat. Festschrift für Theodor Schieder*, ed. Helmut Berding et al. (Munich, 1978), p. 282. On Virchow's medical and scientific ideas, see Wolfgang Jacob, *Medizinische Anthropologie im 19. Jahrhundert* (Stuttgart, 1967).

many of its original members, the loss of its longtime patron in the Education Ministry, the anticlerical Gustav von Goßler, and the eclipse of the society's intimate relationship to liberal politics.[72] After Virchow's death in 1902, German ethnography, and the BGAEU, took a decisively illiberal turn toward racialist speculation and hypernationalist chauvinism.[73]

As we have seen, the DAI, like the BGAEU, had gradually consolidated its relationship with the state. And, as we have also seen, this consolidation was accomplished by a new generation of DAI executives, anxious to disentangle themselves from the inefficiencies and dilettantry of the Hyperborean generation, and fully cognizant that rising Italian nationalism presaged their exclusion from participation in grand new archæological endeavors on Roman soil.[74] It should not, then, be surprising that some members of this body might cast a jealous eye on the German *limes*, whose excavation had turned up much material of interest to classicists. Initially, Mommsen had prevented the DAI from participating in the *limes* excavations, probably as recompense for Conze's reforms in Rome, behind which Mommsen saw Bismarck's hand.[75] But the experience of cooperative work in the investigation of the *limes* gave a new, forceful impetus to found a permanent central institute for Roman-German work, and at the conclusion of the RLK's first campaign in 1897, the DAI saw its chance to enter (and organize) the field. As Eduard Meyer, the most prominent ancient historian from Mommsen's death in 1903 to his own in 1930, later explained the DAI's position, "The idea prevailed that if one wanted to go forward and to overcome the fragmentation and lack of purpose so often predominant in local work and accidental discoveries, the consolidation of the whole area under a new, unified organization was unavoidable."[76]

The Römisch-Germanische Kommission (RGK), however, did not come into the world without a protracted series of disputes among professional factions. The substance of the quarrel lay in control of the new organization, the first central-state institution dedicated to national archaeology. There were two levels of this struggle for control—one political, the other scholarly. The political debate involved the source of funding for the RGK. Those who preferred unification with the DAI wanted to accept the Foreign Ministry's offer of ten thousand marks in start-up money; those who

[72] Ibid., p. 82.

[73] Robert Proctor, "From *Anthropologie* to *Rassenkunde* in the German Anthropological Tradition," in *Bones, Bodies, Behavior: Essays on Biological Anthropology,* ed. George W. Stocking, Jr. (Madison, Wis., 1988), pp. 138–79.

[74] See, e.g., "R.E.," "Römisch-germanische Forschung," *Vossische Zeitung,* Sunday suppl., p. 9 (4 March 1900) in MZStA, Nachlaß Schmidt-Ott, BXIX, vol. 2, p. 175.

[75] Alexander Conze, *Unsern Kindern gewidmet* (Berlin, 1908), pp. 47–48.

[76] Eduard Meyer, "25 Jahre Römisch-Germanische Kommission," in *Fünfundzwanzig Jahre Römisch–Germanische Kommission* (Berlin, 1930), p. 1.

opposed—and here Mommsen was the leader—appealed to the Ministry of the Interior, the body that had funded *limes* research, for double that sum.[77] As he informed the Education Ministry, Mommsen opposed DAI/RGK integration on the grounds that Berlin had no right to dominate an activity whose center belonged in the Rhineland, and that the DAI should be an international, scholarly body, while the RGK would inevitably have to serve national interests and organize local amateurs. "The means and ends [of the two bodies]" Mommsen contended, "are totally different. The institute [DAI] works with and for scholars. The proposed institute must almost exclusively work with dilettantes and the leader or leaders must be personally engaged in a way that cannot occur within the institute."[78] A good liberal, Mommsen was loathe to render unto Bismarck the property of all mankind—that is, classical antiquity, not prehistorical culture. But when a bureaucratic debacle threatened, the Interior Ministry at last relinquished its claim, and the RGK fell to the Foreign Ministry.[79]

The struggle among scholars for control of the RGK was played out between the natural scientists, represented by Virchow and the BGAEU, and the DAI humanists, headed by Conze. Conze clearly intended the RGK to fall under the direction of classicists. Virchow, who had devoted the last thirty years to prehistorical anthropology, distrusted Conze. Perhaps he wanted control himself, or, more likely, he simply resented the claim of the classicist establishment to an area it had scorned for decades, and felt that prehistory required natural-scientific, not humanistic, modes of inquiry. In addition, Virchow opposed on principle the "centralizing tendencies . . . that seek to destroy the whole old organization [of prehistory]"; for despite the elitism of his society, Virchow, like Mommsen, did not want science to have to answer to state officials.[80] A terrific battle for leadership ensued, exacerbated by the quarrel over whether the RGK director was also to head the Roman-German Museum in Mainz. Finally two compromise candidates were selected: Karl von Schumacher, a classical archaeologist with prehistorical interests, would head the museum, and Hans Dragendorff, trained in the philological tradition of the University of Bonn, would direct the RGK in Frankfurt.

However, Schumacher and Dragendorff were still not to the taste of many natural scientists, Germanic philologists and members of provincial *Vereine*. According to Conze, a raging Virchow himself attacked the nominations, in

---

[77] Werner Krämer, "Fünfundsiebzig Jahre Römisch-Germanische Kommission," *Bericht der Römisch-Germanischen Kommission*, suppl. vol. 58 (1977): 9–10.

[78] Theodor Mommsen, untitled, undated [c. January 1899] memorandum to the Education Ministry in MZStA, Nachlaß Schmidt-Ott, B-XIX, vol. 2. A similar document (Mommsen to Felix Hettner, 2 March 1898) appears in Krämer, "Römisch-Germanische Kommission," p. 10.

[79] Ibid., p. 11.

[80] Virchow quoted in Andree, "Geschichte der BGAEU," p. 97.

public as well as in private.[81] The prehistorian Paul Reinecke, in two letters to Adolf Furtwängler, raged over the usurpation of the RGK by bureaucrats who were only interested in Roman remains; the organization, Reinecke felt, deserved an artist and/or a Bismarck, not a pedant or a straw man, for its chief.[82] On the other side, the classicists, who had long ridiculed the dilettantry of those who needed no philological skills to ply their trade, resented this opposition to their beneficent intervention. As Gerhart Rodenwaldt, DAI president throughout the 1920s, later claimed, the "inorganic" separation of the RGK from northern prehistory had been the result of "an accidental clash of personalities," and had been detrimental to the DAI plan to unite and foster prehistorical research in Germany.[83]

The upshot of the RGK controversy was essentially to divide German prehistorical work between those who studied *Germania romana* and those who searched for *Germania libera*, to split research and ideology on geocultural lines.[84] As a result of a compromise with the Interior Ministry, the RGK agreed to limit its scope to the area actually occupied by the Romans.[85] Hereafter, Frankfurt and Mainz would become home to the *romana* faction, the smaller cities in eastern Prussia and Saxony to the *libera* faction; and, at least in the eyes of officialdom, the Mainz contingent would preside over— and more importantly, receive state funding for—the most extensive and most publicized prehistorical digs in Germany.

But the RGK affair also highlighted another fin de siècle phenomenon: the increasing displacement of the *Vereine* in favor of professional archaeologists. As part of its campaign to centralize German archaeological work under its aegis, the DAI had heavily criticized local organizations and amateurs for slovenly restoration and excavation work. Understandably, local *Vereine* resented this censorious posture. In a reply to the criticisms of "Herr U" (Ernst Fabricius) published in the *Darmstädter Zeitung*, a prominent local antiquarian complained bitterly about the ingratitude of the learned community for all the efforts of amateurs. "That previously much was neglected," he wrote, "no one will deny; this, though, occurred at a time at which all of *Altertumswissenschaft* was still at the teething stage. And at that time the scholarly organizations competent to help did nothing at all to encourage *Altertumsvereine* and museum administrations to salvage [arti-

---

[81] Conze, *Unsern Kindern*, p. 49.

[82] Reinecke to Furtwängler, 20 July 1900, and 16 September 1900, in DAI, Nachlaß Furtwängler, Kasten 7.

[83] Gerhart Rodenwaldt, *Archäologisches Institut des Deutschen Reiches, 1829–1929* (Berlin, 1929), p. 43.

[84] Werner Krämer, "Das Römisch-Germanische Zentralmuseum und die deutsche Vorgeschichtsforschung um die Jahrhundertwende," *Jahrbuch des Römisch-Germanischen Zentralmuseums* 25 (1978): 49; Carl Watzinger, *Theodor Wiegand* (Munich, 1944), p. 445.

[85] Krämer, "Römisch-Germanische Kommission," p. 15; Conze, *Unsern Kindern*, p. 49.

facts] but instead looked down on this wheelbarrow work [*Kärrnerarbeit*] with condescending smiles."[86]

Similarly, when the creation of the RGK was discussed at an 1899 general meeting of German *Altertumsvereine* in Straßbourg, it was clear that the *limes* project had not succeeded in establishing much trust between local bodies and the central bureaucracy. Georg Wolff, speaking on behalf of the western German historical societies, warned Conze and the DAI against repetition of the RLK's exclusionary practices. Much local expertise and energy, he contended, had been wasted in not making further use of *Verein* members, and the Reichskommission's high-handed intrusions had recreated feudalistic social stasis in the world of scholarship. "The consciousness," Wolff reported, ". . . that the tasks that they earlier had seen as an *officium nobile* had been taken over by the Reich, had the effect on many of these *Vereine* that fossilized absolutism had on private and communal activity in Prussia before [the battle of] Jena."[87] But this, Wolff insisted, would not happen again; he made it a necessary condition that the *Vereine*, whose efforts and funds traditionally sustained the field, would retain the central role and decision-making power in the new institution. The western *Vereine* were in total agreement with Virchow's suspicions of centralizing tendencies: the "murderous strivings" of centralizers to force local laymen to deliver up finds and relinquish independence, Wolff maintained, were to be fended off at all costs.[88]

Though Conze promised that the local organizations would retain as much freedom of operation as possible, centralized, bureaucratic leadership still had little appeal to the *Vereine*, a number of which had been founded only recently and had little desire to look beyond their own districts.[89] As Karl Lamprecht noted in 1896, these *Vereine* frequently indulged in *kleindeutsch* reveries and shunned the political, "great man" preoccupations of the professoriate, particularly the sort of national histories being written by Heinrich von Treitschke. "They are not much interested in political history," he wrote, "although they in no way exclude it as part of *Landesgeschichte*, but rather they are interested in the development of local conditions."[90] This reentrenchment of amateur cultural organization at the provincial level and the apparently rather lavish patronage accorded to such

---

[86] Dr. Nik, "Auch ein Wort zur Organization der römisch-germanischen Altertumsforschung," *Darmstädter Zeitung*, 11 April 1900, RGK Mappe, 259.

[87] Wolff's speech quoted in Alexander Conze, "Römisch-Germanische Forschung," in *AA* in *Jb des DAI*, 15 (1900): 11.

[88] Ibid., p. 14.

[89] For examples of these, see Braun, "Anfänge der Limesforschung," p. 55.

[90] Karl Lamprecht, "Die Königlich Sächsische Kommission für Geschichte," reprinted in idem, *Alternative zu Ranke: Schriften zur Geschichtstheorie*, ed. Hans Schleier (Leipzig, 1988), p. 344.

efforts by both local governments and private patrons[91] may help to explain the desperate appeals to the Reichstag for national support for professional, supralocal causes like the RGK, the South Polar Expedition, and the Berlin Museums' excavations in Asia Minor.[92] It underscores, in any case, the persistence of overlapping national and provincial institutions and interests, and strongly suggests that the reiteration of "Germanness" of objects discovered on Reich soil and the "national" nature of *Altertumskunde* belonged equally to the campaign for "spiritual and cultural unification," and the pursuit of state-funded, professional scholarship.

Gustav Kossinna and the Radicalization of Prehistory

In founding a German branch—one conceived as equal in status to those in Rome and Athens—the DAI abandoned the aesthetic and temporal bounds set by the Hyperboreans, as well as some part of the claim to practice only "disinterested" scholarship. It now seemed necessary to know and hold title to one's own earliest history, now conceived as a *German* history beginning with the first settlers rather than as human or Western history, beginning with the first writings of the ancients. Taking up where Ratzel, Virchow, and Mommsen left off, professors of classical archaeology, geography, philology, and history evinced a new interest in German *Altertumskunde*. Among archaeologists, the practice of petitioning the ministries for larger subsidies based on their indispensable service to national self-confidence and self-consciousness became common, as even the Kaiser's court, long entranced by classical digs abroad, began to evince interest in prehistorical studies.[93] In 1907, the RGZM informed the Education Ministry that an increase in its Reich subsidy was in order, as its tasks went beyond provincial boundaries, entailing "the elucidation of the earliest cultural beginnings of our *Volk*"[94]; and by 1913, the RGK was speaking of "the national mission, to which the commission is devoted."[95] By 1914, the identity between modern German

---

[91] In 1913, Schumacher reported the recent erection of new museum buildings in at least thirteen locations, and significant enlargements of buildings in nine locations in western Germany alone. See Schumacher, "Aus westdeutschen Museen," *Prähistorische Zeitschrift* 5 (1913): 568. Applegate notes the greatly expanded activities of the historical *Vereine* in the Pfalz during the last two decades of the century; by 1914, there were eleven historical museums for nine hundred thousand inhabitants of the region. See Applegate, *Nation of Provincials*, p. 93.

[92] See, for example, the debate in the 45th session (1 March 1899) of the Reichstag over the propriety of national, as opposed to provincial, cultural patronage. *Stenographische Berichte über die Verhandlungen des Reichstags*, X. Legislaturperiode, I. Session 1898–1900, 2:1221–50.

[93] See chapters 6 and 7.

[94] Dr. L. Beck to Education Ministry, 16 August 1907, in PA/AA/K 24–381, vol. 1.

[95] Dragendorff to Bethmann Hollweg, 4 July 1913, ibid., 42–501, adh. I, vol. 9.

and "Gothic man" (or "Hun," in the mouths of the wartime Allied propagandists) had become self-evident, and ignoring the culture of the *Germanen* was no longer possible, for the RGK or any other group of self-respecting German prehistorians.[96]

Having provided this introductory examination of the ideological and intellectual development of German prehistory, I now want to examine in detail the figure usually associated with the field's most egregious nationalist excesses, Gustav Kossinna. I do not mean to excuse Kossinna's undeniable racism, or qualify the evil uses to which some of his work was put. What I do want to underscore, however, are the peculiar conditions of the context in which he developed his ideas and methods. This context, as I have suggested above, was formed not only of nationalist campaigns to establish Germanic cultural autonomy, but also by K. O. Müller's historicist strictures and Winckelmann's faith in the uniqueness of classical, and especially Greek, cultural achievement. In a letter of 1880 to the American pioneer of social anthropology, L. H. Morgan, the Swiss scholar of primeval Rome J. J. Bachofen sketched out a critique along these lines, deploring the "onesidedness" of German classicists and the calamitous lack of comparativism their aestheticizing narrowness entailed:

> The German scholars, especially the classical philologists, suffer from a regrettable one-sidedness. Rarely does their view stray beyond the borders of the ancient world, or even beyond that of the particular people [they study]. Everything is isolated, every connection broken, and tried, criticized, and at last totally ruined, on the basis of modern coffee-table ideas [*Theetischideen*]. . . . Also, a false admiration of the so-called classicism of the Roman and Greek world, cultivated early in the schools, acts in this direction: Romans and Greeks are treated as a sort of chosen [people], who ought never to be compared to barbarian tribes, and every similarity with other mortals is completely forbidden. For later ages of development, this narrow horizon is not so injurious, but for the understanding of primeval conditions and the first developmental level of peoples, it is quite fatal. For everywhere these follow the same laws and are in all corners of the earth the same.[97]

If, in the years after Bachofen's death, prehistory in Germany—particularly outside the classicist conclave—moved further and further away from the universalism of Morgan and the British anthropologist E. B. Tylor, this is not to blamed on the prehistorians alone. The case of Kossinna may prove an instructive example.

Gustav Kossinna was born on 28 September 1858 in Tilsit, East Prussia—

---

[96] See chapter 7.

[97] Bachofen to L. H. Morgan, 29 October 1880, in *Johann Jakob Bachofens Gesammelte Werke*, ed. Karl Meuli, vol. 10: *Briefe*, ed. Fritz Husner (Basel, 1967), pp. 502–3.

from the cradle, a hypernationalist eulogist noted approvingly, a child of the eastern marches.[98] But if Kossinna had absorbed Germanophilic tendencies with his mother's milk, the signs were slow to manifest themselves. When he began his university career in the later 1870s, he was matriculated as a student of classical philology; his devotion to Germanic languages—and apparently to his patriotic mentor Karl Müllenhoff—evolved rather more gradually than his later pronouncements suggest.[99] But once determined to make German *Altertumskunde* his career, Kossinna persevered in his studies. As paid academic positions in prehistory did not yet exist, Kossinna supported his studies through years of impatient odd-jobbing in libraries and museums, where he developed his interests in archaeology and artifacts. But in 1902, his prayers were answered: as a result, apparently, of a well-received paper Kossinna had presented to a conference of folklorists in 1895, he was offered a new junior professorship of German archaeology at the University of Berlin.

In this paper, Kossinna had announced his intention to "bring together patriotic archaeology and history, and at the same time to end the anonymous status [*Subjektlosigkeit*] of the rich finds that have been collected in our land thanks to a century of work."[100] Kossinna's paper had located the ethnic question at the center of prehistorical reconstructions: the field, he claimed, ought to concentrate on writing of *German* prehistory, not pre-German *history*.[101] To this end, Kossinna hoped to use the work of comparative philologists on the "Indo-German question" as a framework for the interpretation of the myriad anonymous finds languishing in provincial museums. Kossinna, engaged, like Karl Lamprecht, in the attempt to write a "history without names," looked forward to the appearance of a synthetic story about German *Ur*-ancestry.[102]

Kossinna's early essays indicate his ability to combine positivism with patriotism—here in much milder form than this later syntheses would take. His first major essay, "Die indogermanische Frage archäologisch beantwortet" ("The Indo-Germanic question Answered Archaeologically"—1902), published in Virchow's *Zeitschrift für Ethnographie*, did not deal directly with racial questions; the point of the essay was, rather, to show that archaeological evidence could provide a better means for solving the question of the origins and migratory routes of the Indo-Germans (i.e., the Indo-Europeans) than could comparative philology. While the philologists continued to subscribe to the misguided belief in the Asiatic origins of

---

[98] Alfred Götze, "Gustav Kossinnas Leben und Wirken," in *Mannus* 24, no. 1–3 (1932): 7.

[99] Smolla, "Kossinna nach 50 Jahren," p. 10.

[100] Kossinna quoted ibid., pp. 11–12.

[101] Hans Jürgen Eggers, *Einführung in die Vorgeschichte* 3d ed., (Munich, 1986), p. 212.

[102] Smolla suggests some interesting parallels between Lamprecht's school and Kossinna's work; "Gustaf Kossinna," p. 13.

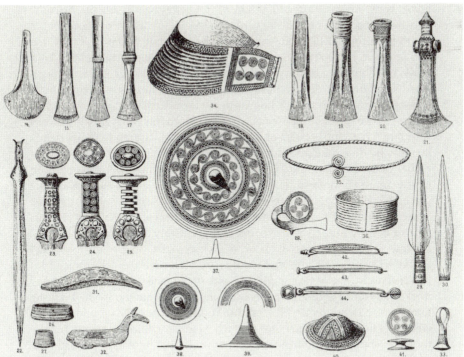

Abb. 114. Typen der zweiten Periode germanischer Bronzezeit aus Dänemark und Südschweden, überwiegend vom Ende dieser Periode (nach Montelius).

Männlich: 14—20. Beillfingen. 21. Arthammer. 22—27. Schwerter und Scheidenortbänder. 28. Gürtelhaken. 29. 30. Lanzenspitzen. 31. Säge. 32. Rasiermesser. 33. Haarzange. 40. Schwertriemenbuckelchen. 41. Doppelknopf.
Weiblich: 34. Halskragen. 35. Halsring. 36. Armband. 37. Gürtelplatte. 38. 39. Gürtelschmuck. 42—44. Gewandfibeln.

19. Page from Kossinna's *Die deutsche Vorgeschichte* (actually borrowed from the Swedish prehistorian, Oskar Montelius). Note the careful attention given to artifact types and ornamentation.

European civilization, all the credible prehistorical archaeologists had adopted the more reasonable theory of a northern primeval home.[103] As the philologists believed that the evolution of words and grammar could be used to write a history of the triumph of Christian Europeans, so Kossinna thought artifacts could tell even deeper, and more patriotic, prehistorical tales. Biology had not yet been added to his already dangerous mixture of scholarly quiddity and nationalist fervor.

But even before the appearance of this essay, there seems to have been a

[103] Gustav Kossinna, "Die indogermanische Frage archäologisch beantwortet," *Zeitschrift für Ethnographie* 34 (1902): 161. Although Kossinna is exaggerating here, it is the case that many early twentieth-century prehistorians had rejected *ex oriente lux*. See Sklenar, *Archaeology in Central Europe*, pp. 144–46.

break between Kossinna and Virchow,[104] after whose death the BGAEU, like Kossinna, grew increasingly interested in questions of race. I have found no record of Kossinna's views on the founding of the RGK, but it is unlikely that he took a generous view of the classicists' triumph; in later years, he adopted an openly hostile attitude toward the organization's members. Nor, however, did established classicists find Kossinna a sympathetic supporter or, though he was known to command a wealth of knowledge, a peer worthy of promotion. He never received from his colleagues the title of "ordinary" (i.e., full) professor, which would have assured him of a steady income. In 1908, much to Kossinna's annoyance, the well-connected biographer of Schliemann, Carl Schuchhardt, received the prestigious position of director of the prehistorical department of the Royal Museums. Kossinna perceived the appointment—and the founding of the *Prähistorische Zeitschrift* without his prior knowledge—as attempts by the classicist satraps to destroy himself in particular and prehistory in general, for he considered Schuchhardt, as a classical archaeologist, to be an "outsider" (*Nichtfachmann*).[105] From this moment we can date the appearance of a new *völkisch* (nationalist, populist, and often racist) note in Kossinna's work, coincident with a new drive for professional autonomy. In 1908, he founded the Deutsche Gesellschaft für Vorgeschichte (DGfV), and his own journal, *Mannus*, in which he courted Germanophiles, younger prehistorians, the provincial bureaucracy, and the all-important local prehistorical organizations.[106] Kossinna's strategy was clear: the excluded scholar spoke to those disinherited by centralization and professionalization, rallying them to take back lost scientific—and patriotic—territory. Classicist hegemony was to be circumvented by romancing the provinces and the old *Vereine*.

If Kossinna's organizational strategy entailed the marshaling of provincial and *völkisch* forces against the classicist establishment, his masterful methodological innovation, which he termed *Siedlungsarchäologie*, also assisted in the accomplishment of both disciplinary autarky and popular appeal. In 1911 he published his first full description of this methodology in *Die Herkunft der Germanen: Zur Methode der Siedlungsarchäologie* (*The Origins of the Germanic People: An Elaboration of the Method of Settlement Archaeology*), a short treatise in which the prehistorian offered his first theoretical discussion of the inseparability of style and race as components of past cultural

---

[104] Günter Smolla, review of Hildegard Gräfin Schwerin von Krosigk, *Gustav Kossinna* (1982), *Germania* 64 (1986): 683.

[105] See, Eggers, *Einführung*, pp. 222–23.

[106] In 1910, for example, Kossinna could be found touting the "wonderful harmony" of science, life, and worldview, and praising the Hanoverian *provincial* bureaucracy for investing money in "great archaeological tasks at home" instead of throwing it away in Babylon and Egypt. Kossinna, report on DGfV meeting in 1910, *Mannus* 1–2, suppl. vol. (1910–11): 10, 8.

life. "Ethnological" conclusions, he argued, could always be drawn from archaeological data, making unnecessary the recourse to written sources for positive proof. By mapping the distribution of, for example, bell-shaped beakers, the prehistorian could chart the westward progress of the racial and linguistic community that made these (i.e., the *Ur*-Germans). He formulated the following programmatic statement: "Cultural areas that are sharply bounded archaeologically always coincide with completely distinct peoples or races (*Völkerstammen*)."[107] The notion that archaeological remains could be used to reconstruct a lost sequence of settlers and settlements certainly was not new; Kossinna differed from earlier prehistorians only in his insistence on *sharply* defined, *coincident* cultural, linguistic, and racial borders. If many prehistorians who came after him would rue this departure from previous practice, many, too, would gratefully acknowledge the usefulness of Kossinna's distributional studies.[108] If Kossinna was anxious to end Germanic prehistory's dependence on (classical) texts, he also developed a method which, stripped of its racial presumptions, has been very valuable in showing archaeologists how to turn material evidence into historical documentation.

Kossinna's most political book was also his most popular. *Die deutsche Vorgeschichte: Eine hervorragende nationale Wissenschaft* (*German Prehistory: A Splendid National Discipline*) appeared in 1912 and in ten months the thousand-copy first edition was sold out. Originally a lecture presented to the Deutsche Gesellschaft für Vorgeschichte in 1911, by 1941 Kossinna's treatise was appearing in its eighth edition—this time with a preface by Alfred Rosenberg. Characteristically, Kossinna packed the volume with highly specific information and a great many extraneous illustrations; but the book's goals were absolutely clear: recovery of German racial pride in the nation's *ur*-history; raising of prehistory over classics as the true "scientific" means for this recovery; and acceptance of national prehistory as the model for the human sciences in the future. The very title of the book indicated that Kossinna's alienation from humanist academia was complete; emphasizing prehistory's "superior present value, its high national significance,"[109] Kossinna sought to expose the unpatriotic, self-interested aims that underlay the classicists' claims to "disinterestedness."

In his introduction, Kossinna modified an axiom of one of his heroes, Paul de Lagarde: "'Germandom lies not in the blood but in the mind.' Today

---

[107] Gustav Kossinna, *Die Herkunft der Germanen: Zur Methode der Siedlungsarchäologie*, 2d ed. (Leipzig, 1920), p. 3.

[108] See Albert Kiekebusch, "Siedlungsarchäologie," in *Reallexikon der Vorgeschichte*, vol. 12 (Berlin, 1928), pp. 102–17; here see especially pp. 104–5; Smolla, "Kossinna nach 50 Jahren," p. 13.

[109] Kossinna, *Die deutsche Vorgeschichte: Ein hervorragende nationale Wissenschaft*, 2d ed. (Würzburg, 1912), p. 5.

we know better and loudly avow: it is blood that makes the mind."[110] German blood and German culture were inseparable and as such provided the basis for Germandom, an ancient, civilized, and independent entity whose greatness could only be established by delving into the prehistorical past. The study of prehistory alone, he argued, circumvented the biased accounts of the German *Volk* handed down by those who up to now had formed the population's historical view—"the men wearing the blinkers of a *Gymnasium* education."[111] Thanks to them, this demeaning treatment of German ancestry and overestimation of the virtues of classical antiquity had become widespread. Modern historians pretended that everything that preceded the Italian Renaissance was *Unkultur*. Medieval art history taught that another Renaissance of the classics, the Carolingian, had first introduced high culture into the desolate Germanic world. Most of all Kossinna decried the misattributions of "the men who rule our higher education system," the classical philologists and archaeologists. "For them," he wrote sarcastically,

> [German] cultural life begins with the moment when, thanks to a merciful, heaven-sent coincidence, Rome marched to and then across the Rhine and thereby the privileged fate befell our forefathers, who were then such wretched, wild barbarians, that they were touched by a ray of the south- classical cultural sun and warmed through and through, and thus at last able to climb out of the eternal monotony of a dull life of pillage without any prospect of improvement.[112]

The whole of this anti-German drivel, Kossinna contended, could be easily countered by evidence available to the prehistorian—the true custodian of Germany's cultural heritage and facilitator of its heroic rejuvenation. The Romanist, on the other hand, had nothing but shopworn, seditious texts to offer.

Predictably, Kossinna's work proved very popular in the 1920s: he gained a large readership and numerous devoted students to replace the many lost on the battlefield. His work became more nationalist than ever and insistent upon the positive autonomy of German culture from southern influences.[113] Along with H. S. Chamberlain and Othmar Spann, he was recruited to speak to radical right-wing student groups.[114] But, if he was more successful than the RGK in attracting a loyal listening audience, he was considerably less capable of winning bureaucratic backing or, importantly, breaking down the geocultural barriers between *Germania romana* and *Ger-*

---

[110] Ibid., pp. 3–4.

[111] Ibid., p. 2.

[112] Ibid.

[113] See Michael Kater, *Das "Ahnenerbe" der SS, 1935–1945* (Stuttgart, 1974), p. 22.

[114] Walter Z. Laqueur, *Young Germany: A History of the German Youth Movement* (New York, 1962), p. 157.

mania libera. Tribalism, the nemesis of the ancient *Germanen,* continued to afflict prehistory right through the Nazi era and into the postwar period.

It is not critical, here, to pass judgment on Kossinna's contribution to the Nazification of his discipline; he clearly bears some responsibility, but surely not all.[115] For our purposes, it is only necessary to understand the ways in which his ideas and career were shaped, in part, by institutions and ideological configurations that belonged to the legacy of German neohumanism, but which had undergone considerable modification after 1871. Their participation in the process of "cultural and spiritual unification" thwarted, nationalist scholars like Kossinna became leaders of an alienated academic faction, eager to wrest power from an elitist cultural establishment, and to replace its passion for "disinterestedness" with their own patriotic fervor. Kossinna, it might be said, represents the first major attempt at generational and cultural revolution against classicist academe in the twentieth century. Seen from this angle, the *furor teutonicus* of the prehistorian and the silent grandeur of the Graecophile appear less opposites than two souls with but a single desire: the right to define German *Kultur,* and to dominate its production. "Augustus" had won the RGK battle, but "Arminius" would not wait long to challenge his rival anew.

[115] See the assessment of Ulrich Veit, "Gustav Kossinna and V. Gordon Childe: Ansätze zu einer theoretischen Grundlegung der Vorgeschichte," *Saeculum* 35 (1984): 326–64.

THE PECULIARITIES OF GERMAN ORIENTALISM

> Look at these stupid foreigners! I pacify them with
> broken stones.
> (*Sultan Abdul Hamid II*)

OF VITAL IMPORTANCE to the understanding of the sacred history of Adam's heirs as well as to the profane history of the progress of nations, European study of the Orient entered the era of hyperimperialism boasting a long and venerable record of philological and exegetical achievements.[1] Christian interest in Hebrew and Islamic texts certainly predates the Reformation, but the rise of interest in the sixteenth century in world religions clearly gave new impetus to forays into these fields. Humanists like Johannes Reuchlin and Philipp Melanchthon studied Hebrew together with Latin and Greek, but by the midseventeenth century, separate chairs began to be devoted to the study of Hebrew texts. If training in Hebrew, as a crucial part of the training of Christian exegetes, fell off in the eighteenth century, the important school of oriental philology under J. Michaelis and J. G. Eichhorn in Göttingen showed scholars of the Enlightenment—including F. A. Wolf—that biblical criticism could provide important models and information for classical scholarship.[2] It was really only after the passing of the Romantic "oriental Renaissance"—featuring Herder's celebration of the beauty of Jewish literature and Creuzer's discovery of *Ur*-monotheism in India—that orientalists and classical neohumanists went their separate ways.[3]

But already in the eighteenth century, specialization, travel, and practical diplomatic concerns had begun to create a subset of orientalists whose interests lay primarily in the secular history of the Orient. An Imperial-Royal

---

[1] See Paolo Rossi, *The Dark Abyss of Time: The History of the Earth and the History of Nations from Hooke to Vico*, trans. Lydia G. Cochrane (Chicago, 1984); Anthony Grafton, *Defenders of the Text: The Traditions of Scholarship in an Age of Science* (Cambridge, Mass., 1991).

[2] Frank Manuel, *The Broken Staff: Judaism through Christian Eyes* (Cambridge, 1992), pp. 106–64; Grafton, "Introduction," in F. A. Wolf, *Prolegomena to Homer*, trans. and introd. Anthony Grafton, Glenn W. Most, and James E. G. Zetzel (Princeton, N.J., 1985), pp. 18–26.

[3] The term "oriental Renaissance" was coined by Raymond Schwab, *The Oriental Renaissance: Europe's Discovery of India and the East, 1680–1880*, trans. Gene Patterson-Black and Victor Reinking (New York, 1984).

Academy of Oriental Languages was opened in Vienna in 1753, primarily in order to provide insightful diplomats and reliable translators for the Austrian state; in 1766, the Danish traveler-scholar Carsten Niebuhr made a well-publicized stop in Persepolis, on his way home from Bombay.[4] Five years later, Abraham Hyacinthe Anquetil-Duperron published the first translation of the *Zend Avesta*; according to Raymond Schwab, this edition "marks the first approach to an Asian text totally independent of the biblical and classical traditions."[5] In 1809, the Austrian orientalist Joseph von Hammer Purgstall announced the founding of a journal for "dilettantes" interested in the Orient; in the opening issue, he insisted that contributors offer essays on mathematics, law, topography, geography, religion, history, and statistics—anything but theology and current politics.[6] Yet, until the later nineteenth century, *Orientalistik* was largely limited to the study of oriental languages and was linked either to the training of travelers (missionaries, entrepreneurs, officials) or to theological pursuits; as was the case in classical studies, material remains (especially coins) helped to establish dates and rulers, but otherwise *Realien* played a very minor, auxiliary role.

Like classical philologists and early archaeologists, German orientalists had rarely ventured beyond Rome in their travels. Prussian Ambassador Bunsen wrote his multivolume *Aegyptens Stelle in der Weltgeschichte* (*Egypt's Place in World History*—1846–57) without leaving his post in Rome; Eduard Sachau, who received his professorship at the University of Vienna in 1869, saw the Orient for the first time a decade after his appointment.[7] In 1863, Georg Ebers even published a set of "Reisebriefe aus Ägypten" ("Letters from an Egyptian Voyage") without having visited the country himself.[8] In part, this lack of real contact was the result of Germany's backwardness in imperial expropriation. But the fact that the Germans lacked, in the words of Edward Said, "a protracted, sustained *national* interest in the Orient,"[9] was also partly the result of *Orientalistik's* inferior institutional position with respect to classical philology. While classicists could generally find jobs in the *Gymnasien*, orientalists had little future outside the university theological faculties. State funding for research on things oriental—especially secular or material things—remained very low

[4] Karl Roider, "The Oriental Academy in the *Theresienzeit*," in *Topic: A Journal of the Liberal Arts* 34 (1980): 19–28; Svend Aage Pallis, *The Antiquity of Iraq: A Handbook of Assyriology* (Copenhagen, 1956), p. 43.

[5] Schwab, *Oriental Renaissance*, p. 17.

[6] Joseph von Hammer Purgstall, "Vorrede," *Fundgruben des Orients* 1 (1809): iv.

[7] Johann Fück, *Die arabischen Studien in Europa bis in den Anfang des 20. Jahrhunderts* (Leipzig, 1955), p. 234.

[8] Hans Fischer, *Der Ägyptologe Georg Ebers: Eine Fallstudie zum Problem Wissenschaft und Öffentlichkeit im 19. Jahrhundert* (Wiesbaden, 1994), p. 101.

[9] Edward Said, *Orientalism* (New York, 1979), p. 19.

until the last years of the century. Despite Lepsius's triumphs, Egyptology remained socially, culturally, and monetarily far behind classical studies.[10] India, though central to comparative philologists and, thanks to Schopenhauer, increasingly popular among neo-Romantics, was too distant and too firmly under British control to appeal to the German bureaucracy. It was, at least initially, the promise of finding rich *classical* remains on the Ionian coast that inspired the Reich to enter the competition for acquisitions in the East.

Carl Humann's excavations at Pergamum, of course, marked the opening of this quest, but in the decades after Humann's great finds, changes in diplomatic relations between the new Reich and the failing Ottoman Empire would permit the undertaking of a grand series of new endeavors. In the 1870s and 1880s, Sultan Abdul Hamid II had suffered a series of humiliating financial setbacks and debilitating military defeats. A breach in Franco-Ottoman relations was followed by a disastrous war with Russia in 1877, the economically paralyzing erection of a European-led committee to administer the Ottoman public debt in 1881, and the humbling extension of British colonial control in Egypt in 1882. Also confronted with ethnic irredentism on the Ottoman peripheries, Abdul Hamid, not surprisingly, began to listen eagerly to overtures from the German Empire, the one great power without any obvious interest in the wholescale or partial dismemberment of the Ottoman state. In 1883 General Colmar Freiherr von der Goltz led a military mission to Turkey; in 1888, two prominent German bankers were awarded the concession to build a railway from Ankara to Constantinople, with a view to extending the line to Baghdad. In 1889, Kaiser Wilhelm II made his first visit to the Ottoman capital, and in the following year the two imperial powers signed a mutually beneficial trade agreement, multiplying German entrepreneurial contact with the southeast and giving new currency to midcentury fantasies about Germany's destiny in *Mitteleuropa*.

This seeming abandonment of German neutrality in the East took place against the fervent opposition of Bismarck, who hoped to play Austrian, Russian, and British interests off against one another without entangling the Reich in Ottoman affairs.[11] Even after the chancellor's departure from office in 1890, and despite increased German investment in Asia Minor, the new Kaiser's sympathy for his Turkish counterpart, and the procolonialist agitation of Pan-Germans, the Foreign Ministry more or less retained the Bismarckian conviction that Germany should preserve its posture as neutral spectator in Asia Minor—in the meanwhile exploiting raw materials and

[10] See Georg Ebers, "Die Ausgrabungen in Aegypten und die deutsche Aegyptologie" [1895], in idem, *Aegyptische Studien und Verwandtes* (Stuttgart, 1900), pp. 124–35.

[11] See Gregor Schöllgen, *Imperialismus und Gleichgewicht: Deutschland, England und die orientalische Frage, 1871–1914* (Munich, 1984), esp. chap. 1.

developing markets for German goods inside the Ottoman state. And even with the further strengthening of German-Turkish economic and diplomatic ties after 1898, Foreign Ministry representatives were careful to preserve the fiction of neutrality in oriental affairs and to cloak colonial or semicolonial ambitions in high-minded rhetoric about German's civilizing mission abroad.[12] Disinterestedness, or at least the illusion of disinterestedness, was believed to be in the state's best interest.

One of the most often-voiced motives underpinning German intervention in Asia was the notion that Germany had been entrusted with a special mission to bring *Kultur* to the unenlightened Turks. The counterpart in the intellectual sphere to the economic modernizing mission of the Baghdad Railway, German cultural activity in the Ottoman Empire allegedly aimed at the creation of a spiritual bond between the two nations as well as the cultivation of a consumer market for German products.[13] This idea was neither new nor specifically German in character. Ever since the Reformation, both Protestant and Catholic missionaries had ventured forth to teach their faiths and German language to heathens worldwide, and the French and the British, of course, had long since shouldered their own variants of the White Man's Burden. But the Germans, as usual, were late in taking up as a national pursuit what had been the preserve of local or denominational groups—so late, in fact, that the bureaucracy felt obliged to intervene in the process to speed and streamline the construction of German-Turkish "friendships." Germany's *"pénétration pacifique"*[14] required state management; even cultural philanthropy, at this stage of imperialist hostilities, was too important to be left to private groups and amateur activists.

The studious cultivation of a disinterested and antiutilitarian reputation had, of course, been the preoccupation of the nineteenth-century German scholarly community: the apolitical neutrality of German scholars had become something of a national bragging point and grounds for asserting Germany's right to a place in the sun. Such qualifications made German scholars ideally suited to assume the duties of overseas cultural emissaries; an exclusively scholarly *Kulturpolitik*[15] complemented the diplomatic strategy of preserving the outward sovereignty and territorial integrity of the regime, offering irreproachable evidence that Germany wished only to contribute to Turkish modernization and the international quest for new and pure knowledge. German scholars, of course, had their own reasons for

---

[12] See Erich Lindow, *Freiherr Marschall von Bieberstein als Botschafter in Konstantinopel, 1897–1912* (Danzig, 1934), p. 43.

[13] See Gregor Schöllgen, "'Dann müssen wir uns aber Mesopotamien sichern!'" *Saeculum* 32 (1981): 142–44.

[14] Schöllgen, *Imperialismus*, p. xiv.

[15] For a full description of *Kulturpolitik*, see chapter 7.

wishing to expand their activities abroad, not least among which was the desire to make material the preeminence Prussia had achieved in the intellectual sphere. As the Reich bureaucracy commenced a policy of subsidizing professorial exchanges, conferences, lecture tours, and costly exhibits at international fairs, and began the process of founding institutes devoted to linguistic and cultural training of bureaucrats and businessmen, the Wilhelmine Empire entered an era characterized by a new interdependence of cultural and political spheres.

Such a confluence of aims was particularly apparent in classical archaeology. As we have seen, the discipline's slow divergence from classical philology had been hastened as Germany's rise to world-power status introduced a desperate desire to bring the Berlin museum collections up to the level of those of the Louvre and the British Museum. But both museum officials and archaeologists wished to preserve the lofty aura of pure scientificness, as they had done at Olympia; not only would this play a critical role in assuaging foreign complaints about Turkish favoritism, but it also reassured a *Gymnasium*-educated elite that their motives were free from the utilitarian spirit they so despised in the anticlassicist school reform movement. Alexander Conze insisted that digs in Asia Minor be performed by the DAI, not by the museums, in order to insure preservation of the artifacts for future generations and to avoid reputation-damaging charges of "interested" acquisitiveness. This arrangement pleased both museum administrators and the diplomatic corps, for it permitted the acquisition of finds without compromising the policy of official neutrality. Ironically, German archaeologists in Asia Minor did indeed carry out the most painstakingly "scientific" excavations of the era, but they did so at the cost of increasing the dependence of scholarly progress in classics on the Kaiser's wiles and the Foreign Ministry's savoir-faire. In proceeding from words to things, from German lecture halls to far-flung eastern locales, German classical studies became ensnarled in the contradictions and covert designs of the *pénétration pacifique*.

The Orientalizing Altruism of Wilhelm II

Like the study of Germanic prehistory, the archaeological exploration of the Orient was not initially the exclusive province of the DAI. Efforts to organize expeditions in the early 1880s were undertaken by several different bodies, with varying amounts of public funding and varying relationships to the academy and/or the state. In 1881, the Education Ministry funded an expedition to Palestine by the Deutscher Verein zur Erforschung Palästinas (German Association for the Study of Palestine), but approved only three thousand marks for the venture; in 1883, the state devoted thirty-five thousand marks to the Prussian Academy of Sciences plan (backed by Helmuth von Moltke) to explore Kurdistan.[16] As the state bureaucracy, especially the chancellor, was still not wholly convinced of the virtues of excavation overseas, the DAI could not depend on state subsidies until after the ascension of Wilhelm II.[17] All manner of efforts were made to raise funds for digs in the Orient, culminating in 1887 with the creation of the Comité behufs Erforschung der Trümmerstätten des Alten Orients (Committee for the Study of the Ruins of the Ancient Orient, or "Orient-Comité"), consisting of what one archaeologist described as "scholars and moneybags."[18] This organization funded several expeditions to Cengerli (in northern Syria) between 1888 and 1902, but its administration by private citizens made its results dissatisfying to the museums, for the acquisitions made during these expeditions belonged to the Orient-Comité, and had to be purchased individually at great cost.[19]

During the 1890s, German archaeological excavation in Asia Minor expanded rapidly, owing much to new state funds as well as Orient-Comité monies now flowing into overseas projects. In addition to the expeditions organized by the Academy of Sciences, the DAI directed digs (funded by the museums and the Kaiser, as well as with budgeted funds from the Foreign Ministry, approved by the Reichstag) at Priene (1895–98), Magnesia (1891–93), and Thera (1895–1902). The Orient-Comité sent five parties to Cengerli between 1888 and 1902; excavations at Troy were recommended with funds allocated by the Kaiser in 1893. DAI and museum administration expenditures grew exponentially, and their budgets increased by leaps and bounds, even though actual excavation costs were often funded separately through bequests from the Kaiser's privy purse. DAI officials, museum bureaucrats, Academy of Science members, politicians, and diplomats in far-flung places descended on the Kaiser with excavation plans, petitions for funding, and earnest assurances of swift national museological triumph. Count Radolin (ambassador in Constantinople, 1892–97) warned the Foreign Ministry that were the Reich not forthcoming with sufficient funds (he estimated three hundred thousand marks) to show their capability of finish-

[16] On the DvzEP dig, see DVzEP to Goßler, 28 October 1882, in PZStA AA/R 37745, pp. 45–6. On Kurdistan see Goßler to Wilhelm I, 27 March 1883, in MZStA 2.2.1–20772, pp. 178–84.

[17] In 1882, Conze told Humann that while renewal of the Pergamum subsidy was in the works, "how we are supposed to find funds for Nemrut Dağ and Sakçagözü only the gods now know. . . ." Quoted in Friedrich Karl Dörner, Kommagene: Götterthrone und Königsgräber am Euphrat (Bergisch Gladbach, 1981), p. 66.

[18] Adolf Erman to Karl Humann, 5 December 1887, in DAI, Nachlaß Humann, Kasten 2. Erman's description was accurate: the Comité treasurer was none other than Bismarck's personal banker Dr. Georg von Bleichroeder, and "scientific" members included Conze, Curtius, Sachau, and Erman.

[19] Ludwig Pallat, Richard Schöne: Generaldirektor der Königlichen Museen in Berlin (Berlin, 1959), pp. 187, 189; Bosse to Wilhelm II, 7 October 1898, in PZStA AA/R 37692, pp. 35–40.

ing a massive excavation at Miletus, the French would surely receive the necessary excavation permit (*firman*). An attached note explained that the dig at Miletus was of vital importance "because here is perhaps the last point where sizeable art treasures in the area in question [Greek settlements on the Turkish coast] are to be found."[20] Even Rudolf Virchow denounced the Reich for its laxity in procuring oriental originals; in a speech to the Prussian Landtag, Virchow angrily contrasted the "extraordinary treasures" collected by the British and French to the paltry cast collections displayed in German museums.[21]

Meanwhile, from still further afield, in Baghdad, Consul Richarz, clearly uncomfortable in an area of French and British predominance, applied regularly to the Foreign Ministry to send German archaeologists to Mesopotamia. In 1896, Richarz proposed a German dig on the site of the ancient city of Uruk and its surrounding settlements. "Frenchmen, Englishmen, and North Americans have overlooked it," Richarz enthused, "just as if by means of fate's decree, the act of unearthing these cultural centers, these schools which produced thousands of years of ancient wisdom, were reserved for the nation of poets and thinkers, the *docta Germania*."[22] Their interests moving further and further eastward, the German scholars and businessmen of the Orient-Comité evinced great enthusiasm for Richarz's plan.[23] Shortly thereafter, the Academy of Sciences took up the cause: "It could only befit the cultural significance of the German Reich," the academy told Education Minister Robert Bosse, "if German work in the future no longer remains unrepresented where there is a world lost from human memory to resurrect and millennia of human histories, sculptural works, and inscriptions to recover." Dispelling fears that the nation might receive no concrete recompense, the academy claimed "that treasures of the previously mentioned types [inscriptions, statues, reliefs], like those that fill the halls of the British Museum and the Louvre, are still there . . . in great quantity." An Uruk expedition, the academy concluded, would be of great profit "to science in general and to German science in particular, as well as to our public collections."[24]

In matters archaeological as in matters naval and imperial, blame for Ger-

---

[20] Radolin to Foreign Ministry, 17 July 1894, ibid., 37718, pp. 2–4. Radolin had reported previously that Humann might be able to tap the industrialist Friedrich Krupp for the necessary funds; what happened to this plan is unclear. See Radolin to Caprivi, 17 June 1894, ibid., pp. 6–8.

[21] Johannes Renger, "Die Geschichte der Altorientalistik und der vorderasiatischen Archäologie in Berlin von 1875–1945," in *Berlin und die Antike*, vol. 1, ed. Willmuth Arenhövel and Christa Schreiber (Berlin, 1979), p. 159.

[22] Richarz to Hohenlohe, 25 August 1896, in PZStA AA/R 37690, pp. 74–75.

[23] Orient-Comité to Hohenlohe, 2 February 1897, ibid., pp. 85–86.

[24] Königliche Akademie der Wissenschaften to Bosse (Education Ministry), 13 February 1897, in ibid., 37691, pp. 11–14.

many's backwardness was placed squarely on the central state; that is, whereas in other countries individuals, private groups, and universities took on much of the burden of keeping pace with international scholarly achievements, in Germany, "keeping up" scientifically became an official imperative, an indispensable aspect of national self-esteem. In 1900, DAI General Secretary Conze informed Chancellor Hohenlohe that the allocation of sufficient funding for German digs was an urgent requirement, "for the sake of our standing among nations."[25] Invocations of national pride and concern for international scholarly standing were not uniquely German, but part of a larger decosmopolitanizing of the study of antiquity—characterized, to take a clear example, by the founding of separate archaeological "schools" in Rome and Athens by the major European powers in the 1870s and 1880s. In addition, the German archaeologists' appeal to patriotic sentiments to obtain funds for *Kulturpolitik* abroad cannot be equated with the frenzied nationalism of the Pan-German or Navy leagues. But once archaeology was established as a realm for the representation of national triumphs, in an era of ever-increasing agitation for colonial conquests and other demonstrations of Germany's newfound international prestige, this logic could hardly be undone.

In the final years of the century, three essential events consolidated this coincidence of state and scientific goals in Asia Minor: the founding of the Deutsche Orient-Gesellschaft (German Orient Society—DOG) in 1898, the Kaiser's second friendship visit to Constantinople and the Levant (also 1898), and the negotiation of a secret exportation treaty between Germany and the Sublime Porte (1899). In the wake of these developments,German archaeological work in the east underwent vast expansion. A "general consulate" for archaeology was established in Cairo in 1899. In 1907, this "consulate" officially became the Institut für ägyptische Altertumskunde; in 1928, it was placed under the administration of the DAI.[26] Excavations were undertaken at a great many sites, funded by numerous state-affiliated agencies including the DAI, the Prussian Landtag, the Academy of Sciences, the Royal Museums, the DOG, and the Kaiser himself. A partial list of the major efforts would include the following digs: Miletus, Baalbek, Pergamum (recommenced in 1901), Kos, Boghazkoi (ancient Hattusa), Didyma, Samos, Borsippa, Far and Abu-Hatab, Ash Shargāt (ancient Assur), Babylon, Axum, Abusir, Jericho, Tel El Amarna, and Warka (ancient Uruk). It is impossible to reckon the total costs of the undertakings to the German state, but a rough idea can be garnered from Wiegand's (conservative) estimate that between about 1899 and 1913, more than four million marks in public and

[25] Conze to Hohenlohe, 31 May 1900, ibid., 37815, pp. 46–53.

[26] Space does not permit a full discussion here of German Egyptological institutions. See Werner Kaiser, *75 Jahre Deutsches Archäologisches Institut Kairo, 1907–1982* (Mainz, 1982).

private funds had been devoted to digs in Asia Minor.[27] Ushering in this era of enormous scholarly, political, and psychological investment in archaeology, each of these three facilitating events were intimately intertwined with progress of Germany's *pénétration pacifique*.

The DOG was officially founded in January 1898, with a presidium that included two well-connected princes, the director of the Deutsche Bank and president of the Baghdad Railway, Georg von Siemens, the under secretary of the Foreign Ministry and director of the Colonial Office, Freiherr Friedrich von Richthofen, Admiral F. Hollmann (a close personal friend of the Kaiser), the archbishop of Breslau, several other powerful politicians and bankers, Althoff, Schöne, Sachau, and Conze. Regular members included important businessmen, well-established professors, diplomats, trade representatives, churchmen of both cloths, and members of the Reichstag.[28] F. A. Krupp pledged a yearly subsidy of 3000 marks; and in 1901, the Kaiser himself took over the official protection of the body. Yet despite the wealth and prominence of its backers, after a few years of heavy private investment, the DOG became more and more a funnel for funds granted by the Kaiser and the Prussian state. Officially, it remained a subsidiary of the museum administration, and thus its finds automatically became state property. After reaching a peak of 307,397 marks in 1903 (the Kaiser, 50,000 marks; Prussia, 88,600 marks), total income began to drop, even though state contributions increased. By 1909, the Reich was paying a total of 150,000 marks of a 215,905-mark budget.[29] What had begun as an association of private patrons had quickly become a holding company for the Reich's cultural investment in the Ottoman Empire.

In the announcements and minutes of the DOG, exhortations to realize Germany's long overdue cultural mission in the Orient played a major role; here the progress of knowledge had clearly become an object of national competition and a less belligerent realm for the expression of resentment at Germany's late leap into colonial activity. The organization's call for membership in late 1897 noted growing interest in Babylonian and Assyrian literature and art worldwide, and the great service to historical understanding performed by "the Anglo-Saxon countries" in taking up with such vigor these studies, so important to the understanding of the Bible. Having established the scholarly contributions and especially the museological conquests of rival nations, the Society went on to register its discontent with Germany's paltry supply of oriental artifacts. "The undersigned are of the opinion," proclaimed the document signed by the organization's most

[27] Wiegand, Promemoria to embassy, Bode, and Helfferich (to be passed on to the Foreign Ministry) 13 November 1913, copy in Wiegand's diary, vol. 2, in DAI, Nachlaß Wiegand, Kasten 23.

[28] DOG membership list in MZStA, Nachlaß Schmidt–Ott, A-XXXIX, vol. 1, p. 18.

[29] See "Jahresberichte," ibid., pp. 107ff.

prominent members, "that the time has come for us Germans to take our part in the great work of opening up and recovering the most ancient Orient by means of systematic excavation and thereby to supply German scholarship with the necessary materials for the expansion of oriental archaeology, as well as [to supply] our public collections with monuments of ancient Asiatic art."[30] Similarly, an announcement in the *National-Zeitung* expressed the need for excavation and collection as the logical and deserved end of German *Orientalistik* and the key to establishing the Orient as a vital field for historical inquiry. The French and the British were unearthing treasures throughout Egypt and the Orient, the article claimed:

> But Germany's inferior position with respect to excavations in Asia Minor, especially in Babylon and Assyria, in no way equivalent [to that of other European nations], stands in the sharpest contrast to the intensive and successful research in philology, general history, and cultural history that we have conducted precisely in this area. This inferior position affects not only our museum collections, but also is reflected in the public's prevailing view [of oriental history and artifacts]. Outside professional and scholarly circles, many regard Babylonian and Assyrian history and culture as curiosities and frequently make fun of them.[31]

The DOG could not be satisfied with grasping Helen's veil, as had Faust in Goethe's great epic; this organization of scholars, bankers, politicians, and churchmen wanted to *possess* material proofs of the grandeur of the oriental past.

On October 18, 1898, Wilhelm II arrived in Constantinople to commence his tour of the Levant. His trip followed German negotiation of peace between Greece and the Ottoman Empire, ending a potentially volatile series of skirmishes over Crete and Macedonia. Taking the part of the Turks against France and Russia, which defended Greece, and Britain, which tried to snatch Crete for itself, the Germans had reasserted their commitment to the preservation of the Ottoman state. Wilhelm's journey also followed four years of Turkish massacres in Christian Macedonia and Armenia, and his friendly bearing toward the Sultan was seen by other European powers as a slap in the face of public morality. Before his departure, Wilhelm had been drawn into the campaign to wrest new permits from the Turks by Reinhold Kekulé von Stradonitz, whose lectures on antiquity had impressed the young Kaiser and who had recently been appointed director of the Sculpture Department of the Royal Museums.[32] In Constantinople, the enterpris-

---

[30] Untitled announcement, ibid., vol. 1, p. 17. See also Friedrich Delitzsch's *Ex Oriente Lux! Ein Wort zur Förderung der Deutschen Orient-Gesellschaft* (Leipzig, 1898).

[31] "Eine Deutsche Orient Gesellschaft," *National-Zeitung* 19 January 1898 (morning edition), in MZStA, Nachlaß Schmidt-Ott, A-XXXIX, vol. 1, pp. 21–22.

[32] Carl Watzinger, *Theodor Wiegand* (Munich, 1944), p. 85.

ing young excavator Theodor Wiegand took up the museums' cause, pleading for the Kaiser's intercession to gain a profitable agreement from the Turks on the distribution of finds from projected digs at Miletus, Baalbek, and Babylon.[33] At a second encounter during the imperial journey, Wiegand urged Wilhelm to support a general expansion of German archaeological work in Asia Minor.[34] On the Kaiser's return to the Reich, Chancellor Bernhard von Bülow spoke before the Reichstag on the subject of Germany's right to extend its protection over its citizens abroad, opening a new campaign to spread German *Kultur* overseas, and Wilhelm faithfully took up Wiegand's cause as part of this cultural calling. He undoubtedly broached the matter of permits for German digs in Mesopotamia with the Sultan,[35] employing his "friendship" with his Turkish counterpart—a tactic he would repeatedly return to in future years—to extract concessions above and beyond those agreed to by the Turkish antiquities administration.

A major concession won by just such imperial intervention was the secret antiquities accord of 1899. In April 1897, Schöne had requested that the matter of acquiring finds to compensate the Royal Museums for their expenditures be broached with Turkish officials. Though the Turkish antiquities law of 1884 specified that all finds became the property of the Ottoman government, the close personal relationship between Carl Humann and Hamdi Edhem Bey, longtime director of the Ottoman Museums, had always enabled the Germans to negotiate more favorable arrangements. Schöne, however, feared this personal tie would be costly as well as unreliable, and pointed jealously to the Austrian excavation at Ephesus, where personal decrees of the Sultan allowed the excavators to retain the choicest finds. Why, then, reasoned the museum director, could not an official agreement, giving Germany at any rate half of all finds, be negotiated between the Sultan and the Kaiser?[36] Months later, the new ambassador in Constantinople, Adolf Freiherr Marschall von Bieberstein, told Chancellor Chlodwig zu Hohenlohe that as soon as the Priene excavations were complete, the arrangement proposed by Schöne should be conveyed to the Sultan as the personal wish of the Kaiser.[37] Joining in the call for an overall treaty, Wiegand reported to the Foreign Ministry that the French and Russians, as well as the Austrians, had made special deals with the Sultan.[38] A year later, Wiegand reiterated his request for Wilhelm's personal intervention to reach

---

[33] See copies of the following letters in Wiegand's diary, vol. 1 (1896–99), DAI, Nachlaß Wiegand, Kasten 22: Kekulé to Wiegand, 11 October 1898 (pp. 40–41); Wiegand to Kekulé, 24 October 1898 (pp. 31–2).

[34] Marschall to Hohenlohe, 7 December 1898, in PZStA AA/R 37693, pp. 75–77.

[35] Bosse to Wilhelm II, 7 October 1898, ibid., 37718, pp. 75–85.

[36] Schöne to Bosse, 27 April 1897, ibid., pp. 59–61.

[37] Marschall to Hohenlohe, 25 January 1898 and 4 March 1898, ibid., pp. 65–67 and pp. 69–70, respectively.

[38] Wiegand to Foreign Ministry, 2 March 1898, DAI, Nachlaß Wiegand, Kasten 13.

an agreement like that enjoyed by the Russians (finds split between the excavaters and the Turks), now especially to be recommended given "the excellent relations between Turkey and the German Empire and the great personal veneration of the Sultan for His Majesty, our most gracious Kaiser."[39] The excavator even made a special trip to Berlin to breakfast with the sovereign, fortifying with photographs of the Greek monuments of Priene and Baalbek the Kaiser's determination to bring home material commemorations of German prowess in the pursuit of knowledge.[40]

Finally, in November 1899, the Sublime Porte issued a *Note verbale* announcing: "The [Turkish] Foreign Ministry has the honor of informing the Ambassador of his Majesty the German Emperor that an *irade* of his Imperial Majesty the Sultan now authorizes the Berlin Museums to keep for themselves half the antiquities that they discover in the course of authorized investigations."[41] This blanket concession meant much to the Royal Museums, for unlike the Russians and Austrians, who invested less state money in archaeological pursuits and acquired fewer sites on which to dig, the Germans could now look forward to years of continuous, fruitful exploitation of the cultural riches of the eastern Mediterranean. And yet, the museum bureaucrats, archaeologists, and diplomats who had hoped this secret agreement would simplify the acquisition of grand monuments found themselves unable to do more than threaten to invoke the treaty when lower-level Turkish officials balked at their demands. For the invocation of this *irade* would have been undesirable for both sides, exposing the Sultan to internal criticism and German diplomats and scholars to attacks on their neutrality. It is testimony both to the Germany's ultimate designs on the Ottoman Empire and to the manifold frustrations entailed in the Reich's "informal" approach, that in 1919 Royal Museums Director Wilhelm von Bode would press for the passage of an explicit exportation law, based on that of colonized Egypt, and the immediate resumption of all excavations halted by Hamdi Bey and the Great War.[42]

Archaeological Diplomacy and Cultural Imperialism, 1900–1905

If the founding of the elite DOG, the newfound friendship between the Sultan and the Kaiser, and the negotiation of a secret acquisitions accord

[39] See Wiegand's Promemoria dated May 1899 in PZStA AA/R 37718, pp. 110–12.

[40] See Watzinger, *Wiegand*, pp. 89–90.

[41] Reprinted in Bernstorff (Embassy Pera) to Reichskanzler Hertling, 11 May 1918, in PA/AA/K 27–468a, vol. 2.

[42] Bode, "Zusammenstellung der bei den Friedensverhandlungen geltend zu machenden dringenden Forderungen der Museen-Verwaltung," passed from the Education Ministry to the Foreign Ministry, 3 February 1919, ibid.

infused German archaeological work in Asia Minor with new funds, force, and political significance, this entanglement of scholarly and quasi-imperialist ambitions posed new problems for the *Altertumswissenschaftler*. A new generation of more assertive mien had joined the campaign in the East, eager to apply imperial pressure on reluctant or simply inefficient Turks. As some archaeologists on the ground quickly realized, however, diplomatic pressures brought to bear on Turkish officials could often be counterproductive, jeopardizing the negotiation of new permissions or lucrative acquisition treaties. The expansion of German undertakings after the century's start, inciting a corresponding rise in Turkish circumspection and internal dissension, would require an archaeological diplomacy of greater finesse—and produce a cultural "friendship" characterized by increasing levels of suspicion and mutual distrust.

Due to the constraints imposed by informal imperialism, the extension of German archaeological work in the East was at every step bound up with changes in international, as well as Turkish domestic political affairs. The Reich depended heavily on the preservation of the personal relationship Humann had established with Hamdi Edhem Bey, sometime Turkish cultural minister and director of the Ottoman Museums from 1881 until his death in 1910. Hamdi was the son of Edhem Pasha, an influential former grand vizier, who had attempted to force the English archaeologist Hormuzd Rassam to donate his finds to the Ottoman Museums. Foreshadowing his sons' frustrations, Edhem Pasha had had his orders revoked by the Sultan, under friendly pressure from the British ambassador, A. H. Layard.[43] Hamdi had been educated in Europe and had absorbed to a considerable degree European tastes and the nineteenth-century—German—scholarly ethos. Part of Hamdi's European experience had included training in oil painting, which he had accomplished in Paris, ironically under the tutelage of France's foremost "orientalist" painter, Jean-Léon Gérôme; in the Sultan's eyes, this artistic training made Hamdi a suitable candidate for the directorship of the museums, a position held by the German classical philologist Anton Déthier until his death in 1881.[44] Halil, Hamdi's younger brother (who would succeed him as museums director, holding the post until 1931), also attended *Gymnasium* in Germany and studied chemistry at the universities of Vienna and Zurich. The brothers came of age in an era of double-pronged Ottoman policy, in which the Sultan sought to emphasize the Muslim, non-Western aspects of his regime, while simultaneously attempting to modernize the army, civil service, and educational system along European lines. It was precisely from this contradictory milieu that the Young Turk movement arose, composed largely of Western-oriented Muslim

---

[43] Rudolf Zehnpfund, "Die Wiederentdeckung Nineves," *Der alte Orient* 5 (1903): 24.

[44] Watzinger, *Wiegand*, pp. 179, 79.

patriots. Both Hamdi and Halil were close to this movement, whose tenets underlay much of their—and by extension, much of the Ottomans state's—archaeological diplomacy.

The passage of the first Ottoman antiquities protection code in 1884—engineered by Hamdi and Halil—followed closely on the heels of several major European expropriations, including that of the Pergamum Altar. Seeking to impose on excavators conditions comparable to those outlined in the Greek antiquities law, the Ottoman statute gave the first signal that the investigation and preservation of historical monuments might be of sufficient value to deserve the state's attention. Even after the flurry of European interest in oriental excavations, however, few native Turks showed great interest in art and archaeology, whether Western or Islamic, though some higher Turkish officials did begin to recognize the touristic value of classical antiquities.[45] As the Ottoman museums did not collect early Christian artifacts at all, many valuable pieces in this style were sent—with Hamdi's connivance—directly to the assiduous director of the *Gemäldegalerie* (the painting collections of the Royal Museums), Wilhelm von Bode.[46] In 1899, Wiegand had astutely noted the Sultan's complete lack of interest in Greek artifacts;[47] the Porte, if not the antiquities administration, was quite willing to dispense with classical artifacts in order to acquire much-needed Western goodwill. Abdul Hamid's inconstancy, suspicious nature, and low regard for art posed endless political dilemmas for those Western-educated individuals who sought to retain Ottoman dominion over cultural treasures found on Turkish soil. Hamdi, for example, though responsible for overseeing the excavation and export of antiquities, was forbidden to pass beyond the walls of Istanbul for more than a decade because Abdul Hamid suspected him (rightly) of sympathizing with the Young Turks.[48] Furthermore, the tiny number of trained officials and the frequent hostility of local populations to excavators' appropriations of land, labor, and building materials made the operation of the antiquities administration a difficult social, as well as political endeavor. Thus Hamdi was required to compel European scholars to comply with their own ethos of disinterested research, using the underdeveloped administrative apparatus of a thoroughly unmodern state, and with no well-defined social support for his maneuvers. Only the advent of Kemal Atatürk would provide the political

[45] Embassy Therapia to Hohenlohe, 24 August 1899, PA/AA/K 27–468, vol. 2. Also, Oleg Grabar, "Islamic Art and Archaeology," in *The Study of the Middle East: Research and Scholarship in the Humanities and the Social Sciences*, ed. Leonard Binder (New York, 1976), p. 242; Pallis, *Antiquity of Iraq*, p. 276.

[46] Watzinger, *Wiegand*, p. 87.

[47] Wiegand, Promemoria dated May 1899, in PZStA AA/R 37718, pp. 110–12.

[48] Gerhard Wiegand, ed., *Halbmond im letzten Viertel: Briefe und Reiseberichte aus der alten Türkei von Theodor und Marie Wiegand 1895 bis 1918* (Munich, 1970), pp. 36, 142.

climate and social basis for an effective campaign against European exploitation.

Ironically, however, the dictates of German-Turkish "friendship" actually allowed Hamdi both to command the deference of German scholars and to profit personally from their transgressions of his decrees. To "compensate" Hamdi for the division of finds at Miletus in 1902, the Royal Museums purchased one of the Turkish official's paintings for the lucrative price of six thousand francs (about five thousand marks) and arranged for Hamdi to receive a decoration from the Kaiser.[49] Under these conditions, it was clear that the delicate negotiations necessary to the extension of archaeological excavation in the Ottoman Empire could not be accomplished by Berlin-based scholars and bureaucrats; daily negotiations with men like Hamdi, whom Humann described as "working himself into a rage over a triviality and ten minutes later dancing the cancan,"[50] required a savvy, adventurous, and well-connected man on the spot, qualities possessed in abundance by Theodor Wiegand.

A poor *Gymnasium* student who came to archaeology by way of modern art rather than through the normal channels of academic classical studies, Wiegand would never hold a university post; he was no philologist, in either the narrowly professional or the broader social definition of the term.[51] He was instead a prodigious organizer and fund-raiser for archaeological projects, due in part to the contacts with big industrialists he established through his in-laws, the von Siemenses. As Humann's successor as head of DAI museum operations in Smyrna after 1897, and as cultural (*wissenschaftlich*) attaché to the German Embassy in Constantinople, Wiegand shouldered most of the burden of mediating between Turkish officials and German museum bureaucrats, diplomats, scholars, and political figures in the crucial years 1897 to 1918; his task was to balance the acquisition lust of the museum administration with the pride and political safety of Germanophile Turkish officials.

Wiegand made his debut as scholar-diplomat in the midst of the discussions leading to the secret German-Turkish accord. In 1898, he advised the German embassy in Constantinople that though Hamdi was devoted in principle to the promotion of German scholarly projects, the powerful Turk could easily make good on his threats to sabotage the Sultan's infringements on his antiquities law.[52] Wiegand was convinced that, secret accord or no, Hamdi's connivance was vital to the successful execution of excavation projects, and especially to the export of artifacts. Although he relocated to

[49] Wiegand to Schöne, 23 May 1903, in StMBZ, IM 7.

[50] Humann's 1888 letter to Schöne, quoted in Pallat, *Schöne*, p. 188.

[51] Watzinger, *Wiegand*, pp. 25–33.

[52] See Embassy Pera (Marschall) to Hohenlohe, 11 June 1898, in PZStA AA/R 37692, pp. 73–77.

Berlin in 1908 to become director of the sculpture collection of the Royal Museums (Kekulé, the previous director, had just died), Wiegand continued to play a major role in negotiations and to base his archaeological diplomacy on the principles of apolitical scholarliness and solicitude for the Turkish museum director.

Owing to Wiegand's careful diplomacy, relations between the DAI the Royal Museums, the Sublime Porte, and Hamdi Bey seem to have been reasonably pacific between 1898 and 1902. Following each excavation, the division of finds was accomplished on site, preventing either side from appropriating all the choice pieces. To avoid future Turkish recriminations, Wiegand even returned Priene material Humann had surreptitiously shipped to Berlin. He had taken this unprecedented step, Wiegand explained in his diary, "first of all because I can't reconcile with my scientific conscience the idea that we would conceal good discoveries for years because of their stealthy importation and not include them in the forthcoming Priene report, and secondly because, for the sake of the future, I must make myself in every way unobjectionable [einwandfrei] in the eyes of the Turks."[53] When the Kaiser dictated a gracious thank-you to the Sultan for granting permission to excavate the sacred site of Ash Shargāt (Assur), he echoed precisely Wiegand's "disinterested" rhetoric:

> Far from wanting to excavate the earth in order to extract treasures or profit, the German Society [the DOG] pursues only purely scholarly ends, and will find the greatest recompense for its labors in succeeding in the discovery of authentic documents that shed light on the foundations and roots of that ancient oriental culture, upon which rests the greater part of modern culture in the Orient as in the Occident.[54]

This brief period of genteel archaeological diplomacy did not, however, last long. According to Wilhelm von Bode, in early 1902 he was approached by the young Byzantinist Josef Strzygowski, who showed him photographs of an elaborate Sassanid castle ruin, known as Mschatta (or "winter quarters") languishing in the deserts of Syria. Convinced that with the completion of the Mecca railway, the monument would be plundered, Bode appealed to the Kaiser for assistance in acquiring the castle's monumental gateway. Wilhelm was impressed by the photos and Bode's pleas: "We must have that, cost what it will!" he averred, and promised to write the Sultan directly about the matter. Bülow, Bode reported, was delighted that the Kaiser was taking an interest in such things, and sped off to inform the embassy in Constantinople.[55] Others in the Reich bureaucracy, however, were less en-

[53] Wiegand's entry dated 20 June 1899, in his diary, vol. 1, p. 49; DAI, Nachlaß Wiegand, Kasten 22.

[54] Wilhelm II to Abdul Hamul, 20 July 1902, in PZStA AA/R 37699, pp. 99–100.

[55] Wilhelm von Bode, Mein Leben, vol. 2 (Berlin, 1930), pp. 155–56.

thusiastic. Schöne feared newspaper reports detailing the Kaiser's interest in the ruin would generate American competition for its acquisition.[56] The Education Ministry and Karl Schumacher, director of the Römisch-Germanisches Zentralmuseum, warned the Kaiser not to intervene in the negotiations, which were being taken care of by the DAI and the embassy in Constantinople.[57] A year later, arrangements for the gateway's exportation had not been resolved, and Wiegand was becoming concerned that the Kaiser's participation in archaeological affairs would produce a Turkish reaction against German high-handedness.[58] Negotiations collapsed when Hamdi, upon seeing photographs of the finds in question, refused to consent to this violation of his antiquities law.[59] Despite Hamdi's resistance, Baron von Wangenheim, second in command at the Constantinople embassy, promised his superiors at the Foreign Ministry that he would see if the Sultan might hand over the Mschatta gate as a personal gift to the Kaiser; Hamdi, he wrote, might be won over later with a "compensation."[60] In June, Wangenheim announced that this gift had been arranged, over the protests of Turkish officials; the ambassador hoped that the German press would not celebrate the victory over the export law too loudly.[61] Finally, Wangenheim recommended that the Kaiser should not, as proposed, give the Sultan an ornate book of illustrations; since Abdul Hamid preferred guns, horses, and dogs to books, pictures, and sculptures, a team of black thoroughbreds should be delivered, to complement the white horses given by Franz Josef of Austria.[62] The horses reached Constantinople in November 1903; several weeks later, the Mschatta Gate arrived in Berlin, packed in 422 cases.

Uncharitable statements in the British press about the gate's acquisition inspired Schöne to attempt to restrain German exultation over Mschatta until tempers cooled.[63] Stifling the Berlin press, however, was to no avail; in Turkey, the damage had been done. The Sultan himself suffered no pangs of conscience; indeed, he is said to have boasted of the painless diplomatic gains made by the Mschatta gift. "Look at these stupid foreigners," he exclaimed to a retainer. "I pacify them with broken stones."[64] Hamdi, how-

[56] Schöne to Otto Puchstein, 23 May 1902, in StMBZ, IM 6.

[57] Studt (Education Ministry) to Wilhelm II, 26 May 1902, MZStA 2.2.1–20775, pp. 51–52.

[58] Wiegand to [Schöne], 26 February 1903, DAI, Nachlaß Wiegand, Kasten 13, Mappe 1903.

[59] Wangenheim to Foreign Ministry, 20 May 1903, in PZStA AA/R 37702, pp. 75–76.

[60] Wangenheim to Foreign Ministry, 16 May 1903, ibid., p. 86.

[61] Wangenheim to Bülow, 15 June 1903, ibid., 37703, pp. 41–43.

[62] Wangenheim to Foreign Ministry, 20 June 1903, ibid., pp. 49–50.

[63] Schöne to von Lucanus, 23 December 1903, in MZStA 2.2.1–20776, p. 3.

[64] Watzinger, *Wiegand*, p. 170.

20. The Mschatta Gate, installed in the basement of the Kaiser Friedrich Museum in 1905, soured relations between German excavators and Turkish officials.
© Bildarchiv, Preußischer Kulturbesitz, 1996.

ever, was outraged by the process and tendered his resignation. His request refused, the museums director turned his wrath on foreign excavators. By August 1903, Wangenheim could already discern a distinct cooling in Hamdi's enthusiasm for German projects. The Mschatta caper, in tandem with a diplomatic crisis between Constantinople and Washington over the refusal of an excavation permit, which the Americans blamed on German intrigue, had prompted Hamdi to repeat dark intimations of the dangers of a "inondation scientifique allemande." Under these conditions, obtaining permits desired by German excavators for digs at Hauran and Palmyra in Syria, Wangenheim suggested, would be very tricky; the extraction of archaeological concessions was beginning to be seen as an incipient form of colonial rule. Pressure should not be applied to gain new permits, wrote the diplomat, "for apart from the complete hopelessness of any prospect of taking steps in this direction after the completion of the negotiations over Mschatta, the Turks could see in this a proof of the real existence of the territorial aspirations in Turkey ascribed to us by our foes and an attempt to make this operative by the inauguration of a kind of *Kolonialpolitik*. To create this sort of impression," Wangenheim added laconically, "would be politically unwise."[65]

His pride hurt and his suspicions aroused, Hamdi imposed new strictures on German excavators. Continuance permits given without hesitation in the past were increasingly refused, pending Hamdi's issuance of a new antiquities law, to which all excavators would be subject. Finds were now required to be reported immediately to the government, rather than awaiting the postexcavation equal division. The Prussian museum administration, of course, was highly distressed at this turn of events, and Schöne appealed to the Education Ministry to pressure the Foreign Ministry and the Constantinople embassy to do something about Hamdi's new measures, which stood in direct contradiction to the provisions of the secret accord.[66] Several weeks later, Marschall reported that in the division of the finds at Ash Shargāt, the secret agreement had not been honored and the Germans would receive nothing; a widely publicized imperial *irade* decreed that everything would remain in the Ottoman museums. "There can be no doubt," the ambassador explained, "that these schemes of Hamdi Bey are to be seen first of all as an act of revenge for the Mschatta affair, from which he still has not recovered." Secondly, Marschall argued, Hamdi now wished to elevate his museum to the level of the great European institutions and had begun to petition the Sultan for state funds for excavations by the Turks themselves; according to the ambassador, Hamdi was apparently employing a most effective appeal to the Sultan's vanity, arguing "that today most of the European sovereigns, including our most gracious Kaiser and the ruler of Austria-Hungary, patronize archaeological undertakings."[67] Hurting Hamdi's pride had simultaneously unleashed his nationalist ambitions, and negotiations hereafter would have to come to grips with both factors—or overcome the museums director's considerable powers of resistance with greater and greater shows of force.

Hamdi Edhem, however, was not the sole object of German archaeological diplomacy. A major preoccupation of professional archaeologists and diplomats in the East was the exclusion of amateur excavators from participation in the cultural colonization of the vast reaches of the Ottoman Empire. As the Orient began to attract the attention of scores of local "scholarly" societies and "friendship" associations, plans for expeditions to the East multiplied with great rapidity. Having recognized the diplomatic advantages of preserving the appearance of scientific disinterestedness, however, fin de siècle scholars feared the extension of privileges to the uninitiated. Particularly as Reich imperialist designs grew larger, attempts were

---

[65] Wangenheim to Bülow, 10 August 1903, in PZStA AA/R 37704, pp. 16–21.
[66] Schöne to Education Ministry, 6 February 1904, ibid., 37705, pp. 65–66.
[67] Marschall to Bülow, 27 March 1904, ibid., pp. 119–21.

made by the DAI, the Royal Museums, and the diplomatic corps to restrict cultural expropriation in the Ottoman hinterlands to licensed members of the classicist establishment.

One good example of this joint crusade against outsiders was the 1902 campaign waged by Wiegand, Schöne, and Wangenheim against the excavation plans of one Dr. Waldemar Belck, head of a newly formed Deutsche Gesellschaft für wissenschaftliche Erforschung Anatoliens (German Society for the Scientific Study of Anatolia—DGEA).[68] Besides his standing in the scientific circles as, according to Wiegand, "a rather arrogant dilettante," Belck also possessed the objectionable qualities of having had a natural-science education and having accepted the patronage of Rudolf Virchow, whom the DAI had recently defeated in the matter of the founding of the Römisch-Germanische Kommission. Wiegand opened his attack on Belck by distancing Conze, Schöne, and others who had attended the founding meeting of the DGEA from Belck's plans and underlining the diplomatic complications caused by Belck's previous trips to the East. "There is present danger," wrote the intrepid excavator, "that the Turkish government's mistrust of Herr Belck will gradually be transferred to the already established major scholarly enterprises of Germany, which have previously known how to keep themselves free from the suspicion of [participating in] political or religious propaganda." Wiegand added that the new DGEA's leadership included several prominent friends of the Armenians, a feature sure to excite Turkish distrust and animosity.[69] Schöne, drawing on the testimony of Conze and a museum assistant, confirmed Wiegand's negative assessment of Belck the chemist, and cautioned against allowing more than one organization to receive digging permits from the Turkish government. "German, especially Prussian, archaeological interests in Turkey," he warned, "would be seriously threatened in all sorts of ways through [the establishment of] a second, competing center of operations."[70]

Seconding the dark intimations of Wiegand and Schöne about Turkish discomfiture at the prospect of the founding of the Anatolian Society, Wangenheim turned the minor issue of Belck's incompetence into a straightforward disquisition on the clandestine means indispensable to the *pénétration pacifique*:

> The idea of Germany's gradual spiritual conquest of Asia Minor is thoroughly sound and capable of development. The intellectual centers already established, or to be established, by our schools, our doctors, and our archaeologists could very well become, in the course of time, the crystalization points onto which German economic and colonizing undertakings are grafted. The eco-

[68] For Belck's background, see Renger, "Geschichte der Altorientalistik," pp. 173–74.
[69] Wiegand to Embassy Therapia, 18 August 1902, PZStA AA/R 37700, pp. 45–48.
[70] Schöne to Education Ministry, 30 September 1902, ibid., 37701, pp. 59–60.

nomic will follow the intellectual conquest as a natural result, and then these two diffused phases will naturally be followed by the third stage, that of political exploitation and consolidation of the cultural values we have created. But for the execution of such a farsighted policy, it is above all necessary that we know when to hold our tongues, that neither at home nor anywhere abroad, to say nothing of among the Turks, do we allow it to be thought that our cultural efforts in Turkey aim at anything else than the satisfaction of German scholarly ambitions and the friendly intention to bring new vitality to the penniless Turkish state coffers. . . . Nothing is more disruptive to the careful and continuing development of our operations than the deportment of German agitators who urge the cultural conquest of the Orient, [and] who are perpetually discussing the subject of Germany's putative future plans in Turkey in public meetings and in the press, and have recently manifested a tendency to come together in associations [like the DGEA]. . . . If our *Altertumsforschung* has been increasingly successful, this is above all to be credited to the tactful and modest behavior of the scholars sent here who have extracted the most precious treasures from the Turkish soil for us, and also who know how to gradually put to rest the Turks' initial mistrust of their activity.[71]

Since Belck did not live up to these standards of tact, modesty, and scholarliness, Wangenheim concluded, he should receive neither the state's blessings, nor its patronage.

Wangenheim's dictum captures in the full the fretful megalomania driving German *Kulturpolitik* in the Orient. Strategically and ideologically, "friendship" with the Ottoman state still suited the Wilhelmine Empire; as a window on Egypt and India, a barrier to Russian expansionist ambitions, and a pacific neighbor on Austria-Hungary's weak eastern border, the sultanate served important defensive purposes, while Wilhelm could not help but approve Abdul Hamid's deeply antidemocratic system of rule. But, craving material enrichment and imperial stature, citizens of imperial Germany could not be contented with mere "friendship," and began to press—in increasing numbers and with rising voices—for concessions, and, finally, conquest. As German entrepreneurs, explorers, and excavators ventured deeper and deeper into the Ottoman hinterlands, this diplomatic contradiction would appear in sharper focus, forcing officials of the Bismarckian school—generally established, older diplomats, businessmen, and scholars—back on assurances of disinterested neutrality, and the equally self-interested proponents of *Weltpolitik* on to acts of expropriative impudence. In the archaeological realm, the culmination of this generational and ideological clash would come at the edge of the text-historical world: Mesopotamia.

[71] Wangenheim to Bülow, 24 August 1902, ibid., 37700, pp. 41–44.

Assur, Babylon, and the Collapse of Disciplinary Solidarity

As noted earlier, by the mid-1890s, numerous voices had been raised in support of commencing German archaeological projects in Mesopotamia. In 1897, following a call from Schöne, a Kommission für die archäologische Erforschung der Euphrat- und Tigrisländer (Commission for the Archaeological Study of the Lands of the Tigris and Euphrates—KaEET) was formed to sell the state on the idea; its members included Schöne (president), Conze, Sachau, the Greek philologist Hermann Diels, the Egyptologist Adolf Erman, and Althoff's protege at the Education Ministry, Friedrich Schmidt (later Schmidt-Ott). The KaEET recommended that an "informational" expedition be sent to the area right away and demanded that diplomatic intervention be used to circumvent the antiquities law once more, giving the Germans a wide area of investigation (embracing the whole vilayet of Mosul, containing the palaces of the Assyrian kings), a long tenure (fifty years), and a large share of the finds. The French had paid the Persians fifty thousand francs for such an all-inclusive arrangement in that region and had thereby benefited greatly; now that Germany was in a favorable political position to extract similar concessions from the Sultan, the KaEET argued, why not seize the opportunity? The commission concluded its appeal with a warning that failure to act now could consign Germany again to a place in the shade, shut out of yet another carving-up of the globe.[72]

Despite the lack of the proposed, absurdly generous fifty-year excavation permit, an archaeological reconnaissance team did survey the Tigris-Euphrates basin during the winter of 1897–98, funded by the Orient-Comité member and cofounder of the DOG, Dr. James Simon.[73] The expedition was headed by Sachau and Robert Koldewey, an eccentric architect who had excavated minor sites under foreign supervision since the early 1880s. Schöne transmitted the party's findings to the Education Ministry, virtually salivating at the prospects for monumental acquisitions. For the modest price of five hundred thousand marks, the museums director argued, a grand-scale excavation at Babylon might be organized, a project that promised abundant and diverse treasures.[74] Bosse passed Schöne's advice to the Kaiser, adding an elaborate appeal to take up the subject of the Babylon permit personally with the Sultan during his upcoming visit to the Orient. The education minister described in glowing terms the prospects of a dig in "the venerable, holy mother city of Mesopotamia," striking a now common competitive tone and, suggesting that Germany's dedication to phi-

[72] Kommission to Bosse, 21 June 1897, ibid., 37691, pp. 15–20.
[73] See Bosse to Wilhelm II, 7 October 1898, ibid., 37692, pp. 35–40.
[74] Schöne (and Kommission) to Bosse, 13 August 1898, ibid., pp. 45–47.

21. Robert Koldewey
proudly poses in
front of the German
excavation house in
Babylon. Deutsches
Archäologisches
Institut, Berlin.

lology might itself be to blame for its archaeological and museological backwardness.[75]

On December 30, 1898, a small party of excavators appointed by the DOG left Damascus for Babylon, following a route that hardly differed from that traveled by Alexander the Great. Despite ongoing building of the Baghdad Railway, the means of transportation were also the same: all equipment and personnel arrived at the site via camel caravan.[76] Despite their remote location and harsh desert conditions, however, by 1902 German archaeologists had succeeded in excavating large sections of the monumental city walls, and had filled six hundred crates with fragments of the tiled Ishtar Gate facade. Koldewey and Assyriologist Friedrich Delitzsch ex-

---

[75] Bosse to Wilhelm II, 7 October 1898, ibid., pp. 35–40.
[76] Walter Andrae, *Lebenserinnerungen eines Ausgräbers* (Berlin, 1961), p. 29.

22. The Ishtar Gate emerges from the desert.

plained to the Foreign Ministry that the relief was to be sent directly to Berlin to prevent damage to the fragments and to facilitate swift reconstruction of the facade by German scholars—allegedly with a view to returning the rebuilt gate to the Ottoman museums.[77]

Aside from the Ishtar Gate and numerous seals, however, Babylon did not yield the rich cache of tablets and sculpture sought by the Royal Museums, Academy of Sciences, and DOG, and by 1902, German attention was straying to other nearby Mesopotamian sites. Delitzsch, whose lecture titled "Babel und die Bibel" ("Babylon and the Bible") had made him a national celebrity earlier that year, in late 1902 submitted a memorandum to the Kaiser and Reich bureaucracy urging the sovereign to arrange a dig at the most important of these sites, Ash Shargāt (ancient Assur) with the Sultan. Delitzsch recommended speedy action on the matter, before the British recovered from the Boer War or the French made a deal with the Ottoman museums. Wilhelm's marginalia confirmed the effectiveness of Delitzsch's

[77] Delitzsch and Koldewey to Foreign Ministry, 8 June 1902, and Education Ministry to Foreign Ministry, 11 August 1902, both in PZStA AA/R 37700, pp. 20–24 and p. 19, respectively.

nationalistic appeal ("That cannot be!" he noted beside the warnings of British or French acquisition of digging rights. "We must do it!"), and the Assyriologist's final plea that German scholars be accorded exclusive rights to publish found materials received the Kaiser's proud endorsement: "Yes! We will carry the light of German genius there too!"[78] And so they did. By early 1903, the DOG had begun excavations at Assur under Walter Andrae. The dig continued for eleven lonely years, employing an average of 180 to 200 workers.[79]

Notwithstanding their remote locations, German digs in Mesopotamia, like those on the Turkish coast, suffered the ill effects of failures in archaeological diplomacy. The Mschatta episode had its impact here too, exacerbated by the haughty behavior of Koldewey and Andrae. The first manifestation of Hamdi's crackdown on antiquities exports occurred in early 1905, when Hamdi's proxy Bedri Bey attempted to confiscate numerous already packed cases of Assur finds. Andrae refused to hand them over, and the Constantinople diplomatic corps, regretting the Reich's failure to instruct scholars on proper behavior overseas, prepared itself for "another Mschatta."[80] A second apocalyptic missive from Marschall to the Foreign Ministry complained that Andrae was behaving as if Assur were "a conquered country" rather than the Sultan's personal property, and he conveyed Wiegand's worries that this conflict would produce a final rupture with Hamdi, just when the Reich "has so many archaeological irons in the fire."[81] The Foreign Ministry did its best to prevent news of the controversy from reaching the Kaiser; Wilhelm's close friend (and DOG president) Admiral Hollmann was sworn to secrecy and Delitzsch was instructed to avoid the subject in an upcoming lecture to the DOG. As the ministry explained to Chancellor von Bülow, Wilhelm had to be restrained from soliciting the Sultan's personal intervention; after Mschatta, this could only further alienate Hamdi and damage German interests.[82]

By mid-1905, German-Turkish cultural relations had reached a nadir. The digs at Babylon, Assur, and Pergamum had been suspended and the status of finds from these sites, plus negotiations over those of Baalbek, Miletus, and Didyma, were in daily flux. Marschall was asked by the Foreign Ministry to use the opportunity of his presentation of a book on Persian poetry to the Sultan to discuss permit renewals and to apply for permission to use a motor boat given to Koldewey by the DOG to transport

[78] Delitzsch's memorandum entitled "Kalat Schirgat" and dated 26 February 1902, ibid., pp. 31–34.

[79] Andrae, *Lebenserinnerungen*, p. 143.

[80] Marschall to Bülow, 1 February 1905, in PZStA AA/R 37708, pp. 6–7.

[81] Marschall to Foreign Ministry, 24 February 1905, ibid., pp. 26–27.

[82] Foreign Ministry to Bülow, 25 February 1905, ibid., pp. 30–32.

equipment and finds to and from the Mesopotamian sites on the Tigris.[83] The ambassador was successful in at least the first of these aims; approval for the boat, however, was denied after Koldewey's secret machinations aroused Turkish suspicion that the Germans either wished to evade the antiquities law or to demand trading privileges in the area equivalent to those held by the British (in the guise of the Lynch Brothers' steamship company).[84]

The course of events in Mesopotamia after 1905 makes evident the increasing development of an important schism in the archaeological world. The DAI and its parent institution, the Foreign Ministry, had pioneered archaeological excavation in the East, and had bombarded the state with requests for patronage and appeals to national pride. Their commitment to discrete diplomacy, however, increasingly vexed the more pugnacious DOG, under the leadership of members of the Kaiser's entourage and backed by the aggressive new General Director of the Royal Museums, Wilhelm von Bode. In spite of its origins as an aristocratic society of dilettantes and diplomats, the DAI had become an exclusive organization of professional classical archaeologists, while the DOG encompassed a much wider and less academically oriented public in its membership lists. The DOG dedicated itself to "opening up and recovering the most ancient Orient," including biblical and prehistorical pursuits, while the DAI, digging mostly in the Ionic and Roman settlements, maintained much of its philhellenic spirit even in its forays into Asia Minor. DOG excavators tended to be younger than those of the DAI, and to have more technical (architectural or engineering) backgrounds than philological ones. Both Andrae and the eccentric Koldewey, as well as Ernst Herzfeld and Julius Jordan (who assisted in Assur and executed numerous other DOG digs and surveys), were architects by training; with the exception of Koldewey, the excavation leaders in Mesopotamia were all born after 1870, and like Koldewey, who regularly performed physiological experiments on himself, were closer to prehistorians with natural-scientific training, like Felix von Luschan, than to any of the DAI classical archaeologists.[85] Koldewey had no interest in inscriptions and did not want to disfigure architectural structures to seek them; his prized personal collection of antiquities consisted not of sculptures but of

[83] Foreign Ministry to Marschall, 18 March 1905, ibid., pp. 30–31; Bülow had previously reassured Wilhelm that Marschall would also convey to the Porte the Kaiser's "lively interest" in German digs. Bülow to Wilhelm II, 12 March 1905, ibid., p. 29.

[84] Embassy Pera to Foreign Ministry, 9 June 1905, ibid., pp. 93–94; Embassy Therapia to Bülow, 11 May 1905, ibid., p. 44; Wiegand to Koldewey, 2 August 1905, in DAI, Nachlaß Wiegand, Kasten 6.

[85] Walter Andrae, *Babylon, die versunkene Weltstadt und ihr Ausgräber, Robert Koldewey* (Berlin, 1952), pp. 242, 208–212.

samples of different sorts of ancient mortar.[86] Andrae was young enough to have read *Rembrandt als Erzieher* as an impressionable student, bored by lifeless Greek and Latin studies, at the Technische Hochschule in Dresden.[87] Touched by the vitalist philosophy of the fin de siècle (*Lebensphiloso-phie*), and later a proclaimed theosophist, Andrae's interests in nature, religion, and art harkened back to a more romantic strain in *Orientforschung*, one that now had little to do with the increasingly specialized pursuits of the DAI.

The clash of the two bodies can be seen as a classic translation to the cultural sphere of the confrontation between an older generation of National Liberals and a rising cohort of new nationalists, with the difference that in the realm of scholarship, the older generation succeeded in using its semimeritocratic credentials to block the access of outsiders for a longer period of time. But soon after the turn of the century, the resentment and politico-acquisitive truculence of newer groups like the DOG began to express itself here too, provoking last-ditch efforts by the classicists and the diplomatic corps to save the Reich's position and German archaeology's scholarly reputation. Koldewey, Andrae, and other DOG excavators, backed by the imperial court, German industrialists, and high members of the clergy, and underwritten by a now established tradition of German scholarly prowess, felt the restrictions of mere Turks to be onerous and the cautious diplomacy of the Constantinople Embassy to be pusillanimous. Rebuffed by the Reich in the matter of the motor boat, and annoyed by the dictates of Wiegand and the diplomats that he modify his behavior toward the "stupid and greedy" members of the Turkish Antiquities Commission, Koldewey vented his frustration to DOG secretary Bruno Güterbock. He had to obey the Turks, Koldewey complained, "Because I have the strict order to do everything that the commission, in the name of its big boss [Hamdi], desires, and if I take the communications from Constantinople seriously, we would do well here, when His Excellence Hamdi Bey slaps us on the left cheek, not only to offer him the right cheek, but to thank him most politely."[88] When Wiegand reproached Koldewey for his hostile statements about the embassy, which had been leaked to the Kaiser by Güterbock, Koldewey apologized to Wiegand personally, but maintained that the diplomats had done nothing to prevent the Turks from treating the Mesopo-

---

[86] Pallis, *Antiquity of Iraq*, p. 308; Adolf Erman, *Mein Werden und mein Wirken: Erinnerungen eines alten Berliner Gelehrten* (Leipzig, 1929), p. 239.

[87] Andrae, *Lebenserinnerungen*, pp. 3–12.

[88] The architect expressed to his friend his opposition to Constantinople's appeasement policy, which had allowed Hamdi to conclude that German archaeologists were no more than his personal slaves. Koldewey to Güterbock, 11 April 1905, PZStA AA/R 37709, pp. 32–36.

tamian excavators "like mangy dogs, to the general amusement of all the other nations and to our own deepest embarrassment."[89]

The stubbornness and arrogance of the DOG excavators was the subject of Marschall's communication to Bülow in late May 1905. Marschall contrasted the behavior of two unnamed younger archaeologists (clearly Koldewey and Andrae) to that of Wiegand, who had just succeeded in wresting the digging permit for Didyma from the French, and DAI veterans Conze and Humann, who had been respectful of Turkish customs, such as petty bribery, for the sake of Germany's long-term archaeological interests.[90] DOG president Hollmann, however, defended Koldewey to his friend the Kaiser, insisting that the Constantinople embassy had overemphasized the architect's role. Hollmann attached a letter from Richarz, who blamed the dispute mostly on the conditions of the far-flung sites, administered by officials exiled from the center and surrounded by local populations of nomads and "thieving bedouins."[91] Down to the World War, DOG members continued to vex the embassy and the DAI by interfering in what the classicist-diplomatic circle believed to be their bailiwick.

The Young Turk revolution of 1907–8 introduced additional complexities into archaeological diplomacy. The rebellion rode in on a wave of pro-British sentiment and anti-German rhetoric: in addition to forcing the Sultan to restore the 1876 constitution and parliament, rebels insisted that pro-German higher officials be removed from their posts.[92] Anglophile enthusiasm proved short-lived, however, as the British refused a large loan for the Young Turks and then, for obscure reasons, backed a brief counterrevolution in April 1909. Germany emerged from the debacle again the most favored nation among Turks in high political (and cultural) circles. In the midst of the rebellion's confusion, Wiegand managed to ship home to Berlin another enormous relic of the Greek past: the market gate of Miletus. Of 533 crates of finds, only 33 went to Constantinople, the remainder to Berlin. In May 1908 Wiegand confided to his diary: "We have succeeded in packing up the entire market gate of Miletus, of which three-quarters of all the ancient dressed stones were found, with the designation 'architectural fragments,' without the Turkish officials having the least idea that they have given us a whole monument the size of Constantine's arch in Rome."[93] This

[89] Wiegand to Koldewey, 18 June 1905; and Koldewey to Wiegand, 18 July 1905, in DAI, Nachlaß Wiegand, Kasten 6.

[90] Marschall to Bülow, 26 May 1905, in PZStA AA/R 37709, pp. 88–90.

[91] Hollmann to Wilhelm II, 10 July 1905, with attached, undated letter from Richarz to Hollmann, ibid., 37710, pp. 58–60.

[92] Lindow, *Marschall von Bieberstein*, pp. 103–6.

[93] Entry dated 15–21 May 1908 in Wiegand diary, vol 2 (July 1907-March 1910), in DAI, Nachlaß Wiegand, Kasten 22.

time, Hamdi apparently connived in the expropriation of the monument;[94] Wiegand still preferred persuasion or bribery to the invocation of the secret accord.

In late February 1910, Hamdi Bey went to his well-deserved rest. He was succeeded by his younger and more nationalist brother Halil Edhem Bey, who proved to be more difficult to manipulate, and more susceptible to internal political pressure than his predecessor. Halil remained sympathetic to German interests down to the time of his retirement in 1931, but the governments he served were deeply divided, and domestic tensions prevented any overt Germanophile behavior on his part. In 1910, the new museum director was denounced in the Turkish parliament for having given a key to the artifacts storehouse at Babylon to Koldewey, and threatened with big cuts in the museum budget if he did not act immediately. Wiegand and the embassy, of course, insisted that Koldewey relinquish the key.[95] Thereafter, negotiations on finds seem to have broken down completely; by 1913, with the finds from Didyma, Babylon, and Assur hanging in the balance, even Wiegand was anxious to invoke the secret accord to save "the enormous scholarly harvest [lying] in German excavation sites in Turkey," though he fully realized that the antiquities question had become a highly sensitive matter of international as well as domestic Turkish politics.[96] It had become easier, the troublesome private excavator Max von Oppenheim complained in 1913, to buy antiquities from local grave robbers than to excavate them. Against all logic, both scholarship and the Royal Museums had suffered as a result of German-Turkish "friendship."[97]

In Germany, *Kulturpolitik* had become a free-for-all; the embassies and Wiegand could no longer control the actions of the more aggressive DOG, the Kaiser, and Bode. In 1912, Wiegand had to force his way onto the DOG presidium, he reported, "since the members did not want to elect me. Still and yet . . . the one-sided mistrust of classical archaeology as the rival of oriental studies persists."[98] The Finance Ministry, which had not been able to strike big archaeological expenditures from the Kaiser's personal budget, now attempted to block the spending of twenty million marks from Prussian state funds, to outbid an American offer to buy artifacts from the Otto-

---

[94] Entry for 11 November 1913 in Wiegand diary, vol. 2 (November 1913-July 1914) ibid., Kasten 23, also quoted in Silke Wenk, ed., *Auf den Spuren der Antike: Theodor Wiegand, ein deutscher Archäologe* (Bendorf am Rhein, 1985), p. 10.

[95] Therapia Embassy (Miquel) to Bethmann, 15 June 1910, in PZStA AA/R 37716, pp. 125–26.

[96] See Wiegand's Promemoria dated 13 November 1913 cited above, n. 27; also Wiegand diary entry, 15–18 March 1914 DAI, Nachlaß Wiegand, Kasten 23.

[97] Oppenheim to Wangenheim, 26 April 1913, StMBZ, VAM 52.

[98] Quoted in Wenk, *Auf den Spuren*, p. 19.

man Museums, sending the Kaiser into a rage.[99] The DOG, Bode, Reich Chancellor Theobald von Bethmann-Hollweg, and Rudolf von Valentini, head of the Kaiser's civil cabinet, all resented Wiegand's direct missives to the Kaiser, circumventing their authority; outraged DOG members, Wiegand said, now considered him "the blackest intriguer on God's earth."[100] In return, Wiegand berated the elite association for allowing information about the dispute over the Assur finds to leak to the public.[101] Wiegand's decision to involve the Kaiser in negotiations also produced a break with Wangenheim, and with Wiegand's friend Karl Helfferich, who resented this new upset in German-Turkish relations just at the moment he was negotiating an important new agreement about the Baghdad Railway. Wangenheim, Wiegand wrote, was so angry with the excavator as to swear that "all the strychnine in the world would not be enough to poison me and my archaeological colleagues."[102] The combination of interministerial backbiting, archaeological infighting, and belligerent nationalist agitation was fast unraveling the diplomat's carefully constructed plans for future conquest.

The status of the Assur finds was still under debate in 1914, when the dig was declared complete. Six hundred crates of artifacts were packed and awaiting shipment to Berlin by early January; but in February, the Constantinople embassy reported that an audience with the grand vizier had resulted in no decision for the present.[103] On March 13, the Kaiser telegraphed the Foreign Ministry, commanding the diplomats to tell the grand vizier that the Kaiser himself wanted the Assur finds; Wangenheim conveyed the message and also promised to discover how the French and the British had evaded the 1907 antiquities law.[104] The ambassador put heavy pressure on the Turks to comply with the secret accord, but told the Foreign Ministry that the matter was endangering the tenure of the pro-German grand vizier, and an ultimatum could cause him to fall, as well as usher in a diplomatic break between the empires.[105] Several days later, the Turkish Foreign Minister Said Halim promised Wangenheim that the government would allow the crates to be sent to Germany, but that this would be concealed from the Ottoman parliament, and hereafter, the 1899 secret accord would be in-

---

[99] See ibid., pp. 19–20; Wiegand diary, vol. 2, 20 February 1914, DAI, Nachlaß Wiegand, Kasten 23.

[100] Wiegand diary, 18 February 1914, ibid.

[101] Wiegand diary, 15–18 March 1914, 22 March 1914, ibid.

[102] Wiegand diary 19 June 1914, ibid.

[103] Civil Cabinet to Foreign Ministry, 13 January 1914, PA/AA/K 27–468a, vol. 1; Constantinople embassy to Foreign Ministry, 3 February 1914, in MZStA 2.2.1–21355.

[104] Wangenheim to Foreign Ministry, 14 March 1914 (includes description of Kaiser's telegram), in PA/AA/K 27–468a, vol. 1.

[105] Wangenheim to Foreign Ministry, 27 March 1914 (telegram), ibid.

valid.[106] Wangenheim was grateful for the concession of the crates, but cryptic on the future of the accord; he reminded the Berlin bureaucrats, however, that taking advantage of the situation to extract further booty would not ultimately be to Germany's benefit. "The political perception of us in Turkey rests on our absolute loyalty [to the Ottoman state]," wrote the ever-calculating Wangenheim. "Therefore we must also remain irreproachable in archaeological matters."[107]

The final irony of the Mesopotamian campaign lies in the fact that the Assur and Babylon finds, the cause of great expenditure and the source of factional rivalries and diplomatic snarls, reached the Reich only after the sun had set on Wilhelmine *Weltpolitik*. The Assur negotiations produced a case of Mschatta redux, for Halil had no intention of allowing the grand vizier to preside over his terrain. In April, Halil informed Bode that he could not stand idly by as the antiquities administration and codes constructed by his brother and himself were destroyed, and refused renewal of all digging permits.[108] On June 7, a telegram arrived in Berlin, confirming that Halil had closed down the Babylon dig; the Kaiser's marginal note on the missive asked, "Have these mad devils gone berserk?" provoking the education ministry bureaucrat Friedrich Schmidt, in passing the missive to the Foreign Ministry, to pose the earnest query: "Who does the Kaiser really mean in this note? The Turks or the Foreign Ministry?"[109] At last, the grand vizier intervened to arrange the shipment of finds and approve new permits for Babylon and Pergamum—but not until July 1914 was the German share of the Assur finds put aboard a steamer in Basra.[110] On August 1, the Assur crates arrived in Lisbon, where they were first impounded and then confiscated when the Portuguese entered World War I on the Allied side in 1915. After the war, the Portugese minister of education had the boxes taken to Porto, where he planned to establish an Assyrian Museum. All efforts to return the finds to Germany (including a half-hearted one conducted by the British Museum in 1923) foundered on the unwillingness of the Germans to compromise; Wilhelm, in exile, recommended sending a warship to Porto to bombard the city until the finds were released.[111] At last in 1926, Andrae and the Foreign Ministry worked out an agreement to share some of the finds with the University of Porto, and the Assur material, together with 536 crates of Babylon finds, impounded by the British in Babylon in 1917

---

[106] Said Halim to Wangenheim, 30 March 1914, ibid.

[107] Wangenheim to Said Halim, 1 April 1914, ibid.

[108] Copy of letter Halil to Bode (undated) in Wiegand diary, vol. 2, 23 April 1914, DAI, Nachlaß Wiegand, Kasten 23; Wiegand to Civil Cabinet, 22 May 1914, in MZStA 2.2.1–21355.

[109] Wiegand diary, vol. 2, 11 June 1914, DAI, Nachlaß Wiegand, Kasten 23.

[110] Wangenheim to Foreign Ministry, 22 June 1914, in PA/AA/K 27–468a, vol. 31.

[111] Andrae, *Lebenserinnerungen*, p. 258; idem, "Der Rückerwerb der Assur-Funde aus Portugal," *Mitteilungen der Deutschen Orient-Gesellschaft* 65 (1927): 1–2.

23. Walter Andrae's sketch for the reconstruction of the Ishtar Gate, 1927.
Staatsbibliothek zu Berlin.

(and secured for the Germans by British archaeologist Gertrude Bell under a new Iraqi antiquities code), finally flowed into the Royal Museums.[112] But even in the Weimar era, the Asia Minor Department only acquired a large exhibition area in the planned Pergamum Museum building when the director of the Egyptian Department decided to leave his collections in the Neues Museum.[113] Only in 1934—long after the *pénétration pacifique* had failed—were the Mesopotamian galleries fully stocked and opened to the public.

The sensation created by the excavation and acquisition of the Pergamum altar in the early years of the Kaiserreich was the product not only of the altar's monumentality, but in large part of its (admittedly Hellenistic) Greekness. The desire to procure grand Greek monuments had driven excavators of the 1890s to investigate Baalbek, Priene, and Miletus, all sites of

[112] Andrae, "Der Rückerwerb der Assur-Funde," pp. 2–3, and idem., "Reise nach Babylon zur Teilung der Babylon-Funde," ibid., 7–27; also Renger, "Geschichte der Altorientalistik," p. 188; and Andrae, *Lebenserinnerungen*, p. 257.

[113] Rainer Michael Boehmer and Ernst Walter Andrae, *Bilder eines Ausgräbers/Sketches by an Excavator: Die Orientbilder von Walter Andrae, 1898–1919* (Berlin, 1989), p. 122.

Ionic settlement. But as archæologists penetrated deeper and deeper into the Orient, leaving behind the Greek colonies on the coast, German ambitions had settled on outstripping other nations in the number, scale, and "scientificness" of their digs, and their celebration of their finds had come more and more to rest on the historical, rather than æsthetic, importance of the objects they uncovered. Digs in Assyria, Egypt, and even Ethiopia (at Axum, 1906) led excavators far beyond Winckelmann's horizons, even beyond Schliemann's "new world," into cultural epochs increasingly less amenable to the philologically based pedagogy institutionalized in German higher education. The progress of German archaeological penetration into Asia Minor confirms the extent to which this nineteenth-century aestheticism, philological bias, and credo of nonutilitarian *Bildung*—the heritage and catechism of German archaeologists before the 1880s—could be set aside in the rush to acquire more objects, more sites, more national glory. If the rise of *Orientforschung* and excavation in Asia Minor and Mesopotamia did not completely divert scholarly attention from the Mediterranean world, or eradicate the neohumanist proclivity for words over things, it did indicate the extent to which the "tyranny of Greece" no longer held the German intelligentsia in its thrall.

German Orientalism and the Critique of the Old Testament

Just as the rising social prominence of German *Altertumswissenschaft* helped to transform the image of Roman antiquity, so too did new forays into the Mesopotamian past alter the status and function of the ancient Orient in Wilhelmine culture. I have written elsewhere about arguments over the relationship between classical and early Islamic art (like the Mschatta Gate),[114] a subject that plays a subordinate role in the history of neohumanism. I will therefore confine myself to a few suggestions about the transformative effects of one of the most consequential new assaults on the deep reaches of the ancient Oriental past: the emergence of Assyriology. Of course, Assyria was not the only ancient Near Eastern civilization to be recovered and feted in this era. In the years before the First World War, scholars also "discovered" the Hittites, and found caches of documents in undeciphered languages in Nubia, Crete, the Sudan, and Chinese Turkestan. Each of these discoveries altered in important ways the conventional image of the preclassical world, largely dependent until this century on classical and biblical sources. But, arriving on the heels of the decoding of Egyptian hieroglyphs and the splintering of the Pentateuch under philologi-

---

[114] Marchand, "The Rhetoric of Artifacts and the Decline of Classical Humanism: The Case of Josef Strzygowski," *History and Theory*, suppl. vol. 33 (1994): 106–30.

cal pressure, Assyriology put the final touches on the liberal Protestant critique of the integrity of the Bible, and especially of the Old Testament. Thus Assyriology played a crucial role in the de-universalizing and demotion of the history of the Hebrews, perhaps the most momentous and ominous shift in the occidental, and especially the German, understanding of the oriental past to occur in recent times.

This tale's prologue begins in the world of midcentury liberal Protestant theology, which had been powerfully shaken by David Friedrich Strauss's *Leben Jesu* (1835). In this long book, the Young Hegelian scholar had attempted to destroy the factual credibility of New Testament accounts of the life of Jesus in order to show that historical events were irrelevant to Christian faith. By demolishing the historical facticity of the gospels, Strauss hoped to clear the way for the reconciliation of biblical philology and speculative philosophy. Strauss's work created an enormous uproar in scholarly circles, and he lost his teaching fellowship at the University of Tübingen.[115] But strikingly, in this same year (1835) Strauss's friend and fellow Young Hegelian Wilhelm Vatke applied the same sorts of philological and philosophical criticism to the Old Testament, and was spared the harsh treatment and wide attention Strauss had received.

It was only in the wake of German unification that the young Semitic philologist Julius Wellhausen took up the arguments in Vatke's *Die biblische Theologie*. To be brief, Wellhausen contrasted the natural religion of the early Israelites, unencumbered by priestly orthodoxy, to the sterile forms of postexilic Judaism; in his most influential book, *Prolegomena zur Geschichte Israels* (1883), he added careful source criticism to Vatke's observations, and concluded that the biblical texts belonged to a period of Israelite history that predated the existence of a written Torah and the conception of a Jewish covenant with God.[116] Initially, Wellhausen's book created the vituperative controversy Vatke had somehow evaded, but his exacting philological analysis and sub-Hegelian portrayal of Judaism's petrifaction on the eve of Christ's birth soon earned him the respect of the anticlerical and largely anti-Semitic theological and classicist communities.

Thanks in great part to the popularity of Wellhausen's "literary-historical" approach, by the end of the century liberal theologians had developed an obsession with the textual authenticity of Jewish holy books, which in turn created new fascination for archaeological discoveries in the East. Wellhausen, whose *Prolegomena* recalled Karl Otfried Müller's strictures on the Creuzerian interpretation of myths, shared the liberal-

[115] On Strauss's *Leben Jesu*, see John Edward Toews, *Hegelianism: The Path Toward Dialectical Humanism, 1805–1841* (Cambridge, 1980), pp. 260–72.

[116] Wellhausen's *Prolegomena* was a revised version of his *Geschichte Israels* (1878). For a summary of Wellhausen's ideas, see Uriel Tal, *Christians and Jews in Germany: Religion, Politics, and Ideology in the Second Reich, 1870–1914* (Ithaca, N.Y., 1975), p. 194.

materialist "cultural protestantism" of his contemporaries Mommsen and Lepsius, and preferred not to discuss revelation, or God's intentions. In 1882, he was so determined to leave the theological faculty in Griefswald, where his historicist studies fit uncomfortably into a program for training Protestant pastors, that he took a demotion in status to move to the philosophical faculty at the University of Halle. After his *Prolegomena*, Wellhausen took up the study of Islam, and especially of nomadic Arab tribes, in order to better understand the ancient Israelites; this venture into historical sociology attracted the interest of two pioneers of the sociology of religion, Max Weber and W. Robertson Smith. It was left, then, to Wellhausen's successors to draw conclusions about the implications of his philological work for believing Christians and Jews; professorial, positivistic "disinterest" held Wellhausen aloof from such practical debates.[117]

The popularity of Wellhausen's work, in addition to the now institutionalized power of historicist philology, may help explain the halting development of Assyriology in Germany. As suggested above, the study of the Orient remained almost exclusively philological until the fin de siècle, and debates over the decipherment of cuneiform long frustrated attempts to introduce new, nonclassical source materials into the study of the Mesopotamian past. Egyptologists, the student of cuneiform Alfred Jeremias complained in 1907, had refused to consider relationships between the people of the Nile and those of the Tigris. "Egyptology," he wrote, "developed as a science in the era . . . in which one proceeded, under the influence of a one-sided philological perspective, on the assumption that different peoples could have pursued lives separate from and independent of one another." Jeremias hopefully pronounced that this false perception had been shattered by recent archaeological finds, and that a new understanding of the common culture of Asia Minor was dawning, but he admitted that Egyptologists had not yet relinquished their "state within a state in the republic of scholarship."[118] Jeremias's colleague Hugo Winckler denounced even more fervently restrictions on comparativism imposed in the name of "prudent scholarship."[119] Winckler, who never received a permanent academic position despite his landmark discoveries at the Hittite capital Boghazkoi, bears a striking resemblance to the alienated, obstreperous Austrian art historian Josef Strzygowski: both bitterly contested the restrictions philologists

[117] On Wellhausen, see ibid.; also, Rudolf Smend, "Julius Wellhausen," in idem, *Deutsche Alttestamentler in drei Jahrhunderten* (Göttingen, 1989), pp. 99–113; Momigliano, "New Paths of Classicism in the Nineteenth Century," *History and Theory*, suppl. vol. 21 (1982): 51–63; Klaus Johanning, *Der Bibel-Babel-Streit: Eine forschungsgeschichtliche Studie* (Frankfurt, 1988), pp. 120–44.

[118] Alfred Jeremias, *Die Panbabylonisten: Der alte Orient und die aegyptische Religion*, Im Kampf um den alten Orient 1 (1907): 21–22.

[119] Hugo Winckler, "Der alte Orient und die Geschichtsforschung," in *Mitteilungen der vorderasiatischen Gesellschaft* 1 (1906): 2.

tried to put on their speculative theories.[120] But in 1908, even Eduard Meyer complained that too many of his fellow scholars lacked the "intellectual elasticity" to come to grips with the fact that Assyrian texts had made the conventional picture of the ancient Orient, based chiefly on Greek texts, wholly untenable. Unwilling to face this realization, the Assyriologists themselves had retreated from the difficult task of developing new ideas into the safer realm of nitpicking linguistic debate.[121]

Both Winckler and Jeremias belonged to the school that came to be called the "Pan-Babylonists," for they firmly believed that many of the myths, architectural forms, scientific practices, and linguistic innovations credited to the Egyptians and Hebrews had in fact been pioneered by the Babylonians. The source materials for the first speculations of this sort came largely from British excavations in the Near East; the sensational discovery and publication of fragments of a Babylonian account of the deluge in the *Daily Telegraph* in 1873 excited biblical scholars and orientalists alike. In Germany, the first attempts at interpreting these new sources were made in Friedrich Delitzsch's *Wo lag das Paradies?* (*Where Did Paradise Lie?*—1881) and Munich professor Fritz Hommel's *Geschichte Babylons und Assyriens* (*History of Babylon and Assyria*—1885); but after the publication of Eduard Stucken's bizarre *Astralmythen* (*Astral Myths*—1896), Assyriological self-assertion began in earnest. Relying upon Babylonian scientific texts and the cache of clay tablets that came to be called the Epic of Gilgamesh, some of these scholars concluded that Babylon's astrological worldview had set its seal on all religions and cultures. Holder of the Berlin chair of Semitic languages, president of the DOG, and director of the Asia Minor Department at the Royal Museums, Delitzsch was by far the most respectable of this group, though by no means the most ardent exponent of Pan-Babylonism. But he did share the group's excitement about newly available source materials and their frustrations over academia's unwillingness to draw theological conclusions from these. In the end, it was not a great philological breakthrough or a fantastic archaeological find, but Delitzsch's conveyance of his conclusions in a public lecture that gave Assyriology the social recognition and theological purchase it had long been denied.

In 1902, Delitzsch gave a lecture at a DOG meeting entitled "Babel und die Bibel" to an audience consisting of highly placed theologians, businessmen, bureaucrats, and naval officers. Also attending the meeting was Kaiser Wilhelm II—the titular head of the Lutheran Church. Accompanying his philological argument with material evidence presented in slides, Delitzsch proudly announced the falling away of the walls that had previously con-

---

[120] See Marchand, "Rhetoric of Artifacts," and Winckler, "Der alte Orient." On Winckler's archaeological work, see C. W. Ceram, *The Secret of the Hittites: The Discovery of an Ancient Empire*, trans. Richard and Clara Winston (New York, 1956), pp. 49–66.

[121] Meyer quoted in Renger, "Geschichte der Altorientalistik," pp. 154–56.

fined theological study of the Orient to the Old Testament. New artifacts and documents—like the Code of Hammurabi, found by French excavators in Susa only weeks before Delitzsch's lecture—showed that many biblical stories had Babylonian precursors; concepts like the "Sabbath," "sin," "paradise," and even the Jewish name for God, "Yahweh," had originated in Mesopotamia.[122] Delitzsch's Jewish and conservative Christian listeners bridled at the professor's ruthless philological dissections, but Wilhelm II enjoyed the lecture so much that he demanded Delitzsch repeat it for him privately. A year later, Delitzsch offered a second, even more inflammatory, paper on the subject, before an even more distinguished audience of friends and foes. The Kaiser's fascination with the subject and the controversies that surrounded the first and second lectures made Delitzsch and Assyriology hot topics in the Reich. By 1905, Delitzsch's first lecture had sold sixty thousand copies and inspired the publication of more than 1,650 articles and twenty-eight pamphlets in Germany alone.[123] Karl May wrote his only drama on the subject (*Babel und Bibel*, 1906), and in 1908 the Kaiser ordered the performance of the pantomime-play *Assurbanipal*, for which he recruited Andrae, Delitzsch, and other DOG scholars to ensure that props, costumes, and hairdos were stylistically accurate.[124] Bablomania, one might say, had seized the Wilhelmine Empire.

As the foregoing suggests, the part played by Wilhelm II in what came to be called the *Babel-und-die-Bibel-Streit* (Babylon and the Bible affair) contributed heavily to the high profile of the controversy. When, in his second lecture, Delitzsch extended his argument for Babylonian precedence and denied the Old Testament revelatory content, Wilhelm came under heavy pressure from religious conservatives to distance himself from these claims. That the German sovereign did so in language borrowed from his virulently anti-Semitic friend Houston Stewart Chamberlain[125] is telling: to placate his Christian critics, it was sufficient only that he demonstrate his belief that the coming of Christ had been properly foretold.[126] For his part, Delitzsch stuck to the liberal historicist conviction that going to the root was the indispensable prerequisite of true understanding. It would be showing ingratitude to God, he wrote in 1907, if we did not use our knowledge to purify our faith, as well as our conceptions of the past:

---

[122] Delitzsch, *Babel und Bibel: Ein Vortrag* (Leipzig, 1902), pp. 29–47.

[123] Reinhard G. Lehmann, *Friedrich Delitzsch und der Babel-Bibel-Streit* (Göttingen, 1994), p. 50; Delitzsch, *Babel und Bibel: Ein Rückblick und Ausblick* (Stuttgart, 1904), p. 3.

[124] Wilhelm invited dignitaries foreign and domestic to the play's opening night and proceeded to offend the British and French by adding to the archaeological spectacle a speech praising Assyria's lack of parliaments. Andrae, *Lebenserinnerungen*, pp. 180–82. In 1913, Wilhelm also staged—with Wiegand's assistance—a costume drama about Corfu. Watzinger, *Wiegand*, pp. 265–66.

[125] Lehmann, *Delitzsch*, pp. 222–26.

[126] See copy of letter reprinted in Johanning, *Bibel-Babel-Streit*, pp. 408–11.

Thus the results of the Babylonian-Assyrian excavations powerfully contribute to freeing us from the old, deeply rooted errors of our religious thought and to helping us to prepare the ground, on foundations of unshakable historical knowledge, for that further development of religion to which our age is ever more irresistibly drawn. . . . For the sake of this endeavor, we may also be obliged by science to remove with reverent hands a great number of manmade accretions from the Old as well as the New Testament, in order to grasp the kernel of eternal truth the more frankly and joyfully; so too we want to accept openly and thankfully the new discoveries we have been granted, to welcome as the harbinger of a new day the light from the East![127]

Delitzsch was perfectly willing to abandon corrupted scriptures, and especially the Old Testament, as a means to complete the Reformation; it is hardly surprising that by 1908, he, like Wilhelm, had moved toward the Germanic Christianity of the radical right-wing theologian Wilhelm Schwaner.[128] In spite of the conservatives' disapproval, and (unfounded) suspicious of Delitzsch's socialist leanings, the two men kept up their friendship, and Delitzsch retained his prestigious institutional positions until his death in 1921, by which time he had become a virulent, outspoken anti-Semite.[129]

Although a number of recent writers have emphasized the importance of the *Babel-Bibel-Streit* for the study of theology in Germany, its wider cultural ramifications have not really been studied. I would suggest that it might be seen as the German equivalent of the Scopes Trial, in which the long-standing contest between science and religion for social and intellectual hegemony came most forcefully into public view. The facts that in the German case, the science which took on the Bible was *philology*, and that Delitzsch's attack on "antiquated, ancient-oriental perceptions" had more than an undertone of anti-Semitism, are instructive peculiarities of the German case. Clearly, the controversy had its greatest impact on the clergy and on the schools, both of which felt compelled to respond to the new scholarly findings. Furious that they had not been prepared for Delitzsch's shocking claims, clerics denounced their teachers and superiors; pastors, respected for their expert understanding of the scriptures, had had their distance from the Olympus of academia rudely exposed to public view.[130]

---

[127] Delitzsch, *Mehr Licht: Die bedeutsamen Ergebnisse der babylonisch-assyrischen Grabungen für Geschichte, Kultur, und Religion* (Leipzig, 1907), pp. 53–54; quotation, p. 55.

[128] Lehmann, *Delitzsch*, p. 266–68.

[129] Ibid., p. 242; By 1921, Delitzsch was emboldened to argue that the Old Testament was not merely pure literature, but the fictional product of a murderous and deceitful Jewish nation. Delitzsch also trotted out an explanation for the Aryan Christ hypothesis, favored by Chamberlain and the Kaiser; Jesus, he insisted, had been a Galilean by blood, and a convert to the Jewish faith. Delitzsch, *Die große Täuschung* vol. 1 (Stuttgart, 1921); pp. 53–54; 96.

[130] See the letters collected in Delitzsch, *Babel und Bibel: Ein Rückblick*.

Yet when teachers of religion did incorporate the new knowledge into the curricula, the laity turned on the educators; as Friedrich Paulsen remarked in 1911, the population had begun to suspect the schools of creeping materialism.[131] Inevitably, the interpretation of Assyrian artifacts and inscriptions, like the interpretation of Germanic prehistory, was much more controversial, and much less monopolized by professional experts, than the explication of classical antiquity.

The *Bibel-Babel* affair exposed the fragility of the social consensus upon which the progress of specialized scholarship depended and the increasingly antiliberal politics behind its claims to "disinterestedness." In this way, it parallels the fragmentation of *Kulturpolitik* in Asia Minor; so many groups expected so many grandiose and conflicting solutions to social and political problems from the cultural sphere that no solution, literally, would have pleased everyone. The quest for more and more materials left little time for interpretation; but when interpretation commenced at last, scholars found that the wider population, schooled in Greek classicism and the sanctity of the Bible, could not easily digest their results, nor could the state provide sufficient funds to exhibit all their finds. Hyperhistoricism and archaeological acquisitiveness had made professional *Altertumswissenschaft* dependent on state funding at the very time that the German military was preparing for new sorts of conquest, and that the Marxist Social Democratic party was rapidly increasing its presence in the Reichstag. Notwithstanding the Kaiser's enthusiasm for archaeology (he began his own excavations on the island of Corfu in 1911),[132] and his affection for Delitzsch, it was clear that both classicists and orientalists would find it more and more difficult to find patrons willing and able to support their specialized endeavors in the years to come.

But, seen in retrospect, quarrels over the meaning of Babylonian texts and artifacts had more distressing cultural implications as well. There is some dispute about the point at which Delitzsch actually became an anti-Semite, but none that, as a result of his philological perorations, the sanctity of the Old Testament had certainly been diminished. Delitzsch's scholarly colleagues certainly recognized this, as quickly as did Wilhelm and Chamberlain, and many objected to his attempts to deny Israel a central role in the development of monotheism.[133] But they did not, on the whole, object to the simultaneous historicization of the Jewish holy books and the rejection of their historical reliability. If both Old and New Testaments were to be subjected to further philological and rationalist critiques, it was clear which of the two testaments the liberal Protestantism establishment would

---

[131] Lehmann, *Delitzsch*, p. 231–36.

[132] See chapter 7.

[133] See Rudolf Kittel, *Die babylonischen Ausgrabungen und die biblische Urgeschichte*, 4th ed. (Leipzig, 1903); Johanning, *Bibel-Babel-Streit*, pp. 249–57.

wish to rescue from theological irrelevance. Their attempts to clarify, by historical-philological purgation, the "essence" of Protestantism led them away from, rather than toward, reconciliation with their Jewish liberal brethren.[134] Similarly, orientalists, now privy to a vast mass of Egyptian, Hittite, and Assyrian monuments, lost interest in the study of the Israelites, whose history had come to seem rather shallow.[135] The *Bibel-Babel* controversy was only one episode in the history of the degeneration of German tolerance, but it represents, perhaps, a little-appreciated warning sign that the pursuit of knowledge for its own sake had begun to take on the protective coloring of its reactionary patrons and grow reckless about its social costs.

[134] Tal, *Christians and Jews*, p. 298.
[135] See Delitzsch, *Babel und Bibel: Ein Vortrag*, p. 7; Erman, *Mein Werden*, pp. 252–53.

KULTUR AND THE WORLD WAR

In the country of Kantian aesthetics, it is above all advisable
to emphasize that one desires a German victory in a
disinterested way.
(*Thomas Mann*)

THE TWO DECADES that preceded the outbreak of the Great War present a puzzling blend of vastly expanded international cultural contact and enormously increased nationalist chauvinism. Bitter colonial rivalries and the British-German naval arms race broke out just as Europeans of the middling sort were seeing more of one another than ever before, in photographs and at international exhibitions, by means of faster, cheaper transportation routes and the expanding embrace of the popular press. Commerce among European and American scholars accelerated as international conferences and scholarly organizations grew in number. The reverse side of this expansion, however, was the demand for equal access to information (and, as we have seen, equivalent ownership of objects) by national groups and institutions previously dependent on others for scientific and cultural materials.[1] Paradoxically, as scholarly advancement became more and more dependent upon international contact, it also came increasingly to be regarded as a national bragging point. On the eve of the First World War, then, *Kultur* and *Wissenschaft* were both more international in scope and more nationalist in sentiment than ever before.

Coinciding with and complexly related to the rise of this curious mixture of extended contact and narrowed mind-set was the increasing activity of the German state in cultural affairs, as patron, organizer, and publicizer. During the tenures of Richard Schöne and Friedrich Althoff, the Reich had vastly increased both its generosity and its control in the cultural sphere. But the state had not acted alone or without encouragement from cultural interest groups that saw the state as the guarantor of scholarly autonomy against the incursion of party-political demands.[2] In fact, much of the cul-

---

[1] See, e.g., the correspondence denouncing French domination of the antiquities bureau in Egypt, beginning with the Foreign Ministry's "Notiz" of 9 March 1881, in PZStA AA/R 37106, p. 5.

[2] See Bernhard vom Brocke, "Hochschul- und Wissenschaftspolitik in Preußen und im Deutschen Kaiserreich 1882–1907: Das System Althoff," in *Bildungspolitik in Preußen zur Zeit des Kaiserreiches*, ed. Peter Baumgart (Stuttgart, 1980), p. 89.

tural reorganization in the late nineteenth and early twentieth centuries took place at the insistence of commercial interests or para-academic organizations like the Prussian Academy of Sciences, the DAI, and the Royal Museums. Of course, these groups did not turn to the state merely to avoid the politicization of their causes; specialization and escalating international rivalries required high levels of investment to build laboratories and provide research materials, particularly in "applied" fields such as electromagnetics, medicine, and agronomy. Engaged in a furious naval arms race, the Reich could hardly fund all applicants, but could not easily turn down those who emphasized their contributions to German prestige and empowerment. The principle that *Kultur* should serve the state and, correspondingly, that the state should promote *Kultur*, had become the shared conviction of academia and the Reich bureaucracy.

Noting the changing parameters of patronage, however, does not explain *why* late Wilhelmine Germans took such avid interest in the modernization and promotion of *Kultur*. New forms of organization for the pursuit of knowledge were not only spawned by internal, institutional demands for modernization and expansion but can also be linked to the rise of new, broader, and more subtle forms of imperialist activity. As the product of national institutes and public-private joint ventures, cultural enrichment and the progress of scholarship provided endless opportunities for non-belligerent self-congratulation, a particular delight to a German nation that had long called itself one of "poets and thinkers." It also offered an excuse for Germans to patronize or even colonize other nations by means of gradual cultural influence, as Hans von Wangenheim and Theodor Wiegand planned to do in the Ottoman Empire. Something of the same mentality lay behind Friedrich Althoff's founding of universities in newly Germanized Straßburg and in Polish-dominated Posen.[3] Here the pursuit of knowledge served as a kind of nationalist propaganda, without, however, losing any of its merit as good scholarship; in carrying the German *Kulturmission* abroad, the patron and/or the scholar could be philanthropist, patriot, and professional all at once.

It should not be imagined, however, that *Kulturpolitik* sprang fully formed from the minds of a few elite manipulators. It would be a grave misrepresentation of its diverse origins and wide appeal to construe it as a superstructural excrescence of internal imperialism, for prewar *Kulturpolitik* remained chaotic in its intentions and undisciplined in its practice. Increasing interest in cultural diplomacy in the years before the war owes

---

[3] On Althoff's work in Alsace see John E. Craig, *Scholarship and Nation Building: The Universities of Strasbourg and Alsatian Society, 1870–1939* (Chicago, 1984); on his involvement in *Polenpolitik*, see Arnold Sachse, *Friedrich Althoff und sein Werk* (Berlin, 1928), p. 123. On later, more insidious scientific intervention, see Michael Burleigh, *Germany Turns Eastward: A Study of Ostforschung in the Third Reich* (Cambridge, 1988).

less to a concerted effort to instrumentalize scholarship and culture than to the proliferation of groups sensitized to the importance of Germany's image abroad.[4] The Foreign Ministry's notorious factionalization and ambivalence left the operation of *Kulturpolitik* by and large open to all comers, from Pan-German agitators to the left liberals of the school of Friedrich Naumann, who hoped to replace *Machtpolitik* with a more benign conquest of new territory through *Kulturexport*.[5] "Friendship" societies were composed of scholars like Karl Lamprecht, proponents of economic (or worse) colonialism like Paul Rohrbach, influential overseas businessmen like Georg von Siemens, and Education Ministry bureaucrats in Berlin, like Friedrich Althoff. Scores of organizations dedicated to *Kulturpolitik* were formed, devoting their activities to specific areas (Deutsch-Asiatische Gesellschaft [German Asiatic Society]), particular causes (Flottenverein im Ausland [Supporters of the Navy League Abroad]), individual industries (Buchgewerbe-Verein [Society of Book Traders]), or philanthropic goals (Deutsche Bagdadkomitee für Humanitätszwecke [German Humanitarian Society of Baghdad]). Each group pursued its own ends, employing the means available; no central authority existed to coordinate disparate plans.[6] The disjunction of views and aims represented here would find full and bitter expression in venomous wartime disputes over Germany's proper territorial and cultural spoils.

This appropriation of *Kultur* as a kind of ersatz diplomacy is merely one example of the changes in form, content, and social proprietorship underway in the cultural sphere. Urbanization, industrialization, and the rise of the popular press also allowed other groups to organize separate cultural spheres against the official culture of universities and academies. Inside the universities, scholars in fields like geography, ethnography, modern art history, and prehistory pressed for more positions and begged the Reich for fieldwork support. Language study—beyond the classics, French, and English—was ever more in demand; the social sciences blossomed and acquired new prestige. Increased demand for bureaucrats and businessmen fueled the great expansion and diversification of lower education in the years before the war, provoking frightened warnings from the elite against

---

[4] See Rüdiger vom Bruch, *Weltpolitik als Kulturmission: Auswärtige Kulturpolitik und Bildungsbürgertum in Deutschland am Vorabend des Ersten Weltkrieges* (Paderborn, 1982).

[5] Lamar Cecil, "Der diplomatische Dienst im kaiserlichen Deutschland," in *Das diplomatische Korps, 1871–1945*, ed. Klaus Schwabe (Boppard am Rhein, 1982), p. 36; Jürgen Kloosterhuis, "Deutsche auswärtige Kulturpolitik und ihre Trägergruppen vor dem Ersten Weltkrieg," in *Deutsche auswärtige Kulturpolitik seit 1871*, ed. Kurt Düwell and Werner Link (Vienna, 1981), p. 15.

[6] For other examples of such *Vereine*, see vom Bruch, *Weltpolitik als Kulturmission*, p. 82; for an interesting parallel in the political sphere, see Geoff Eley, "Some Thoughts on the Nationalist Pressure Groups in Imperial Germany," in *Nationalist and Racialist Movements in Britain and Germany before 1914*, ed. Paul Kennedy and Anthony Nicholls (London, 1981), pp. 40–67.

the "proletarianizing" of the higher education.[7] Meanwhile, beyond the world of officially sanctioned arts and sciences, semiofficial or popular groups gained large followings. The youth movement, the Social Democrats, and Catholics all sought to organize their sectors of the cultural sphere, while at the same time, provincial patriots recruited members for their local associations. In short, academic culture, particularly humanistic academic culture, had become more and more obviously a parochial rather than a national possession. An exclusive garden tended by aged men, classical studies were fated to suffer the wrath of contentious new groups.

Thus the coming of the war seemed to spell doom for *Altertumswissenschaft*. Both domestically and internationally, the world war figured as a kind of *Existenzkampf* for neohumanist academe as well as for the German monarchy. The classicist establishment owed the continuation of its preeminence to the Wilhelmine state. Not only did archaeologists and the museum administration depend on the success of *Weltpolitik* for the furtherance of their ambitions (and acquisitions), but philologists needed the backing of the Education Ministry to stave off further progress by school reformers. As we have seen, the philhellenist resort to *Anschauungsunterricht* and celebration of archaeological triumphs succeeded, at least to some extent, in reinvigorating classical education. This tactic, however, tied the preservation of domestic cultural predominance to expansionist *Kulturpolitik*. As we trace below the participation of classicists in the German war effort, we must keep in mind archaeology's peculiar investment in and dependence on the carefully controlled exercise of German foreign policy. For the vehement expansionism of the academic propagandists and the dedicated preservation work of the field archaeologists cannot be explained by nationalist sentiment alone; *Altertumswissenschaft*, too, had come to believe that life without conquest was equivalent to death.

Classicists at War

One of the major, though surely unintended, effects of the Entente's atrocity propaganda campaign proved to be the arousal of the ferocious patriotism of the German professoriate. This is not to say that the vast majority of Wilhelmine academics, nominated by their conservative peers and approved by the local ministries of education, had been ambivalent at the war's outbreak. German scholars, especially since the passing of the liberal generation of Theodor Mommsen and Rudolf Virchow, by and large ap-

---

[7] Bernd Zymek, "Perspektive und Enttäuschung deutscher Gymnasiasten," in *"Neue Erziehung," "Neue Menschen": Ansätze zur Erziehungs- und Bildungsreform in Deutschland zwischen Kaiserreich und Diktatur*, ed. Ulrich Herrmann (Basel, 1987), p. 237.

proved of the monarchy, saw the justice in Germany's pursuit of *Weltpolitik*, and felt themselves in duty bound to defend the state that had done so much to promote the interests of *Wissenschaft* and *Kultur*. The Allies' accusations that the land of Goethe and Beethoven had become the land of Bismarck and Attila, however, stirred the embers of state loyalism into a patriotic bonfire, igniting proclamation after appeal after counterpropaganda effort by Germany's leading scholars.

Two charges rankled most: that the essential character of the German state lay in its military power; and that beneath a thin layer of scholarly prowess and Romantic poetry, the Germans themselves remained barbarians, uncivilized descendants of the murderous Vandals and Huns. In the first instance, the professoriate simply could not endure the charge that pure militarism had taken over the German soul, even in the midst of the nation's "struggle for existence." Germany was "about" *Kultur*, not militarism; or at least about the symbiosis of the ascetic soul and the strong body. The famous "two Germanies" argument excited the patriotic passions of both conservative and reform-minded scholars, ensuring the eternal recurrence of Wilhelm von Humboldt and the Weimar poets in wartime addresses. Reminding audiences of Germany's foremost renown as the "nation of poets and thinkers," these invocations of the world of Goethe and Kant also underscored the special role German cultural nationalism had played in throwing off the French yoke.[8] For example, in a late 1914 press release directed at American readers, Paul Clemen, Bonn art historian and head of monument protection for the German occupation government in Belgium, attacked the false opposition made by propagandists between

> the genocidal spirit of the new militarism and the spirit of the old Germany of poets and thinkers. Are you the descendants of Goethe or of Attila? asks Romain Rolland. We can't defend ourselves enough against such a false understanding of German *Geist*—the Berlin literary historian Gustav Roethe has recently said that in this hour, Goethe's *Faust*, Beethoven's *Eroica*, Kant's categorical imperative, and Jacob Grimm's *Deutsche Grammatik* do battle with our enemies just as do Krupp's cannon and Zeppelin's aircraft, to [the production of] which German science also contributed. In this war, all of German *Kultur*, of German *Geist* stands united.[9]

[8] See, e.g., Ulrich von Wilamowitz-Moellendorff, "Militarismus und Wissenschaft," in idem, *Reden aus der Kriegszeit* (Berlin, 1915), p. 87; Lamprecht also returns ceaselessly to the *Goethezeit* in his three public lectures published in *Krieg und Kultur* (Leipzig, 1914). For more on the "two Germanies" problem see Bernhard vom Brocke, "'Wissenschaft und Militarismus': Der Aufruf der 93 'An die Kulturwelt!' und der Zusammenbruch der internationalen Gelehrtenrepublik im Ersten Weltkrieg," in *Wilamowitz nach 50 Jahren*, ed. William M. Calder et al. (Darmstadt, 1985), p. 653, n. 4.

[9] Paul Clemen, "Der Krieg und die Kunstdenkmäler," dated 31 December 1914 and intended for the American press, in MZStA 2.2.1–20793, p. 24.

In fact, it proved not to be the case, as the war raged on, that even *Geist* remained united, to say nothing of the social, political, and regional divisions that tore apart the civil peace. By 1915, the professoriate had become embroiled in war aims debates so vituperative as to all but banish the rhetoric of "*Kultur* united" to the land of wishful thinking.[10]

The second charge, that the barbaric Germans had destroyed European cultural treasures, evoked even deeper scholarly distress, perhaps partly because the legacy of the Huns and Goths had previously been invoked by so many patriotic Germans, including Wilhelm II.[11] The upholders of *Wissenschaft* and *Bildung* in an age of increasing materialism and utilitarianism—barbarians? The suffering of the soldiers, the vast scale of the fighting, the introduction of new war technology, the social effects of the conflict, the events surrounding the war's outbreak, even the virulently debated issue of unlimited submarine warfare: all these subjects paled in comparison to the determination to prove Germany undeserving of the epithet "barbarian." Even local politicians believed this particular accusation required refutation in deeds as well as in words. No less than three representatives of the Prussian Landtag, including the Social Democrat (and later Education Minister) Konrad Haenisch, explicitly claimed the maintenance of the cultural budget for 1915 at near peacetime levels to be a vital weapon of war as it provided proof positive that Germans were not barbarians.[12] Clearly reports about the sacking of Louvain and looting at Reims struck a raw nerve, or perhaps two: the vehement denials of the scholarly community testify to both offense at the slighting of their honor and fear that they might indeed be superfluous in the emerging, war-torn world.

Thus *Kultur* quickly took its place in the struggle, asserting its indispensability to German prestige abroad and its inseparability from the fortunes of the German military. "Intellectual weapons" (*Waffen des Geistes*), claimed the scholars and their bureaucratic supporters, were absolutely essential to defend against the French "terrorism of public opinion" and the British "tyranny of cant."[13] The practice of what was termed *Kulturpropaganda* by individuals or private groups was related to but not identical with *Kulturpolitik*: the latter implies the general cultivation of good feeling through philanthropic deeds and mutually beneficial exchanges of information, while the former aims at arousing sympathy for a particular cause by trading on established reputations. The prevalent mode of scholarly participation in the war, *Kulturpropaganda* could be exercised in various ways, the most common and attractive of which appears to have been what Aby War-

---

[10] On these debates, see Klaus Schwalbe, *Wissenschaft und Kriegsmoral* (Göttingen, 1969).

[11] See chapter 5.

[12] Reported in [Eugen Grünewald], "Die höheren Lehranstalten in den preußischen Landtagsverhandlungen am 2. und 3. März 1915, *Das humanistische Gymnasium* (1915): 77–78.

[13] Wilamowitz, "Militarismus und Wissenschaft," p. 92.

burg called *Personalpolitik*, or the attempt to sway friends and colleagues overseas by means of personal appeals.[14] Manifestos and press releases, too, offered intellectuals the opportunity to lend their credibility to the proclamations of their leaders, particularly with an eye to influencing policy decisions in neutral countries.

If German professional and also literary participation in *Kulturpropaganda* was vigorous and widespread, however, the Reich really never recovered from early Entente broadsides and remained, for the most part, on the defensive. Several factors can be adduced to explain this. Practically speaking, the Germans had little access to important neutral presses: in the case of the United States, the Reich's overseas telegraph cable was cut on 5 August 1914, giving the British publicists a monopoly on war reportage to America.[15] In Greece, the press was hostile from the outset due to German alliance with the country's arch-enemy, the Ottoman Empire; in Italy, opportunities to cultivate pro-German sentiment were missed due to lack of funds and knowledgeable propagandists on the scene.[16] By October 1914 twenty-seven bureaus handling propaganda abroad had sprung up,[17] but cooperation among these was sporadic at best. The situation was no better on the home front. The agency responsible for domestic morale building, the Kriegspresseamt, was founded under the Prussian War Ministry only in October 1915, and concentrated on supplying the German press with war news rather than counteracting the effects of Allied insinuations.[18] Ludendorff was apparently still trying to centralize Germany's propaganda efforts in March 1918;[19] here too, it seems, the specter of German cultural disunity rose to plague the nation's leaders.

But if disunified, relatively ineffectual, and largely defensive, Germany's *Kulturpropaganda* effort performed several important internal functions. Most obviously, it gave scholars itching to contribute to the cause an outlet for the expression of their convictions. More importantly, it provided intellectuals with an explanation of what the war was about, one unsullied by the materialistic designs of commerce or the purely political aim of propping up two decaying empires. If exhilarated by the coming of the war, scholars with extensive foreign ties and experience were also deeply wounded and embittered by the visceral enmity of their new foes. The liberal theologian Ernst Troeltsch, for example, pointed with angry incom-

---

[14] See Warburg's letters, especially to Bode, in WI, Kopierbuch Nr. 6, 1915–18.

[15] Vom Brocke, "'Wissenschaft und Militarismus,'" p. 676.

[16] See Delbrück to Wiegand, 1 April 1915, DAI, Nachlaß Wiegand, Kasten 2.

[17] Claus Conrad, *Krieg und Aufsatzunterricht: Eine Untersuchung von Abituraufsätzen vor und während des Ersten Weltkrieges* (Frankfurt, 1986), p. 75.

[18] George G. Bruntz, *Allied Propaganda and the Collapse of the German Empire in 1918* (Stanford, Calif., 1938), p. 194.

[19] Ibid., p. 198.

prehension to "a crusade against the German spirit, a moral continental boycott against Germany, an intellectual hell of lack of understanding and hatred toward that which we believe to be our best."[20] An inconsolable Eduard Meyer believed Germans "manly enough" to bear the revelation that "the era of internationalism is buried and will not return," but was not alone in shedding a tear over its passing.[21] Casting political opposition in intellectual terms, as Bernhard vom Brocke has argued, explained and justified this alienation of Germany from her "civilized" neighbors as a product of essential national-cultural differences, establishing thereby the contours of the *Sonderweg* ideology.[22] Troeltsch's "German idea of freedom" and Thomas Mann's famous opposition of Western, political *Zivilisation* and German, moral and aesthetic, *Kultur* did not, of course, appear in every pamphlet, but the working out of enmities in philosophical terms did make sense of the conflict—at least for the largely unregenerate professoriate of the 1910s and 1920s.[23]

Not surprisingly, much counterpropaganda touted Germany's humanist credentials, its special role as protector of European culture from the hegemonic and decadent forces of Western domination and from the apocalyptic threat of slavic or oriental inundation. The annexationist "Seeberg Adresse," signed by 352 university teachers, pledged Germany to the defense of European culture "against the barbarian flood from the East and the lust for vengeance and mastery from the West."[24] Hans von Arnim explained that atrocity charges against the German nation merely reflected the chauvinism and ignorance endemic in French and English culture (as opposed to German tolerance and knowledge), while Wilamowitz denounced the lure of English customs and manners as the witchery of a nation of Dorian Grays.[25] In another wartime address, Wilamowitz turned accusations of German barbarism around to show how the destruction of the orientalized Roman Empire had actually saved and revived European civilization by throwing off the dead hand of single-culture rule.

> The tyranny of any single one of [the European peoples] must necessarily have as its consequence the extinction of *Kultur*, just as *Kultur* died out in the Roman Empire. If we are hopeful that the day of the Germans is dawning, only

[20] Ernst Troeltsch, *Das Wesen des Deutschen* (Heidelberg, 1915), p. 5.

[21] Eduard Meyer, *England: Seine staatliche und politische Entwicklung und der Krieg gegen Deutschland*, 7th ed. (Stuttgart, 1915), pp. 208, 207.

[22] See vom Brocke, "'Wissenschaft und Militarismus,'" pp. 687–88, 704ff.

[23] On the lack of an overall consensus on meaning, see the powerful book by Robert Whalen, *Bitter Wounds: German Victims of the Great War, 1914–1939* (Ithaca, N.Y., 1984).

[24] "Seeberg Adresse" (20 June 1915) in *Aufrufe und Reden deutscher Professoren im Ersten Weltkrieg*, ed. Klaus Böhme (Stuttgart, 1975), p. 125.

[25] See Hans von Arnim, "Humanismus und Nationalgefühl," *Das humanistische Gymnasium* (1915): 10; Wilamowitz, *In dem zweiten Kriegswinter* (Berlin, 1915), p. 13.

shortsighted and narrow-minded chauvinists see in this the repression of others: we value our *Volk* more highly and trust it to establish world peace in order that the individuality of each *Volk* can unfold freely side by side for the good of all.[26]

Similarly, Thomas Mann's *Reflections* outlined Germany's role as European protester against and protectress of variety and depth in the face of Roman-French leveling universalisms.[27] Not for its own sake, but for the sake of Europe, Germany must emerge triumphant.

A favorite German counterpropaganda tactic entailed the application of the repellent charge of barbarism to Entente forces composed of "culture-less" colonial peoples and Slavs. For example, the famous "Aufruf an die Kulturwelt" ("Appeal to the Civilized World") of 4 October 1914, signed by ninety-three eminent cultural figures including Wiegand, Dörpfeld, Bode, Wilamowitz, Eduard Meyer, and Karl Robert, directly confronted the "lies and slanders" being spread about Germany's heartless behavior in Belgium. The appeal first attacked the "two Germanies" thesis, denying that German cultural life could have flourished without the army, as well as the idea that militarism represented an autonomous force that could be defeated without bringing down German *Kultur* and the German *Volk* as well. The violent countercharges made in the document, however, suggest both the urgency of deflecting the "barbarism" accusation, and also the terror inspired by the way in which the war was exceeding the bounds of a heroic battle between "civilized" men:

> It is not true that our war leaders ignored the dictates of international law. They know nothing of wild atrocities. In the east, however, the earth is soaked with the blood of women and children murdered by the Russian hordes, and in the west, dumdum bullets rip apart the chests of our fighters. Least of all do those who ally themselves with Russians and Serbs and offer the world the tasteful spectacle of Mongols and Negroes incited against the white race have the right to pose as the defenders of European civilization.[28]

The "ninety-three" could endure, and even welcomed, a "struggle for exis-tence," but not categorization with Russians and black Africans. "Believe us!" the appeal concluded; "Believe that we will fight to the end as a *Kultur-volk*, to whom the legacies of a Goethe, a Beethoven, [and] a Kant are just as sacred as its hearth and its soil."[29]

An odd, but interesting variation of the struggle for control of the title of

[26] Wilamowitz, "Orient und Okzident," in his *Reden aus der Kriegszeit*, p. 235–36.

[27] Thomas Mann, *Reflections of a Nonpolitical Man*, trans. Walter D. Morris (New York, 1987), p. 33.

[28] "An die Kulturwelt!" My copy comes from DAI, Nachlaß Dörpfeld, Kasten 16, Mappe 2.

[29] Ibid.

defender of European culture was the German claim to be liberator of the Orient. Politicized orientalists had, of course, already perfected this rhetorical trope, but others now joined in the chorus. Wilamowitz, the doyen of classical philology, composed an essay titled "Orient und Okzident," in which he praised the Islamic world for its preservation of Greek culture ("Metamorphosis into a mosque hurt the Parthenon less than [metamorphosis] into a Christian church")[30] and declared Germany's disinterested role in the encouragement of autonomous Islamic culture. "The oriental who denies his inborn essence and wants to play the European would be a very unpleasant bastard creature," he wrote; fortunately, however, Germany's Hellenic roots would once again guide her (and thence the rest of the world) to recognition of the rights of self-determination for all.[31] In some cases, German anticolonial propaganda apparently slid over into outright provocation of *jihad*; the Dutch orientalist C. Snouck Hurgronje found this departure from prevailing scholarly ethics on the part of his German colleagues particularly reprehensible.[32] But generally speaking, orientalists like Hamburg Professor Carl Heinrich Becker put their efforts into popularizing the two nations' "community of interests," hoping to win the Turks' hearts by maintaining oriental culture (especially Islam) while pouring in badly needed European investment.[33] In the wartime rhetoric of Becker and his colleagues, the antiannexationist claims of oriental *Kulturpolitik* met humanistic insistence on disinterested universalism.

Employing their erudition to legitimate the drawing of such analogies, the humanists, especially the historians, national economists, and classicists, seem to have taken the leading role in propaganda campaigns.[34] Of the fifty-eight professors who signed the "Aufruf an die Kulturwelt," only twenty-two belonged to the natural science and medical faculties, and of the sixteen signers (of seventy-five still living) who still unconditionally supported the "Aufruf" after the war, a large proportion were classicists (including Meyer, Robert, Dörpfeld, and Friedrich von Duhn).[35] Albert Einstein, himself an outspoken pacifist, underlined this division of the faculties in a letter to the Dutch physicist H. A. Lorentz: "In Berlin, things are

[30] Wilamowitz, "Orient und Okzident," p. 248.

[31] Ibid., p. 250 (quotation), p. 251.

[32] See Hurgronje to Ignaz Goldziher, 27 January 1915, and 10 February 1915 in P. Sj. von Koningsveld, ed. *Scholarship and Friendship in Early Islamwissenschaft: The Letters of C. Snouck Hurgronje to I. Goldziher* (Leiden, 1985), pp. 430–34.

[33] See, e.g., Becker, "Deutsch-türkische Interessengemeinschaft," in *Bonner vaterländische Reden und Vorträge während des Krieges*, no. 2 (Bonn, 1914); idem, *Deutschland und der Islam*, Der Deutsche Krieg, vol. 3, ed. Ernst Jaeckh (Stuttgart, 1914).

[34] In England, according to one recent account, the historians and philosophers took the leading role in academic propaganda efforts. See Stuart Wallace, *War and the Image of Germany: British Academics, 1914–1918* (Edinburgh, 1988), p. 44.

[35] vom Brocke, "'Wissenschaft und Militarismus,'" p. 661, n. 18.

strange. The natural scientists and mathematicians are as scholars deeply internationally minded and watch carefully that no unfriendly steps be taken against colleagues in enemy countries. The historians and philologists, however, are for the most part chauvinists and hotheads."[36] To explain their more aggressive participation in propaganda, a number of humanists argued that their expertise in construing the events of the past accorded them a more objective view of the present than that available to the natural scientists and laymen. This was clearly the self-understanding of a group of Bonn historians who called on their foreign colleagues not to credit tales of German aggression. "Those abroad who value our scholarly work," the address concluded, "should not refuse to attend also to this expression of our historical-political convictions!"[37]

But belief in the adage *historia magistra vitae* cannot fully explain the extreme vehemence of the *Geisteswissenschaftler*, and in particular, the classicists. Vom Brocke notes that the spirit of internationalism burned brighter not only in natural scientists as opposed to humanists, but in scholars of the modern world as opposed to experts in antiquities.[38] Why this should have been so cannot be answered definitively; motivations, like intentions, are in the final analysis susceptible only to case by case consideration. But we can suggest a few factors that may have contributed to the especially virulent patriotism of the classicists. One might begin by suggesting that in addition to functioning as a disinterested explanation of Germany's isolation from the other European powers, *Kulturpropaganda* also served as a kind of ersatz machismo. The leading classicists at the war's outbreak belonged by and large to the generation of the 1880s, not the 1910s; by 1914, most were nearer to retirement than to enlistment age.[39] This meant that their burning desire to demonstrate their patriotic loyalty and their manliness would have to express itself in words rather than deeds. Such a restriction was especially vexatious to a generation that had come of age too late for the wars of unification, and whose nationalist credentials had been repeatedly challenged by vigorous reform movements. Now, it had to endure the sight of the *Jugendbewegung* marching off to glorious battle and the specter of its own sons fallen on the field of glory.[40] In September 1914, C. H. Becker (rather younger and less conservative than most of his colleagues) told his

---

[36] Quoted in ibid., p. 689.

[37] "Aufruf Bonner Historiker" (1 September 1914), in *Aufrufe und Reden*, pp. 50–51.

[38] vom Brocke, "'Wissenschaft und Militarismus,'" p. 690.

[39] Schwalbe, *Kriegsmoral*, p. 21.

[40] The two most prominent scholars of the ancient world, Eduard Meyer and Wilamowitz, both had sons who died in the conflict. Their contemporary, Eduard Schwartz (also a classicist) lost two sons, and a third returned maimed; Schwartz was apparently proud of his family's patriotic sacrifice. See Arnaldo Momigliano, "New Paths of Classicism," *History and Theory*, suppl. vol. 21 (1982): 61. Archaeologist Paul Wolters's son was killed at Verdun.

friend and teacher Theodor Nöldecke: "As a nonserving reservist over thirty years old no one has yet considered me; but I have never found it so painful as now not to have served. All auxiliary work is only a weak substitute."[41] With the outbreak of war, the sixty-four-year-old philologist-archaeologist Karl Robert immediately offered himself to the state for active duty, and was bitterly disappointed to get no response.[42] Archaeologists turned down for regular service, as we will see below, anxiously applied for service in preservation units at or near the front. Wiegand, for example, could not wait to get into the war. His application for service deferred on August 11, Wiegand voluntarily attached himself to the 48th Reserve Regiment in Küstrin two weeks later; the forty-nine-year-old museum director, however, was sent home to assist in military administration and cultural propaganda.[43]

Second, if other intellectuals had begun to worry about their credentials as members of the German *Volk*, classicists had reason to be even more anxious. Comparing the lives of two leading philologists of the generation described above, a near-contemporary made the following generalization about their experience and his own: "The charge is often made against university teachers that they show no interest in the prospering of the *Volk* and bury themselves in their disciplines like moles. Above all representatives of classical scholarship are often reproached for this."[44] Lacking modern economic, political, and historical (not to mention natural-scientific) expertise valuable in the execution of the war, classicists had more to fear from the "two Germanies" thesis than other academic "moles." The concerted patriotic efforts of Wilamowitz, a man who frequently took all his discipline's problems on his own shoulders, indicate something of this ivory tower anxiety. In his 1915 address as newly appointed rector of the University of Berlin, the eminent philologist assured his "fellow students" of the dependence of the university on German arms and the ardent patriotism of "those of us who are condemned to sit here," despite the academic formality that dered their expressions of loyalty.[45] Similarly, Karl Robert, in a late 1915 lecture on *Seven Against Thebes*, a play ideally suited to a nation fearful of sabotage and encirclement, confessed that his discipline "is under siege. Don't we read everyday that our students in the trenches have convinced themselves of the uselessness of Greek and Roman phrases and that they will all turn to practical professions upon their return home, to the army,

[41] Becker to Nöldecke, 17 September 1914, GStAPKB, Nachlaß Becker, Mappe 3138.

[42] Otto Kern, *Hermann Diels und Carl Robert: Ein biographischer Versuch*, Jahresbericht über die Fortschritte der klassischen Altertumswissenschaft, ed. Karl Münscher (Leipzig, 1927), p. 126.

[43] See Silke Wenk, ed., *Auf den Spuren der Antike: Theodor Wiegand, ein deutscher Archäologe*, (Bendorf am Rhein, 1985), p. 20.

[44] Kern, *Hermann Diels und Carl Robert*, p. 117.

[45] Wilamowitz, *In dem zweiten Kriegswinter*, pp. 22–23.

the navy, and aeronautics, to technology, industry, and trade, and that this world war also signifies the end of philology?"[46] Robert encouraged all youngsters so inclined to take up useful jobs for the sake of "our great and dear Fatherland," but denied that world war could extinguish "eternal" philology as a pure science. As Wilamowitz admitted the insufficiency of scholarship to speak for the heart, Robert confessed the narrowing appeal and impractical nature of his field. The war may not have killed philology, but it did administer the dose of humility that the classicist professoriate had been unwilling to receive from the school reformers.

The retreat from classical ideals was particularly evident in pedagogical debates, which raged throughout the war despite the Education Ministry's attempt to proclaim a temporary truce on the issue.[47] Pedagogical thinking during the war emphasized more and more the necessity for the renewal of *Bildung* by means of deeper concentration on specifically German values and past deeds: as theorist Georg Kerschensteiner testified in a letter to the philosopher Eduard Spranger, "German as the foundation of our *Bildung*" had become a catchphrase by late 1915.[48] In 1917, Ernst Troeltsch agreed with the Germanist Konrad Burdach that classical humanism needed to be reconciled with the "Gothic" side of German character to form a new educational ideal based on *German* selfhood. "This means that the standpoint that antiquity contains at the same time the *ur*-forms of nature and the absolute ideal must be relinquished, just as must the exclusively backward-looking character of inquiry and the isolation of classical from Germanic philology and vice versa."[49] Germans could no longer depend on the Greeks for living ideals; Euphorion, the half-Greek, half-German product of Faust's brief marriage with Helen of Troy, was not the doctor's legitimate heir.[50]

Even the argument for classical civilization's formative historical role, as Werner Jaeger came to realize, did not suffice as a defense: historical significance, he averred, did not assure the classics of meaning and vitality in the present.[51] The annexationist geographer Albrecht Penck made a similar argument about the coming demise of Rankean historical consciousness. Concluding his essay with the typical paralleling of the Great War and the Wars of Liberation, Penck looked forward to the end of debilitating *Gymna-*

---

[46] Quoted in Kern, *Hermann Diels und Carl Robert*, p. 126.

[47] Eugen Grünewald, "Die höheren Lehranstalten in den preußischen Landtagsverhandlungen am 15. und 16. März 1916," *Das humanistische Gymnasium* (1916): 160.

[48] Kerschensteiner to Spranger, 20 December 1915, in KBA, Nachlaß Spranger (182), Mappe 366.

[49] Ernst Troeltsch, *Humanismus und Nationalismus in unserem Bildungswesen* (Berlin, 1917), p. 19.

[50] Ibid., p. 31.

[51] See Jaeger's "Der Humanismus als Tradition und Erlebnis," (1919) in his *Humanistische Reden und Vorträge*, 2d ed. (Berlin, 1960), p. 25.

sium education and the arrival of future-oriented geographic studies. After this war, he wrote,

> things will stand differently than after the Wars of Liberation. Then the foreign yoke was cast off, but no unity was won. Hopes for the future grew from the soil of historical remembrance. At that time the German *Gymnasium* arose in its current form. This war will assure us of a place in the sun. In the future we will live more in the present than previously and true humanism will consist in clear recognition of this. The cultivation of geographic knowledge will make an essential contribution to furthering [this humanism].[52]

This new orientation to the future, product of expansionist dreams, war-weariness, and *Jugendbewegung* longings, posed a major challenge to the defenders of traditional schooling. As one of the leaders of the *Jugendbewegung*, Gustav Wyneken, contended, school reform would have to be a matter of changing not only the content of but also the pedagogical approach to learning as a whole. "It is a question," he commented, ". . . of educating a generation that does not think in historical terms."[53]

If the social disruption engendered by total war aided the cause of reform, still the conflict did not work entirely to the detriment of the status quo. Most crippling to the reformist cause were the vast numbers of *Gymnasium* graduates who gleefully volunteered for service and quickly acquitted themselves of the charge of lack of patriotic devotion and unfitness for battle. If reform might be used to strengthen the system, proclaimed a liberal Landtag member in 1916, "In the war our youth has shown its worth, and drawing any kind of conclusions about the necessity of a reform of secondary education from the performance of our young men in the field should now finally stop."[54] "By their fruits ye shall know them," quoth Saxon State Secretary Beck, recounting the valiant deeds of the *Gymnasiasten* on the front.[55] Humanism and patriotism could not be seen as contradictory, others argued; after all, the Greeks had been first to develop the concept of dying for the Fatherland and the words of Horace, *Dulce et decorum est pro patria mori*, could hardly have weakened the student body's will to self-sacrifice.[56] Other arguments for the preservation of the status quo

[52] Albrecht Penck, "Der Krieg und das Studium der Geographie," *Zeitschrift der Gesellschaft für Erdkunde zu Berlin* 64, no. 3–4 (1916): 45.

[53] Quoted in R. H. Samuel and R. Hinton Thomas, *Education and Society* (London, 1947), p. 31.

[54] Quoted in Grünewald, "Die höheren Lehranstalten . . . am 15. und 16. März 1916," p. 162.

[55] Beck in "Landtagsverhandlungen der II. sächsischen Kammer," *Das humanistische Gymnasium* (1916): p. 175.

[56] Wilamowitz, "Heroentum," in idem., *Reden aus der Kriegszeit*, p. 105; Representative Cassel quoted in Grünewald, "Die höheren Lehranstalten . . . am 15. und 16. März 1916," p. 172.

were adduced. From the field, *Gymnasium* defender Captain Paul Brandt employed the rather tenuous argument that strenuous drilling in Latin and Greek had prepared the troops for the hard, tedious labor of trench digging.[57] Finally, in a speech to the Verein der Freunde des humanistischen Gymnasiums (Friends of the Humanistic Gymnasium) in 1916, the President of the Bavarian Academy of Sciences Otto Crusius returned to the philhellenism of the Napoleonic era to emphasize Greek literature's contribution—even greater than that of Tacitus's *Germania*—to cultural self-sufficiency: "Since the end of the eighteenth century," Crusius enthused, "the Greeks have been fellow combatants against the imposed dominion of French-Latin pedantry, and leaders of national autonomy and independence. This they are still; they, who like the Romans held the Orient for more than a millennium, set a magnificent example for a people [the Germans] that continually develops the form that was impressed on it at the hour of its birth, but never will renounce it."[58]

Still, for the defenders of classical education, the handwriting was on the wall. If it had not been for the continued support of the state bureaucracy, the war would have ensured the obsolescence of Greek and Latin studies and the ruination of the *Gymnasium's* social and cultural centrality. Eduard Meyer's wartime response to the Education Ministry's moderate reforms in secondary-level historical training make this dependence clear. Though he blamed officialdom for allowing the *Gymnasien* to decay, he directed his long entreaty for the reinvigoration of classical learning to the bureaucracy; popular sentiment, he acknowledged, was all on the side of reform.[59] Only the state's support could prevent further erosions in classical hegemony; the rhetoricians' emphasis on national self-promotion and the military's reliance upon "relevant" modern skills simply exposed the obsolescence of the historicist defense of classical *Bildung*. Despite the effusive declarations of the cultural propagandists, *Kultur*, *Bildung*, and *Wissenschaft*, after the World War, would never be the same.

Archaeological *Kulturpolitik* and the World War

While *Kulturpropaganda* aimed at the dissemination of flattering self-images, *Kulturpolitik* directed its attention to cultivating influential contacts and securing favorable advantages for future exploits. As even the high-minded professoriate was eager to emphasize, the German state did mean to secure new territories for economic (and other) exploitation by means of

[57] Paul Brandt, "Krieg und Schule," *Das humanistische Gymnasium* 5 (1916): 178.

[58] Otto Crusius, *Der griechische Gedanke im Zeitalter der Freiheitskriege* (Vienna, 1916), p. 11.

[59] Eduard Meyer, *Die Aufgaben der höheren Schulen und die Gestaltung des Geschichtsunterrichts* (Leipzig, 1918), pp. 33, 37.

waging war, and archaeologists, familiar with foreign terrain, languages, and officialdoms, provided a cadre of established, unsuspicious reconnaissance men ready to provide information necessary to expansionist plans. The approach here, particularly in dealing with the Reich's antiquities-rich ally, the Ottoman Empire, had to be quite different from that of the speech-makers and manifesto signers at home. Whereas attempts to explain the war and to influence neutral populations needed to be rhetorically persuasive and widely conveyed, attempts to secure cultural concessions—like those to gain economic concessions—were better carried on in silence.

Before we take up the wartime activities of archaeologists and museum bureaucrats, a caveat must be issued. While German archaeologists did play an important role in cultural reconnaissance, none participated in the kind of espionage and intrigue practiced by T. E. Lawrence, who also began his career as an excavator. Against the insinuations made by Fritz Fischer, Wilhelm Treue has demonstrated that the amateur archaeologist Max Freiherr von Oppenheim actually did not play a major part in spying or in policymaking in Asia Minor.[60] But Treue does note that it was Oppenheim, not university Arabists like Enno Littmann or Eduard Sachau (who did volunteer their services), whom the Foreign Ministry chose to head up its Eastern information bureau, while the War Ministry chose Wiegand over other equally willing academic candidates.[61] If their effect on the general conduct of the war was negligible, the expansion of the archaeologist's role from that of cultural ambassador to that of cultural secret agent (*Kulturagent*) warrants scrutiny. Now devoted to the protection and extension of German interests abroad, archaeologists could now hardly claim to inhabit an international Hyperborea.

By 1914, archaeologists held a prominent position at court as well as in German society at large. Wiegand, Dörpfeld, Kekulé, and Conze were all intimates of the Kaiser; these men, as well as other leading DAI figures, all either held museum posts themselves or worked closely with Schöne and his successors. Despite increasing expenditures on weaponry, the Reich continued to fund DAI budgets at higher and higher levels, and requests for special grants from the Kaiser's privy purse were rarely refused. In fact, between 1911 and 1914, Wilhelm II had conducted his own excavations on the grounds of the royal summer palace on the island of Corfu; with the "assistance" of his friend Dörpfeld, the Kaiser, to his great excitement, had unearthed a large clay statue of an ancient pagan goddess whom the monarch called "Gorgo."[62] Wiegand, son-in-law to Georg von Siemens and

---

[60] See Wilhelm Treue, "Max Freiherr von Oppenheim: Der Archäologe und die Politik," *Historische Zeitschrift* 209, no. 1 (1969): 37–74.

[61] See ibid., p. 73.

[62] Wilhelm announced his find in a telegraph to Museums Director Bode, 12 April 1911, in printed form in DAI, Nachlaß Dörpfeld, Kasten 7, Mappe 4. Naturally, his excavation caused much consternation in diplomatic circles. Karo to Wangenheim, 20 May 1911, ibid., Mappe 2.

24. The Kaiser's dig at Corfu, ca. 1911. Wilhelm is pictured at center.
SuperStock.

friend (and later brother-in-law) to Karl Helfferich (Deutsche Bank executive and treasury secretary during the war), solicited contributions from Arthur Gwinner, of the Deutsche Bank, and Friedrich Krupp, among others, for DAI digs.[63] In 1913, Wiegand formalized his patronage circuit by founding the Vereinigung der Freunde antiker Kunst (Friends of Ancient Art Society) under Wilhelm's protection.[64] Socially and financially secure, and committed to a practical policy of scholarly disinterestedness, the DAI could put its energies into streamlining its bureaucracy and boasting of its contributions to Germany's international reputation.[65]

But the DAI also lived in constant fear of being bested by its foreign rivals, and therefore continued to apply regularly to the Reich for supplemental monies. These prewar petitions show a competitive anxiety and a patriotic vehemence unequaled in the period before 1898–99, and were sometimes addressed to the Kaiser himself. In 1911, Georg Karo, Dörpfeld's underling and the real administrator of the Athens branch, petitioned the monarch for ten thousand marks to supplement the Athens institute bud-

[63] See Conze to Wiegand, 14 February 1907 and 14 April 1907 in DAI, Nachlaß Wiegand, Kasten 2.

[64] C. Weicker, "Theodor Wiegand," in *Gedächtnisreden für Theodor Wiegand* (Berlin, 1937), p. 26.

[65] On bureaucratic streamlining, see Reichskanzler to Bundesrat, 5 September 1913 in PA/AA/K 42–501 adh II, vol. 2.

get, assuring him that this sum would suffice "to remedy our plight in a single stroke, to restore our administration and secure our ascendancy in our competition with sister institutes on the excavation fields. This is not only a matter of scholarly interests, but also of our national prestige."[66] As usual, Wilhelm was convinced. The adjustment made, the DAI budget for 1912 totaled 226,495 marks, a substantial rise from the 5,840 talers (17,520 marks) provided in 1871.[67]

The DAI greeted the outbreak of hostilities on 1 August 1914 with a patriotic flourish. On 11 August, Wiegand reported in his diary that in a spurt of generosity, the Royal Museums had returned 2 million marks from their budget to the state coffers, including 90,000 marks set aside for excavations and 110,000 marks dedicated to the Antiquities Department.[68] By 1 October the new RGK director had gone to the front (and would soon be killed); the second assistant at the Rome institute, E. Schmidt, had already fallen, and the central directorate's business manager Burghardt had gone to work in a munitions factory.[69] By no means, however, did the DAI simply shut its doors for the war's duration. Later in October, Dragendorff informed the chancellor that a new central directorate had been formed, whose activity commenced simultaneously with "Germany's mighty struggle for its existence and culture. Your Excellency should be assured," the DAI chief continued, "that the central directorship staff will find its honor at this time in keeping up the work of the institute, to show the world in its small way that Germany is strong enough to continue its peaceful cultural tasks even during its struggle for existence."[70]

The DAI commitment to this policy of maintaining high levels and standards of scholarly activity as a means of "spiritual" propaganda never flagged. After all, it allowed the institute to contribute to the cause without sacrificing its professional interests or the entirety of its income. The DAI's budget for 1915 totalled 212,241 marks; in 1916, the total rose to 245,890 marks, where it hovered for the remainder of the war.[71] The institute did return large sums in "savings" to the Reich, with the promise that these funds would be available for scholarly work after the war. In 1915, for example, the DAI returned 70,000 marks, a full one-third of its budget, to the

---

[66] Karo to Wilhelm II, 30 March 1911, in PZStA AA/R 37828, p. 103.

[67] "Etat 1911," ibid., pp. 115–24.

[68] Wiegand diary, vol. 3, 11 August 1914, in DAI, Nachlaß Wiegand, Kasten 23.

[69] Dragendorff to Central Directorate, 1 October 1914, in DAI, Nachlaß Dörpfeld, Kasten 3.

[70] Dragendorff to Bethmann and Foreign Ministry, 19 October 1914, PA/AA/K 42–501, vol. 40.

[71] Foreign Ministry to DAI Central Directorate, 14 April 1915, and Staatssekretär des Reichsschatzamts to Foreign Ministry, 29 July 1915, ibid.; "Bericht des Generalsekretärs für das Jahr 1915," 30 June 1916, in DAI, Nachlaß Wiegand, Kasten 28. Total for 1917: 244,970 marks; 1918 proposed: 244,920 marks. See "Etatsentwurf 1918," PA/AA/K 42–501, vol. 41.

Reich coffers.[72] Even so, some big projects continued to be funded. In late autumn 1915, construction of the new Royal Museum building was continuing swiftly and the new Berlin University museum for casts was nearly complete; Wiegand, director of the Antiquities Department of the Royal Museums, was still purchasing golden jewelry and most spectacularly, a monumental Greek statue of an enthroned goddess, priced at 1.35 million marks.[73] Excavation progressed where possible; the Babylon project continued as did excavations at Tiryns, Dipylon, and Olympia (Tiryns to 1916, the others to 1917). Wiegand, reporting to the Archäologische Gesellschaft on Winckelmann's Day 1915, explained that excavation had been halted at Samos, Miletus, and Didyma less because of the war than because of strict implementation of the Turkish antiquities law. In compensation, archaeological investigations were, however, being made at Laon, Arras, Soissons, and Bucy le Long in occupied French territory. Emphasizing again the patriotic nature of preservation work and archaeological investigation, Wiegand boasted that "the whole scholarly crew has devoted itself to service in the army."[74]

This is not to say, however, that the DAI and the Royal Museums simply went about their usual business while the war raged around them. The Athens institute in particular was in a fortuitous position to engage in *Kulturpropaganda*. German meddling in Greek internal affairs could boast a pedigree stretching back to at least the 1820s, and German archaeologists had long enjoyed privileged access to court society (with the exception of the period between the 1843 revolution and the commencement of the Olympia dig). And, as in Rome, German archaeologists in Athens had often played actual or unofficial ambassadorial roles. The first director of the DAI branch office in Athens, Otto Lüders, left this position to become tutor to Crown Prince Constantine; he would later become Ambassador to Athens. His successor, Ulrich Köhler, began his career as an interpreter at the Prussian embassy, moving to the Athens institute in 1874.[75] Dörpfeld, who was appointed deputy director in 1885 and director of the Athens DAI in 1887, had regularized this ambassadorial function by developing close ties to both Greek and German courts. His cultural diplomacy had been so successful, in fact, that the DAI had declined his request to retire from his position in

---

[72] Dragendorff to Chancellor and Foreign Ministry, 28 August 1916, ibid., vol. 40. By means of arranging its own forced savings, the DAI was generally able to keep control of its own budget. See Dragendorff to Chancellor Michaelis, incorrectly dated 19.19.1917 (probably 19 September 1917) ibid., vol. 41.

[73] See Wiegand to William Buckler, 29 October 1915, in DAI, Nachlaß Wiegand, Kasten 1; and Wiegand diary, vol. 3, 26 December 1915, ibid., Kasten 23. Most of the money for the goddess came from private sources.

[74] Wiegand's speech recorded ibid., 11 December 1915.

[75] Ulf Jantzen, *Einhundert Jahre Athener Institut, 1874–1974* (Mainz, 1986), p. 16.

1909, fearing that the loss of his prestige in Greek circles would do the institute grievous harm.[76]

When the war broke out, Dörpfeld, by this time back in Germany, went to work for the navy's information services; soon thereafter, he joined the Kriegspresseamt.[77] He made many appeals to his Greek friends to remember Germany's dedication to Hellas and European culture. As a cofounder of the Deutsch-Griechische Gesellschaft (whose membership included Wilamowitz, Paul Wolters, Friedrich Freiherr von Bissing, and several other professors and bankers), Dörpfeld signed an open letter to Greek members and friends in which the Germans dismissed accusations of German "Vandalismus" and deplored the "numerous members of the black and yellow races" recruited by the Entente in purported defense of European civilization. Unable to use the Greek War of Independence as a parallel—because of the touchy matter of Germany's alliance with the Turks—the committee fell back on the example of the Persian Wars to stir Greek sympathy: "What can anyone have against the supposed "militarism" of Germany, that uncomprehending catchphrase that our enemies try to use to stir opinion against us? The *Volk* in arms, schooled and equipped to defend the Fatherland and the homeland. The civilian army. The same spirit that millennia ago in Hellas defeated the Persians in victorious battles."[78] Like many of his fellow humanists, Dörpfeld belonged to the "ninety-three," was devoted to the Kaiser, and after the war became a vehement opponent of the Versailles Treaty. Dörpfeld's precise wartime activities remain shadowy, and it is possible that the death of his wife in 1915 reined him in, but in 1917 he went to Berlin to deliver a series of honorary lectures, something he might never have done had his relations with the new Greek leaders remained harmonious.[79]

Georg Karo's machinations, on the other hand, are rather less mysterious. Karo, offspring of a cosmopolitan Jewish couple, realized early on that Allied atrocity propaganda would be difficult to counter given the hostility of the Greek press and the general disgust engendered by Germany's alliance with the Ottoman Turks. A quiet approach, the deputy director of the Athens institute believed, was required.[80] Karo's actions—which included the editing of an ardently pro-German war chronicle[81]—however, proved

---

[76] Ibid., pp. 32–33.

[77] See Dörpfeld to DAI, 4 September 1939 in DAI Nachlass Dörpfeld, Kasten 3; Peter Goessler, *Wilhelm Dörpfeld: Ein Leben im Dienste der Antike* (Stuttgart, 1951), p. 170.

[78] "An die Mitglieder und Freunde der deutsch-griechischen Gesellschaft in Hellas," (Munich, December 1914). In DAI, Nachlaß Dörpfeld, Kasten 17, Mappe 3.

[79] See Goessler, *Dörpfeld*, pp. 173–74.

[80] Karo to Otto Crusius, copy to Dörpfeld, 11 November 1914, in DAI, Nachlaß Dörpfeld, Kasten 3, Mappe 1.

[81] Georgios I. Thanopulos, *Das deutsche Neugriechenland-Bild, 1918–1944* (Neuried, 1987), p. 152.

not subtle enough to save him, despite the Greeks' generally favorable view of the DAI and the Greek queen's personal wish that Karo be allowed to remain at his post. In late 1916, under pressure from the French and the antimonarchist Venizelosists, the Athens branch was entrusted to the Greek Education Ministry for the duration of the war. Other institute members were permitted to continue work (under the aegis of the Greek Archaeological Society) at the Kerameikos and Dipylon Gate sites in Athens and at Olympia, but the excavations at Dodona, for which the Kaiser had donated ten thousand marks, would have to wait for the peace.[82]

In Rome, the young First Secretary Richard Delbrück railed at the clumsiness and meanness of German *Kulturpolitik* in neutral Italy. In a series of letters to Wiegand, Delbrück denounced the Reich's lack of skilled cultural advocates and journalists, charging the current "system of methodical self-deception" with forfeiting crucial opportunities to influence Italian popular opinion.[83] Delbrück remarked on the confusion engendered by the wide variety of agencies sponsoring cultural advocates, none of which informed the Rome embassy of their minions' activities, thereby forcing the diplomats to turn to Delbrück for information.[84] The latter, apparently, was able to provide a great deal of information on the subject, as he and other German classicists had become deeply involved in *Kulturpolitik*. Potentially more damaging to his reputation and that of German scholarship, however, was the participation of DAI members in illegal smuggling of goods. In defiance of the Italian government's export ban, Dr. Weege, an assistant at the Institute, busily organized illegal exports of woolen blankets and grain, while Delbrück himself helped send Italian cotton back to the fatherland.[85] Delbrück took care that his activities were obscured by surrounding himself with a protective layer of Italian middlemen, but worried that his colleagues' carelessness would destroy the Reich's political and scholarly standing. "It is to be feared," he told Wiegand in early 1915, "that the exporting activity of these men cannot remain concealed and that it will endanger the pro-German movement by connecting rice smuggling with our work of historical-philosophical enlightenment."[86] All the first secretary's efforts, however, went for naught, and the Rome branch was taken over by the government when Italy joined the Allies in May 1915. A year after the signing of the Versailles Treaty, the original branch office and library of the DAI

---

[82] Karo to General Headquarters, 30 January 1917, in MZStA 2.2.1–20781, pp. 3–4; "Deutsche Archäologie in Griechenland," in *Frankfurter Zeitung*, 15 June 1917, in PA/AA/K 46–531, vol. 1. See also Karo's report to the Archäologische Gesellschaft, reported in *AA* 31 (1916): 239–44.

[83] See, e.g., Delbrück to Wiegand, 1 April 1915, in DAI, Nachlaß Wiegand, Kasten 2.

[84] Delbrück to Wiegand, 2 January 1915 (date mistyped as 2 January 1914), ibid.

[85] Delbrück to Wiegand, 30 December 1914, ibid.

[86] Delbrück to Wiegand, 2 January 1915, ibid.

had not been returned. Delbrück's fears for the confusion of scholarly outposts with nationalist conventicles had indeed been realized.

The RGK, initially crippled by the war in the west and decreases in local and private contributions, soon discovered patriotic tasks for its associates in areas under German control. The commission itself pressed the Foreign Ministry for more funds to cover unforeseen costs of caring for the monuments and collections in the occupied western territories[87] and lent its students to assist in scholarly duties, but other bodies took over most of the organizational work. Gerhard Bersu and Wilhelm Unverzagt, both young prehistorians, as well as Ludwig Borchardt, head of the DAI branch office in Cairo, served in Belgium in the German civil government's monument protection group, organized by Paul Clemen (the military had dominion over finds at the front). Clemen's high-minded campaign to steer troops away from cultural treasures and to lend Teutonic experts to the cause of preservation was conceived as a response to charges that the Germans had destroyed Reims and Louvain. This disinterested gesture, Clemen told the Civil Cabinet, would show the rest of the world how German scholarship, "free from all chauvinism, does its all to defend art monuments in enemy territory."[88] Clemen continued his work up to the war's end and even afterward; as cultural counterpropaganda, preservation work, he believed, could not be rivaled.[89]

Wilhelm von Bode, too, had a share in *Kulturpolitik* in the west, though his interests lay more in acquisition than in counterpropaganda. Already in early September 1914, Bode had foreseen a chance to repossess German treasures taken by Napoleon and held in Parisian museums; by late 1915, he impatiently suggested that a collection of French art from the occupied northern regions could instead be held as ransom for the "stolen" German items.[90] In April, the Foreign Ministry strongly advised the Kaiser and his cabinet against this idea, but the army, on the orders of the Education Ministry and the Kaiser, was proceeding with Bode's plan in December 1916 when another unwelcome interlocutor entered the discussion.[91] Crown

---

[87] Dragendorff to Michaelis and Foreign Ministry, 30 October 1917, in PA/AA/K 42–501, vol. 41. Officially, the RGK kept its thirty-seven-thousand-mark Reich subsidy throughout the war, though it returned a good portion of this (e.g., fourteen thousand marks in 1916) to the state in the form of "voluntary" savings.

[88] Clemen to Valentini, 31 May 1917, MZStA 2.2.1–20793, pp. 123–28.

[89] See, e.g., Paul Clemen, "Der Krieg und die Kunstdenkmäler," dated 31 December 1914 and intended for the American press, ibid., pp. 23–29. On postwar use of *Kulturpropaganda*, see Clemen to Wiegand, 1 November 1918, and 25 July 1919, in DAI, Nachlaß Wiegand, Kasten 2.

[90] Bode to Civil Cabinet, 5 September 1914, and Bode and to Valentini, 27 December 1915, both in MZStA 2.2.1–20793, pp. 1a–b, and 85a–b, respectively.

[91] Foreign Ministry to Valentini, 15 April 1916, and Steindorff (Generalquartiermeister) to Civil Cabinet, 7 December 1916, both ibid., pp. 85d–f and p. 97, respectively.

Prince Ruprecht of Bavaria, Bode reported, had refused to allow museum representative Dr. Demmler to plunder French collections in the area occupied by his army.[92] The director of the Royal Museums requested that the Kaiser intercede with German military officials to assist him in changing Ruprecht's mind, and judging by the army command's cooperation with Bode's plan and Wilhelm's appropriation of 35,000M from his disposition fund for an inventory of Belgian art works in August 1917,[93] the ransom note would probably have been delivered had it not been for the aggressive opposition of the Foreign Ministry.[94] In October 1918, General Headquarters had already arranged for artworks hidden in Valenciennes to be moved to Brussels, but hesitated to implement the Kaiser's order to move these on to Germany.[95] Fortunately for the Reich, the Foreign Ministry, playing constantly on fears of negative propaganda (and the potential commandeering of German property in Entente-controlled areas), managed to forestall the united efforts of the Kaiser, the Royal Museums, the Education Ministry, and the army command long enough for the war to end before such an obvious catastrophe for *Kulturpolitik* occurred.[96]

The subject of the DAI's wartime activities in Asia Minor deserves a rather more lengthy discussion than that given to the involvement of the other branches in *Kulturpolitik*. Persistent suspicion on the part of the Turks necessitated very careful maneuvers in the cultural sphere. The 1913 military mission sent by the Reich had not converted the Ottomans into docile allies, and despite the presence of large numbers of German troops on Ottoman soil in the later years of the war, the Turks retained control of their own forces to the bitter end. The Baghdad Railway lay unfinished in 1914, thus rendering it only marginally useful for the purposes intended, which included: extracting raw materials, permitting the settlement and perhaps colonization of Mesopotamia, threatening India and Egypt, and most importantly, moving troops from the center to unruly areas on the periphery.[97] In

---

[92] Bode to Valentini, 28 December 1916, ibid., p. 110.

[93] Clemen to Valentini, 31 May 1917, and proclamation of Wilhelm II, 23 August 1917, ibid., pp. 123–28, 139.

[94] Elsewhere, similarly, the DOG was pressing the idea of holding French and Belgian artwork hostage in exchange for the Assur finds marooned in Portugal. See [Heinrich] Schäfer, president of the DOG, to Foreign Ministry, 14 July 1916, PA/AA/K 27–468a, vol. 32.

[95] Generalquartiermeister to Civil Cabinet, 5 October 1918, in MZStA 2.2.1–20793, p. 167.

[96] As newspaper articles and documents in the Munich Education Ministry files show, however, the French did claim compensation for art objects removed or destroyed by German troops. See, e.g., Dr. Rudolf Berliner, "Kunstraub," in *München-Augsburger Abendzeitung*, 4 March 1919, in BHStA, MK 41226.

[97] One commentator has estimated that the Germans spent something on the order of 360 million marks between 1914 and 1918 on Ottoman railroads, all of which was lost with the war's conclusion and the Kemalist takeover. Ulrich Trumpener, *Germany and the Ottoman Empire, 1914–1918* (Princeton, N.J., 1968), p. 316.

defiance of German wishes, in November 1916 the Ottoman government declared the abrogation of its treaty commitments of 1856 and 1878, thereby casting off restrictions against territorial aggrandizement; in September 1918, the Ottoman army occupied Baku and proclaimed the creation of an Azerbaijani buffer state in the Transcaucasian area, a move the Germans found so vexatious that the alliance nearly collapsed.[98]

Back in the Reich, Turkish entry into the conflict on 31 October 1914 was greeted with a deluge of literature from Vereine and Orient-propagandists celebrating the new opportunities this military friendship would offer to merchants, religious institutions, and industrialists in search of cheap raw materials and markets for finished goods. In Leipzig, the Deutsches Vorderasienkomitee and the Vereinigung zur Förderung deutscher Kulturarbeit im islamischen Orient (German Asia Minor Committee, Union for the Furtherance of German Culture in the Islamic Orient) distributed hundreds of thousands of books, pamphlets, and maps of the Turkish Empire; a Near East Institute (Nah-Ost Institut) also offered lectures and courses, while an information bureau for businessmen, operated by the same Leipzig orientalist clique, published pamphlets on commercial and industrial opportunities in the Orient and established German libraries at key spots along Baghdad Railway routes.[99] Beginning in February 1916, the Reich began a major new effort to exploit Turkish resources, in the process of which it crossed swords with its other ally, Austria. Vienna clearly resented Germany's proprietorial bearing with respect to Turkish booty, and mounted its own resistance to "German imperialism in Turkey."[100]

In this atmosphere of expanding popular interest in and increasing commercial designs upon the Islamic world, maintaining a centralized and "disinterested" *Kulturpolitik* was more difficult—and more consequential—than ever. The Foreign Ministry, the DAI, the Education Ministry, and the Royal Museums all hoped that the war would increase, rather than abolish, German influence in Asia Minor. In 1916, the liberal C. H. Becker received a call to join the Education Ministry in a permanent position (he had served as adviser since 1913); neither a lawyer nor a policy expert, Becker was an unusual choice, but his linguistic skills and wide circle of orientalist contacts allowed him unusual insight into developments in oriental *Kulturpolitik*.[101] Bode, too, dabbled in Ottoman cultural affairs, proposing, typ-

---

[98] Ibid., pp. 198ff.

[99] Edward M. Earle, *Turkey, the Great Powers, and the Bagdad Railway: A Study in Imperialism* (London, 1923), p. 281.

[100] Trumpener, *Germany and the Ottoman Empire*, pp. 322–24.

[101] On Becker's orientalism, see chapters on him in Jean-Jacques Waardenburg, *L'Islam dans le miroir de l'occident* (Paris, 1963); Ludmila Hanisch, ed., *Islamkunde und Islamwissenschaft im Deutschen Kaiserreich: Der Briefwechsel zwischen Carl Heinrich Becker und Martin Hartmann (1900–1918)* (Leiden, 1992).

ically, to Georg Karo (en route from Greece to monument protection service in Anatolia) that the latter steal the Sarcophagus of Sidon for the Berlin Museums in recompense for unpaid Turkish war debts.[102] But undoubtedly the most successful campaign of *Kulturpolitik*, diplomatically as well as scientifically, was that conducted by Theodor Wiegand, director of the Antiquities Department and special liaison to the commander of the Fourth Turkish Army, Djemal Pasha.

Although Wiegand's official reception in the scholarly world was halting (he became an ordinary member of the Prussian Academy of Sciences only in 1923), in 1914 he was already a powerful figure in Berlin, where he belonged to an exclusive group of artists and their patrons, including Richard Strauss, Max Slevogt, Peter Behrens, Max Reinhardt, and Gerhart Hauptmann. After the war, he was accepted into the intimate Mittwochs-Gesellschaft (Wednesday Society), whose membership included Wilhelm Gröner, Johannes Popitz, Friedrich Meinecke, Hermann Onken, Eugen Fischer, Eduard Spranger, and Ludwig Beck.[103] In Asia, his influence was unparalleled. As we have seen, his intimacy with Hamdi and Halil Edhem and his close ties to the German embassy in Constantinople put him in an excellent position to extract concessions from the Turks as well as to guide German *Kulturpolitik*. His efforts were highly regarded by the Kaiser and frequently subsidized by his friends in heavy industry. Georg Karo's tribute to his colleague sums up Wiegand's remarkable appeal: "He knew how to interest the widest variety of men in his aims: Kaisers and sultans, ministers and governors, leaders of industry and scholars, Turkish nobles as well as Anatolian and Greek peasants. . . . Hardly has a European held such a position in western Asia Minor."[104]

Following his failed attempts to get to the front, in early September 1914 Wiegand was contacted by the Foreign Ministry to assist with "information services" in Greece and the Orient and to plead Germany's case to foreign scholars; he and his friends immediately sent off personal appeals to their contacts abroad, and Wiegand composed several articles for the Greek press.[105] Two days later, the excavator of Priene and Miletus declared himself ready to serve his country in Belgium and France as a member of a monument protection and preservation corps. Retaining his dedication to the avoidance of recriminations, Wiegand described the high-minded task

---

[102] Georg Karo, *Fünfzig Jahre aus dem Leben eines Archäologen* (Baden, 1959), pp. 96–98. The Kaiser denied Bode's claim that he had endorsed the idea, and Wiegand, upon hearing of the plot, quashed the plan immediately.

[103] Ludwig Hoffmann, *Lebenserinnerungen eines Architekten* (Berlin, 1983), p. 244; Kurt Aland, ed., *Glanz und Niedergang der deutschen Universität: 50 Jahre deutscher Wissenschaftsgeschichte in Briefen an und von Hans Lietzmann* (Berlin, 1979), p. 150.

[104] G. Karo, "Theodor Wiegand zum Gedächtnis," *Forschung und Fortschritte* 13, no. 4 (February 1937): 55.

[105] Wiegand diary, vol. 3, 2 September 1914, in DAI, Nachlaß Wiegand, Kasten 23.

25. Theodor Wiegand on patrol with the German-Turkish Monument Protection Commando, ca. 1917. Deutsches Archäologisches Institut, Berlin.

of his unit: "We were agreed that the [corps] must concern itself with monument preservation and the protection of threatened works of art, not with pillaging à la Denon."[106] But he was needed more urgently in the East, and after a stint as section chief (for Turkey and the Balkans) in the Kriegspresseamt, in August 1916 he received a call to head up a transport of troops being sent to fortify Djemal Pasha's Fourth Army. His official purpose in Turkey, as his sponsors the War Ministry and the Education Ministry wished it to appear, was to conduct topographical, historical, and archaeological studies in the service of preservation.[107] His unofficial purpose remains unclear, but almost certainly involved reconnaissance for the Royal Museums, which, as Bode and the Kaiser frequently reminded the Education Ministry, should profit rather than suffer from the Central Powers' alliance.[108] Wiegand stuck to his "beyond suspicion" policy, following care-

[106] Ibid., 4 September 1914. Dominique Vivant Denon was the knowledgeable antiquarian who accompanied Napoleon's armies and advised the general on which artistic works to take back to France.

[107] See ibid., vol. 1, 29 August 1916, copy of letter von Wriesberg (War Ministry) to unknown, in DAI, Nachlaß Wiegand, Kasten 24.

[108] See, eg., Valentini to Education Ministry, 11 March 1917, in MZStA 2.2.1–20781, p. 14; and Bode to Foreign Ministry, 28 March 1917, in PA/AA/K 27–468a, vol. 2. Schmidt also wrote to Wiegand praising his efforts and hoping they would be to the benefit of "the museums' goals, which are close to both of our hearts." Schmidt to Wiegand, 16 April 1917, MZStA, Nachlaß Schmidt-Ott, A-LXXIII, p. 91.

fully the program outlined by his protégé Martin Schede just before the latter's reassignment from the French front to preservation service in the Ottoman Empire:

> The Turks want to use the war for the emancipation of their nation, and therefore it is hardly clever for us to indicate now that we might sometime be their masters. . . . One shouldn't remind the Turks in any way that we have a museum and they have the antiquities, but should stress the commonality of our national interests. Under this condition I would gladly fight in the Turkish army. If the peace agreement looks like what we all hope and desire, we can permit ourselves everything; we can extend our privileges. . . .[109]

Wiegand's first mission was to survey the early Byzantine monuments of the Sinai region, a task he undertook under the command of the Bavarian General Kress von Kressenstein.[110] This expedition, however, must have raised Turkish suspicions, for in November, in order to prevent discovery of his "true purposes," the ambassador in Damascus arranged Wiegand's attachment to the Fourth Army, where he was to serve directly under Djemal Pasha, a personal friend of the ambassador.[111] Halil Edhem remained convinced that the German archaeologist was covertly engaging in collecting activities, but within the year, Wiegand's "strictly scientific" bearing had earned him the army commander's deepest trust.[112] Wiegand's travels through Syria, Jordan, the Sinai, and his visits to Palmyra, Petra, Jerusalem, Damascus and other ancient centers resulted in several publications, including a popular volume featuring 150 photographs of the ruins of Syria and Palestine, with text in German and Turkish, as well as in reams of information about the condition, location, and significance of scores of oriental monuments, filed away for peacetime use. He may also be credited with having been first to use aerial photographs in archaeology, having persuaded the military—when and where convenient—to photograph ancient sites for the Antiquities Department's collection.[113]

Wiegand, however, was not the only *Kulturagent* at work in the Ottoman Empire. Schede commenced work in May 1917, and Karo, freshly evicted from his abode in Athens, arrived to assist the monument protection effort at about the same time. Karo and Wiegand did not get on at all well, due in part to Wiegand's concern that Karo's reputation and careless behavior would reignite the Turkish suspicions Wiegand had worked so hard to dis-

[109] Schede to Wiegand, 21 February 1915, in DAI, Nachlaß Wiegand, Kasten 8.

[110] Theodor Wiegand, "Denkmalschutz in Syrien," *Klio* 15 (1918): 422–23.

[111] Damascus Consulate to Bethmann Hollweg, 13 November 1916, in PA/AA/K 27–468a, vol. 31.

[112] Pera embassy (Istanbul) to Reich Chancellor Michaelis, 12 September 1917, ibid.

[113] Wenk, *Auf den Spuren*, p. 22.

sipate.[114] But also, in July 1917, Wiegand accidentally got wind of a plan—backed by the German embassy in Constantinople and involving Karo—to establish a new "Culturgeschichtliches Institut" ("Institute for Cultural History") to oversee all acquisitions, excavations, and museum officials in the Ottoman Empire. The Education Ministry, museum administration, the Academy of Sciences, and even the Kaiser, apparently, had been completely ignorant of the plot, a circumstance Wiegand credited to the fickleness and self-interested motivations of the diplomats:

> Prussia and the museums, and with them the Kaiser, are urging that the current vexatious Turkish antiquities law be softened, in order that monuments can again be legally sent to Germany. This, like all acquisition questions is an extremely burdensome business. Therefore, when Karo turned up and proclaimed the principle of pure "scholarship without interest in acquisition" for the [Royal] Museums, he was received with enthusiasm.[115]

Fortunately for Wiegand, such effrontery, not to mention generosity, would not be tolerated by Karo's powerful Prussian friends and employers. After being chastised by Wilamowitz—whom, Wiegand reported, "still, thank God, had enough of a Prussian heart not to misconstrue the interests of the Berlin museums"—Karo, crestfallen, departed Turkey for a vacation in Switzerland.[116]

Schede, incited by this event, by Koldewey's behavior in Babylon, and by another Becker-backed proposal to found a Byzantine Institute without the participation of the Royal Museums,[117] reflected Wiegand's worries about the fragmentation of *Kulturpolitik* in the Orient. The Academy of Sciences and the DAI, Schede suggested, increasingly opposed the interests of the Royal Museums, but careful preparation could insure the museums full control of German scientific exploits in the East: "After the war, a great stream of German scholars will come to Turkey, and we must take care that *we* provide the only entrance gate. Therefore we must draw together other branches of study as much as possible and turn them to the museums' account, before the idea occurs to them to establish for themselves their own "disinterested" existence."[118] Despite his dedication to "disinterestedness," Wiegand also took the part of the Royal Museums. In May 1918, he

[114] Rodenwaldt to Ernst Buschor, 1 February 1926, in BSB, Nachlaß Rodenwaldt, Mappe 386; Schede to Wiegand, 2 October 1918, in DAI, Nachlaß Wiegand, Kasten 30; and Schede to Wiegand, 21 May 1917, ibid, Kasten 8.

[115] Wiegand diary, vol. 4, 25 July 1917, ibid., Kasten 23.

[116] Ibid. In late 1918, however, Karo was back in Turkey; the Turks, Schede told Wiegand, suspected that he had come to spy on the condition of the Greek population. See Schede to Wiegand, 2 October 1918, ibid., Kasten 30.

[117] On the latter, see Schede to Wiegand, 21 May 1917, ibid., Kasten 8.

[118] Schede to Wiegand, 26 August 1917, ibid.

composed a memo for the embassy on the subject of postwar Ottoman archaeological concessions, much of which was lifted verbatim by the embassy and forwarded to Chancellor von Hertling. To Wiegand's familiar complaints about the 1906 antiquities law, the embassy added a framing argument about the Turks' debt to the Reich and underlined the incalculable "political seesawing" of the Ottoman government, which required that Germany have concessions set down in writing. As no danger remained (after Russia's capitulation) that the Turks, who depended on German funds and political backing for their pan-Islamic plans, would conclude a separate peace, pressure could now be applied to win concessions for German *Kultur*. "It is believed that this time scholarly interests cannot be allowed to lag behind other objectives of the negotiations," Count Bernstorff of the embassy in Constantinople told the chancellor,

> and the conviction has been very widely expressed that [in exchange] for the billions that flow into Turkey, a final establishment of archaeological concessions must be reached, especially as this desire has been expressed by the supreme authority so repeatedly and emphatically that the lack of such [an agreement] would be taken as a discourtesy on the part of the Turks toward the German monarch.[119]

In view of the funds and defensive forces the Reich had lavished on its Ottoman ally, the Turks could at least offer cultural concessions in return.

As the prospect of grand territorial and cultural spoils in the Ottoman lands faded with defeats and increasing Turkish uncooperativeness in late 1918, Wiegand and the Royal Museums turned their attention to another potentially culturally rich weak spot in the East, an area also targeted for exploitation by German politicians and businessmen: the Ukraine.[120] As early as March 1918, Wiegand had petitioned the Education Ministry to negotiate with the provisional government in Russia for permission to dig in the Ukraine when the war was finished. Naturally, the Ukrainians could keep all items dated later than the sixth century A.D.; the Germans' share would be composed of classical and preclassical artifacts only.[121] In April, Wiegand asked that specific excavation sites be secured for the Royal Museums under this partitioning agreement, and a month later, Schede was musing excitedly about the possibility of bringing the entire Black Sea region into the museums' "sphere of influence."[122] Wiegand seems to have reactivated plans for Russian excavations in the fall of 1918, when the Reic-

---

[119] Bernstorff (embassy Pera) to von Hertling, 11 May 1918, in PA/AA/K 27–468a, vol. 2.

[120] See Fritz Fischer, *Griff nach der Weltmacht* (Düsseldorf, 1962), pp. 708ff.

[121] See Wiegand diary, vol. 5, 28 March 191[8], in DAI, Nachlaß Wiegand, Kasten 24.

[122] Civil Cabinet to Reich Chancellor, 5 April 1918, in PA/AA/K 24–377B.5, and Schede to Wiegand, 14 May 1918, in DAI, Nachlaß Wiegand, Kasten 8.

hsbank announced it had opened a seventy-five-thousand mark account in his name at the Central Office for Russian Currency.[123] In late September, Wiegand wrote the German-speaking president of the Society for the Study of History and Antiquities in Odessa, sympathizing with the latter over the plight of the Black Sea city of Olbia, where "as a result of current political conditions, grave robbery on a great scale will occur." Wiegand then offered his own expertise and Germany's support for immediate systematic excavation and protection of the area, promising European plaudits for the Ukrainians' organization of such an endeavor.[124] The excavator's diary records the following gloss on these negotiations: "from my experience in Turkey I know how careful one must be in 'friendly' countries that the suspicion never arise that one is dealing with a conquered nation."[125] Veteran of many an intrigue with Turkish officials, Wiegand knew his overtures would have to be versed in the language of disinterested scholarship, hedged by appeals to reciprocal "cultural friendship."

Wiegand's hopes for a dig at Olbia, however, were dashed when the Ukrainians swung to the Allied side with Germany's capitulation in early November, and Wiegand was forced to flee, along with the remainder of German and Austrian personnel and the leaders of the Turkish wartime government, all of whom had been evacuated from Constantinople to Black Sea ports between 26 October and 2 November.[126] In the course of his two-month stay in the Crimea, however, Wiegand had managed to amass a collection of ancient vases, bronzes, and gold pieces for the Royal Museums, purchased at bargain prices.[127] Returning to Berlin, Wiegand gave up his lifelong commitment to liberalish apoliticism and joined the newly founded right-of-center Deutschnationale Volkspartei (DNVP).[128] Perhaps Wiegand himself sensed then that the halcyon days of grand archaeological *Kulturpolitik* would never return; in any event, his next years would be spent paying tribute to the grand achievements of the DAI's past and battling the Education Ministry for funds with which to refurbish the Berlin Antiquities Department and to build a Pergamum Museum. On receiving the *Pour le mérite* in 1931, Wiegand indulged in a bit of nostalgic reflection on the delights of a bygone age of archaeological triumphs. "Before the war we did not know how lucky we were," he commented to a friend. "Now, after the

---

[123] Reichsbank to Wiegand, 9 September 1918, ibid., Kasten 30, Mappe 1.

[124] Wiegand to Warnecke, copy in Wiegand diary, vol. 5, 24 September 1918, ibid., Kasten 24.

[125] Ibid., 18 September 1918.

[126] Trumpener, *Germany and the Ottoman Empire*, p. 357.

[127] See Wiegand to Bode, 10 February 1919, in DAI, Nachlaß Wiegand, Kasten 13, Mappe "1919" and Wiegand diary, 11 November 1918, in DAI, Nachlaß Wiegand, Kasten 24, Mappe 6.

[128] Ibid., 15 and 22 December 1918, in DAI, Nachlaß Wiegand, Kasten 23.

defeat, we must try to bring the pieces together and make the vessel whole again."[129] With the demise of *Weltpolitik*, archaeology, like Wiegand, had been stranded in republican Weimar, doomed to suffer the onslaught of the modern world.

Cultural Consequences of the Peace: Philhellenism Confronts the Republic

In the months following the armistice, German academics felt irresistibly drawn into another sort of "struggle for existence": the grand battle, as they saw it, against the eradication of German *Geist*. Reversing their position on the "two Germanies" thesis, professors argued that intellectual life had not died with the army's defeat: indeed, *Geist* was threatened not from without, but from within, by the "maggots of anarchism" Wiegand pictured, or the flatterers and cowards Wilamowitz feared. Eduard Meyer was only one among many to recall Friedrich Wilhelm III's exhortation to replace physical losses with intellectual power,[130] but this time he, like most of his classicist colleagues, resisted "reform from above" as well as the de facto reform from below seeping into the universities as enrollments boomed and hungrier, more career-minded students invaded German campuses. The professoriate preferred to beat a hasty, hostile retreat from the modern world; German spiritual unity, in their view, depended upon the restoration of hierarchical dispensation of scientific truths and the resurrection of traditional ideals, not on democratization and innovation in the academy.

Not surprisingly, the war's dismal end and the democratic revolution in Germany came as bitter disappointments to the classicist establishment, and classical philology became a hot bed of monarchist nostalgia and apoplectic reaction. With the demise of the monarchy, the relinquishing of the leadership of the Education Ministry to the Social Democrats, and the collapse of dreams of cultural expansion in Asia, the powerful props supporting the institutional and social prominence of *Altertumswissenschaft* were kicked away. Unquestionably, the events of November 1918 came as a dreadful shock to the professoriate in general and the classicists in particular, and they emerged from the experience more conservative and more "political" than ever before. Meyer and Wilamowitz had been among the founders of the annexationist Vaterlandspartei in 1917; they subsequently became members of the DNVP, as did Wiegand and the much younger philologist Ulrich Kahrstedt, who presided over the party's Göttingen sec-

---

[129] Wiegand to Hiller von Gärtringen, 16 March 1931, ibid., Kasten 13.
[130] See Eduard Meyer's "Rede beim Antritt des Rektorats der Friedrich-Wilhelms-Universität Berlin am 15. Oktober 1919," in *Kleine Schriften*, vol. 2 (Halle, 1924), pp. 539–67.

tion.[131] Kahrstedt also belonged to the Stahlhelm, a right-wing veterans' organization, as did Althoff's deputy Friedrich Schmidt (now Schmidt-Ott). The latter's two sons joined the paramilitary Freikorps and participated in the Kapp Putsch.[132] Hostility toward the republic became de rigueur for *Gymnasium* teachers and academic philologists, scions of the old regime whose position in the brave new Weimar world would only grow increasingly precarious.

For the defeated cultural propagandists, the collapse of the monarchy meant national emasculation and, worse, foretold Germany's—and their own—spiritual extinction. As usual, Wilamowitz's view was most poignant: "I have had to experience the self-destruction, the self-castration of my *Volk*. In this ochlocracy and under the cowardly or corruptible flatterers that are to be found in all classes there is no longer a place for an old man who cannot allow any man or any god to tear his Prussian honor from his heart. He has only to become extinct."[133] Meyer shared his colleague's sentiments—and even his metaphors—without hesitation. "In the list of remembrance days of the German nation," he wrote of 9 November, the day the Weimar Republic was proclaimed, "it can never be erased; but instead of a day of celebration, that day, on which our *Volk* castrated itself and threw itself into an abyss, will become a great national day of repentance."[134] Confronted with Germany's new international impotence—and their own powerlessness in preventing what they perceived to be national self-mutilation—the aging classicists' imaginations teemed with scenes of sexual disfigurement and imminent death.

With the signing of the Versailles Treaty, despondency and satire turned into anger and vengeful oaths. The archaeologists joined the clamor in earnest, for their hopes that prewar conditions and concessions could be resurrected abroad had now been dashed.[135] Archaeologists had self-interested reasons for opposing the treaty, for with its conclusion, the pros-

[131] Cornelia Wegeler, "Das Institut für Altertumskunde der Universität Göttingen 1921–1962: Ein Beitrag zur Geschichte der klassischen Philologie seit Wilamowitz," in *Die Universität Göttingen unter dem Nationalsozialismus,* ed. Heinrich Becker and Hans-Joachim Dahms (Munich, 1987), p. 251.

[132] Friedrich Schmidt-Ott, *Erlebtes und Erstrebtes, 1860–1950* (Wiesbaden, 1952), p. 173. Meyer also backed Kapp.

[133] Wilamowitz, "Nachwort zu Band II," (1918) in idem, *Platon,* vol. 1: *Leben und Werke* 2d ed. (Berlin, 1920), p. vi.

[134] Quoted in Bernd Sösemann, "'Der kühnste Entschluß führt am sichersten zum Ziel': Eduard Meyer und die Politik," in *Eduard Meyer: Leben und Leistung eines Universalhistorikers,* ed. William M. Calder III and Alexander Demandt (Leiden, 1990), p. 468.

[135] See Dragendorff to Reich Chancellor Hertling, 14 January 1918, in PA/AA/K 42–501, on prospects for the Rome and Athens branches; see also Bode's *Denkschrift* on desired archaeological concessions to be inserted in the peace treaty, sent to the Foreign Ministry by the Education Ministry, 3 February 1919, ibid., 27–468a, vol. 2.

pects for overseas expeditions looked grim. Many of the DAI's facilities overseas had been occupied, and taking possession again would require careful
diplomatic negotiations, as well as hefty sums to replace staff and repair
damages. Many of the excavation houses in the Orient had been looted or
demolished. In Egypt, the guest house and other property of the Institut für
ägyptische Altertumskunde in Thebes was demolished by British military
officials who claimed it had been a center for illicit antiquities trading; in
Cairo, the institute's office itself had been taken over by U.S. diplomats
during the war.[136] The *Vossische Zeitung* reported in December 1919 that
the Rome branch, still occupied by the Italians, would be turned into a
housing facility for students at the Italian national school of art.[137] In 1920,
the Athens branch remained in the possession of the pro-French Greek
government, and one of the archaeologists' residences had been converted
into a girls' school.[138] It was suggested that Karo and Delbrück not return
"at first" to their respective branch directorships, given their wartime political activities.[139] As the Turkish revolution doomed the last lingering hopes
for new German archaeological victories in the East and budget shortfalls
forced new cutbacks, an unwelcome era of modest ambitions, international
impotence, and bureaucratic bickering opened before archaeologists' eyes.

The violence of the language with which archaeologists greeted the peace
comes as a surprise from men whose sense of professional decorum or bureaucratic propriety had previously prevented them from ranging beyond
the disinterested serenity of archaeological reportage or the rhetorical conventions of the lecture hall. Incensed by the Versailles agreement, Wiegand
wrote to his diary:

> Germany is like a beast shot in the belly that suffers in silence and cannot
> defend itself, while eagles and foxes threaten it from the outside and the mag-
> gots of anarchism gnaw on its smarting wounds. . . . What I most regret is that
> my adolescent sons will not, as I did, grow up in a victory-conscious, strong
> Germany and will not be allowed to cherish *Siegfriedsgedanken* (ideas of a
> Siegfried, of victorious peace). . . . My sons, you must perpetually think of
> this, to make Germany great and respected again, and to avenge all of today's
> disgrace. You should be responsible for this to my future memory, and when I
> am dead, you and your children must always think of me in this sense.
> Siegfried must change himself into the more ominous Hagen.[140]

[136] See Director of IfAA to Foreign Ministry, 16 December 1916, ibid., 42–501 adh II,
vol. 2.

[137] *Vossische Zeitung* 11 December 1919, in PA/AA/K 24–377B.5.

[138] "Bericht von Hr. Karo" (1920) in DAI, Nachlaß Dörpfeld, Kasten 6. Information in this
report on political opinion and cultural affairs in Greece came from Karo's secret encounter
with his promonarchist friends in Switzerland.

[139] On Karo, see ibid. On Delbrück, see Dragendorff to Central Directorate, 31 January
1920, in DAI, Nachlaß Wiegand, Kasten 28.

[140] Quoted in Wenk, *Auf den Spuren*, p. 24.

Dörpfeld, who by June 1919 had already been to visit the choleric Kaiser in exile,[141] commenced a fierce campaign to convince British scholars to press for the revocation of the offending treaty.[142] Karo set about virulent publicizing of his views on German war guilt (none) and the legitimacy and popularity of the new Greek government (ditto).[143] In his short *Die Verantwortung der Entente am Weltkrieg* (*The Entente's Responsibility for the World War*), the ex-director of the Athens DAI insisted upon the necessity of opposing the Versailles war-guilt clause, for only by revision of this paragraphs "can we emerge from the penal colony of our enemies a free *Volk* again."[144] And in May 1919, the long-time *limes* excavator Ernst Fabricius led a university-sponsored rally in Freiburg to protest the "inhumane and shameful" treaty. Speaking to between eight and ten thousand listeners, Fabricius condemned the robbery and enslavement proposed by the Entente, and extracted from the audience a pledge to refuse the treaty, regardless of the consequences—including a new war.[145]

Thus we find on the brink of a new era our Wilhelmine classicists, pondering their exclusion from the international scholarly community and the extinction of their expansionist dreams, their irrelevance as political commentators and their obsolescence as national cultural mentors. As professional scholars and former grandees, they could neither tolerate nor afford the enforced asceticism of reformist, impoverished Weimar. Specialization and archaeological, chronological, and geographical expansion had put paid to the unity-of-antiquity thesis; in recapitulating this shopworn conception, Wilamowitz remarked, Spengler was as naive as had been the young Friedrich Schlegel.[146] Aestheticism, too, would need to be revised for the younger generation; the "temple of art" metaphor used by Friedrich Noack on Winckelmann's Day 1917 could hold little appeal for the children of the Great War.[147] With the coming of peace, classicists seem to have had little left but their threats—and their determination to endure a brief period of national and intellectual decline in order to prepare for the inevitable philhellenic revival to come. In the afterword to the second volume of his

---

[141] See Wiegand diary, vol. 5, 6 June 1919, in DAI, Nachlaß Wiegand, Kasten 23.

[142] See, eg., Gilbert Murray to Dörpfeld, 4 January 1923 and Dörpfeld to Murray, 7 January 1923, ibid., Nachlaß Dörpfeld, Kasten 2; also see responses to Dörpfeld's letters from Jane Harrison, 1 January 1922 (probably misdated; should be 1923) and Walter Leaf, 14 December 1924, ibid., Kasten 1.

[143] See Karo's many articles, mostly published in the *Münchener Neueste Nachrichten* between 1920 and 1923 and collected ibid., Kasten 16, Mappe 2.

[144] Karo, *Die Verantwortung der Entente am Weltkrieg* (Halle, 1921), p. 6.

[145] "Die Freiburger Protestkundgebung gegen den Gewaltfrieden," in *Freiburger Zeitung*, 12 May 1919, p. 1, in DAI, Nachlaß Dörpfeld, Kasten 16, Mappe 2.

[146] Wilamowitz, "Die Geltung des klassischen Altertums im Wandel der Zeiten," (1921) in idem, *Kleine Schriften*, vol. 6 (Berlin, 1972), p 151.

[147] See Noack's speech to the Archäologische Gesellschaft reprinted in *AA-JbdDAI* 32 (1917): 163.

Platon (1919), Wilamowitz declared a private war on this un-Prussian age of "mob rule." There might indeed be no place left for men of his kind, the philologist confessed; "But the empire [Reich] of eternal forms, which Plato unlocked, is indestructible, and we will serve it with our scholarship: the miasmas of putrefaction cannot penetrate its pure ether. . . . As long as I breathe, I will fight on under the sign of Plato."[148] Admitting temporary defeat on all sides, German philhellenists retreated into reactionary idealism, vowing, however, to rise again.

[148] Wilamowitz, "Nachwort zu Band II," p. vi. Wilamowitz's book had already sold ten thousand copies by early 1919. Eduard Norden to Werner Jaeger, 5 March 1919, in Jaeger Papers, Houghton, Box I.

THE PERSISTENCE OF THE OLD REGIME

> Behind all the present discussions of the foundations of the
> educational system, the struggle of the "specialist type of
> man" against the older type of "cultivated man" is hidden at
> some decisive point. This fight is determined by the
> irresistibly expanding bureaucratization of all public and
> private relations of authority and by the ever-increasing
> importance of expert and specialized knowledge. This fight
> intrudes into all intimate cultural questions.
>
> (*Max Weber*)

AT THE FOUNDING of the Weimar Republic, several signs indicated
that reform in the realm of *Wissenschaft* and *Bildung* might be under
way. A new generation, cut off from the Wilhelmine culture of their
parents by four years of war, returned to the universities from the trenches.
The Prussian Education Ministry,[1] now directed by a prominent Social
Democrat politician, Konrad Haenisch, began to issue statements in favor of
wholesale remodeling of the hierarchical decision-making structure of the
universities and readjustment of academic mores to suit present-day (republican) needs.[2] Under secretary C. H. Becker, his reformist stance
strengthened by his contact with *Lebensphilosophie*, devoted himself to a
policy of overcoming the particularisms, "pure intellectualism," and compartmentalized learning of the past.[3] Becker's advocacy of a conciliatory,
streamlined, and progressive cultural policy (*Reichskulturpolitik*) helped to
shape the new constitution, which established the basis for the creation of a
more unified and democratic system of national education as well as for
greater Reich competency in the cultural sphere.[4]

---

[1] As of 1919, the Prussian *Kultusministerium* was officially retitled the *Ministerium für
Wissenschaft, Kunst, und Volksbildung*.

[2] See, for example, Konrad Haenisch to Senate and Faculties of the Universities, 17 May
1919, GStAPKB, Nachlaß Becker, Mappe 939.

[3] See his *Kulturpolitische Aufgaben des Reiches* (Erfurt, 1919), and Becker to Theodor
Nöldecke, 9 December 1920 in GStAPKB, Nachlaß Becker, Mappe 3138; for some discussion
of Weimar pedagogical debates and Becker's role in these, see chapter 9.

[4] See Fritz Ringer, *The Decline of the German Mandarins: The German Academic Community,
1890–1933* (Hanover, N.H., 1990), pp. 67–69; and Bernhard vom Brocke, "Preußen—Land
der Schulen, nicht nur Kasernen: Preußische Bildungspolitik von Gottfried Wilhelm Leibniz

And yet, the few hopeful portents that appeared in the wake of the war were more than offset by signs that the bureaucratic-academic cadre of the previous era had maintained much of its predominance in educational and scientific affairs. In the universities, the continued predominance of prewar elites made the appointment of younger, left-leaning and/or Catholic scholars arduous. The Haenisch-Becker plan to break the stranglehold of arch-conservative full professors by promoting lower-ranking professors as swiftly as possible foundered on the bleak beach of Weimar-era finance. Within the ministries, a kind of "silent battle" raged between newly appointed but inexperienced reformers and conservative lower-level functionaries, masters of bureaucratic details and unwilling minions of the new regime.[5] The ravages of hyperinflation induced the republic to take over major portions of the funding for scholarly bodies over which it could exert no discretionary influence; this restructuring, however, did nothing to clarify the issue of administrative authority in cultural policy. Where the lower bureaucracy was weak or overburdened, as in the new Cultural Section of the Reich's Interior Ministry, special-interest groups were able to appropriate central funding and control to their own purposes.[6] The new constitution had provided "principles" for the reform of lower-level education, but, owing to particularist dissension, the Weimar Reichstag never managed to pass a nation-wide school law, leaving the implementation of reformist precepts up to the impoverished localities and their often conservative or clerical elites. These failures—of will, of opportunity, or of savoir-faire—opened the way for the reentrenchment of traditional forces and the collapse of *Reichskulturpolitik.*

I have taken this chapter's title from Arno Mayer's provocative survey of European culture and politics between about 1890 and 1930 (*The Persistence of the Old Regime*) to underscore the endurance of prewar patterns of organization and cultural norms. Perhaps nowhere else is this persistence so marked as in the realm of classical scholarship and education; but further investigation of the Weimar bureaucracy would undoubtedly illuminate other areas in which complex cultural and political forces combined to stifle innovation and reform. In any event, my analysis departs from Mayer's in attributing this persistence not only to willed domination, but also to structural stagnation, the product of economic hardship, the tenacity of particularistic interests, and institutionalized commitments to an aristocratic *Bildungsideal* and "pure," specialized, scholarship. Together these

---

und Wilhelm von Humboldt bis Friedrich Althoff und Carl Heinrich Becker (1700–1930)," in *Preußen: Eine Herausforderung,* ed. Wolfgang Böhme (Karlsruhe, 1981), p. 92.

[5] See "Der stille Kampf in den Ministerien," in *Die Neue Zeitung* (Berlin), 16 June 1919, in GStAPKB, Nachlaß Becker, Mappe 7679.

[6] Erich Wende, *C. H. Becker: Mensch und Politiker* (Stuttgart, 1959), p. 95.

forces doomed the liberal-republican project of national reconciliation through unified and reinvigorated *Bildung* by rendering innovation impracticable and centralization unacceptable.

The effect of structural—and ideological—barriers to academic-scholarly reform in the realm of classical studies was, in general, to forestall once more the demotion of the Greeks and the disempowerment of the philological establishment. Despite the constitutional provisions for the establishment of national school types, education remained highly fragmented; one commentator reports the existence of as many as seventy types of secondary schools in Germany during the 1920s.[7] This condition allowed the *Gymnasium* to retain much of its prestigious position and preindustrial character, although its percentage of enrollments fell off considerably. Continuing hostility to school reformers and socialists recemented old associational linkages among philologists, and new organizations mobilized resistance to the democratization of admissions or regularization of curricula. The united opposition of the *Gymnasium* and university teachers squelched a movement—backed by Becker—that would have increased the prestige and salaries of lower educators by requiring them to hold university degrees.[8] The Notgemeinschaft der deutschen Wissenschaft (Emergency Association for German Science and Scholarship) helped to fund research projects and DAI excavations, while the institute's parenting Foreign Ministry, too—still itself a haven of aristocratic pedigree and esprit—did its utmost to protect archaeologists from budgetary cuts and the state's periodic trimming of the civil service. The classicist establishment did not intend to allow Germany's change in government to disrupt its prewar practices, and circumstances, at least initially, connived to favor institutional stasis.

As exemplary representatives of scholarly achievement, archaeologists naturally hoped to participate prominently in the campaign to restore German prestige. Accustomed to placing excavation ahead of interpretation, however, these scholars could see no other means to recuperate their international standing than by recommencing their grand-scale digs overseas. For Weimar archaeologists, excavation had become an urgent requirement for "scientific" progress as well as for the DAI's survival as a national cultural institution; an extended delay in undertaking a grand project, like the twenty-year postponement forced on Ernst Curtius by Bismarck's hostility to his Olympia dig, would now undermine the social and scientific legitimacy of German archaeology. The first imperative for postwar archaeologists, then, was not organizational reform, but the reconstruction of a pa-

---

[7] Andreas Fritsch, "Die altsprachlichen Fächer im nationalsozialistischen Schulsystem," in *Schule und Unterricht im Dritten Reich*, ed. Reinhard Dithmar (Neuwied, 1989), p. 135.

[8] Instead, a rather unsatisfying compromise was reached in which elementary-school teachers were sent to special pedagogical institutes for additional training. See vom Brocke, "Preußen—Land der Schulen," p. 96.

tronage network suitable for supporting the costs of "big archaeology" and the refurbishing of old arguments for the pursuit of cultural diplomacy.

From Revolution to Hyperinflation: Patronage Problems, Self-Monumentalization, and the Future of *Kulturpolitik*

Germany's provincial governments, traditionally the major patrons of education and culture, emerged from the World War in desperate financial straits. Exacerbated by the inflation of 1919–20, this condition encouraged the Länder to put their meager funds into the overcrowded schools and to trim already diminished budgets for research, libraries, equipment, and salaries. Practical research continued to be organized by the Kaiser-Wilhelm-Gesellschaft (KWG), a collection of specialized agencies founded in 1911 and dedicated largely to medicine and the applied sciences. The prewar KWG was funded both by the state and by heavy industrialists, and actually expanded its purview during the war. Even the KWG, however, fell on hard times in the 1920s, and by mid-decade, a much-reduced organization was receiving half its income from Prussia and the republic.[9] For the social sciences and the humanities, the outlook was even more disturbing. A rising number of provincially supported organizations were transferred to the budget columns of the Reich's Interior Ministry and Foreign Ministry, and the Prussian Education Ministry during the 1920s to prevent their financial collapse. Already alienated from the international scholarly community—and barred from participation in its conferences—German scholars and their patrons became ever more alarmed about the parlous state of national *Geist*. From the academies, universities, and scientific institutes, a clamor arose for central state intervention to restore German culture and with it Germany's intellectual *Konkurrenzfähigkeit* (ability to compete).

In April 1919, Friedrich Schmidt-Ott, now excluded from the Education Ministry after thirty years of service, published an essay recommending that the Reich contribute "significant monies" to sustain scholarship in its time of need.[10] Schmidt-Ott's arguments in many ways resembled those used by Becker in his pleas for the creation and implementation of national cultural policy; both men pointed to the limited resources, self-interested policies, and inefficient administrations of the Länder to justify the transference of responsibility for cultural organization to the central state. One crucial difference, however, was evident in the ultimate aims of the new policies they

---

[9] J. L. Heilbron, *The Dilemmas of an Upright Man* (Berkeley, Calif., 1986), p. 96.

[10] See Schmidt, "Die Kulturaufgaben und das Reich," reprinted from *Internationale Monatsschrift für Wissenschaft, Kunst, und Technik* 13, no. 5 (April 1919): 451–64; copy in GStAPKB, Nachlaß Schmidt-Ott, Mappe 8.

proposed: while Becker's program centered chiefly on domestic reconciliation and reform, Schmidt-Ott's plan aimed mostly at the rehabilitation of
overseas prestige. Schmidt-Ott's approach to postwar cultural reconstruction, then, concentrated on the perpetuation of "big scholarship" and traditional areas of German expertise. In restricting the republic's cultural responsibilities to the promotion of specialized scholarship, he and his
entourage were able to ignore Becker's warnings about cultural disintegra-
tion and academic irrelevance.

The idea for the Notgemeinschaft der deutschen Wissenschaft was apparently developed by Schmidt-Ott and another leading figure in the KWG,
Fritz Haber, as they calmly awaited the start of a meeting, delayed by the
outbreak of the Kapp Putsch.[11] Their plan called for the formation of a
nonpartisan, autonomous, national organization under the aegis of the Interior Ministry that would distribute funds to the neediest and most deserving
research projects of national scope and import, leaving the Länder the responsibility for schooling and for studies of purely provincial interest.[12]
Haber, director of the KWG Institut für physikalische Chemie and a Nobel
Prize winner, presented the idea to university rectors and academies of science across Germany in March 1920, and quickly won the backing of the
professoriate for the plan. Acclaim came also from heavy industry, to which
both Schmidt-Ott and Haber had some connection; the prospect of preventing the destruction of corporatist self-administration threatened by the
socialist-led government appealed to the captains of industry as well as to
the satraps of academia.[13] By 12 October Schmidt-Ott could report to a
meeting of Notgemeinschaft founders that the Finance Ministry had approved a one-time grant of 20 million marks, while industry had promised
35 million, the banks 24 million, and the chemical industry 15 million.[14]

Despite the initial enthusiasm of heavy industrialists, it quickly became
evident that the Reich would have to fund the bulk of the Notgemeinschaft's
needs. The formation of an industrialist-led contributors' committee resulted primarily in the circumstance that private donors were now able to

[11] See the account given in Kurt Zierold, *Forschungsförderung in drei Epochen* (Wiesbaden,
1968), pp. 8–10. The Kapp Putsch was a short-lived attempt by several right-wing leaders in
the *Reichswehr* to dissolve the Republic. Two of Schmidt-Ott's sons and his soon-to-be assistant
Eduard Wildhagen participated in the coup attempt.

[12] Schmidt, "Aus dem Werden der Notgemeinschaft," Sonderdruck aus *Bericht der Notgemeinschaft der Deutschen Wissenschaft* 9 (1930): 9, copy in GStAPKB, Nachlaß Schmidt-Ott,
Mappe 8.

[13] Gerald D. Feldman, "The Private Support of Science in Germany, 1900–1933," in *Formen
außerstaatlicher Wissenschaftsförderung im 19. und 20. Jahrhundert*, ed. Rüdiger vom Bruch and
Rainer A. Müller (Stuttgart, 1990), pp. 100–101.

[14] Report on Notgemeinschaft meeting of 12 October 1920, in GStAPKB, Nachlaß Schmidt-
Ott, Mappe 2. For a more detailed account of the founding of the agency, see Zierold, *Forschungsförderung*, pp. 14–20.

allocate their gifts to utilitarian ends, precisely the eventuality Schmidt-Ott wished to avoid. In addition, private donations to the Notgemeinschaft dwindled swiftly after a first round of large pledges, and patrons insisted that only the interest on their munificence be spent (the principal itself disappeared during the hyperinflation). Clearly, despite its altruistic rhetoric, private industry could not be induced to support precisely the impractical, humanistic projects the professoriate believed to be vital to national cultural recovery.

The Reich, as usual, was petitioned to make up the deficit, and through the beneficence of Weimar President Friedrich Ebert, Finance Minister Rudolf Hilferding, and the Reichstag, the agency received 40 million marks in 1921 (2.5 million goldmarks), 440 million in 1922, 900 billion (plus 500,000 goldmarks) in 1923, 3 million rentenmarks in 1924, and RM 8 million in 1925.[15] Between 1924 and 1933, the Notgemeinschaft received RM 1.3 million in private donations, as compared with RM 59.2 million in Reich funds.[16] As Haber intimated, however, selling nonutilitarian scholarship to the Reich as well as to private industry would require delicacy, or perhaps even trickery. The Reich bureaucracy, too, now shied away from funding specialized preoccupations too reminiscent of the *Kaiserreich*. In a private letter to Schmidt-Ott, Haber noted that the finance minister's "willingness to provide 20 million in the budget to be passed in September is exclusively thanks to his faith in the future success of chemistry. I avoided mentioning philology and everything connected with it."[17] Employing the *kulturpolitische* rhetoric of the past and defending themselves masterfully against charges of superfluity and/or obsolescence, the Notgemeinschaft supporters prepared a forceful argument for the resuscitation of Wilhelmine *Wissenschaft*.

In general, until the final years of the republic, such rhetoric sufficed to win Reichstag, as well as ministerial, support for the agency. The organization did not, however, propel its budgets through the Reichstag without suffering a good measure of criticism, particularly from the left. In a 1922 budgetary debate, for example, the Social Democrat (and medical doctor) Julius Moses agreed that science was essential to rebuilding the cultural and economic life of the German nation. But Moses could not understand the private sector's abdication from its duty to patronize new ideas. "Where is our heavy industry," he asked, "where are the big banks, which are swim-

[15] Schmidt, "Aus dem Werden," p. 24; Thomas Nipperdey and Ludwig Schmugge, *50 Jahre Forschungsförderung in Deutschland: Ein Abriß der Geschichte der deutschen Forschungsgemeinschaft, 1920–1970* (Berlin, 1970), p. 23.

[16] Gerald D. Feldman, "The Politics of Wissenschaftspolitik in Weimar Germany: A Prelude to the Dilemmas of Twentieth-Century Science Policy," in *Changing Boundaries of the Political*, ed. Charles Maier (Cambridge, Mass., 1987), p. 269.

[17] Haber to Schmidt, 2 August 1920, quoted ibid., p. 268.

ming in money?", while Communist Representative Heydemann demanded an end to the "educational monopoly of the propertied."[18] Comrade Wegmann of the Bavarian Communist Party commenced his complaint with a damning reminder of the participation of the professoriate in obfuscating real conditions during the war. He then argued that repetitious paeans to the grandeur of knowledge had simply concealed the fact that conservative, capitalist forces were able to determine precisely what *kind* of knowledge would be fostered.[19] Within the Catholic Center party, too, respect for scholarship was mingled with resentment of the exclusive, aristocratic, and Prussophile bearing of the professoriate.[20] But, like the smaller liberal parties, the Center hoped that scholars would reform their institutions of their own accord; reverence for the august attainments of "disinterested" scholarship outweighed the attractions of structural reorganization.

Reforming the academy, however, did not figure in the Notgemeinschaft's statutes, and so long as Catholics and liberals voted with the Right to approve the budget, the principle of self-administration sufficed to deflect pressures for change. The structure and staffing of the Notgemeinschaft virtually ensured that prewar biases and penchants would prevail in the organization's distribution of funds. The board of directors (Schmidt-Ott plus four others) and the eleven-member executive committee changed little between 1920 and 1929. The twenty faculty committees, responsible for reviewing projects in their areas of expertise, were chosen by university faculties, who selected chiefly conservative, established scholars to represent them. Technically, the Interior Ministry retained veto power over the financial decisions of the Notgemeinschaft, but this prerogative was little used until the late 1920s, when reformist bureaucrats grew impatient with the organization's exclusivity.

The Notgemeinschaft's significance for Weimar scholarly and scientific affairs lay not in the quantity of funds it dispensed but rather in the supplementary nature and conservative function of its monies. Notgemeinschaft expenditures between 1924 and 1933 totalled only 60 million marks, as compared with a total Reich budget for science and art of 496.5 million in 1927/8.[21] More to the point, however, is the fact that the annual budget of the Prussian Education Ministry included only 180,000 marks for direct

---

[18] Moses in *Verhandlungen des Reichstags* (1. Wahlperiode 1920) vol. 357, 268. Sitzung (16 November 1922), p. 9004; Heydemann, ibid., pp. 9023–27.

[19] Wegmann, ibid., p. 9028.

[20] As the Interior Ministry's delegate to the Reichstag Budget Committee, Msgr. Georg Schreiber proved instrumental in Catholic support for the Notgemeinschaft. Schreiber, himself a professor of church history at the University of Münster, feared the total degradation of German prestige but also advocated greater social accountability for science and scholarship. See Schreiber's speech, ibid., 267. Sitzung (15 November 1922), p. 8987.

[21] Nipperdey and Schmugge, *50 Jahre Forschungsförderung*, p. 40.

financing of research.[22] In these circumstances, the Notgemeinschaft's ability to fund particular projects, laboratories, and publications made it the center of attention for a large cadre of highly skilled experts, all eager to recreate their prewar prominence. Of course, by funding research needs, the agency did promote path-breaking research in many areas, particularly in medicine and the natural sciences. Yet those who stress the innovative qualities of the Notgemeinschaft frequently fail to appreciate the ways in which its practices, modeled on those of Schmidt-Ott's mentor Friedrich Althoff, had, by 1920, become the means of conservative preservation of Wilhelmine styles of scholarship. In Schmidt-Ott's day, the senior members of the professoriate—and especially Schmidt's confidantes—were on the whole less liberal than they had been in Althoff's early years.[23] Importantly, the Notgemeinschaft quickly came to represent the interests and biases of the established members of German academia *against* the Education Ministry's attempts to modernize the educational system. Notgemeinschaft funds allowed established scholars to enhance their reputations, expand their operations, and ignore the efforts of Becker and others to introduce much-needed institutional reforms.[24]

Challenges to the Notgemeinschaft's modernity reflected in large part discontent with the agency's apparently indulgent support for the humanities. In 1926, Fritz Haber did his utmost to correct the misapprehension that the bulk of Notgemeinschaft funds had slipped into humanists' pockets; though 63.2 percent of individual grants had gone to the humanities, as against 36.8 percent to the natural sciences, he averred, the major part of funds for research groups had gone to the latter, pushing its total far above the former.[25] In later years, as the advocates of utilitarian science grew more vocal, the Notgemeinschaft's expenditures on the natural sciences increased considerably; between 1928 and 1933, the humanities received 30 percent, medicine and natural science 50 percent, engineering and agriculture 15 percent, and miscellaneous projects 2 percent of the annual budget.[26]

[22] Kurt Düwell, "Staat und Wissenschaft in der Weimarer Epoche: Zur Kulturpolitik des Ministers C. H. Becker," *Historische Zeitschrift*, suppl. vol. 1 (1971): 60.

[23] Althoff's advisers had included Rudolf Virchow, Theodor Mommsen, and Friedrich Paulsen; Schmidt-Ott's advisers included Wiegand, Meyer, Wilamowitz, Reinhard Seeberg, Werner Sombart, and Otto Hoetzsch.

[24] The close ties between the wartime annexationists, opponents of reform, and Schmidt's agency were no secret to Becker and his entourage. Becker secured his unpopularity in conservative university circles by seeking to abolish lecture fees, from which established professors earned considerable supplementary income, and by supporting elementary teachers in their attempts to improve their social and economic positions. See Friedrich Glum, *Zwischen Wissenschaft, Wirtschaft, und Politik* (Bonn, 1964) pp. 314–15.

[25] Feldman, "Politics of Wissenschaftspolitik," p. 274.

[26] Nipperdey and Schmugge, *50 Jahre Forschungsförderung*, p. 95.

26. A festive meeting of the Notgemeinschaft der deutschen Wissenschaft.
Obviously, this was not an organization that catered to the younger generation.
© Bildarchiv, Preußischer Kulturbesitz, 1996.

Within the humanities, funded projects often reflected the Notgemeinschaft's desire to demonstrate its contributions to German spiritual
renewal. Schmidt-Ott favored projects that enhanced the international re-
pute of German scholarship; such projects included deep-sea and polar exploration, *Ostforschung* (research into Eastern Europe), prehistory, and
most particularly, archaeology, an interest he shared with his exiled friend,
Kaiser Wilhelm II.[27] In executive sessions of the Notgemeinschaft,
Schmidt-Ott was surrounded by forceful advocates of overseas excavation,
including Adolf Deißmann, the papyrologist who headed the faculty committee for theology, Wiegand (who headed the committee for art history
from 1921 to 1929), and Rodenwaldt (who succeeded Wiegand). Elected to
chair the faculty committee for oriental and classical philology in 1921,
Eduard Meyer also championed the projects of archaeologists. Meyer's continued concern for reestablishing international prestige for German *Alter-*

---

[27] Schmidt-Ott spent four weeks with Wilhelm in 1921, during which time their discussions turned frequently to matters archaeological. See Friedrich Schmidt-Ott, *Erlebtes und
Erstrebtes, 1860–1950* (Wiesbaden, 1952), pp. 189ff.

tumskunde as well as his desire to take advantage of available research opportunities overseas led him to give high priority to projects "in Indian, East Asian, Semitic, and Islamic areas;"[28] excavation and exotic cultural studies suited both the historian's resolve to restore national prestige and his barely concealed desire to renew German cultural imperialism in the East. The noble tradition of German classical archaeology and the continuing significance of excavation abroad for the revival of German cultural diplomacy ensured that the Notgemeinschaft would not allow archaeology to languish in postwar penury.

In fact, the Notgemeinschaft was not the only body concerned with the fortunes of German archaeology and the future of the archaeological treasures collected before the war. As before 1914, financing for digs and projects remained a hodgepodge of private and public, openly debated and covertly transferred monies. In 1920, the Reich supplemented the DAI budget with thirty thousand marks to finance the preparation and publication of excavation reports.[29] After the war, Dörpfeld managed to convince the Weimar government to continue to pay him the stipend he had been granted by Wilhelm II.[30] In 1920, the Foreign Ministry sent the Swedish consulate in Smyrna twenty-five thousand marks to pay German excavation personnel in Asia Minor; the ministry also provided tens of thousands of marks to employ watchmen for former German dig sites.[31]

Public monies could not match DAI desires, however, and in January 1920, Dragendorff announced the necessity for the institute to pursue private funds with greater energy and ingenuity. He suggested to the central directorate that the RGK be separated from the main institute in order to allow the latter—appealing to a much different public and undertaking more pressing national tasks (presumably defense of Germanic culture in the Rhineland)—to seek out funds on its own.[32] In 1922, the new DAI director Gerhart Rodenwaldt made a suggestion—likewise anathema to prewar philhellenes—that a stipend for Christian archaeology and a working arrangement with Italian Catholic scholars be established.[33] Like Dragendorff's plan to divest the DAI of the RGK, this tactic aimed at increasing the DAI's circle of patrons, and also at cultivating Center party support for

---

[28] Quoted in Wolfhart Unte, "Eduard Meyer und die Notgemeinschaft der deutschen Wissenschaft," in *Eduard Meyer: Leben und Leistung eines Universalhistorikers*, ed. William M. Calder and Alexander Demandt (Leiden, 1990), p. 516.

[29] Eduard Meyer, "Fünfundzwanzig Jahre Deutsche Orient-Gesellschaft," *Mitteilungen der Deutschen Orient-Gesellschaft* 62 (1923): 6.

[30] Rodenwaldt to Dörpfeld, 22 January 1924, in DAI, Nachlaß Dörpfeld, Kasten 3, Mappe 2.

[31] Swedish Consulate, Berlin, to Foreign Ministry, 14 March 1920, and Foreign Ministry to Legationskasse, 23 August 1921, in PA/AA/K 27-468a, vol. 32.

[32] Dragendorff to Central Directorate, 31 January 1920, in DAI, Nachlaß Wiegand, Kasten 28, Mappe 1.

[33] Rodenwaldt to Foreign Ministry, 28 August 1922, in PA/AA/K 52-557, vol. 2.

the institute. In the end, the RGK remained bound to the DAI—in part to retain the sympathetic parentage of the Foreign Ministry for Roman-German studies, in part to retain the domestic appeal of Germanic archaeology for the DAI as a whole—while both Catholics and Pan-Germans received new solicitude from a politically shrewd central directorate.

Prohibited or limited in the undertaking of new projects, Weimar archaeologists drew on their heroic past to underscore the profound significance of their institutions and activities for the revival of *Kulturpolitik*. In early 1920, Georg Karo, on behalf of the DAI central directorate instructed the Foreign Ministry that if the DAI budget were not increased by approximately 758,300 marks, the Rome and Athens branches would have to be dissolved. The abandonment of the Rome institute, Karo argued, would not only deal a great blow to German prestige, but would also result in the loss of "a proven means, cultivated over generations, of reestablishing good relations with the Italians." Similarly, amputation of the Athens branch would entail the Reich's loss of a choice political and cultural position in the Balkans. "For archaeology now forms the only passable bridge to Asia Minor and Constantinople, through the mediation of [the study of] Greekdom in Turkey, which is bound by many threads to our institute."[34] The Foreign Ministry passed this dire message along to the Finance Ministry, adding the following gloss: "A voluntary abandonment of institutions of such recognized international significance as the archaeological institutes in Rome and Athens for financial reasons will be seen abroad as a declaration of bankruptcy by Weimar scholarship and the German economy, and will be correspondingly exploited by our foes."[35]

In addition to organizing the financial resurrection of its overseas affiliates, the DAI also set about the reconstruction of its politically neutral, ambassadorial reputation. Karo, in view of Greek demands that the reopened Athens institute avoid political meddling, resigned his directorship in July 1920 for a professorship at Halle.[36] From Halle, Karo continued his political propagandizing; by 1924, he had published nine sizable pamphlets or books on the war guilt question and had become a regular on the right-wing lecture circuit. But by 1929, when he returned to the Athens office, he had curtailed his political activism, at least in public.[37] As projected, Rich-

---

[34] "Auszug aus einem Antrag der ZD des Archäologischen Instituts an das Auswärtige Amt auf Erhöhung des Etats für 1920 . . ." 3 April 1920, in DAI, Nachlaß Wiegand, Kasten 28, Mappe 1.

[35] Unterstaatssekretär in Foreign Ministry to Finance Ministry, 11 April 1920, in PZStA AA/K 69494, pp. 14–15.

[36] Karo to DAI, 27 July 1920, ibid., 69574, pp. 183–84.

[37] Karo boasted of his publications in a letter to the Archivdienst, Berlin Charlottenberg, 15 August 1924, in ADAI, Nachlaß Karo, Mappe 804. As early as 1922, Rodenwaldt had (erroneously) described Karo's decision to cease his political propagandizing. Rodenwaldt to Wiegand, 9 January 1922, DAI, Nachlaß Wiegand, Kasten 8.

ard Delbrück did not return to his post in Rome, and with the help of Benedetto Croce, the Germans managed to effect the reopening of the original institute. Affirmations of the therapeutic effects of Germanic *Altertumskunde* abounded as Roman-German archaeologists prescribed immersion in national history as a tonic for social fragmentation. Banishing political and particularistic interests from its halls, the DAI set the stage for the recommencement of archaeological *Kulturpolitik*.

Financial hardship, however, continued to frustrate the institute's plans for the recovery of its prewar prestige. If the World War had not done irreparable damage to the organization, by 1919, hard times had unquestionably set in. In that year, even under self-imposed savings restrictions, the DAI had run 91,000 marks over its 223,041-mark budget (210,621 marks of which had been supplied by the Reich).[38] The finance minister excised funds for stipends and for excavations in the East from the 1920 budget, which very soon needed considerable amending just to keep salaries in pace with inflation.[39] In July 1920, the finance minister demanded that the DAI return funds saved during the war to Reich coffers, an action Dragendorff was able to prevent only by demonstrating left-over funds to be private donations and gifts of the Kaiser.[40] For 1920 and 1921, the DAI requested subsidies of approximately 1.5 million marks per year from the Reich, but had consistently to ask for supplementary funds as the value of the mark fell. As of 23 January 1923, the Reich had given the DAI 10,598,990 marks for 1922, some 48 million short of the institute's actual expenditures.[41] Thereafter, inflation proceeded so rapidly that budgets had to be adjusted first by the month, then biweekly, then daily. Projects and publications were temporarily suspended, and funds were chiefly given over to paying salaries and pensions.

Unluckily for the new DAI general director Gerhart Rodenwaldt, this new inflationary cycle coincided precisely with his attempts to restore and re-staff branch offices abroad. In Asia, the situation appeared hopeless; Halil Edhem reported that excavation houses in Smyrna, Pergamum, Miletus, and Didyma had been essentially destroyed,[42] and prospects for receiving or renewing dig permits looked grim. In Rome and Athens, personnel shortages crippled efforts to restore the institutes' former eminence; whereas the

[38] Wolters to Education Ministry, 26 April 1920, and "Haushalt des Archäologischen Instituts für das Rechnungsjahr 1919," both in PZStA AA/K 69574, pp. 56–57 and 26–33, respectively.

[39] Finance Ministry to Foreign Ministry, 6 December 1919, and Dragendorff to Foreign Ministry, 9 June 1920, both ibid., pp. 15–16 and 77–80, respectively.

[40] Finance Ministry to Foreign Ministry, 14 July 1920, and Dragendorff to Foreign Ministry, 17 December 1920, both ibid., pp. 88 and 294–96, respectively.

[41] Finance Ministry to Foreign Ministry, 24 February 1923, ibid., 69576, p. 93.

[42] Halil Edhem Bey to Wallenberg (Swedish Minister) 4 June 1923, copy in PA/AA/K 27-468a, vol. 11.

Athens branch before 1914 employed two secretaries, one librarian, and one architect, in 1922, the staff was composed solely of a first secretary. In addition, the Reich Salary Law of April 1920 had recategorized DAI higher bureaucrats as state officials (*Beamte*), reducing their salaries relative to those of full professors.[43] Finally, frustrated with the Finance Ministry's refusal to allow old staff positions to be refilled, in April 1923 Rodenwaldt proposed that in lieu of appointing second deputy directors, annual professorships at the branches be created, as professorial encounters with original artifacts had now become essential to German archaeology's *Konkurrenzfähigkeit*.[44] This plan, too, however, fell victim to the rapid devaluation of the mark, and with the passage of the severe Personnel Reduction Decree in October 1923—an emergency measure that eliminated 24.9 percent of public-sector positions[45]—it became clear that the reconstruction of archaeological prestige would have to await economic stabilization.

In the DAI's bureaucratic transactions of the immediate postwar period, the reestablishment of ties to Greece seems to have taken top priority. As Rodenwaldt's proposals indicated, travel to Greece and direct encounter with original artifacts had now become the sine qua non of archaeological progress as well as a vital component of German prestige. Rodenwaldt, who had established close ties with important personages in the military and civil administrations during the World War,[46] certainly pressed the Reich bureaucracy on this point, while Wilhelm Dörpfeld supplied reports to the DAI and Foreign Ministry on the Reich's cultural and political standing in his second homeland.[47] If the endangered status of the Rome library caused consternation in Berlin, campaigns to reconstruct prestige here were lackluster by comparison to those carried out on behalf of the Athens branch. In his autobiography, Ludwig Curtius described the technical, as well as intellectual concerns underlying the inferior position the original institute had assumed by the mid-1920s:

> The Roman museums are indeed richer in Greek originals than the passing visitor believes, but they cannot at all be compared with the treasures in the Greek museums, and their endless rooms filled with Roman copies disappoint the eye seeking the magic of the original, immediate work of the Greek chisel. The Rome institute too has never during the entire time of its existence undertaken major excavations, while the tradition of independent excavation be-

[43] See undated document on *Reichsbesoldungsgesetz* in DAI, Nachlaß Wiegand, Kasten 28, Mappe 1.

[44] Rodenwaldt to Foreign Ministry, 28 April 1923, in PZStA AA/K 69576, pp. 130–35.

[45] Jane Caplan, *Government without Administration: State and Civil Service in Weimar and Nazi Germany* (Oxford, 1988), p. 53.

[46] See Borbein, "Gerhart Rodenwaldts Bild der römischen Kunst," in *L'Impero Romano fra Storia generale e Storia locale*, ed. E. Gabba and K. Christ (Como, 1991), p. 184.

[47] Dörpfeld to Central Directorate, 27 November 1923, PZStA AA/K 69495, pp. 153–56.

longs to the Athenian [institute] just as does the [tradition of] the most intimate collaboration with Greek scholars and their excavations. Thus Rome was a place to do scholarly work, but compared with Athens, it was a sidetrack.[48]

The original home of the Hyperboreans had become less a vital center for innovative researches than a museum commemorating the Romantic, philological, and aesthetically inspired origins of modern European humanism. The question remained, however, whether without state subsidies and overseas sites sufficient for grand-scale excavation, the DAI itself would share the same fate.

Stabilization and Its Discontents, 1924–1929

Ironically, the period of economic stabilization ushered in by the reissuing of the currency, the French withdrawal from the Ruhr valley, and the rescheduling of the German debt engendered increases in bureaucratic infighting and scholarly grumbling in the field of classical studies. The hyperinflation multiplied the circle of the republic's cultural clients, and fear of its recurrence inspired scholars to seek new assurances and more autonomous positions (less subject to political changes) from the state bureaucracy. Following the German economy's recovery, ideas for new, state-funded projects proliferated, stimulating a resurgence of factionalization. As archaeologists pressed for reinstatement of their former projects, the desire for state protection and professional control resurfaced, reconsolidating both their commitment to *Kulturpolitik* and their dependence on the good will and munificence of the state bureaucracy.

However valuable its activities and insights in the field of *Kulturpolitik*, the DAI could not persuade the Foreign Ministry to finance all of its projects.[49] Thus, numerous archaeological schemes, most particularly those launched by Wiegand and his intimates, sought backing from the para-bureaucratic prestige seekers of the Notgemeinschaft. With Wiegand and then Rodenwaldt as head and Ludwig Curtius and Dragendorff as members of the faculty committee for art-historical affairs, many projects in the field received Notgemeinschaft funding, often given in conjunction with monies allocated by the other bodies. Excavations at Ephesus—still officially under Austrian control—were restarted in 1927 with joint Notgemeinschaft and Foreign Ministry support, later to be supplemented by funds from the

---

[48] Ludwig Curtius, *Deutsche und antike Welt: Lebenserinnerungen* (Stuttgart, 1950), p. 433.

[49] The real barriers to DAI funding came from the Finance Ministry and the DAI-hostile lower reaches of the Foreign Ministry. See Rodenwaldt to Gerkan, 30 May 1927, in BSB, Nachlaß Rodenwaldt, Mappe 424.

Rockefellar Foundation, the Interior Ministry, and the Austrian Archaeological Institute itself.[50] When Wiegand failed for the third time to extract funds for new Pergamum investigations from the Education Ministry, he turned to the Notgemeinschaft, from which he received the generous sum of 35,000 rentenmarks per year.[51] By the mid- to late 1920s, Germans were participating in American excavations at Troy and Alisar, in the Swedish excavation at Larissa, in Greek excavations at Tiryns and in Athens, and in the Austrian excavations at Ephesus. German excavators were leading digs in Aezani (Phyrgia), on Aegina, in Sichem (Palestine), at Numantia (Spain), at Pergamum, at Giza (Egypt), at Ctesiphon (ancient Seleucia), on the island of Samos, and in hundreds of locations within Germany itself. Yet for each of these endeavors, all modest in comparison to prewar undertakings, significant funds had to be marshaled—by dint of extensive petitioning, persistent lobbying, and occasionally intrigue.[52] Unfortunately for the archaeologists of the Weimar era, there was no longer a sympathetic Kaiser with a plentiful privy purse ready to hand.

Recovering prewar riches and international prestige, however, was not the sole occupation of the mid-1920s. Both the DAI and the RGK, in this period, faced grave threats to their bureaucratic and budgetary autonomy, posed by the divergent forces of centralization and particularistic envy. The DAI's difficulties owed to efforts to bring all national research organizations under the supervision of a single agency, namely the Interior Ministry. The first campaign for unification was launched in early 1924 and caused renewed consternation that the DAI's overseas branches would be robbed of the life-giving sustenance of quasi-diplomatic status and participation in *Kulturpolitik*.[53] Deflected once, the Interior Ministry's bid for unification recurred in 1926, apparently backed by the Center party.[54] In this case, too, however, the Interior Ministry received a forceful rebuff, this time from Foreign Minister Gustav Stresemann:

> The necessity of retaining the closest connection between the overseas work of the archaeological institute and the Foreign Ministry has in fact increased, since, in full agreement with the demands of broad sections of the population and the repeated suggestions of the Reichstag, a more active German *Kultur-*

[50] See A. Deißmann to Foreign Ministry, 7 April 1927, and Deißmann to Terdenge (Foreign Ministry), 17 July 1929, both in PA/AA/K 114-2 Türkei, vol. 1.

[51] Wiegand to Hiller von Gärtringen, 2 June 1927, in DAI, Nachlaß Wiegand, Kasten 13; Rodenwaldt to L. Curtius, 21 June 1927, in BSB, Nachlaß Rodenwaldt, Mappe 393. Official Turkish permission to restart excavations in Pergamum was given in February 1927.

[52] For one account of Wiegand's machinations, see Erich Boehringer, *Leben und Wirken*, ed. Robert Boehringer (Düsseldorf, 1973), p. 20.

[53] Rodenwaldt to Dörpfeld, 8 January 1924, in DAI, Nachlaß Dörpfeld, Kasten 3, Mappe 1.

[54] See Rodenwaldt to Karo, 8 June 1926, BSB, Nachlaß Rodenwaldt, Mappe 475.

politik is to be exercised, in the execution of which the Reich's archaeological institute is simply indispensable.[55]

When the Interior Ministry remonstrated, insisting that its supervision would not impair the republic's cultural diplomacy, the Foreign Ministry replied that DAI operations abroad would need to be supervised by diplomats in any case; transference of bureaucratic control would simply result in duplication of effort.[56] Both the Foreign Ministry itself and its favored client institute wished to remain as distant as possible from entanglement in domestic politics.

The threat to the RGK stemmed not from centralizing tendencies but rather from the resurgent provincialism of the postwar period. Great new enthusiasm for provincial studies (*Heimatkunde*), folklore, and local prehistory engendered vigorous campaigns to add these subjects to university curricula; local *Vereine*, however, did their utmost to ensure that these positions went to regional, rather than Roman-German, specialists.[57] The efflorescence of Weimar-era *Heimatkunde*, Koepp averred, had not much benefited national prehistorical institutions: "We can't conceal from ourselves" he wrote in 1923, "the fact that this devotion fixes itself powerfully on the narrower, even the narrowest *Heimat*, for today no German can find joy in [devoting his passion to] the whole Fatherland, and we cannot fail to recognize that in this *Heimatliebe* not only patriotism, but also particularism, has its roots."[58] The most troubling aspect of this continued fragmentation, Koepp argued, was that local groups had become most uncooperative where money was concerned; their renewed provincialism had fueled the founding of many new *Heimatblätter* [local journals] while the RGK had insufficient funds for digs, travel, publishing costs, and even postage.[59]

But it was not local groups alone who contributed to the coffers of these particularistic organizations. The Interior Ministry, not surprisingly, tended to favor non-RGK groups. In 1926, it established in Leipzig its own Stiftung für deutsche Volks- und Kulturbodenforschung (Foundation for the Study of Ethnic and Cultural Areas), an interdisciplinary organization devoted to studying border areas; in 1930, it founded the Institut für ostbairische Heimatforschung (Institute for East Bavarian Studies), or Südostinstitut, in

---

[55] Stresemann to Interior Ministry, 5 May 1926, in PZStA AA/R 38042/4, pp. 207–8.

[56] See unsigned, undated memoranda, "Die Zusammenfassung aller wissenschaftlichen Institute beim Reichsministeriums des Innern," and "Zu der Aufzeichnung des Reichsministeriums der Innern bezüglich des Archäologischen Instituts des Deutschen Reiches, Berlin," in PZStA AA/K 69502 Arch 1, pp. 161–71.

[57] See Josef Oswald, "Bayerische Heimatbewegung und -forschung zwischen den zwei Weltkriegen," in *Zwischen Wissenschaft und Politik: Festschrift für Georg Schreiber*, ed. Johannes Spörl (Munich, 1953), pp. 609–10.

[58] Fr. Koepp, "Am Jahresschluß," *Germania* 6, no. 3 (March 1923): 137–38.

[59] Ibid., pp. 136–44.

Munich.[60] The Notgemeinschaft and even the DAI's own patron, the Foreign Ministry, too, often funded particular projects not administered by the DAI/RGK, much to the organization's dismay.[61] In 1928, Rodenwaldt had made a formal complaint to the Foreign Ministry over the Notgemeinschaft's independent—and reckless—funding policy. Undiplomatic amateurs and bunglers, the director lamented, had received funds without regard to scholarly credentials and/or effectiveness in the realm of *Kulturpolitik*, and threatened to give the external impression of "internal German fragmentation and aimlessness."[62] Raising again the specter of dilettante usurpation, the DAI insisted that only nonpartisan, national professionals should set the standards (and allocate the funds) for research.

Not surprisingly, archaeologists saw the reconstruction of their international prestige as the best defence against domestic threats to their cultural prominence and autonomy. After 1924, DAI officials commenced an informal campaign to improve relations with Spanish, Russian, and Swedish scholars, hoping thereby to expand excavation possibilities and the scientific influence of the German state. More than ever, DAI employees seemed to consider themselves cultural ambassadors—and reconnaissance men. In September 1925, Rodenwaldt, apparently on the instructions of the Foreign Ministry, had four stipend recipients produce reports on the exercise of foreign *Kulturpropaganda* in Greece and Italy.[63] The director and branch leaders increasingly added intelligence on the conduct of political affairs, the stance of the press, the status of foreign influences, and, occasionally, aspects of trade relations to their official reports of visits to conferences abroad.[64] In this atmosphere, even the inroads made by the French into Bulgarian archaeological circles could become a subject of concern[65]—as never before, archaeologists felt themselves to be national *Kulturagenten*, emissaries and advance men for the reconstruction of German *Kulturpolitik*.

Prehistorians were especially avid in promoting their information-gathering services and advertising the political import of their scientific efforts. During the French occupation of the Ruhr, both the RGK and the RGZM had capitalized on fears that the French would usurp not only political but also scholarly control of the Rhineland, substituting a false Celtic-

---

[60] Michael Burleigh, *Germany Turns Eastward: A Study of Ostforschung in the Third Reich* (Cambridge, 1988), p. 25; Oswald, "Bayerische Heimatbewegung," p. 612.

[61] Drexel to Eduard Meyer, 5 June 1928, in RGK, Mappe 41; Bersu to Rodenwaldt, 7 August 1930, in BSB, Nachlaß Rodenwaldt, Mappe 18.

[62] Rodenwaldt to Foreign Ministry, 11 January 1928, in PZStA AA/K 69502 Arch 1, pp. 110–12.

[63] Rodenwaldt to Heilbron (Foreign Ministry), 18 September 1925, ibid., 69577, p. 164.

[64] E.g., Rodenwaldt to Foreign Ministry, 17 June 1925, in PA/AA/K 21-359, vol 1., on his visit, with Noack and Wiegand, to an archaeological conference in Tripoli.

[65] German consulate, Sofia, to Foreign Ministry, 10 December 1925, (on Rodenwaldt's recent visit to the city), in PZStA AA/K 69577, p. 177.

Gallic past for the Roman-German one German scholars had carefully traced out. Were state support not forthcoming, an RGZM advocate had warned during the crisis, the French were anxious to snap up the museum and bend its historical evidence to the purposes of "Frenchification."[66] In July 1922, Rodenwaldt had advised the Foreign Ministry to raise its RGK subsidy in order that the organization might effectively counter the "feverish" work of French scholars in the field. This, he maintained, would be of great value from the point of view of scholarship; but also "from a national and political standpoint" the investment would not be wasted.[67]

In the eastern border regions, prehistorians devoted themselves with particular fervor to upholding Germandom against Slavic-Polish inroads. The most fanatical of nationalist prehistorians worked in this area, including the future Nazi appointee to the chair of prehistory in Königsberg, Bolko Freiherr von Richthofen, and Berlin Associate Professor Gustav Kossinna, who was furious to find his ex-student, Josef Kostrzewski, employing *Siedlungsarchäologie* to defend Polish claims to what Kossinna believed to be *Ur*-German territory. Accused by Kossinna and Richthofen of putting prehistorical work to political ends, Kostrzewski in 1930 was able to illustrate the egregious distortions perpetrated by German scientists in proclaiming Upper Silesia part of the original Germanic homeland. "People who live in glass houses," Kostrzewski concluded, "shouldn't throw stones."[68] But this group continued to cast aspersions on Polish scholars and Roman-German specialists alike, referring disdainfully to the latter as "*Römlinge*" ("minions of Rome"). By 1928, Kossinna was drawing heavily on the work of the infamous racial hygienist H. F. K. Günther to underwrite his claims about primeval Germanic conquests.[69]

Archaeologists did not, however, supply such information and render such patriotic services without reminding the Foreign Ministry at every turn of the importance of their profession to German security at home and prestige abroad. When attempts were made by the Finance Ministry to force the DAI to save 20 percent of its nonsalary budget, Rodenwaldt bombarded his diplomat-patrons with apocalyptic prophecies until the Foreign Ministry at last cleared the way for the removal of the spending restrictions.[70] Pleading for budgetary increases rather than decreases, the director reaf-

---

[66] Reichsvertretung in Darmstadt to Foreign Ministry, 29 October 1922, in PA/AA/K 24-381, vol. 1.

[67] Rodenwaldt to Foreign Ministry, 27 July 1922, in PZStA AA/K 69576, p. 8.

[68] Josef Kostrzewski, *Vorgeschichtsforschung und Politik* (Poznań, 1930), p. 28.

[69] See, e.g., Kossinna, *Ursprung und Verbreitung der Germanen in vor- und frühgeschichtlicher Zeit* (Leipzig, 1928).

[70] See Foreign Ministry to Rodenwaldt, 20 September 1924; Rodenwaldt to Foreign Ministry, 22 November 1924; Foreign Ministry to Finance Ministry, 12 December 1924; and Rodenwaldt to Foreign Ministry, 10 February 1925; all in PZStA AA/K 69506, pp. 206, 229–31, 232–33, and 278, respectively.

firmed the discipline's national significance and warned against the inflic-
tion of permanent losses in scholarly status for the sake of short-term
savings:

> There can hardly be another area in which international scholarly cooperation
> has so broadly developed again and in which German scholarship has again
> achieved so strong an international position as in archæology. . . . With the
> projected reduction, many undertakings would have to be interrupted, discon-
> tinued, or limited, and the damage thereby incurred would be not only tempo-
> rary but irreparable, since due to sharp international competition in this area,
> other nations would soon take steps to take over the work described here.[71]

By dint of such arguments, the DAI managed to reverse the effects of the
Reich Salary Law and eventually to regain the positions struck from the
budget.[72]

In February 1927, the Foreign Ministry and the DAI reached tentative
agreement on their mutual obligations and cooperative goals. The institute,
represented at a meeting with Foreign Ministry officials by familiar old-
guard *Kulturpolitik* activists (Karo, Eduard Meyer, Wilamowitz, and Wiegand, in addition to Rodenwaldt and Paul Wolters), thanked the Foreign
Ministry for its recent efforts on behalf of the archaeologists, "by means of
which [special assistance]," Rodenwaldt reportedly averred, "the institute
now promises to become an organic part [*Glied*] of German *Kulturpolitik*."
The Foreign Ministry representative, Freytag, responded that the DAI could
indeed become "one of the great instruments of *Kulturpolitik*"—but only if
the organization became more inclusive and its enterprises became more
extensive. "Relations with the Notgemeinschaft der deutschen Wissenschaft
and to the museums in individual Länder must be made closer," Freytag
insisted. "Without occupying territory already belonging to other groups,
the institute must extend itself beyond the narrower bounds of archaeology
([into] prehistory, Christian archaeology) in order to lend its activity inclu-
siveness and completeness." Both officials and scholars expressed the conviction that prehistorical research, in particular, should be increased, and
many enthused excitedly about prospects for renewing German excavations
in Asia Minor. The Foreign Ministry promised a budgetary increase of
166,000 rentenmarks plus RM 20,000 for the library in Rome, and Wolters
rejoiced that the Germans could now exercise "an intellectual propaganda
campaign" on the model of recent French efforts.[73]

---

[71] Rodenwaldt to Foreign Ministry, 28 March 1925, ibid., 69507, pp. 6–7.

[72] See Rodenwaldt to Foreign Ministry, 25 February 1925 and 2 September 1925, ibid.,
69506, pp. 282–88 and 289–80, respectively.

[73] All the above information is contained in "Sitzung des engeren Ausschusses des Archäologischen Instituts am 19. Feb. 1927," ibid., 69502 Arch 1, pp. 23–26. The quotations given
above are actually paraphrases of the remarks of the attending persons.

Freytag's advocacy of the extension of the institute's activities and interests suited perfectly the DAI's awakening desire to embrace north German prehistory, now endowed with a new, nobler aura as a "documentary" source for territorial claims. By 1926, the RGK had begun to feel constricted by its 1902 statutes, confining its official purview to the regions of Germany "that had long been under Roman control." In 1902, an RGK memorandum argued, prehistory had been dilettantish and the "knowledge potential" of non-Roman prehistory had been overlooked; it had now become clear that the field must embrace whole cultural areas and be conducted by a centralized scholarly institute with international standing.[74] Though he loathed the "woeful amateurishness" of north German prehistory, Drexel insisted on the necessity of unifying "northern" and "southern" factions and extending the RGK's work into *Germania libera*.[75] In a letter to the DAI and Foreign Ministry, adducing the inability of local bodies to finance necessary prehistorical work, Drexel gave another, less practical, reason for the commission to rethink its premises: "In order to avoid the accusation that the study of the supposedly essentially different Roman era is more important to the Reich institution than that of its own past, [the RGK statutes] cannot remain as they are in the future."[76] Weary of continual attacks on its "internationalism," the RGK now wished to shrug off the mantle of cosmopolitan classicism—or at least its unpatriotic ambience.

The attempted revision of the statutes was not a little reminiscent of the debates on the founding of the RGK—so much so, in fact, that Rodenwaldt later confessed privately that he had modeled his actions on those of Conze.[77] Once again, there was a dispute over patronage; the Interior Ministry envisioned an independent organization under its control, but cofunded by the DAI, while the DAI opposed the erection of a new prehistorical institute.[78] Once again, the classicists claimed professional competence in a field most of them had recently scorned, and once again, the localist prehistorians resented such incursions into their territory. Drexel and Gerhard Bersu, the new vice director of the RGK, seem to have tried their best to bring northern prehistorians into the work of the commission. In 1927 and 1928, they proposed both establishing stipends for the students of northern prehistory and redressing the lack of northerners on the institute's membership rolls; in 1929, Bersu applied to the Foreign Ministry to fund an *Ostinstitut* to give an institutional basis to German prehistorical work on the Polish border.[79] But most of the northern prehistorians continued to view

---

[74] RGK to DAI, 2 April 1927, in DAI, Nachlaß Wiegand, Kasten 28, Mappe 1.

[75] Drexel to Dr. Cremer (Reichstag deputy), 6 December 1926, in RGK, Mappe 22.

[76] Drexel to Rodenwaldt and Foreign Ministry, 9 July 1926, ibid.

[77] Rodenwaldt to Carl Watzinger, 3 May 1945, DAI, Nachlaß Rodenwaldt, Kasten 2.

[78] Rodenwaldt to Bersu, 12 June 1926. in BSB, Nachlaß Rodenwaldt, Mappe 367.

[79] See Drexel to Rodenwaldt, 27 April 1927; and Drexel to DAI, 24 February 1928, in RGK, Mappe 22; Bersu to Terdenge, 24 May 1929, in PZStA AA/K 69522, pp. 82–83. Bersu was

classicists with a jaundiced eye, and preferred forming their own organizations to joining the RGK.[80] As the northern critics of *Römlinge* gravitated
toward political radicalism, the expansionist campaign of the classicist prehistorians collapsed under the pressure of irreconcilable ideological differences and a highly fragmented system of patronage.

Somewhat more successful—if similarly reminiscent of prewar classicist
expansionism—was the renewal of discussions on Germany's archaeological future in Asia Minor. The Royal Museums most particularly wished to
resurrect the DAI's "station" (a step below the branch offices in Rome and
Athens) in Turkey, the direction of which had passed from Humann to
Wiegand and then to Martin Schede. The circumspection of the Ankara
government, however, and the archaeologists' familiar desire not to arouse
suspicions that Germany was receiving preferential treatment, caused the
campaign to proceed slowly, beginning with the reconstruction of the "station" library, the inspection of former sites, and the encouragement of
young Turks to undertake their archaeological training in Germany.[81] But
several Germans noted with concern repeated attempts by the French to
found independent archaeological institutes as well as the aspirations of the
Italians to take over the Austrian dig at Ephesus;[82] action was necessary to
reassert the Reich's prerogatives before others seized the initiative. In early
1926, Schede announced to the Constantinople embassy that were the
Turkish government to give its consent and were sufficient funds to be made
available, the time had come to refound the German archaeological outpost.

Schede recommended a grand undertaking, complete with funds for digs,
library help, cleaning staff, photographers, and four section directors (plus
assorted underlings) to supervise the four areas of study practicable in Turkey: classical archaeology, Byzantine studies, Turkology, and preclassical
Altertumskunde. Still pursuing his wartime plan in which the Royal Museums would guard the gate through which all German scholars passed
eastward, Schede underscored the economic and especially the diplomatic
imperative that all branches of inquiry be united in a single institution. He
also proposed a hierarchy among branch directors, based on age and length
of service, knowledge of local conditions, and "also, especially, [on] the

---

himself trained as a prehistorical rather than a classical archaeologist, and he was the first RGK
president to be so trained when appointed to the post in 1931.

[80] Examples include the Berufsvereinigung deutscher Prähistoriker, founded in 1922; the
Arbeitsgemeinschaft für Erforschung der nord- und ostdeutschen vor- und frühgeschicht-
lichen Wall- und Wehranlagen (1927), and the Ostdeutscher Verband für Altertumsforschung,
created in 1928.

[81] Copy of Schede to general director of the museums, 29 January 1925, and attached
"Beilage," written by Wiegand and dated 20 February 1925, in PA/AA/K 27-468a, vol. 32. Also,
Becker to Foreign Ministry, 6 March 1925, ibid., 52-557, vol. 2.

[82] E.g., Schede to Nadolny (German embassy, Constantinople), 16 January 1926, in PZStA
AA/K 69527, pp. 31–35 (on the French).

circumstance that classical archaeology, which would sacrifice its previous highly experienced and successful organization to such an institute, cannot be denied a deciding influence and the leadership, at least at first."[83] Roden-waldt agreed that the new institute should also embrace Islamic, Byzantine, and prehistorical studies, and in June 1927, the Education Ministry approved Schede's proposal, so reminiscent of prewar triumphs and so suitable a vehicle for postwar cultural diplomacy.[84]

Foreign Ministry negotiations with the Ankara government, however, dragged on for two years, and it was not until the autumn of 1928 that a personnel budget was drawn up, and a date set—1 April 1929—for the opening of the new office. Having at last arranged the matter with the trying Turks, archaeologists and diplomats were surprised and dismayed to discover domestic dissension, both in the Reichsrat and in the Reichstag. A scholarly propaganda campaign commenced, in which Eduard Meyer circulated petitions to be presented to the Reichstag and Foreign Ministry, and August Heisenberg, the renowned Byzantinist, publicly called on the Bavarian government to use its influence in Berlin.[85] Endorsed by the academies of science in Berlin, Göttingen, Heidelberg, and Leipzig, all major classical antiquities societies, and the two major *Gymnasium* associations, Meyer's petition touted the "glorious excavations of the Berlin museums in Pergamum, Magnesia, Priene, and Didyma" and warned that were Germany to decline this offer, such an opportunity to renew the Reich's proud tradition would not present itself again. Of course, not only would scientific interests be gravely damaged; "German prestige in the Orient," the elderly historian threatened, "would suffer a colossal blow."[86]

Such rhetorical exhortations on behalf of such esteemed institutions could only fail to win Reich backing under the most exceptional of circumstances. Unfortunately for the supporters of the Constantinople institute, late 1928 and 1929 proved to be just such an exceptional era in the realm of cultural affairs. In November 1928, seeking to take advantage of the appointment of Carl Severing, a sympathetic Social Democrat, to the post of interior minister, Becker—who had been education minister since 1925—launched a campaign to force "autonomous" scholarly bodies to allow greater participation by both national and provincial bureaucracies in funding decisions. Becker had long opposed the haughty independence of the

---

[83] Schede to Nadolny, 16 January 1926, ibid., pp. 31–35.

[84] Rodenwaldt to Foreign Ministry, 7 March 1927, ibid., p. 14; Rodenwaldt to Schede, 24 June 1927, BSB, Nachlaß Rodenwaldt, Mappe 595.

[85] See [Meyer], "Gefährdung der deutschen wissenschaftlichen Arbeit im Orient" (January 1929) in DAI, Nachlaß Wiegand, Kasten 28, Mappe 1; and August Heisenberg, "Ein archäologisches Institut in Konstantinopel," *Münchener Neueste Nachrichten*, 31 January 1929, in PZStA AA/K 69527, p. 140.

[86] [Meyer], "Gefährdung."

KWG, the Cultural Section of the Foreign Ministry, and especially the Not-gemeinschaft, and feared "a dissolution of the state into self-administering bodies."[87] He was now prepared to form a "working committee" composed of members of the relevant Prussian and German ministries to stave off the danger that "with the further growth of these [autonomous] organizations, political difficulties could arise through the potentially hostile attitude of scholarly circles toward the state."[88] When the Interior Ministry demurred on the grounds that the other Länder would have to be represented in the "working committee" too, Becker resorted to financial threats, regaling the Notgemeinschaft's unofficial treasurer Arthur Salomonsohn with his criticisms of the autocratic practices of the funding agency.[89] A meeting of professors, Notgemeinschaft officials, and state bureaucrats on 1 December put further pressure on Schmidt-Ott to reform his organization or face its dismemberment, a threat Schmidt-Ott and the professors countered with warnings about the harmful appearance of bureaucratic tampering with the freedom of research.[90] As Schmidt-Ott was unwilling to grant more than minor concessions, the bureaucracy allowed the controversy to spill over into the public sphere, where the abiding foes of the academic insularity—including leftists and school reformers—joined the attack.

As quickly became evident from the reproaches leveled at the Notge-meinschaft, however, growing hostility to autonomous research agencies—and especially to those that patronized the humanities—was not simply a matter of inappropriate form. One of the chief motives behind Becker's attacks on the Notgemeinschaft was the agency's deference to the interests of (in Salomonsohn's paraphrase) "a clique of old men, whose average age is 68½ years."[91] These "old bigwigs" (*alte Bonzen*) had dominated decision-making, appointments, and fund distribution to the benefit of their fellows and had failed to give any assistance to younger, and especially to more liberal, scholars. The same issues were addressed by socialist deputies in Reichstag debates on the Notgemeinschaft budget in June 1929. Julius Moses chastised the agency for favoring older scholars, excluding Social Democrats, and especially for preferring to fund philological, theological, and historical projects with little relevance for or benefit to the bulk of the German population.[92] In a follow-up article, Moses went straight to the

---

[87] See Düwell, "C. H. Becker," pp. 59–60; and Feldman, "Politics of Wissenschaftspolitik," pp. 274–75; Becker quoted in Zierold, *Forschungsförderung*, pp. 117–18.

[88] Becker to Interior Ministry, 22 November 1928, KBA R73/17, p. 277.

[89] See "Aktennotiz betr. Notgemeinschaft der deutschen Wissenschaft," 29 November 1928, signed by Salomonsohn, ibid., R73/17.

[90] See "Vermerk," 8 December 1928 (report on 1 December 1928 meeting in Dresden), ibid.

[91] See note 89 above.

[92] See his speech in *Verhandlungen des Reichstags*, IV. Wahlperiode (1928), vol. 425, 82. Sitzung (10 June 1929), pp. 2264–66.

heart of the matter: academic immunity from political or bureaucratic inter-vention had allowed the reactionary Notgemeinschaft to dispose of the re-public's funds in a highly prejudicial manner. Moses underlined the neces-sity that research remain free and nonpartisan, but denied that this could be the case under the administration of the reactionary, inbred professoriate. Particularly in times of hardship, the interests of the economy and the soci-ety at large, rather than those of individual specialists, should be served.[93]

Classical philology, of course, had by now become exemplary of "useless" or "obsolete" science, a highly visible symbol of the *zwecklose* predilections of yesteryear and the persistence of the old regime. Not so archaeology, however; despite the voicing of private concerns that costly excavations should have been postponed for better financial weather,[94] archaeological expeditions did not appear amongst projects lampooned by Notge-meinschaft opponents for abstruseness or triviality, while the prestige-enhancing triumphs of German excavations did play a prominent role in defenses of the emergency association's importance.[95] In fact, the Prussian Academy of Science's 1929 memorandum, written by Eduard Meyer to be circulated to the ministries in defense of the beleaguered Notgemeinschaft, singled out archaeological excavation for special commendation. Scholar-ship, Meyer contended, should not be restrained by utilitarian demands but should set higher goals for itself—for, as the example of archaeology indi-cated, studies commenced on the basis of purely *zwecklose* interests could eventually reap rich national rewards:

> The claim that these [excavations] bring no profit is completely erroneous. He who has taken the most superficial of glances at this area realizes at every turn what it means for German scholars energetically to uphold the renown and prestige of the German *Volk*, and [sees] that German scholarship has consis-tently achieved a position of high esteem in this field. Directly as well as indi-rectly, this [esteem] brings rich rewards for our trade and industry in all these nations, even if this cannot be expressed in definite figures.[96]

Archaeological activity, for the academy, was a safe, popular sphere in which to argue the merits of "unproductive" science; no other field of the human-ities offered such powerful, material expressions of scholarly success or such satisfying glimmers of Germany's imperial past—and, perhaps, future.

---

[93] Moses, "Verknöcherte Wissenschaft," in *Sozialistische Bildung*, August 1929, pp. 225–32. See also Feldman, "Politics of Wissenschaftspolitik," p. 277.

[94] See, e.g., those raised in the 1 December 1928 meeting between the Notgemeinschaft and its bureaucratic critics. See "Vermerk," 8 December 1928, in KBA R73/17.

[95] See "Die Nothilfe der deutschen Wissenschaft," in *Berliner Tageblatt*, 4 September 1929, ibid., which attacks many Notgemeinschaft projects, and especially criticizes scholarly travel; in defense, see [Meyer], "Gefährdung."

[96] [Meyer], "Denkschrift der Preußischen Akademie der Wissenschaften," (May 1929) in KBA R73/17.

The Notgemeinschaft itself certainly did not feel expending large sums on excavation to be a political liability. While attacks on its patronage of *zwecklose* projects and aged clients may indeed have inspired increases in proportional spending for the natural sciences and for student stipends, archaeological subsidies continued to consume large percentages of Notgemeinschaft funds. Late in the decade, Schmidt-Ott and his wife spent a busy three weeks visiting the German excavation sites along the Turkish coast. Their guides to the ruins included Germany's three most prestigious living archaeologists: Dörpfeld, Wiegand, and Schede.[97] In Pergamum itself, Schmidt-Ott and Wiegand devised a plan for new Notgemeinschaft-funded excavations, and Schmidt did not fail to pay homage to Halil Edhem's Ottoman Museum in Istanbul.[98] In 1929, Meyer convinced Schmidt-Ott to dispense a twenty-thousand-rentenmark-a-year publication subsidy to the DOG, and on the eve of forced Notgemeinschaft reform, the agency approved a sixty-thousand-rentenmark grant to Berlin professor Bruno Meißner for the purpose of recommencement of the excavation of Warka (ancient Uruk), halted in 1914 with the advent of war.[99] Despite its humanistic origins and affiliations, archaeology's continued contribution to prestige exempted the science from direct assault.

Of course, the arena in which archaeology's contributions to German prestige were most likely to be observed by the general population was the museum, and Weimar classicists eagerly anticipated the beneficial effects to be offered by a project dating back to 1907, the completion of a grand new antiquities museum in Berlin. The new museum was designed to replace the structurally unsound original Pergamum Museum and to be placed on the so-called Museums Island on the Spree. As early as 1921, in an essay for the newspaper *Der Tag*, Wiegand contended that the opening of a new Pergamum museum, the centerpiece of the island, would be of great assistance in reinvigorating domestic "spiritual values" as well as in restoring international prestige for the Wilhelmine capital.[100] Naturally, Wiegand also recognized the potential for increasing the status of his field by means of monumental exhibitions of German-owned and German-excavated antiquities. But Wiegand, the consummate cultural politician, had to use all his influence—social and institutional—and his cunning to win the so-called "museums war." If the wresting of millions of marks from public and private donors in years of economic turmoil demonstrates that the heirs of Ernst Curtius still possessed considerable domestic prestige, the severity

---

[97] See Schmidt, *Erlebtes*, where this trip is lovingly described, pp. 247–64.

[98] Ibid., pp. 250–51.

[99] Unte, "Eduard Meyer," pp. 534–35; Schmidt-Ott to Meissner, 1 October 1929, KBA R73/274.

[100] Wiegand in *Der Tag*, 12 April 1921, quoted in Silke Wenk, *Auf den Spuren der Antike: Theodor Wiegand, ein deutscher Archäologe* (Bendorf am Rhein, 1985), p. 25.

and breadth of the criticisms of the project indicate the extent to which the philhellenist elite's grasp on cultural institutions had slipped.

Anhäufungspolitik and the Pergamum Museum

In 1907, the Pergamum Altar sculptures had been removed from display to await the erection of a grand museum complex on the banks of the Spree. Thought to be among Germany's greatest national treasures, they were destined for a long wait for a suitable home. The building of a new "Pergamon-museum" was one of the largest and most bitter controversies over cultural policy to occur in Prussia since the school reform conference of 1890, and involved a number of the same combatants. Already in the early planning stages, it was clear that the dispensation of space in the new structure or structures would be hotly debated; although the need to provide a home for the Pergamum Altar was the original motivation for adding new buildings to the existing ones on the banks of the Spree, facing the Royal Palace, it was also clear that new exhibition space was desperately needed to showcase the nation's recently acquired or expanded collections. The struggle for space on what came to be called the "Museums Island" engaged the proponents of Egyptian, Islamic, East Asian, Germanic, medieval, prehistorical, Near Eastern, and classical arts and antiquities, and by the 1920s had grown so fierce as to be described as the "Museums War." For the battle over exhibition space, of course, was simply part of a larger struggle over state funds for excavations, acquisitions, and domestic prestige, a struggle, as we have seen, usually won by the classicists. The "Museums War," though bitterly fought, was no exception to this rule.

The origins of this "war" lay in the conflict between Richard von Schöne and Wilhelm von Bode, the director of the Nationalgalerie, who assumed Schöne's position as general director of the Royal Museums in 1905. As the nonclassical collections of the museums burgeoned in the period after 1890, Bode eagerly advocated the building of new museums on the Spree, while Schöne, an ardent Graecophile, insisted that these collections should be housed in the Museum für Völkerkunde (Museum of Ethnography), located in Prinz-Albrecht-Straße.[101] After Schöne's departure in 1905, Bode developed an elaborate plan for a complex of new buildings that would link together the Near Eastern, classical, and Germanic collections, creating a magnificent national museum, in which these three central departments were to play an equal role in reflecting the glory of the Reich. The new Germanic wing, which Bode designed first, was to be divided into chronologically defined period rooms, each decorated with appropriate wall cover-

---

[101] Renate Petras, *Die Bauten der Berliner Museumsinsel* (Berlin, 1987), p. 138.

ings and enhanced with plaster casts; to his frustration, however, in attempting to purchase new artifacts, he encountered the same sorts of provincial opposition to museological centralization that the RGZM had encountered decades earlier.[102] And, of course, the Mesopotamian artifacts had not yet reached Berlin, and would not do so for another twenty years. Creating the grand imperial museum Bode envisioned would not, it seemed, be an easy task.

But Bode's greatest adversaries were not to be provincial curators, Turkish officials, or the Prussian Landtag, which willingly dedicated 11 million marks to the project in 1907. Rather, Bode's nemesis was to be Theodor Wiegand, the great excavator who had just acquired an enormous new monument he wished to exhibit (the Miletus Gate), and who knew how to use his influence at court to promote his plan to make the new museum a grand exhibition of ancient architecture.[103] Thus, despite the fact that he was general director of the museums, by 1911, Bode, who preferred oriental carpets and medieval paintings to Greek antiquities, was still complaining to the Education Ministry about the overdependence on private funds of the Near Eastern, Egyptian, medieval, East Asian, and Islamic departments, and to a lesser extent, the collections of paintings and German art. Everything but classical antiquities, he implied, was still being slighted by the state.[104] Building on the new museums complex had been fitful, and was halted in 1915 for the duration of the war. When at last construction on the island recommenced in 1921, Bode had been forcibly retired from the museums directorship—though he remained director of the Nationalgalerie and head of the Museumsbaukommission (Museums Building Commission). By this time, Wiegand, of course, had returned from monument protection duty in Asia Minor, and was ready to reassert his right to shape the Pergamum plan.

Money, of course, posed the greatest problem, and in 1921, Bode, as head of the Museumsbaukommission, asked Wiegand to identify some objects from his collection for possible sale to buoy up the building fund. Wiegand, wily as ever, responded that American dealers now cared little for classical antiquities, but that Islamic, East Asian, and medieval works were said to command amazingly high prices.[105] But, as this example suggests, insufficient funding was not the only reason for the delays in the completion of the new complex; ideology and museological aesthetics also played a role. As Thomas Gaehtgens has shown, already by 1915, the project's architect, Ludwig Hoffmann, had begun to lean toward a simplification of the complex's interior design that saved money, but also conveyed a quite different

[102] Thomas W. Gaehtgens, *Die Berliner Museumsinsel im Deutschen Kaiserreich* (Berlin, 1987), pp. 102–4, 109–11.

[103] Ibid., pp. 107–8.

[104] Bode to Education Minister, 28 March 1911, in StMBZ, IM 15.

[105] Wiegand to Baukommission President [Bode], 24 January 1921, in StMBZ, AS 13.

27. Building proceeds, slowly, on the Museums Island. The state of the project in 1916. © Bildarchiv, Preußischer Kulturbesitz, 1996.

aesthetic and museological philosophy. The rooms were to be white in color, cool, and suitable for the display of any collection; the viewer was to be encouraged to concentrate on the works of art, and no casts or copies were to be displayed. When the Prussian Landtag embraced this design in 1925, it was not only money, but a new sort of asceticism and aestheticism that had decided the question.[106]

Interior design did not, however, completely resolve the question of space allocation in the new complex, and the battle between the supporters of Bode and Wiegand continued to rage. In 1921, the influential art critic Karl Scheffler published a blistering attack on the Wilhelmine *Anhäufungspolitik* (policy of heaping things up) and *Fassadengesinnung* (facade mentality) exemplified in Wiegand's plan. The archaeologists, Scheffler charged, were attempting to usurp enormous exhibition spaces, which they would fill according to their own style-historical inclinations rather than according to the actual interests of the viewing public.[107] Like Bode, Scheffler resented

---

[106] Gaehtgens, *Berliner Museumsinsel*, p. 114. See also chapter 9, below.

[107] Karl Scheffler, *Berliner Museumskrieg* (Berlin, 1921), pp. 44–46, 74–78. Scheffler makes the acute comment: "If the era of the Kaiserreich had lasted fifty years longer, if the war had come later and excavations had continued, we would surely have had to make room in the museum for an entire Greek city." Ibid., p. 76.

the fact that the artworks of highly cultivated Asian and Islamic cultures were still lodged with the tools and relics of modern "primitives," or with the decorative arts, rather than joining Greek and Roman works in the galleries of art.[108] Fearful that this assault would doom his plans, Wiegand bombarded the Education Ministry with declarations of support for his project from *Gymnasium* philologists, the DAI, and influential members of his Vereinigung der Freunde antiker Kunst (for example, C. F. von Siemens and Emil Stauß). By 1922, Wiegand's plan seemed to have prevailed—just in time, however, for building again to be postponed by the onset of hyperinflation.[109]

While the Weimar Republic struggled to bring its finances under control, both work on the Museums Island and debates over its contents largely subsided. Finally, in July 1925, an impatient Wiegand circulated a memorandum in the attempt to speed the completion of the island and to establish his right to appropriate large areas of the new buildings for his exhibit of ancient architectural styles. In the memorandum, Wiegand emphasized the popularity of the Pergamum Altar and the prestige to be gained by establishing a new trend in museum display. The reconstruction to scale of sections of monuments (many of them excavated by Wiegand in Asia Minor) would offer the public the experience of total *Anschauung* and make up for years of misleading displays of isolated objects; the new exhibits would also, he hoped, enhance the status of archaeology as the science of cultural wholes. "In Germany, particularly among the wider public," Wiegand lamented, "the impression seems to be rampant that archaeology is the study of damaged and no longer useful objects."[110] The public had the right not to be led astray; the state had the obligation to put before them the most scientifically correct exhibits.

A few days later, a memorandum signed by the heads of all the departments of the Royal Museums reached the general director's desk. The memo complained about the large sums (770,000 rentenmarks) diverted from the Museums Island project to the refurbishing of the Ethnography Museum and the Museumsbaukommission's lack of sensitivity to their space requirements. Noting that recent quarrels had resulted in mistrust among department heads and unfavorable portrayals of the project in the daily press, the scholar-bureaucrats asked for a new general plan and increased funding to finish the building quickly.[111] Presumably, the general director took these grievances to the Prussian Education Ministry where, however, sympathy for the interminable project, and especially for Wiegand's grand ambitions, ran low. The Education Ministry possessed a powerful ally in the Prussian

[108] See ibid., pp. 44–46, 7–19.
[109] Watzinger, *Wiegand*, pp. 354–55.
[110] [Wiegand], "Pergamon-Museum," 15 July 1925, in StMBZ, VAM 17.
[111] Bode, Demmler, Sarre, Friedländer, Weber, Wiegand, Schäfer, Zahn to general director of the Museums, 22 July 1925, ibid. See also Watzinger, *Wiegand*, pp. 376–77.

finance minister, who balked at providing the requested funds, but Wiegand skillfully countered bureaucratic opposition by launching a propaganda campaign in his own influential circles. In early 1926, the *Zentralblatt der Bauverwaltung* (*Building Administration Gazette*) issued a strong declaration in support of Wiegand's plans—including the full-scale erection of the Miletus Gate. Signed by more than a hundred leading scholars, architects, and DAI bureaucrats, the document proclaimed the great public service promised by a grand museum displaying the historical development of Greek and Roman architectural styles.[112] Appended to this pronouncement were affirmations issued by various art-historical, archaeological, and *Gymnasium Vereine*, precisely those with the greatest interest in the success of this new form of *Anschauungsunterricht*.

In March 1926, the Education Ministry called a meeting to discuss the dispensation of exhibition space in the new museum building. Wiegand remonstrated vigorously against plans to put the Mschatta Gate in the same room with his monumental Miletus facade and accused the ministry of stirring up opposition in the press. Ministerial counselor Wilhelm Waetzoldt (who would become general director of the museums in October 1927) reminded Wiegand that not all of his desires could be realized, especially as there was a large sector of the general public that opposed—as the report paraphrased his words—"the heaping up of dead art in an age in which we can no longer sufficiently support living art."[113] Scheffler, the voice of this opposition, likewise denounced the classicists' imperious attitude to the building plan, describing their desire to fill enormous spaces with monumental artifacts as "the archaeologists' expansionist drive."[114] In an April 1926 essay in the *Frankfurter Zeitung*, Scheffler broadened the issue of museological Graecocentrism and took stock of the costs to the nation of its persistence, arguing that neoclassicism "has made our art academic and conventional [and] it has made [Germany] other-worldly [weltfremd], self-righteous, and arrogant."[115] In an essay in the *Preußische Jahrbücher*, the hypernationalist art historian and Viennese professor Josef Strzygowski transformed a number of Scheffler's complaints into a howl of outraged Aryanism. Charging the Prussian Education Ministry with making a deliberate attempt to denigrate Nordic art, Strzygowski concluded by making the shocking suggestion that if the Pergamum Altar and Mschatta Gate were to remain in Berlin only to reinforce the false conviction that all culture originated in the Mediterranean, the monuments should be shipped back to the East.[116]

[112] See "Pergamonmuseum," *Gnomon* 2, no. 5 (May 1926): 303–4.

[113] Report on meeting over Antikenabteilung, 18 March 1926, in StMBZ, AS 14.

[114] Scheffler quoted in Watzinger, *Wiegand*, p. 382.

[115] Scheffler quoted from *Frankfurter Zeitung*, 20 April 1926, in Wenk, *Auf den Spuren*, p. 28.

[116] See Strzygowski, "Schicksal der Berliner Museen," pp. 181–84.

In spite of these journalistic assaults, by mid-1926 Wiegand's plan seemed to have triumphed at last as Becker, weary of the controversy, took the archaeologist's part. Building began again, but was halted within a year when it was discovered that the designer of the display area for the Miletus Gate fragments had underestimated the required space by more than three meters. Quarrels broke out again as it was revealed that the error would add three-quarters of a year and two million marks to the building project. Scheffler and others argued for the completion of the project without the additional three meters. Wiegand, however, was persuaded by arguments in favor of authentic reconstruction and eventually won the concurrence of the Museumsbaukommission.[117] In 1928, the archaeologist proudly announced to the Prussian Academy of Sciences the forthcoming exhibit of original architectural fragments, including the Miletus Gate, "in their true proportions," a scientifically correct reconstruction that would display the grandeur of the ancients to the unfortunate masses who could not afford to visit ancient Greek sites in person. The archaeologist also revealed his plan for an exhibition on the evolution of writing, including displays on the development of the Greek alphabet, which would draw those with "technical" interests as well as those "who have remained true to Greekdom and the humanist ideal."[118] Created in the face of rapid technological change and social upheaval, the Pergamum Museum would epitomize the enduring institutional power of positivist philhellenism.

Appropriately, the first Germans to visit the new Pergamum Museum were archaeologists, who were permitted to take a special tour of the classical exhibits in honor of the centennial of the DAI in April 1929. The museum was, of course, hailed as a great achievement by the entire classicist community, which bruited its prestige-enhancing effects abroad and its popularizing functions at home. Displaying the great classical facades appropriated by German archaeologists in Asia Minor, the otherwise nearly empty museum exuded Wilhelmine typological positivism and Graecophile aesthetics, offering the viewer a succinct statement of German archaeology's philosophical heritage. Perhaps the final act of philhellenist vengeance for archaeology's exposure of a vast array of complexly interrelated world cultures was the discovery in 1929 that the latest architect had far exceeded his budget. Completion of the Asiatic and Islamic exhibits had to be postponed once more, allowing the classical artifacts sole occupation of the grand new national museum for several more years.[119]

After touring the completed Pergamum Museum in Wiegand's company, Wilamowitz is reported to have said: "You people of the spade have suc-

[117] See Watzinger, *Wiegand*, pp. 392–94.

[118] Wiegand, "Untergang und Wiedererstehen antiker Kulturdenkmäler," *Sitzungsberichte der Preußischen Akademie der Wissenschaften*, Phil.-Hist. Kl. (1928): xxxvi–xxxvii.

[119] Watzinger, *Wiegand*, p. 432.

ceeded better than we ancient philologists; we have failed."[120] Such an admission from philology's most venerable defender underscores not only archaeology's superior social status, but also the old mandarin's recognition that his campaign to reestablish philologically based classical *Bildung* had miscarried. The visual force represented by the museums' sculptures was the last, best argument for the present-day importance of antiquity; the lessons of the beautiful Greeks now resided in their monuments alone.

Isolation, Old Age, and the End of Prestige 1930–1933

Autonomous—or now, more properly, semiautonomous—research institutions experienced the frustrating hardships, profound anxieties, and deep resentments, if not the grinding poverty, of the depression years. The Notgemeinschaft's budget, which had been slashed by a million rentenmarks (to 7 million) during the bureaucratic struggles of 1928–29 now fell to 5.1 million for 1931, then to 4.4 million in 1932, and to 4 million in 1933.[121] In 1930, the KWG, reprimanded by the Education Ministry for misrepresenting its needs and assets, reported a shortfall of 1 million marks.[122] Chancellor Brüning's emergency measures, imposed in July 1930, cut civil service pay by nearly 23 percent,[123] a staggering blow to institutes that had only recently regained prewar staffing and salary levels. For the DAI, the early 1930s brought endless financial audits, numerous complications in its *Kulturpolitik* activities, and considerable reductions in its projects. Sheltered by the Foreign Ministry and the Notgemeinschaft, archaeologists continued their endeavors abroad until national economic crises, political chaos, and finally, Nazi purges put an end to *Kulturpolitik* based on prestige and ambassadorial deportment.

Following the reforms forced on the Notgemeinschaft in 1929, the Interior Ministry obtained five of fifteen seats on the executive committee, one of which went to Julius Moses, the socialist deputy who had so vehemently attacked the reactionary practices of the agency in the Reichstag.[124] Yet new elections to the faculty committees returned 65 percent of previous members, and in 1930, the Interior Ministry, now under Josef Wirth (Center), decorated and praised Schmidt-Ott for his service to the Reich.[125] In 1932,

---

[120] Wilamowitz quoted in Watzinger, *Wiegand*, p. 423.

[121] Nipperdey and Schmugge, *50 Jahre Forschungsförderung*, p. 38.

[122] See previous note and Richter to Max Planck, 7 August 1930 (copy), and also Planck to KWG members, dated December 1930, both in GStAPKB, Nachlaß Becker, Mappe 2341.

[123] Harold James, *The German Slump: Politics and Economics, 1924–1936* (Oxford, 1986), p. 67.

[124] Carl Severing (Interior Minister) to Notgemeinschaft, 10 December 1929, KBA R73/17.

[125] Nipperdey and Schmugge, *50 Jahre Forschungsförderung*, p. 31; Schmidt-Ott, *Erlebtes*, p. 277.

yet another interior minister revoked the "bureaucratization" of the Notgemeinschaft by waiving his right to appoint executive committee delegates,
completing the agency's return—albeit with less plentiful coffers—to administrative normalcy.[126]

In late 1930 Schmidt-Ott issued a plea to all members of the faculty
committees to conserve funds, scale back requests, and pay careful attention to the interests of society at large in choosing projects for funding, in
order to avoid further parliamentary recriminations.[127] This policy, however, seems largely to have benefited *völkisch* and/or provincial groups
rather than the leftist interests the Education and Interior Ministries had
wished to include in the republic's benevolence. Classical archaeology certainly did not suffer—at least in proportion to other fields—from this new
commitment to the common weal: in 1930, 1931, and 1932, Wiegand received 10,000 rentenmarks for Pergamum; Gabriel Welter received 5,000
rentenmarks for Sichem in 1929, 20,000 rentenmarks in 1930, and 15,000
rentenmarks in 1931; and Schmidt-Ott insisted that the apportioning of
40,000 rentenmarks for the continuance of the Warka dig in 1932 was "indispensable."[128] Between 1928 and 1933, the Notgemeinschaft spent 51
percent of its travel and excavation fund, 20 percent of its publication allowance, and 8 percent of its stipend fund on projects in the fields of *Altertumswissenschaft* and *Orientalistik*; these two fields thus consumed one-
third of the agency's budget for the humanities and one-tenth of its funds
overall.[129] Notgemeinschaft subsidies for classical studies in 1932
amounted to 350,500 rentenmarks, the fifth highest award among the research areas, placing the field below medicine, physics, chemistry, and combined funds for history, political science, and law, and above biology, agri-
cultural studies, and the remaining humanities, social sciences, and
engineering fields.[130]

As we have seen, the Education Ministry did not share the Notgemeinschaft's narrow commitment to preserving research and protecting
German prestige. In late May 1930, Richter proposed to the Reichsrat pay
cuts for overseas DAI members.[131] The measure was temporarily scuttled by

[126] Ibid.

[127] Schmidt-Ott to Members of Fachausschüsse, 17 November 1930, DAI, Nachlaß Wiegand, Kasten 29.

[128] Schmidt-Ott to Wiegand, 23 November 1931, and Schmidt-Ott to Welter, 3 January
1931, both ibid.; Schmidt-Ott to Presidium, 10 September 1931, in KBA R73/72. Schmidt was
convinced that were the Germans unable to dig, the permit would be issued instead to the
Americans.

[129] Nipperdey and Schmugge, *50 Jahre Forschungsförderung*, pp. 118–19. Modern philology
and art history received a further 25 percent of the publications fund and 8 percent of the
stipend allowance.

[130] See "Niederschrift über die Beratung des Präsidiums der Notgemeinschaft am Montag,
den 12. September 1932," in KBA R73/72.

[131] Rodenwaldt to Karo, 30 May 1930, BSB, Nachlaß Rodenwaldt, Mappe 475.

the DAI's long-time defender in the Foreign Ministry, Hermann Terdenge, and by Wiegand, who used his considerable influence on friendly Reichstag members.[132] A parliamentary review followed in June, but the matter remained unresolved into July, when Rodenwaldt conveyed to Curtius his concerns about the "mood of panic" prevailing at the Foreign Ministry. "The only certain thing," he wrote, "is a profusion of new work, anxiety, and difficulties. I fear that the result will be catastrophic, as much due to the reduction of funds as to the impossibility of making plans."[133] In September, Rodenwaldt spread the bad news to his colleagues abroad: their salaries would indeed be reduced.[134] DAI heads deprived of full pay and left to handle their own housekeeping by the dismissal of lower office holders bridled at the republic's imposition of overly precise accounting practices, instituted to curb unapproved expenditures and the transference of funds among categories. Bersu, complaining that he now had to explain why a staff member had taken an express rather than a slower, cheaper train, argued: "This kind of verification of expenses takes away all the joy in having responsibility and in time will cause us to leave important scholarly work undone in order to avoid absurd complications."[135] Embittered and constrained by the republic's poverty and distrustfulness, the DAI began to lose its faith in the bureaucracy's traditional dedication to *Wissenschaft* and apolitical neutrality.

At home and abroad, German archaeological privilege and prestige were under siege. The DAI branch office in Constantinople, whose founding had at last been permitted, was restricted to a tiny budget and required to excavate only with foreign (or private) donations; the retirement of the accommodating Halil Edhem in early 1931 and the rising tide of Turkish nationalism further doomed German ambitions for the renewal of *Orientpolitik*.[136] In Athens, the Greek archaeologist Arvanitopoulos, who had received German support, was implicated in the theft of antiquities.[137] In Rome, jealous backers of the local German school attacked the extravagance of the DAI, declaring that German funds should be directed to the interests of Germans abroad, not to classical scholarship.[138] Rodenwaldt took this criticism very seriously, forecasting that were an article to appear comparing the hard-

---

[132] Rodenwaldt to L. Curtius, 16 May 1930, ibid., Mappe 393.

[133] Rodenwaldt to Curtius, 22 July 1930, ibid.

[134] See Rodenwaldt to Karo, 22 September 1930, ibid., Mappe 475; Rodenwaldt to Curtius 22 September 1930, ibid., Mappe 393.

[135] Bersu to Rodenwaldt, 31 December 1930, ibid., Mappe 255.

[136] Schede to Rodenwaldt, 18 July 1931, ibid., Mappe 255; on Halil, Wiegand et al. to Halil, 31 March 1931, in DAI, Nachlaß Wiegand, Kasten 3.

[137] Karo to Rodenwaldt, 28 December 1930, and copy of Karo to Wiegand, 2 February 1931, in BSB, Nachlaß Rodenwaldt, Mappe 131.

[138] See Gerkan to Rodenwaldt, 27 July 1931, ibid., Mappe 79; and Rodenwaldt to Gerkan, 30 July 1931 ibid., Mappe 424.

ships suffered by the school to the luxuriousness of Curtius's salary, there would be a 95 percent chance that the already eager finance minister would abolish, at the very least, the extra allowances afforded to overseas scholar-bureaucrats. "The situation is different now than it was three years ago, when we had the support of Herr Popitz in the Finance Ministry," Roden-waldt remarked with sober concern: "The Foreign Ministry will let us fall flat if we seem a burden in the pursuit of *Kulturpolitik* rather than a benefit. We will find no support among the public, and just as little from our colleagues in the universities [whose salaries had suffered deeper cuts than those of DAI officials] and probably not even [the support] of the central directorate."[139] Were its leaders to be stripped of their ability to maintain an ambassadorial lifestyle, the director foresaw the ruin of the institute and the collapse of archaeological *Kulturpolitik*.

In the face of such challenges, archaeologists responded with their usual tactics of self-defense. In April 1931, Rodenwaldt had lectured the Foreign Ministry on the importance to German prestige of attracting influential personalities to overseas posts. "The eyes of the nation are focused on the activities of foreign scholars," he maintained. "If the German institute is to fulfill its scholarly tasks, and also its role in *Kulturpolitik* as the center of highly conspicuous German projects and also the hub of Germandom [abroad], this is only possible if top positions are occupied by leading personalities, whose efforts will enjoy international recognition."[140] Reminiscent of Conze's approach to the school reform challenge of the 1890s, Curtius suggested expanding the pedagogical role of the institute.[141] Again, educational vacations in the Mediterranean for schoolteachers were planned in the hopes that the institute could shed its growing reputation as an elitist preserve, catering only to the special interests of unproductive humanists. To no avail, however, were invocations of virtually defunct *auswärtige Kulturpolitik* and unaffordable invitations to popular participation in classical pursuits. In November 1931, Rodenwaldt implored his colleagues overseas to cut their budgets beyond the 10 percent required by the Finance Ministry to show the institute's good will; in any event, he could be confident that their suffering would not be too great, as he had deliberately overstated the organization's penury.[142] In March of the following year, more personnel cuts were enforced at the Rome branch as the DAI budget

---

[139] Rodenwaldt to Curtius, 4 August 1931, ibid., Mappe 393.

[140] Rodenwaldt to Foreign Ministry, 18 April 1931, ibid., Mappe 643.

[141] Curtius to Rodenwaldt, 5 March 1931, ibid., Mappe 53.

[142] Rodenwaldt noted that the Foreign Ministry itself had suffered a more than 30 percent decrease in its nonsalary budget in November. Rodenwaldt to Curtius, Junker, Karo, and Schede, 17 November 1931, ibid., Mappe 475. Rodenwaldt admitted that he had overstated the DAI's penury as a "propaganda measure" in a letter to Carl Watzinger, 3 May 1945, DAI, Nachlaß Rodenwaldt, Kasten 2.

fell from 957,550 rentenmarks in 1930 to a total of 738,150 rentenmarks in 1932, and a team of Americans took over excavations at Schliemann's Troy site, symbolizing the end of an archaeological era.[143]

The remainder of 1932 brought only a new series of financial and bureaucratic crises to the DAI/RGK. Richter continued to lobby in the Reichsrat for budget reductions, now contending that since Mussolini had forbidden foreigners to dig on Italian soil, the Rome institute had no reason—or right—to continue its existence.[144] Bersu vented his fears that the RGK's budgetary constraints would cause its eventual isolation from those local amateurs who still did the bulk of archaeological work and whose patriotic zeal knew no bounds: "It will not be understood by the public," he explained, "if the commission fails to participate in these sorts of tasks, about whose import to national interests propaganda is often spread."[145] The rising popularity of the Nazi party did little to brighten the institute's hopes; Georg Karo, like most of his colleagues, fervently desired victory for Hindenberg in the March elections, fearing Hitler's selection would endanger the DAI.[146] Armin von Gerkan, similarly, remarked that "if a Third Reich commences or even if only the preliminary stages come to pass, non-Germanic archaeology may be sacked." In the event of such an insalubrious occurrence, the Rome deputy director suggested that archaeology be entrusted to the protection of natural scientists; geologists, he thought, "especially the *Privatdozenten* [junior lecturers] who deal with fossils," might succeed in rescuing classical *Altertumskunde* from the malice of the new Teutonic hordes.[147] This was no longer a matter of autonomy, much less one of increasing German prestige, but of institutional and scholarly survival.

Survival, indeed, was not merely a metaphorical threat for the classicists of the late 1920s and early 1930s; the period 1928–33 saw the deaths of many of the profession's most influential promoters and erudite scholars. The generation of the 1880s, whose academic tenure and social prestige had outlasted war, revolution, and inflation, at last was at an end. Eduard Norden died in 1927. Wilhelm von Bode, the assiduous general director of the Royal Museums, the leading classical scholar Franz Studniczka, and the ancient historian K. J. Beloch passed away in 1929. In 1930, Eduard Meyer, Adolf von Harnack, Friedrich Drexel, and Franz Winter threw off their mortal coils; the next year stole away August Heisenberg, Ferdinand Noack, and Wilamowitz, the bitterness of whose loss Wiegand could only compare

---

[143] Rodenwaldt to Curtius, 1 March 1932, BSB, Nachlaß Rodenwaldt, Mappe 393.

[144] E.g., Rodenwaldt to Gerkan, 31 May 1932, and 9 May 1932, both ibid., Mappe 424.

[145] Bersu, "Jahressitzung der Römisch-Germanischen Kommission am 11 Juli 1932," PZStA AA/K 69523, pp. 23–34.

[146] Karo to Rodenwaldt, 12 March 1932, BSB, Nachlaß Rodenwaldt, Mappe 131.

[147] Gerkan to Rodenwaldt, 30 April 1932, ibid., Mappe 79.

to that of Richard Wagner.[148] Even Kossinna, a late and rebellious member of this generation, did not live to see the founding of the Third Reich, having passed away in 1931. Those who were left—Wiegand, Dörpfeld, Rodenwaldt, and Dragendorff (as well as the somewhat younger Karo, Schede, Ludwig Curtius, and Werner Jaeger)—still commanded respect from the state bureaucracy and from scholarly circles abroad, but could offer no representative with the encyclopedic knowledge of Meyer or the universal recognition of Wilamowitz; hereafter, German prestige would depend even more heavily on bureaucratic intrigue and politically irresistible "big scholarship" than on great names.

When Rodenwaldt announced his intention to vacate the DAI directorship in favor of a professorship at the University of Berlin in mid-1932, deliberations on his successor turned precisely on the question of the candidates' ability to ensure the survival of the organization. Whereas previous directors had required something like a balance between diplomatic, bureaucratic, and scholarly talents, most important now were qualities like zest for battle, high bureaucratic and political connections, tactical cunning, tenacity, and close attention to detail. Karo, a popular choice among members, withdrew his name on the grounds that, though he was well respected abroad and well informed as to the needs of all the DAI branches, his ineptitude in administrative savoir faire would ultimately damage the institute's prospects. Karo estimated that administration had now become ten times as significant as scholarship in the direction of the DAI.[149] For just such reasons, Rodenwaldt threw his support to Wiegand, believing him to be best able to defend the institute in political and bureaucratic circles.[150] Gerkan considered Wiegand too egotistical for the job, and Bersu feared the famous excavator would only expend his energy for grand projects, neglecting vital if mundane paperwork,[151] but Wiegand did, finally, receive the call. If Wiegand, habitué of high military, industrial, and conservative political circles, can in some sense be seen as the DAI's strong man, he did not need to be so strong; before his departure, Rodenwaldt had secured the positions of the leading DAI officials in the republic's civil-service structure in perpetuity.[152]

Yet another blow, however, fell in September. Hermann Freytag, the sym-

---

[148] Wiegand to Hiller von Gärtringen, 26 September 1931, in DAI, Nachlaß Wiegand, Kasten 13.

[149] Karo to unnamed "non-archaeological friend," n.d., copy included in Karo to Rodenwaldt, 12 August 1932, BSB, Nachlaß Rodenwaldt, Mappe 131.

[150] Rodenwaldt to Curtius, 21 August 1932, ibid., Mappe 393; and Rodenwaldt to Wolters, 21 August 1932, ibid., Mappe 682.

[151] Gerkan to Rodenwaldt, 27 July 1932, ibid., Mappe 79; Bersu to Rodenwaldt, 23 August 1932, ibid., Mappe 18.

[152] Rodenwaldt to Carl Watzinger, 3 May 1945, DAI, Nachlaß Rodenwaldt, Kasten 2.

pathetic head of the Foreign Ministry Cultural Section, announced that as of 1 January 1933, he would assume the post of German ambassador in Lisbon. His deputy Hermann Terdenge had previously been promised the appointment in case of Freytag's resignation, but, as Rodenwaldt explained to Paul Wolters, given current, extremely tense, political conditions, such promises were not to be trusted. "In the Foreign Ministry," the pessimistic DAI director continued, "Terdenge is seen as an unpleasant intruder and the Cultural Section as a superfluous appendage." But were someone else to receive the call, Rodenwaldt indicated, Terdenge would resign, leaving the Cultural Section and the DAI to Interior Ministry control.[153] Rodenwaldt requested that Paul Wolters, full professor in Munich, use his connections to bring high Bavarian influence to bear on the appointment, assuring his correspondent that Terdenge, like the Foreign Ministry in general, followed a policy of giving special consideration to Center Party desires in determining the practice of *Kulturpolitik*.[154] Wolters agreed to lend his assistance, and commiserated with Rodenwaldt on the probable apocalyptic outcome should efforts in Terdenge's behalf fail.[155]

In his autobiography, Ludwig Curtius reflected on the seminal importance for the DAI of Terdenge's rise and fall. The coincidence of Terdenge's ambition with Rodenwaldt's desire to reconstruct the DAI, Curtius argued, had been the basis for the expansion of archaeological efforts in the postinflation period:

> The result [of this coincidence] was not only the almost magnificent endowment of the already existing institutes in Rome and Athens in the midst of the Reich's financial tribulations, but also the generous enlargement of the Roman-German Commission in Frankfurt am Main to become an independent institute, which now also took on the great task of studying Central European prehistory, the founding of the Egyptian Institute in Cairo, and of the Archaeological Institute in Istanbul, which organized work in Asia Minor. Only the fall of Terdenge and the difficult position into which the DAI was put with the victory of the Nazis prevented the fulfillment of two further grand projects: the founding of an archaeological institute for Spain in Madrid and one for China in Peking. Had these [plans] been achieved, Germany would have possessed a complete organization for archaeological research under unified leadership unlike that of any other country in the world.[156]

If Curtius undoubtedly overstressed the import of Terdenge, perhaps he alone recognized the essential, recapitulative function performed by the Weimar bureaucracy. Much more deeply committed to the reconstruction of

---

[153] Rodenwaldt to Wolters, 28 September 1932, BSB, Nachlaß Rodenwaldt, Mappe 682.

[154] Ibid.

[155] Wolters to Rodenwaldt, 30 September 1932, ibid., Mappe 345.

[156] Curtius, *Deutsche und Antike Welt*, p. 426.

national prestige than to the modernization and democratization of internal cultural affairs, and more interested in the promotion of grand exhibitions of undefeated German *Geist* than in the encouragement of new cultural forms, the bureaucrats and scholars of the 1920s managed to preserve much of the aristocratic insularity and imperialist élan of the prewar era. The near establishment of this grand Euro-Asian archæological combine in the midst of the political, economic, and social crises of the Weimar Republic's final years is a fitting indication of the final bankruptcy of the Humboldtian educational ideal and German philhellenist humanism; the persistence of the old regime insured that German high culture would survive even if democracy, liberal capitalism, and even common decency failed.

THE THIRD HUMANISM AND THE RETURN

OF ROMANTIC AESTHETICS

Erudition is not humanism.
(*Werner Jaeger*)

THE WAR'S END opened an era of profound, diverse, and sometimes bizarre reflections on antiquity and the European past. Anxieties expressed during the conflict resurfaced in new forms; old historiographical and generational disputes took on new urgency. Classicizing aesthetic standards coexisted uneasily with new "morphological" treatments of cultural history that stressed the insularity and nontranslatable nature of individual cultures. The relatively stable prewar borders between works of art and ethnographic objects, historical and nonhistorical peoples, *Kultur* and culture, had been destroyed by the advent of modern art, scholarly scavenging raids into prehistorical terrain, travel, photography, and finally, by the world-shattering experience of total war. What role, classicists began to wonder, could the ancients play in this brave new world?

At stake for conservative classicists were not only worldviews but also museological conceptions and museum funding, the social prestige and self-conception of the humanistic disciplines, and last but certainly not least, the uniqueness, autonomy, and cultural integrity of Europe, threatened by "orientals" and Slavs. Moreover, they stood before the apparently imminent demise of that seminal philhellenist institution, the *Gymnasium*. The *Gymnasium* still formed the primary gateway to university studies in the humanities; it maintained semimeritocratic nineteenth-century standards of refined personhood, and German classicists were desperate to preserve it. Yet only a philosophical formulation seemed capable of countering the thoroughgoing *Humanismusfeindschaft* (hostility toward humanism) now issuing from the socialist, ultranationalist, and youth movement camps and threatening to shake even middle-class confidence in the value of classical education. As *Gymnasium* teachers and academic specialists continually reminded one another in the pages of professional journals, in this half-utilitarian, half-existentialist era, humanism's right to exist required justification beyond historical significance and aesthetic interest.[1]

Most importantly, classicists needed to find some way to defend their studies before their students, for even Wilamowitz had discovered to his dismay that his students found philology unsatisfying as an end in itself. What was worse, the students looked to Wilamowitz's old foe, Friedrich Nietzsche, to justify their searches for the value and significance of scholarship for life.[2] "What is left of the grand Wilamops?" asked the Graecophile poet-prophet Stefan George. "Perhaps the dirt that Nietzsche shook from his coattails."[3] Even insiders like Ernst Howald suggested that in renouncing Creuzerian Romanticism in the 1820s, philology had cut itself off from life; this overly rationalist higher criticism had resulted, he wrote regretfully, in "the disappearance of the feel for artworks from archaeology, for religiosity from the study of religion, [and] for poetry from literary scholarship."[4] But, as Howald recognized, professional classicists could not simply abandon the specialized scholarship that legitimized their place in the social order. "There were three possible ways in which one could free classical philology from the petrifaction of the fin de siècle," philologist Karl Reinhardt wrote in retrospect. "First, one could reject the classical ideal in favor of the scholarly one. This was the course Wilamowitz followed, all contradictions notwithstanding. Second, one could have abandoned scholarship for the sake of the classical ideal. But that flew in the face of scholarly conscience; that is what the fiction writers did. Third, finally, one could try to reconcile the two. That is what Werner Jaeger did."[5] It is the tragedy of Weimar humanism that the first of these options was hedged around with a deep, antidemocratic pessimism, the second became the realm of vitalist Nietzscheans like George, and the third was saddled with both the elitism of the first and the antihistorical ambitions of the second. Despite the warnings of liberal reformers like C. H. Becker, moderate solutions to the manifold crises facing humanistic education and scholarship were spurned both by new prophets and by entrenched philologists.

In the Weimar-era works of Wilamowitz, Jaeger, and their colleagues, anxieties about the disunity, weakness, and moral-cultural degeneration of

[1] See, for example, Otto Regenbogen's review of Eduard Fraenkel's *Die Stellung des Römertums in der humanistischen Bildung*, *Gnomon* 3, no. 4 (April 1927): 226–41.

[2] See Ernst Vogt, "Wilamowitz und die Auseinandersetzung seiner Schüler mit ihm," in *Wilamowitz nach 50 Jahren*, ed. William M. Calder et al. (Darmstadt, 1985), pp. 613–31.

[3] George quoted in Edgar Salin, *Um Stefan George: Erinnerung und Zeugnis* (Munich, 1954), p. 251.

[4] Ernst Howald, *Der Kampf um Creuzers Symbolik: Eine Auswahl von Dokumenten* (Tübingen, 1926), p. 3.

[5] Reinhardt, "Die klassische Philologie und das Klassische" [1942] in idem, *Vermächtnis der Antike* (Göttingen, 1966), p. 348.

the democratic state are quite near the surface. Increasingly, as the Weimar era lapsed into the Nazi regime, Jakob Burckhardt's condemnation of the polis for suppressing individual genius was turned into praise for the power of the unified, *völkisch* state.[6] "Democracy is the harbinger of tyrannies," wrote Wilamowitz in 1932, noting also that it was tyranny that twice saved Greekdom, and democracy that nearly ruined it before its time.[7] According to Jaeger, the neohumanists of the early nineteenth century, "living in an unpolitical age," had presumed Greek pedagogy to aim at the cultivation of the independent, individual personality. "But our own intellectual attraction to the state has opened our eyes again to the fact that for the Greeks of the Golden Age, mind divorced from the state was as unthinkable as state divorced from mind. . . . The coming third humanism is essentially derived from the basic fact of all Greek education: that humanity, human nature, for the Greeks, is profoundly bound up with man's essential, political character."[8] As it happened, Jaeger's "third humanism" barely outlived the Weimar Republic itself—though not for lack of trying. Jaeger's attempt to revive the German philhellenic tradition represents a final step in neohumanism's abdication of social responsibility in pursuit of its own, "disinterested" ends.

If Weimar-era classicists generally subscribed to antidemocratic opinions and pursued their own interests with little thought to the good of the polity, however, most, to their credit, participated rather little in racist speculation. In part, this was due to the fact that most classicists continued to concentrate their efforts on post-Homeric events. The world hedged in by texts simply offered less room for racist speculation than did the prehistorical world, where skull-types and pot styles could be made to document tribal movements. But also, for the humanists, the geocultural exceptionalness and physical beauty of the Greeks had been an accepted truism since Winckelmann's time. When the question was posed, the Greeks were always categorized as "Indo-European" or "Aryan"—the name came directly from comparative linguistics, though it did, often, also suggest physiognomic traits. It was not at all difficult for most classicists to acknowledge Greek racial superiority—not purity—but, importantly, for these men, admiration of Hellas was of necessity primarily cultural, not biological. If these men bear a measure of responsibility for the failure of the Weimar Republic, it lies in their resistance to progressive reform and their willingness to listen only to the cultural critiques of the vitalists, nationalists, and cultural pessimists. Employing the arguments of the new Right to defend the status quo, they failed to lay the foundations for a nonelitist, liberal humanism which

[6] Beat Näf, *Von Perikles zu Hitler? Die athenische Demokratie und die deutsche Althistorie bis 1945* (Bern, 1986), p. 237.

[7] Wilamowitz, *Glaube der Hellenen*, 2 vols. (Berlin, 1931–32), 2: 219.

[8] Jaeger, *Paideia*, vol. 1: *Die Formung des Griechischen Menschen*, (Berlin, 1934), p. 16.

could offer resistance to the biological fatalism of the Nazi regime and form the basis for a democratic educational system in the post-1945 era.

Philhellenism and Pessimism

One of the dubious accomplishments of the Great War was to underscore, particularly for the losers, the fragility of civilization and the power of sub-rational desires: Sigmund Freud was certainly not the only postwar writer to reflect on humankind's inability to tame its bestial instincts. Even amongst humanism's torchbearers, this sort of pessimism made deep inroads, transforming Wilamowitz's warnings about the jackals howling in Ephesus into a fatalist acceptance of a coming age of renewed barbarism. The fact that Italy and, most painfully, Greece had joined the Allied cause only reinforced German skepticism about Mediterranean-centered Europe's influence and integrity, both in the past and in the future. Thus the prophesied death of the West opened the way for the enormous welter of specialized scholarship, plunging deep into the ancient oriental past and wide across the continents, to organize itself into separate, non-Western narratives. Increasingly, *Kultur*—defined universally, as mankind's sum of achievements—was replaced by *Kulturen*, organically conceived *cultures*, each driven by the sort of instinctive "will to form" that art historian Alois Riegl had postulated for the purposive (but nonpredictable) evolution of artistic designs. Under the dual pressure of postwar skepticism and culture-historical specialization, the philosophical foundations of aristocratic, universalist humanism disintegrated into dust.

The critique of objectivity and universal values began effectively with Nietzsche, but required the war's crippling lessons in the crude brutality of civilized nations to flourish. Naturally, for classicists, this abandonment of universal values had implications first and foremost for the Greek ideal, so much a part of their affective attachment to their field as well as a fundamental element of its institutional underpinnings. As we shall see below, very many of Weimar's classicists, particularly philologists and archaeologists, could not relinquish their philhellenic idealism. Here, however, we have to do with those who took Wilamowitz's path, as Reinhardt described it: the rejection of the classical ideal for the scholarly (historicist) one, a path that entailed the integration of a vast corpus of orientalist, prehistorical, and even ethnographic work into the German portrait of the ancient world. It is highly significant that this work, much of which had been marked by its exclusion from the charmed humanist world, was finally taken up in an era in which classical education and specialist scholarship had suffered great losses in social status. For humanist academia's appreciation of the nonclassical world, when it finally did arrive, was very much colored by cultural despair.

Oswald Spengler's extremely popular *Decline of the West* (1918) both reinforced and helped to create the maudlin conclusions about Europe's future that German intellectuals drew from the loss of the Great War. Acknowledging debts only to the "philosophies" of Goethe and Nietzsche, Spengler's book coupled themes from *Lebensphilosophie* with a vehement attack on the self-absorption and progress fixation of nineteenth-century Europeans. Spengler insisted that individual cultures should be represented as organisms, each with its own, predetermined life span; each culture proceeded through the predictable stages of youth, middle age, and old age (or becoming, being, and decaying) regardless of the value of its philosophical insights, the justness of its political institutions, or the beauty of its art. In fact, Spengler disavowed the possibility of the existence of such timeless standards. "For other men, there are other truths," he wrote; "There are no eternal truths."[9] Spengler did not, however, believe that even recognition of his organic—or to use his term, "morphological"—laws of cultural waxing and waning could halt the inevitable decline of Western civilization. His was a sublime pessimism modelled on late Roman Stoicism; the best he could do was to fortify his contemporaries with the observation that their inevitable decline followed a typical pattern of cultural dissolution. From coherence, closeness to the soil, and inner-orientation, cultures indefatigably overripened into "civilized" materialism and urban anomie, mass society and intellectual fragmentation.

Spengler used several supposedly analogous cultural morphemes to point up this unavoidable slide from *Kultur* into *Zivilisation*, but one parallel dominated the comparison: the Western world's decline since the happy coherent years of the baroque (Rembrandtian) age paralleled the transition from the Greek polis to Caesarist Rome. For Spengler, however, this recapitulation was a matter of form alone; if his delineation of autonomous cultural epochs was reminiscent in some ways of Hegelian *Universalgeschichte*, his world-historical schema was at base emphatically nondialectical and deeply antiteleological. There was no hope that *Geist* would eventually achieve self-conscious actuality for more than a fleeting moment, nor that contradictions could be overcome and yet preserved in the amber of universal reason; mankind, as Spengler announced, like all other species, had no goal and would never escape the eternal return of civilized decay.[10]

Spengler could not abide the common tripartite sequence antiquity–Middle Ages–modernity, a temporal and ideological differentiation that

[9] Oswald Spengler, *Der Untergang des Abendlandes: Umrisse einer Morphologie der Weltgeschichte*, vol. 1: *Gestalt und Wirklichkeit* (Munich, 1921), pp. 34, 58.

[10] See, e.g., Ibid., p. 28.

mistook the evolution of the West for the history of the world.[11] The West's periodizations and particular cultural developments were irrelevant as characterizations of other historical morphemes, possessed of their very own languages, truths, and gods, and headed eventually for their very own, unique deaths.[12] "What does Tolstoy, who rejects from his deepest humaneness the whole thought-world of the West as foreign and distant, have to do with the 'Middle Ages,' with Dante, with Luther; what does a Japanese have to do with Parsifal and Zarathustra, or an Indian with Socrates?"[13] For Spengler, all cultures operated according to self-referential systems of significance; since each of these systems remained incomprehensible to outside observers, none—including "the West"—could offer a valid foundation for universal norms.

Spengler's radical critique of the imposition of Western values, standards, and chronological frames on world history had perforce to emphasize the essential differences that divided modernity from antiquity, Germany from Greece. Spengler's critique of both optimistic and nostalgic Graecophilia forms the centerpoint of his critique of cross-cultural imitation; his plea for the liberation of modern *Geist* turns on the abandonment of conventional, classical norms:

> We West Europeans have offered up to "the ancients" the purity and self-sufficiency of our art, which we only dare to create with a sidelong glance at the majestic "model"; our images of the Greeks and Romans have always possessed the contents and feelings that we lacked or longed for in the depths of our own souls. One day an intelligent psychologist will recount for us the story of our fateful illusion, the history of what we have in each case revered as ancient. There are few tales more instructive for the intimate knowledge of the Western soul from Emperor Otto III, the first, to Nietzsche, [who was] the last, victim of the South.[14]

In claiming German victimization by "the South," Spengler was not simply reviving the nineteenth-century theme of Romandom versus Germandom. To defend his gloomy relativist historiography, he was willing to dismiss Graecophilia too—even that of his hero Nietzsche—as a vitality-sapping delusion.

But Spengler was by no means the only man of his age to attempt to write humanism's epitaph. In his deranged *Mythus des zwanzigsten Jahrhunderts* (*Myth of the Twentieth Century*—1930), Alfred Rosenberg announced the end of universalizing projects, including the "Christianizing of the world" and the "humanist dream of 'Mankind.'" "Both ideals," he proclaimed,

[11] Ibid., pp. 29–30.
[12] Ibid., p. 29.
[13] Ibid., p. 38.
[14] Ibid, p. 41.

"have been buried in the bloody chaos of the Great War and in the subsequent rebirth out of this calamity despite the fact that now one, and now the other, still find increasingly fanatical adherents and a venerable priesthood. These are processes of petrifaction and no longer of living tissue: A belief which has died in the soul cannot be raised from the dead."[15] Moreover, the prehistorians, *Ostforscher*, orientalist art historians, geopoliticians, and romantic ethnographers of the 1920s, heirs to prewar nationalist and positivist critiques of classical humanism, now felt free to vent their contempt for their classicizing colleagues and blithely to retell history according to their own needs and prejudices. The art historian Josef Strzygowski condemned philological humanism for its elitist concentration on written records and its obsession with representational art, both of which prevented true appreciation of the profundity of the Nordic folk.[16] The antihumanist reaction had truly come of age.

These challenges did not fail to strike a chord in academia. Spengler's pessimistic pronouncements appealed to many, though defenders of the neohumanist tradition by and large could not accept his delineation of self-contained cultural epochs, for the obvious reason that this destined classical antiquity to the mists of inevitable misunderstanding.[17] A few specialists, like Paul Wolters, dismissed Spengler as a "crass ignoramus,"[18] but prominent students of ancient history like Eduard Meyer and C. H. Becker realized that Spengler was the product of a hypertrophied historicism induced by scholarly specialization. Like many of their peers, Meyer and Becker took Spengler's pronouncements seriously, if they ultimately rejected his morphological method and insistence on cultural closure.[19] Some scholars, like Ulrich Kahrstedt, derived from Spengler the frightful proph-

---

[15] Rosenberg, *The Myth of the Twentieth Century*, trans. Vivian Bird (Torrance, Calif., 1982), pp. 2–3.

[16] Strzygowski, "Die Stellung des Islam zum geistigen Aufbau Europas," in *Acta Academiae Aboensis Humaniora* vol. 3, no. 3 (Abo, 1992), pp. 22–23; idem, "Natur und Unnatur in der bildenden Kunst," *Mannus* 20 (1928): 5, 7; see also Suzanne Marchand, "The Rhetoric of Artifacts and the Decline of Classical Humanism: The Case of Josef Strzygowski," *History and Theory*, suppl. vol. 33 (1994): 106–30.

[17] Jaeger was prepared to concede that prehistorical and non-European cultures might defy comprehension, but neither he nor Spranger would concede the "foreignness" of the ancients—or give up the Faustian metaphor of spiritual wedlock. See Spranger, "Kulturzyklentheorie," and "Vom Neuhumanismus bis zur Gegenwart," in *Vom Altertum zur Gegenwart* (Berlin, 1921), p. 78; Jaeger, "Der Humanismus als Tradition," in *Humanistische Reden und Vorträge*, 2d ed. (Berlin, 1960), p. 20; and idem, "Antike und Humanismus," ibid., p. 104. Both essays are discussed below.

[18] Wolters to Ludwig Curtius, 16 March 1921, in DAI, Nachlaß L. Curtius, Biographische Mappe.

[19] See Eduard Meyer, "Spenglers Untergang des Abendlandes," *Deutsche Literaturzeitung* 25 (1924): 1759–80; C. H. Becker, "Spenglers magische Kultur: Ein Vortrag," in GStAPKB, Nachlaß Becker, Mappe 818.

ecy that the self-destruction of the West in its internal struggle for imperialist domination would call forth "the awakening of the East, of the colored
peoples, with emancipation as the mildest and the extermination of the
whites and the educated classes as its strongest form. . . ."[20] For his part,
Spengler developed over the course of the Weimar era a fascination for
classical and prehistorical archaeology, making him less an enemy than a
troublesome, morose fellow traveler.

In the postwar period, scholars with humanistic training increasingly
opted to specialize in nontraditional periods or places. Despairing of the
West's prospects to save itself from impending barbarism, many turned their
attention to the manifold local cultures that had resisted, outlasted, and
overwhelmed Europe's classical heritage. Of course, specialized work on the
Byzantine, Carolingian, Germanic, Slavic, and early Islamic worlds had
begun before the war; the leading figures in these fields, however, now acquired new prominence and attracted new audiences. Scholars such as Konrad Burdach, Alfons Dopsch, August Heisenberg, and Albert Brackmann
now occupied important bureaucratic and academic posts; in their books
and essays, they evoked the unconventional beauties and strengths of forgotten cultures, rarely missing the chance to emphasize the frailty of the
much more familiar ancients.[21]

The despairing mood of the time was captured most poignantly in Eduard Meyer's "Blüte und Niedergang des Hellenismus in Asien," ("Flowering
and Decay of Hellenism in Asia"—1925) in which Hellenism's celebrated
conquests, like those of European culture in the nineteenth century, prove
both Pyrrhic and fleeting.[22] But the same sentiment runs through Franz
Boll's fatalistic history of the eternal recurrence of astrology—the "titanic"
backlash of the Orient, which destroyed this-worldly Greek philosophy[23]—
and through Friedrich Freiherr von Bissing's racist parable *Das Griechentum
und seine Weltmission* (*Greekdom and its World Mission*—1921). "Although
the Greeks achieved so many wonderful things for humankind," Bissing
warned, "their political structures all collapsed in the face of the assault of
native, ancient oriental forces and the domination of Rome, supported by
Italian peasant hardiness."[24] More anti-Semitic and militant than most of
his peers, Bissing concluded his book by urging the Germans to behave

---

[20] Kahrstedt, review of Eduard Meyer, *Blüte und Niedergang des Hellenismus in Asien*, *Deutsche Literaturzeitung* 41 (1925): 2001. See also Meyer, "Spenglers Untergang," p. 1779.

[21] See, e.g., August Heisenberg's "Das Problem der Renaissance in Byzanz," *Historische
Zeitschrift* 133 (1926): 393–412; Alfons Dopsch, *Der Wiederaufbau Europas nach dem Untergang der alten Welt* (rectorial address, University of Vienna, 26 October 1920) (Vienna,
1920).

[22] Reprinted in Franz Altheim and Joachim Rehork, eds., *Der Hellenismus in Mittelasien*
(Darmstadt, 1969), pp. 19–72.

[23] See Franz Boll, *Sternglaube und Sterndeutung: Die Geschichte und das Wesen der Astrologie*
(Leipzig, 1918), pp. 22–26.

[24] Bissing, *Das Griechentum und seine Weltmission* (Leipzig, 1921), p. 4.

more like the strong-willed Romans and less like the feckless Greeks.[25] If most ancient historians scorned such overt political dictates, the tragic demise of Hellenism, in the 1920s, remained a favorite theme—against the backdrop, it must be remembered, of Kemal Atatürk's simultaneous expulsions of the Greeks of Anatolia from the newly founded Turkish state.

This emphasis on Greek frailty went hand in hand with new interest in and appreciation of Greek religious life, a subject marginalized by the anticlerical, rationalizing philhellenes of the nineteenth century. This theme, however, had never really disappeared entirely: Ernst Curtius had taken an interest in Graeco-Christian linkages, and Erwin Rohde's very popular *Psyche* (1894) had made a deep impression on the *Gymnasium* generation of 1914. Ever since the 1880s, the Bonn philologist Hermann Usener, whose pupils included Hermann Diels, Wilamowitz, Eduard Norden, Eduard Schwartz, Aby Warburg, and Hans Lietzmann, had helped to revive academic enthusiasm for the subject through his studies of Greek religion on the one hand, and of Christian saints and festivals on the other.[26] But perhaps German classicists required the bitter experience of military defeat to awaken their interest in cults of the dead, the philosophical elaboration of the soul, and portrayals of the afterlife. Here too, the emphasis was placed on the Orient's—but not the Jewish—contribution to the religious basis of Greek culture, and here, the study of myth, nearly banished since the time of K. O. Müller, was revived in a peculiarly expressionist, vitalist, and anticomparativist mode. Diverging here from the much more social-scientific Cambridge Ritualists and French scholars, German classicists cultivated a new, antirationalist, appreciation for Greek culture.[27]

The best known exponent of this new view was Frankfurt professor Walter F. Otto, who purported to actually believe in the Greek gods.[28] Associated with the neo-Romantic circle of Stefan George, Otto combined a kind of Schillerian nostalgia for the "young and not yet fragmented culture" of Hellas with a Nietzschean attraction to the daemonic passions of the Greeks.[29] He celebrated, on the one hand, the anthropocentric message of Greek religion ("What man wills and achieves is himself and is God"); but on the other hand, like Nietzsche, he saw the coming of rationalism (in the form of Euripides) and the demand for systematic justice as the lamentable

[25] Ibid., p. 174.

[26] See Arnaldo Momigliano, "New Paths of Classicism in the Nineteenth Century," *History and Theory*, suppl. vol. 21 (1982): 33–47.

[27] See Walter Burkert, "Griechische Mythologie und die Geistesgeschichte der Moderne," in *Les Études classiques aux XIXᵉ et XXᵉ siècles: Leur place dans l'histoire des idées*, ed. Willem den Boer (Geneva, 1980), pp. 187–207.

[28] Siegfried Morenz, *Ägyptische Religion* (Stuttgart, 1960), p. ix. Thanks to Gavin Lewis for this reference.

[29] Walter F. Otto, *Die Götter Griechenlands: Das Bild des Göttlichen im Spiegel des griechischen Geistes* (Bonn, 1929), pp. 173, 102–4.

end of healthy religiosity.[30] In 1933, he published a full-length study of his favorite god, Dionysus, in which he paid more explicit homage to the heroic vitalism of the Right. Without question, Otto's gods descended less from a Schillerian Olympus than from a Nietzschean Valhalla;[31] but he did not give up the attempt to secure a place for the classical world in the reborn Reich. In 1940, Otto cofounded the *Jahrbuch für geistige Überlieferung (Journal of Intellectual Traditions)*, in whose second volume Martin Heidegger's celebrated essay, "Plato's Doctrine of Truth," first appeared.[32] Otto's neo-Romantic sympathy for the ritualistic and subrational aspects of Greek culture had once put him in the company of conservative mavericks like Leo Frobenius and Stefan George; by the time of the outbreak of World War II, he had graduated into the company of the most highminded of German and Italian collaborators.

A number of other major works on Greek religion and neo-Platonic "theology" appeared during the Weimar era, including Karl Reinhardt's pathbreaking study *Poseidonios* (1921).[33] Perhaps the most revealing of these studies, however, was Wilamowitz's two-volume *Glaube der Hellenen (Beliefs of the Greeks)*, left still partially unfinished at his death in 1932. Like Otto, Wilamowitz emphasized the need to take the Greek gods seriously, as objects of religious reverence rather than as means for mere artistic expression. For Wilamowitz, this departure from the "rationalism" of the scholars of the previous century was bound up with the decline of aestheticizing Graecophilia and the new value accorded to inward-oriented and religious eras over the previously exalted, externalizing artistic epochs. "We have learned to see differently than did Winckelmann and Goethe," the great philologist contended, "and this corresponds to the fact that we are also able to comprehend [*nachzuempfinden*] the ancient, authentic religion."[34] Like other students of the subject, Wilamowitz concentrated his attention on the "unripe" and "decadent" eras of Greek history, in which he found the greatest faith and the most numerous anticipations of Christian beliefs. But if he inverted the philhellenist's usual period preferences, Wilamowitz still stuck doggedly to the philological-historicist tradition, refusing to introduce cross-cultural comparisons or information about peoples whose lan-

---

[30] Ibid., pp. 237, 331.

[31] On Otto's right-wing leanings, see Hubert Cancik, "Dionysos 1933: W. F. Otto, ein Religionswissenschaftler und Theologe am Ende der Weimarer Republik," in *Die Restauration der Götter: Antike Religion und Neo-Paganismus*, ed. Richard Faber and Renate Schlesier (Würzburg, 1986), pp. 105–23.

[32] For the journal's context, see Victor Farias, *Heidegger and Nazism*, ed. Joseph Margolis and Tom Rockmore (Philadelphia, 1987), pp. 260–68.

[33] For some examples and commentary, see Franz Josef Brecht, *Platon und der George-Kreis*, Das Erbe der Alten, vol. 17 (Leipzig, 1929).

[34] Wilamowitz, *Glaube der Hellenen*, 1: 5.

guages he had not studied. "About other peoples, I have no opinion," Wilamowitz demurred, "I know the Greeks."[35]

Despairing of the mass culture of the present and impressed by the findings of historicist scholarship, Wilamowitz accepted the demise of the classical ideal. He would not, however, abandon his commitment to the pursuit
of specialized classical scholarship, and could not understand why his
students—many of them war veterans—and the Weimar state did not share
his dedication to this ascetic ideal.[36] It was not Wilamowitz who attempted
to save classical normativity, but his nemesis, Stefan George, who rejected
precisely the demythologizing sterility of historicist scholarship in favor of
an eroticized philhellenism that emphasized the body (*der Leib*) and the
here and now. As one of George's many devotees commented in 1929, "It is
the writer's opinion that the new German humanism . . . comes from the
longing and desire for the total human renewal of our state of being, which
has been stamped by that of antiquity, that thus its true sources do not lie in
scholarship." This critic was probably correct in identifying the sources of
humanistic revival outside the halls of academia, but he also, properly, gave
credit to Wilamowitz's student Werner Jaeger, "who is definitely to be
thanked for grasping, in essence, the sense and the structure of the new
humanism."[37] For, unlike his mentor, Jaeger and a number of his peers
realized that, in the wake of the youth movement, the lost war, and school
reform, the asceticism of the historicist ideal could no longer generate reverence for the ancients or support for *Gymnasium* education. Like George,
whose antiestablishment classicism lies beyond the bounds of this study,
Jaeger rejected pessimistic historicism and took his cues from another
school of thought with its origins in the fin de siècle: *Lebensphilosophie*.
Perhaps, this classicist hoped, a little "life" would suffice to save the educational system from what otherwise promised to be inevitable democratization and debasement.

Philology and *Lebensphilosophie*: Classical Schooling under Siege

As the aging professoriate returned to its specialized research and pursuit
of prestige, a much larger and somewhat broader student population,
schooled in wartime and restless under the "dictated" peace, also resumed
its studies. Never before had the gap between scholarly research and the

[35] Ibid., p. 288; see also p. 10.

[36] After the war, Wilamowitz grudgingly gave up teaching his seminars in Latin because, to
his disgust, his students were no longer able to conduct discussions in that tongue. Friedrich
Solmsen, "Wilamowitz in his Last Ten Years," *Greek, Roman, and Byzantine Studies* 20, no. 1
(Spring 1979): 95, n. 8.

[37] Brecht, *Platon und der George-Kreis*, p. x.

cultivation of the individual seemed so wide; never before had the Humboldtian aim of reconciling the interests of both within the German system of higher education seemed so implausible. Perhaps the two could never be harmonized, as C. H. Becker concluded in 1931, owing to a fundamental antinomy that von Humboldt had failed to perceive. "Scholarship," Becker averred, "must according to its essence become increasingly depersonalized, while *Bildung* is the most powerful expression of personality."[38] The German system's comprehensive identification of education and scholarship, Becker believed, actually distorted the Greek *Bildungsideal*; like many other critics of "pure intellectualism," Becker advocated the reconstruction of humanistic education, cured of its stultifying obsession with historical and linguistic detail and infused with new significance for *life*.[39]

Becker's critique, drawing on contemporary strains in *Lebensphilosophie* as well as on his frustrating experience at the Prussian Education Ministry, was by no means the first nor was it the only attack on Humboldtian humanism during the Weimar era. Heavily influenced by Nietzsche's insistence upon the desiccation of scholarship when not directed to enhancing life, the prewar youth movement had criticized the scholarly community for destroying vitality and meaning in obsessive concentration on details and facts. Ludwig Hatvany's *Die Wissenschaft des nicht Wissenswerten* (*The Field of Knowledge Not Worth Knowing*—1908), for example, a parody of philological lectures conveyed in the form of a student's diary, expressed deep discontent with the "objectivity" of classical studies, described at one point as "the nineteenth century's enslavement to facts."[40] During and particularly after the war, this critique of scholarship for its own sake found a large and increasingly diverse circle of advocates; by 1923, for example, the young philosopher Karl Jaspers was suggesting that the "will to objectivity" in German academia had something "inhumane" about it.[41] By 1932, the literary scholar Ernst Robert Curtius had come to see the "asceticism" of German *Bildung* as a danger to the moral and mental health of his people:

[Our] wholly idealistic system of *Bildung* has been dominated by an ascetic ideal and has created a highly one-sided type of man, which has put the equilibrium of human faculties in great danger. Ascetic is Kantian philosophy and all its idealistic later developed forms [*Spätformen*]. Ascetic is the German scholarly ideal, as perhaps it was represented to us in Wilamowitz, its last great embodiment. Ascetic and idealistic is Schiller's ethos, but also the thin mountain air of the classicizing aesthetic. All these cultural forces have sundered

---

[38] Becker, draft of speech to be given at opening of internationale Hochschulkurse in Davos, 22 March 1931, p. 29; in GStAPKB, Nachlaß Becker, Mappe 8131.

[39] Ibid., p. 8; Becker, "Bildung und Kulturkrise" (1930), ibid., Mappe 7776.

[40] Ludwig Hatvany, *Die Wissenschaft des nicht Wissenswerten* (1908; reprint ed., Oxford, 1986) p. 24.

[41] Karl Jaspers, *Die Idee der Universität* (Berlin, 1923), p. 15.

man from the fundamental ground of his existence, from the vital, the instinctive, and the sensual, and that has had a fearful effect on him.[42]

For the cosmopolitan Curtius (grandson of the excavator), the real threat to German *Geist* was not corruption by external influences but self-inflicted, idealist, paralysis.

Critics charged the scholarly community of the 1920s with abdicating its role in establishing social values and building character. The scapegoating of "specialists" for the "soullessness" of modern German culture went hand in hand with the conviction that "pure intellectualism" would destroy social unity—as well as the integrity of the human character. The appearance of this caricature of the specialist as pedant, skeptic, and passive bookworm in an era hungry for heroes, prophets, and strongmen was telling and troubling for the typical German academic, devoted to *zwecklos* scholarliness but equally dedicated to the resurrection of German national puissance. Most scholars would not prove so resistant to such criticism as Max Weber, whose much-criticized *Wissenschaft als Beruf* (*Science as a Vocation*—1919) turned a stoical countenance on the "disenchantment of the world" and the amorality of scholarly inquiry.[43]

Connected to the problem of the specialist's inability to convey values was the question of reform in secondary education. The secondary schools, now more than ever, were entrusted with the task of unifying the *Volk*. No longer were they simply university preparatory schools, argued Otto Boelitz, who served as education minister between 1921 and 1925; they were now called upon to prepare students for practical life and to foster leadership qualities without separating students from the life of the *Volk*.[44] The desire to unite the nation and dissolve class, confessional, and provincial boundaries through the creation of a single secondary-school type (*Einheitsschule*) had been significantly augmented by the experience of the war, and reformers were emboldened by the sympathetic stance of the education ministries of the various Länder. In 1924–25, beginning in Prussia, a series of curriculum reform measures was passed in most of the German states. Based on the ideas of DVP Prussian Landtag representative Hans Richert, these reforms allowed for the continuing existence of different school types, but sought to impose on all a set of "kulturkundlichen Kern-fächer" (cultural core areas), including German language, history, religion, and geography. Aiming at the regeneration of national unity and the reestablishment of traditional "German" values, this reformist agenda promised the retention of classical works in translation, but threatened to attenuate

---

[42] E. R. Curtius, *Deutscher Geist in Gefahr* (Stuttgart, 1932), p. 13.

[43] Max Weber, "Science as a Vocation," in *From Max Weber: Essays in Sociology*, ed. H. H. Gerth and C. Wright Mills (New York, 1946), pp. 129–56.

[44] See Otto Boelitz, *Der Character der höheren Schule* (Leipzig, 1926).

instruction in Latin and Greek. Though considerably less radical than other proposals, the Richert reforms, for the philologists, represented an unwelcome "political" intrusion into their domain.[45]

Attacks on *Gymnasium* elitism from the socialists, *Realschulmänner*, and the radical nationalists, of course, were hardly new, and their complaints seemed to run along familiar lines. For the socialists, humanism was elitist, and outdated: it failed to provide a common critical perspective suitable for comprehending modern social relations and did not provide students with appropriate training for modern jobs. For the school reformers, similarly, *Gymnasium* humanism did not recognize changes in the nature of the world economy that demanded that students learn geography, modern languages, economics, and especially natural science rather than Greek grammar: humanism was an ideal whose currency had elapsed. Nationalists still believed humanism to be too "international": despite efforts by philologists and archaeologists to prove the distinctively German aspects of *Altertumswissenschaft*, the continued centrality of the Mediterranean lands was seen as a kind of self-effacement and pandering to the enemy.

The critique from the standpoint of *Leben*, however, came frequently from those who wished to preserve, not destroy, the classical foundations of German *Bildung*, and hence posed a particular problem for classical scholars.[46] The assertion that classical humanism had lost touch with life came primarily from those schooled in and still committed to the *Gymnasium* tradition: they did not challenge the essential validity of antiquity as the basis of secondary schooling (though a few, like Becker, did wish to revise the curriculum somewhat). Hatvany's parody, for example, caricatured the dry-as-dust approach taken by historio-critical philologists, but the author still clearly believed that the ancients merited profound study. Ever harkening back to the Humboldtian era, Hatvany's student could never have attended a meeting of the *Realschulmänner*; it was laughable, as Hans Blüher wrote of the vitalist, antiurban wing of the youth movement, to suggest that the *Realschulen* could have produced this profoundly humanistic crusade.[47] The danger for the philologists was not that these proponents of *Leben* would join the reformer enemies, but rather that they would seek

---

[45] Ute Preuß, *Humanismus und Gesellschaft: Zur Geschichte des altsprachlichen Unterrichts in Deutschland von 1890 bis 1933* (Frankfurt, 1988), pp. 117–31.

[46] These critics all emphasized the necessity of transcending rationalism, mechanization, and other modern forces fragmenting the individual and his creative powers, but the remarkably similar language they borrowed from Nietzsche, Schiller, and Goethe often obscured the wide variety of vantage points, scapegoats, and ultimate ends pursued by critics as diverse as Theodor Litt, Hans Blüher, Oswald Spengler, and Max Scheler.

[47] Hans Blüher, "Die humanistische Bildungsmacht" (1925), in idem, *Die humanistische Bildungsmacht* (Heidenhein an der Brenz, 1976), p. 9 of "Anhang." For more on the middle-class origins and complaints of the youth movement, see Walter Z. Laqueur, *Young Germany: A History of the German Youth Movement* (New York, 1962).

to modernize neohumanism by breaking its ties to scientific philology. Such a move would have ended the marriage of text criticism and anthropocentric philosophy begun in the Renaissance, as well as attenuating professorial influence over the *Gymnasium*, and *Gymnasium* teachers' privilege over other instructors. *Lebensphilosophie* and its scholarly relative philosophical anthropology threatened to take humanism away from the traditional humanists, to dissociate discussion of man's nature from scholarly inquiries into his classical past, a prospect which could not help but horrify—and preoccupy—the committed *Philolog*.

Thus, paramount in the debate over the future of humanism under the Weimar Republic was the issue of grammatical training in Greek and Latin. "Philology" had become a metaphor for numbing drudgery, authoritarian discipline, and pedantic obscurantism, while classical language training remained, for the bulk of the professoriate, the sine qua non of both *Bildung* and humanistic *Wissenschaft*. This combination of declining social status and the increasing sense that the *Gymnasium* alone held back a culture-destroying flood of superficiality, decadence, and utilitarianism prepared the backdrop for a kind of classicist morality play, in which philologists were sacrificed on the altar of modern materialism. The Richert reforms seemed to the institution's backers to prove their encirclement by enemies and detractors. Otto Regenbogen's 1927 description of the embattled *Gymnasium* instructor accurately reflects this self-portrayal as lonely warrior on the field of humanist glory:

> The *Humanismusfeindschaft* of life presses in on him more closely and powerfully than it generally does on university teachers; daily he leads the fight against the indifference or disinclination of parents who frequently have long since lost their connection to and understanding for intellectual values. . . . [He leads] the fight also against the prejudice and distractedness of the young, whose friends and relations, in addition to the clamorous, unruly press, are constantly bending their ears about the senselessness of their lessons and [school]work. He has to struggle and to defend himself not only against lack of participation and lack of understanding on the part of his colleagues in other fields—the worst battle of all, however, is that of standing firm against his own cowardice and his own faintheartedness.[48]

The favorite metaphor of the 1920s—the heroic struggle of the unappreciated savior against evil forces and overwhelming odds—had come to humanism as well.

If the maintenance of philology was a crusade for some, the practice of conveying the abstruse grammatical interests of the academic community to

---

[48] Regenbogen, review of Eduard Fraenkel's *Die Stellung des Römertums in der humanistischen Bildung*, in *Gnomon* 3, no. 4 (April 1927): 226.

the *Bildungsbürgertum*-in-training, too, could hardly be jettisoned by higher secondary teachers, for whom this semischolarly function still served an essential, status-enhancing role. Yet both professors and *Gymnasium* philologists recognized that nineteenth-century defenses of the services of linguistic education in the disciplining of the mind and refining of rhetorical skills would no longer suffice. In an extensive joint declaration on school reform published in 1931, the Verband der deutschen Hochschulen and Deutscher Philologenverband (Association of German Secondary Schools and Association of German Philologists) acknowledged that formalist pedagogy and nonpurposive scholarship no longer appealed to a utilitarian epoch. However, the philologists then proceeded to translate the problem into the more familiar language of *Leben* and to argue the problem against opponents within, rather than outside, the *Bildungsbürgertum*: "Even among those with scholarly credentials," the philologists' remonstrance read, "the voice of skepticism can be heard, for pure scholarship has supposedly shown itself unable to grasp the creative forces in life and to put [these] productively to work in the service of man, and also unable to give answers to the final and greatest questions of human existence." The remainder of the declaration demonstrated that scholarly pedagogy was not necessarily *lebensfern* (remote from life); indeed, only the "objective" teacher, devoted to facticity and reality, could truly induct students into "the world of values."[49] Thus Becker's plans to modernize the training of all school teachers were unnecessary and impracticable; having translated the debate over relevance into one over vitality and values, the *Gymnasium* instructors were able to justify both their exceptionalness and their method.

Yet another defense of classical education, the patriotic, seems to have been the choice of Latinists, undoubtedly the most maligned by the antihumanist faction. Whereas Greek literature arose from the Greek populace, Otto Regenbogen argued, Roman literature reflected the essence of Latium only in a much less direct way. Rome could be paradigmatic, as Eduard Fränkel had suggested, only by being seen as the first nation to consciously construct a *Bildungsideal* around Greek culture.[50] As we have seen, this denigration of Roman creativity, a recurrent tendency in German classical studies despite the pioneering research of Germans in the field, usually entailed new emphasis on Rome's military power and patriotic ethos, chiefly as a means to explain her conquest of the ever so much more imaginative Greeks. As a chorus of critics assembled to denounce Rome's domineering place in Germany's past, Weimar Latinists returned to the double defense of Roman martial virtues and good (Graecophile) taste.

---

[49] *Hochschulreform und wissenschaftliche Ausbildung der Philologen* (Denkschrift des Verbandes der Deutschen Hochschulen und des Deutschen Philologenverbandes) (Leipzig, 1931), pp. 15, pp. 16–21.

[50] See Regenbogen, review of Fraenkel's *Die Stellung des Römertums*, pp. 232–40.

In a public lecture given in 1919, Eduard Norden, the eminent Berlin Latinist, used Graecophile arguments to defend the lasting value of Latin learning. He compared Greek and Latin to spring versus piped water or wine versus schnapps. Greek was sweet while Latin was merely fortifying; in Rome, Norden contended, "the light of originality did not glow, which in the truest sense of the word, only one single Volk belonging to the European cultural area, the Greeks, can claim."[51] But the Romans did have something to offer, Norden insisted, namely their patriotism and ethical sense, which his students in 1914 had found inspiring as they expired on the fields of Belgium and northern France. Norden ended by expressing the hope that, fortified by the expressions of patriotic devotion of Horace, Tacitus, and Fichte, Germany would live up to its obligation to "the preservation and lasting renewal of the ancient Siegfried nobility from the era of [Germanic] migrations."[52] If Rome had not the intellect-forming powers of the school of Athens, at least it offered sustenance for the disciplining of the will.

Without doubt, Werner Jaeger played the major role in this classicist counterreformation. One Gymnasium activist emphasized in Gnomon the important part Jaeger's 1925 lecture "Antike und Humanismus" could play in "propaganda work" for classical schooling and described the book of similar pieces in which Jaeger's text had appeared as "our vademecum and our confession of faith [Bekenntnisbuch]."[53] "In philology, dear Jaeger, you are our Führer," an appreciative archaeologist told his hero in 1933.[54] Jaeger assisted in the founding (and editing) of Gnomon and Die Antike, founded and helped direct annual congresses of philologists (the Weimarer Fachtagungen) and the nonprofessional Gesellschaft für antike Kultur, and delivered numerous addresses to humanist associations, in addition to offering regular lecture courses at the University of Berlin. Academic classicists and Gymnasium teachers looked to him for philosophical props and tactical cues; the influence of his revivalist philhellenism reached far and wide, touching even M. I. Finley in England, who remarked in 1968: "Werner Jaeger was for my generation the central (and ambiguous) figure in the latest chapter of the story [the tradition of Humboldtian classical scholarship]."[55] Thus Jaeger's writings deserve special attention: without coming to grips with this new Winckelmann of the word, we will not fully grasp the

[51] Eduard Norden, *Die Bildungswerte der lateinischen Literatur und Sprache auf dem humanistischen Gymnasium* (Berlin, 1920), p. 5; quotation, p. 20.

[52] Ibid., p. 42.

[53] Max Krüger, review of *Das Gymnasium* (ed. Otto Morgenstern) in *Gnomon* 3, no. 10 (October 1927): 601, 600.

[54] Ernst Bickel to Jaeger, 28 July 1933, in Houghton Library, Jaeger Papers, AM5, Box D.

[55] M. I. Finley, review of Arnaldo Momigliano, *Terzo contributo alla storia degli studi classici e del mondo antico*, *History and Theory* 7 (1968): 359.

28. The young
Werner Jaeger in Kiel,
ca. 1915. Theresa
Ried Jaeger.

Weimar philhellenist reaction, its ascetic nuances and its amoral implications, its noble aspirations and its ignoble collapse.

Werner Jaeger: *Paideia* and the Politicization of *Bildung*

Werner Jaeger was born in 1888 in Lobrerich am Niederrhein near the
Dutch and Belgian borders, a heavily Catholic town still graced by much
medieval architecture. A Protestant and an only child, Jaeger was a preco-
cious learner of languages (Latin at nine, Greek at thirteen) and a challenge
to his *Gymnasium* instructors.[56] His enthusiasm for classical studies was
sharpened at the University of Marburg after 1907, where he discovered
neo-Kantian philosophy—and Plato. From Marburg, Jaeger proceeded to
Berlin, the philological Mecca of early twentieth-century Europe, to sit at

[56] William M. Calder, "Werner Jaeger," in *Berlinische Lebensbilder*, vol. 4: *Geisteswissenschaftler*, ed. Michael Erbe (Berlin, 1989), pp. 345–46.

the feet of the "Dioscuri" Wilamowitz and Hermann Diels, and to learn text-critical skills from Johannes Vahlen and Adolf Lassen. It was Wilamowitz who exerted the most influence on the young student. From this mentor, Jaeger acquired his dedication to teaching over research, his passion for the Greek language, and his conviction that classical studies formed a vital, indispensable part of national cultural life.[57] Upon completing his doctorate, Jaeger took a post first at the University of Basel and then in Kiel, and in 1921, having been fourth on the Berlin faculty's list of candidates, received the call to fill Wilamowitz's grudgingly vacated chair.

Becker, it seems, had long been plotting to bring Jaeger to Berlin. Already in mid-1919, the under secretary had pleaded with the Kiel philologist not to accept an offer from Hamburg, in anticipation of a call to the capital.[58] In a 1920 letter to the orientalist Theodor Nöldecke, Becker had reassured his colleague that the Education Ministry's interest in reform did not entail its abandonment of the *Gymnasium* or of classical studies, and had indicated the ministry's keen interest in Jaeger's proposals for classical renewal. "The value of humanistic *Bildung* is clear to us here in the ministry," Becker explained, "and we especially allow Werner Jaeger to advise us; [he] is certainly the Wilamowitz of the future, except that he possesses, in my view, a deeper and more authentic understanding of antiquity."[59] Becker saw in Jaeger a member of his own generation, who had recognized the difficulties of restoring the "relevance" of the Greeks, and he was anxious to have Jaeger on hand to assist him in his reformist projects (Jaeger would ultimately disappoint Becker in this). But, of course, Becker could not make the appointment single-handedly, and Jaeger would not have won his position had he not proven himself a careful and insightful literary scholar.[60] Although I emphasize in this section Jaeger's pedagogical *Lebensphilosophie*, it should not be forgotten that his scholarly work—particularly his work on Aristotle, not on his beloved Plato—is still widely read and respected by classical scholars.[61]

---

[57] Ibid., p. 349.

[58] Becker to Jaeger, 30 June 1919, in GStAPKB, Nachlaß Becker, Mappe 2061.

[59] Becker to Nöldecke, 9 December 1920, ibid., Mappe 3138. After his appointment, Jaeger and Becker became neighbors as well as good friends. For more documentation on Jaeger's appointment, see William M. Calder III, "12 March 1921: The Berlin Appointment," in *Werner Jaeger Reconsidered*, ed. William M. Calder III (Atlanta, 1992), pp. 1–24.

[60] Upon Jaeger's induction into the Prussian Academy of Sciences in 1924, Gustav Roethe claimed that the philosophically oriented philologist represented a link to the tradition of Schleiermacher and Adolf Trendelenburg as well as an unswerving defender of text-critical accuracy. See Roethe's "Erwiderung," in *Sitzungsberichte der Preußischen Akademie der Wissenschaften* (1924): lxxxviii–lxxxix.

[61] See Charles H. Kahn, "Werner Jaeger's Portrayal of Plato," in *Werner Jaeger Reconsidered*, p. 69.

In previous chapters, I have underscored the importance of generational cohorts and their defining historical experiences; nowhere are these so significant as in the Weimar period. Although Jaeger did not suffer the torments of the trenches (he was disqualified from military service on medical grounds),[62] he took up the problem of "relevance" from the standpoint of a generation whose links to the past had been destroyed. After four years at the front, the return to specialized philology had become problematical even for dedicated younger scholars. In 1921, the philologist Paul Friedländer told his mentor Wilamowitz that he simply could not take up text editing with the same enthusiasm he had felt in 1914. "I haven't enough strength, my life is just too short, for me to edit things of peripheral importance just for the sake of editing," Friedländer wrote.[63] Jaeger, to his credit, understood that German cultural institutions had to respond to this "crisis of values"; already in 1914, upon assuming Nietzsche's former chair at the University of Basel, Jaeger had argued for the freeing of philology from the tyrannical thrall of historicism, which had been sapping its vitality since about 1850.[64] Jaeger's so-called "Third Humanism"—a term that he used only twice but which was frequently applied to his philosophy by contemporaries[65]—was a deeply felt attempt at the overall reinvigoration of German cultural life, not just a slogan devised to cloak philological self-protection (though it certainly did serve that purpose as well). But his concessions to Lebensphilosophie—in general an antihistoricist and frequently antiacademic stream of thought—were made at a considerable cost, both to himself and to German classical scholarship. His Third Humanism recapitulated the ascetic urges, philological proclivities, and etatist convictions of the founders of neohumanism, this time, however, as reaction rather than peaceful revolution.

In July 1924, Jaeger, Rodenwaldt, and Hans Lietzmann met in the offices of the publisher Walter de Gruyter to discuss the founding of a journal to complement the newly established Gesellschaft für antike Kultur. This society, whose charter members included Johannes Popitz (under secretary in the Finance Ministry), the leading Center politician (and chancellor, 1930–

[62] Calder, "12 March 1921," p. 4.

[63] Friedländer quoted in William Musgrave Calder, "The Credo of a New Generation: Paul Friedländer to Ulrich von Wilamowitz-Moellendorff," Antike und Abendland 26 (1980): 97.

[64] Werner Jaeger, "Philologie und Historie," (1914) in Humanistische Reden und Vorträge, pp. 1–16.

[65] The term was actually coined by Eduard Spranger in his 1921 lecture Der gegenwärtige Stand der Geisteswissenschaften und die Schule (Leipzig, 1925), p. 7, and was meant to announce a rebirth of classical studies in the 1920s, comparable (he hoped) to the Italian Renaissance and the German neohumanist era. Jaeger himself used the term only in his 1933 essay for Volk im Werden (see below, no. 82) and in the 1934 edition of Paideia; thereafter, he insisted that it did not apply at all to his work.

32) Heinrich Brüning, Emil von Stauß, director of the Deutsche Bank, a Krupp, and a retired major general,[66] sought to cultivate humanistic learning beyond the circle of specialists and also, clearly, to rally political support and raise money for the pursuit of classical scholarship. The mission of *Die Antike*, declared Jaeger the following year in the preface to the first issue, "is to make the scholarly knowledge of ancient culture fruitful for the intellectual life of the present and to secure for [this knowledge] a fitting place in German *Bildung*."[67] Jaeger suggested that works of art (masterpieces) be used to speak directly to the reader. Literary works would appear too—but not in translation. Most of all, he recommended a kind of intellectual history, one that accentuated great personalities and emphasized the unique achievements of Greece and Rome but did not shrink from historical research, an approach he believed essential were antiquity to yield new "life-norms."[68] *Die Antike* might, then, rejoin *Wissenschaft* to *Bildung*, historical research to the generation of values, and modern "rootless" Germans to the serene and morally superior Greeks; a new German Golden Age, a Third Humanism, might commence in the shadow of military defeat and political chaos. If it seems not to have made many converts amongst the school reformers, *Die Antike* quickly became the preferred venue for established scholars to express their solidarity with Jaeger's program and to lecture a wider readership on the indispensability of neoclassical *Bildung*.

The key to Jaeger's classicist revival lay in his attempt to retrieve the conception of *Kultur* from its increasingly common "anthropological" definition, and his use of Diltheyan hermeneutics to defend the project of reviving the Greeks and to limit the content of this revival to European—and especially Greek—literature. A number of mainstream classicists of the previous generation, including Eduard Meyer and Wilamowitz himself, had moved toward an anthropological culture concept as they moved away from the isolated, aestheticized conception of "classical" Greece. But for Jaeger, "culture" was "not the objective, unconscious stylistic unity that infuses the creations of a people, including those at primitive stages of development, but rather the conscious system of creative intellects which are unified in the pursuit of common goals in the highest of all cultural endeavors: the education of man."[69] The Greek conception of culture formed the kernel of European history, he contended; the great Greek ideal around which each nation formed itself was the structural principle underlying European unity

---

[66] See Donald O. White, "Werner Jaeger's 'Third Humanism' and the Crisis of Conservative Cultural Politics in Weimar Germany," in Calder, *Werner Jaeger Reconsidered*, p. 282, n. 44.

[67] Jaeger, "Einführung," *Die Antike* 1 (1925): 2; a report of the meeting (2 July 1924) can be found in DAI, Nachlaß Rodenwaldt, Kasten 7.

[68] Jaeger, "Einführung," pp. 3–4.

[69] Jaeger, *Humanismus und Jugendbildung* (Berlin, 1921), p. 9.

(and the exclusion of Indians, Egyptians, and "orientals").[70] Europe, in fact, was the product of a continuous series of renaissances; if his contemporaries wished to recover their lost faith in "the autarky of our own European culture" and root out materialistic Americanization and mystical envy of the Orient, they needed only to recall the continent's unique indebtedness to Greek *Bildung*.[71]

Furthermore, for Jaeger, Europeans could really only understand those who shared this conscious cultural ideal. The philologist distinguished an "anthropological" method—which could be used to study the remotest of peoples and races—from real history, "which has as its precondition an active and fateful intellectual solidarity still alive in us, be it with one's own people or among a closely related group of peoples. Only this kind of history allows understanding [Verstehen] from within, a truly creative contact with the other."[72] Proper understanding also required the very sorts of linguistic competence Jaeger advocated as proper elementary pedagogy: only by experiencing the linguistically conceived other world of the Greeks, Jaeger wrote in 1925, could one emerge as a full self—or, historically, as a true nation.[73] Thus the imposition of hermeneutical restrictions allowed Jaeger to justify European self-consideration and philological training as the only means to true cultivation.

Jaeger's preface to the first issue of *Die Antike* underlined the importance of art as a direct medium for conveying classical ideas and explicitly included *Realien* in its list of proper objects for norm-inspiring *Geistesgeschichte*. Yet Jaeger, in the years after 1925, grew increasingly less confident that material culture could be an appropriate object of humanist concern. If Wilamowitz, as Jaeger argued in his eulogy for his great teacher, "studied material remains to augment the written [remains] on papyrus, parchment, and stone,"[74] Jaeger himself in his student days apparently made no attempt to attend lectures on archaeology or ancient history and throughout his life showed little interest in *Realien*: he ventured onto Greek soil for the first time long after he had been called to fill Wilamowitz's chair in Berlin—and then primarily to receive an honorary degree.[75] Jaeger's emphasis on culture as a *conscious* process of communal self-formation could not embrace the independent testimony of objects, for objects had not been

[70] See Jaeger, "Platos Stellung im Aufbau der griechischen Bildung" (1927), in *Humanistische Reden und Vorträge*, p. 129.

[71] Jaeger, "Antike und Humanismus," pp. 103–4, 111–16.

[72] Jaeger, *Paideia*, 1:4–5.

[73] Werner Jaeger, "Die Antike im wissenschaftlichen Austausch der Nationen," *Die Antike* 6 (1930): 85–92.

[74] Jaeger, "Ulrich von Wilamowitz-Moellendorff" (1932), in *Humanistische Reden und Vorträge*, p. 218.

[75] See Calder, "Werner Jaeger," p. 350.

consciously passed down through the generations, they did not possess the sort of past-ness suited to humanist revival. The ambiguity and fragmentary nature of their testimony simply could not conjure up an organic whole, as could literature, which, Jaeger contended, "represents a historical-intellectual unity, an organically unfolded *Bildungswelt*, complete in itself, a gradual development of human values."[76]

In addition, the study of art, Jaeger argued, had fallen prey to the great nineteenth-century surge of specialized historical research; after having seen the "moving" sculptures of the Pergamum Altar and experienced the "preclassical, harsh severity" of the Olympia pediments, even the admirers of "noble simplicity and serene grandeur" began to sense the limitations of traditional aesthetic ideals.[77] Though classical art, Jaeger averred, would continue "to translate the *Geist* of antiquity into the dimension of the visible," Jaeger doubted that his contemporaries, their perceptions contorted by modern and "exotic" art, still possessed the proper semantic sensitivity to "read" this translation correctly.[78] "The classical and its sublime harmony," Jaeger continued,

> is no longer obviously apparent, or is almost banal. It has again become a problem. One cannot emphasize enough in this regard the increasing familiarity of our age with the form-worlds of exotic and pre-Greek peoples, for this has made us truly conscious, for the first time, of the uniqueness of the phenomenon of Greek form. But the moment when the true artistic will of our age shall, from its innermost needs, return to the Greeks is, if I see rightly, apart from a few exceptions, not yet in sight. As I said before: this time the aesthetic will not be the point of departure for our return to antiquity. . . . An aesthetic sensorium in which all may be groped with sensitive fingers—Chinese, Indian, Egyptian—is already too specialized, too divorced from the intellectual totality of the human essence, to achieve the embracive vantage point appropriate to the great ethical and religious orientation of Greek art. A modern Winckelmann would not seek in art, in the *morphē*, the way to the Hellenic, but find his point of departure in the spiritual production in which this indivisible unity of all the powers of *Geist* achieves surely a less universally sensible, but an explicit expression: in literature, in the Logos.[79]

Thus, certainty of the ancient world's unity and ideality would have to be secured in the realm of the word; the aesthetic realm had become too varied, too colorful, too sensuous for a new Winckelmann to ground a spiritual renaissance in its forms.

---

[76] Jaeger, "Die geistige Gegenwart der Antike," (1929) in *Humanistische Reden und Vorträge*, p. 160.

[77] Ibid., p. 167.

[78] Ibid., p. 173.

[79] Ibid., p. 174.

In abandoning the cluttered material sphere, Jaeger shifted the defense of the classics from an aesthetic to an ethical vantage point, from a historicist orientation to a philosophical one. Particularly in essays of the later Wiemer era, Jaeger expressed a growing desire to overturn Humboldt's overly individualistic concept of *Bildung*; he now looked to conservative moral philosophy for a means to overcome culteral fragmentation. This shift suited Jaeger's interests and talents, but it was also a product of his attempt to place neohumanism above and beyond the reach of party politics. In a 1932 lecture titled "Staat und Kultur" (and subsequently published in *Die Antike*), Jaeger argued that the liberal era of cultural hyperindividualism and hostility to the Bismarckian *Machtstaat* (state built on power) was a thing of the past. Now, as in the era of Plato—which followed a similar age of atomization— culture had regained consciousness of its social functions, but German intellectuals all too often turned the new social orientation into party politics, rather than, like the Greeks, into philosophical ethics. For Jaeger, the real task of the modern intellectual was to reinforce and propagate the Platonic "idea of the state, which is independent from changes in human opinions and endeavors and from the fate of the state at any given time."[80] He did not attack the Weimar Republic, although he did express concern about "the acute danger of the eradication of the best [minds]'" as a result of Weimar's attempts to democratize education and cultural affairs, and he warned his readers explicitly against the instrumentalizing of culture for national ends.[81] In his desire to leave behind the noisy tumult of the marketplace and Reichstag for the calm serenity of the Platonic ideal state, however, Jaeger had failed to recognize the already existing interdependence of the cultural and political spheres. By recommending indifference to "the fate of the state at any given time," Jaeger was offering his colleagues both a false assurance of scholarship's autonomy and an idealism unto quietism.

Jaeger's most compromising essay, "Die Erziehung des politischen Menschen und die Antike" ("Antiquity and the Education of Political Man"), appeared in the Nazi pedagogical journal *Volk im Werden* (*A Folk in the Making*) in mid-1933. Summarizing the main points of a conversation between the Nazi official Bernhard Rust (appointed Reich minister of education in 1934), Jaeger, and Emil Kroymann (Director of the Berlin Steglitz *Gymnasium* and president of the Deutscher Altphilologenverband), the essay represents a rather pathetic attempt to prove the relevance of the *Gymnasium* to the goals of the Third Reich. Like the ten theses on the future of *Gymnasium* education approved by the Verband in September 1933, this short piece turned its back on the pan-European inheritance of Greek culture Jaeger had so assiduously expounded in the Weimar-era essays. In-

---

[80] Werner Jaeger, "Staat und Kultur," in *Die Antike* 8 (1932): 71–89.
[81] Ibid., pp. 88–89.

stead, Jaeger stressed here the importance of the encounter with antiquity for the formation of Germany's "spiritual constitution," which, like "the basic features of a national race [*Volksrasse*]," remained constant over time.[82] The author underscored the apoliticalness of the Weimar poets and of German literature in general as a means of defending the retention of the classical curriculum. Greek literature provided "a gallery of incomparable monuments to heroic-political mankind," Jaeger averred; from its coffers, numerous lessons on the virtues of hard work, strong leadership, and civil obedience could be drawn. Here scholarship could assist, by abandoning its life-destroying historicism and positivism and returning again to its Platonic form, in which the setting of values and teaching of ethics played an essential role.[83] Clearly Jaeger also hoped to make use of this Nazification for his own philosophical-pedagogical ends, for the piece concluded with an attack on the "leveling and materializing of true humanistic training [*Zucht*] and energy [*Kraft*]" instituted in the school reform program of 1924. Instead of the "false idol of culture studies [*Kulturkunde*]," in Jaeger's conception, "the indispensable, fundamental learning of both ancient languages, because it strives toward general education in its true, ancient sense, would be given back its fixed and secure foundation in the building of national education."[84] To all appearances, Jaeger was offering the state a compromise: political *Gleichschaltung* in exchange for the preservation of philologically based philhellenism.

A cursory glance at the theses passed by the Altphilologenverband in September suffices to indicate Jaeger's prominent role in their composition.[85] As in his essays of the late 1920s, the state is described as the source of ethical norms; the theses add explicit denunciations of "merely individualistic self-cultivation" (thesis 7). Thesis 5 defends the centrality of the Greeks, "who stand at the threshold of European history and who, by means of their fundamental conception of human self-cultivation [*Menschenbildung*], have established the highest aim of educational efforts for all time." The following paragraph extends the argument for Greece's significance by linking Germany's "fateful encounter with Greekdom" during the *Goethezeit* to the nation's liberation from the "predominantly Roman-influenced culture of the age of Enlightenment"; the Greeks, the philologists' declaration asserts, had played an instrumental role in the Germans'

---

[82] Jaeger, "Die Erziehung des politischen Menschen und die Antike," *Volk im Werden* 1, no. 3 (1933): 43.

[83] Ibid., p. 44.

[84] Ibid., p. 49.

[85] The theses were later revised by Rust. Both versions have been reprinted by Andreas Fritsch in "Die altsprachlichen Fächer im nationalsozialistischen Schulsystem," in *Schule und Unterricht im Dritten Reich*, ed. Reinhard Dithmar (Neuwied, 1989), pp. 155–59.

narrow escape from pan-European petrifaction (thesis 6). Finally, in response to an old accusation, the organization insisted that the arduous effort required to learn Latin and Greek would not imperil national self-consciousness, but rather strengthen it (thesis 10). If these compromising tenets were meant to establish the association's autonomy, they failed, for by March 1935, the Altphilologenverband had been absorbed into the Nationalsozialistisches Lehrerbund.[86] The theses stand, however, as profound testimony to the initial adaptability of Jaegerian pedagogy to the National Socialist world view.

Like Jaeger's 1933 essay, the first volume of *Paideia*, published in 1934, announced the coming of a third, political humanism. The culmination of the philologist's revivalist efforts of the 1920s, Jaeger's book sought to establish a new basis for the appreciation of the Greeks by crediting the latter with the invention of a now peculiarly community-oriented form of *Bildung*. Jaeger identified the origins of the Western educational ideal in the earliest known Greek portrayal of the educational process; Homer's narrative of the coming of age of Telemachus, the son of Odysseus, in the *Odyssey*. Here, the philologist emphasized the purely Greek origin and timeless qualities of what he took to be a single concept; Jaeger's use of the term *Paideia* (in Greek, literally: education) consolidated into a single mass, as Karl Reinhardt later commented, the following subconcepts: "The Greek educational ideal, the process of character formation [Formung], *Bildung*, the education of youth, humanity, dedication to the polis, tradition, civility [*Gesittung*], and Kultur."[87] Most important, of course, was Jaeger's elision of *Paideia* and *Bildung*; by this means, classical philology was granted special access to the history of the European (or better, German) mind—and, hopefully, would receive new formative power in modern cultural affairs. *Paideia* was intended to establish precisely this sort of relegitimizing legacy, to restore vitality to an elitist school system and outdated scholarly habitus by creating a hypothetical history of the European mind based on the ascetic, neohumanist philosophy of *Bildung*. In collapsing the distinctions between Greek and German educational ideals, *Paideia* subtly claimed a continuity between Homer and Humboldt (and Plato and Werner Jaeger) which made studying or teaching the rest of human history superfluous.

In fact, *Paideia* marked Jaeger's final abandonment of the historicism of his mentor Wilamowitz. The advent of National Socialism, Jaeger suggested in the introduction to the book, made it impossible for classical studies to defend itself with the weak weapons provided by historical research. Ab-

---

[86] Ibid., p. 141.

[87] Karl Reinhardt, "Die klassische Philologie und das Klassische," (1941), in idem., *Vermächtnis der Antike: Gesammelte Essays zur Philosophie und Geschichtsschreibung* (Göttingen, 1960), p. 349.

sorption in historical questions had prevented nineteenth- and early twentieth-century scholars from recognizing the extent to which specialized studies had undermined the ideality of the Greeks:

> Antiquity came to be simply another—if still a favorite—fragment of history, whose more immediate significance one was reluctant to treat. . . . The scholarly community made no attempt to reestablish the ideal, whose classicizing historical conceptions had been destroyed by research. But at the present time, when our whole culture, shaken by an enormous, unique historical experience, has begun to examine its foundations anew, *Altertumsforschung* must once again assess the educational value of the ancient world as its own final and fateful question.[88]

If the study of the classics were to retain anything of its previous social status, it would have to reestablish its role as provider of cultural norms. The only means to preserve the tradition, for Jaeger, was to abandon its modern, historicist modesty and to recreate for itself a corpus of timeless ideals and "permanent" values.[89]

As the Hamburg philologist Bruno Snell indicated in an insightful review, Jaeger had applied an anachronistic definition of his key term to the works of Homer, Hesiod, and others, its Greek definition obscured in order to compose an ancient equivalent to *Bildung*. Snell noted that Jaeger's literary examples failed to articulate in any strict sense this supposedly ubiquitous concept of man as the object and end of education; furthermore, the reviewer suggested, Plato himself might not fully conform to Jaeger's view.[90] But for Snell, this scholarly laxity simply obscured a more serious failing: the vacuousness of Jaeger's new "political" humanism. In praising the Greek as political man, Jaeger had refused to take a stand with respect to current ethical and political questions, Snell lamented; even Winckelmann, albeit in the aesthetic sphere, had not invoked the Greeks without indicating against whom their example should be raised. In addition, in order to preserve the normative function of Greek culture, Jaeger had ignored the concrete historical conditions that had produced the actual forms of Greek political life. Jaeger's empty, but still exemplary, Hellenism, then, was destined to political instrumentalization on the one hand, and scholarly petrifaction on the other, while for Snell, the better part of philological valor lay in retreat from philosophical defenses of classical normativity.[91]

But Snell remained in Germany throughout the Nazi years, as did an-

---

[88] Jaeger, *Paideia* 1:19–20.

[89] See Jaeger's later reflections on this problem in his "Introduction to 'Scripta Minora': 'An Intellectual Autobiography,'" in *Five Essays*, trans. Adele M. Fiske (Montreal, 1966), p. 41.

[90] See Bruno Snell, review of Jaeger, *Paideia*, in *Göttingische Gelehrte Anzeigen* 197, no. 9 (September 1935): 332–33.

[91] Ibid., p. 353.

other critic of Jaeger's book, Karl Reinhardt.[92] In 1934, Jaeger gave the Sather Lectures at Berkeley, and in 1936, he resigned the most prestigious chair in Germany and took a position at the University of Chicago.[93] It is possible that his departure was accelerated by the fact that his second wife, Ruth, was Jewish, but it is also probable that some aspects of the philologist's reclassicizing project might have seemed threatening to the new regime, and that Jaeger had recognized earlier than many the incompatibility of Nazism and *paideia*.

If elitist, Jaeger's work was not particularly racist—and certainly less so than that of many of his contemporaries. The attempt to establish "permanent" values by someone outside the regime, and particularly someone so imbued with the *Gymnasium* culture .of the hated academic elite, also cannot have been entirely pleasing to the Nazi leadership; "permanence" could easily become a source of resistance. In fact, proponents of the new regime continued to fear Jaegerian humanism's reentrenchment late into the Nazi period. In 1942, with the blessing of the Nationalsozialistischer Dozentenbund (Nazi Lecturers' Union), Göttingen professor Hans Drexler published a long diatribe against the liberal, ahistorical, and anti-*völkisch* Third Humanism. Echoing Spengler and Rosenberg, Drexler complained that Jaeger had foresworn his nation's autonomy and unique mission by attempting to make Germans mere epigones of the incomparable Greeks.[94] Like many another conservative scholar, Werner Jaeger discovered that the Nazi regime had its own plans for "cultural renewal," but he—unlike, for example, Martin Heidegger—was either foresightful or fortunate enough to escape the evils and embarrassments of internal exile.

Paideia saved—in the short run—German philhellenism less by politicizing classical studies than by dehistoricizing the Greeks. Jaeger's attempt to make classical values "relevant" to an antihistorical generation ultimately required him to throw overboard the perceptual experience and detailed knowledge gained by the expansion and professionalization of classical studies in the nineteenth and early twentieth centuries. It was perhaps this dematerializing impulse that Frau von Wilamowitz decried in asking a brilliant young scholar who had never been to Greece (possibly Jaeger himself): "Do you really want to turn the clock back?"[95] The problem was not that Jaeger failed to recognize the research imperative implicit in the self-conception of modern scholarship, or, on the other hand, the vanishing

---

[92] Jaeger's Third Humanism had already been denounced in mid-1933 by Nazi pedagogical philosopher Ernst Krieck. White, "Jaeger's 'Third Humanism,'" pp. 286–87.

[93] See Calder, "Werner Jaeger," pp. 356–58.

[94] Hans Drexler, *Der Dritte Humanismus: Ein kritischer Epilog*, Auf dem Wege zum nationalpolitischen Gymnasium, vol. 10 (Frankfurt, 1942), p. 25.

[95] "Wollen Sie eigentlich alles rückgängig machen?" Quoted in Solmsen, "Wilamowitz," p. 105.

significance of Greek culture for modern life; as early as 1919, Jaeger had described the progressive "dematerialization and spiritualization of our Faustian courtship of Helen, the Greek bride."[96] But his response to this dematerialization of the German-Greek courtship had been the refurbishing of spiritual ties between two no longer existent nations, the idealized Greece of the neohumanist generation and the liberal-aristocratic world of nineteenth-century Germany. Thus the greatest failing of this devoutly anti-modern pedagogy was its inability to confront nationalist and racialist classical studies with a credible, embracive cultural history; in insisting upon the *Ur*-originality of the Greeks in all things and relinquishing the task of coming to grips with a century's worth of prehistorical and non-Greek artifacts, Jaeger and his followers simply allowed themselves to become straw men—or uncomprehending internal émigrés like Thomas Mann's Serenus Zeitblom—under the reign of the antihumanist advocates of Aryan supremacy.

Weimar Archaeology: *Winckelmann als Erzieher*

Like philologists and ancient historians, the archaeologists of the 1920s found themselves caught between the desire to press on with their specialized, nonaestheticizing, scholarship, and the fear that classical *Bildung* and Graecophile aesthetics might be destroyed if not immediately shored up by revitalization. Archaeologists like Rodenwaldt recognized that decades of grand-scale excavation had transformed their discipline, reducing the importance of works of art as they strove to reconstruct cultural wholes. "The earliest excavators," the DAI director mused in 1930,

> had as their goal the rediscovery of ancient works of art. The more the task of archaeology and its sister sciences became the achievement of an overall picture of past cultures, the more universal its area of study became. If the history of art will always stand at the center of archaeological scholarship, its task, to make history from the preserved traces of the past, can only be achieved if [archaeology] investigates the entire realm of human activity: a primitive hut and a water pipe are just as much objects of excavation as a temple or a prince's castle.[97]

And yet, Rodenwaldt and other classical archaeologists themselves exhibited profound ambivalence at the nonaestheticizing, anthropological prospects opened by their own science. Hoping, like their philologist colleagues, to preserve the foundations of classical *Bildung*, they were drawn to Jaeger's

[96] Jaeger, "Humanismus als Tradition," p. 20.

[97] Gerhart Rodenwaldt, "Einführung," in *Neue deutsche Ausgrabungen*, ed. idem (Münster, 1930), pp. 8–9.

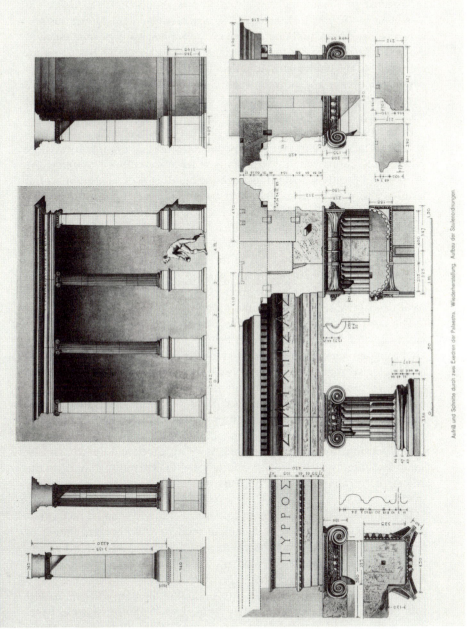

29. Page from the DAI's publication on the Pergamum gymnasium. In contrast to
the sketched layouts in illustration 4, here the exact measurements of
architectural elements are given.

reclassicizing program; but they also did not wish to abandon their work in Mesopotamia, Egypt, Turkestan, and Roman-German prehistory. It was perhaps the fact that penury and diplomatic powerlessness prevented much in the way of new grand-scale excavations that led archaeologists to return more fully to the philhellenist fold than did the historians. In archaeology, a new emphasis on art and on visuality, or *Anschauung*, paralleled Jaeger's stress on the exemplary beauty of Greek literary and philosophical masterpieces.

By the 1920s, archaeological positivism had clearly gone out of fashion—at least in the expanding realm of popular treatises and museum catalogs. Where excavations were undertaken, site reports continued to follow the Dörpfeldian-positivist pattern, delineating building materials, architectural layouts, and pottery styles. But with the curtailment of opportunities for excavation abroad after 1918, DAI archaeologists began to prepare interpretive treatments of their prewar finds that partook of a rather different scholarly—and social—ethos. No longer did observation of formal details suffice to describe cultural entities or to illuminate the historical background of the single artifact. In the pages of *Gnomon* and other classicist journals, calls came for popular, interpretive art histories that ventured beyond descriptive style histories into discussions of essence and meaning.[98]

The most striking evidence of this altered approach was offered by the multivolume *Propyläen-Kunstgeschichte*, an art-history series published by the Propyläen-Verlag, which appeared for the first time after the world war. Archaeologists wrote the text for most sections in the volumes that treated art before medieval times and undoubtedly selected the illustrations—which formed the bulk of the books' pages—to complement their essays. Intended for a popular but prosperous audience, the leatherbound series commenced with a volume on ethnographic and prehistorical art and included introductions to Egyptian and Assyrian, Greek and Roman, and Islamic art, offering archaeologists a long-sought opportunity to impress the *Bildungsbürgertum* with the virtuosity and vitality of the science of the spade.

The authors of these sumptuous tomes had clearly composed their interpretations under the heavy influence of modern art's experimentation in perspective; the conversion of style-historical thinking into a kind of history of national *mentalités* by modern art historians—most notably Alois Riegl, Wilhelm Wörringer, and Heinrich Wölfflin—also helped them to formulate their essentialist arguments. Several of the non- and preclassical volumes explicitly described changes in modern "Sehform" (forms of seeing) that revealed classical and Renaissance perspectival realism to be

[98] See, e.g., B. Schweitzer, review of Arnold von Salis, *Kunst des Altertums*, in *Gnomon* 2, no. 3 (March 1926): 129–36.

merely one way of seeing and rendering nature. Heinrich Schäfer, director of the Berlin Egyptian Museum, argued that Greek and Renaissance artists rendered the world as it might be seen in a single glance (*sehbildmäßig*) while Egyptian and all other non–Greek-influenced artists, as well as children, untutored adults, and *Naturvölker*, operated instead on the basis of direct, total conceptualization (*geradansichtig-vorstellig*). Schäfer decried the long-held belief that nonperspectival art was simply inept, bad art—a myth perpetuated by the suffusion of the Western visual world with diagonal vistas and foreshortened forms. Contrasting Greek "naturalism" as *learned* behavior to the instinctive qualities of immediate conceptualization, Schäfer debunked the long-held belief in the naïveté and universality of the Hellenic eye.[99]

If other *Propyläen* authors also described the fundamental dissimilarities between Western and oriental *Sehformen*, Rodenwaldt made language the key to comprehending each of these internally coherent, cultural units. In this, Rodenwaldt's *Die Kunst der Antike: Hellas und Rom* differed in profound ways from Furtwängler's *Meisterwerke*, ignoring, for the most part, the issues of authorship, authenticity, and formal evolution so dear to the fin de siècle scholar's heart. But Rodenwaldt's aesthetic predilections, ultimately, did not differ significantly from those of Furtwängler,[100] and his essentialist intellectual history allowed him to return to another favorite claim of nineteenth-century archaeologists: the autonomy and originality of the Greeks, from the Geometric age into the Hellenistic period.[101]

Returning to these prepositivist pursuits brought archaeologists like Rodenwaldt closer to philological-philosophical interests than the discipline had been since the death of August Böckh in 1869. In this atmosphere, Jaeger's Third Humanism exerted strong influence on archaeological–art historical writing, particularly in publications intended for popular audiences. Privately, archaeologists admitted that Jaeger's reclassicizing quest had displaced the historicizing tendencies of the late nineteenth century (which had been spurred, in large part, by the maturing of their discipline). In a letter of late 1929, for example, Rodenwaldt rebuked Martin Schede, the director of the newly formed DAI branch in Constantinople, for his insis-

[99] See Schäfer, "Einleitung," in idem and Walter Andrae, *Die Kunst des Alten Orients*, Propyläen-Kunstgeschichte, vol. 2 (Berlin, 1925), pp. 11–19.

[100] Rodenwaldt, like Winckelmann, believed Greek art to be the measure of all other forms, and, as usual, power, will, and politics dominated his nonaestheticizing interpretation of the evolution of Roman forms. Adolf Borbein, however, perhaps goes too far in asserting that Roman art awakened Rodenwaldt's passion only insofar as it recapitulated Greek forms. See Rodenwaldt's "Antrittsrede," *Sitzungsberichte der preußischen Akademie der Wissenschaften* (1933): cix; Adolf H. Borbein, "Gerhart Rodenwaldts Bild der römischen Kunst," in *L'Impero romano fra storia generale e storia locale*, ed. E. Gabba and K. Christ (Como, 1991), p. 199.

[101] Gerhart Rodenwaldt, *Die Kunst der Antike: Hellas und Rom*, Propyläen Kunstgeschichte, vol. 3, 4th ed. (Berlin, 1927), p. 56.

tence on the ecumenical nature of modern classical studies. Addressing
Schede, who had spent most of the 1920s in Asia Minor, Rodenwaldt emphasized Jaeger's role in the field's retreat from positivist historicism:

> When you write that scholarship today is dominated by the tendency to recog-
> nize no preference for classical epochs, this really does not correspond to the
> facts. For the whole movement of the younger generation in *Alter-
> tumswissenschaft*, under Jaeger's leadership—the founding of *Die Antike*, the
> Weimar Fachtagung, etc.—is dictated by the conviction of the absolute superi-
> ority of classical epochs over any other period of history. Wilamowitz ex-
> pressed the same ideas at the institute's [centenary] celebration in putting him-
> self on the side of newer *Altertumswissenschaft* against [his own] previous
> remarks.[102]

Jaeger's intellectual leadership and organizational skills, the DAI director
averred, had galvanized an inspiring generational counterreaction that had
enticed even Wilamowitz to cast aside his historicist convictions.

Schede's response indicated that he, too, sided with this younger generation, but could not condone their approach to what Rodenwaldt had termed
"the problem of the classical." "In my opinion and experience" wrote the
excavator, "one can only really establish the legitimacy of the supremacy of
classical cultural eras—which I too fully recognize in my heart—when one
is obliged to give the other [eras] formal equality from the beginning. I
hope that our [Constantinople] institute will provide, over the course of
time, proof of the correctness of such tactics."[103] In return, Rodenwaldt
assured his deputy that he, too, preferred a policy of outward organizational
neutrality despite his inner devotion to high classicism.

> As a representative of *Altertumswissenschaft*, of course I believe it right to es-
> pouse the humanistic superiority of these fields, while I am likewise convinced
> that the institute as such must support all fields equally. . . . An institute like
> ours, in my opinion as in yours, must be of assistance to all fields and not act as
> a missionary outpost for a worldview. The latter is much more a matter for
> individuals and for scholarly associations. In any case, that the institute sup-
> ports all these efforts seems right to me. Therefore I have personally supported
> all the Weimar gatherings and set the journal *Die Antike* in motion, but I have
> intentionally not allowed these [projects] to establish organizational ties to the
> institute.[104]

If the Hyperborean humanistic ideal had become a "problem," owing to
specialization and archaeological expansion, the DAI director remarked in

[102] Rodenwaldt to Schede, 2 December 1929, in BSB, Nachlaß Rodenwaldt, Mappe 595.
[103] Schede to Rodenwaldt, 9 December 1929, ibid., Mappe 255.
[104] Rodenwaldt to Schede, 21 December 1929, ibid., Mappe 595.

his 1929 centenary history of the institute, the rearticulation of humanism and classicism could not be a task for a purely scholarly institute; instead, great "personalities" were needed to impress their élan on the archaeology of the future.[105]

Though Rodenwaldt officially maintained the institute's neutrality toward this reclassicizing impulse—fearing he would offend prehistorians of Germany beyond the *limes* and orientalists—privately he agreed with Ludwig Curtius that Jaeger represented "our most valuable possession." "It would be terrible," Curtius added in a letter to the DAI director, "if that—pardon me—horrid Berlin wears [Jaeger] out. Everything should be done to help him."[106] "What you say about Jaeger," Rodenwaldt responded, "is precisely my view and indeed that of most of his fellow specialists. We must preserve his energies as much as possible, though on the other hand, it is a particular bit of luck that in addition to his scholarly work he champions general ideas, which will necessarily involve him in organizational tasks and multiple personal relationships."[107] Wiegand, too, applauded the founding of *Die Antike* and of scholarly associations dedicated to promoting (and patronizing) classical studies, whose united strength he hoped to employ to reverse the curriculum reforms of 1924.[108] Still conscious of its debts—historical and historiographical—to philology, archaeology could not fail to side with the classicists, despite their increasing dissociation of material culture and historical *Realien* from their pedagogical programs. Devotion to the Greeks and hostility to school reform laid the basis for the consolidation of a new, nostalgic *Altertumswissenschaft*, unified in reaction to the threatened dissolution of the classical ideal.

But there was more than merely interest-group politics behind the widespread rejection of historicist positivism by Weimar-era archaeologists. Karl Schefold has recently traced three trends of the 1920s in archaeology to the impact of Stefan George's poetry: (1) careful study of preclassical and postclassical monuments; (2) emphasis on creative genius in classical art; (3) recognition of the religious content of great art. Although all three of these tendencies actually had origins closer to home—in the later nineteenth-century work of Schliemann, Conze, Furtwängler, and Usener—Schefold convincingly demonstrates manifold linkages between Weimar-era archaeologists and the George circle, and he is surely correct in claiming that George had a greater impact on classical studies than on any other field of

---

[105] Rodenwaldt, *Archäologisches Institut des Deutschen Reiches, 1829–1929* (Berlin, 1929), p. 51.

[106] Curtius to Rodenwaldt, 10 January 1926, BSB, Nachlaß Rodenwaldt, Mappe 53.

[107] Rodenwaldt to Curtius, 28 January 1926, ibid., Mappe 393.

[108] See Theodor Wiegand, "Festrede zum 85. Jahrestag der Archäologischen Gesellschaft" (1925), pp. 2–3, in DAI, Nachlaß Wiegand, Kasten 10, Mappe 24.

art history.[109] In George, many younger classicists found an antidote to the uninspiring historicism of Wilamowitz, as well as a nonspecialist with whom they could share their devotion to Greek beauty, their contempt for the unlettered masses, and their longing for German cultural regeneration.

One signal indication of the Weimar archaeologists' sympathy for Georgean-Jaegerian classicizing revival can be found in their frequent return to Winckelmann for inspiration if not for detailed information. Of course, since the instigation of *Winckelmannstag* in 1831, the honorary disciplinary ancestor had been continually reconjured to mark the profession's progress or—as in the case of Furtwängler—to condemn its misdirection. In the 1920s, however, Winckelmann took on a new allure for embattled classicists: his passion, will, youthful opposition to decadent tastes, and courage in his convictions appealed to those attacked for their obsolescence, skepticism, and will-numbing bookishness. To cite just two examples, in a lecture presented in 1926, Ludwig Curtius praised Winckelmann's contribution to moral philosophy, claiming for the shoemaker's son the invention of the conception of life-enhancing education prior to Rousseau. Behind Winckelmann's poetic-prophetic words, Curtius announced, "there flamed a new passion, that sought not only knowledge, but life, not just scholarliness but the freedom of a new humanity."[110] Ernst Buschor, first secretary at the Athens DAI office between 1921 and 1929, emphasized the revolutionary qualities of Winckelmann and his contemporaries in their attempts to use the revival of Greece to regenerate mankind. Unlike other disciplines, Buschor claimed in 1932, "classical archaeology is not only a historical discipline, it can participate in a still greater task: the conquest of history itself."[111] To revive Winckelmann now was not to pander to dilettantism but to resurrect passion, value, and cultural unity in the midst of specialized scholarship's incremental gains, aesthetic agnosticism, and pedagogical fragmentation. *Winckelmann als Erzieher* was the classical archaeologists' best defense against attacks on the field's "irrelevance."

Naturally, in this context, Greek sculpture received new, eroticized and politicized, attention. Oddly, the most disfiguring war of all time had contributed to the cult of the healthy body, popularized by the "life reform" movement of the previous decades; the George circle and the youth movement, both hedged around with homoerotic mannerisms and yearnings, devoted considerable attention to the beauty of the nude Greek body. Sculptors celebrating sports and fitness—linked to national strength by patriotic

---

[109] Karl Schefold, "Wirkungen Stefan Georges auf drei neuen Wegen der klassischen Archäologie," *Castrum Peregrini* 35 (1986): 72–97.

[110] Ludwig Curtius, *Die antike Kunst und der moderne Humanismus* (Berlin, 1927), p. 4.

[111] Ernst Buschor, "Begriff und Methode der Archäologie," in *Allgemeine Grundlagen der Archäologie*, ed. Ulrich Hausmann (Munich, 1969), p. 10.

school reformers and revanchists—invariably took classical works for their models. War memorials, too, frequently portrayed German heroes in the form of beautiful, nude Greeks, as did the reproduction of Polycleitus's "Spear Carrier," set up at the University of Munich to commemorate fallen students in 1921–22. This monument, whose erection was fervently backed by Munich archaeology professor Paul Wolters, so clearly associated itself with the monarchical past and the "stab-in-the-back" legend that it provoked vociferous opposition from the left.[112] Winckelmann's words were, of course, frequently invoked; but in this context, rapturous admiration of pure, white, Greek masterworks signified not antiaristocratic cultural revolution, but nationalist, and even racist resistance to the modern art and democratic politics of the postwar world.

Another indication of the return of Winckelmannian ascetic aestheticism was the post-1930 surge in popularity of Graecophile photography. Photography had first become part of archaeological studies in the era of high positivism, as a means for Schliemann to show off the wealth of his finds and for Adolf Furtwängler to demonstrate the formal peculiarities of each sculpture. At the fin de siècle, photographs had been employed to promote classicizing Anschauungsunterricht against the inroads made by school reformers; the editors of the Propyläen series, too, had recognized the appeal of the genre, and had filled their books with hundreds of carefully produced pictures. Inexpensive travel guides, featuring photos of ruins, also flourished.[113] Increasingly, Weimar archaeologists employed photos to document their claims and, especially, to appeal to a popular audience; the Nazi years simply accelerated this trend. Only 119 pages in length, Ernst Buschor's Die Plastik der Griechen (The Sculpture of the Greeks—1936) contained 101 photos; only 19 pages of this book were unrelieved by photographs, while 49 pages offered only pictures.[114] Photographs also played an important part in archaeological self-defense against Nazi anti-intellectualism and Germanophilia. In a letter recommending that Rodenwaldt exploit the planned Olympia dig by publishing an illustrated volume to commemorate it, Martin Schede exclaimed: "I am again and again impressed by the observation that one is never more useful to our field, and especially to the cause of excavation abroad, as when one spreads before an educated lay public our results, in a comprehensible, up-to-date, and trustworthy account with good pictures. The situation of classical archaeology today, in my opinion, particularly requires us to pursue this form of pub-

---

[112] Kathrin Hoffmann-Curtius, "Der Doryphoros als Kommilitone: Antikenrezeption in München nach der Räterepublik," Humanistische Bildung 8 (1984): 92–93.

[113] Georgios I. Thanopulos, Das deutsche Neugriechenland-Bild, 1918–1944 (Neuried, 1987), pp. 489–502.

[114] Ernst Buschor, Die Plastik der Griechen (Berlin, 1936).

lication."[115] The importance of the appeal to the eye now equaled that of the address to the ear: visual immediacy was fast replacing flowery descriptions as a means to convince the spectator of the glories of Greek art—and German archæology.

During the 1930s, 1940s, and 1950s, a number of Germany's most prominent photographers and filmmakers turned to Greek landscapes and statuary for inspiration. Leni Riefenstahl's *Olympia* film is, of course, the most famous work in this genre, but the work of one of her collaborators on the movie, Walter Hege, must also have reached numerous Nazi homes. Hege, who began his career as a photographer of medieval cathedrals, journeyed to Athens in 1928 to photograph Greek architecture and sculptures for an American patron. An unpaid aide at the DAI in Berlin during the 1920s, Hege had sent Rodenwaldt copies of his experiments with lighting before his departure, and had kept in contact with the DAI president during his two-year trip. Thus, when the photographer returned to Germany with no patron but some notoriety and a position at the Staatliche Hochschule für Baukunst, bildende Kunst und Handwerk (National Academy for Architecture, Plastic Arts, and Crafts) in Weimar, Rodenwaldt himself consented to write the text to accompany the striking images of the Acropolis Hege had made. Appearing in 1930, the same year Hege joined the Nazi party, the first edition of their *Die Akropolis* received rave reviews; a second edition appeared in 1935, a third in 1937, a fourth in 1941, and a fifth in 1956.[116] The popular success of this heavily illustrated book undoubtedly persuaded Rodenwaldt to collaborate with Hege on two other similar volumes, *Olympia* (1936) and *Griechische Tempel* (1941), and to give further voice to the quasi-racist *Strukturforschung* with which he had been experimenting in the early years of Nazi rule.[117] Undoubtedly, like Schede, he also saw the cultivation of lay audiences as a necessary defensive measure in an era of undependable bureaucratic patronage.

In introducing *Die Akropolis*, Rodenwaldt converted Jaeger's insistence upon art's inferior instructional value into an argument for the replacement of museological classicism with the revitalizing power of captured light. "It is said, not without justice," he wrote, paraphrasing the philologist, "that a modern Winckelmann should seek the path to the Hellenic not through art

---

[115] Schede to Rodenwaldt, 17 March 1935, in BSB, Nachlaß Rodenwaldt, Mappe 255, pp. 48–49.

[116] Maren Hobein, "Monument und Ideal: Die Griechenlandphotographien von Walter Hege," *Fotogeschichte* 8, no. 29 (1989): 48–50. On Hege's politics, see Friedrich Kestel, "Walter Hege (1893–1955): 'Rassenkunstphotograph' und/oder 'Meister der Lichtbildkunst'?" *Fotogeschichte* 8 (1989): 65–73.

[117] On *Strukturforschung* see Gunnar Brands, "'Zwischen Island und Athen': Griechische Kunst im Spiegel des Nationalsozialismus," in *Kunst auf Befehl? 1933–1945*, ed. Bazon Brock and Achim Preiß (Munich, 1990), pp. 120–26.

30. The Acropolis, in the aestheticizing view of Walter Hege. Deutsches
Archäologisches Institut, Athens.

or forms [*morphē*] but through creations of the mind, the Logos. He who
seeks real understanding must chose this path, for the mere perceiving of
forms does not easily penetrate the inner essence [of the Greeks]." But for
Rodenwaldt, it was not the forms themselves, but their lack of authentic
illumination that made them poor conductors of Hellenic *Geist*. "Even the
originals of the highest quality appear dead in the dank atmosphere of western and northern museums, for in these the life-element is lacking with
which and for which [the monuments] were created, the Attic light."[118]
Hege's photography, however, could re-create this lost world, and thereby
win a new public for Greek art and German scholarship.[119] The Olympia
sculptures conveyed, for Rodenwaldt, a familiar (Nordic) energy, harshness,
and struggle for self-definition, while the landscape and the light remained
essentially untouched by time.[120] Cropping out all people and modern
buildings and enhancing light/dark distinctions with colored lens filters,
Hege created timeless, mythical scenes suffused with a uniquely Wagnerian

118 Rodenwaldt in idem and Hege, *Die Akropolis*, 2d ed. (Berlin, 1935), p. 2.
119 Rodenwaldt in idem and Hege, *Olympia*, 2d ed. (Berlin, 1937), p. 7.
120 Ibid., pp. 47, 10.

drama. Greek normativity had been preserved and Greek art's special validity reestablished at the cost of abandoning all historical distance and detail.[121]

Thus, popularizing attempts by archaeologists, like Jaeger's Third Humanism, failed to accomplish the neohumanist hermeneutical task: the creation of new forms of self-consciousness on the basis of an ever-expanding horizon of historical and philosophical discovery. In failing this task, but in demanding allegiance to an outdated system of educational norms and aesthetic preferences, Jaeger's movement simply recapitulated the aristocratic, ascetic ideals of the century before. Rather than accepting, as did Max Weber, the disenchantment of the world and a limited role in the shaping of young minds, Weimar classicists wanted to recreate humanism's cultural and pedagogical monopoly in a world increasingly characterized by academic specialization, industrial production, and slow but steady destruction of aristocratic forms. To do so, they had to abandon the cluttered realm of historicist scholarship and the painful realities of Weimar politics. Jaeger and Rodenwaldt are certainly not Weimar's greatest villains; they may even be counted among the most influential intellectual opponents of the regime that followed. But the vitalist strains of the "third humanism" did, in my view, open the way for a more general abandonment of what Walter Otto in 1940 sneeringly called "historical fact-finding."[122] In failing to come to grips with a century of political, demographic, institutional, and intellectual change, the Weimar-era proponents of neoclassical revival tried to rescue their prewar prerogatives and aesthetic ideals, and by so doing, sacrificed the very principles and practices upon which humanism was based.

[121] Herbert List's *Licht über Hellas* (Munich, 1953) represents a final, highly significant work in this genre. A devotee of Friedrich Gundolf in his youth, List worked in Athens between 1937 and 1941, when he returned to Germany to escape internment ahead of the German invasion. See Boris von Brauchitsch, "Licht über Hellas: Griechenland als visionäres Erlebnis: Die Photographien von Herbert List," *Fotogeschichte* 8, (1989): 59. The short text that accompanied List's pictures was written by Freiburg professor Walter Schuchhardt.

[122] W. F. Otto, "Die Frage der geistigen Überlieferung," *Geistige Überlieferung: Ein Jahrbuch* 1 (1940): 15.

THE DECLINE OF PHILHELLENISM, 1933–1970

> Man now stands in the midst of the dissolution of a world
> determined by Christianity and antiquity, completely
> abandoned by God, [and] facing the threat of sinking
> into bestiality, revives the question of the essence
> and goal of humanity.
> (*Helmuth Plessner*)

DURING the Third Reich, the *Gymnasien* were not disbanded, but Nazi disdain for non-utilitarian education hastened the demise of the classical schools. The Nazi curriculum emphasized "modern" subjects to the detriment of "ancient" ones; biology, recent history and literature, physical education, and geography, all suffused with racist conceits, took classroom hours away from traditional subjects. There were some surprising reversals, as in Reich Education Minister Rust's 1936–37 instructions on the reorganization of the schools which, while closing a number of *Gymnasien*, reinstituted Latin as an obligatory subject for all secondary school students.[1] By 1938, Greek language instruction had been restricted to a few schools, and the *Gymnasien* enrolled only 11 percent of the student population.[2] But even where classical language training endured, the content of the lessons emphasized Aryan supremacy and racial purity. Clearly, antiquity, under the National Socialist regime, no longer represented the source of European norms, but had become merely a storehouse of forms to be ransacked for aesthetic effect or political self-legitimation.

In many ways, this final devolution of philhellenism into mere formal associationism represents the culmination of the antihistoricist pedagogy and aestheticizing Winckelmania of the late 1920s. The incorporation of *Lebensphilosophie* into the classicists' defensive program, too, helped to convert the neohumanist philosophy of imitation into a literal-minded cult of the Germano-Greek body—though racist nationalists were obviously more

---

[1] Fritsch, "Die altsprachlichen Fächer im nationalsozialistischen Schulsystem," in *Schule und Unterricht im Dritten Reich*, ed. Reinhard Dithmar (Neuwied, 1989), p. 146.

[2] R. H. Samuel and R. Hinton-Thomas, *Education and Society in Modern Germany* (London, 1949), p. 50; Cornelia Wegeler, "Das Institut für Altertumskunde der Universität Göttingen 1921–1962: Ein Beitrag zur Geschichte der klassischen Philologie seit Wilamowitz," in *Die Universität Göttingen unter dem Nationalsozialismus*, ed. Heinrich Becker and Hans-Joachim Dahms (Munich, 1987), p. 260.

culpable here than the conservative members of the Altphilologenverband. But Nazi educational policy also represents the victory of antihumanistic forces that had been gathering since the school conference of 1890. The Nazis did not invent the idea that the "German man"—rather than the abstract "man" discussed by the ancient Greeks or Renaissance Italians— should stand at the center of all education; the utility of natural-scientific training, too, had impressed itself on the populace long before Nazi-era rearmament and war pushed aside the humanities for more "practical" scientific investment.[3] The radical instrumentalizing of education to the demands of the command economy and the ideology of the Nazi party attempted after 1933 was the joint product of extreme resentment on the part of the modernizers and stubborn, persistent resistance to change on the part of the classicists. We miss a critical aspect of the radicalization of the school reform movement if we fail to see the persistence of institutionalized philhellenism as its dialectical twin.

If we can trace certain features of Nazi educational policy to Wilhelmine debates, we can also uncover continuities in pedagogical thought that link the Weimar era to the period after the Second World War. As Jaeger recognized, the advent of the modern world had diminished Europeans' cultural dependence on historically generated models, and most post-1945 policymakers, too, came to believe that the moral dilemmas of the present could not be solved by the reiteration of classical exemplars. If economic hardship and the return to prominence of some members of the Weimar-era elite permitted the partial reconstitution of pre-Nazi norms, there remained a pervasive sense that the world beyond Europe and before the Greeks could not be excluded from "humanity," and that practical education did not deserve the scorn heaped upon it by previous generations of educators. The singular propaideutic power of the Greeks, under siege since 1890, by the 1960's had decisively been broken.

If classical *Bildung* as normative national enterprise did not survive the 1930s, classical *Wissenschaft* did endure the Nazi era. At least in the zone occupied by the western powers, classicists emerged from the debacle relatively free from the stigma of participation in Nazi crimes, and ready to resume their specialized pursuits. In the eastern zone, the adjustment of nonutilitarian study of the ancients to socialist goals required more dexterity, but was possible.[4] Yet the survival of *Altertumswissenschaft* came at a

---

[3] By 1941–42, the Deutsche Forschungsgemeinschaft, the great patron of excavations in the 1920s, was devoting a mere two percent of its 1,875,906-reichsmark budget to excavations and art history; the overwhelming majority of the funds went to technical-scientific—especially war-related—research. See Forschungsgemeinschaft report for 1941–42 in GStAPKB, Nachlaß Schmidt-Ott, no. 10. Of course, the Nazis also spent large sums on nonutilitarian projects, but generally, expenditure seems to follow Weimar trends away from the humanities and toward the natural and social sciences.

[4] See, e.g., Johannes Irmscher, *Das Antikebild unserer Gegenwart: Tendenzen und Perspektiven*, Sitzungsberichte der Akademie der Wissenschaften der DDR (Berlin, 1979).

price. Those who pursued strictly historicist studies had lost their prestige, state patronage, and in some cases, their jobs; those who had attempted to make their work "relevant" to Aryan historiography had produced embarrassingly politicized books that twisted or ignored the massive new materials provided by a century of specialized scholarship. The portrait of the ancient past the latter had presented to the general public had diverged radically from the historicists' sequence of particularized cultural wholes. This radical disjuncture between synthetic treatments of Greek history and the continued "heaping up" of specialized details surely lies behind the crisis in Greek history writing identified by Arnaldo Momigliano in the early 1950s, at least insofar as this crisis has its sources in the German-speaking world.[5] During the 1930s and early 1940s, only those whose politics coincided with those of the regime, and whose conviction outweighed their fear of their colleagues' disdain for "popularizers," dared to put forward accessible general works for public consumption.

Fortunately for the classicists, the immediate postwar era remembered their patient positivist labors and the slights suffered by the *Gymnasien* much better than it recalled the racist enthusiasm of some members of the profession. Fortunately, too, postwar Germans came quickly to connect technology, materialism, and barbarism, and to oppose this set of modern evils to the otherworldly, antimodern virtues of neohumanism and Christianity. If in the years after 1945 classicists had to give up their claim to be purveyors of universal values and providers of national norms, they could at least play the role of victims rather than villains, those who had resisted the nationalist perversions of scholarship rather than the perpetrators of this heinous crime against German *Kultur*. It was this stance as "victims" of modernity and defenders of the noble tradition of German philosophy and poetry that ensured the classicists' continued prominence late into the postwar era. This is not to say, of course, that there was not a kernel of truth to their claims: had there not been, the trick would not have worked so well. But it took a new generation to come to grips with the sins of quiescence and "disinterestedness" in the face of fascism, and to begin to look elsewhere for the foundations of a new, ethnographic, humanism.

Philhellenism in a New Key

In certain ways, the classicists who subscribed to dematerialized, Jaegerian humanism may have prepared the way for collaboration with the Nazi regime. This does not mean, however, that all, or even many, classicists rejoiced at the ascension of Adolf Hitler. Philologists had good reason to fear

---

[5] See Momigliano, "George Grote and the Study of Greek History," in idem, *Contributo alla storia degli studi classici* (Rome, 1955), pp. 213–31.

displacement at the hands of the Nazis, who unquestionably stood for sudden and violent Germanophile school reform, and who had shown little evidence of their love for ancient art before their seizure of power.[6] Numerous important scholars, including Jaeger himself, eventually went into exile. Classical archaeologists, for their part, hesitated to welcome a regime that promised to promote their arch internal opponents, the prehistorians of *Germania libera*, to positions of power and academic influence. Already in 1930, the architecturally trained DAI archaeologist Armin von Gerkan had predicted that the advent of Nazi rule would impose a new era of penury on the institute. "Archaeology would in any case be significantly weakened," Gerkan prophesied in a private letter; "probably half of the professorships would be dissolved, though patriotic prehistory will begin to bloom—first of all those [prehistorians] like Kossinna and [Hermann] Wirth."[7] Wiegand apparently expressed reservations about the National Socialist attitude to humanistic education and lack of respect for scholarly credentials to his pro-Nazi friend Rudolf Herzog.[8] Rodenwaldt, though guilty of a mild form of collaboration, certainly did not welcome the dissolution of the DAI's long-cherished connection to the Foreign Ministry and its subordination to the newly created Reich Ministry of Research, Education, and Public Instruction (Reichsministerium für Wissenschaft, Erziehung, und Volksbildung) in 1934.[9] In March 1933, Ludwig Curtius wavered at the brink of endorsing Germany's new political departure, admiring the domestic idealism inspired by the new sovereign.[10] Several months later, however, Curtius conveyed to Wiegand his worries about the impression Nazism was making abroad, and by the mid-1930s, Curtius's scruples had resulted in his forcible retirement from his post as first secretary in Rome.[11]

Others, however, greeted the arrival of the Third Reich with rather more enthusiasm, particularly, it seems, at the Athens institute. In early 1933, Karo had already eagerly set about the business of buttressing the regime's prestige abroad. In a letter to the DAI dated 30 April 1933, the Athens first

[6] Kathrin Hoffmann-Curtius, "Der Doryphoros als Kommilitone: Antikenrezeption in München nach der Räterepublik," in *Humanistische Bildung* 8 (1984): 98.

[7] Gerkan to Wiegand, 1 October 1930, in DAI, Nachlaß Wiegand, Kasten 3. Hermann Wirth was a dilettante folklorist and prehistorian who had been excluded from academia and became an early collaborator in the setting up of Himmler's Race and Settlement office. See Michael Kater, *Das "Ahnenerbe" der SS, 1935–1945* (Stuttgart, 1974), pp. 14–16, 24–26.

[8] See Herzog to Wiegand, 28 July 1932, DAI, Nachlaß Wiegand, Kasten 4. Herzog responded to Wiegand's disparagements with a vigorous campaign to convince the important scholar (as well as other academics) of the advantages of Nazi academic policy over Weimar reformist practices. See this letter and others in the collection.

[9] See Rodenwaldt to Wiegand, 13 March 1933, ibid., Kasten 28, Mappe 2.

[10] Ludwig Curtius to Wiegand, 21 March 1933, ibid., Kasten 2.

[11] Curtius to Wiegand, 21 December 1933, ibid.

secretary—and son of Jewish parents—reported his efforts to counter "atrocity propaganda" in Greece. Karo assured his colleagues that the Greeks were favorably inclined to the new German regime, and French and British officials of his acquaintance had at least listened with sympathy to his impassioned accounts of Germany's maltreatment and encirclement.[12] Karo's deputy, Walter Wrede, who had spent most of the Great War interned in a Russian prison camp, joined the party and rose quickly to become the highest-ranking member of the NSDAP in Greece; Wrede became first secretary at the DAI office when Karo was forced from his post in 1936.[13] Dörpfeld, who had been deeply discontented with the Versailles Treaty and the simultaneous collapse of imperial rule and his celebrity status, likewise welcomed the fascist seizure of power. Later he would also greet the coming of the Second World War, which he believed to be justified by Germany's need for security and a steady supply of groceries.[14]

As Gerkan had predicted, the advent of the Third Reich did cause Germanic prehistory to bloom. Between 1933 and 1935, at a time of deep reductions in university staff (partly due to the exclusion and/or emigration of Jewish professors), five new professorships for prehistory were established—all of which were, in fact, filled with anticlassical advocates of *Germania libera* prehistory. *Volkskunde*, too, boomed after 1933; long the popular preoccupation of regional groups and the object of scholarly ridicule, folkloric studies now gained new academic stature and national currency.[15] At the same time, classical studies suffered enormous losses; of eighty-six professors lecturing in classical philology in the winter of 1932–33, twenty-one were removed by the new government; five of twenty-three holders of chairs in ancient history fell victim to Nazi racial policies.[16] Many new agencies, some of which are discussed below, devoted considerable effort, personnel, and funds to prehistorical and folkloric studies. Even the Notgemeinschaft put new emphasis on prehistory, eugenics, and folklore—spurred, as Schmidt-Ott announced in late 1933, to devote new energy to "the practical aims of the present . . . which the Führer has set

---

[12] Karo to DAI, 30 April 1933, PZStA AA/K 69496, pp. 111–14.

[13] On Wrede's war service, Rodenwaldt to Foreign Ministry, 30 April 1928, in ibid., pp. 22–23; on Wrede's participation in Nazi activities, see Mark Mazower, *Inside Hitler's Greece: The Experience of Occupation, 1941–1944* (Yale, 1993), pp. 5–8; Ulf Jantzen, *Einhundert Jahre Athener Institut, 1874–1974* (Mainz, 1986), p. 50.

[14] See, e.g., Dörpfeld to Heinrich Rüter, 2 December 1939, in DAI, Nachlaß Dörpfeld, Kasten 2.

[15] See, e.g., Rolf Wilhelm Brednich, "Volkskunde—die völkische Wissenschaft von Blut und Boden," in Becker and Dahms, *Die Universität Göttingen unter dem Nationalsozialismus*, pp. 313–20.

[16] Wegeler, "Institut für Altertumskunde," p. 259; Reinhold Bichler, "Neuorientierung in der alten Geschichte?" in *Deutsche Geschichtswissenschaft nach dem Zweiten Weltkrieg (1945–1965)*, ed. Ernst Schulin and Elisabeth Müller-Luckner (Munich, 1989), p. 63.

31. Archaeologist Walter Wrede shows some fellow Nazis the glories of Greece, ca. 1937. Bundesarchiv, Koblenz.

out for the German people and the German economy."[17] In 1935, Schmidt-Ott reasserted the organization's commitment to two main branches of "research essential to life": medical, technical, and natural-scientific research (essential to the economy), and prehistory, racial science, and folklore (essential, presumably, to the soul).[18] Undoubtedly, prehistory had now become, as Kossinna had dubbed it, "a supremely national field."

Ironically, however, the very popularity and political importance of these quintessentially *völkisch* fields doomed the project of *Gleichschaltung* almost from the outset. Prehistory became the battleground for three agencies with recognizable roots in the 1920s—Rosenberg's Reichsbund für deutsche Vorgeschichte (Reich League for German Prehistory), headed by the pugnacious Hans Reinerth and heavily composed of members of the Kossinna circle, Himmler's *Ahnenerbe*, home to many members of the less fanatical (but anticlassicist) Ostdeutscher Verband für Altertumsforschung,

[17] Schmidt-Ott to Notgemeinschaft members, 10 November 1933, in GStAPKB, Nachlaß Schmidt-Ott, Mappe 3.

[18] Schmidt-Ott to Dr. Schumann (director of the scientific department of the Education Ministry) 22 March 1935 (copy), in DAI, Nachlaß Wiegand, Kasten 29.

and the humanistically inclined RGK.[19] The story of bureaucratic infighting amongst prehistorians during the Nazi period has been recounted by Michael Kater, Helmut Heiber, Alain Schnapp, and Reinhard Bollmus, so I shall not rehash the details here.[20] Most significant to our story is the fact that in this bitter battle between prehistorical institutions, all the factions were identified with various state organizations: years of local-central strife and the economic deprivations of the 1920s had left no independent, centralized base for cultural organization. Whether the institutes that remained carried on truly scholarly work during the Nazi era is a separate issue; it is undoubtedly the case that the DAI/RGK did its best to retain its scholarly credentials. But ultimately it still had to drink from the same poisoned well as its more politicized opponents. As a *Reichsinstitut* it could hardly be an effective source of resistance.

One interesting aspect of Nazi prehistory should, however, be noted: as before, particularly in Reinerth's more political Reichsbund für deutsche Vorgeschichte, attacks on humanism's attachment to Rome and its disdainful attitude to *Germania libera* continued unabated. Even those obsessed with proving the nation's *Ur*-historical Aryan racial purity were equally, if not rather more, intent on establishing Germanic cultural autonomy—and equal validity—as if frantically seeking final absolution and vindication for having sacked Rome in the fifth century. Declaring its intention to build on Kossinna's "scientific" foundations, in 1934, the hypernationalist prehistorical journal *Mannus* announced its resolve "to solidify and give new meaning to German prehistory. It will serve Nordic thinking, refute Romanism in all its guises, and fight tirelessly for the discrediting of the lies about the culturelessness of our Germanic ancestors."[21] Similarly, the introduction to Walter Frank's 1941 German history textbook conjured the spirit of Kossinna to lament the Mediterranean-centeredness of the past: "Before prehistorical studies made a change in [historical writing], it was believed that *Kultur* arose in the South alone and only was later brought to the North, last of all to the *Ur*-Germans. The *Ur*-Germans' benefactors were supposed to have been the Romans. Kossinna made the following complaint about this [theory]: "All that we had before, according to this view, was not *Kultur* but *Unkultur*."" Fortunately, however, Frank argued, archaeology had made it possible to redress this surviving prejudice; the science of the spade

---

[19] On the Ostdeutscher Verband, see Mechthilde Unverzagt, *Wilhelm Unverzagt und die Pläne zur Gründung eines Instituts für Vorgeschichte Ostdeutschlands* (Mainz, 1985).

[20] See Kater, *Ahnenerbe*; Helmut Heiber, *Walter Frank und sein Reichsinstitut für Geschichte des neuen Deutschlands* (Stuttgart, 1966); Reinhard Bollmus, *Das Amt Rosenberg und seine Gegner* (Stuttgart, 1970); and Alain Schnapp, "Archéologie et nazisme," *Quaderni di Storia* 5 (January–June 1977): 1–26.

[21] "Einleitung," *Mannus* 29 (May 1934).

had bestowed on the German nation a cultural self-consciousness and pride unattainable by means of elitist philology.[22]

If Rome-centeredness continued to be assailed, however, philhellenism, a much more widespread and consequential passion, rarely received harsh criticism during the Nazi years. Orientalists struggled with their portrait of the Hellenistic East; able to blame neither the Greeks nor the "Aryan" Persians for the decline of the Achaemenid Empire, many hit on racial miscegenation as an explanation for Eastern decay.[23] Classicists, like Rodenwaldt, attempted the rhetorical rescue of Graecophilia at the expense of Roman studies. In a 1943 lecture on Roman art at the time of Augustus, Rodenwaldt dealt the following blow to his own area of expertise:

> For us, Roman architecture on German soil reminds us of battles and foreign domination. The concept "Rome" for us is burdened with memories, whose present-day political significance does not always allow us easy access to the eternal value of Rome. By contrast, Greekdom offers us a sphere that lies beyond partisan affinities and hatreds. We approach it fearlessly and with light hearts, and are happy to perceive the present-day relevance [*Gegenwartsnähe*] of its art. . . . Homer will always mean more to us than Virgil, the Acropolis more than the Roman Forum, the sculptures of Olympia more than Roman historical portraits.[24]

German access to Rome, for Rodenwaldt, was complex and controversial, while Greece permitted immediate appropriation and faction-free embrace. Given Nazi claims to German cultural autonomy and *völkisch* unity, it was clearly safer for classicists to exalt Greece, even if the philhellenic culture of the *Gymnasien* and universities had not already inclined them to do so.

Devout Germanophiles, in fact, preferred to assert German-Greek racial commonality than to debunk philhellenism as a self-serving humanist delusion. In 1936, the racist art historian Josef Strzygowski declared himself in favor of retaining compulsory Greek lessons in the secondary-school curriculum, for Greece, he wrote, "next to Iran, will be the most important basis for the knowledge of all Nordic Being."[25] Here some classicists and Nordic

---

[22] Walter Frank and Johannes Silomon, *Volk und Führer: Deutsche Geschichte für Schulen* (Frankfurt, 1941), p. 2.

[23] Josef Wiesehöfer, "Das Bild der Achaimeniden in der Zeit des Nationalsozialismus," *Achaemenid History*, vol. 3: *Method and Theory*, ed. Amélie Kuhrt and Heleen Sancisi-Weerdenburg (Leiden, 1988), pp. 1–14.

[24] Rodenwaldt, *Kunst um Augustus*, Sonderdruck aus *Die Antike* 13 (Berlin, 1937), p. 3.

[25] Josef Strzygowski, *Aufgang des Nordens: Lebenskampf eines Kunstforschers um ein deutsches Weltbild* (Leipzig, 1936), p. 74. Strzygowski had previously suggested that Humboldtian humanism had been a "beautiful idealism" that had degenerated into boring, overfed, fossilized *Gymnasialphilologie*; the practitioners of this perverse form not only clove to the dogma of the ancient (Roman) *Patentvölker*, but also failed to appreciate the true value of the Greeks. See

prehistorians could find common ground, for several classically trained scholars easily accommodated themselves to the transposition of the German-Greek special relationship from the realm of *Geist* to the dominion of blood. In 1942, a memorandum produced by the Philosophical Faculty at the University of Tübingen emphasized the virtues of a new, nonformalist, Greek philology in preparing students for the coming of a racially defined and German dominated *Großeuropa*; "Increasing Greek lessons in the Württemberg schools is a necessary prerequisite for . . . the comprehension of the formation of the Aryan spirit in Greekdom and its continuous, fertile impact on Germandom up to the present day. In the struggle for a racial entity of our own, we cannot dispense with the assistance that Greekdom offers us."[26] Fritz Schachermeyr, Richard Harder, Helmut Berve, Franz Altheim, and Carl Schuchhardt—all respectable classical scholars— subscribed to some form of this racial linkage theory.[27] In fact, racialist classical studies provided perhaps the ideal means to reassert the metaphor of German-Greek spiritual wedlock as well as to preserve Greek cultural autonomy in the face of archaeological and literary evidence to the contrary; whatever contacts with "orientals" and other *Untermenschen* appeared in the historical record, Hellenic purity was maintained where it really counted: in the blood.[28]

DAI archaeologists did not balk at advertising new *völkisch* efforts; a budget submitted to the Education Ministry in 1935 apparently asked for 220,000 reichsmarks for prehistorical work (as against 80,160 reichsmarks for other projects) "in consideration of its significance for the National Socialist worldview."[29] But Nazi-era archaeologists were ultimately less successful in trying to gain control of *Germania libera* or in articulating new world-historical theories than in retreating to a long-lost world of Winc-

---

Strzygowski, *Forschung und Erziehung: Der Neuaufbau der Universität als Grundlage aller Schulverbesserung an den Verfahren der Forschung über bildende Kunst* (Stuttgart, 1928), pp. 18–20.

[26] "Denkschrift der Philosophischen Fakultät der Universität Tübingen über Ergänzungsprüfungen in Latein und Griechisch, über die Lage des gymnasialen Unterrichts in Württemberg und ihre bedrohlichen Auswirkungen auf die Zukunft der Hochschulen des Landes," dated 31 July 1942, signed by Dekan Weinreich, in DAI, Nachlaß Rodenwaldt, Kasten 7.

[27] See Alain Schnapp, "Archéologie et nazisme, II," in *Quaderni di Storia* 6 (1980): 19–33; Schuchhardt, "Die Indogermanisierung Griechenlands," *Die Antike* 9 (1933): 303–19; and idem, *Alteuropa: Kulturen-Rassen-Völker*, 3rd ed. (Berlin, 1935). On Schachermeyr and Berve, see Beat Näf, *Von Perikles zu Hitler? Die athenische Demokratie und die deutsche Althistorie bis 1945* (Bern, 1986), esp. pp. 135–59.

[28] See Volker Losemann, *Nationalsozialismus und die Antike* (Hamburg, 1977), p. 111. For an ideal example of the genre, see W. Aly, "Das griechisch-römische Altertum im Rahmen der nationalsozialistischen Erziehung," *Volk im Werden* 2, no. 4 (1934): 226–35.

[29] Max Wegner to Theodor Wiegand, 25 May 1935, in DAI, Nachlaß Wiegand, Kasten 28.

kelmann's aesthetics and Goethe's poetry.[30] Here, the classical archaeologists had in their favor the fact that the Führer revered Greek and Roman art and architecture and took a dim view of the prehistorical and folkloric fixations of Himmler, Rosenberg, and Walther Darré.[31] It did not take classicists long to discover the new leader's aesthetic biases. Already in March 1933, Curtius was conveying the hopeful news to Wiegand: "Hitler himself is a passionate admirer of Greek art," Curtius noted amongst suggestions for defensive tactics the DAI might take against *völkisch* fanatics. "He declares it to be the only art there is."[32] If the *völkisch* set continued to promote Germanic arts, one has only to look at the 1937 Haus der Künste in Munich and Albert Speer's designs for the rebuilding of Berlin to see that the venerable tradition of state preference for classical styles was never abandoned.

Fortunately for the classicists, Hitler had expressed his reverence for Mediterranean art in print. This enabled Wiegand and Carl Schuchhardt, for example, to employ the Führer's own words to defend their own opposition to the *Germania libera* prehistorians' appropriation of the RGK.[33] Rodenwaldt composed a list of Hitler's proclassicist quotations from *Mein Kampf*, perhaps to prepare himself in advance for attacks on the irrelevance and disloyalty of *Altertumswissenschaft*.[34] Archaeologists would play this trump time and again against their *völkisch* rivals; the Führer's words served as a sort of protective incantation against total expropriation.[35]

Playing to Hitler's conception of Greek art, however, would require concentration on the familiar monumental forms of classical sculpture and architecture; this was no time for developing evolutionary-typological sequences. Thus the resurgence of romantic aesthetics begun in the late Weimar years continued into the Nazi period unabated, infused with a new emphasis on the white, pure, naked masculine body so central to Winckelmannian aesthetics. If other fields like ethnography, prehistory, or folklore studies could stress their importance in binding and strengthening the

---

[30] Despite new efforts in the mid-1930s, the DAI never managed to establish a branch for northern and eastern prehistory, as had been envisioned in 1927.

[31] Kater, *Ahnenerbe*, p. 23; Gilmer W. Blackburn, *Education in the Third Reich: Race and History in Nazi Textbooks* (Albany, N.Y., 1985), p. 48. It seems clear that if Hitler permitted an upsurge in prehistorical work and sometimes even employed prehistorical "evidence" in his speeches, this was more of a concession to the *völkisch* element in the party than a wholehearted embrace of the discipline. See eg. Kater, *Ahnenerbe*; Carl Watzinger, *Theodor Wiegand* (Munich, 1944), pp. 448–52.

[32] Curtius to Wiegand, 21 March 1933, DAI, Nachlaß Wiegand, Kasten 2.

[33] This remonstrance from the defenders of the DAI appeared as a privately circulated pamphlet in 1934. See Silke Wenk, ed., *Auf den Spuren der Antike: Theodor Wiegand, ein deutscher Archäologe* (Bendorf am Rhein, 1985), p. 51.

[34] See typed list, "Hitler über die Antike," in BSB, Nachlaß Rodenwaldt, Mappe 718.

[35] See Wenk, *Auf den Spuren*, pp. 51–52.

Volk with lessons in cultural cohesion, archaeology could offer the new Reich exemplary warriors, unnamed heroes of the state, Aryan strongmen masquerading as Olympic athletes. The renewal of the Olympia excavations in 1936 reinforced this archaeological/eugenic parallel, as two exhibitions of athletic sculptures were mounted in Berlin which linked the dig to the Berlin Olympics. Rodenwaldt served as organizer for the smaller exhibit of Olympic casts (at the Berlin University Museum);[36] the other, grander, display, was mounted by Wiegand (now DAI president) and Theodor Lewald, veteran of the Weimar Interior Ministry. Entitled "Sports of the Greeks," the latter exhibition gathered together numerous original sculptures from Berlin collections, in joint celebration of German museological prowess and of the ideal of Greek corporeal beauty.

Wiegand's speech at the opening of "Sports of the Greeks," which proved to be his last public address, claimed—not indefensibly—a long German tradition of collecting "works that represent ancient life in its care for the body and sporting competition."[37] Wiegand pointed out various examples of "noble figures of youth" owned by German galleries, but offered no obvious indications of archaeological capitulation to the new regime. This was left to Education Minister Bernhard Rust, who condemned the humanistic *Gymnasium*'s "one-sided" obsession with *Geist* (and especially Latin texts!) and disregard for the body, the key to understanding German-Greek racial relatedness. "Concern for Latin writings," he lamented,

> is greater than the feeling of responsibility for the truth that Hellas remains essentially lifeless, so long as the harmony of body and soul as the vital force behind all its great cultural creations is not perceived and is not recognized by the defenders of [Greek] *Bildung*. With such a [philological] view predominating in the circles of those responsible for education, the Hellenic world can find no acceptance amongst the *Volk*, though in its related blood, it bears the same powers that unfolded in so marvelous a way in Hellas. National Socialism has for the first time decided this question and enlarged the narrow access of scholars and artists for [the benefit of] the whole *Volk*.[38]

Similarly, Rodenwaldt's speech at the opening of the new Olympia excavations proclaimed the arrival of a new—and even more reverent—German view of Olympia, arising from renewed appreciation of "the harmonious development of body and soul" rather than the "purely intellectual training" that had inspired the excavators of the 1880s.[39] If the archaeologists of the 1920s had been content to leave the philosophical defense of classical

---

[36] Universitätskurator, Berlin, to Education Ministry, 30 July 1936, in PZStA, RMfWEV 1361, Allgemeine Hochschulsachen Abt. X, No. 75, 3:260.

[37] Wiegand quoted in Wenk, *Auf den Spuren*, p. 53.

[38] Rust quoted ibid.

[39] Rodenwaldt, sketch for "Olympia," in DAI, Nachlaß Rodenwaldt, Kasten 7, Mappe 19.

culture to the philologist Jaeger, they now allowed an anti-intellectual racialism to rescue their beloved Greeks. In many ways a continuation of the late 1920s return to romantic aesthetics, this capitulation to eugenics and vitalist thought is indicative of institutionalized philhellenism's final moral vacuity.

Archaeologists under the Third Reich were able to employ with some success the bureaucratic and diplomatic skills developed in the course of a half-century of "big archaeology." Most reminiscent of older tactics was the reversion to dependence on the Kaiser—now replaced by the Führer—to defend their unpopular interests against the masses on the one hand and the nonhumanist party machine and business interests on the other. The Führer, as we have seen, was frequently invoked to ward off enemy spirits, and even served as ultimate patron, as had Wilhelm II in the past; funds for the Olympia dig (50,000 reichsmarks per year for six years) had been appropriated from Hitler's personal disposition fund.[40] Karo, who had long wished to recommence excavations at Olympia and to build a badly needed new institute office in Athens, was overjoyed at the news that the Führer had approved money for both plans. "I don't need to tell you how much the fulfilling of two long-cherished desires pleases me," Karo wrote to Wiegand in April 1936.[41] Of course, the Nazi establishment, even more forcibly than the DAI's bureaucratic patrons of old, attempted to define the aims of the institute's work and to use its support for classical archaeology to demonstrate the grandeur and generosity of the new regime.[42] But, ironically, at least in the case of the Olympia excavations, Nazi interference proved partly beneficial. Pressed against their better instincts to dig in the stadium by the demands of Reichssportführer Tschammer und Osten, the excavators were to find there very rich caches of artifacts.[43] By skillful use of their ambassadorial heritage and the venerable tradition of German philhellenism, DAI archaeologists were able to continue digging at Olympia until 1943.[44]

Archaeologists under the NSDAP regime, too, used to some effect the policy of cultivating friends in high places; their first reaction upon hearing of the Nazi seizure of power seems to have been frantic scanning of their address books for colleagues who might represent their interests to Hitler

---

[40] See Interior Ministry to Foreign Ministry, 24 July 1936, titled "Zusammenfassung der Besprechung über die geplanten Ausgrabungen in Olympia vom 15. Juli 1939," in PA/AA/K 114 Europa III, vol. 1.

[41] Karo to Wiegand, 10 April 1936, in ADAI, Korrespondenz und Berichte, vol. 41.

[42] For example, Education Minister Rust, in his speech at the University of Athens celebrated the Nazi regime's intention "to be true to the great tradition of German classical studies." Rust, "Rede in der Universität Athen am 8. April 1937," ibid.

[43] Jantzen, Einhundert Jahre Athener Institut, pp. 49–52.

[44] Rust declared an official end to the dig in March 1943. Rust to DAI Berlin and DAI Athens, 29 March 1943, in ADAI, Korrespondenz und Berichte, vol. 41.

and the new regime.[45] Now that the pursuit of patronage had become less a matter for rational argument than for backstage bargaining and symbolic display, Wiegand turned his connections to the world of heavy industry and the upper bureaucracy—and the honors bestowed on him by Nazi officials—into defensive weapons, threatening, for example, to give back his Prussian Order of the Eagle if the RGK was forcibly divorced from the DAI and handed over to Alfred Rosenberg's minions.[46] Wiegand also planned to organize a group of industrialists—headed by his friend Gustav Krupp von Bohlen und Halbach—to support his archaeological efforts; evidently, he intended to make Göring the protector, or at least an honorary member.[47] But playing this game required some tragic compromises: the DAI did allow the Jewish prehistorian Gerhard Bersu to be dismissed from the directorship of the RGK and removed the sixty-six-year-old Eduard Norden (also of Jewish descent) from the central directorate in 1934.[48] We should not forget that the preservation of scholarly status in the Nazi period was in many cases accompanied by such sins—and worse—against innocent men.

Even the argument from national prestige was used, as the Nazi troops marched triumphantly into conquered Greece. In July 1941, Martin Schede—who had succeeded Wiegand as DAI president upon the latter's death in December 1936—sent an ambitious proposal to the sympathetic Education Minister Rust. According to Schede, a grand new archaeological era had already commenced in Greece. German excavations at several locations had been restarted, the taking of aerial photographs of ruined sites had been organized with the Luftwaffe, and the salvaging of pieces of a famous Greek frieze, sunk in Piraeus harbor, had begun, with the help of naval warships. Now Schede wished to add a Byzantine section to the Athens branch, and hoped that funding could also be found for the reorganization and reopening of Greek museums, as well as the continuance of the aerial archaeological reconnaissance, excavations, and salvaging efforts. The total cost, the DAI president estimated, would amount to 1.5 million

[45] See e.g., Rodenwaldt to Wiegand, 13 March 1933, in DAI, Nachlaß Wiegand, Kasten 28, Mappe 2. Rodenwaldt immediately consulted Ambassador Stieve (now head of the Cultural Section in the Foreign Ministry) and Johannes Popitz, and suggested that Wiegand approach Hjalmar Schacht, the Nazi financial wizard. Currius suggested Freiherr von Bissing, an archaeologist and a long-time NSDAP member, and Wilhelm Furtwägler, the orchestra conductor much admired by Hitler and also the son of the now long-deceased archaeologist Adolf Furtwängler. See Curtius to Wiegand, 21 March 1933, ibid., Kasten 2.

[46] Theodor Wiegand, *Halbmond im letzten Viertel: Archäologische Reiseberichte*, ed. Gerhard Wiegand (Mainz, 1985), p. 18.

[47] See Paul Kempner to Ludwig Adam Graf Strachwitz, 17 December 1935, and Kempner to Wiegand, 13 January 1936, in DAI, Nachlaß Wiegand, Kasten 28, Mappe 2.

[48] On Bersu, see Bollmus, *Das Amt Rosenberg*, pp. 159; 204–7; on Norden, see Bernhard Kytzler, "Eduard Norden," in *Berlinische Lebensbilder*, vol. 4: *Geisteswissenschaftler*, ed. Michael Erbe (Berlin, 1989), p. 338.

reichsmarks, but offered great benefits in exchange for its costs. "Thereby," he proclaimed, "the uncontested hegemony of Germany in the study of Greek monuments would be secured, an event that doubtless is worth so high an expenditure. . . . It would be so grand a gesture by the conqueror," Schede concluded, "who shows himself conscious of his cultural calling in Europe, [that] it could not fail to make an impression on the whole world. Thus, all this [planned activity] must take place very soon, so that Italy or even America does not beat us to it."[49] Philhellenists by tradition and aesthetic education, opportunists by professional necessity, archaeologists could not fail to seize one last chance to exalt themselves and their nation in appropriating the culture of ancient Greece.

Universalism and Neohumanism in the Postwar Period

It may well be the case that the destruction of antiutilitarian neohumanism in the GDR after 1945 contributed, curiously, to a preponderance of classical allusions in East German literature. In a recent essay, Bernd Seidensticker has shown how East German writers, following the trail blazed by Bertholt Brecht, enrolled the ancients in veiled criticisms of their own society, and more open attacks on Western capitalist culture.[50] Clearly, however, this literary appropriation of classical figures was linked to scholarly and institutional trends only insofar as these realms of intellectual activity shared a similar disdain for the elitist and antiutilitarian neohumanism of the recent past. In Eastern Germany after 1945, the meaning of humanism was entirely altered by its new, modifying adjective "socialist," and by the self-conscious effort of the state to break the old elite's monopoly on education and to make education and research serve the needs of the successive five-year plans for economic recovery.[51] Institutionalized philhellenism, here, was at an end—though the East German government was eager to reconstruct the prestigious Pergamum Museum (the artifacts, however, remained in the Soviet Union until late 1958).[52] From a post-1989 standpoint, moreover, it is all the more evident that we will have to look westward in order to gauge the continuities and changes in the philhellenist legacy that have helped to shape the German cultural institutions that exist today.

For those wrestling with the problem of reconstructing German *Bildung*

[49] Schede to Rust, 22 July 1941, in MZStA, Rep. 151/1C Nr.7108/1.

[50] Bernd Seidensticker, "Metamorphosen: Zur Antikerezeption in der deutschen Literatur nach 1945," in *Antike Heute*, ed. Richard Faber and Bernhard Kytzler (Würzburg, 1922), pp. 128–54.

[51] See Hannelore Belitz-Demiriz and Dieter Voigt, *Die Sozialstruktur der promovierten Intelligenz in der DDR und in der Bundesrepublik Deutschland 1950–1984*, part 1 (Bochum, 1990), pp. 107–224.

[52] Renate Petras, *Die Bauten der Berliner Museumsinsel* (Berlin, 1987), pp. 184–88.

in the zone of Western occupation after 1945, the return to some variety of humanistic education seemed inescapable. Even the socialist Adolf Grimme, who had served as Prussian education minister between 1930 and 1933, in 1948 defended the continuation of Latin and even Greek lessons in the secondary schools.[53] Humanism still seemed the antidote to barbarism, and what the Greeks lacked in appropriate moral sentiment was more than made up for with ecumenical Christian sermonizing. Despite a general commitment on the part of cultural officials to build democratic values and root out racialist and nationalist ideas, the practical problems of providing sufficient classrooms, schoolbooks, and teachers intervened in the campaign to reform education. Old provincial patterns reemerged, and with them, the *Gymnasien* and the philologically centered lesson plans. The onset of the Cold War, too, opened up some space for classical scholars to defend the Greeks as the ancestors of "Western" democracy. Thus material and mental constraints thwarted radical pedagogical departures and tended to reinforce nostalgic longings for the philhellenist past. The oft-repeated motto of the postwar classicists—that world is past, but it is not dead—at least in the first two decades after Hitler's demise, rang true.[54]

In the immediate postwar period, many academic classicists of the old school, including DAI bureaucrats, simply absolved themselves of guilt for the debacle. The DAI's struggles with Reinerth and Rosenberg had prepared an ideal alibi for the organization's continuance throughout the Nazi era, as a 1946 report illustrates: "Even during the Hitler era, the DAI never forsook its cultural and scholarly stance, which dates back to J. J. Winckelmann, and fought successfully, for example, against the Nazi-managed falsification of prehistory. The circles that fostered this pseudoscience were hostile to the institute and tried to thwart its operation."[55] Portraying the DAI—more or less accurately—as the victim of pseudoscientific attacks by prehistorians, such accounts omitted mention of the institute's collusion with Rust's plans, accommodation with Himmler's projects, and cultivation of Hitler's classicist tastes. Ludwig Curtius's autobiography, similarly, left the impression that Germanists and Germanic prehistorians had been the sole perpetrators of collaborationist scholarship, though he did admit the existence of a deep urge to nationalist self-assertion in the respectable *Bildungsbürgertum*.[56] Curtius even composed a rather odd modern fable about a soldier who restored his ties to Germany and Europe—and his feeling for

---

[53] Grimme quoted in Manfred Overesch, "Die Gesamtdeutsche Konferenz der Erziehungsminister in Stuttgart am 19./20. Februar 1948," *Vierteljahreshefte für Zeitgeschichte* 28, no. 2 (April 1980): 280.

[54] For example, see Otto Regenbogen, *Humanismus heute? Ein Vortrag* (Heidelberg, 1947), p. 28.

[55] "Bericht über das DAI 1946" in DAI, Nachlaß Rodenwaldt, Kasten 11.

[56] See Ludwig Curtius, *Deutsche und antike Welt: Lebenserinnerungen* (Stuttgart, 1956), pp. 489–64.

human value, destroyed by technological total war—by repeated visits to the Apollo Belvedere. The moral of Curtius's story was, ostensibly, the healing force of nude Greek sculpture, perhaps a novel variation on the theme of statuary's formative aesthetic power, but clearly headed toward predictable philhellenist-neohumanist conclusions.[57]

But if philhellenism, in places, had survived the war, so, too, had its enemies. When *Gymnasium* teacher Arnold Bork identified the opponents of the study of Greece in 1951, these fell into five groups, the last three of which recapitulated the anticlassicist coalitions of the previous decades: the know-nothings, the small-minded men, the proponents of all that is modern (*Realschulmänner*), the Europe-weary (orientalists), and the misguided Christians (clerics).[58] Some modernizers, like natural scientist Max Hartmann, were willing to offer a compromise to the classicists, proposing yet another return to that mythical epoch of scientific and humanistic harmony in the wake of the catastrophes of 1806–13.[59] But, as many occasional essays and letters to (who else?) Werner Jaeger indicate, classical scholars by and large recognized that in the late 1940s, they faced far greater challenges than they had faced even in the chaotic Weimar era. Having experienced the destruction of their worlds—both intellectual and physical— several of these men poignantly lamented the war's cultural costs. In a February 1947 letter to Jaeger, Ludwig Curtius wrote: "You should know that in the past few years I have thought of you thousands of times; for the European catastrophe did not only destroy city halls and industrial towns, castles and cathedrals, but it also has made a ruin of the edifice of our humanistic ideas, and we will have to start all over from the beginning."[60] The events of the world war caused Eduard Fraenkel to question not his dedication to specialized scholarship but his faith in mankind. As he confessed to Jaeger in early November 1945:

> The fate of our "science" [philology] and all that goes with it, is only a negligible, tiny particle of the wrenching events that are occurring around us and which often take away my breath and rob me of every sort of primitive joy in life. I will certainly never doubt the correctness and necessity of our specialized work; it is more important than ever to, as you say, "make people realize what living tradition is." And if truly the "decline of the West" is coming, I would rather be the most modest companion of the Symmachi and Nicomachi [late Roman patrician families persecuted for their paganism] than

[57] Ludwig Curtius, "Begegnung beim Apollo von Belvedere," (1947) in *Humanistisches und Humanes: Fünf Essays und Vorträge* (Basel, 1954), pp. 13–38.

[58] Arnold Bork, "Griechentum und Abendland" [1951], *Gymnasium: Zeitschrift für Kultur der Antike und humanistische Bildung* 59 (1952): 4–19.

[59] Max Hartmann, "Naturwissenschaft und humanistische Bildung," in *Erziehung zur Menschlichkeit: Die Bildung im Umbruch der Zeit: Festschrift für Eduard Spranger* (Tübingen, 1957), pp. 39–51.

[60] Curtius to Jaeger, 11 February 1947, in Houghton Library, Jaeger Papers, AM 5, Box E.

desert to the new gods. But what I find almost unbearable is that the systematic persecution of millions of men (a real Inferno) goes ever forward and there is no end in sight.[61]

In letters to his old friend Eduard Spranger, who had endured "internal exile" and even imprisonment under Nazi rule, Jaeger himself expressed his own heartfelt sorrow for the sad fates of Europe and German *Kultur*. "The sufferings of Europe tear at my heart, and I am often without hope," wrote Jaeger in 1947. "In my heart of hearts, I still believe in European culture's spiritual mission in the world, although I also think that this continent has now, politically, become a [mere] province. We have now become Hellenistic exiles or imprisoned Greeks." Yet, Jaeger noted, like the Greek philosopher whose home and library had been expropriated by King Demetrius, the exiles still had their *paideia*.[62] Although he insisted that he had given up on the Germans as readers of the second and third volumes of his *Paideia*, and had grown quite fond of his life at Harvard, Jaeger clearly felt marooned in a post-humanistic world alien to his sensitivities and relatively unimpressed by his credentials.[63]

This sorrowing group's adoption of a new philhellenic ancestor is a telling indication of changes in the German cultural climate. Already in 1943, DAI president Carl Weickert had opened a gathering of the Archäologische Gesellschaft by quoting a mournful stanza from Friedrich Hölderlin's early poem, "Brot und Wein."[64] Hölderlin, a favorite of Nietzsche's whose fame had risen through the 1920s and '30s, reached his apogee in the late '40s and early '50s; the one hundredth anniversary of his death in 1943 spawned more than three hundred Nazi-backed festive commemorations, the publication of new editions of his work, and Hitler's visit to the poet's grave. For some, Hölderlin symbolized the struggle for the realization of Germany's essence; for Martin Heidegger, who published an important essay on Hölderlin in this year, the Romantic poet represented the promise of transcendental homecoming, which was also an explicitly Germanic one.[65] But Hölderlin was perhaps nowhere so highly regarded as amongst classicists of

---

[61] Eduard Fraenkel to Werner Jaeger, 7 November 1945, ibid., Box F.

[62] Jaeger to Spranger, 16 February 1947, in KBA, Nachlaß Spranger, 182/199. Also see Jaeger to Spranger, 3 November 1946 and 1 June 1955, both ibid. Jaeger presumably was referring to a story briefly told in Plutarch's *Lives*; here, Demetrius, son of Antigonus and later king of Macedonia, having just captured Megara, summons the philosopher Stilpo to ask whether or not anyone has robbed him. Plutarch has Stilpo respond: "'No one,' said Stilpo, 'for I saw nobody carrying away knowledge.'" Plutarch does not use the word *paideia*. Plutarch, "Demetrius," 9.5–6, in *Plutarch's Lives*, vol. 9, trans. Bernadotte Perrin, Loeb Classical Library (London, 1950), pp. 22–23.

[63] Jaeger to Spranger, 16 February 1947, KBA, Nachlaß Spranger, 182/199.

[64] Weickert quoted from 8 June 1943 meeting, in *JdesDAI, AA* 59–60 (1944–45): 116–17 ("Brod und Wein," lines 55–64).

[65] See Victor Farias, *Heidegger and Nazism*, ed. Joseph Margolis and Tom Rockmore (Philadelphia, 1987), pp. 268–75.

this era, who saw in the poet a reflection of their own melancholic stoicism and otherworldly longings. In a 1957 essay (for Spranger's Festschrift), Jaeger lovingly described Hölderlin's courageous attempt to revive the Greeks in spite of the ignorance of his age.[66] Clearly this analogy struck a chord for Spranger, who wrote to thank Jaeger for his tribute and to commiserate with his friend's sense of homelessness in an age of cultural decline. Spranger was not surprised that the philologist had now taken up Hölderlin, whose Graecophilia paid tribute less to the fifth-century pagans than to the early Church fathers. "For in no other German author," Spranger averred, "does one perceive so clearly how understanding of the Greeks springs from a truly religious root and makes itself into a religion."[67] Jaeger and Spranger retained their faith in the redemptive promise of the Germano-Greek spiritual marriage to the last, though they now conceived the foundations of the match to lie less in the aesthetic union of Faust and Helen than in the Greeks' philosophical prefiguration of Christian faith.

As we saw in the last chapter, Platonic "religion" had been the subject of a number of Weimar-era treatises, many of them bearing the impress of the school of Stefan George. But Jaeger's work, after his departure from Germany in late 1936, reflects the more sober, less aestheticized, work on Graeco-Christian spirituality characteristic of the postwar era. Where his previous essays had emphasized the place of creative individuals in the (pagan) Greek polis, Jaeger's later works emphasize the proto-Christian aspects of pre-Socratic and especially Platonic philosophy and the otherworldly qualities of humanistic thought.[68] In a 1960 article entitled "Humanism and Theology," Jaeger refuted those who believed humanism to be essentially agnostic and anthropocentric. "The true paideia," he insisted, "be it education or legislation, is founded on God as the supreme norm. It is—to speak with Plato's *Republic*—'conversion' from the world of sensual self-deception to the world of the one true being which is the absolute good and the one desirable. Or in the words of Plato's *Theaetetus*: true human virtue is assimilation to God."[69] If he was, as a former student recalled, a kindly if serenely detached and highly paid teacher during his years at Harvard, Jaeger in America had clearly lost his crusading spirit and interest in reforming the world around him. It is indicative of his abandonment of *Leben* for the afterlife that even this admiring student could only describe

[66] Werner Jaeger, "Friedrich Hölderlins Idee der griechischen Bildung," in *Erziehung zur Menschlichkeit: Die Bildung im Umbruch der Zeit* (Tübingen, 1957), pp. 53–63.

[67] Spranger to Jaeger, 8 September 1957, in Houghton Library, Jaeger Papers, AM 5, Box K.

[68] For two more examples of his early "political" interests, see his "Solon's Eunomia" and "Tyrtaeus on True Arete," both translated in Jaeger, *Five Essays*, trans. Adele M. Fiske (Montreal, 1966), pp. 75–100, 101–42; for examples of the latter mode, see his "Humanism and Theology" [1943], in *Humanistische Reden und Vorträge*, 2d ed. (Berlin, 1960), pp. 300–334, and his Gifford lectures of 1936, published under the title *The Theology of the Early Greek Philosophers* (Oxford, 1947).

[69] Jaeger, "Humanism and Theology," p. 320.

her mentor in the following way: "What comes to mind, rather than any image, is a color—a steady, shining grey, so milky and so luminous that it is hardly a color at all."[70]

In Germany, the most characteristic response of the classicists to the challenges of the postwar period was the efflorescence of Christian *Universalgeschichte*. Having foundered on the rocks of antihistoricist "relevance," many classicists in the postwar period turned their attention—and certainly their rhetorical talents—to the cultivation of a kind of benevolent globalism. Catholic scholars in particular advocated abandoning the narrowly defined *Antike* of the Third Humanists, as well as the racially defined Aryan sphere, for a more UNESCO-friendly world view. It was incumbent upon Germans, Würzburg professor Hermann Bengtson announced in 1963, to abandon Graecocentrism for a healthier appreciation of all of the historical actors in the ancient world. Today, Bengtson proclaimed, the composition of universal histories had become a moral duty as well as a professional necessity: "We have finally learned, taught by our very painful experiences, to look beyond the borders of our own Fatherland, and we have seen that beyond the hills live men whose fate cannot be a matter of indifference to us."[71] Similarly, Tübingen professor Joseph Vogt announced in 1957:

> The task stands before us of searching out the connections between antiquity and the cultures that preceded and followed it, those that surrounded and suffused the *orbis antiquus*. All motivating forces that affect historical understanding lead in this direction. It is a singular characteristic of the course of ancient history itself that it tended toward universality and now can be conceived in connection with the whole; it is the uninterrupted process of archaeological discovery and the expansion of our sources that has broken down the barriers between classical antiquity and the ancient Orient, as well as the barriers between these civilized peoples and the nomads and half-nomads of prehistory. Finally, it is our generation's desire, after political catastrophes and spiritual debacles [*geistigen Zusammenbrüchen*], to regain our bearings in a historical world that embraces all of mankind. In this situation, the problem of the ancient world's contacts with neighboring cultural areas has become a problem of singular significance.[72]

Obviously, this sort of "universalism" differed considerably from the materialist conceptions circulating in the GDR; cultural contact, not socioeconomic stages, formed the basis for this sort of globalist historiography. Of course, the widely shared conviction that *Universalgeschichte* was a

---

[70] Clara Claiborne Park, "At Home in History: Werner Jaeger's Paideia," *The American Scholar* 52 (1983): 382.

[71] Hermann Bengtson, "Zum Problem der Universalgeschichte des Altertums" [1963], in idem, *Kleine Schriften zur alten Geschichte* (Munich, 1974), p. 46.

[72] Joseph Vogt quoted in Karl Christ, "Joseph Vogt," in idem, *Neue Profile der alten Geschichte* (Darmstadt, 1990), p. 110.

crucial means to promote universal human understanding and prove western Germany's abandonment of radical nationalism did not mitigate the continuing influence of older forms of thought. This is hardly surprising in light of the continuity in the classicist teaching corps between the Nazi era and the late 1960s: as Reinhold Bichler has shown, the large majority of professional ancient historians in the two decades after the war—including Bengtson and Vogt—had completed their studies, or even held teaching positions, during the Third Reich.[73] Vogt had imbibed a number of Karl Hausofer's geopolitical conceptions as well as elements of Helmut Berve's racialist classicism; after 1945, Arnold Toynbee's work was instrumental in redirecting a kind of geopolitical intellectual history toward universalist historiography.[74] Bengtson, a student of the orientalist Walter Otto (not to be confused with the Hellenist of the same name), owed much not only to Eduard Meyer, but also to Spengler, to whom he credited the discovery that it was no longer possible to establish the eastern boundaries of the ancient world.[75] The Europo-pessimism of Meyer and Spengler, reinforced by the process of decolonization, suffuses the work of the specialists of the postwar era. In 1960, Bengston wrote: "None of us have any doubts that today decisive changes are going on around us. The suffusion of the world with European *Geist* is at an end, today we see the waves, that once Europe sent out, flooding back towards us."[76]

Even the composition of pessimistic *Universalgeschichte*, however, presented technical difficulties for professional classicists. Given the vast increase in source materials and secondary treatments now available to the classical scholar, writing a "scientific" universal history of the ancient past had become an impossible task for a single individual. This was particularly the case in the postwar era, in which the predominant trend was the retreat into specialized, uncontroversial studies. Bengtson himself warned explicitly against lapses into dilettantism, emphasizing the importance of source work, "in which philology has the first word. The path to knowledge leads through languages."[77] The solution was simply to resort to the model of cooperative scholarship pioneered in the nineteenth century and continued in the *Propyläen-Weltgeschichte* and *Cambridge Ancient History* series of the 1920s and 1930s. During the 1950s, two major universal histories—the *Saeculum-Weltgeschichte* and *Historia mundi*—and several minor handbooks were launched on the popular history market. The editors of these multivolume compilations clearly recognized the urgency of commencing their

[73] Bichler, "Neuorientierung in der alten Geschichte?" pp. 63–86.

[74] See Christ, "Joseph Vogt," pp. 84–108.

[75] Bengtson, "Zum Problem der Universalgeschichte," p. 57.

[76] Bengtson, "Barthold Georg Niebuhr und die Idee der Universalgeschichte des Altertums" [1960], in *Kleine Schriften zur alten Geschichte*, p. 41.

[77] Ibid., p. 39.

universal histories in the prehistorical past; one series, in fact, opens with a discussion of theories of the physical origins of the universe.[78] In these handbooks, Greece and Rome appeared as stages in one continent's development, not as the single legitimate model for civilized existence.[79] In the absence of the normative aesthetics and liberal optimism of the nineteenth century, prehistory became the one moment in which mankind's shared history could be described and praised.

Of course, students of Greece and Rome still held a privileged position in academia, their prominence underwritten by the familiar historicist defense of Graecocentrism. But this defense now had a new, chastened air, as the conclusion of Richard Benz's *Wandel des Bildes der Antike in Deutschland* (*Changes in Germany's View of Antiquity*—1948) nicely illustrates:

> Antiquity is no longer for us the only primal past, as it was for our [German] classic writers; the Middle Ages and the Romantic era have since then stepped up beside it, and in the ancient world itself we have had our eyes opened to a series of other cultures, which we no longer see as primitive and less worthy precursors of the Hellenic world, since vibrant cultures have also unfolded before us, like the East Asian, which do not stem from [classical antiquity] at all. It is perhaps the fact that for us, antiquity's image stands among the other great images of history and no longer represents the single supreme image that most divides us from the classical *Bildung* of the nineteenth century. Still, because of its role in European development, [classical antiquity] will always have to remain particularly near and dear to us, since throughout the centuries, so much of ourselves and our lives have been bound up with antiquity.[80]

If Jaeger and Spranger continued to compose tracts in favor of their brand of humanistic education,[81] the moral weight seemed to have shifted away from fifth-century Athens; it is not by chance that many of these postwar spokesmen possessed expertise in fields beyond the confines of high classical philology. Bengtson, for example, was trained as an orientalist, while Vogt specialized in the late Roman Empire. Latium, the pan-European classical past, rather than Hellas, the unspoiled *Kulturnation*, now came to the fore, as most notably illustrated in E. R. Curtius's magnificent *Europäische Literatur und lateinisches Mittelalter* (*European Literature and the Latin Middle Ages*—

---

[78] *Handbuch der Weltgeschichte* vol. 1, ed. Alexander Randa (Olten, 1954), pp. 13–34.

[79] See, e.g., the 1961 edition of the *Propyläen-Weltgeschichte*, edited by Alfred Heuß and Golo Mann.

[80] Richard Benz, *Wandel des Bildes der Antike in Deutschland: Ein geistesgeschichtlicher Überblick* (Munich, 1948), p. 149.

[81] See, e.g., Jaeger, *The Greeks and the Education of Man* (Annandale on Hudson, N.Y., 1953); idem, "Im Zeichen eines neuen Humanismus," in *Eduard Spranger: Bildnis eines geistigen Menschen unserer Zeit*, ed. Hans Wenke (Heidelberg, 1959), pp. 24–30; and letters between the two men collected in KBA, Nachlaß Spranger.

1948). What Vassilis Lambropoulos has provocatively described as a sort of "NATO-humanism" had arisen, underlining the coherence and continuity of Western thought.[82]

Archaeology, as numerous of these postwar commentators observed, played a crucial role in destroying belief in Greek cultural primacy and autonomy—although, as we have seen, it also played a significant role in the perpetuation of that myth. What now would be its role? Could it save some cultural salience for Greek art? In an important 1956 article (reprinted in 1970), the art historian/archaeologist Ernst Langlotz openly acknowledged the postwar "disempowerment of classical *Bildung*." Given a world in which it seemed easier to get children to appreciate prehistorical cave paintings than the Greek sculpture worshiped by the *Goethezeit*, Langlotz doubted that many would follow him back to the fifth century.[83] Langlotz was certain that the aestheticizing humanistic tradition, which had seen in Greek sculpture the reflection of its own anthropomorphic worldview, had reached its end. He attributed its passing largely to archaeological excavation, which had put before the public actual works of authentic Greek art, replacing those hedonistic Roman copies so prized by Italian humanists and eighteenth-century Graecophiles. The "one-sidedness" of their image of the Greeks could now be appreciated:

> Excavations in Greece and Asia Minor have made available to us works of Greek art of the early and mature eras, rather than works from the decline and the Roman period. From inscriptions, which illuminate the unfamiliar side of the ancient world, we now understand the spiritual backdrop to these works more deeply than Winckelmann could have done. We now comprehend the religious fundament from which these works arose. In particular, the excavations of the early Greek sanctuaries at Olympia, Delphi, and Samos have given us an image of Greek art and religion before which our classicizers would have shrunk in horror. . . . Eyeballs made of colored stone, eyelids rendered by scalloped bronze sheets, the polychromy of sculpted marble of this age, make all the images of later periods in antiquity seem to us bloodless, powerless—like beautiful ghosts.[84]

Real Greek sculpture, however, by virtue of its pious religiosity and pessimistic view of mankind, still held special significance for postwar men.

---

[82] See Vassilis Lambropoulos, *The Rise of Euro-Centrism: Anatomy of Interpretation* (Princeton, N.J., 1993), pp. 89–90, 337, n. 16. Classing Curtius and especially Erich Auerbach as part of this school of thought, Lambropoulos describes it as "anti-Hellenic," and instead "Hebraic," to the core. I must admit to some confusion over Lambropoulos's categories, but his argument here, I think, is consistent with mine.

[83] Ernst Langlotz, "Antike Klassik" (1956) reprinted in *Humanismus*, ed. Hans Oppermann (Darmstadt, 1970), pp. 365, 410.

[84] Ibid., pp. 368–70.

In fact, it alone could bring us face to face with our limits and our depravity. In a striking inversion of Schiller's philhellenic chiliasm, Langlotz described Greek sculpture's power as that of teaching man his inevitable hopelessness (*Ausweglosigkeit*), his inability to elude the fate of his benighted species.

In general, archaeologists, like other classical scholars, gave up normative Graecophilia for more uncontroversial specialized pursuits. But the latter, of course, still entailed the collection, study, and publication of artifacts, and consequently state funding. The relatively few acts of overt collaboration committed by DAI classicists made the institute's transition to the Federal Republic's budgetary rolls unproblematical. A full return to the specialized pursuits of even the penurious Weimar age was, however, thwarted by national poverty, diplomatic circumspection, and constraints imposed by the destruction of numerous libraries, university buildings, and museums—including large sections of the Pergamum Museum. But already by 1960, the Wissenschaftsrat—an advisory body founded in 1957 to coordinate funding for research—was recommending the expansion of classical archaeology;[85] five years later, this agency's call to expand the DAI, "which today belongs amongst the most significant institutions in the humanities," so as to cover more Byzantine, Islamic, and early Christian archaeology, might have been scripted by bureaucrats of the Weimar era.[86] In 1963, the central directorate and its eight satellite branches received DM 7,263,000 from the state, and employed 158 persons, 56 of them described as "specialist personnel."[87] Funding for archaeology still outpaced funding for most other humanistic fields but had fallen even farther behind the natural sciences, especially atomic physics, which received in the same year a total of DM 242,468,000.[88] Archaeology remained a prestigious science, but not one vital for national self-representation.

The reconstruction of the Glyptothek in Munich provides a neat instance of both the changes and the continuities in archaeology's relationship to state power. It had been heavily damaged by Allied bombing, and in 1945 little more than an empty shell remained of Leo von Klenze's lavishly decorated museum. The collections, however, had been stored in cellars for safekeeping, and emerged from the debacle unscathed but virtually inaccessible, as they remained for some years following the nation's defeat. As the Russians tightened their grip on East Berlin and the collections of the Pergamum Museum, however, classicist scholars became convinced of the urgency of displaying what was now the finest collection of ancient sculpture

[85] *Empfehlungen des Wissenschaftsrates zum Ausbau der wissenschaftlichen Einrichtungen,* Teil 1: *Wissenschaftliche Hochschulen* (Tübingen, 1960), p. 89.

[86] Ibid., Teil 3: *Forschungseinrichtungen außerhalb der Hochschulen,* vol. 1 (Tübingen, 1965), pp. 112–13.

[87] Ibid., 3:45.

[88] Ibid., 46.

32. The central gallery of the Pergamum Museum in 1948. The altar itself was packed in crates and shipped to the Soviet Union. © Bildarchiv, Preußischer Kulturbesitz, 1996.

left to West Germany. In late 1949, the Verband deutscher Kunsthistoriker (Association of German Art Historians) exhorted the Bavarian Education Ministry to reconstruct Ludwig I's museum immediately, insisting upon the state's obligation to fund the perpetuation of classical *Bildung.* "The West [*das Abendland*] cannot do without the formative power of ancient art. It is therefore a high duty of the state to provide a worthy abode for these works of art, the earliest and purest testaments of Western culture."[89]

[89] Verband deutscher Kunsthistoriker (Munich) to Bavarian Ministry of Education, 14 November 1949, in BHStA, MK 50904-I.

33. Cemented to its base, the Mschatta Gate was blown to bits by bombs in 1944. © Bildarchiv, Preußischer Kulturbesitz, 1996.

But by 1952, the museum had received only a partial roof, and even the intervention of the DAI in 1956 could not budge the education minister, who was already overwhelmed by bills for the reconstruction of the Alte Pinakothek and the Residenz.[90] When some funds did become available in

[90] Erich Boehringer (DAI president) to H. Diepolder, 12 June 1956, containing copy of Bavarian Education Minister Panholzer's response to Boehringer petition, ibid.

34. The Roman Room of the Glypthothek, as it appeared in the nineteenth century. Glypthothek München (Foto Museum).

1957, a long and vituperative controversy began over the museum's future form, which bore some resemblance to the "Museums War" of the 1920s, and whose outcome would prove to be in some respects quite similar. One faction was led by Hans Diepolder, the director of the nonexistent museum and a classical archaeologist who had belonged to the DAI community in Athens in the Weimar era. The other was commanded by Rudolf Esterer, president of the General Building Commission. Diepolder defended the position that the museum should be rebuilt in an architecturally correct fashion, but without the glamorous interior decoration Ludwig had commissioned. His reasoning was twofold: first, this simplified plan would be considerably cheaper and faster to follow; and second, perceptions of Greek art had changed since the Bavarian monarch built his Romanizing exhibition hall. Esterer, on the other hand, insisted upon full and accurate reconstruction of Klenze's masterpiece.[91] The real question, as a 1962 memorandum on the still unresolved issue pronounced, was which tradition to

[91] See "Protokoll" of meeting on reconstruction of the Glyptothek, 17 December 1957, ibid.

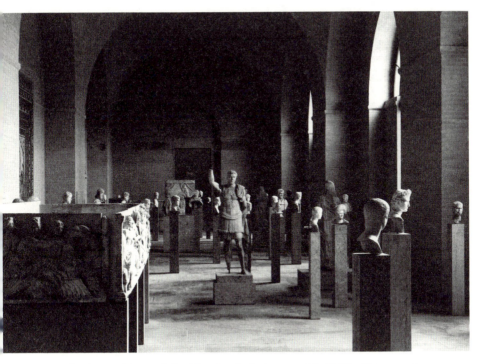

35. The Roman Room of the Glypthotek, in its post–World War II incarnation.
Glypthotek München (Foto Museum).

conserve: that of the Glyptothek as one of the most important collections of
Europe, or that of the Glypthotek as imperial showplace, a sort of museum
of the museum style of the *Vormärz*.[92] The latter program, while more expensive, promised greater returns from the tourist trade; the former plan
relied on the tried and true appeal to the international prestige to be gained
by demonstrating Germany's dedication to pure scholarship. The moral
value of Greek sculpture did not, for perhaps the first time since 1810, play
a prominent role in the debate.

The final decision on the museum's interior dispensation was at last
taken in 1964, and proved to be one Adolf Furtwängler, at least in his
positivist-realist moments, would have applauded; Diepolder, though he
had vacated his directorship in frustration two years earlier, finally triumphed. "We have learned to see ancient art without depending upon the
images of completeness that dominated the age of Ludwig I," correspondent

[92] "Niederschrift" of the Bayrischer Landesbaukunstausschuß meeting, 2 March 1962,
ibid., 50905.

Doris Schmidt reported in the *Süddeutsche Zeitung*; "our image of antiquity is no longer determined by the nineteenth century's tame idea of the beautiful. . . . We also now know that in the preservation and reconstruction of historic buildings, we must be content to do what is possible for our age."[93] Despite this sadder-and-wiser modesty and the asceticism of its interior furnishings, by 1967, the year of its reopening, the interior of the Glyptothek alone had cost upward of DM 6,400,000.[94]

As in the case of the Pergamum battles of the 1920s, the professional archaeologists had won, with the result that the Glyptothek, like the Pergamum Museum, has a distinctly intellectual and even antiseptic feel. Importantly, the Glyptothek reconstruction took even longer to complete than did that of the Pergamum Museum, and it had to wait for the Residenz and the Alte Pinakothek to be completed before it received a full measure of state support. Without the Faustian marriage metaphor and cultural clout of a Wiegand or Dörpfeld, the classicists had only international prestige and a vague sort of NATO-humanism on which to base their claims to cultural significance, and the Glyptothek, today, has become merely one cultural institution (and a little-visited one) among many.

Farewell to Antiquity? The Cultural Revolutions of the 1960s and 1970s

The demotion of classical antiquity in German culture was accelerated by demographic, philosophical, and historiographical trends that burst onto the scene in the late 1960s. This decade saw not only the passing or retirement of the Weimar and Nazi era professoriate but also a population boom and the "economic miracle," West Germany's return to economic prosperity a mere fifteen years after its devastation in World War II. All of these factors contributed to a movement to democratize higher education in the Federal Republic, though demographic forces probably provided the greatest impetus to change, for initial reforms almost exclusively addressed insufficient output of teachers and limitations on access to higher education. In 1963, the *Kultusminister-Konferenz* (Commission of Cultural Ministers—KMK) received a report predicting a deficit of three hundred thousand teachers by 1970. At the current rate of graduation, the report noted, only about the same number of students would finish college during the same period—all graduates would have to take up teaching to fill the vacant positions. The KMK in conjunction with other organizations set about doubling the num-

---

[93] Doris Schmidt, "Glypthotek: Würfelgefallen," in *Süddeutsche Zeitung*, 21 August 1964, ibid.

[94] See documents ibid.

ber of those who would pass the *Abitur*; this project coincided with new calls to end the upper-class monopoly on *Gymnasium* education. By the 1970s, the child of independently wealthy parents was only six times more likely to attend a *Gymnasium* than a child of working-class parents, as against 33 to 1 in 1931.[95] To accommodate the ensuing expansion of higher education—between 1960 and 1970, the total number of students at this level in West Germany rose from 291,000 to 510,000—eleven new universities were created between 1962 and 1970. But overcrowding continued, as did, according to those who joined the student revolts in 1968, the authoritarian, repressive, and frustratingly antipolitical orientation of the teaching staffs.[96]

Crucially, the 1960s and 1970s saw the retirements and/or deaths of those who had begun their careers in the Weimar era and managed to survive both Nazi and anti-Nazi purges. Of course, demise had come earlier for some of our protagonists of the previous generation: Wiegand and Paul Wolters departed in 1936; Wilhelm Dörpfeld died at age eighty-seven in 1940. Gerhart Rodenwaldt committed suicide in 1945, and Martin Schede died in a Russian prison camp in 1947. The next decade saw the deaths of Ludwig Curtius (1954), Walter Andrae (1956), and both Walter F. Otto and Karl Reinhardt (1958). But the real change came with the retirements of men like Ernst Buschor in 1961, Helmut Berve in 1962, Ernst Langlotz in 1963, Walter H. Schuchhardt and also Wolfgang Schadewaldt in 1968.[97] The departure of these scholars opened the way for fresh consideration of the discipline's past and the rethinking of the place of classical studies in the changed social and political conditions of the postwar era.

In fact, philosophical reflection on these issues had already begun by the early 1960s, often initiated by classicists whose formative experiences lay in the Weimar and Nazi eras. Perhaps chastened by Jaeger's failures, these self-critical spokesmen possessed neither the will nor the desire to reassert classicist hegemony. By 1962, Bruno Snell felt he had to invent new terminology to defend (basically on historicist grounds) the relevance of the Greeks. He would have spoken of "humanistic cultivation [*Bildung*]," Snell noted, "But the concept . . . is so vague and so burdened with obsolete conceits and suspect ideologies (in both parts, both "humanistic" and "cultivation") that I would rather avoid it."[98] Even Jaeger's collaborationist student Wolfgang Schadewaldt, by 1960, was prepared to admit that Humboldt's notion

[95] Margret Kraul, *Das deutsche Gymnasium, 1780–1980* (Frankfurt, 1984), pp. 207–15.

[96] Rosalind M. O. Pritchard, *The End of Elitism? The Democratization of the West German University System* (New York, 1990), pp. 71–87.

[97] For profiles of more archaeologists, an astonishing number of whom retired or died during this era, see Reinhard Lullies and Wolfgang Schiering, *Archäologenbildnisse* (Mainz, 1985).

[98] Bruno Snell, *Die alten Griechen und wir* (Göttingen, 1962), p. 3.

that the essence of mankind could be conveyed in *Gymnasium* study of classical languages was a delusion, backed by an unwarranted belief in the "mystical powers" of Greek and Latin.[99] Announcing the final decline of the *Gymnasium* in 1965, Uvo Hölscher, finally, linked humanism to nationalist right-wing politics, to the Romantic "fear of the present," and to outdated belief in the autonomy of individuals, heroes, and reason. In the disenchanted postwar world, Hölscher averred, "No one believes any longer in the possibility of resurrecting the Greeks, in which even the Third Humanism trusted. The younger people have become sensitive to the preacher's tone in philology, the credos of older people sound strange to their ears, they don't seem to need proofs of meaning."[100] The philology of the future would be a much more modest—and, Hölscher added, much less self-deceiving—member of the *Geisteswissenschaften*.

Wider confirmation of classicism's change in status is available from a remarkable series of interviews collected in 1963–64 and published in the journal *Wort und Wahrheit* under the title "Abschied von der Antike?" Respondents to the survey, who ranged from Konrad Adenauer to philosophy professor Arnold Gehlen, were to give their views on whether or not the classical world still had any value or meaning for the present. Although the great majority of the respondents defended antiquity's role in education—particularly as an antidote to the new utilitarianism of the natural sciences—given the discoveries of the last hundred years, these leading *Bildungsbürger*, like the philologists themselves, could not envision a simple return to the Humboldtian *Bildungsideal*. The historicization of the Greek world, several noted, had destroyed the unique status once enjoyed by the Greeks and Romans. "Historicism has robbed this classical *Bildungswelt* of its claim to exert a normative force,"[101] commented Josef Derbolev, professor of philosophy and pedagogy at the University of Bonn. "He who seeks historical clarification of the development of our modern world will always have to return to its ancient foundations," insisted the sinologist Herbert Francke. "But historicism has also taught us the uniqueness and contingency of every cultural phenomenon. The unconditional positing [*Verabsolutierung*] of ancient forms of art and thought as a single valid ideal

[99] Wolfgang Schadewaldt, "Ziel und Gestaltung des Unterrichts in den alten Sprachen auf der Oberstufe unserer altsprachlichen Gymnasien," in idem, *Hellas und Hesperien*, vol. 2 (Zürich, 1960), p. 954. Schadewaldt, according to Hugo Ott, had been "a devoted supporter of the new [Nazi] regime." Hugo Ott, *Martin Heidegger: A Political Life*, trans. Allan Blunden (London, 1993), p. 143.

[100] Uvo Hölscher, *Die Chance des Unbehagens: Drei Essays zur Situation der klassischen Studien* (Göttingen, 1965), pp. 53f.; quote p. 76.

[101] Josef Derbolev quoted in "Abschied von der Antike?" *Wort und Wahrheit* 19 (1963–64): 17.

no longer seems possible. The concept of the classical today can no longer be solely applied to the authors of [classical] antiquity."[102]

Germanophilia, at the same time, never really recovered from its Nazi-era biologization. In places, racialist thought and radical rightist archaeologists —especially prehistorians—did survive denazification.[103] Some right-wing proponents of national reunification tried to revive the cult of Arminius; but their efforts do not seem to have created much of a following, and by 1970s, the German "barbarian," as national folk figure, was dead.[104] In general, postwar prehistorians have avoided grand claims—and even theoretical debates[105]—especially when these involve Indo-European migrations. Instead of insisting upon cultural purity, as did Kossinna, most would endorse the conclusion of classicist Alexander Demandt: "That which is typically Germanic consists of clearly un-Germanic elements; "Germanic" is in any event a mixed bag."[106] The *furor teutonicus*, along with rapturous Graeco-philia, had at last been exhausted.

Historiographically, new interest in modern history and social history, as well as major self-critical assessments of modern German developments like Fritz Fischer's highly controversial treatment of German diplomacy on the eve of the First World War, *Griff nach der Weltmacht* (*Grab for World Power*— 1961), drew practitioners and especially audiences away from classical subjects. The focus, in recent years, has been on the use and abuse of power in the modern world and on "forgotten" actors—workers, women, and peasants—and little-studied areas and periods in the deeper past. By the late 1970s, the DAI felt it had to come to grips with these developments, and did so, as usual, by creating another subdepartment. On the 150th anniversary of the founding of the IfAK (1979), the Kommission für Allgemeine und Vergleichende Archäologie (Commission for General and Comparative Archaeology) was created to redress Germany's neglectful treatment of archaeological inquiry in Asia, Africa, and America. The following statement about the founding of this body should indicate the ways in which the philhellenic institute had come to terms with postwar developments:

---

[102] Herbert Francke quoted ibid., p. 22.

[103] See Alain Schnapp and Jesper Svenbro, "Du nazisme à nouvelle école: Repères sur la prétendue nouvelle droite," in *Quaderni di storia* 6 (1980): 107–19.

[104] Völker Losemann, "Arminius und Augustus: Die römisch-germanische Auseinandersetzung im deutschen Geschichtsbild," in *Römische Geschichte und Zeitgeschichte*, vol. 1: *Caesar und Augustus*, ed. E. Gabba and K. Christ (Como, 1989), pp. 145–63.

[105] Härke, "All Quiet on the Western Front? Paradigms, Methods, and Approaches in West German Archaeology." in *Archaeological Theory in Europe: The Last Three Decades*, ed. Ian Hodder (New York, 1991), pp. 187–222.

[106] Alexander Demandt, "Was wäre Europa ohne die Antike?" in *Alte Geschichte und Wissenschaftsgeschichte*, ed. Peter Kneissl and Volker Losemann (Darmstadt, 1988), p. 116.

Western culture rests on the inheritance of the ancient high cultures of the Mediterranean region. It is therefore understandable and even necessary for intellectual history, that the study of these cultures was given priority. However, with the process which Oswald Spengler termed, negatively, the decline of the West—which can, positively, be seen as the broadening and evolution toward a world culture—the archaic cultures that have helped to shape the nations of the Americas, Asia, and Africa and that had already been included in *Universalgeschichte* in Humboldt's sense, can now move the scholarly interests of the modern world in new directions. Allowance for this has been made with the founding of the Kommission für Allgemeine und Vergleichende Archäologie of the Deutsches Archäologisches Institut.[107]

The DAI could not entirely give up its neohumanist heritage, but it now committed itself to the comparative historicism of Humboldt's later years. Institutionally, it had endured many reversals in thought, but this winsome acceptance of "the decline of the West" was perhaps its most momentous, if hardly conspicuous, change in scholarly worldview.

Looming behind these postwar changes of heart lays a larger intellectual event, whose contours we can only sketch here: the collapse of faith in man's ability to rise above barbarism, to possess a special moral essence and a universal moral goal. Voiced in the philosophy, philosophical anthropology, and theology of the postwar era, this anthropo-skepticism was compounded by the sense that the *Naturvölker*, unsullied by technological hubris and abstract will to violence, had much to teach the *Kulturvölker*. Karl Jaspers looked explicitly to prehistory, hoping that it could function as a propaideutic to human solidarity. Max Horkheimer and Theodor Adorno identified a false step in humanity's past already apparent in the Homeric epics.[108] These thinkers offered no Rousseauist utopia of the "natural" man, but rather undertook torturous descents into the depths of the modern psyche, without the teleological comfort of religious salvation, self-justification by cultivation, or even imminent Marxist revolution. Here the Greeks were useless (except, as Horkheimer and Adorno use them, as exemplars of a critical moment in human estrangement from nature). Their long-touted beauty, truth, and goodness had all become suspect in a world wary of returning to old ideals.

Thus it is, perhaps, the prehistorians, ethnographers, and folklorists—predisposed to perceiving the flaws in classical humanism—to whom the right to speak with scholarly authority about the human condition has

---

[107] Quoted in B. Andrae, "Zur Einführung," in *Archäologie und Gesellschaft: Forschung und öffentliches Interesse*, ed. idem (Stuttgart, 1981), pp. 25–26.

[108] See Karl Jaspers, *The Origin and Goal of History*, trans. Michael Bitlock (London, 1949), p. 43; and Max Horkheimer and Theodor Adorno, *Dialectic of Enlightenment*, trans. John Cumming (New York, 1986).

largely been bequeathed. As early as 1943, the British prehistorian Graham Clark was preparing for the postwar arrival of such an "ethnographic" humanism:

> Community of sentiment can only be founded upon the appreciation of a common past. Education everywhere must be based on the common experience of humanity. Hellenism and Christianity are common to only a small section of the world's population, but anthropology and prehistory have in the last hundred years shown the age-long struggle for betterment which lies behind the whole of the human race. . . . Had the German, Italian, and Japanese peoples received a grounding in the natural and cultural history of mankind, they would never have been led astray by the crazy dreams of racial and cultural dominations which to-day are sweeping them to ruin.[109]

Disseminated and encouraged by UNESCO and the Wenner-Gren Foundation after the war, this ethnographic universalism has become more and more entrenched in Europe and America, and may even be said to form a sort of subconscious moral paradigm in today's human sciences.

In its German guise, this new universalism sprouts from the consciousness of a sort of biblical fall from grace, and is not easily reconcilable with nineteenth-century neohumanist aspirations. The testimony of the prehistorian Herbert Kühn is perhaps one of the most profound expressions of this strain of thought.

> Man in our time has experienced two of the most dreadful wars that mankind has ever had to endure. The First World War, 1914–18, reached 3.2 million dead [sic], the second, 1939–45, reached 40 million dead. Approximately 10 million men were held in concentration camps, in Auschwitz alone 4 million died, and the number of dead in the camps comes to approximately 6 million.
>
> What numbers, what fearsome numbers. Numbers from the continent of Europe, which sees itself as the most developed of mankind and which considers itself so perfect, that it wants to lift the other peoples of the world to its heights. . . .
>
> More powerfully in such an era as in a tranquil epoch the eternal question presents itself: what is man, how is it possible that men can carry these horrors within themselves? What is man, when he hides in himself such evil, such abysses, such joy in killing? Man stands there, accursed, dismembered, despairing for himself. He has done the worst that man can do: he has committed an assault on the ideal of humanity, and thus on the [spark of] divinity that man carries in himself.
>
> Such an age must ask about the meaning of man, his essence, his being, his

---

[109] J. D. G. Clark, "The Contribution of Archaeology to the Post-War World," in *Conferences on the Future of Archaeology* (University of London, 6–8 August 1943), University of London Institute of Archaeology, Occasional Paper no. 5, (London, 1943), p. 7.

value, and his lack of value—and thus the gaze must be more powerfully directed to earlier epochs, to the original man, to the *Ur*-man. Our gaze must rest on the era when man was still simple, not yet corrupted and broken by ideas and illusions, not yet fixed to the rails of a particular thought, not yet seized by struggles for one idea against another; the age in which man was still man: the prehistorical era. What is a man, that such paths are possible for him, what is it, that in our age, which we see as the most perfect, allows him to become a wild beast, boundless in murder, robbery, and destruction?

[These are] questions that always recur in the difficult eras of history, [questions] that Christianity puts, when it speaks of Adam, of his fall from God, of sin. Questions that the Renaissance puts, the Reformation; questions that Erasmus of Rotterdam asks, [along with] Melanchthon, Roger Bacon, [and] Hugo Grotius.[110]

In the wake of such self-inflicted barbarism, Europeans had to look beyond the classical age to understand their nature. The question, What is man? in the late twentieth century seemed to Kühn one that only the ethnographer or prehistorian could answer.

Of course, Kühn was plumping here for his own field of study; but the anguish expressed in his reflections was widely shared, and may lead us to reexamine from another angle the question with which we opened this volume: What happened to German philhellenism? Over the course of this long book, I have tried to suggest some of the other components of this answer. German philhellenism, I have argued, was destroyed by a combination of internal and external forces: specialization, institutional inertia, demographic and economic changes, nationalism, hyperaestheticization, and the social irresponsibility of those who benefited from the perpetuation of "disinterested" learning. Kühn's insightful linkage of the terrors of the twentieth century to the search for a new, "barbarian" common ancestor provides another explanation for the end of Greece's tyranny over Germany.

Being a man of wide *Bildung*, in addition to scholarly treatises and diplomatic memos, Wilhelm von Humboldt also wrote poetry. In his "Rom" of 1806 he paid tribute to his beloved city, among whose greatest accomplishments was the preservation of Greek art and poetry:

> Ewig hätt' Homeros uns geschwiegen,
> Hätte Rom nicht unterjocht die Welt . . .
>
> Homer would never have sung to us,
> Had not Rome conquered the world . . .[111]

---

[110] Herbert Kühn, *Geschichte der Vorgeschichtsforschung* (Berlin, 1976), pp. 3–4.

[111] Wilhelm von Humboldt, "Rom," in *Wilhelm von Humboldts Werke*, ed. Albert Leitzmann et al., vol. 9 *Gedichte* (Berlin, 1912), p. 35.

Indeed, we do have Roman conquest to thank for the preservation of much of Greek antiquity, and, in the same way, we have largely Germans to thank for the nineteenth century's "conquest of the ancient world by scholarship" as Wilamowitz described the professionalization of classical learning.[112] But perhaps we have had enough of conquests for the present, and enough of the sort of ascetic, aestheticizing, and aristocratic humanism that shaped German cultural institutions until very recently. We may still worship the Greeks, and admire the German scholars who have uncovered and recovered so much of their strange and marvelous world. Yet the unflattering record of German philhellenism's entanglement with imperialist, elitist, and even racist state policy makes it likely that even those who make the study of Greece their life's work will now keep a cool, scholarly distance from their subject, and be wary of the excessive attachment and flaunting of ordinary morals our age sees in the spiritual marriage of Faust and Helen. The Greek gods, it seems, have come down from Olympus, and philhellenic neohumanism has lost its privileged place in German culture. And though the nostalgic may yet mourn the losses entailed by this process of double demystification, it is certain that the way has been cleared for the creation of more inclusive—if ever imperfect—forms of individual cultivation and more varied—if less "pure"—ideals of beauty.

[112] Ulrich von Wilamowitz-Moellendorff, *History of Classical Scholarship*, trans. Alan Harris (London, 1982), p. 105.

SELECTED BIBLIOGRAPHY

MANUSCRIPT SOURCES

Athens, Archiv des Deutschen Archäologischen Instituts. Internal correspondence (Korrespondenz und Berichte) of the DAI, Athens; Nachlaß of Georg Karo.

Berlin, Archiv der Akademie der Wissenschaften. Records of the Prussian Academy of Sciences.

Berlin, Archiv des Deutschen Archäologischen Instituts. Nachlasse of Alexander Conze, Ernst Curtius, Ludwig Curtius, Wilhelm Dörpfeld, Karl Humann, Otto Puchstein, Gerhart Rodenwaldt, Kekulé von Stradonitz, Theodor Wiegand.

Berlin, Staatliche Museen zu Berlin, Zentralarchiv. Records of the Islamic Department, Near Eastern Department, and Antiquities Department (Islamisches Museum, Vorderasiastisches Museum, Antikensammlung).

Berlin, Geheimes Staatsarchiv, Preußischer Kulturbesitz. Nachlasse of Carl Heinrich Becker and Friedrich Schmidt-Ott.

Berlin, Staatsbibliothek. Nachlasse of Walter Andrae, Gustav Kossinna, Eduard Meyer, Gerhart Rodenwaldt.

Bonn, Politisches Archiv des Auswärtigen Amtes. Records of the Foreign Ministry, Cultural Affairs Section (Auswärtiges Amt, Kulturabteilung).

Cambridge, Mass., Houghton Library, Harvard University. Papers of Werner Jaeger (AM 5).

Frankfurt am Main, Archiv der Römisch-Germanischen Kommission. Internal correspondence of members of the Römisch-Germanische Kommission and Deutsches Archäologisches Institut.

Koblenz, Bundesarchiv. Record group R73 (records of the Notgemeinschaft der deutschen Wissenschaft). Record group NS 8/244 (records of the Nazi-era Reichsministerium des Innern). Nachlaß of Eduard Spranger.

London, British Museum. Papers of A. H. Layard.

London, Warburg Institute. Papers of Aby Warburg.

Merseberg, Zentrales Staatsarchiv. Record group 2.2.1 (records of the Kaiser's Civil Cabinet [Zivilkabinett]). Record group 151C (records of the Finance Ministry [Finanzministerium]). Nachlasse of Friedrich Althoff and Friedrich Schmidt-Ott.

Munich, Bayerisches Hauptstaatsarchiv. Records of Bavarian Education Ministry (Kultusministerium).

Potsdam, Zentrales Staatsarchiv. Records of the Foreign Ministry, Legal Affairs Section (Auswärtiges Amt, Rechtsabteilung), and Cultural Affairs Section (Auswärtiges Amt, Kulturabteilung).

PRINTED SOURCES

Aarsleff, Hans. *From Locke to Saussure: Essays on the Study of Language and Intellectual History.* Minneapolis, 1982.

Abelein, Manfred. *Die Kulturpolitik des Deutschen Reiches und der Bundesrepublik Deutschland.* Cologne, 1968.

Albisetti, James. *Secondary School Reform in Imperial Germany*. Princeton, N.J., 1983.

Althoff, Marie. *Aus Friedrich Althoffs Berliner Zeit*. Jena, 1918.

Andrae, B., ed. *Archäologie und Gesellschaft: Forschung und öffentliches Interesse*. Stuttgart, 1981.

Andrae, Walter. *Babylon: Die versunkene Weltstadt und ihr Ausgräber, Robert Koldewey*. Berlin, 1952.

————. *Lebenserinnerungen eines Ausgräbers*. Berlin, 1961.

Andree, Christian. "Geschichte der Berliner Gesellschaft für Archäologie, Ethnographie, und Urgeschichte." In *Festschrift zum hundertjährigen Bestehen der Berliner Gesellschaft für Archäologie, Ethnologie und Urgeschichte, 1869–1969*, 1:9–142. Berlin, 1969.

Applegate, Celia. *A Nation of Provincials: The German Idea of Heimat*. Berkeley, Calif., 1990.

Barth, Wilhelm, and Max Kehrig-Korn. *Die Philhellenenzeit*. Munich, 1960.

Becker, Carl H. *Deutschland und der Islam*. Der deutsche Krieg, ed. Ernst Jaeckh, vol. 3. Stuttgart, 1914.

————. *Gedanken zur Hochschulreform*. 2d ed. Leipzig, 1920.

————. *Islamstudien*. Vol. 1. Leipzig. 1924.

————. *Kant und die Bildungskrise der Gegenwart*. Leipzig, 1924.

————. *Kulturpolitische Aufgaben des Reiches*. Erfurt, 1919.

Behrens, Gustav. "Das Römisch-Germanische Zentralmuseum von 1927 bis 1952." In *Festschrift des RGZM in Mainz zur Feier seines hundertjährigen Bestehens 1952*, 3:182–93. Mainz, 1953.

Bernal, Martin. *Black Athena: The Afroasiatic Roots of Classical Civilization*. Vol. 1: *The Fabrication of Ancient Greece, 1785–1985*. New Brunswick, N.J., 1987.

Blok, Josine. "Quest for a Scientific Mythology: F. Creuzer and K. O. Müller on History and Myth." *History and Theory*, suppl. vol. 33 (1994): 26–52.

Böckh, August. *Encyklopädie und Methodologie der philologischen Wissenschaften*. 2d. ed., edited by Ernst Bratuscheck. Leipzig, 1886.

Böhner, Kurt. "Das Römisch-Germanische Zentralmuseum—Eine vaterländische und gelehrte Gründung des 19. Jahrhunderts." *Jahrbuch des Römisch-Germanischen Zentralmuseum, Mainz* 25 (1978): 1–48.

Böhme, Klaus, ed. *Aufrufe und Reden deutscher Professoren im Ersten Weltkrieg*. Stuttgart, 1975.

Bollmus, Reinhard. *Das Amt Rosenberg und seine Gegner*. Stuttgart, 1970.

Borbein, Adolf. "Klassische Archäologie in Berlin vom 18. bis zum 20. Jahrhundert." In *Berlin und die Antike*, edited by Willmuth Arenhövel and Christa Schreiber, pp. 99–150. Berlin, 1979.

Braun, Rainer. "Die Anfänge der Limesforschung in Bayern." *Jahrbuch für fränkische Landesforschung* 42 (1982): 1–70.

————. "Die Erforschung der 'Teufelsmauer' in Württemberg bis 1890." *Fundberichte aus Baden-Württemberg* 10 (1985): 37–75.

Brocke, Bernhard vom. "Hochschul- und Wissenschaftspolitik in Preußen und im Deutschen Kaiserreich 1882–1907: Das System Althoff." In *Bildungspolitik in Preußen zur Zeit des Kaiserreiches*, edited by Peter Baumgart, pp. 9–118. Stuttgart, 1980.

————. "Preußen—Land der Schulen, nicht nur Kasernen. Preußische Bildungspolitik von Gottfried Wilhelm Leibnitz und Wilhelm von Humboldt bis Friedrich Althoff und Carl Heinrich Becker (1700–1930)." In *Preußen: Eine Herausforderung*, edited by Wolfgang Böhme, pp. 54–99. Karlsruhe, 1981.

———. "'Wissenschaft und Militarismus': Der Aufruf der 93 'An die Kulturwelt!' und der Zusammenbruch der internationalen Gelehrtenrepublik im Ersten Weltkrieg." In *Wilamowitz nach 50 Jahren*, edited by William M. Calder et al., pp. 649–719. Darmstadt, 1985.

Bruch, Rüdiger vom. *Weltpolitik als Kulturmission: Auswärtige Kulturpolitik und Bildungsbürgertum in Deutschland am Vorabend des Ersten Weltkrieges*. Paderborn, 1982.

Bruch, Rüdiger vom, and Rainer A. Müller, ed., *Formen außerstaatlicher Wissenschaftsförderung im 19. und 20. Jahrhundert: Deutschland im Europäischen Vergleich*. Stuttgart, 1990.

Bruer, Stephanie-Gerrit. *Die Wirkung Winckelmanns in der deutschen klassischen Archäologie des 19. Jahrhunderts*. Akademie der Wissenschaften und der Literatur Mainz: Abhandlungen der geistes- und sozialwissenschaftlichen Klasse 1994, Nr. 3. Stuttgart, 1994.

Bruford, W. H. *The German Tradition of Self-Cultivation*. Cambridge, 1975.

Brunn, Heinrich. *Archäologie und Anschauung*. Munich, 1885.

———. *Geschichte der griechischen Künstler*. 2 vols. Braunschweig, 1853; Stuttgart, 1859.

———. *Griechische Kunstgeschichte*. 2 vols. Munich, 1893–97.

———. *Heinrich Brunns Kleine Schriften*, edited by Heinrich Bulle und Hermann Brunn. Leipzig, 1905.

Buddensieg, Tilmann, Kurt Düwell, and Klaus-Jurgen Sembach, eds. *Wissenschaften in Berlin*. Berlin, 1987.

Burkert, Walter. "Griechische Mythologie und die Geistesgeschichte der Moderne." In *Les Etudes classiques aux XIXe et XXe Siècles: Leur place dans l'histoire des idées*, edited by Willem den Boer, pp. 159–207. Geneva, 1980.

Burleigh, Michael. *Germany Turns Eastward: A Study of Ostforschung in the Third Reich*. Cambridge, 1988.

Butler, Edith May. *The Tyranny of Greece Over Germany*. Cambridge, 1935.

Calder, William. "Werner Jaeger." In *Berlinische Lebensbilder*. Vol. 4: *Geisteswissenschaftler*, edited by Michael Erbe, pp. 343–63. Berlin, 1989.

Calder, William M., ed. *Werner Jaeger Reconsidered*. Illinois Studies in the History of Classical Scholarship, vol. 2. Atlanta, 1992.

Calder, William M., et al., eds. *Friedrich Gottlieb Welcker: Werk und Wirkung*. *Hermes*, vol. 49. Stuttgart, 1986.

Calder, William M., and Alexander Demandt, eds. *Eduard Meyer: Leben und Leistung eines Universalhistorikers*. Leiden, 1990.

Calder, Willam M., and David A. Traill, eds. *Myth, Scandal, and History*. Detroit, 1986.

Ceram, C. W. *The Secret of the Hittites: The Discovery of an Ancient Empire*. Translated by Richard and Clara Winston. New York, 1956.

Christ, Karl. *Neue Profile der alten Geschichte*. Darmstadt, 1990.

———. *Römische Geschichte und Wissenschaftsgeschichte*. Vol. 3: *Wissenschaftsgeschichte*. Darmstadt, 1983.

―――. *Von Gibbon zu Rostovsteff: Leben und Werk führender Althistoriker der Neuzeit.* Darmstadt, 1972.

Constantine, David. *Early Greek Travellers and the Hellenic Ideal.* Cambridge, 1984.

Conze, Alexander. "Pro Pergamo." Reprinted in *Entdeckungen in Hellas,* edited by Heinrich A. Stoll, pp. 475–92. Berlin, 1979.

―――. *Unsern Kindern gewidmet.* Berlin, 1908.

―――. "Zur Geschichte der Anfänge griechischer Kunst." In *Sitzungsberichte der Kaiserlichen Akademie der Wissenschaften in Wien* (Phil.-Hist. Kl.) 64 (1870): 505–534; 73 (1873): 221–50.

Craig, John E. *Scholarship and Nation Building: The Universities of Strasbourg and Alsatian Society, 1870–1939.* Chicago, 1984.

Creuzer, Friedrich. *Aus dem Leben eines alten Professors.* Part 5, vol. 1 of *Friedrich Creuzer's Deutsche Schriften.* Leipzig, 1848.

Curtius, Ernst. *Alterthum und Gegenwart.* Berlin, 1877.

―――. *Unter drei Kaisern.* Berlin, 1889.

Curtius, Friedrich, ed. *Ernst Curtius: Ein Lebensbild in Briefen.* Berlin, 1903.

Curtius, Ludwig. *Die antike Kunst und der moderne Humanismus.* Berlin, 1927.

―――. *Deutsche und antike Welt: Lebenserinnerungen.* Stuttgart, 1956.

―――. *Humanistisches und Humanes: Fünf Essays und Vorträge.* Basel, 1954.

Delitzsch, Friedrich. *Babel und Bibel: Ein Vortrag.* Stuttgart, 1902.

―――. *Babel und Bibel: Ein Rückblick und Ausblick.* Stuttgart, 1904.

―――. *Mehr Licht: Die bedeutsamen Ergebnisse der babylonisch–assyrischen Grabungen für Geschichte, Kultur, und Religion.* Leipzig, 1907.

Döhl, Hartmut. *Heinrich Schliemann: Mythe und Ärgernis.* Munich, 1981.

Dörpfeld, Wilhelm. *Alt-Olympia: Untersuchungen und Ausgrabungen zur Geschichte des ältesten Heiligtums von Olympia und der älteren griechischen Kunst.* Vol. 1. Berlin, 1935.

―――. *Troja und Ilion: Ergebnisse der Ausgrabungen in den vorhistorischen und historischen Schichten von Ilion, 1870–1894.* Athens, 1902.

Düwell, Kurt. "Staat und Wissenschaft in der Weimarer Epoche: Zur Kulturpolitik des Ministers C. H. Becker." *Historische Zeitschrift,* suppl. vol. 1 (1971): 31–74.

Ebers, Georg. *Richard Lepsius: A Biography.* Translated by Zoe Dana Underhill. New York, 1887.

Eggers, Hans Jürgen. *Einführung in die Vorgeschichte.* 3d ed. Munich, 1986.

Ehrhardt, Wolfgang. *Das Akademische Kunstmuseum der Universität Bonn unter der Direktion von Friedrich Gottlieb Welcker und Otto Jahn.* Opladen, 1982.

Erman, Adolf. *Mein Werden und mein Wirken: Erinnerungen eines alten Berliner Gelehrten.* Leipzig, 1929.

Esch, Arnold. "Limesforschung und Geschichtsvereine: Romanismus und Germanismus, Dilettantismus und Facharchäologie in der Bodenforschung des 19. Jahrhunderts." In *Geschichtswissenschaft und Vereinswesen,* edited by Hartmut Boockmann et al., pp. 163–91. Göttingen, 1972.

Feldman, Gerald D. "The Politics of Wissenschaftspolitik in Weimar Germany: A Prelude to the Dilemmas of Twentieth-Century Science Policy." In *Changing Boundaries of the Political,* edited by Charles Maier, pp. 255–85. Cambridge, Mass., 1987.

Ferber, Christian von. *Die Entwicklung des Lehrkörpers der deutschen Universitäten und Hochschulen, 1864–1954.* Göttingen, 1956.

Field, Geoffrey G. *Evangelist of Race: The Germanic Vision of Houston Stewart Chamberlain.* New York, 1981.

Fischer, Hans. *Der Ägyptologe Georg Ebers: Eine Fallstudie zum Problem Wissenschaft und Öffentlichkeit im 19. Jahrhundert.* Wiesbaden, 1994.

Forman, Paul. "Weimar Culture, Causality, and Quantum Theory, 1918–1927: Adaptation by German Physicists and Mathematicians to a Hostile Intellectual Environment." *Historical Studies in the Physical Sciences,* 3:1–115. Philadelphia, 1971.

Freier, Elke, and Walter F. Reineke, eds. *Karl Richard Lepsius (1810–1884).* Schriften zur Geschichte und Kultur des Alten Orients, vol. 20. Berlin, 1988.

Fuchs, Reinhold. "Zur Geschichte der Sammlungen des Rheinischen Landesmuseums." In *Rheinisches Landesmuseum Bonn: 150 Jahre Sammlungen,* pp. 1–158. Düsseldorf, 1971.

Fück, Johann. *Die arabischen Studien in Europa bis in den Anfang des 20. Jahrhunderts.* Leipzig, 1955.

Führ, Christoph. "Die preußischen Schulkonferenzen von 1890 und 1900: Ihre bildungspolitische Rolle und bildungsgeschichtliche Bewertung." In *Bildungspolitik in Preußen zur Zeit des Kaiserreichs,* edited by Peter Baumgart, pp. 189–223. Stuttgart, 1980.

Fuhrmann, Manfred. "Die 'Querelle des Anciens et des Modernes,' der Nationalismus und die deutsche Klassik." In *Deutschlands kulturelle Entfaltung: Die Neubestimmung des Menschen,* edited by Bernhard Fabian, Wilhelm Schmidt-Biggemann, and Rudolf Vierhaus, pp. 49–67. Munich, 1980.

Furtwängler, Adolf. *Kleine Schriften,* edited by Johannes Sieveking and Ludwig Curtius. Vol. 1, Munich, 1912.

———. *Masterpieces of Greek Sculpture.* Edited and translated by Al. N. Oikonomides. Chicago, 1964.

Gaehtgens, Thomas W. *Die Berliner Museumsinsel im Deutschen Kaiserreich: Zur Kulturpolitik der Museum in der Wilhelminischen Epoche.* Munich, 1992.

Gerhard, Eduard. *Thatsachen des Archäologischen Instituts in Rom.* 2d ed. Berlin, 1834.

Ginzburg, Carlo. *Clues, Myths, and the Historical Method.* Translated by John and Anne Tedeschi. Baltimore, 1989.

Glum, Friedrich. *Zwischen Wissenschaft, Wirtschaft, und Politik.* Bonn, 1964.

Goessler, Peter. *Wilhelm Dörpfeld: Ein Leben im Dienst der Antike.* Stuttgart, 1951.

Gollwitzer, Heinz. "Zum politischen Germanismus des 19. Jahrhunderts." In *Festschrift für Hermann Heimpel,* 1:282–356. Göttingen, 1971.

Gombrich, E. H. *Aby Warburg: An Intellectual Biography.* London, 1970.

Gossmann, Lionel. *Orpheus Philologus: Bachofen versus Mommsen on the Study of Antiquity.* Transactions of the American Philosophical Society, vol. 73, pt. 5. Philadelphia, 1983.

Grabar, Oleg. "Islamic Art and Archaeology." In *The Study of the Middle East: Research and Scholarship in the Humanities and the Social Sciences,* edited by Leonard Binder, pp. 229–263. New York, 1976.

Grafton, Anthony. *Defenders of the Text: The Traditions of Scholarship in an Age of Science, 1450–1800*. Cambridge, Mass., 1991.

―――. *Forgers and Critics: Creativity and Duplicity in Western Scholarship*. Princeton, N.J. 1990.

―――. "Polyhistor into Philolog: Notes on the Transformation of German Classical Scholarship, 1780–1850." In *History of Universities* 3 (1983): 159–92.

Griewank, Karl. "Wissenschaft und Kunst in der Politik Kaiser Wilhelms I. und Bismarcks." *Archiv für Kulturgeschichte* 34 (1952): 288–307.

Gummel, Hans. *Forschungsgeschichte in Deutschland. Vol. 1: Die Urgeschichtsforschung und ihre historische Entwicklung in den Kulturstaaten der Erde*. Edited by Karl Jacob-Friesen. Berlin, 1938.

Härke, Heinrich. "All Quiet on the Western Front? Paradigms, Methods, and Approaches in West German Archaeology." In *Archaeological Theory in Europe: The Last Three Decades*, edited by Ian Hodder, pp. 187–222. New York, 1991.

Hammer, Karl. "Preußische Museumspolitik im 19. Jahrhundert." In *Bildungspolitik in Preußen zur Zeit des Kaiserreiches*, edited by Peter Baumgart, pp. 256–77. Stuttgart, 1980.

Hardtwig, Wolfgang. "Strukturmerkmale und Entwicklungstendenzen des Vereinswesens in Deutschland, 1789–1848." In *Vereinswesen und bürgerliche Gesellschaft in Deutschland*, edited by Otto Dann. *Historische Zeitschrift*, suppl. vol., n.s. 9 (1950): 1–50.

Hatvany, Ludwig. *Die Wissenschaft des nicht Wissenswerten*. 1908. Reprint, Oxford, 1986.

Hauser, Christoph. *Anfänge bürgerlicher Organisation: Philhellenismus und Frühliberalisms in Südwestdeutschland*. Göttingen, 1990.

Haym, Rudolf. *Wilhelm von Humboldt: Lebensbild und Charakteristik*. Osnabrück, 1856.

Heiber, Helmut. *Walter Frank und sein Reichsinstitut für Geschichte des neuen Deutschlands*. Stuttgart, 1966.

Heilbron, J. L. *The Dilemmas of an Upright Man*. Berkeley, Calif., 1986.

Heimpel, Hermann. "Geschichtsvereine einst und jetzt." In *Geschichtswissenschaft und Vereinswesen im 19. Jahrhundert*, edited by Hartmut Boockmann et al., pp. 45–73. Göttingen, 1972.

Herder, Johann Gottfried. *Sämtliche Werke*. 33 vols. Edited by Bernhard Suphan. Berlin, 1877–1913.

Heuss, Alfred. *Theodor Mommsen und das 19. Jahrhundert*. Kiel, 1956.

Hochschulreform und wissenschaftliche Ausbildung der Philologen (Denkschrift des Verbandes der deutschen Hochschulen und des deutschen Philologenverbandes). Leipzig, 1931.

Hieronimus, Ekkehard. "Von der Germanen-Forschung zum Germanen-Glauben: Zur Religionsgeschichte des Präfaschismus." In *Die Restauration der Götter: Antike Religion und Neo-Paganismus*, edited by Richard Faber and Renate Schlesier, pp. 241–57. Würzburg, 1986.

Hölscher, Uvo. *Die Chance des Unbehagens: Drei Essais zur Situation der klassischen Studien*. Göttingen, 1965.

Hoffmann, Maximilian. *August Böckh*. Leipzig, 1901.

Honour, Hugh. *Neoclassicism*. Harmondsworth, Middlesex, 1968.

Howald, Ernst. *Der Kampf um Creuzers Symbolik: Eine Auswahl von Dokumenten.* Tübingen, 1926.

Irmscher, Johannes. *Das Antikebild unserer Gegenwart: Tendenzen und Perspektiven.* Sitzungsberichte der Akademie der Wissenschaften der DDR. Berlin, 1979.

Jacob, Maurice. "Etude comparative des systèmes universitaires et place des études classiques au 19ᵉ siècle en Allemagne, en Belgique, et en France." In *Philologie und Hermeneutik im 19. Jahrhundert.* Vol. 2, edited by Mayotte Bollack and Heinz Wismann, pp. 108–40. Göttingen, 1983.

Jaeger, Werner. "Die Antike im wissenschaftlichen Austausch der Nationen." *Die Antike* 6 (1930): 85–92.

———. "Die Erziehung des politischen Menschen und die Antike." *Volk im Werden* 1 (1933): 43–49.

———. *Five Essays.* Translated by Adele M. Fiske. Montreal, 1966.

———. *The Greeks and the Education of Man.* Annandale on Hudson, N.Y., 1953.

———. *Humanismus und Jugendbildung.* Berlin, 1921.

———. *Humanistische Reden und Vorträge.* 2d ed. Berlin, 1960.

———. "Im Zeichen eines neuen Humanismus." In *Eduard Spranger: Bildnis eines geistigen Menschen unserer Zeit,* edited by Hans Wenke, pp. 24–30. Heidelberg, 1959.

———. *Paideia.* Vol. 1: *Die Formung des griechischen Menschen.* Berlin, 1934.

———. "Staat und Kultur." *Die Antike* 8 (1932): 71–89.

———. *Stellung und Aufgaben der Universität in der Gegenwart.* Berlin, 1924.

Jahn, Otto. "Über das Wesen und die wichtigsten Aufgaben der archäologischen Studien." *Berichte über die Verhandlungen der Königlichen Sächsischen Gesellschaft der Wissenschaften zu Leipzig* 2 (1848): 209–226

James, Harold. *The German Slump: Politics and Economics, 1924–1936.* Oxford, 1986.

Jenkyns, Richard. *The Victorians and Ancient Greece.* Cambridge, Mass., 1980.

Johanning, Klaus. *Der Bibel-Babel-Streit: Eine forschungsgeschichtliche Studie.* Frankfurt, 1988.

Jorns, Marie. *August Kestner und seine Zeit, 1777–1853.* Hannover, 1964.

Justi, Carl. *Winckelmann und seine Zeitgenossen.* 2 vols. 1943. Reprint, Hildesheim. 1983.

Karo, Georg. *Fünfzig Jahre aus dem Leben eines Archäologen.* Baden, 1959.

Kater, Michael. *Das "Ahnenerbe" der SS, 1935–1945.* Stuttgart, 1974.

Kekulé von Stradonitz, Reinhard. *Eduard Gerhard.* Berlin, 1910.

———. *Die Vorstellungen von griechischer Kunst und ihre Wandlung im neunzehnten Jahrhundert.* Berlin, 1908.

Kern, Otto. *Hermann Diels und Carl Robert: Ein biographischer Versuch.* Jahresberichte über die Fortschritte der klassischen Altertumswissenschaft. suppl. 215, edited by Karl Münscher. Leipzig, 1927.

Kloosterhuis, Jürgen. "Deutsche auswärtige Kulturpolitik und ihre Trägergruppen vor dem Ersten Weltkrieg." In *Deutsche auswärtige Kulturpolitik seit 1871,* edited by Kurt Düwell and Werner Link, pp. 7–36. Vienna, 1981.

Kossinna, Gustav. *Die deutsche Vorgeschichte: Eine hervorragende nationale Wissenschaft.* Würzburg, 2d ed., 1912.

————. *Die Herkunft der Germanen: Zur Methode der Siedlungsarchäologie.* 2d ed. Leipzig, 1920.

————. "Die indogermanische Frage archäologisch beantwortet." *Zeitschrift für Ethnographie* 34 (1902): 161–222.

————. "Der Ursprung der Urfinnen und Urindogermanen und ihre Ausbreitung nach Osten." *Mannus* 1 (1909): 17–52, 225–45, 2 (1910): 59–108.

Kostrzewski, Josef. *Vorgeschichtsforschung und Politik.* Poznań, 1930.

Krämer, Werner. "Fünfundsiebzig Jahre Römisch-Germanische Kommission." *Bericht der Römisch-Germanischen Kommission,* 58 (1977), suppl. vol., pp. 5–23.

————. "Das Römisch-Germanisch Zentralmuseum und die deutsche Vorgeschichtsforschung um die Jahrhundertwende." *Jahrbuch des Römisch-Germanischen Zentralmuseums, Mainz* 25 (1978): 49–73.

Kraul, Margret. *Das deutsche Gymnasium, 1780–1980.* Frankfurt, 1984.

Kühn, Herbert. *Geschichte der Vorgeschichtsforschung.* Berlin, 1976.

La Vopa, Anthony. *Grace, Talent, and Merit: Poor Students, Clerical Careers, and Professional Ideology in Eighteenth-Century Germany.* Cambridge, 1988.

————. "Specialists against Specialization: Hellenism as Professional Ideology in German Classical Studies." In *German Professions, 1800–1950,* edited by Geoffrey Cocks and Konrad H. Jarausch, pp. 27–45. New York, 1990.

Landfester, Manfred. *Humanismus und Gesellschaft im 19. Jahrhundert.* Darmstadt, 1988.

Ledebur, Leopold von. *Das Königliche Museum vaterländischer Alterthümer im Schlosse Monbijou in Berlin.* Berlin, 1838.

Lehmann, Reinhard G. *Friedrich Delitzsch und der Babel-Bibel-Streit.* Göttingen, 1994.

Leifer, Walter. *Hellas im deutschen Geistesleben.* Herrenalb, Schwarzwald, 1963.

Lepenies, Wolf. "Fast ein Poet: Johann Joachim Winckelmanns Begründung der Kunstgeschichte." In idem, *Autoren und Wissenschaftler im 18. Jahrhundert,* pp. 91–120. Vienna, 1988.

Levine, Joseph M. *The Battle of the Books: History and Literature in the Augustan Age.* Ithaca, N.Y., 1991.

————. *Dr. Woodward's Shield: History, Science, and Satire in Augustan England.* Ithaca, N.Y., 1977.

Lindow, Erich. *Freiherr Marschall von Bieberstein als Botschafter in Konstantinopel, 1897–1912.* Danzig, 1934.

Littmann, Enno. *Der deutsche Beitrag zur Wissenschaft vom Vorderen Orient.* Stuttgart, 1942.

Losemann, Volker. "Arminius und Augustus: Die römisch-germanische Auseinandersetzung im deutschen Geschichtsbild." In *Römische Geschichte und Zeitgeschichte,* edited by E. Gabba and K. Christ. Vol. 1: *Caesar und Augustus,* pp. 129–63. Como, 1989.

————. "Aspekte der nationalsozialistischen Germanenideologie." In *Alte Geschichte und Wissenschaftsgeschichte: Festschrift für Karl Christ,* edited by Volker Losemann and Peter Kneissl, pp. 256–84. Darmstadt, 1988.

————. *Nationalsozialismus und die Antike.* Hamburg, 1977.

Ludwig, Emil. *Schliemann: The Story of a Gold-Seeker.* Translated by D. F. Tait. Boston, 1931.

Lullies, Reinhard, and Wolfgang Schiering, eds. *Archäologenbildnisse*. Mainz, 1985.

Lundgreen, Peter. "Differentiation in German Higher Education." In *The Transformation of Higher Learning, 1860–1930*, edited by Konrad Jarausch, pp. 30–57. Chicago, 1983.

McClelland, Charles. "The Aristocracy and University Reform in Eighteenth-Century Germany." In *Schooling and Society: Studies in the History of Education*, edited by Lawrence Stone, pp. 146–74. Baltimore, 1976.

————. *The German Experience of Professionalization: Modern Learned Professions and their Organizations from the Early Nineteenth Century to the Hitler Era*. Cambridge, 1991.

————. *State, Society, and University in Germany, 1700–1914*. Cambridge, 1980.

Mann, Thomas. *Reflections of a Nonpolitical Man*. Translated by Walter D. Morris. New York, 1987.

Marchand, Suzanne. "Professionalizing the Senses: Art and Music History in Vienna, 1880–1920." *Austrian History Yearbook* (1985): 23–57.

————. "The Rhetoric of Artifacts and the Decline of Classical Humanism: The Case of Josef Strzygowski," *History and Theory*, suppl. vol. 33 (1994): 106–30.

Mejcher, Helmut. "Die Bagdadbahn als Instrument deutschen wirtschaftlichen Einflusses im Osmanischen Reich." *Geschichte und Gesellschaft* 1 (1975): 447–81.

Mercklin, Eugen. "Archäologische Institute." In *Forschungsinstitute: Ihre Geschichte, Organisation und Ziele*, edited by Ludolph Brauer et al., 1:280–301. Hamburg, 1930.

Meyer, Eduard. *Die Aufgaben der höheren Schulen und die Gestaltung des Geschichtsunterrichts*. Leipzig, 1918.

————. "Fünfundzwanzig Jahre Deutsche Orient-Gesellschaft." *Mitteilungen der Deutschen Orient-Gesellschaft* 62 (1923): 1–25.

————. *Kleine Schriften*. Vol. 2. Halle, 1924.

————. "Spenglers Untergang des Abendlandes." *Deutsche Literaturzeitung* 25 (1924): 1759–80.

Meyer, Ernst, ed. *Heinrich Schliemann: Briefwechsel*. Vol. 1 (*1842–1875*); vol. 2 (*1876–1890*). Berlin, 1953, 1958.

————. *Wilhelm Dörpfeld: Werk und Mensch*. Wuppertal, 1955.

Michaelis, Adolf. "Die Aufgaben und Ziele des Kaiserlichen Deutschen Archäologischen Instituts." *Preußiche Jahrbücher* 63 (1889): 21–51.

————. *Geschichte des Deutschen Archäologischen Instituts, 1829–1879*. Berlin, 1879.

————. *Ein Jahrhundert kunstarchäologischer Entdeckungen*. 2d ed. Leipzig, 1908.

Momigliano, Arnaldo. *The Classical Foundations of Modern Historiography*. Berkeley, Calif., 1990.

————. *Contributo alla storia degli studi classici*. Rome, 1955.

————. *Essays in Ancient and Modern Historiography*. Middletown, Conn., 1977.

————. "New Paths of Classicism in the Nineteenth Century." *History and Theory* suppl. vol. 21 (1982): 1–64.

————. *Sesto Contributo alla storia degli studi classici e del mondo antico*. Vol. 1. Rome, 1980.

Mommsen, Theodor. *Reden und Aufsätze*. Berlin, 1905.

Most, Glenn W. "Zur Archäologie der Archaik." *Antike und Abendland* 35 (1989): 1–23.

Moyano, Steven. "Quality vs. History: Schinkel's Altes Museum and Prussian Arts Policy," *The Art Bulletin* 72, no. 4 (December 1990): 585–608.

Müller, Karl Otfried. *Ancient Art and its Remains*. Edited by F. G. Welcker. Translated by John Leitch. London, 1852.

———. *Introduction to a Scientific System of Mythology*. Translated by John Leitch. 1844. Reprint, New York, 1978.

———. *Karl Otfried Müllers kleine deutsche Schriften*. Edited by Eduard Müller. Vol. 2. Breslau, 1848.

Müsebeck, Ernst. *Das Preußische Kultusministerium vor hundert Jahren*. Stuttgart, 1918.

Näf, Beat. *Von Perikles zu Hitler? Die athenische Demokratie und die deutsche Althistorie bis 1945*. Bern, 1986.

Nipperdey, Thomas. *Gesellschaft, Kultur, Theorie: Gesammelte Aufsätze zur neueren Geschichte*. Göttingen, 1976.

Nipperdey, Thomas, and Ludwig Schmugge. *50 Jahre Forschungsförderung in Deutschland: Ein Abriß der Geschichte der deutschen Forschungsgemeinschaft, 1920–1970*. Berlin, 1970.

Norden, Eduard. *Die Bildungswerte der lateinischen Literatur und Sprache auf dem humanistischen Gymnasium*. Berlin, 1920.

O'Boyle, Lenore. "Klassische Bildung und Soziale Struktur in Deutschland zwischen 1800 und 1848." *Historische Zeitschrift* 207, no. 3 (December 1968):584–608.

Ottaway, J. H. "Rudolf Virchow: An Appreciation." *Antiquity* 47 (1973):101–08.

Otto, Walter F. *Die Götter Griechenlands: Das Bild des Göttlichen im Spiegel des griechischen Geistes*. Bonn, 1929.

Pallat, Ludwig. *Richard Schöne: Generaldirektor der Königlichen Museen in Berlin*. Berlin, 1959.

Pallis, Svend Aage. *The Antiquity of Iraq: A Handbook of Assyriology*. Copenhagen, 1956.

Paulsen, Friedrich. *German Education Past and Present*. Trans. T. Lorenz. New York, 1908.

———. *The German Universities and University Study*. Translated by Frank Thilly. New York, 1906.

Petras, Renate. *Die Bauten der Berliner Museumsinsel*. Berlin, 1987.

Pletsch, Carl. *The Young Nietzsche: Becoming A Genius*. New York, 1991.

Podro, Michael. *The Critical Historians of Art*. New Haven, Conn., 1982.

Potts, Alex. *Flesh and the Ideal: Winckelmann and the Origins of Art History*. New Haven, Conn., 1994.

Preuß, Ute. *Humanismus und Gesellschaft: Zur Geschichte des altsprachlichen Unterrichts in Deutschland von 1890 bis 1933*. Frankfurt, 1988.

Proctor, Robert. "From *Anthropologie* to *Rassenkunde* in the German Anthropological Tradition." In *Bones, Bodies, Behavior: Essays on Biological Anthropology*. Edited by George W. Stocking, Jr., pp. 138–80. Madison, 1988.

Pyenson, Lewis. *Neohumanism and the Persistence of Pure Mathematics*. Philadelphia, 1983.

Ratzel, Friedrich. *Deutschland: Einführung in die Heimatkunde*. Leipzig, 1898.

Renger, Johannes. "Die Geschichte der Altorientalistik und der vorderasiatischen

Archäologie in Berlin von 1875 bis 1945." In *Berlin und die Antike*, vol 1, edited by Willmuth Arenhövel and Christa Schreiber, pp. 151–92. Berlin, 1979.

Ringer, Fritz. *The Decline of the German Mandarins: The German Academic Community, 1890–1933*. 1969. Reprint, Hanover, N.H., 1990.

———. *Education and Society in Modern Europe*. Bloomington, Ind., 1979.

———. "A Sociography of German Academics, 1863–1938." *Central European History* 25 (1992): 251–80.

Rodenwaldt, Gerhart. *Archäologisches Institut des Deutschen Reiches, 1829–1929*. Berlin, 1929.

———. *Die Kunst der Antike: Hellas und Rom*. Propyläen Kunstgeschichte, vol. 3. 4th ed. Berlin, 1927.

Rohde, Erwin. *Afterphilologie: Sendschreiben eines Philologen an Richard Wagner*. Leipzig, 1872.

———. *Psyche: Seelencult und Unsterblichkeitsglaube der Griechen*. 2d ed. 2 vols. Freiburg im Breisgau, 1898.

Rüegg, Walter. "Die Antike als Begründung des deutschen Nationalbewußtseins." In *Antike in der Moderne*, edited by Wolfgang Schuller, pp. 267–81. Konstanz, 1985.

Rüster, Brigitte. "Geschichte des Museums von 1884 bis 1912." *Jahresschrift für mitteldeutsche Vorgeschichte* 67 (1984): 72–86.

Sachse, Arnold. *Friedrich Althoff und sein Werk*. Berlin, 1928.

Samuel, R. H., and R. Hinton Thomas. *Education and Society in Modern Germany*. London, 1949.

Sandys, John Edwin. *A History of Classical Scholarship*. 3 vols. New York, 1964.

Scheffler, Karl. *Berliner Museumskrieg*. Berlin, 1921.

Schelsky, Helmut. *Einsamkeit und Freiheit: Idee und Gestalt der deutschen Universität und ihrer Reformen*. Reinbeck bei Hamburg, 1963.

Schiering, Wolfgang. "Zur Geschichte der Archäologie." In *Allgemeine Grundlagen der Archäologie*, ed. by Ulrich Hausmann, pp. 11–161. Munich, 1969.

Schlesier, Renate. *Kulte, Mythen und Gelehrte: Anthropologie der Antike seit 1800*. Frankfurt, 1994.

Schlette, Friedrich. "Die Anfänge einer Ur- und Frühgeschichtsforschung in Halle bis zur Gründung des Provinzialmuseums." *Jahresschrift für mitteldeutsche Vorgeschichte* 67 (1984): 9–27.

Schmidt-Ott, Friedrich. *Erlebtes und Erstrebtes, 1860–1950*. Wiesbaden, 1952.

Schnapp, Alain. *La Conquête du passé: Aux origines de l'archéologie*. Paris, 1993.

Schöllgen, Gregor. "'Dann müssen wir uns aber Mesopotamien sichern!'" *Saeculum* 32 (1981): 130–45.

———. *Imperialismus und Gleichgewicht: Deutschland, England und die orientalische Frage, 1871–1914*. Munich, 1984.

Schöne, Richard. "Die Gründung und Organization der Königlichen Museen." In *Zur Geschichte der Königlichen Museen in Berlin: Festschrift ihres fünfzigjährigen Bestehens am 3. August 1880*, pp. 31–58. Berlin, 1880.

Schreiber, George. *Zwischen Demokratie und Diktatur: Persönliche Erinnerungen an die Politik und Kultur des Reiches, 1919–1944*. Regensberg, 1949.

Schuchhardt, Carl. *Aus Leben und Arbeit*. Berlin, 1944.

———. *Schliemann's Excavations*. Translated by Eugenie Sellers. Chicago, 1974.

Schuchhardt, Carl, and Theodor Wiegand, eds. *Der Entdecker von Pergamon: Carl Humann*. Berlin, 1931.

Schuchhardt, Walter. *Adolf Furtwängler*. Freiburg im Breisgau, 1956.

Schumacher, Karl. "Das Römisch-Germanische Central-Museum von 1901–1926." In *Festschrift zur Feier des fünfundsiebzigjährigen Bestehens des Römisch-Germanischen Central-Museums zu Mainz 1927*, pp. 53–88. Mainz, 1927.

Schwalbe, Klaus. *Wissenschaft und Kriegsmoral*. Göttingen, 1969.

Seeberg, Reinhold. "Friedrich Schmidt-Ott und die deutsche Wissenschaft." In *Aus fünfzig Jahren deutscher Wissenschaft: Festschrift für Friedrich Schmidt-Ott*, edited by Gustav Abb, pp. 1–8. Berlin, 1930.

Seidl, Wolf. *Bayern in Griechenland*. Munich, 1981.

Sherman, Daniel J. *Worthy Monuments: Art Museums and the Politics of Culture in Nineteenth-Century France*. Cambridge, Mass., 1989.

Sklenar, Karel. *Archaeology in Central Europe: The First 500 Years*. New York, 1983.

Smith, Woodruff D. *The Ideological Origins of Nazi Imperialism*. New York, 1986.

———. *Politics and the Sciences of Culture in Germany, 1840–1920*. New York, 1991.

Sösemann, Bernd. " 'Der kühnste Entschluß führt am sichersten zum Ziel': Eduard Meyer und die Politik." In *Eduard Meyer: Leben und Leistung eines Universalhistorikers*, edited by William M. Calder and Alexander Demandt, pp. 446–83. Leiden, 1990.

Solmsen, Friedrich. "Wilamowitz in his Last Ten Years," *Greek, Roman, and Byzantine Studies* 20, no. 1 (Spring 1979): 89–122.

Spengler, Oswald. *Der Untergang des Abendlandes: Umrisse einer Morphologie der Weltgeschichte*. Vol. 1: *Gestalt und Wirklichkeit*. Munich, 1921.

Spranger, Eduard. *Das humanistische und das politische Bildungsideal im heutigen Deutschland*. Berlin, 1916.

———. *Kultur und Erziehung: Gesammelte pädagogische Aufsätze*. 4th ed. Leipzig, 1928.

———. *Das Ministerium der geistlichen und Unterrichtsangelegenheiten*. Berlin, 1917.

Stern, Fritz. *The Politics of Cultural Despair*. Berkeley, Calif., 1961.

Strzygowski, Josef. *Aufgang des Nordens: Lebenskampf eines Kunstforschers um ein deutsches Weltbild*. Leipzig, 1936.

———. "Mschatta II. Kunstwissenschaftliche Untersuchung." *Jahrbuch der Königlich Preußischen Kunstsammlungen* 25 (1904): 225–373.

———. "Das Schicksal der Berliner Museen." *Preußische Jahrbücher*, no. 203 (March 1926): 163–90.

Tal, Uriel. *Christians and Jews in Germany: Religion, Politics, and Ideology in the Second Reich, 1870–1914*. Ithaca, N.Y., 1975.

Thanopoulos, Georgios I. *Das deutsche Neugriechenland-Bild, 1918–1944*. Neuried, 1987.

Treue, Wilhelm. "Max Freiherr von Oppenheim: Der Archäologe und die Politik." *Historische Zeitschrift* 209 (1969): 37–74.

Troeltsch, Ernst. *Humanismus und Nationalismus in unserem Bildungswesen*. Berlin, 1917.

———. *Das Wesen des Deutschen*. Heidelberg, 1915.

Trumpener, Ulrich. *Germany and the Ottoman Empire, 1914–1918*. Princeton, N.J., 1968.

Turner, R. S. "The Growth of Professional Research in Prussia, 1818 to 1848: Causes and Consequences." *Historical Studies in the Physical Sciences* 3 (1971): 137–82.

————. "Historicism, *Kritik*, and the Prussian Professoriate, 1790 to 1840." In *Philologie und Hermeneutik im 19. Jahrhundert*, vol. 2, edited by Mayotte Bollack and Heinz Wismann, pp. 450–77. Göttingen, 1983.

Unte, Wolfhart. "Eduard Meyer und die Notgemeinschaft der deutschen Wissenschaft." In *Eduard Meyer: Leben und Leistung eines Universalhistorikers*, edited by William M. Calder and Alexander Demandt, pp. 505–37. Leiden, 1990.

Vidler, Anthony. *The Writing of the Walls: Architectural Theory in the Late Enlightenment*. Princeton, N.J., 1987.

Wahle, Ernst. "Geschichte der prähistorischen Forschung." *Anthropos* 45, no. 4–6 (July–December 1950): 497–538, 46, no. 1–2 (January–April 1951): 49–112.

Watzinger, Carl. *Theodor Wiegand*. Munich, 1944.

Wegeler, Cornelia. "Das Institut für Altertumskunde der Universität Göttingen 1921–1962: Ein Beitrag zur Geschichte der klassischen Philologie seit Wilamowitz." In *Die Universität Göttingen unter dem Nationalsozialismus*, edited by Heinrich Becker and Hans-Joachim Dahms, pp. 246–71. Munich, 1987.

Wegner, Max. "Geschichte der Archäologie unter dem Gesichtspunkt der Methode." *Studium Generale* 17 (1964): 191–202.

Weil, Rudolf. "Geschichte der Ausgrabung in Olympia." In *Olympia: Die Ergebnisse der von dem deutschen Reich veranstalteten Ausgrabung*. Text vol. 1: *Topographie und Geschichte*, edited by Ernst Curtius and Friedrich Adler, pp. 101–54. Berlin, 1897.

Wende, Erich. *C. H. Becker: Mensch und Politiker*. Stuttgart, 1959.

Wenk, Silke, ed. *Auf den Spuren der Antike: Theodor Wiegand, ein deutscher Archäologe*. Bendorf am Rhein, 1985.

Whitman, James Q. *The Legacy of Roman Law in the German Romantic Era: Historical Vision and Legal Change*. Princeton, N.J., 1990.

Wiegand, Theodor. *Halbmond im letzten Viertel: Archäologische Reiseberichte*. Edited by Gerhard Wiegand. Mainz, 1985.

————. "Zur Geschichte der Ausgrabungen von Olympia." *Sitzungsberichte der Preußischen Akademie der Wissenschaften*, Phil.-hist. Klasse (1926): 14–22.

Wilamowitz-Moellendorff, Ulrich von. *Erinnerungen, 1848–1914*. 2d ed. Leipzig, 1928.

————. *Glaube der Hellenen*. 2 vols. Berlin, 1931–32.

————. *History of Classical Scholarship*. Translated by A. Harris, edited by Hugh Lloyd-Jones. London, 1982.

————. *Reden aus der Kriegszeit*. Berlin, 1915.

————. *Reden und Vorträge*. 3d ed. Berlin, 1913.

————. *Zukunftsphilologie! Eine Erwiderung auf Friedrich Nietzsches "Geburt der Tragödie."* Berlin, 1872.

————. *Zukunftsphilologie! Zweites Stück: Erwiderung auf die Rettungsversuche für Fr. Nietzsches "Geburt der Tragödie."* Berlin, 1873.

Wolf, Friedrich A. "Darstellung der Altertumswissenschaft." In *Kleine Schriften*, edited by G. Bernhardy, 2:786–875. Halle, 1869.

————. *Prolegomena to Homer*. Translated and introduced by Anthony Grafton, Glenn W. Most, and James E. G. Zetzel. Princeton, N.J., 1985.

Zierold, Kurt. *Forschungsförderung in drei Epochen*. Wiesbaden, 1968.

INDEX

Aarsleff, Hans, 29 n. 96

Abdul Hamid II, 190, 208; and Hamdi Edhem, 200, 201, 202, 206; relations with Germans, 102, 197, 198, 199, 203; mentioned, 209, 211

Abitur, 27, 137

Adler, Friedrich, 50, 84, 87

Adorno, Theodor: *Dialectic of Enlightenment,* 372

Aeschylus, 127

Albisetti, James, 31

Altenstein, Karl Freiherr von, 59, 166

Altertumswissenschaft, 22–24; conservative turns in, 76–77, 230–31, 258–62, 302–05; generational structure of, 50–51, 60, 298–99, 321, 369–70; narrowing of, 44–48, 50, 51; and Nazism, 342–54; and opposition to school reform, 117–18; philhellenic prejudices of, 21, 116, 181; and prehistorical archaeology, 154–55; and WWI propaganda, 231–42

Altheim, Franz, 349

Althoff, Friedrich, 136, 172, 196, 209, 228, 229, 230, 270

Andrae, Walter, 212, 213, 214, 218, 224, 369

Anquetil-Duperron, Abraham Hyacinthe, 189

antiquarians, 7, 11, 40

archaeology, classical, 48, 49; and antiquarianism, 40; and dependence on state, 231, 265–66, 300–01; as focus of book, xix–xxi; and *Kulturpolitik,* 192–220, 242–58; and museums, 73–74, 288–94; and Nazism, 344–45; normative v. historicist dimensions of, 42, 49, 91, 111–12, 115, 151, 330–40; and philology, xx, 40–41, 42–43, 46–49, 58, 142–46, 143 n. 99, 293–94; and photography, 106–07, 337–40; and prehistory, 162–80, 282–83; and private patronage, 53, 118, 193; and professional techniques in 87, 97–98, 104–08; school reform, 142–51; state funding of, 83–87, 192. *See also* DAI; IfAK

archaeology, prehistorical (*Vorgeschichte*),

154–55, 162–63, 170–72, 172–80; post-war situation of, 278–80; *Vereine* for, 163–65, 167–70, 174, 177–80

Archäologische Gesellschaft, 58, 173

Aristotle, 128, 139, 320

Arnim, Hans von, 235

art, Greek, xix, 43, 60, 70, 90–91; and Egypt, 44, 47, 110–11, 122; exhibition space 67, 69–70, 288–94, 363–68; post–1945 interpretation of, 362–63; sculpture, 5, 15, 67, 336–37; and Weimar aesthetics, 323–25, 330–40

Assyriology, 221–27

Augustus the Strong, 24, 67

Babel-und-die-Bibel-Streit, 224–27

Bachofen, J. J., 102, 108, 181

Becker, Carl Heinrich: and Jaeger, 320; and Spengler, 308; and Weimar reforms, 263–67, 270, 284–85, 293, 303, 313, 315, 317; and WWI, 237, 238–39; 251

Belck, Waldemar, 207, 208

Beloch, K. J., 109, 141, 298

Bengston, Hermann, 359, 360, 361

Benz, Richard: *Wandel des Bild der Antike in Deutschland,* 361

Bernal, Martin, xxii, 44

Bersu, Gerhard, 249, 282, 296, 298, 353

Berve, Helmut, 349, 369

Beseler, Georg, 160

Bethmann-Hollweg, Theobald von, 217

Beyme, K. F., 22

BGAEU (Berliner Gesellschaft für Archäologie, Ethnographie, und Urgeschichte), 173, 174–76, 177

Bichler, Reinhold, 360

Bildung, xix, xxiii, 26–28, 240, 341–42. *See also* Gymnasium; Humboldt, Wilhelm von; school reform

Bismarck, Otto von, 17, 71; opposition to Olympia dig, 82, 85–86; Orient policy of, 92, 190; mentioned, 95, 128, 150, 170, 173, 176, 177, 178, 265

Bissing, Friedrich Freiherr von, 247; *Der Griechentum und seine Weltmission,* 309–10